HANDBOOK

FOR LITURGICAL STUDIES

V

Liturgical Time and Space

THE PONTIFICAL LITURGICAL INSTITUTE

HANDBOOK FOR LITURGICAL STUDIES

VOLUME V

Liturgical Time and Space

ANSCAR J. CHUPUNGCO, O.S.B.

EDITOR

A PUEBLO BOOK

The Liturgical Press   Collegeville Minnesota

A Pueblo Book published by The Liturgical Press

Design by Frank Kacmarcik, Obl.S.B.

Library of Congress Cataloging-in-Publication Data

Handbook for liturgical studies / Anscar J. Chupungco, editor.
p. cm.
"A Pueblo book."
Includes bibliographical references and index.
Contents: v. 1. Introduction to the liturgy.
ISBN 0-8146-6161-0 (vol. I)
ISBN 0-8146-6162-9 (vol. II)
ISBN 0-8146-6163-7 (vol. III)
ISBN 0-8146-6164-5 (vol. IV)
ISBN 0-8146-6165-3 (vol. V)
1. Liturgics—Study and teaching. 2. Catholic Church—Liturgy—Study and teaching. I. Chupungco, Anscar J.
BV176.H234 2000
264—dc21 97-20141
CIP

Contents

* translated by Lisa A. Twomey
** translated by Renée Domeier, O.S.B.
*** translated by David Cotter, O.S.B.
**** translated by Bethany Lane
***** translated by Madeleine Beaumont
****** translated by Matthew J. O'Connell

Introduction

In the preceding volumes the study of liturgy focused on the history, sources, theology, and the ritual and euchological components of the different liturgical celebrations, particularly the Eucharist, sacraments, and sacramentals. Evidently these considerations do not exhaust the study of liturgy. Rites are not only made up of actions, words, and material things; they are also bound to a given time and a given space. This last volume of the series is devoted to the study of the time and space components of the liturgy.

Although the Eucharist, sacraments, and sacramentals are all celebrated in time and space, there are three types of liturgical celebrations on which time and space have a direct and particular bearing. These are the Liturgy of the Hours, the liturgical feasts and seasons in the course of the year, and the dedication of churches. The first two relate to time; the third, to space. It is useful to note that while the Liturgy of the Hours is by its nature and purpose a celebration in time, the feasts of the liturgical year require the Eucharist and the Liturgy of the Hours as their normal components. The dedication of churches, on the other hand, refers to the rite of setting apart a suitable place for worship.

This volume, which opens with a preliminary notion of liturgical time and space, has three parts. The first deals with the Liturgy of the Hours. This topic is developed in the light of the early Christian tradition until the fourth century and its subsequent forms in both East and West. The Western form includes both the Roman and the non-Roman Offices. Stress is given to the constitutive elements of the Liturgy of the Hours, particularly the psalms. The reform of the Roman Office envisaged by *SC* 89–97 is given special attention because of its impact on the spiritual life of the Church's ministers and faithful. This part concludes with the theology of the Liturgy of the Hours, which is seen as a sanctification of Christian life in the context of the day and the night, but especially at the beginning and end of each day.

The second part is a study of the liturgical year, traditionally called the *anni circulus.* The term applies to the celebration of Sunday, which *SC* 106 calls the "original feast day," the feasts of the Lord and the saints, and the seasons of the year with their particular disciplines. The second part begins with a review of the development of the liturgical year during the first four centuries. This is followed by a detailed study of the Byzantine, Roman, and non-Roman Western traditions.

SC 102 teaches that the celebrations of the liturgical year center on the paschal mystery and unfold the entire mystery of Christ in the course of the year. However, in the spirit of *SC* 103, this volume reserves a special place for the cult of Mary, the Mother of God, who is "inseparably linked with her Son's saving work." Attention is also given to the cult of saints, for as *SC* 104 affirms, "By celebrating their anniversaries the Church proclaims achievement of the paschal mystery in the saints who have suffered and have been glorified with Christ." This part concludes with the theology and spirituality of the liturgical year, wherein the mystery of Christ as a saving event is made present in time, so that the faithful may lay hold of it through the word and the sacraments.

The third part of this volume addresses the question of the space reserved for the worship of the Christian community. The first and obvious consideration is the impressive rite for the dedication of the place for worship. Although this rite is not a daily occurrence and few might know that it exists, its relationship to the worshiping community as *domus ecclesiae* should not be ignored. In this connection it is necessary to examine the structure, purpose, function, and symbolism of church architecture. Liturgical architecture has its own canons based on the nature of the Church and its liturgical celebration. *SC* 128 has important things to say about this. In conclusion, the theology of liturgical space is drawn from the mutual interaction between the assembled community, which gives meaning to the place of assembly, and the place itself, which upholds and signifies the community.

This volume contains the concluding material for an integral study of the liturgy. In five volumes the Pontifical Liturgical Institute has made a serious attempt to offer the necessary elements both for the information of the reader and the formation of future liturgists. It is hoped that those who have journeyed, as it were, through the liturgical time and space represented by these five volumes will have acquired a deeper theological and spiritual appreciation of the Christian mystery that the Church celebrates and proclaims in the liturgy.

Anscar J. Chupungco, O.S.B.
Editor

Abbreviations

A	*Ambrosius*. Milan, 1925–.
AA	Vatican II, decree *Apostolicam actuositatem* (Decree on the Apostolate of the Lay People). *AAS* 58 (1966) 837–864; Abbott, 489–521; Flannery, 766–798.
AAS	*Acta Apostolicae Sedis*. Rome, 1909–.
AB	*Analecta Bollandiana: Revue critique d'hagiographie*. Brussels, 1882–.
Abbott	Walter M. Abbott, S.J., ed. *The Documents of Vatican II*. New York, 1966.
ACC	Alcuin Club Collections. London, 1899–.
ACW	Ancient Christian Writers. New York, 1946–.
A.Dmitr	A. Dmitrievskij. *Opisanie liturgiceskich rukopisej hransjascihsja v bibliotekach pravoslavnago Vostoka*, 2 vols. Kiev, 1895, 1902.
AG	Vatican II, decree *Ad gentes* (Decree on the Church's Missionary Activity). *AAS* 58 (1966) 947–990; Abbott, 584–630; Flannery, 813–856.
AGreg	Analecta Gregoriana. Rome, 1930–.
AH	Analecta hymnica. Leipzig, 1886–1922; rpt. New York, 1961.
AL	Analecta liturgica. Rome (see SA).
ALW	*Archiv für Liturgiewissenschaft*. Regensburg, 1950–. Supersedes *Jahrbuch für Liturgiewissenschaft*. Münster, 1921–1941.
Anàmnesis	*Anàmnesis: Introduzione storico-teologica alla liturgia*. Edited by the professors at the Pontificio Istituto Liturgico S. Anselmo, Rome, under the direction of S. Marsili and others. Casale Monferrato, 1974ff. Vol. 1, *La liturgia: Momento nella storia della salvezza*. 2nd ed. Genoa, 1979. Vol. 2, *La liturgia: Panorama storico generale*. Genoa, 1978. Vol. 3/1, *La liturgia: I sacramenti. Teologia e storia della celebrazione*. 3rd ed. Genoa, 1992. Vol. 3/2: *La liturgia eucaristica: Teologia e storia della celebrazione*. Genoa, 1989. Vol. 5, *Liturgia delle ore*. Genoa, 1990. Vol. 6, *L'anno liturgico: Storia, teologia e celebrazione*. 3rd ed. Genoa, 1992. Vol. 7, *I sacramentali e le benedizioni*. Genoa, 1989.
ASE	*Annali di storia dell'esegesi*. Bologna.

AST	*Analecta sacra Tarraconensia.* Barcelona, 1925–.
BA	Bibliothèque Augustinienne. Oeuvres de S. Augustin. Paris, 1949–.
BAR	S. Parenti and E. Velkovska, *L'eucologio Barberini gr. 336* (BELS 80). Rome, 1995.
BEL	Bibliotheca Ephemerides liturgicae. Rome, 1932–.
BELS	Bibliotheca Ephemerides liturgicae Subsidia. Rome, 1975–.
Bugnini	A. Bugnini, *The Reform of the Liturgy: 1948–1975.* Collegeville, Minn., 1990.
ButLitEc	*Bulletin de littérature ecclésiastique.* Toulouse, 1899–1936.
CAO	*Corpus antiphonalium officii.* Rome, 1963–1979.
CBL	Collectanea biblica Latina. Rome.
CCC	*Catechism of the Catholic Church.* Vatican City, 1994.
CCL	Corpus Christianorum. Series Latina. Turnhout, 1954–.
CCCM	Corpus Christianorum Continuatio Mediaevalis. Turnhout, 1971–.
CD	Vatican II, decree *Christus Dominus* (Decree on the Pastoral Office of Bishops in the Church. *AAS* 58 (1966) 673–701; Abbott, 396–429; Flannery, 564–590.
CL	*Communautés et liturgies.* Ottignies, Belgium.
CLLA	*Codices liturgici Latini antiquiores.* Freiburg/Schweiz. 1968.
CNRS	Centre National de Recherches Scientifiques.
Conc	*Concilium.* Paris, 1965–.
CP	Martimort, A.-G., ed. *The Church at Prayer.* 4 vols. Collegeville, Minn., 1986–1987; one vol. ed., 1992.
CPG	*Clavis Patrum Graecorum.* Turnhout, 1974–.
CPL	*Clavis Patrum Latinorum.* Steenbruge, 1995.
CSCO	Corpus scriptorum Christianorum orientalium. Louvain, 1903–.
CSEL	Corpus scriptorum ecclesiasticorum Latinorum. Vienna, 1886.
CSIC	Consejo superior de investigaciones científicas. Madrid, 1940–1941.
DACL	*Dictionnaire d'archeologie chrétienne et liturgie.* Paris, 1907–1953.
DB	*Rituale Romanum, De benedictionibus* (Kaczynski). Vatican City, 1984.
DCA	*Didascalia et Constitutiones Apostolorum.* Ed. F. Funk. Paderborn, 1905; reprint Turin, 1962.
DMP	*Directorium de Missis cum pueris* (*Directory for Masses with Children*). Vatican City, 1973. *EDIL 1*, ##3115–3169, pp. 968–980; *DOL* 276.

DOL	International Commission on English in the Liturgy, *Documents on the Liturgy 1963–1979: Conciliar, Papal and Curial Texts.* Collegeville, Minn., 1982.
DPAC	*Dizionario patristico e di antichità cristiane.* 3 vols. Casale Monferrato, 1983–1988.
DS	H. Denzinger and A. Schönmetzer, *Enchiridion symbolorum.* 32nd ed. Freiburg, 1963.
DSp	*Dictionnaire de spiritualité ascétique et mystique.* Paris, 1932–.
DSPB	*Dizionario di spiritualità biblico-patristica.* Turin, 1993.
DV	Vatican II, dogmatic constitution *Dei verbum* (Dogmatic Constitution on Divine Revelation). *AAS* 58 (1966) 817–835; Abbott, 111–128; Flannery, 750–765.
EDIL 1	*Enchiridion documentorum instaurationis liturgicae* 1 (1963–1973). Ed. R. Kaczynski. Turin, 1976.
EDIL 2	*Enchiridion documentorum instaurationis liturgicae* 2 (1973–1983). Ed. R. Kaczynski. Rome, 1988.
EO	*Ecclesia Orans.* Rome, 1984–.
EP 1961	A.-G. Martimort, ed. *L'Église en prière: Introduction à la liturgie.* Paris, 1961.
EP 1983	A.-G. Martimort, ed. *L'Église en prière,* Paris, 1983. English text: *The Church at Prayer.* 4 vols. Collegeville, Minn., 1986–1987; one vol. ed., 1992.
EphLit	*Ephemerides liturgicae.* Rome, 1887–.
EstTrin	*Estudios trinitarios.*
ET	English translation.
FCh	Fontes Christiani. Freiburg–New York, 1990–.
Flannery	Austin Flannery, O.P., ed. *Vatican Council II: The Conciliar and Post Conciliar Documents.* Collegeville, Minn., 1975; rev. ed., 1992.
FOP	Faith and Order Papers. Geneva.
FS	Festschrift.
GaF	*Missale Francorum.* Ed. L. C. Mohlberg. Rome, 1957.
GCS	Die griechischen christlichen Schriftsteller der ersten drei Jahrhunderte. Leipzig.
GE	Vatican II, declaration *Gravissimum educationis* (Declaration on Christian Education). Vatican City, 1965. Abbott, 637–651; Flannery, 725–737.
GeA	*Liber sacramentorum Engolismensis (Le sacramentaire Gélasien d'Angoulême).* Ed. P. Saint-Roch. CCL 159C. Turnout, 1987.
GeG	*Sacramentarium Gellonense.* A. Dumas, ed. *Liber Sacramentorum Gellonensis.* CCL 159. Turnhout, 1981.

GeV *Sacramentarium Gelasianum Vetus.* L. C. Mohlberg, ed. *Liber Sacramentorum Romanae Æcclesiae ordinis anni circuli.* Rome, 1960.

GILH General Instruction of the Liturgy of the Hours *(Institutio generalis Liturgiae Horarum).* Vatican City, 1971. *DOL* 426.

GIRM General Instruction of the Roman Missal (*Institutio generalis Missalis Romani).* 4th ed. Vatican City, 1969, 1975. *DOL* 208.

GLNT *Grande lessico del nuovo testamento.*

GrH *Sacramentarium Gregorianum Hadrianum.*

GrS *Sacramentarium Gregorianum Supplementum.*

GS Vatican II, constitution *Gaudium et spes* (Pastoral Constitution on the Church in the Modern World). *AAS* 58 (1966) 1025–1120; Abbott, 199–308; Flannery, 903–1001.

HBS Henry Bradshaw Society. London, 1891–.

HDG *Handbuch der Dogmengeschichte.*

HGK *Handbuch der Kirchengeschichte.*

HJ *Heythrop Journal.* Oxford, 1960–.

HS *Hispania sacra.* Madrid, 1948–.

IEHE *Instituto español de historia eclesiástica.* Rome.

IGLH *Institutio generalis liturgia Horarum* (General Instruction of the Liturgy of the Hours). Vatican City, 1971. DOL 426.

IGMR *Institutio generalis Missalis Romani* (General Instruction of the Roman Missal). Vatican City, 1969, 1975. *EDIL* 1, ##1381–1736, pp. 469–546; DOL 208.

Irén *Irénikon.* Chevetogne, 1926–.

JAC *Jahrbuch für Antike und Christentum.* Münster, 1958–.

JLw *Jahrbuch für Liturgiewissenschaft.* Münster, 1921–1941, 1973–1979.

JThS *Journal of Theological Studies.* London, 1900–1905; Oxford, 1906–1949; n.s., Oxford, 1950–.

Jungmann J. A. Jungmann, *Missarum sollemnia.* 2 vols. Casale Monferrato, 1963. English translation: *The Mass of the Roman Rite: Its Origins and Development.* Trans. F. Brunner. Christian Classics. Westminster, Md., 1986. Originally published New York, 1951–1955.

KB *Katechetische Blätter.* Munich, 1875–.

Lat *Lateranum.* Rome, 1919–.

LeV *Lumière et vie.* Lyon, 1951–.

LG Vatican II, dogmatic constitution *Lumen gentium* (Dogmatic Constitution on the Church). *AAS* 57 (1965) 5–71; Abbott, 14–96; Flannery, 350–423.

Lit *Liturgia.* Rome, n.s., 1967ff.

LJ	*Liturgisches Jahrbuch.* Münster, 1951–.
LL	A. Nocent, "I libri liturgici." *Anàmnesis* 2: *La liturgia: Panorama storico generale.*
LO	Lex Orandi. Paris, 1944–.
LQF	Liturgie- (until 1957: geschichtliche) wissenschaftliche Quellen und Forschungen. Münster, 1909–1940; 1957–.
LThK	*Lexikon für Theologie und Kirche.* Freiburg, 1957–1965.
LV	*Lumen vitae.* Brussels, 1946–.
MA1981	*Missale Ambrosianum.* Iuxta ritum sanctae Ecclesiae Mediolanensis ex decreto Sacrosancti Oecumenici Concilii Vaticani II instauratum. Milan, 1981; new ed. 1990.
Mansi	J. D. Mansi, *Sacrorum conciliorum nova et amplissima collectio.* 31 vols. Florence–Venice, 1757–1798; reprinted and continued by L. Petit and J. B. Martin, 53 vols. in 60. Paris, 1889–1927; reprinted Graz, 1960–.
MD	*La Maison-Dieu.* Paris, 1945–.
MEL	Monumenta Ecclesiae liturgica. Paris, 1890–1912.
MelScRel	*Mélanges de science religieuse.* Lille, 1944–.
MGH	Monumenta Germaniae historica. Berlin, 1826.
MHS	Monumenta Hispaniae sacra. Madrid, 1946–.
ML	C. Vogel, *Medieval Liturgy: An Introduction to the Sources.* Washington, 1986.
MR1570	*Missale Romanum* ex decreto Sacrosancti Concilii Tridentini restitutum Pii V Pont. Max. iussu editum (various editions; here *Missale Romanum* ex decreto Sacrosancti Concilii Tridentini restitutum Summorum Pontificum cura recognitum. Editio XIX iuxta typicam. Turin–Rome, 1961).
MR1962	*Missale Romanum* ex decreto Sacrosancti Concilii Tridentini restitutum Summorum Pontificum cura recognitum. Editio prima iuxta typicam. Vatican City, 1962.
MR1970	*Missale Romanum* ex decreto Sacrosancti Oecumenici Concilii Vaticani II instauratum auctoritate Pauli PP. VI promulgatum. Editio typica.Vatican City, 1970.
MR1975	*Missale Romanum* ex decreto Sacrosancti Oecumenici Concilii Vaticani II instauratum auctoritate Pauli Pp. VI promulgatum. Editio typica. Vatican City, 1970; 2nd editio typica, 1975. English text: *The Sacramentary.* Trans. International Committee on English in the Liturgy. Collegeville, Minn., 1973, 1985.
MS	*Medieval Studies.* Toronto–London, 1938–.
MuS	*Musicam sacram. EDIL 1,* ##733–801, pp. 275–291; *DOL* 508.
NBA	Nuova biblioteca Agostiniana. Rome.

NDL	*Nuovo dizionario di liturgia.* Rome, 1984.
NDM	*Nuovo dizionario di mariologia.* Cinisello Balsamo, Milan, 1985.
NHL	*Neues Handbuch der Literaturwissenschaft.* Frankfurt-am-Main.
Not	*Notitiae.* Vatican City, 1965–.
NRT	*Nouvelle revue théologique.* Louvain, 1869–.
OB	*Rituale Romanum, Ordo benedictionum.* Vatican City, 1984.
OBP	*Rituale Romanum, Ordo baptismi parvulorum.* Vatican City, 1969, 1973.
OC	*Ordo confirmationis.* Vatican City, 1971.
OCA	Orientalia christiana analecta. Rome, 1935–.
OCM	*Rituale Romanum, Ordo celebrandi matrimonium.* Vatican City, 1969.
OCP	*Orientalia christiana periodica.* Rome, 1935–.
OCV	*Ordo consecrationis virginum.* Vatican City, 1970.
ODEA	*Pontificale Romanum, Ordo dedicationis ecclesiae et altaris.* Vatican City, 1977.
OE	Vatican II, decree *Orientalium Ecclesiarum* (Decree on the Catholic Eastern Churches). *AAS* 57 (1965) 76–89; Abbott, 373–386; Flannery, 441–451.
Oe	*Rituale Romanum, Ordo exsequiarum.* Vatican City, 1969.
OICA	*Rituale Romanum, Ordo initiationis christianae adultorum.* Vatican City, 1972; rev. ed. 1974.
OKS	*Ostkirchliche Studien.* Würzburg, 1952–.
OLM	*Ordo lectionum Missae.* Editio typica, Vatican City, 1969. 2nd editio typica, Vatican City, 1981. *EDIL* 2, ##4057–4181, pp. 337–370; English text: *Lectionary for Mass.* Collegeville, Minn., 1970, 1981, 1998.
OM	Order of Mass *(Ordo Missae).* Vatican City, 1969.
OP	*Rituale Romanum, Ordo paenitentiae.* Vatican City, 1974.
OPR	*Rituale Romanum, Ordo professionis religiosae.* Vatican City, 1970; rev. ed. 1975.
OR	*Ordines Romani.* In M. Andrieu, ed. *Les Ordines romani du haut moyen âge* Spicilegium sacrum Lovaniense 11, 23, 24, 28, 29. Louvain, 1931–1961.
OS	*L'Orient syrien.* Paris, 1956–1967.
OSA	Opera Sancti Augustini.
OUI	*Rituale Romanum, Ordo unctionis infirmorum.* Vatican City, 1972.
PatOr	*Patrologia orientalis.* Paris, 1904–; Turnhout, 1969–.
PCS	*Pastoral Care of the Sick: Rites of Anointing and Viaticum.* In *The Rites of the Catholic Church.* New York, 1983[2].

PDOC	*Petit dictionnaire de l'Orient chrétien.*
PG	J. P. Migne, Patrologia cursus completus: Series Graeca. Paris, 1857–1866.
PGD	*Pontificale Guglielmi Durandi.* In M. Andrieu, ed. *Le Pontifical romain au moyen âge* III: *Le Pontifical de Guillaume Durand.* Vatican City, 1940.
Ph	*Phase: Revista de pastoral liturgica.* Barcelona, 1961–.
PL	J. P. Migne, Patrologia cursus completus: Series Latina. Paris, 1844–1855.
PO	Vatican II, *Presbyterorum ordinis* (Decree on the Ministry and Life of Priests). *AAS* 58 (1966) 990–1024; Abbott, 532–576; Flannery, 863–902.
PR	*Pontificale Romanum.* In M. Andrieu, ed. *Le Pontifical romain au moyen âge* I: *Le Pontifical Romain du XIIe siècle.* ST 86. Vatican City, 1939; reprint 1984.
PRG	*Pontificale Romano-Germanicum.* In C. Vogel and R. Elze, eds. *Le Pontifical romano-germanique du Xe siècle.* Vatican City, 1963.
QL	*Questions liturgiques.* Louvain, 1910–.
QLP	*Les questions liturgiques et paroissiales.* Louvain, 1919–1969.
RAC	*Reallexikon für Antike und Christentum.* Stuttgart, 1950–.
RB	Rule of Benedict *(Regula Benedicti).*
RBib	*Revue biblique.* Paris, 1892–.
RBén	*Revue bénédictine.* Maredsous, 1884–.
RCT	*Revista catalana de teología.* Barcelona, 1976–.
RED	Rerum ecclesiasticarum documenta. Rome, 1954.
RET	*Revista Española de teología.* Madrid, 1940–.
Rev Lit Monastique	*Revue de liturgie e monastique.* Maredsous, 1911–1940.
REB	*Revue des Etudes Byzantines.* Paris, 1943.
RG	*Revue grégorienne.* Paris, 1911–.
RHE	*Revue d'histoire ecclésiastique.* Louvain, 1900–.
Righetti	*Manuale di storia liturgica.* Vol. 1 (2nd ed., 1950); vol. 2 (2nd ed., 1955); vol. 3 (1949); vol. 4 (1953). Milan.
RL	*Rivista liturgica.* Praglia-Finalpia, 1914–.
RM	Rule of the Master *(Regula Magistri).*
RPL	*Rivista di pastorale liturgica.* Brescia, 1963.
RSPT	*Revue des sciences philosophiques et théologiques.* Paris, 1907–.
RSR	*Recherches de science religieuse.* Paris, 1910–.
RTAM	*Recherches de théologie ancienne et médiévale.* Louvain.
SA	Studia Anselmiana. Rome, 1933–.
SAEMO	*Sancti Ambrosii Episcopi Mediolanensis Opera.*

SC	Vatican II, constitution *Sacrosanctum concilium* (Constitution on the Sacred Liturgy). *AAS* 56 (1964) 97–138; Abbott, 137–78; Flannery, 1–36.
SCA	Studies in Christian Antiquity. Washington, 1941–.
ScC	*Scuola cattolica.* Milan, 1873–.
SCh	Sources chrétiennes. Paris, 1941–.
SE	*Sacris erudiri.* Steenbruge, 1948–.
SF	Spicilegium Friburgense. Fribourg, 1957.
SFS	Spicilegii Friburgensis Subsidia.
SL	*Studia liturgica.* Rotterdam, 1962.
ST	Studi e testi. Vatican City, 1900–.
StudPad	*Studia patavina.* Padua, 1954.
TDNT	*Theological Dictionary of the New Testament.* Grand Rapids, Mich., 1964–1976.
ThRv	*Theologische Revue.* Münster, 1902–.
ThS	*Theological Studies.* Woodstock, 1940–.
TQ	*Theologische Quartalschrift.* Tübingen, 1819–.
TRE	*Theologische Realenzyklopädie.* Berlin, 1947–.
TS	*Typologie des sources du moyen âge occidental.*
TTZ	*Trierer theologische Zeitschrift.* Trier, 1945–.
TU	Texte und Untersuchungen zur Geschichte der altchristlichen Literatur. Berlin, 1882–.
TuA	Texte und Arbeite. Beuron, 1917–.
UR	Vatican II, decree *Unitatis redintegratio* (Decree on Ecumenism). *AAS* 57 (1965) 90–112; Abbott, 341–366; Flannery, 452–470.
VC	*Vigiliae Christianae.* Amsterdam, 1947–.
Ve	*Sacramentarium Veronense.*
ViSpi	*Vie spirituelle.* Paris, 1947–.
Wor	*Worship.* Collegeville, Minn., 1951–. Formerly *Orate Fratres,* 1926–1951.
WUNT	Wissenschaftliche Untersuchungen zum Neuen Testament. Tübingen, 1950.
ZAW	*Zeitschrift für Alttestamentliche Wissenschaft.* Berlin, 1881–.
ZKTh	*Zeitschrift für katholische Theologie.* Vienna and Innsbruck, 1877–.
ZRGRA	*Zeitschrift der Savigny-Stiftung für Rechtsgeschichte (Romantische Abteilung).* Weimar.

Anscar J. Chupungco, O.S.B.

Liturgical Time and Space

1. THEOLOGICAL PREMISE

By the mystery of the incarnation God broke into cosmic time and human history; God dwelt as one of us in the cosmic and human space. Jesus, the Word made flesh, was born in the little town of Bethlehem in Judea in the days of King Herod (Matt 2:1). He spent his early years in the town of Nazareth, where he was subject to his parents (Luke 2:51). With them he celebrated the Jewish festivals (see Luke 2:41-42). He roamed the streets of cities and the countryside of Palestine, climbed its hills and mountains, crossed its lake.

The Gospels, when narrating Christ's mission, inform us of the circumstances, sometimes of the day and hour, when he did or said something. He praised the God of his ancestors, preached, forgave sinners, defended the oppressed, healed the sick, and raised the dead to life at specific times and places. When the hour came for him to complete his messianic work of preaching and healing, he delivered himself to the cross on a Friday, at around three o'clock in the afternoon, on a hill called Golgotha (see Matt 27:46; John 19:31). His disciples would later announce that he had risen from the dead and had appeared to the women disciples in the early morning of the first day of the week (Mark 16:2). To crown his saving work, he sent the Holy Spirit to the disciples on the Jewish day of Pentecost at nine o'clock in the morning (Acts 2:1, 15). As *AG* 10 teaches, "Christ by his incarnation committed himself to the particular social and cultural circumstances of the people among whom he lived."

In the person of Christ, God lived and accomplished human salvation in time and space. In Christianity time and space are the stage where God and humankind meet each other. That is why Christianity is a historical religion that moves in a spiral, different from the closed cycles of mythological religions. We know for certain, though always in the light of faith, that God entered the sphere of human history. This certainty allows us to respond to him, equally in faith, through acts that recall his wonders and express our praise and thanksgiving.

God's action of breaking into time and space is essential to our understanding of the liturgy. Our liturgical anamnesis deals with God's interventions in human history, centering on Christ's own mission. Our Eucharist brings us back to the night before he died, when he took bread. Our baptism recalls Christ's burial and resurrection. Our prayers in the course of day and night remind us of Christ's own prayer to God. Our liturgical feasts unfold the different aspects of Christ's life and mission. Our places of worship tell us that God has made us his place of dwelling.

The epiclesis, on the other hand, calls upon God to be present in our world to save and heal it, as once he did in times past. When we invoke God to send us the Holy Spirit, we profess that every day is a day of Pentecost. Lastly, our participation in the liturgy brings us face to face with the *mirabilia Dei* as these are recorded for us in Scripture; now we become partakers of the divine mystery as this is made present to us in the liturgical rites. All our encounters with God in worship must take place in time and space, because it was in time and space that God proclaimed his word and offered his human life in sacrifice.

With this in mind we are able to understand the deeper implications of *SC* 7, when it says that "the liturgy . . . is rightly seen as an exercise of the priestly office of Jesus Christ." Through the ministry of the Church and in sacramental or liturgical form, Christ continues the priestly work he accomplished during his lifetime on earth. This work, being priestly, focuses on his sacrifice on the cross and on its culmination, which is the bestowal of the Holy Spirit, or in short, on the paschal mystery and the mystery of Pentecost. However, Christ's priestly work is the crowning of his messianic mission. As Messiah he first preached, especially to the poor, healed the sick, and freed those enslaved by evil powers, and only then as priest did he offer to God a perfect worship by giving up his life in sacrifice for all. All these actions of Christ, both messianic and priestly, took place in history. The Church now celebrates them "in mystery" as she performs their rites in determined times and places.

The liturgy celebrates everything that Christ has said and done for our sake. This explains why the liturgy is not confined to the Eucharist, the sacraments, and the sacramentals. The liturgy also consists of other celebrations in time and space whereby the Church recalls Christ's so many other words, prayers, and miracles. In the words of Pope Leo the Great, "What was visible in Christ passed on to the sacraments of the Church" (*Sermo* 74, 2). Nevertheless, every liturgical celebration is ultimately centered on the paschal mystery; every liturgical prayer is ultimately joined up with the worship of Christ on the cross; every liturgical feast ultimately commemorates Christ's death and resurrection; and every liturgical space reminds us ultimately of Christ's human body, which hung on the cross, as well as of the Cenacle, the hill of Calvary, the tomb, and the places where he appeared to his disciples after the resurrection.[1] This is so because all the messianic activities of Christ found their completion and perfection in his paschal mystery.

Because of Christ's incarnation, time is no longer merely cosmic and historical; it has acquired a soteriological dimension. For Christians, time is no longer the simple succession of day, night, week, month, and season of the year (κρόνος). Time has become the privileged moment in which, through the liturgy, Christians experience the presence and saving power of Christ's mystery (καιρός).[2] The "time of Christ," that is, the time he spent for his messianic and priestly activity, gave birth to the "time of the Church," that is, to the liturgical time that embodies the "time of Christ."[3] That is why, when we celebrate the liturgy, we are able to experience the presence and power of Christ's salvation in the here-and-now of the "time of the Church." To this the liturgy often refers when it solemnly proclaims *hodie,* "today."

Liturgical time is thus the "time of Christ," which extends itself into the "time of the Church" as it engages in daily prayer and feasting. Since the "time of Christ" signifies his work as Messiah and priest, the "time of the Church" expresses the continuing concerns of Christ for his people. Daily prayer and liturgical feasts cannot be divorced from the mission Christ entrusted to the Church: they are the ecclesial forms expressing not only his death and resurrection but also his work of preaching, healing, and liberation. Liturgical time does not alienate

[1] S. Marsili, "La teologia della Liturgia nel Vaticano II," *Anàmnesis* 1:96–100.

[2] Angelini applies this concept to the monastic Liturgy of the Hours: "La liturgia delle ore: tra 'Chronos' e 'Kairos' nella 'figura' della esperienza monastica," in *Liturgia delle ore: Tempo e rito* (Rome, 1994) 141–180.

[3] Marsili, "La teologia della Liturgia nel Vaticano II," 90–91.

the Church from historical time; rather it urges her, in imitation of the incarnate Word, to be profoundly involved in what goes on in history and to transform the κρόνος of human misery into the καιρός of divine grace.

In a similar way, because of the incarnation, space and environment take on a soteriological meaning when they are used by Christians as places of encounter with God in worship. The building which is called "house-church" *(domus Ecclesiae)* becomes the figure of that community called Church, the ἐκκλησία, which God "assembled out of darkness into his marvelous light" (1 Pet 2:9). This community is made up of "living stones" with which the spiritual house is built as a holy priesthood offering up spiritual sacrifices to God (see 1 Pet 2:5). *LG* 6 points out that this community is an edifice that has many names to describe it: "the house of God in which his family dwells; the household of God in the Spirit (Eph 2:19, 22); the dwelling-place of God among people (Rev 21:3); and, especially, the holy temple." *LG* 6 continues to explain that "this temple [is] symbolized in places of worship built out of stone." One can rephrase this by saying, "built out of any material with which people construct their houses." In the thinking of *LG* 6, liturgical space is not only a place for assembly but also the image of the worshiping community that God gathered through the sacrament of water and the Spirit.

Since the Body of Christ is the true temple where God dwells in the Spirit, our sole justification for building churches and other places of worship is that the community assembled in them expresses the presence of Christ among the two or three gathered together in his name (Matt 18:20).[4] In this sense the community gathered in worship is the "extension" and presence of Christ's glorified body; it is the visible form of Christ who is the temple of God. The liturgical assembly is thus the liturgical "space" par excellence. Wherever it gathers in worship, there is the place where God encounters his people. This is one implication of Christ's statement regarding the worship of God "in Spirit and in truth" (John 4:23-24).

The theology of liturgical space allows us to connect places of worship with the earthly places visited by Christ. Thus the house-church

[4] C. Valenziano: *Architetti di chiese* (Palermo, 1995 68–69; see J. Boguniowski, *Domus Ecclesiae: Der Ort der Eucharistiefeier in den ersten Jahrhunderten* (Rome, 1986); N. Duval, "Le space liturgique dans les églises paléochrétiennes," *MD* 193 (1993) 7–29.

evokes the houses, streets, hilltops, fields, desert places, and lakesides where Christ was present to his disciples or where they experienced his presence. As he was present there, so he is present now in our assembly. Liturgical space always brings us back to those places where the incarnate Word walked among us, but especially to the three places where he ate his final meal with his disciples, where he slept the sleep of death, and where he rested for three days before the resurrection. Christ's death, burial, and resurrection are the object of Eucharistic and baptismal anamnesis. No wonder, then, that in the tradition of the Church the two principal liturgical spaces are the house-church for the Eucharist and the baptistery.

2. THE CELEBRATIONS IN TIME AND SPACE

When we speak of liturgical time and space, we normally refer to the celebration of the Liturgy of the Hours, to the liturgical days, feasts, and seasons of the year, to church architecture, and to liturgical environment and furnishings. However, we need to take an important premise into consideration. The Eucharist, sacraments, and sacramentals are also celebrated in time and space. On the other hand, the Liturgy of the Hours and the liturgical year are always celebrated with reference to the Eucharist and the sacraments, while the liturgical space is dedicated to the celebration of the Eucharist, the sacraments, and the Liturgy of the Hours.

a) The first type of celebration in time is the Liturgy of the Hours.[5] The shift from the appellation "Divine Office" to "Liturgy of the Hours" indicates the will of the Church to restore the time dimension of this prayer. *SC* 84 states that "the divine office, in keeping with ancient Christian tradition, is so devised that the whole course of the day and night is made holy by the praises of God." According to *SC* 83, by his incarnation Christ the high priest introduced into our time the timeless liturgy of the halls of heaven. Seated at the right hand of God, Christ continues to intercede for us as he did on the cross. One earthly form of that heavenly liturgy is the Divine Office, whereby

[5] Congregation for Divine Worship, *General Instruction of the Liturgy of the Hours* (Vatican City, 1971), in *Documents on the Liturgy 1963–1979: Conciliar, Papal, and Curial Texts* (Collegeville, Minn., 1982) pp. 1091–1140; E. Bettencourt: "The Reformed Divine Office, A Font of Spiritual Life," *The Liturgy of Vatican II* (Chicago, 1966) 2:188–208; A.-G. Martimort, "The Liturgy of the Hours," *The Church at Prayer* (Collegeville, Minn., 1986) 4:153–275.

Christ "continues his priestly work through his Church" (*SC* 83). In this sense the Liturgy of the Hours should be considered a principal ecclesial form of Christ's priestly office. It is the counterpart in time of Christ's "singing his divine song of praise" in eternity. As the General Instruction of the Liturgy of the Hours (GILH) explains: "When the Church offers praise to God in the Liturgy of the Hours, it unites itself with that hymn of praise sung throughout all ages in the halls of heaven; it also receives a foretaste of the song of praise in heaven" (no. 16).

Basically the Liturgy of the Hours is the Church's prayer to and about Christ; it is an *opus operantis Ecclesiae,* composed and performed by the Church. But because of the Church's union with Christ, the Head, he claims the Church's prayer as his own, so that when the Church sings the Liturgy of the Hours, he himself is wholly engaged before God. That is why *SC* 84 affirms that "it is the very prayer which Christ himself together with his Body addresses to the Father." The General Instruction gives this explanation: "In the liturgy of the hours the Church exercises the priestly office of its Head and offers to God 'without ceasing' a sacrifice of praise, that is, a tribute of lips acknowledging his name" (no. 15). In synthesis, we may say that the Liturgy of the Hours recalls and proclaims the priestly work of Christ, that is, his death and resurrection. At the same time, it embodies his priestly prayer then on the cross and now at the right hand of God for the salvation of the world.

b) The second type of celebration in time is the liturgical year. According to *SC* 102, "Holy Mother Church believes that it is for her to celebrate the saving work of her divine Spouse in a sacred commemoration on certain days throughout the course of the year." While the Divine Office refers to the hours of the day, the liturgical year is concerned with days, weeks, and seasons of the year.[6] It is useful to note that the liturgical year is not merely the sum total of liturgical feasts, nor is it merely a functional distribution of feasts in the course of the year. Rather, it is the extension in the "time of the Church" of the "time of Christ," which, by his incarnation, was inserted into the cosmic and historical time. Thus the cosmic time, which is regulated by nature's cycles and seasons, and the historical time, wherein recorded events

[6] M. Augé, "Teologia dell'anno liturgico," *Anàmnesis* 6:13–21; for the concept of sacred time, see: G. Van der Leeuw, *Religion in Essence and Manifestation* (New York, 1963); A. Rizzi, "Categorie culturali odierne nell'interpretazione del tempo," *L'Anno liturgico* (Casale Monferrato, 1983) 11–22.

take place, become the locus of God's saving interventions. The succession of days and nights, of weeks and months, and of the various seasons of the year, which the ancient Greeks called κρόνος, became the Christian καιρός.

When God became incarnate, God broke into our time, our cosmic time, our historical time. God's saving acts in the person of Jesus Christ took place in time. We might say that they could be "calendared" or recorded because they happened in the course of time, in a given year, in a given month, in a given week, on a given day or night, at a given hour. That is why, every year is A.D.—*Anno Domini,* "in the year of the Lord." At every Easter Vigil the celebrant traces on the candle the sign of the cross, the Greek letters A and Ω and the current year, as he declares: "Christ yesterday and today, the beginning and the end, alpha and omega, all time belongs to him and all ages." These words are a profession of faith that Christ is the key to the Christian understanding of time.

The passion and death of Christ are recorded in cosmic and historical time. Tradition has it that he suffered and died during the week when the Jews celebrated their Passover in memory of the historical Exodus. Furthermore, we are informed that it happened at the cosmic occurrence of the equinox of spring and when it was full moon. The Synoptic Gospels add that he died at around three o'clock Friday afternoon. In short, history and cosmos merged in order to provide a backdrop for Christ's celebration of the paschal mystery.[7]

Though the liturgical year is grafted onto the cosmic year, it follows a peculiar calendar year. It has its own system of determining the beginning and end of the year; of reckoning the paschal month, which consists of thirty-five days from March 22 to April 25; of considering the fifty days of Easter as if they were all one day; of declaring on Sunday that Christ ascended to heaven on this fortieth day, when in reality it is the forty-third day; and of extending Sunday from the afternoon of the previous day to the midnight of the following day.

The Constitution on the Sacred Liturgy sums up the essential elements of the liturgical year: "Once each week, on the day which [the Church] has called the Lord's Day, she keeps the memory of the Lord's resurrection. She also celebrates it once every year, together with his blessed passion, at Easter, that most solemn of all feasts. In

[7] A. Chupungco, *Shaping the Easter Feast* (Washington, 1992).

the course of the year, moreover, she unfolds the whole mystery of Christ from the incarnation and nativity to the ascension, to Pentecost and the expectation of the blessed hope of the coming of the Lord" (no. 102). In this we should include the other articles of the Constitution on the Liturgy that deal with the yearly celebrations of Mary, the saints, and the seasons of the liturgical year.

In conclusion, we may say that the celebrations of liturgical days, feasts, and seasons render the "time of Christ" present and accessible to the people of our time. As *SC* 102 aptly puts it, "Recalling thus the mysteries of redemption, [the Church] opens up to the faithful the riches of her Lord's powers and merits, so that these are in some way made present for all time; the faithful lay hold of them and are filled with saving grace."

c) The celebrations connected with liturgical space are the dedication of a church and an altar and the rites for the blessing of a baptistery, ambo, tabernacle, and confessional room.[8] These are spaces reserved for liturgical celebrations. Their dedication or blessing sets them apart as places where God encounters his people through the sacraments and the preaching of the word. *SC* 128 desires that regulations on the construction of such places be updated: "These laws refer especially to the worthy and well-planned construction of sacred buildings, the shape and construction of altars, the nobility, placing, and security of the Eucharistic tabernacle, the suitability and dignity of the baptistery, the proper ordering of sacred images, and the scheme of decoration and embellishment."

According to the decree *Dedicationis ecclesiae,* "the rite for the dedication of a church and an altar is rightly considered to be among the most solemn of liturgical services."[9] And rightly so, since the house-church "stands as a special kind of image of the Church itself, which is God's temple built from living stones."[10] This explains why liturgical tradition regards the dedication of a church as a feast of the Church

[8] *Rite of Dedication of a Church and an Altar* (Vatican City, 1977); *De benedictionibus* (Vatican City, 1985) 322–357.

[9] Sacred Congregation of Divine Worship, decree *Dedicationis ecclesiae: Not* 13 (1977) 364.

[10] Ibid. GIRM, no. 253, requires that "churches and other places of worship should be suited to celebrating the liturgy and to ensuring the active participation of the faithful. Further, the places and requisites for worship should be truly worthy and beautiful, signs and symbols of heavenly realities."

with the rank of a solemnity. The record of the dedication mentions the day, month, and year, the name of the bishop who celebrated the rite, and the titular of the church. An inscription in a suitable location in the church should be placed stating these details. The record and inscription are not just for historical or archival purposes; they are a solemn declaration that on a given day, month, and year a particular space was transformed into a house-church, "in which the Christian community gathers to hear the word of God, to pray together, to receive the sacraments, and to celebrate the Eucharist."[11]

In a sense, the holy places, especially the area of the Anastasis in Jerusalem, where Christ celebrated his mysteries, are evoked by every house-church and place of worship. For it was in those places that the incarnate Word accomplished what he now renews in our midst. This probably explains why in the Middle Ages churches far away from the Holy Land tried to imitate those places, like the holy sepulcher, the Martyrium, and the Cenacle, and named their lateral or inside chapels after them."[12]

Besides the house-church, there are other spaces used for the liturgy. Prominent among them is the baptistery, whether built inside or outside the church, because of its connection with the sacrament of baptism."[13] The baptistery with its font reminds us of that holy place which is Christ's own sepulcher. That is why baptism is the sacrament whereby "we are buried with him into death" (Rom 6:4). The tradition of baptism by immersion heightens the symbolism of entering into the tomb with Christ and rising to a new life with him. Thus the baptistery stands out as a liturgical space where the paschal mystery takes effect in the life of the baptized. From the seventh to the thirteenth century, it was the practice at the Lateran Basilica during the octave of Easter to hold a procession at Vespers to the baptistery and to the chapel of the Holy Cross, named *Ad Sanctum Andream.* It gave expression to a desire to visit the holy places in Jerusalem, which are represented by the baptistery and the chapel of the Holy Cross.[14]

[11] Introduction, *Rite of Dedication of a Church,* chap. 2, no. 1.

[12] C. Valenziano: "Mimesis anamnesis: Spazio-temporale per il triduo pasquale," in *La celebrazione del triduo pasquale: Anamnesis e Mimesis,* SA 102 (Rome, 1990) 13–54.

[13] *De benedictionibus,* no. 832.

[14] See A. Chupungco, "Anamnesis and Mimesis in the Celebration of Easter Sunday," in *La celebrazione del triduo pasquale: Anamnesis e Mimesis,* 259–271.

CONCLUSION

The mystery of the incarnation is the basis for the theology of liturgical time and space. The incarnate Word broke into human time and space and made them the locus of his saving work. Today he continues to accomplish it in times and places the Church has dedicated to the celebration of the liturgy. Liturgical time and space are "sacraments" recalling and making the messianic and priestly office of Christ present in our midst.

Bibliography

Adam, A. *The Liturgical Year* (New York, 1981).

Augé, M. "Teologia dell'anno liturgico." In *Anàmnesis* 6:11–34.

Bonaccorso, G. *La liturgia: celebrazione del mistero* (Padua, 1996).

Bouyer, L. *Liturgy and Architecture* (Notre Dame, Ind., 1967).

de Reynal, D. *Théologie de la Liturgie des heures* (Paris, 1978).

Taft, R. *The Liturgy of the Hours in East and West: The Origins of the Divine Office and Its Meaning for Today* (Collegeville, Minn., 1986).

Talley, T. *The Origins of the Liturgical Year* (New York, 1986).

Terrin, A. "Il rito come scansione del tempo: Per una teoria del rito come 'indugio simbolico.'" In *Liturgia delle ore: Tempo e rito* (Rome, 1994) 15–44.

Valenziano, C. *Architetti di Chiese* (Palermo, 1995).

White, J., and S. White. *Church Architecture* (Nashville, 1988).

Part I

Liturgy of the Hours

Rubén M. Leikam, O.S.B.

1

The Liturgy of the Hours in the First Four Centuries

INTRODUCTION

The Liturgy of the Hours forms part of a living complex that we call "liturgy." The Eucharist, the other sacraments and sacramentals, and the liturgical year are also included in this complex. By its very nature, the Liturgy of the Hours has the special role of guiding Christians to a progressive participation in the saving mystery of Christ through prayer. It is original in that it is a fully Christian celebration based on the New Testament. In it, as in many other liturgical celebrations, the mystery of Christ is made real. This liturgy has a structure of *hourly prayer,* created and organized so that by sanctifying the whole day, the liturgy becomes an expression of the prayer of each participant and, above all, of the entire ecclesial community. The importance of the Liturgy of the Hours in the life of the Church lies in the fact that "public and common prayer by the people of God is rightly considered to be among the primary duties of the Church" (*GILH* 1). The Liturgy of the Hours is essentially prayer organized by the Church but always carried out through the personal prayers that each participant offers in the celebration.

I. BIBLICAL PRECEDENTS

Prayer is a universal phenomenon in world religions. There is no religion in any level of culture that does not recognize the phenomenon of prayer. The custom of praying at certain times of the day, especially in the morning and afternoon, goes way beyond the history of the religion of Israel and Christianity. It can be verified that similar acts took place in other cultures of the past and present. By looking at prayer externally, it can also be considered simply an observance of natural religion.

In this chapter we will focus on Christian prayer, which developed in the wake of the prayers of the Jewish people. By studying the *ideological presumptions* of Christian liturgical prayer, the *objective* of prayer, and the *manner* in which prayer is carried out, we see that all these aspects indicate a *tradition.* The origins of this tradition certainly come from before the time of Jesus Christ, who "came from a people who knew how to pray."[1] The origin of the Liturgy of the Hours lies in a spiritual ideal that is proposed to us in the New Testament: incessant prayer. The Church hoped to accomplish this ideal by establishing specific times of prayer in order to give a kind of rhythm to the days. This rhythm was developed through the spiritual currents of the first centuries and was influenced by Jewish practices, but above all it evolved according to the teaching and example of Jesus and the apostolic community.

1. From Jewish Prayer to Christian Prayer[2]

The primitive Christian community began its path in history without having its own structure of prayer or a heritage of texts that could be considered a concrete expression of the preaching and teaching of Jesus. This gap was filled by the first Christian communities, which looked deeper into the teachings and example of Jesus Christ in the context of the Hebrew tradition, a tradition in which Jesus himself had built his relationship with the Father through prayer. Jesus was born and lived among people who had a long and deep experience of prayer. Many of the formal elements—the psalms, for example—and content of the prayers of Jesus and the first Christians come from the human and religious environment of these people.

[1] J. Jeremias, *The Prayers of Jesus,* Studies in Biblical Theology, 2nd series, no. 6 (London, 1967) 66.

[2] For this part we have followed the excellent work of R. De Zan, "Il tempo della preghiera nel Nuovo Testamento," *Liturgia delle Ore: Tempo e rito,* Atti della XXII Settimana di Studio dell'Associazione Professori di Liturgia, Susa (TO), August 29–September 3, 1993 (Rome, 1994) 89–106; J. Cassien and B. Botte, eds., *La prière des heures,* Semaine d'Etudes Liturgiques de Saint-Serge 1961, LO 35 (Paris, 1963), which contains the following articles on this subject: B. Cassien, "La prière dans le Nouveau Testament," J. Jeremias, "La prière quotidienne dans la vie du Seigneur et dans l'Eglise primitive," 43–58; and K. Hruby, "Les heures de prière dans le judaïsme à l'époque de Jésus," 59–84.

The Gospels demonstrate an awareness of the Jewish influence on Christian prayer. The great teacher of prayer, St. Luke, begins his Gospel with a description of a liturgy of prayer that developed in the Temple of Jerusalem at the time when the angel of the Lord appeared to Zechariah (see Luke 1:8-23); he concludes with a specific reference to Jesus' disciples continuing to go to the Temple to pray after the ascension of the Lord (Luke 24:52-53). Also, in Acts 3:1-11, Luke says that John and Peter used to go to the Temple for the evening prayer. However, references to the first Christians' participation in the Temple prayers become successively less frequent and finally disappear completely (see Acts 2:46).

We will now focus on *prayer* as a *ritual* moment at *set times*. The three areas of testimony are: (1) the ritual Jewish prayer in Jesus' time; (2) the experience and teachings of Jesus; (3) the ritual prayer of the believing community (of the Church of Jerusalem and the Church of Paul). The sources we have used include the biblical text and the rabbinic writings. The *Berakot,* either that of the Mishnah or the corresponding *Tosefta,* is particularly useful.

a) Ritual Jewish prayer in the time of Christ

The most complete known documentation about the practice of prayer in Jesus' time is found in the work on the blessings *(berakot)* of the Mishnah, a rabbinic code compiled between the second and third centuries of the Christian era.

We know of five kinds of prayers in Jesus' time that can be considered "ritual," given that they were officially prescribed. These are the three daily prayers, the prayer for feast days, the prayers of the *maʿamad,* the meal prayers, and the prayer proper to the sect.

The three daily prayers. In general terms, prayer at three specific times of the day is believed to have occurred in the time of Jesus. The text of *Berakot* 4, 1 confirms this, naming the *tefillat shaḥar* (morning prayer), the prayer of the *minḥa* sacrifice, and the *tefillat haʿerev* (afternoon prayer). The morning prayer could be said until noon or, according to Rabbi Judah, not later than the "fourth hour" (ten o'clock in the morning). The afternoon prayer could last until sunset[3] or not past twilight

[3] A direct testimony could be Psalm 140:2: "Let my prayer be counted as incense before you / and the lifting up of my hands as an evening sacrifice (*minhat ʿareb*)." See L. Rost, "Ein Psalmenproblem," *Theologische Literaturzeitung* 39 (1968) 241–246.

and began two and a half hours before nighttime. The prayer at sunset did not have a fixed time.

These three daily prayers are different from the morning and evening recitation of the *Shemaʿ* (Deut 6:4, 5-9; 11:13-21; Num 15:41), which should be considered more a profession of faith (Israelite creed) than a prayer.[4] These three prayers already seem to have been witnessed to in Daniel 6:10 ("Daniel . . . continued to go to his house . . . and to get down on knees three times a day to pray to his God") and perhaps in Psalm 54:16-17 as well:

But I call upon God,
and the LORD will save me;
Evening and morning and at noon
I utter my complaint and moan,
and he will hear my voice.

Since the time of Jesus and even before him, two of the three prayers were combined with the hour of sacrifice in the Temple.[5] Ezra (Ezra 9:5) prays the splendid *todah* (a prayer asking for forgiveness) at the time of the *minḥat haʿerev* (afternoon offering). Daniel also prays and confesses his sins and those of his people at the hour of the evening sacrifice (Dan 9:21). The same thing is found in Judith 9:1 (during the evening offering of incense). Peter, in Acts 3:1, goes up to the Temple with John to pray at three o'clock in the afternoon: this is the *tefillat minḥah,* or *tefillah* par excellence. This afternoon prayer, the oldest according to earlier biblical testimonies, is thus attested in Acts 3:1; at the end of the first century A.D. it was enriched with the eighteen benedictions.[6]

The origin of the close relationship between the two daily prayers and the daily sacrifices could come from the fact that during the morning sacrifice, at the time of the offering of perfume, those present in the Temple prayed (see Sir 50:1-21). The same thing occurred during the evening incense offering (see Luke 1:10). When the people could not participate directly in the Temple sacrifices, the rabbis recommended that they withdraw themselves in prayer, wherever they were, at the

[4] See Jeremias, *Prayers of Jesus,* 70. Years before, the same author, in his lecture at the Conference of Saint-Serge in 1961, had maintained the close relationship of origin between the daily prayer and the *Shemaʿ*.

[5] See *Bar. Berakot* 26b: "The rabbis coordinated the prayers with the sacrifices."

[6] See Jeremias, *Prayers of Jesus,* 70.

same time that the sacrifices were being offered in the Temple. In fact, in accordance with a rabbinic ruling, "the chant (the prayer) confirms the sacrifice and is a part that cannot be omitted, since the sacrifice without the chant (the prayer) is not pleasing to God."[7] The prayer was, therefore, a way for people to unite themselves to the sacrificial action and, at the same time, give meaning to it.

The feast day prayer or supplementary prayer. Along with the three daily prayers, *Berakot* 4, 1 refers to the additional or supplementary prayer called *mussaf* (supplement), which is the same name as the sacrifice. It was said during the days of the *ma'amad* and on the days that the sacrifice called for, which were Saturdays, new moons, and other holy days.

The prayers of the "ma'amad." In Jesus' time the priests and levites were divided into twenty-four classes *(mishmarot),* with a leader at the head of each class (see 1 Chr 24:1-31). Each class *(mishmar)* was made up of six priestly families, one for each day of the week. On Saturday the six families served together. According to 1 Chronicles 9:25, each week the classes changed. The *mishmar* that arrived in Jerusalem was accompanied by a delegation of the people, who were blessed four times a day, as many times as they prayed (the three daily prayers as well as the supplementary prayer). The other people who remained in their respective towns came together in the center of the town four times a day in order to pray (morning prayer, afternoon prayer, evening prayer, and the supplementary prayer), listen to the reading of the Torah, and fast four times during that week.

The meal prayer. This fourth prayer, very important to the faith experience of the people of Israel in the time of Jesus, is a very complex text that is attested to in the rabbinic texts.[8] It is not easy to identify with certainty the original basis of the prayer in the time of Jesus, even though the text was passed on with a high degree of fidelity. Looking beyond these difficulties, it is interesting to note how the meal prayer at Easter *remembers* the past (the nation) and also the future that will come (the Messiah and salvation).

The prayer of the sect. In Jesus' time each religious group had a special and characteristic prayer. This is true of the Pharisees, the Essenes, and the disciples of John. This prayer was taught to the disciples by

[7] Hruby, "Les heures de prière," 61.

[8] *Berakot J.* 8, 12a, 45; 6, 10a, 49, 63.

their teacher. In Luke 11:1 the followers of Jesus address him as their teacher: "Lord, teach us to pray, as John taught his disciples." What is important here is not the teaching of the experience but rather the "formula" of the prayer.

To summarize, of the five kinds of ritual prayer in Jesus' time, the first three (the threefold daily prayer linked to the triple recitation of the *Shemaʿ*, the four daily prayers of the *maʿamad*, the supplementary prayer or *mussaf*) correspond either to the sacrificial worship in the Temple or to the liturgical time. This indicates two things: (1) the close relationship between Temple worship and prayer; (2) the close relationship between prayer outside the assembly and the liturgical assembly being present in the sacrifices. The other two forms of prayer were related to the personal environment of the believer: the meal prayer and the prayer of the sect.

b) The experience and the teaching of Jesus

From the little information that the Gospels offer about the prayer of Jesus, we know for certain that he frequently went to the synagogue (see Luke 4:16) and that he participated in the three daily prayers and in the recitation of the *Shemaʿ*. In addition to the typical prayer life of all devoted Hebrews of that time, Jesus also prayed with an apparent spontaneity in certain situations. He used a prayer that was new in that it was the prayer that the Son offered to the Father, although an Old Testament background can be observed in the form and expressions of the prayer.

Jesus acted with great freedom in his practice of the threefold Hebrew prayer, as he demonstrates in his teaching. He teaches his followers to pray "in his name" (John 15:7, 9; 16:23-24, 26-27), to pray alone (Matt 6:5-8) or at least in pairs (Matt 18:19), but always with the attitude that their prayers would be heard (Mark 11:24; Matt 7:7-11; Luke 11:5-8; John 15:7). The admonition about when to pray is also very important: Jesus teaches his disciples to pray "always" (Luke 18:1-7; 21:36).

In the New Testament we find the framework of an actual precept about uninterrupted prayer. We also witness the great Pray-er, Jesus, who gives us examples of prayer, teaches us how we ought to pray, and "institutes" Christian prayer. Jesus establishes a new relationship between humankind and God, which is about adopting an attitude of acceptance of the plans of the Father. This acceptance is transformed into praise and recognition of the will of God. Those who pray must then know that they have a part in the saving plan of God for humanity and for themselves.

With the prayer of the Our Father, Jesus teaches his disciples to pray by relating the content of his own prayer so that when Christians say it, Jesus himself will continue to pray with them and in them. The interest that the first generations of Christians had in this prayer seems to be reflected in the *Didache* (8, 3), where, after giving the complete text of the Our Father, it says "in this way you should pray three times a day."[9] The substitution at the end of the first century of the old profession of faith, the *Shemaᶜ*, by the Our Father in the three daily prayers, at least in Judeo-Christian circles, symbolizes the fact that this new situation or relationship of humankind with God, introduced by Christ, should correspond to a new prayer that expresses and conserves it.

c) The prayer of the community

The early Church, which was still linked to the Jewish world, seems to have respected Jesus' faithful use of the threefold daily prayer. One testimony of this is found in Acts 3:1, where "Peter and John were going up to the Temple at the hour of prayer, at three o'clock in the afternoon." This is a reference to the evening prayer. In Acts 10:9 we may have testimony of the morning prayer when reference is made to Peter, who prays "about noon."[10] Although faithful to the Jewish tradition, in the early Church both men and women were obligated to participate in prayer.[11] The leaders of the community had a specific duty to pray (see Acts 6:4). The twelve apostles prayed before laying their hands on the seven (Acts 6:6), before receiving the Spirit (Acts 8:15), and before reviving Tabitha (Acts 9:40).

[9] The Judeo-Christian tradition of the threefold daily prayer continues in the Church even after the destruction of Jerusalem, according to the testimony of the *Didache* (8, 3), which instructs the Christians to pray the Our Father three times a day. In this case the Judeo-Christian Church had made a combination of the Hebrew daily prayer (three times a day) and the "prayer of the sect" taught by the Teacher.

[10] See *Berakot* 4, 1. It is clearly stated that the morning prayer "can be recited until midday."

[11] In Acts 1:14 it is said: "All these were constantly devoting themselves to prayer, together with certain women, including Mary the mother of Jesus. . . ." We must

This fidelity to the Jewish tradition underwent great changes. We see in Romans 12:12 and Colossians 4:2 how Paul urges his readers to persevere in prayer. The verb that was adopted to describe this perseverance is προσκαρτερεῖν, which indicates fidelity and constancy in time. The theme of continuous prayer without interruption is repeated often, with abundant expressions such as "always," "assiduously," "day and night" becoming almost commonplace in the language of Paul and the Acts of the Apostles. These expressions try to encourage constancy, not so much in the repetition of acts as in the persistence of a prayerful attitude. We no longer find references to the three daily prayers of the Hebrew world. The old Christian tradition paid particular attention to this doctrine, and, at the same time, the precept of uninterrupted prayer played an important role in the formation of the times and rhythms of prayer.

The prayers of the Christian community were normally directed to the Father, following the command and example of Jesus, but they used Christ as mediator. According to Paul in 2 Corinthians 1:20, ". . . it is through him that we say the 'Amen' to the glory of God." But Christ is not only an intercessor (see 1 John 2:1) and intermediary before the Father; he also receives the prayers of the primitive community and is the object of their praise. This is an aspect of singular importance for the theology of Christian prayer, particularly liturgical prayer.

In summary, in the New Testament we discover three dimensions of the role that Christ played in prayer: first, Christ appears as a praying person, as a living example of a man of prayer; second, Christ is shown as mediator of our prayer with the Father; third, Christ is also the object of Christian praise and prayer. Christ will be the essential subject of the filial dialogue of the Christians with the Father. The hymns of the apostolic letters (Col 1:3-20; Eph 1:3-14; 1 Pet 1:3-12) assume the character of a great benediction to God through Christ, not only because he is the mediator of Christian praise for the Father, but above all because Christ is the motive of this praise. For this reason the Christians progress, at the same time that they pray, in their knowledge of the mystery of Christ.

---

remember that only men were obligated to recite the *Shemaʿ*, while women, children, and slaves also were obligated to pray (*Berakot* 3, 3).

II. ECCLESIAL PRAYER OF THE CHRISTIAN AUTHORS OF THE FIRST THREE CENTURIES

The first period in the history of the daily prayer of Christians, up to its first structuralization at the end of the fourth century, is characterized by a preoccupation to "justify" the times of prayer. Each hour takes on a religious and spiritual meaning, taken not only from the natural symbolism of the different parts of the day and night but also and above all from the act of recalling certain biblical episodes or moments in the lives of Jesus and the apostles. In this way a true theology of time began to form, demonstrating how each and every one of the hours has a symbolic and sacramental value; in other words, they are *signs* of salvation. The Fathers of that time agreed that in order to carry out the ideal of incessant prayer, it was necessary to set specific times of prayer. These times can be interpreted as a visible expression and symbolic action of what should be, in light of the New Testament ideal, the *mystery of prayer* as a permanent reality in the life of the believers.

1. *The Hours of Christian Prayer and Their Symbolism*

The *Didache* (from the end of the first century) is the first testimony before the third century that specifically refers to some hours of Christian prayer. In chapter 8, 2-3 it says: "Do not pray as the hypocrites, but as the Lord commanded in his Gospel; pray thus: 'Our Father, who are in heaven. . . .' Pray thus three times a day." In the *Didache* we observe the Jewish ritual custom of praying three times a day, but the content of the prayers is replaced by the Christian prayer of the Our Father. In this document it is not clear if the three daily times of prayer were private or communal, as in the synagogues. Nor is it clear when the three times were, but they probably were similar to the Jewish times. In any case, the practice of praying the Our Father three times a day constitutes one of the first links of the cyclical Christian prayer.[12]

[12] At the beginning of the second century we have other testimonies, such as the letter of Pliny the Younger to Trajan around the year 112, where he states that the Christians of Bithynia came together at sunrise, probably on Sundays, to sing hymns to Christ as they would to a god (see *Epist.* 10, 96, 7). In his *Apology* 15:10 (second century), Aristides says that the Christians glorified and praised God for the blessings they had received and gave thanks for their nourishment every morning and at every hour.

In his first letter to the Corinthians in the last decade of the first century, Pope Clement (92–101) was the first to affirm that the Christian celebrations should be done at *fixed times and hours:* "We ought to do in order all things which the Master commanded us to perform at appointed times. He commanded us to celebrate sacrifices and services, and that it should not be thoughtlessly or disorderly, but at fixed times and hours."[13] Another fragment of this same letter to the Corinthians is also interesting, containing an interpretation of the resurrection that will very soon be attributed to the morning celebration.[14]

The first three centuries were marked by insistence on the precept of praying without interruption and the spiritual tension that this caused. In this time period there were four teachers and witnesses of prayer: Clement of Alexandria, Tertullian, Origen, and Cyprian. To these four we can also add another source, the *Apostolic Tradition,* attributed to Hippolytus of Rome. Below we present the common doctrine and writings of these sources.

a) Incessant prayer

Almost all the writers make reference to the Lord's command and the Pauline text.[15] A person's life should always include prayer, at all times and in all places. With respect to this, the *De dominica oratione* (35–36) of St. Cyprian is particularly important for spirituality. Cyprian introduces a different idea on the subject, explaining why we should always pray: it is not necessary for us to pray always because we are needy, but rather because, having already been introduced through baptismal rebirth to the glory of being the children of God, we are brought to incessant praise by the very reality of our life in Christ. In this way we imitate on earth how we will later be in the eternal afterlife. Prayer is a defense against temptation, and a lack of prayer will make room for an evil spirit.[16]

[13] *1 Clement* 40, 1-2: PG 1:287–288.

[14] *1 Clement* 24, 1-3: PG 1:259–262.

[15] See Clement of Alexandria, *Stromata* 7, 40, 3 (GCS 17) 30; Tertullian, *De oratione* 25: CCL 1, p. 272, and *De ieiunio* 10, 3: CCL 2, p. 1267; Hippolytus, *Apostolic Tradition* 36, 1; Origen, *De oratione* 12: PG 11:452–453.

[16] We see this particularly in the *De oratione* 12 of Origen, for whom prayer is energetically active. Arrows fly out from the minds of those who pray, piercing the evil spirits and driving them away. This "defensive-aggressive" concept of prayer was already present in the writings of St. Ignatius of Antioch (see *Letter to the*

b) The specification of some precise times of prayer

The authors mentioned above specify the command to pray always and at fixed hours. In Book 7 of his *Stromata*, a work on worship and prayer, Clement of Alexandria mentions for the first time the third, sixth, and ninth daily hours, together with the morning Office. Clement notes that some Christians have established these set hours for prayer but that the perfect Christian, the spiritual person who has a deeper knowledge of God, prays always, in all places, alone or with others of the faith during his or her whole life.

The ecclesial celebration of the morning Office is associated with the appearance of Christ, who is the light that shines in the darkness. Clement does not mention the evening prayer, but that does not mean that he did not know of it; in fact, we can see an implicit reference to the prayer when he quotes Psalm 140:2.[17] The lesser or private hours (third, sixth, and ninth) are presented as being suitable for making Christian prayer continuous. Clement of Alexandria was the first author to recognize the symbol of the Trinity in the threefold number of the times of prayer. It is important to note that he does not base the custom of prayer on any biblical text or any tradition. His work is also the first patristic testimony of the eschatological character of Christian prayer in the nocturnal vigil. In his work *The Pedagogue*, 2, Clement uses many biblical quotations as he writes of the baptized who, like children of the light and of the day, keep watch during the night, waiting for the coming of the Lord. The character of the vigil consists in waking up and praising God. In this way the believers are similar to more spiritual beings, the angels, that is to say, the guards par excellence, whose essential function is to praise God. For Clement, the "angelic life" of Christians consists in being similar to the angels through prayer, vigil, and praise.

Tertullian was the first writer to try to find a basis for the three lesser hours (third, sixth, and ninth) in the Bible, discovering one model in Daniel.[18] For Tertullian, the importance of the three daytime hours comes from their connection to the principal saving events. The third hour is connected to the descent of the Holy Spirit (Acts 2:1-15); the sixth hour, to the prayer of Peter in Joppa (Acts 10:9); and the ninth

Ephesians 13:1), and it will have a certain influence in the spirituality of the first monks of the desert.

[17] See *Stromata* 7, 7: PG 9: 456–457.

[18] See Tertullian, *De ieiunio* 10, 4: CCL 2, p. 1267.

hour, to the healing of the paralytic man by Peter (Acts 3:1). With these links to biblical events and people, Tertullian attempts to justify the sacredness of the three hours of prayer.[19] He thus advocates a program that recognizes the necessity of prayer and establishes a kind of law that sets a time to satisfy the obligation to pray. But by referring to the sacred traditional numbers of the hours as third, sixth, and ninth, he bases his idea on a double historical error related to Daniel (6:10-11) and Acts (2:16), since we know for certain that the prayer on the day of Pentecost was the morning prayer, and the prayer of Peter and John was in the evening.[20] Nevertheless, the origin of the practice of prayer at the third, sixth, and ninth hours does not come from a mistaken interpretation of Tertullian nor from the explanation of the *Apostolic Tradition* regarding the hours of Christ's passion.[21] This practice was already taking place before these writings, just as Clement of Alexandria witnessed to earlier.[22]

Tertullian himself specifies the true historical motive for the three daytime hours when he verifies that they were the same hours that marked the divisions of the day. What he does is simply consecrate a practice of fact by supporting it with biblical texts.[23] However, the fact that Tertullian turns to the Acts of the Apostles to do this has substantial justification, transcending the invalid sacredness he gives to third and ninth hours.

Credit must be given to Tertullian for having opened the way to discovering an "apostolic tradition" as a basis and justification for the ecclesial tradition in the liturgy of praise. St. Cyprian agrees with Tertullian in part and corrects his historical error in some way. His reasoning is better developed, and although he uses an excessive allegorical interpretation, he does show that each of the three daytime hours is strengthened by three others, and that this set of threes clearly connects to the Trinity.[24]

[19] See Tertullian, *De oratione* 25, 1–4: CCL 1, p. 272; *De ieiunio* 10, 3: CCL 2, p. 1267.

[20] This historical error, which biblical studies have sufficiently clarified, was passed down through the centuries to our day. This we know because the GILH 1 and some of the same final prayers for these hours from the actual Roman Liturgy of the Hours still make reference to it.

[21] See *The Apostolic Tradition* 41. We are following the numbering of B. Botte, *La Tradition apostolique*, 2nd ed. rev. (Paris, 1984).

[22] See Clement of Alexandria, *Stromata* 7, 7: PG 9:456–457; 461–463.

[23] See Tertullian, *De ieiunio* 10: CCL 2, p. 1267.

[24] See Cyprian, *De dominica oratione* 34: CCL 3A, p. 111.

Origen identifies the divine command of prayer done three times a day, and he makes reference to Daniel, Peter, and Psalms 5:3-4 and 140:2. For the three daily hours he follows the Jewish use: in the morning, at midday, and in the evening. Using as a foundation Psalms 118:62 and Paul and Silas singing psalms at midnight in prison, Origen adds an invitation to pray at night, something that is known to be a typically Christian practice.[25] Origen recognizes the private practice of the lesser hours, and in the morning and evening hours he discovers the specification of a sacred command. In reference to the evening prayer, in Origen we find a testimony of the use of Psalm 140, which will later be converted into the nucleus of the evening prayer for all Christianity. In his work on prayer, Origen states that there is no opposition between continuous prayer and prayer at determined hours. The established times for prayer are an integral part of incessant prayer, which tries to unite prayer to work and work to prayer in daily life; a person's life is in this way inspired by the intention of fulfilling the will of God in all that one does. This adherence, this profound union with God, truly constitutes uninterrupted prayer.

For Tertullian and Cyprian, two other hours exist, together with the third, sixth, and ninth. These hours are called *legitimatae orationes,* and unlike the others, they are obligatory. These hours need no justification, given that they are perfectly institutionalized.[26] Tertullian also mentions the vigil as a time of prayer when Christians interrupt their sleep in order to dedicate themselves to prayer.[27]

In the *Apostolic Tradition,* chapters 25, 35, and 41 are important. The times of Christian prayer during the day and the night are discussed with more detail in chapter 41. First the *lucernarium* or blessing prayer is mentioned when presenting the lamp in the room where the *agape* is celebrated. This prayer is the oldest text known of for the *lucernarium* prayer. It is introduced with a dialogue similar to the preface of the Eucharistic Prayer. The bishop presides after the deacon brings the lamp into the room.[28] The following is the text of the prayer:

"We give you thanks, Lord, through Jesus Christ your Son and our Lord, through whom you illuminate us, revealing to us the light that

[25] See Origen, *De oratione* 12: PG 11:452–453.

[26] See Tertullian, *De oratione* 25: CCL 1, pp. 272–273; also Cyprian, *De dominica oratione* 34-36: CCL 3A, pp. 111–113.

[27] See Tertullian, *Ad uxorem* 4, 2; 5, 2: CCL 1, pp. 388–389.

[28] *Apostolic Tradition* 25.

has no darkness. After having completed a day, we approach the beginning of the night. You have filled us with the light of the day. We praise you and glorify you through Jesus Christ, your Son and our Lord, through whom you receive the glory, power and honor, with the Holy Spirit, now and forever from age to age. Amen."

In this prayer we see the beginnings of the first thematic blossoms that will be converted into the great branches of the later euchology of the Liturgy of the Hours: light of day, light of light, light of Christ; God creates the world, ordering the phases of the invisible light; God reveals the invisible eternal light in Christ. Facing the sign of the light, the Church prays, recognizes, proclaims, gives thanks, praises, and glorifies. The blessing of the lamp in the *Apostolic Tradition* is converted into the first model for the prayer of the hours in the form of thanksgiving. Thus we have the first reference to the *Eucharistic* dimension of the prayer of ecclesial praise.

In chapter 35 of the *Apostolic Tradition* private prayer is mentioned as one of the obligations of Christians after they awaken from sleep and before beginning their work. If by chance there was a meeting in the church dedicated to catechetical training, Christians are recommended to attend. But the subject of prayer is treated with more detail in chapter 41. It begins with an invitation to the morning prayer, just after waking. If that day there is a synaxis of listening to the Word and catechism, the believer should go. When there is no catechism, it is recommended that all Christians pick up a holy book at home and read it for their benefit.

The *Apostolic Tradition* goes on to describe the times of private prayer that are advisable to practice, whether at home or in another place: the third, sixth, and ninth hours. At the same time the doctrinal reasons that justify these hours are explained, referring to the passion of the Lord, understood in all its paschal dynamism—in other words, united to the resurrection. The third hour alludes to the crucifixion (Mark 15:25); the sixth is related to the cry of Jesus crucified and the darkness that came upon the earth in that moment (Matt 27:45; Mark 15:33; Luke 23:44-45); the ninth hour makes reference to the spear that slashed the side of Christ on the cross (John 19:33-37). The last lights of the day, at twilight, are an image that announce the coming of the resurrection. Christians are invited not only to unite their personal piety to the memory of the death of Christ on the cross but also to identify themselves with the reasons and manner of his prayer.

In the next part we will discuss further the prayer before going to sleep, the prayer at midnight, and the prayer at cockcrow. In reference to the prayer at midnight, done in private, the action of the Holy Spirit is mentioned, as well as the prayer in communion with the cosmic praise; the night hours also make reference to the eschatological waiting of the Spouse and the resurrection of the dead.

2. *Principles of the Theological Meaning of the Hours*

The Fathers of the third century explain the meaning of the Christians' daily prayer with two kinds of principles:

a) Principles related to the wholeness of daily prayer, which includes the theology of the hours:

1) The first principle consists in all the hours of the day being connected to the risen Christ, the light of the Church. The hour at sunset is a reference to Christ through the lamp of the *lucernarium.*

2) The second principle refers to the symbolic and sacrificial character of prayer: the Christians present their prayers to God as an offering of a spiritual sacrifice.

b) Principles concerning the three daily hours:

1) The first principle tries to explain why there are three hours and not more or less. The reason is based on the symbolism of the Trinity.

2) The second principle refers to the prayer of the apostles during these hours according to the testimony of Acts, as a basis for an apostolic tradition of ecclesial prayer.

3) The third principle refers to the connection of these three hours to the paschal mystery of Christ. This principle also is applied in order to give meaning to the two main hours of the ecclesial prayer.

All the principles of the third-century writers that give meaning to the different hours of prayer can be summarized in the following way:

The mystery of the Trinity: Clement, Tertullian, and above all Cyprian take the meaning of the three daily hours and extend it to all the hours of the Office. According to Cyprian, because there are three hours between each of the hours of prayer, these three daily hours reveal the *sacramentum Trinitatis,* veiled in the prayer of the just of the Old Testament.[29]

[29] See Cyprian, *De dominica oratione* 34: CCL 3A, p. 111.

The "apostolic tradition": The example of the apostles as a principle is applied primarily to the three daily hours, later being extended to the whole *cursus.* Tertullian, Cyprian, and Origen use this example. The people who are specifically cited as the founders of an apostolic tradition of prayer include the disciples on the day of Pentecost, Peter at Joppa, Peter and John going up to the Temple, and Paul and Silas in prison. This apostolic tradition will be the foundation and justification of the ecclesial tradition of the hourly liturgy of praise.

Memorial of the paschal mystery of Christ: This principle of the Lord's passion as a basis for the daily hours seems to come from the *Apostolic Tradition.* The passion is synonymous with all parts of the paschal mystery (passion, death, and resurrection) as an inseparable unity. The third hour draws meaning from the crucifixion; the sixth, from the cry and prayer of Christ, his death, and the darkness after; and the ninth hour finds meaning in the spear, the flowing of blood and water, the final breath of the Lord, and his lying in the tomb. According to Hippolytus, the resurrection of the Lord is foreshadowed in the image of the last light at dusk. The prayer at cockcrow is a reference to the hope of eternal light in which, through the denials of Peter in that hour, the memory of the resurrection is evoked without, however, forgetting the passion. According to the *Apostolic Tradition,* the hours are not only a memorial of the passion of Christ but also a participation in the actions and prayers of the Lord. In this we find the foundation of the theology and spirituality of the Divine Office. Its celebration is the liturgy: the prayer of the Hours is a memorial of the paschal mystery, as well as a saving event.

For Tertullian, the time that corresponds to the hour of Vespers is the laying of the Lord in his tomb *(tempus dominicae sepulturae).*[30] The death of the Lord is the *sacrament* that should always be in the memory of Christians.

According to Clement of Alexandria, Tertullian, Cyprian, and the *Apostolic Tradition,* the threefold daily prayer is set in relation to the mysteries of Christ, emphasizing in this way the christological and soteriological character of liturgical prayer. In the text of the *Apostolic Tradition* the prayer is brought to an *anamnestic* level; in other words, it is a *memorial celebration.* In fact, this prayer is a memorial celebration of the mystery of Christ, which means that the prayer is at the same time

[30] Tertullian, *De ieiunio* 10: CCL 2, p. 1268.

a concrete memory and sacramental interpretation of the salvation that Christ fulfills on the cross as a praying and sacrificing priest.

All the authors tend to associate the prayer of Christians with Christ's passion or with Christ the light. These two principles come together to form one: the prayer of the Church as a memory of the work of salvation.

Christ, light without darkness. The light of the lamp is a symbol of the risen Christ in the same way that it is a symbol of the light of dawn. We see this in the blessing prayer of the lamp in the *Apostolic Tradition*, which corresponds to the prayer of the *lucernarium.*[31] This text is enriched by the hymn φῶς ἱλαρόν[32] along with the hymn that Paul recounts in Ephesians 5:14, as well as the hymn that Clement of Alexandria gives.[33] Through St. Cyprian we find an explanation of the meaning of the evening Office through the image of Christ, the sun that never sets.[34] In the fourth century both Eusebius of Caesarea and St. Hilary, who bases his ideas on those of Eusebius, bring the two completely ecclesial Offices to the same level in a festive sense.[35] Cyprian explains the foundation of the vigils in reference to the theme of light. In his work he tells us that if we remain always in the light of Christ, day and night, we will feel the eternal joy of the heavenly city, where there is no sun because God is the light that illuminates all through Christ. This state of total illumination causes us to break out in incessant praise, imitating how we will be in eternal life.

Prayer, a spiritual sacrifice: Tertullian describes the prayer of the Christian as a true spiritual sacrifice, a substitute for the sacrifices of earlier times.[36] Later John Cassian also will present the morning and evening prayers as substitutes for the old sacrifices.[37]

[31] See B. Botte, ed., *La tradition apostolique,* 64; see also J. Pinell, *Vestigis del lucernari a Occident,* Liturgica I. Scripta et Documenta 7 (Montserrat, 1956) 93–94.

[32] See E. Smother, *"Fos ilarón," RSR* 19 (1929) 266–283.

[33] See Clement of Alexandria, *Exhortatio ad nationes* 9: PG 48:196. The theme of Christ as light, sun of justice, was certainly very fitting at the time in which the cult of the sun developed in the Roman Empire, but it was deeply tied to the revelation that will always be valid: "The true light, which enlightens everyone, was coming into the world" (John 1:9).

[34] See Cyprian, *De dominica oratione* 34: CCL 3A, pp. 111–113.

[35] See Eusebius of Caesarea, *In Ps. 64:* PG 23:639; Hilary, *Tractatus in Ps. 64,* 12: CSEL 22, p. 244.

[36] See Tertullian, *De oratione* 28: CCL 1, p. 273.

[37] John Cassian, *De institutis coenobiorum* 3, 3: CSEL 17, 37–38.

III. THE FIRST ATTEMPTS AT ORGANIZATION

1. *The Cathedral Office and the Monastic Office*

In the fourth century the prayer of the hours was organized almost everywhere in two ways, which are clearly described by A. Baumstark: the prayer of the Christian community together with the bishop and his presbytery, called the *cathedral* Office, and the prayer of the monastic community, called the *monastic* Office.[38]

The cathedral Office celebrates the main hours of the morning and evening, which are called Lauds and Vespers. In addition to these two prayer times, the faithful gathered for Sunday and holy day for prayer vigils. This cathedral liturgy consisted of an Office for all people, characterized by symbols and rites (lights, incense, processions, etc.), chants (hymns, responsorials, antiphons), the diversity of ministers (bishop, presbyter, deacon, reader, psalmist, chanter), and the psalmody, which was limited to selected psalms that were not continuous and complete as in the monastic celebration. The monastic Office, in addition to Lauds and Vespers, also included the daily hours of Terce, Sext, and None; later Prime (today eliminated) and Compline were added. The monks also institutionalized the prayer vigils as a daily Office. The monastic ideal is the complete recitation of the Psalter.

The two traditions do not oppose but rather complement each other. However, the distinction between the cathedral and monastic Offices will soon disappear in the West because of the general monasticization of the Liturgy of the Hours. The meeting and the union of the two traditions, monastic and cathedral, constitutes the foundation of the traditional patrimony of the Divine Office that has reached our time.

2. *The Cathedral and Parish Office*

The first news of a cathedral type of Office is given by Eusebius of Caesarea (ca. 263–339). In his commentary on Psalm 64, while explaining verse 9b he says that the hymns and praises that are offered, like true divine pleasures, at dawn and at dusk in the churches of God all over the world are certainly more than just a small sign of God.[39] In the same text Eusebius quotes Psalm 140:2, which will later be the traditional evening psalm, common to all the Offices of the diverse traditions. The traditional morning psalm will be Psalm 62, as Eusebius

[38] A. Baumstark, *Comparative Liturgy*, rev. ed. B. Botte, trans. F. L. Cross (Westminster, Md., 1958) 111ff.

[39] See Eusebius, *In Ps. 64:* PG 23:639–640.

suggests in his commentary on Psalm 142:8.[40] In fact, from the fourth century onward there are abundant testimonies describing the daily meetings not only in Palestine but also in Antioch, Constantinople, and Africa. They formed part of the daily duties of a Christian, as St. John Chrysostom affirms when he teaches the catechesis to the newly baptized.[41] The Councils of Spain and Gaul of the fifth and sixth centuries dealt with specifying the details of these meetings, and they urged the clergy and the lay people to attend them.[42]

During the morning Office, which was for all the people, Psalms 50, 62, 66, 117, and 148–150 were sung. These last three are the so-called Lauds or morning psalms. Biblical canticles, hymns, prayers, and, in some cases, almost daily preaching were also added. The celebrations closed with prayers of intercession, the Our Father, and a collect recited by the bishop or the presbyter.

Since the fourth century the evening celebration consisted principally of an Office of the light or *lucernarium* and included Psalm 140 as its most meaningful psalm.

Another important testimony is that of John Chrysostom, who was in Antioch around the year 390. In his *Baptismal Catecheses* (8, 17-18) he refers to the reasoning behind the daily meetings for ecclesial prayer. The purpose of the morning prayer, to which all are invited, is to give thanks and praise to God for the benefits received, as well as to ask for God's presence in daily activities. The evening prayer is the opportune moment to ask for God's forgiveness for wrongs committed during the day. To this is added a petition for the protection of God during the night, and for time to pass quickly so that all may again be present at the morning praise.[43] In his *Commentary on Psalm 140,* 1, Chrysostom refers to the daily chanting of Psalms 140 and 62. For him, Psalm 140 has a penitential meaning: spiritual chant and healthy medicine in order to free ourselves from sins committed during the day. Psalm 62[63], on the other hand, lights the soul with longing for God, filling it with goodness and love, making it immune to sin.[44] In his *Homily 6*

[40] See Eusebius, *In Ps. 142:* PG 24:49.

[41] See John Chrysostom, *Catechesis octava:* SCh 50, 256–257.

[42] See J. Fernández Alonso, *La cura pastoral en la España romanovisigoda* (Rome, 1955) 341–344.

[43] See A. Wenger, ed., *Jean Chrysostome: Huit catéchèses baptismales inédites,* SCh 50 (Paris, 1957) 256–257.

[44] See PG 55:427–432.

on 1 Timothy, 1, John Chrysostom also gives information about the intercessions that formed part of the two daily Offices.[45] Besides the community prayer, Christians were invited to pray frequently during the day, wherever they were, kneeling and with their hands raised high.[46]

As typical examples of the cathedral Office, we must quickly consider some documents from the Eastern liturgy that have had some influence on Western liturgies.

One writing that has reached our time is the *Apostolic Constitutions*, a Syrian document of a canonical-liturgical character that goes back to the end of the fourth century or the beginning of the fifth. Book 8 includes a description of the complete structure of daily prayer.[47] Also included is the fundamental structure of the Divine Office, with the two primary times of prayer in the morning and at sunset (Lauds and Vespers), the three lesser hours (Terce, Sext, None), and the nocturnal prayer at cockcrow. In Book 2, 59 we read that the nucleus of the morning and evening prayers is Psalms 62 and 140. A Sunday vigil was also celebrated with the Gospel of the resurrection and three prayers in honor of Christ's rising on the third day, followed by the liturgy of the Word, the anaphora, and communion. Book 7, 47 holds the text of the hymn *Gloria in excelsis*, which will later be converted into the common element of all the Eastern morning Offices. Chapter 48 of this same work contains the nocturnal hymn *Te decet laus* and the *Nunc dimittis* of Luke 2:29-32. Chapters 35–39 of Book 8 describe the two daily liturgical celebrations and also include the texts of the long intercessions, to which the response *Kyrie eleison* was used, as well as the collect prayers that were said by the bishop.

As in the patristic testimonies that we studied earlier, in this document strong christological references can also be found. The hours or times of prayer are linked to the great happenings of the redemption: the christological and paschal reference is what sanctifies time or makes it sacred. In exceptional cases the morning and evening celebration can be carried out privately at home or, even better, with a small group of believers. It is a profoundly ecclesial act, given that it is

[45] See PG 62:530. Other information from Chrysostom about the intercessions is found in his homily *On the Obscurity of the Prophecies* 2, 5: PG 56:182.

[46] See John Chrysostom, *Sermon on Hannah* 4, 5–6: PG 54:666–668.

[47] See *Constitutiones Apostolorum* 8, 34–39, ed. F. X. Funk, *Didascalia et Constitutiones Apostolorum* (Paderborn, 1905) 540–548.

normally celebrated in the church, with all the people attending. The structure of the morning and evening Office is identical:

1. Chanting of the *lucernarium* psalm, Psalm 140, at Vespers and of the morning psalm, Psalm 62, at Lauds;
2. The prayers of the catechumens;
3. Dismissal of the catechumens;
4. The deacon invites all to pray. This is an admonition of specific content;
5. Prayer of the bishop;
6. Diaconal admonition for the laying on of the hands;
7. Prayer of blessing said by the bishop before dismissing the people;
8. Dismissal by the deacon, ending the celebration.

In the evening and morning prayers of the *Apostolic Constitutions* (Book 8, 37–38) we find an important advance in the development of the thematic already presented in the blessing prayer of the lamp in the *Apostolic Tradition.* Composed in the form of pleading, these prayers define both celebrations as a giving of thanks: God is asked to accept the gift of the evening and morning "ecclesial Eucharist." In the petitions the attributes of God are listed, which is a sign not only of an accentuated theological sensitivity but also of a greater consciousness of the anthropological dimension of prayer. The attribute of Creator and the multiple applications of this notion not only serve to reveal God but also to bring him closer to humankind. God orders the night so that humans may rest, and he is anxious to provide a peaceful night free from sin. There is a clear conviction that God is the Creator of the universe, the Lord of the day and of the night, the owner of time. The morning prayer, also directed to the Father, through Christ the creator of time and of things, is transformed into an act of thanksgiving for the gift of life and a redeemed existence. In addition, there is a clear and explicit confession of the transcendence and eternity of God, which cannot be contained within the limits of time and space. The community pleads with God to continue maintaining them, keeping them in a joyful existence.

Another document to consider is *Egeria's Travels.* In her account, the pilgrim Egeria describes the monastic and cathedral Offices of Jerusalem at the end of the fourth century. Chapter 24 describes the functions of an ordinary week. In the description, the importance of the celebration of the morning, the *lucernarium,* the vigils, and the nocturnal

Office are especially emphasized. This liturgy developed in the Basilicas of the Anastasis and the Martyrium, where groups of monks, ascetics, and virgins participated, especially in the nocturnal Offices. They have contributed in a decisive way to the introduction and continuation of the nocturnal prayer in the Church. The bishop, the clergy, and the people especially celebrate the morning Office and the *lucernarium*. In this way two kinds of assemblies have been superimposed: one monastic, which celebrates the vigils, and another, presided over by the bishop and with the attendance of the clergy, which can be called ecclesial. Besides these important times of community prayer and the great prominence of Sunday, Egeria indicates the celebration of Sext and None but only refers to Terce when describing the Lenten celebrations (27:4-5), without mentioning the christological intentions of these times of prayer. The Sunday celebration started at cockcrow with a very solemn Office of the resurrection, which was for all the people. The structure was as follows:

Three responsories or antiphons with collects in honor of the resurrection on the third day
General intercessions
Incensing
Sunday Gospel of the resurrection
Procession of the cross with psalmody
Station of the cross: psalm and collect, blessing and dismissal

Vespers opens with a rite of light: lamps are lit with the light taken from the Holy Sepulcher. This rite symbolizes the risen Christ who comes out of the tomb in order to bring the light of salvation to the world darkened by sin. After the singing of the evening psalms, including Psalm 140, the celebration concludes with a brief stational Office in the place of the cross.

In this cathedral liturgy we find the predecessor of the "appendixes" —devotional visits to holy places—added to the evening and morning Offices, which we will later find in the liturgies of the Ambrosian and Hispanic rites.

With regard to these cathedral liturgies, in chapter 25:5 Egeria emphasizes the fact that the psalms used are always fitting, adapted and chosen with a logic that corresponds to the circumstance.[48]

[48] See the description of the Offices in *Egeria's Travels*, trans. J. Wilkinson, 3rd ed. (Warminster, England, 1999) 146.

3. "Pure" Monastic Office and Urban Monastic Office

Through his works, especially the *Institutes* and the *Conferences*, John Cassian (360–435) has had a decisive influence on the monastic life of the West and East. Books 2 and 3 of the *Institutes* are about the monastic celebration of the Divine Office. Cassian describes, above all, the usages of the Divine Office in the monasteries of Egypt and, indirectly, those of Marseilles in Gaul.

In his work Cassian indicates a variety of usages, referring above all to the number of psalms recited in the nocturnal Office. This variety will be eliminated with the establishment of the so-called "rule of the angel": the recitation of twelve psalms in the nocturnal Offices.[49] The Egyptian monks, most of whom were anchorites, maintain a reduced version of the community celebrations called the "pure" monastic Office—evening and morning prayer—insisting upon solitary uninterrupted prayer united to manual labor.[50]

In his *Institutes* (3, 3, 8–11), Cassian refers to the morning and evening Offices and comments on the meaning of Psalms 140 and 62 of the respective celebrations. In this fragment he makes an explicit relationship between Christian praise, the old sacrifices and the sacrifice of Christ. Quoting Psalm 140:2, Cassian affirms that in the evening celebration a profound meaning can be understood if we consider the celebration in two ways: first, as the true evening sacrifice, instituted by the Lord on the evening of the Last Supper with his apostles, when he founded the sacred mysteries of the Church; second, as the evening sacrifice of the following day, when Christ extended his hands on the cross as a sacrifice for the salvation of the world. For Cassian, the relationship between ecclesial praise and Christ's sacrifice does not come from a pious evocation but rather from the discovery of the true content *in mysterio* of the liturgy.[51]

In the Palestinian area, Cassian gives testimony of a mixed urban-monastic Office in which the monastic and cathedral traditions are united. In Book 3, 3 of his *Institutes,* he refers to the daily celebration of Terce, Sext, and None. He also mentions the hour of Prime, which was established in the monastery to prevent the monks from returning to their beds to sleep after the morning and night Offices.[52] According to Cassian, the daily Office of Bethlehem included:

[49] See *De institutis coenobiorum* 2, 2–6.

[50] See *De institutis coenobiorum* 3, 2.

[51] See J. Pinell, "Liturgia delle Ore," *Anàmnesis* 5:67.

[52] *De institutis coenobiorum* 3, 4, 2.

From cockcrow to just before daybreak: nocturnal psalmody as in Egypt, followed by Lauds (Psalms 148–150).

At sunrise: morning prayer, made up of Psalms 50, 62, and 89 with other prayers.

At the hours of Terce, Sext, None: lesser hours, each with three psalms and three prayers.

Evening: monastic evening psalmody, as in Egypt, probably with some cathedral elements.

On Friday nights a vigil was celebrated that lasted until dawn.[53]

The structure of the daily Offices was adjusted to the symbolism of the numbers, establishing seven times of prayer: nocturnal vigil, Lauds, Prime, Terce, Sext, None, and Vespers. Of all these, Cassian attributes special importance to the nocturnal prayer celebrated communally in an environment of contemplative silence and alert vigilance. Its very simple structure includes a combination of twelve psalms and two readings—one from the Old Testament and another from the New Testament. The pauses of silence and the collect prayer are intercalated into the psalmody.[54] He also speaks of "canonical vigils," which were celebrated as a community, and the "private vigils" that the monks observed in their cells. For Cassian, this continuous prayer during the whole day, even while working, becomes a kind of uninterrupted spiritual offering to God, an expression of a docile and humble heart, a recognition of the sovereignty of God, and an expression of vigilance and constant struggle. The objective was to always keep lips and hearts occupied in spiritual meditation.[55] It is evident that the modern problem of the relationship between liturgical and individual piety, which posed a great dilemma for later generations, not only was not a worry for those monks but rather seems to have been resolved for them. For Cassian, prayer and work, liturgy and life, community and individual are harmonized and complement each other, forming a unitary and organic synthesis.[56]

Through the writings of St. Basil († 379) we know about the monastic Office of Cappadocia. His two great *Rules* contain abundant infor-

[53] *De institutis coenobiorum* 3, 4, 2.

[54] See *De institutis coenobiorum* 2, 4, 6, 7, 10.

[55] See *De institutis coenobiorum* 2, 12, 13, 15.

[56] See the extensive, detailed description of the monastic Egyptian Office of the fourth century, like the monastic urban Office in the East in R. Taft, *The Liturgy of the Hours in East and West*, 2nd rev. ed. (Collegeville, Minn., 1993) 75–91.

mation on the morning and evening celebrations of the monks. But because of the fact that Basil rejects the word "monks," reasoning that this word only included Christians who took things seriously, the Offices imitated in large part the cathedral celebrations, adding the hours of Terce, Sext, None, and later Compline. Basil introduced the novelty of a nocturnal vigil celebrated not at cockcrow, as in Palestine and Antioch, but rather at midnight. In his *Rules* (37, 2–5) we find the reasoning behind the daily hours: he says they are traditional hours, quoting the well-known texts of the Acts of the Apostles. For the morning and evening Offices of the cathedral hours the meaning is the same as that which we found in John Chrysostom.[57] Basil also gives us the wonderful information on the "giving of thanks through light," constituted by the evening hymn φῶς ἱλαρόν. In his treatise *On the Holy Spirit* 29, Basil says that this hymn was already old in his times.

CONCLUSION

The great wealth of documentation from the fourth century allows us to verify that in Palestine, Syria, Asia Minor, and Constantinople a defined and permanent *cursus* of the cathedral Office was being organized and structured. This Office was celebrated by all the community: the bishop, clergy, and lay people. The community and ecclesial dimension of prayer was strongly cultivated by those Christians, who felt that their strength came from realizing that they were the Body of Christ. Being absent from the liturgical community meant that the Body of Christ would be weakened, depriving others of feeling that they were members.

The morning and evening Offices constituted the principal celebrations of daily prayer. The morning prayer, a Christian form of beginning and consecrating the new day, was a service of thanksgiving and praise for the current day as well as for the salvation received through Jesus Christ. Vespers was the Christian end of the day, a time to thank God for the benefits received and to ask forgiveness for the wrongs done during the day; added to this was a petition for the grace and protection of God and for a peaceful night, free of sin.

These celebrations included elements for all the people, such as certain psalms and canticles suitable for each hour and carried out with the participation of all the people through responsories and antiphons. The schedule of the celebration developed with light, incense,

[57] See PG 31:1012ff.

processions, prayers, and intercessions. The symbol of the light was common at both times of prayer: the sunrise and the new day, with its passing from darkness to light, made reference to the resurrection of Christ, the Sun of justice, and the lamp in the evening was a symbol of the light in the world that shines in the darkness.

The monastic Office was generally characterized by the celebration of seven hours of community prayer, as well as continuous individual prayer. Toward the end of the fourth century the monks developed a monastic *cursus* with the introduction of the lesser hours and constructed a combination of monastic and cathedral elements of the morning and evening Offices; in these they conserved the continuous monastic psalmody at the beginning as well as at the end of the monastic rhythm of the day. They introduced the new hour of Compline. The vigils and the psalmody had an ascetic character, developing at the same time the contemplative aspect. Worth noting is the harmonization of prayer, work, and monastic life.

Bibliography

AA.VV. *Liturgia delle Ore: Tempo e rito.* Atti della XXII Settimana di Studio dell'Associazione Professori di Liturgia, Susa (TO), August 29–September 3, 1993). Rome, 1994.

Beckwith, R. T. "The Daily and Weekly Worship of the Primitive Church in Relation to Its Jewish Antecedents." *Evangelical Quarterly* 56 (1984) 65–80.

Bradshaw, P. F. *Daily Prayer in the Early Church: A Study of the Origin and Early Development of the Divine Office.* New York, 1982.

De Gennaro, G., ed. *La preghiera nella Bibbia.* Naples, 1983.

Koenig, J. *Rediscovering New Testament Prayer: Boldness and Blessing in the Name of Jesus.* San Francisco, 1992.

Pinell, J. "Liturgia delle Ore." *Anàmnesis* 5.

Salmon, P. "La oración de las horas." In *La Iglesia en oración: Introducción a la liturgia,* 855–955. 2nd ed. Barcelona, 1967.

Sigal, P. "Early Christian and Rabbinic Liturgical Affinities: Exploring Liturgical Acculturation." *New Testament Studies* 30 (1984) 63–90.

Taft, R. *The Liturgy of the Hours in East and West: The Origins of the Divine Office and Its Meaning for Today.* 2nd ed. rev. Collegeville, Minn., 1993.

Robert F. Taft, S.J.

2

The Liturgy of the Hours in the East

I. INTRODUCTION

The accepted taxonomy for the Liturgy of the Hours divides the numerous Offices that developed in the Christian East from the end of the fourth century into three types: monastic, cathedral, and urban monastic or mixed.[1] These are not just three Offices, much less three successive chronological stages of the development of the same Office, but three distinct kinds of Offices that evolved in three separate areas of Church life. The first two types evolved simultaneously from the mid-fourth century. The third, a synthesis of the first two, is already visible in the last quarter of the same century.

1. *Monastic Offices*

"Pure" monastic-type Offices characteristic of Egyptian monasticism had no special relation to the time of day when they were celebrated but were simply a stimulus to the monk's uninterrupted prayer. They comprised continuous psalmody according to the numbering of the psalter. Each unit of psalmody was followed by a prostration for private prayer and ended with a collect. Scripture readings concluded the synaxis.

2. *Cathedral Offices*

The cathedral Hours of Morning Praise and Evensong were popular services with rituals that developed the symbolism of the rising sun and the evening lamp as images of Christ, the Light of the world.

[1] R. Taft, *The Liturgy of the Hours in East and West: The Origins of the Divine Office and Its Meaning for Today,* 2nd rev. ed. (Collegeville, Minn., 1993) = *La Liturgia delle Ore in Oriente e in Occidente: Le origini dell'Ufficio divino e il suo significato oggi,* Testi di teologia 4 (Milan, 1988) = *La Liturgie des Heures en Orient et en Occident: Origine et sens de l'Office divin,* Mysteria 2 (Turnhout, 1991).

Unlike monastic Offices, they were clearly related to the time of celebration, with psalms, chants, and symbols chosen to suit the hour. Evensong, for instance, opened with a *lucernarium,* or ritualization of the evening lamp, at the coming of darkness, a symbol of Christ illuminating the sin-darkened world. The lamplighting was often accompanied by a Hymn of Light. Then followed the evening psalm, Psalm 140/141, with an offering of incense, a symbol of praise rising to the throne of God, as in Psalm 140/141:2. This opening was more or less standard, as were the concluding intercessions and dismissal. Within this fixed framework one could find other elements, depending on the tradition: additional psalms, collects, a canticle or responsory, perhaps a lesson.

Morning Praise began with a penitential psalm (Psalm 50/51) or a matutinal psalm (Psalm 62/63) and ended with an Old Testament canticle, the psalms of Lauds (Psalms 148–150), the *Gloria in excelsis* on Sundays and feasts, and the usual concluding intercessions and prayers. In between, other elements such as variable psalms, a hymn in praise of the morning light, or a lesson could be found, depending on the tradition.

Cathedral vigils had three basic forms:

1. The weekly resurrection vigil of three antiphons, incensation, and the proclamation of the paschal gospel.

2. Occasional vigils, consisting of the repetition of a liturgical unit comprising, though not necessarily in this order, cathedral psalmody (responsories and antiphons), lessons, prostration for prayer followed by collects and, often, preaching. This type of vigil, found usually as an extension of Vespers, could be longer or shorter to suit the occasion.

3. The vigil of readings, an extended Word service, as at Easter and some other feasts.

3. Hybrid Urban Monastic Offices

Monks living near urban centers in Palestine, Mesopotamia, Syria, and Cappadocia were in contact with the life of the secular churches and adopted cathedral usages into their Offices without, however, abandoning the continuous monastic psalmody inherited from Lower Egypt. This is how hybrid, mixed Offices evolved from the end of the fourth century, a development that carried the evolution of the Liturgy of the Hours three steps further:

a) The urban monks filled out the daily horarium by turning the traditional fixed times of Christian private prayer at the third, sixth, and ninth hours into formal liturgical services—the "Little Hours" of Terce, Sext, None.

b) They effected a synthesis of monastic and cathedral usages by adopting elements of cathedral Morning Praise and Evensong, while retaining the continuous monastic psalmody at the beginning and end of the monastic order of the day.

c) They introduced a new Office, Compline, as bedtime prayer, thus duplicating Vespers, which ended the day in both the cathedral and pure monastic cursus.

These hybrid urban monastic horaria and Offices were not the same everywhere. The sources agree that three psalms formed the core of the Little Hours and that Compline included Psalm 90/91. Our information on Vespers is less explicit, but Cassian implies that urban monastic Vespers in Bethlehem was not just a replica of the Egyptian monastic psalmody, so it probably had incorporated at least such classic cathedral elements as the *lucernarium* with a hymn, Psalm 140/141 with incense, and intercessions, giving the following tentative and ideal structure repeated in later hybrid Eastern vesperal rites:

Continuous monastic psalmody
Light ritual with Hymn of Light
Psalm 140 with incense
Intercessions
To this skeleton responsories, lesson, and canticles were later added.

But the most significant differences among the hybrid traditions occur in the Offices that open the monastic day: Nocturns and Matins or cathedral Lauds. In Palestine and Antioch, Lauds was appended to the nocturnal Office, which went from cockcrow (around 3 A.M.) to before dawn. Later another Matins service was added at daybreak, comprising morning psalms and, in Antioch, other elements borrowed from cathedral Morning Praise, such as the *Gloria in excelsis* and concluding intercessions. But in Cappadocia, the Office of cathedral Matins, celebrated at dawn, apparently retained its integrity, including the psalms of Lauds, while a separate monastic vigil of continuous psalmody was introduced at midnight. So it seems that the Palestinian monks started with an essentially Egyptian monastic system into which they introduced cathedral elements. The Cappadocian ascetics took as their point of departure cathedral Matins-Lauds at dawn and added a vigil service of continuous monastic psalmody at midnight.

In sum, then, from the desert monastics of Egypt the later, mostly hybrid Hours inherited the practice of "continuous" or "monastic" psalmody, that is, recitation of the psalms in numerical order without regard to their content and the meditative reading of other Scriptures. The "cathedral" usages of the secular churches furnished the "select" psalmody—psalms suited by their content to a particular time of day (Psalm 62/63 in the morning, Psalm 140/141 in the evening)—as well as the hymns and ceremonial embellishment shunned by the desert monks, and the intercessions for, and dismissal of, various categories already customary at the Eucharist. Different urban monastic centers combined the systems in various ways, adding cathedral elements to a monastic framework or vice versa, to create the hybrid Offices.

4. The Hours in the East Today

In the Christian East these developments evolved a full cursus of canonical Hours in seven distinct traditions. At one end of the spectrum are the Armenian and East Syrian or Assyro-Chaldean Offices, which have best retained their pristine cathedral character unalloyed. At the other extreme is the Coptic tradition, strongly monastic in its history and hence in its liturgy, which has kept its monastic and cathedral Offices juxtaposed and separate, not synthesized. Other traditions, especially the Byzantine, are clear hybrids, the product of the fusion of monastic and cathedral usages.

Our brief description of these Offices will concentrate on the principal Hours at the beginning (Nocturns-Matins-Lauds) and end (Vespers) of the day in the several traditions. The Little Hours, with their original core of three psalms, remain common to most traditions and present no particular historical or structural problems.

II. THE ARMENIAN OFFICE

1. History

The historical cradle of Christian Armenia lies around Lake Van in Asia Minor, just east of Greek Cappadocia and north of Syriac Mesopotamia, and the earliest Christian influences in the third to the fifth century flowed in from both streams, first Syriac, then Greek. From the fifth to the seventh century, when the indigenous Armenian Christian tradition had reached the Golden Age of its formation, there was strong liturgical influence from Jerusalem. A period of Byzantinization followed, from the ninth to the thirteenth century, when Constantinopolitan political and ecclesiastical influence was especially strong. Finally, during the Crusades, from the twelfth through the fourteenth century, the Latin presence in Asia Minor also left its traces on the liturgical uses of Armenia.

2. *The Offices*

The Armenian Office has seven Hours, but not the exact same seven we are used to:

Night Hour (Nocturns)	*giśerayin żam*
Morning Hour (Matins)	*arawōtean żam*
Sunrise Hour (Prime)	*arewagali żam*
Midday Hour *(Typika)*	*caśu żam*
Evening Hour (Vespers)	*erekoyean żam*
Hour of peace	*xałałakan żam*
Hour of rest (Compline)	*hangstean żam*

a) Nocturns

The Armenian night Office, the only one with no continuous monastic psalmody, is structured as follows:[2]

Opening prayers:	Doxology
	Our Father
Invitatory:	Doxology (Psalm 50:17)
	Psalms 3, 87, 102, 142
	Chant
	Biddings
	Chant
	Collect
Psalmody:	Doxology
	Variable psalms
	[Office of the Dead—later addition]
	Old Testament canticle
	Refrain of the canticle
Conclusion:	Intercessions
	Collect
	Concluding chants and prayers

[2] Reconstruction after G. Winkler, "The Armenian Night Office," I: *Journal of the Society of Armenian Studies* 1 (1984) 93–113; II: *Revue des études arméniennes* 17 (1983) 471–551.

b) Matins

Our Father
Introit: Psalm 89:14-17
Doxology
(original beginning of Sunday cathedral vigil)
Old Testament canticles: Dan 3:26-45 + refrain; Dan 3:52-88 + refrain
Biddings
New Testament canticles: *Magnificat-Benedictus-Nunc dimittis*
Litany and collect

(Cathedral vigil on Sundays)
Psalm 112:1-3
Psalm 43:26, 24
Psalm 145:10, 1
Gospel of the Myrrhophores
Gospel refrain
Biddings

Psalm 50 + refrain
Biddings
Psalms 148–150 + refrain
Gloria in excelsis
Kataxioson (Dignare Domne)
Refrain of the Resurrection
Intercessions:
Litany and collect
Angel of peace petitions and collect
Prayer of Blessing
Trisagion

To this original conclusion of the Office the following have been appended:

Bidding
Responsory
Gospel of healing
Refrain of the gospel
Bidding
Blessing

c) Vespers

Armenian Vespers is a purely cathedral service with no monastic psalmody:

Our Father	Psalm 54:17-18; Psalm 84
Invitatory	Psalms 139, 140, 141
Fixed vesperal psalms	Prayer of blessing of the light
Lucernarium	Hymn of light (= φῶς ἱλαρόν, on Sundays)
	Prayer of thanksgiving for the light
	Biddings
	Responsory 1
	Responsory 2: *Dirigatur* (Psalm 140:2)
Intercessions	Litany
	Angel of peace petitions
	Collect
	Prayer of blessing

As at Matins, other material has been appended to this original conclusion of the Office:

Trisagion
Biddings
Psalm 121
Refrain of Psalm 121
Biddings
Collect
Psalms of dismissal (two or three)
Biddings
Collect of dismissal
Our Father
Dismissal

3. Present Usage

Today in Armenian parishes, Vespers is usually celebrated only on Saturday evening, though many parishes still celebrate daily the night and morning Offices together in the morning. Within the Patriarchate of Constantinople, during Lent parishes in the same town take turns celebrating alternately on weekdays the Peace and Rest (Compline) Services and the Sunrise Service (Prime).

III. THE ASSYRO-CHALDEAN OFFICE

There are three Syriac liturgical families: East Syrian, West Syrian, and Maronite, all different, all related. Three principal liturgical centers had a major influence in the origins of these rites: Antioch, Jerusalem, and Edessa. Of these, only Edessa was a center of Syriac language and culture; the other two were Greek cities with Syriac-speaking minorities.

The East Syrian or Assyro-Chaldean Rite, used today by the members of the "Church of the East," who call themselves "Assyrians," as well as by the Chaldean and Malabar Catholics, is the ancient usage of the Mesopotamian Church in the Persian Empire, formerly centered in the Catholicosate of Seleucia-Ctesiphon on the Tigris River, about fifty kilometers downriver from Baghdad, Iraq.

1. *History*

Though we know very little about the early shape of the liturgy of Mesopotamia that developed into the Assyro-Chaldean Rite, it is indigenously Syriac in origin, that is, it is not an adaptation of earlier Greek usages, and so its roots can be traced to Edessa.

The reform instigated by Catholicos Igo ʿyahb III in 650–51 at the Upper Monastery or Convent of Mar Gabriel in Mosul established the norms for the cathedral Office that fixed it in more or less the shape in which it has come down to us, while leaving the monks free to organize their nightly vigils according to their own customs. It is the usage of this Upper Monastery that has been preserved until today in the Assyro-Chaldean Liturgy of the Hours.

In modern times the Hours have been gathered in the three-volume *Breviarium iuxta ritum Syrorum Orientalium id est Chaldaeorum* (Paris,[3] 1938) of the Chaldean Vincentian (Lazarist) Paul Bedjan (1838–1925), from Khosrova in Persia.

2. *The Liturgical Disposition of the Church*

To understand the ancient ceremonial of the Assyro-Chaldean Offices, one must recall that until the fourteenth century, East Syrian churches were equipped with a bema, or large enclosed platform in the center of the nave.[4] This enclosure, connected to the sanctuary by a narrow

[3] 1886–1887, reprint Rome.

[4] On the bema and its liturgical use, see R. Taft, "Some Notes on the Bema in the East and West Syrian Traditions," *OCP* 34 (1968) 326–359; idem, "On the Use of the Bema in the East-Syrian Liturgy," *Eastern Churches Review* 3 (1970) 30–39; both updated in the same author's *Liturgy in Byzantium and Beyond,* Collected Studies

pathway, the *bet-šqaqona*, contained the bishop's throne, seats for the concelebrating priests, and pulpits for the Scripture readings.

The East Syrian liturgical commentators have provided us with a description of the use of the bema in the celebration of the Offices. The opening procession of the services was an exit rather than an introit, not proceeding into sanctuary but in the reverse direction, out from the sanctuary to the bema in the nave. This was true not only of the Eucharist but also of the Hours: all three cathedral services in this tradition are rich in ceremonial as befits their popular character, and this ceremonial is centered on the bema and the comings and goings to and from it. When the bema fell into disuse around the end of the fourteenth century, the popular ceremonial of these Offices lost their raison d'être and just evaporated.

3. The Offices

The Assyro-Chaldean Liturgy of the Hours, like the Armenian, has remained largely cathedral in character. Though today's Office does bear some traces of monastic influence in the lesser Hours, the three cathedral Hours of Matins, Vespers, and the festal cathedral vigil have retained their cathedral purity unalloyed. Indeed, in today's Assyro-Chaldean breviary these are the only extant Hours outside of Lent, except for *Subbaʿa* or Compline or certain saints' days and feasts apart from Sunday.

The East Syrian monks also had the three Little Hours and Compline, which eventually entered the Assyro-Chaldean cursus, then later disappeared except for Terce and Sext on Lenten ferias and some extant remnants during the rest of the year.

Since the Middle Ages the weekday propers for the daily cathedral Offices have been arranged in two "choirs" or "weeks," that is, a series of twelve propers divided into two "weeks," depending on whether they follow an even or uneven Sunday in the calendar numbering. Each week has six sets of propers, one for each day, Monday through Saturday, for the Offices of *Lelya, Ṣapra,* and *Ramša* (Nocturns, Matins, Vespers). Two choirs alternate intoning the services, the First Choir on Monday, Wednesday, and Friday of uneven weeks, the Second Choir on Tuesday and Thursday, with the order reversed for even weeks. These propers are gathered in the *Book of Before and After,* which takes

Series (London, 1995), chaps. 7–8 and pp. 3–6 of the "Additional Notes and Comment."

its name from the variable "*śurraya* (Alleluia psalm) before" and the "*ʿOnita* (refrain or antiphon) before" and the parallel pieces "after," that is, before and after the cathedral psalmody of Vespers (Psalm 140/141, etc.).

a) Nocturns (Lelya)

There are several types of monastic vigils in the Assyro-Chaldean Office, depending on the day or feast. On ferial days the monks rise for a nocturnal Office at midnight, followed by another period of rest before Matins. This night Office has the classic structure of a monastic vigil:

Invitatory: Psalm 3:6-9 and Psalm 113
  or Psalm 118:62-64
  or Psalm 118:57-58 and Psalm 91
Continuous monastic psalmody: seven *Hullale* (sections of the psalter)
ʿOnyata d-mawtba (poetic strophes)
Select psalm with refrain
Hymn
Litany

On days when there is Compline, this Nocturns or *Lelya* follows Compline immediately and there is no rest beforehand. And on Sundays, instead of returning to bed after Nocturns or *Lelya,* the monks add two more sections of the psalter, then proceed directly to the cathedral vigil *(Qale d-šahra),* Matins *(Ṣapra),* and Sunday Eucharist. Finally, on the eve of three feasts—Christmas, Epiphany, and Good Friday—there is a vigil that lasts through the whole night.

b) Cathedral Vigil (Qale d-šahra)

The cathedral vigil, or *Qale d-šahra,* celebrated in the narthex of the church since the disappearance of the bema, formerly comprised:

Opening of sanctuary doors and veil
Procession of the bishop to the bema
Three *marmyata* (originally composed of Old Testament canticles),
  followed by prayers
Procession from the bema to the sanctuary and chant of the *ʿOnita šubbaha* (psalm with refrain)
Tešbohta (= *Gloria,* a poetic composition)
Litany and prayer

c) Matins (Ṣapra)

Matins, or *Tešmešta d-ṣapra,* at dawn has a pure cathedral shape. The following general outline does not include all possible variants:

Fixed morning psalms with refrains: Psalms 99; 90; 103:1-16a; 112; 92[5]
Lauds psalms: Psalms 148 (149 on ferias only); 150; 116
Collect
ʿOnita d-ṣapra (Incense Antiphon of Matins, with solemn incensation) or the hymn *Laku Mara* (on ferial days)
Nuhra (festal Hymns of Light)
Benedicite (festal) or *Miserere* (ferial)
Gloria in excelsis (festal) or *Tešbohta* (hymn)
Trisagion and Our Father
Trisagion prayer
Prayer of blessing

At the beginning of the Office, the bishop and clergy were in the sanctuary for the chanting of the opening psalms with their refrains, usually referring to the theme of light. Psalm 99 is a psalm of entrance, suited to open the service: "Praise the Lord all the earth . . . come into his presence with exultation . . . enter into his gates with thanksgiving." The others are all psalms of praise, some of which (for example, Psalms 103:2; 112:13) were chosen because of their reference to light or sunrise. During the chanting of Psalm 112 all the lamps were lighted, and the bishop and clergy went out in solemn procession to the bema for Lauds and the rest of the service.

d) Vespers (Ramša)

In *Ramša,* or Vespers, too, we see a pure cathedral service, if we prescind from the remains of None that have become attached to the beginning of Vespers:

Marmita (psalmody: remnant of None)
ʿOnita of incense
Laku Mara Hymn and its collect

[5] The "classic" cathedral Matins Psalm 62 is missing here because the Psitta version of Psalm 62 makes no references to the ὀρθρίζω of LXX Psalm 62:1 and translates the LXX "in the mornings" (ἐν τοῖς ὄρθροις) of verse 6 as "in the nights." Psalm 90 in Matins, the traditional psalm of Compline and Sext in other traditions, is an Assyro-Chaldean peculiarity.

šurraya da-qdam (Alleluia psalm before the vesperal psalmody)
ʿOnita da-qdam (antiphon before the vesperal psalmody)
Fixed vesperal cathedral psalms: Psalms 140; 141; 118:105-112; 116
šurraya d-batar (Alleluia psalm after the vesperal psalmody)
ʿOnita d-batar (antiphon after the vesperal psalmody)
Intercessions: *karozuta* (litany) + angel of peace petitions
Trisagion and its collect
Prayer of blessing

Stational procession:
(On feasts of the Lord and memorials: *Suyyake* = Psalms 93–98)
ʿOnita d-basiliqe (antiphon of the procession)
šurraya (Alleluia psalm)
Our Father
Final prayers

This is the outline of festive *Ramša.* Ferial Vespers omits the *ʿOnyata da-qdam* and *d-batar* and concludes as follows:

Trisagion and collect
ʿOnita d-ramša (antiphon of the evening)
šurraya (Alleluia psalm)
Procession, with *ʿOnita d-sahde* (antiphon of the martyrs)
Subbaʿa (Compline)
Final prayers

So *Ramša* began, like Mass and Matins, with the raising of the outer sanctuary veil. Then, while the bishop and clergy proceeded to the bema, the *ʿOnita* of incense, with its theme resumed from Psalm 140/141:2, was chanted between the verses of Psalm 83, a psalm of love and longing for God's temple ideally suited for such an introit procession.

This was followed by the *lucernarium,* when the evening lamp on the qestroma, or platform before the sanctuary door, was lighted with flame brought from the ever-burning lamp within the sanctuary, as in Egeria (24:4), and a prayer was said to Christ the Light of the world. Then came the prayer of incense and the incensation, the hymn *Laku Mara* ("To you, Lord"), the vesperal psalms and accompanying ecclesiastical poetry.

The service concluded with the customary intercessions and final benediction or Prayer of Inclination, all at the bema. Then the veil of the sanctuary was closed, indicating the true end of *Ramša*. The stational service that followed, similar to the one at the end of Byzantine festive Vespers, took place only on Sundays and was not an integral part of *Ramša*.

4. Present Usage

The Churches of this rite have by and large retained in parish worship the daily celebration of the integral cathedral cursus. In Syro-Malabar usage the parish Office has died out, but some efforts are being made to restore it.

II. THE WEST SYRIAN AND MARONITE TRADITIONS

The West Syrian or Syro-Antiochene Rite is the tradition of the Syrian Orthodox in the Patriarchate of Antioch and in India, as well as of the Syrian and Malankarese Catholics.

1. History

The West Syrian Rite is a synthesis of native Syriac elements, especially hymns and other choral pieces, with material translated from Greek liturgical texts of Antiochene and hagiopolite provenance. This synthesis was the work of non-Chalcedonian monastic communities in the Syriac-speaking hinterlands of Syria, Palestine, and parts of Mesopotamia, beyond the Greek cities of the Mediterranean littoral. These Syriac-speaking Christians were organized into an independent church under Bishop Jacob Baradai († 578), which is the reason why they are sometimes called "Jacobites."

The Maronite Rite, once considered just a Latinized variant of the Syro-Antiochene tradition, is in fact an independent synthesis by Syriac-speaking Chalcedonian communities which in Syria (though not in Palestine) managed to establish themselves independently of the Greek-speaking coastline and to preserve their ancient Syriac usages. Later most of these Syriac-speaking Chalcedonians were Byzantinized, but the ancient Syrian rites and traditions were preserved and developed by monks who had taken refuge in the mountains of Lebanon at the beginning of the eighth century, thus laying the foundations for the Maronite Church. This Church came into contact with the Crusaders in the Middle Ages and underwent progressive Latin influence. But the Office was not tarnished by this, and the Mass has recently been restored.

2. *The Offices*

The Maronite and Syrian traditions both have a full complement of the customary seven canonical Hours: Nocturns, Matins, Terce, Sext, None, Vespers, and Compline.[6] Matins, or *Safro,* has absorbed the remains of the cathedral vigil. In Nocturns, or *Lilyo,* the replacement of the continuous nocturnal psalmody by ecclesiastical poetry and the doubling of Matins created by the juxtaposition in the same service of monastic and cathedral usages have created structural problems that need not concern us here.

a) Matins (Safro)

The following schema reveals the affinity of the morning Office in the two related traditions. The various Syriac pieces—*Nuhro, Sogito, Boʿuto, Qolo*—are all strophic chants, ecclesiastical poetry in one form or another, in spite of the literal meaning of their names, which at times betrays the original liturgical unit they have replaced. The *Boʿuto* ("supplication") at the end of the Offices is a paradigmatic instance.

Maronite:	*West Syrian (Sundays)*
REMNANTS OF CATHEDRAL VIGIL	
Magnificat	Psalm 50
Psalm 62	Psalm 62
Psalm 90 (festive)	Psalm 18
	Canticle of Isaiah 42:10-13; 45:8
CATHEDRAL MATINS	
Psalm 50 (festive)	
Nuhro (Hymn of St. Ephrem)	
Benedicite	*Magnificat*
Fixed psalms of Lauds: 148, 149, 150, 116	
Sogito	Beatitudes
Ḥussoyo (Prooemion and *Sedro)*	
Mazmuro (Lessons: festive)	
Hussoyo (Prooemion and *Sedro)*	

[6] On these Offices, see the bibliography in Taft, *The Liturgy of the Hours,* 239–247, 379–381.

Boʿuto	*Qolo, Boʿuto*
	Hullolo (Alleluia psalm)
	Gospel

Maronite Vespers today comprises:

Opening prayers
[Monastic synaxis:]
Prayer (before the psalmody)
(formerly: variable monastic psalmody)
Alleluia (after the psalmody)
[Cathedral Vespers]
Invitatory: Prayer
Psalm 50 with refrains
Fixed cathedral psalmody: Psalms 140; 141; 118:105-112; 116

3. Present Usage

Though it is impossible to generalize, given the wide variety of usage from country to country in the West Syrian, Syro-Malankarese, and Maronite traditions, these Offices are still used in both monastic and parish worship throughout the world today.[7]

V. THE COPTIC OFFICE

The Coptic Rite, celebrated today in Bohairic, the dialect of Lower Egypt, is the liturgical tradition of native Egyptians or Copts ("Copt" is the "gypt" of Egypt). It is a highly penitential, contemplative rite, long, solemn, even monotonous, with much less speculative poetry, symbolic splendor, and sumptuous ceremonial than, for example, the Byzantine tradition.

1. History

There had always been two Egypts: that of the indigenous Copts, concentrated chiefly along the Nile in Upper Egypt, and that of the Greek-speaking population of the Delta and along the coast. Egyptian Christianity began in Alexandria and was Greek. By the third century, however, there were numerous converts among the Copts, and the Scriptures and liturgy were already in the native tongue. Not until the rise of monasticism, however, did the Coptic Church solidify as a native counterbalance to the cosmopolitan, theologically sophisticated,

[7] Details in Taft, *The Liturgy of the Hours*, 243–247.

Hellenic Church of Alexandria, whose speculative, spiritualizing intellectualism stood in marked contrast to the popular, traditionalistic piety of the South, a largely oral culture transmitted through sayings, proverbs, and ritual rather than through theological treatises.

In the aftermath of the Council of Chalcedon (451), the non-Chalcedonian Copts underwent fierce persecution and were driven from their churches. The patriarchate, forced to leave Alexandria, took refuge in the Monastery of St. Macarius, still functioning today in the desert of Scetis, halfway between Cairo and Alexandria. This banishment from Alexandria emancipated indigenous Egyptian Christianity from the tutelage of its Hellenic overlords of the Mediterranean littoral and the Nile Delta. Thereafter the Monastery of St. Macarius became perforce the center of the Coptic Church, and Coptic monastic culture—concrete, popular, ascetic—created the liturgy and Offices of the Coptic Rite.

2. *The Monastic Cursus of the* Horologion

Today's Coptic Rite is basically the usage of the monasteries of Scetis somewhat modified by later reforms. The basic structure of its services, described by Cassian's *De institutis coenobiorum,* is still clearly visible in the eight Hours of the present Coptic *Horologion:* Morning Prayer, Terce, Sext, None, the Eleventh Hour (Vespers), and Compline, plus the "Prayer of the Veil" and a Midnight Hour comprising three nocturns. These last two Hours are later additions that repeat psalmody already distributed throughout the other six Hours. The Prayer of the Veil, a doubling of Compline used only in monasteries, appears first in *Abuʾl-Barakat ibn Kabar* around 1320, exists only in Arabic sources (a sure sign of its late origin), and is composed of elements from the other Hours.

With the exception of these two later additions, the basic structure of all these Hours is the same:

Fixed initial prayers
Twelve psalms (ideally)
Gospel lesson
Troparia (poetic refrains)
Kyrie eleison (41 or 50 times)
Trisagion
Our Father

Dismissal prayer of absolution
Final prayer

Variety among the Hours is minimal. Morning Prayer has the Great Doxology *(Gloria in excelsis)*, as one would expect, and the Creed. Other Hours also have certain minor peculiarities: the later addition of seven further psalms to the original twelve at Morning Prayer and some variety in the final prayers. This is the structure of all the traditional Hours from Morning Prayer to Compline. If we prescind from the refrains, or *troparia*, a later addition of Palestinian origin, we see an Office that is almost pure Cassian.

3. *Cathedral Remnants*

In addition to these monastic Hours, we find other services, the Offering of Incense morning and evening, and the threefold *Psalmodia* of the night, the morning, and the evening, which contains elements apparently of cathedral provenance.[8]

4. *Present Usage*

The Coptic Orthodox Church is at present undergoing a remarkable monastic renewal, and its Offices are in vigorous use in both monasteries and parishes, where the morning and evening Offering of Incense and the *Psalmodia* are celebrated.[9]

VI. THE ETHIOPIAN OFFICES

Like the Coptic Rite, the Ethiopian tradition has separate parallel cathedral and monastic Hours that have not been synthesized into one hybrid Office.[10] More surprising still, the Ethiopians have not just two but several *Saʿātāt* traditions of monastic-type Hours.

[8] See the schema of these Hours in Taft, *The Liturgy of the Hours*, 253–256.

[9] Details in Taft, *The Liturgy of the Hours*, 256–259; idem, "Praise in the Desert: The Coptic Monastic Office Yesterday and Today," *Wor* 56 (1982) 513–536; idem, "A Pilgrimage to the Origins of Religious Life: The Fathers of the Desert Today," *The American Benedictine Review* 36 (1985) 113–142 = "Peregrinaje a los origines de la vida religiosa: los Padres del Desierto hoy," *Cistercium* 38 (1986) 31–61.

[10] The fundamental work on the Ethiopian Hours is Habtemichael Kidane, *L'ufficio divino etiopico: Studio storico-critico con particolare riferimento alle ore cattedrali* (Rome, 1996). See also B. Velat, *Etudes sur le Meʿerāf: Commun de l'office divin éthiopien. Introduction, traduction française, commentaire liturgique et musicale, PatOr* 33, passim.

1. Cathedral Services

The native Ethiopian cathedral Office comprises the three chief Hours of Vespers, Nocturns, and Matins, except at certain times of the year such as Lent, when one also finds the Third, Sixth, and Ninth Hours as well as some special occasional Offices. These cathedral Hours, celebrated in the larger churches on days of special solemnity, are executed by the *dabtara,* professional cantors or "masters" of the *qumet,* or complex Ethiopian sacred chant. This chant is executed *aquaquam* (from *quoma,* "to stand"), that is, standing, keeping time with the *maquomeya,* or choir cane, held in the right hand and accompanying the chant with bodily movements to the beat of drums and the shaking of sistrums. These movements are the famous "liturgical dance" of the Ethiopians.

a) Wāzēmā (Solemn Vespers)

An Ethiopian festive celebration opens in the early afternoon of the vigil with the chanting of Vespers, a service of four or five hours duration. Here is the structure of festive Vespers:

Fixed opening prayer
Wāzēmā (proper hymn)
Psalm 23
Baḥāmestu (proper antiphon)
Ḳenē wāzēmā (Vesper hymn) 1
Prayer for rain
Psalm 92
Baḥāmestu (proper antiphon)
Ḳenē wāzēmā (Vesper hymn) 2
Prayer for the sovereign
Psalm 140
Baḥāmestu (proper antiphon)
Liṭon (prayer of evening thanks)
Epistle lesson
Yetebārak (canticle of Daniel 3:52-56)
Yetebārak (antiphon of the canticle)
Two or three *Ḳenē* (hymns)
Mesbāk (Alleluia psalm)
Gospel
Kidān (prayer of evening)
Psalm 101 with *Salast* (antiphon)
Psalm 84 with *Salām* (antiphon)

"Christ Lord, have mercy on us" (three times)
Final prayer
Creed
Our Father

On ferias the two variable psalms of the initial psalmody are part of the continuous psalter, as can be seen from a glance at the Lenten ferial Office.[11] But on festive days these two variable psalms and Psalm 50 are replaced by Psalms 23, 92, and 140, the last of which is a traditional element of cathedral Evensong.

b) Nocturns (Mawaddes) *and Matins or Lauds* (Sebehāta nagh)
This same pattern, in which psalms are alternated throughout the Office, interspersed with chants, prayers, and lessons, is common to the other Hours, though with different psalms and other pieces and with a structure that varies considerably according to the liturgical feasts and seasons.[12] Thus, after a period of repose, Vespers is followed at first cockcrow by Nocturns, or *Mawaddes,* a series of units of psalmody, prayers, and other elements in which both monastic and cathedral elements are intermingled.

Matins (Lauds), or *Sebehāta nagh,* also found in several forms (ferial, festive, for the Marian season, for Holy Week, for Holy Saturday), and Eucharist follow Nocturns without interruption. At *Sebehāta nagh,* two choirs of *dabtara* chant the psalms alternately, intercalated with proper antiphons and interspersed with prayers, litanies, doxologies, hymns, invocations, and intercessions. Among the pieces the classical elements of cathedral Matins are immediately recognizable: Psalm 62, the canticle of Daniel 3, and the Lauds Psalms 148–150.

Another service of the sung Office, *Kestat za-āryām,* is celebrated only on the thirty greatest feasts of the Marian and sanctoral cycles, including the Finding of the Holy Cross, which in the Ethiopian tradition is not considered a Christological solemnity. This Office is the longest Ethiopian Hour and the richest in ecclesiastical, that is, nonbiblical, compositions. It replaces the other morning Offices on feasts when it is celebrated and includes psalms and the entire Ethiopian corpus of fifteen Old and New Testament canticles with antiphons, along with numerous invocations, readings from the *Senkessār*

[11] Schema in Velat, *Etudes sur le Meʿerāf,* 140a.
[12] Schemata in Taft, *The Liturgy of the Hours,* 264–265.

(synaxarium), from *The Book of Miracles of Mary*, from the Gospels, *The Praises of Mary*, and various prayers reserved to the priest.

c) The Saʿatat *Ethiopian Hours*

In addition to the cathedral services, the Ethiopians also have not one but several other cursus of daily prayers preserved in Office books called *Saʿatata* or *Horologia*. Not only are these distinct Offices separate from the cathedral services, but—and this is completely novel and peculiar to Ethiopia—there is not one but four independent and competing types of Ethiopian *horologion:*

1. The *Saʿatat za-Gebs*, or "*Horologion* of the Copts."
2. The *Saʿatat* of Abba Giyorgis Saglawi.
3. A *Saʿatat* that includes the entire psalter in the daily *pensum*.
4. The cursus of prayers found in the manuscript *Vatican Ethiopic 21*.

d) The Saʿatat za-Gebs

The *Saʿatat za-Gebs*, or "*Horologion* of the Copts," is a translation of the Coptic *Horologion* with the addition of Byzantine elements. This cursus has the traditional sevenfold cycle of Offices before the addition of Prime: Nocturns, Matins, Terce, Sext, None, Vespers, Compline.

e) The Night Office

The same is true of the Ethiopian nocturnal service in the *Saʿalat za-Gebs*. It is simply an adaptation of the Coptic *Psalmodia* of the Night. But in the Ethiopic redaction this Matins or "Prayer at Cockcrow" appends considerable additional material not found in present Coptic usage, including three gospels with eschatological themes of watching and vigilance in expectation of the parousia. Here is an outline of this additional material:

New Testament canticles: *Magnificat-Benedictus-Nunc dimittis* (Luke 7:46-55, 68-79; 2:29-32)
Old Testament canticle of Hezekiah (Isaiah 38:10-20)
Gloria in excelsis
Dignare Domine (Kataxioson)
Psalm 91:2-3
Trisagion
Our Father
Creed with its *prooemion*
Prayer and blessing before the gospel

Gospel: Luke 11:5-13
Troparia
Kyrie eleison (fifty-one times)
Absolution
Prayer
Psali
Prayer and blessing before the gospel
Gospel: Mark 13:32-37
Gospel: Matthew 25:14, 30
Kyrie eleison (three times)
Invocation of the Trinity
Prayer of blessing of St. Basil
Invocation of the King of Peace
Deacon: intercession for the Church
Concluding doxology

f) The Eleventh Hour (Vespers)
Even more cathedral elements not found in Coptic usage are interspersed after the monastic psalmody and gospel lesson of the eleventh hour (Vespers) in the Ethiopic recension of the Coptic *Horologion.* These elements peculiar to the Ethiopic recension are italicized in the following outline:

Initial prayers
Monastic psalmody (twelve psalms): Psalms 116–117, 119–128
Gospel lesson
Psalm 129:7-8 with refrain
Psalm 116:1, refrain; verse 2, refrain; glory . . . both now . . . refrain
Hymn of light (= φῶς ἱλαρόν)
Kataxioson (after *Nunc dimittis* in the Coptic recension)
Psalm 91:1 with refrain
Psalm 122:1 with refrain
Troparia
Nunc dimittis
Psalm 140:1, refrain; verse 2, refrain
Trisagion
Evening thanks

Then the Coptic *Horologion* resumes with the customary concluding prayers.

g) The Saʿātāt *of Abba Giyorgis Saglawi*

Abba Giyorgis, nicknamed Baʿāla Saʿātāt, "Composer of the Book of Hours," was a liturgical reformer from the small town of Sagla in Amhara. He died around 1426. He composed the Office that bears his name.[13] This *Saʿātāt* is apparently the only one still in common use, having replaced the Hours of Coptic provenance as the common *horologion* of the Ethiopian Orthodox Church. It comprises Nocturns and the Eleventh and Twelfth Hours.

The Twelfth Hour is a devotional Office in praise of Mary, but Nocturns and the Eleventh Hour, or Vespers, are little more than a series of four Scripture lessons, with a responsorial psalm before the last, always a gospel, at Nocturns. This lection unit is enclosed in a framework of opening prayers and concluding intercessions, hymns, orations, canticles, etc. Thus the Ethiopians can lay claim to having transformed the Hours into a Liturgy of the Word centered on Scripture lections a century before Luther mistakenly concluded that this was the purpose of the Hours.[14]

These Hours, though not celebrated privately but only in church, do not require the participation of the *dabtara,* or trained cantors, needed for the sung Office, and so they are celebrated daily in churches and monasteries throughout the land.

h) The Saʿātāt *of the Psalter*

Another Ethiopian *Saʿātāt* has the customary seven Hours of the Office, with no psalms at Compline *(Newam)* or the Midnight Office *(Lelit),* but with thirty psalms and three canticles in each of the other five Hours, so that the entire Ethiopian psalter, including fifteen biblical canticles, is recited each day.[15]

[13] "On Abba Giyorgis and his *saʿātāt,* see Taddesse Tamrat, *Church and State in Ethiopia* 1270–1527 (Oxford, 1972) 222ff.; Getatchew Haile, "*Fekkare Haymanot* or the Faith of *Abba* Giyorgis Saglawi," *Le Muséon* 94 (1981) 236–237; idem, "Writings of *Abba* Giyorgis Saglawi from Two Unedited Miracles of Mary," *OCP* 48 (1982) 65–91, esp. 65–66, 71, 81, 85.

[14] See Taft, *The Liturgy of the Hours,* 319–20, and the entry "readings" in the Index.

[15] See mss. *Val. Aeth. 15,* in S. Grébaut and E. Tisserant, Codices Aethiopici Vaticani et Borgiani (Vatican City, 1935) 1:45–48; EMML 2097, in Getatchew Haile and W. F. Macomber, *A Catalogue of Ethiopian Manuscripts Microfilmed for the Ethiopian Manuscript Microfilm Library, Addis Ababa, and for the Hill Monastic Manuscript Library, Collegeville* (Collegeville, Minn., 1976) vol. 6.

i) The Saʿātāt *of* Codex Vaticanus Aethiopicus 21

The fifteenth-century manuscript Office in *Codex Vatican Ethiopic 21* gives a cursus with not only the usual midnight, morning, and evening prayers but with prayer for each of the twelve daylight Hours,[16] a practice seen also in the Iberian monastic usage described by Fructuosus of Braga.[17]

In this cursus the morning and day Hours are just a series of nonbiblical prayers without psalmody, canticles, or lessons. But the Midnight Hour and Vespers have four and five biblical readings respectively, and Vespers includes the light ritual with its dialogue and prayer of blessing from *Apostolic Tradition* 25.

j) The Midnight Hour

Opening prayer
Lessons: Ephesians 6:10-24; 2 Peter 3:8-14; Acts 12:6-11; Mark 13:32-36
Prayer to Christ
Prayer of imposition of hands
Profession of faith

k) Vespers

Vesperal "Prayer of Ephrem"
Lucernarium from *Apostolic Tradition* 25
Three vesperal prayers
Lessons: Zechariah 14:5-9; Ephesians 2:19-22; James 4:7-12; Acts 10:34-38; Luke 23:50-56
Prayer of imposition of hands
Creed with anathemas
Final prayer

2. *Present Usage*

Today in the Ethiopian Orthodox Church, the full Office is celebrated only in monasteries. In parish usage on the eve of Eucharistic days (Sundays and feasts), Vespers is celebrated in the evening, followed at about 1:00 A.M. by Nocturns, Matins (Lauds), and Eucharist, all in succession without interruption. But of course only the *dabtara* and other

[16] Grébaut and Tisserant, *Codices Aethiopici Vaticani,* 1:85–105. A translation can be found in S. Salaville, "La prière de toutes les heures dans la littérature éthiopienne," in *Studia orientalia liturgico-theologica* (Rome, 1940) 170–185.

[17] See Taft, *The Liturgy of the Hours,* 119.

clergy, exceedingly numerous in the Ethiopian Orthodox Church, are present for the whole of the Offices.

VII. THE BYZANTINE OFFICE

The present Byzantine Hours are "Byzantine" only in part: the original cathedral Office of Hagia Sophia fell into disuse sometime after the fall of the city to the Latins during the Fourth Crusade in 1204, and was gradually replaced by the present Office, a monastic synthesis of Constantinopolitan and Palestinian uses.

1. *History*

It is to the monasteries of Constantinople, and beyond them to those of Palestine, that we must look for the origins of the present "Sabaitic" Office of the Byzantine Rite.[18] After the Persians destroyed the Holy City in 614, a remarkable period of creative restoration followed, in which the monks of St. Sabas Monastery produced a new rite via a massive infusion of new poetic compositions into the former staid and sober monastic Offices.

This Sabaitic monastic Office was then adopted by the monasteries of Constantinople in the restoration following the first wave of iconoclasm (726–775), when another new monastic synthesis was in formation under the leadership of the great Byzantine monastic reformer St. Theodore Studite († 826). In this "Studite" synthesis a basically Palestinian structure was adapted to the prayers and litanies of the Constantinopolitan Offices of Vespers and Matins found in the euchologion of the capital. This hybrid urban monastic Office spread to the Byzantine monasteries of Mount Athos, Georgia, Rus', and Southern Italy.

Meanwhile the monks at St. Sabas in Palestine, while adopting many of these new developments, had retained a more sober usage that is the ancestor of our present Byzantine Office. This "Neo-Sabaitic" synthesis ("neo" because the "Studite" synthesis was also "Sabaitic"), for which we have evidence from the twelfth century, then made its way back to Constantinople a century later, reached Mount Athos, and had taken over even in Rus' by the end of the fourteenth century.

Sometime after the fall of Constantinople to the Latins in 1204, this monastic Office replaced the more elaborate cathedral rite even in the

[18] See R. Taft, *The Byzantine Rite: A Short History*, American Essays in Liturgy (Collegeville, Minn., 1993).

secular churches of the capital, and it is this synthesis of Palestino-Constantinopolitan monastic uses with the euchology of Constantinople that is our Byzantine Office today.

2. *The Offices*

The Byzantine cursus has the full complement of eight Hours—the traditional seven plus Prime—and, in monastic usage, *mesoria* or intermediate Little Hours for some seasons and "Little Vespers."

a) Vespers

Vespers in this tradition is basically a hagiopolite cathedral *lucernarium* interpolated with Constantinopolitan prayers and litanies, to which a monastic synaxis of continuous psalmody has been prefixed. The presidential prayers now bunched at the beginning of both Vespers and Matins were, of course, meant to be distributed throughout the Office, each in its proper place.

PART I: MONASTIC SYNAXIS
Fixed opening
Initial blessing and prayers
Monastic psalmody
Invitatory Psalm 103
Seven vesperal prayers said silently by priest during Psalm 103
Great *synapte* litany
Monastic psalmody

PART II: CATHEDRAL EVENSONG
Lucernarium
Vesperal psalmody and offering of incense:
Psalms 140, 141, 129, 116, with intercalated strophes
Incensation
Introit:
At Great (Festive) Vespers: Entrance with thurible and Introit prayer
Hymn of Light: φῶς ἱλαρόν
Responsory and readings:
Prokeimenon
On the vigil of some feasts: Three Old Testament or Epistle lessons
(Lenten ferias: Two Old Testament lessons with *Prokeimenon* before each)
Intercessions
Ektene litany

Kataxioson (Dignare Domine)
Great *synapte* litany with *Aiteseis* ("biddings")
Peace to all
Prayer of inclination
On the vigil of some feasts: Rogation *(litę)*
Aposticha and concluding prayers:
Aposticha refrains
Nunc dimittis
Concluding prayers and *troparia*
Dismissal *(Apolysis)*

b) Orthros *(Matins)*

In its present form, ὄρθρος, or Matins, is really a conflation of four distinct Offices. Part I is the so-called Royal Office, a brief service for the sovereign celebrated originally in imperial monastic foundations. This is really a separate service, extraneous to the structure of Matins. Part II is a monastic Nocturns of continuous psalmody. Part III is a cathedral vigil of the type described in Egeria (24:9-11) and the *Apostolic Constitutions* (II, 59), inserted on Sundays and feasts. Part IV, cathedral Lauds, begins with Psalm 50 and concludes, as we would expect, with Psalms 148–150, intercessions, a blessing, and the dismissal, followed, on ferias, by a brief appendix.

But between the Invitatory (Psalm 50) and the Lauds psalms, nine poetic Odes make up the bulk of the service." These Odes, called the "Canon," have for the most part supplanted the corresponding nine biblical canticles of the Byzantine liturgical psalter except in the Lenten-paschal season, where the original three-canticle structure has been preserved. At other times only the *Magnificat* has been retained.

Originally the practice of doing all nine canticles daily was customary only in the monastic ἀγρυπνία. Normally the nine canticles were distributed throughout the week, two per day, one variable and one fixed (the ninth: *Magnificat/Benedictus*), with three on Sunday, as follows:

DAY	CANTICLE
Monday:	2, 9
Tuesday:	3, 9
Wednesday:	4, 9
Thursday:	5, 9
Friday:	6, 9

Saturday:	7, 9
Sunday:	1 (cathedral Vigil)
	8, 9

As with Vespers, the hybrid cathedral-monastic nature of Byzantine ὄρθρος is evident from the following schema.

Daily	MATINS	Festive
	PART I: ROYAL OFFICE	
	Fixed opening prayers Psalms 19, 20 *Trisagion* Our Father *Troparia* *Ektene* litany	
	PART II: NOCTURNS	
	Invitatory *Hexapsalmos:* Psalms 3, 37, 62, 87, 102, 142 Twelve Matins prayers said by priest during *Hexapsalmos* Great *synapte* litany	
Verse from Psalm 117 (In Lent: Isaiah 26) *Troparion*		Verse from Psalm 117 *Troparion*
	Monastic Psalmody	
	PART III: CATHEDRAL VIGIL	
	Psalm 118 or *Polyeleos:* Psalms 134–135 (+ 136 in Lent)	
	On feasts in some usages: icon enthroned, *Megalynarion* chanted	
	Incensation *Eulogitaria* (Sundays) Small *synapte* litany *Hypakoe* (Sundays) or Sessional hymns Gradual hymns *(anabath-moi)*	
	Responsory: *Prokeimenon* "Let us pray to the Lord!" *Ekphonesis* "Let everything that breathes bless the Lord!"	
	Gospel on Sundays and Feasts (On Sundays: Resurrection *troparia*)	

PART IV: MORNING PRAISE

	Invitatory	
	Psalm 50	*Troparia*
(Lent: Intercessions)		Intercessions
	Canon of nine Odes[19]	
	Lauds: *Exaposteilarion*	
		(On Sunday: "Holy is the Lord our God!")
(Lent: *Photogogikon*)		
		+ strophes indicated
	Psalms 148–150	
	"Glory to You who have shown us the light!"	
		Great Doxology
Doxology		
	Kataxioson	*Trisagion* *Troparion/Apolytikion*
	Intercessions and Dismissal	*Ektene* *Synapte* litany with *aiteseis* Prayer of inclination *Apolysis* (Dismissal)
Synapte litany with *aiteseis* Prayer of inclination *Aposticha* and Concluding prayers: *Apostica* refrains *Trisagion* "Most Holy Trinity . . ." Our Father *Troparion* *Theotokion* *Ektene* litany *Apolysis* (Dismissal)		

3. *Present Usage*

Today the Byzantine Sabaitic Office is the most widely used Liturgy of the Hours in the Christian East. Nor is its use confined to monasteries. The celebration of Morning Praise and Evensong has remained an integral part of parish worship at least on weekends and feast days in much of the Byzantine East.

In 1976 the Monks of New Skete, a monastery in Cambridge, New York, published a reformed Byzantine Office which, though not without defects, is a move in the right direction toward correcting

[19] Only eight are used outside Lent: Ode 2 is suppressed during the rest of the year.

some of the inconsistencies in present Byzantine usage of the Liturgy of the Hours.[20]

[20] For a critique of this reform, see R. Taft, "The Byzantine Office in the *Prayerbook* of New Skete," *OCP* 48 (1982) 336–370.

Bibliography

Arranz, M. "Office divin. II. En Orient." *DSp* 11:707–720.

Cassien, B., and B. Botte. *La prière des heures.* LO 35. Paris, 1963.

Dalmais, I-H. *Les liturgies d'Orient.* 2nd ed. Rites et symboles 10. Paris, 1980. Chap. 10: "L'Office Divin," pp. 163–181.

Hanssens, J.-M. *Aux origines de la prière liturgique: Nature et genèse de l'office des matines.* AGreg 57. Rome, 1952.

Martimort, A.-G. "The Varied Forms of the Liturgy of the Hours. § 1: In the East." *CP* 4:233–242.

Mateos, J. "Les matines chaldéennes, maronites et syriennes." *OCP* 26 (1960) 51–73.

____. "The Morning and Evening Office." *Wor* 42 (1968) 31–47.

____. "L'office monastique a la fin du 4e siècle: Antioche, Palestine, Cappadoce." *Oriens christianus* 47 (1963) 53–88.

____. "Prières initiales fixes des offices syrien, maronite et byzantin." *OCP* 26 (1960) 489–498.

Raes, A. "Les complies dans les rites orientaux." *OCP* 27 (1961) 281–312.

____. *Introductio in liturgiam orientalem.* Rome, 1947. Reprinted Rome, 1962. Chap. 6: "De Officio vespertino," pp. 178–206.

Taft, R. *The Liturgy of the Hours in East and West: The Origins of the Divine Office and Its Meaning for Today.* Collegeville, Minn., 1986.

____. *The Liturgy of the Hours in the Christian East: Origins, Meaning, Place in the Life of the Church.* Cochin, Kerala (India), 1984.

Winkler, G. "Über die Kathedralvesper in den verschiedenen Riten des Ostens und Westens." *ALW* 16 (1974) 53–102.

Rubén M. Leikam, O.S.B.

3

The Liturgy of the Hours in the Roman Rite

I. FROM THE MONASTIC-BASILICA OFFICE OF THE ANCIENT ROMAN RITE TO THE CAROLINGIAN REFORM

1. *The Ancient Roman Office*

There are very few sources that allow us to reconstruct the structures of the cathedral and the monastic Office in Rome in the fourth and fifth centuries. Nor do we think such a distinction is worth making here between the two forms of the Office, given the fact that in the fifth century there existed monastic communities to which was entrusted the liturgy of the Roman basilicas.[1] Some sources give clear reference to the existence of such monastic groups in the city of Rome. In his letters, St. Jerome speaks of the prayer or psalmody offered at dawn, at the third, sixth, and ninth hours, at the beginning of evening and during the night.[2] In his communication with Leta (*Letter* 107, 9), he refers to some elements that could relate to the cathedral Office, such as the morning hymns, and to the offerings of "an evening sacrifice" with a burning lamp.[3] Also, vigils were sometimes celebrated in

[1] The oldest monastic foundation in Rome was the monastery of St. Sebastian *in catacumbas* founded by Sixtus III (432–440). There was a more or less organized monastic life prior to that date, although it is not exactly known whether everyone lived in community. It is certain, however, that there were many Roman virgins and ascetics who lived in their own homes. In the fifth century the Lateran Basilica as well as St. Peter's Basilica began to be served by small monastic communities, and their Office was that of the churches in which it was celebrated for the people.

[2] Cf. L. Gutierrez, "El monaquismo romano y San Jerónimo," *Communio* 4 (1971) 49–78.

[3] *Epist.* 107, 9: CSEL 55, 300.

Rome: at Easter time, the Saturday after Pentecost, which brought the Easter time to an end, on the anniversary of some martyrs, on the feast of SS. Peter and Paul, and Saturday fastdays. In the *Cautio episcopi* of the *Liber diurnus* 74—a kind of "oath of office"—a bishop had to promise to fulfill certain obligations of his office, among which was the daily celebration of the vigils in the church in the midst of all his clerics.[4]

Tradition attributes the organization of prayer in the Roman Church either to Pope St. Damasus I[5] or to Pope St. Celestine I. It is certain, however, that between the fourth and seventh centuries, there took place in the Roman basilicas an initial systematization of the Office, keeping as an original element the recitation of the psalter, thus bringing together some of the ancient Eastern influences, in large measure of monastic origin. The ancient Roman Office was characterized by the weekly recitation of the psalter, a principle that would hold until the reform of Vatican II. The psalter was divided into two large groups: the first, Psalm 1 to 108, was destined for prayer at the morning hours, which concluded with the three traditional psalms: 148, 149 and 150; the second group, Psalm 109 to 147, was to be prayed throughout the week at the evening Office. This division of the psalter has left its traces in the Ambrosian liturgy and in the Benedictine monastic liturgy. With respect to the psalmody and the readings, the ancient Roman rite presents the following structure:

a) *Vespers*
Five psalms with an antiphon
Magnificat
Prayer

b) *Ferial Vigil*
Six psalms
Three readings with responsory
Three psalms
Three psalms
Total:
Twelve psalms and nine readings

c) *Sunday Vigil*
Twelve psalms
Three readings with responsory
Six psalms

Three readings with responsory
Six psalms
Three readings with responsory
Three readings with responsory
Three readings with responsory
Total:
Twenty-four psalms and nine readings

[4] Cf. PL 105, 71.

[5] Cf. L. Duchesne, ed., *Liber Pontificalis* I (Paris, 1885) 214: "Hic constituit ut psalmos die noctuque canerentur per omnes ecclesias, qui hoc praecepit presbyteris vel episcopis aut monasteriis."

d) *Morning Office*
Psalm 50
A variable morning psalm
Morning Psalms 62 and 66
Canticle from the Old Testament
Laudate Psalms 148–150
Canticle of Zacharias
Prayer

Psalms for the morning Office were selected with a specific purpose in mind. Psalm 50, for example, opens the celebration of the morning Office in many traditions as a true penitential act, to which is attributed a purifying, almost sacramental quality. Of the three morning psalms, one of which is changeable and two are fixed: Psalm 62, already selected according to the schema of the *Apostolic Constitutions,* and Psalm 66. The canticle from the Old Testament follows, a second universal tradition. Then the three psalms of praise, *Laudate,* also called *Alleluiatici,* from which the name of the morning hour, *Laudes,* was later taken. These psalms will be peculiar to the Divine Office and always present as an inseparable triad in all the Eastern and Western rites. They are present as a compact and daily group in the Roman Office up until the reform of St. Pius X (1911).

The part of the psalter reserved for Vespers (Psalms 109–116, 119–147) contains those psalms that first the Eastern liturgies and later the other Western rites assigned to accompany the *lucernarium,* or lamp-lighting. The more archaic festive antiphons in the Roman Office—Second Vespers of Christmas, Vespers of the Sacred Triduum, Second Vespers of the feasts of SS. Peter and Paul—show that in Rome as well there was a selection of "evening" psalms. The Little Hours are made up of sections of Psalm 118, and at Compline, Psalms 4, 30 (vv. 1-6), 90, and 133 are prayed.

The ancient Roman rite also formed a cycle of seven canticles of the Old Testament, to be distributed each day of the week during the Office of Lauds.[6] The Roman basilica liturgy will pray a particular distribution of the Gospel canticles: the *Magnificat* (Luke 1:46-55) for Vespers; the *Benedictus* (Luke 1:68-79) for Lauds; and the *Nunc dimittis* (Luke 2:29-32) for Compline. As for the hymns, we find no trace of

[6] Sunday: Dan 3:57-88; Monday: Isa 12:1-6; Tuesday: Isa 38:10-20; Wednesday: 1 Sam 2:1-10; Thursday: Exod 15:1-9; Friday: Hab 3:2-19; Saturday: Deut 32:1-43.

them in the ancient Roman liturgy, given the fact that they enter the choral Office around the eleventh century.

2. The Divine Office in the Rule of St. Benedict

St. Benedict (480–547), who carefully arranged the schedule of the monks to be equally divided by the triad of work, holy reading, and choral Office, attributed the greatest importance to what he called the *opus Dei,* to which no other work should be preferred.[7] This service to the glory of God, which ought to be carried out with the greatest attention and spiritual sensitivity, takes a place of prominence in Benedict's Rule. Of the seventy-three chapters, twelve are dedicated to the Divine Office. More than other legislators, St. Benedict describes in detail the Divine Office which is outstanding for its balance and the finely elaborated character of its schema:

a) *Vespers*
Verse: O God, come to my assistance
Four psalms with antiphons
Short reading
Short responsory
Hymn
Verse
Magnificat
Litany *(Kyrie eleison)*
Our Father
Concluding prayer

b) *Ferial Vigils*
Verse: O Lord, open my lips
(three times)
Psalm 3 (in its entirety)
Psalm 94 (responsorial)
Hymn

c) *Sunday Vigils*
Verse: O Lord, open my lips
Psalms 3 and 94
Hymn
Six psalms with antiphon
Verse
Four readings with responsory
Six psalms with antiphon
Verse
Four readings with responsory
Three canticles from the Old Testament (prophets) with Alleluia
Verse
Four readings with responsory
Te Deum laudamus
Gospel reading
Te decet laus
Blessing

d) *Morning Office*
Verse: O God, come to my assistance

Psalm 66 (in its entirety)
Psalm 50 with antiphon
Two morning psalms with antiphon

[7] Cf. RB 43, 3.

Six psalms with antiphon

Verse
Three readings with response
Six psalms with Alleluia
Reading from the Apostle
Litany of supplication *(Kyrie eleison)*
Concluding prayer

Canticle from Old Testament with antiphon
Psalms 148–150 with antiphon
Short reading
Hymn
Verse
Benedictus
Litany *(Kyrie eleison)*
Our Father
Concluding prayer

St. Benedict, in addition to knowing the monastic-basilica Office of the Roman rite, knew the monastic-Byzantine Office from which he took the gospel of the Sunday vigils and the doxology *Te decet laus,* which the *Apostolic Constitutions* VII, 48 was reproducing. Following the example of St. Caesarius of Arles, he introduced the hymn, which he called the Ambrosian, and the *Te Deum laudamus.* The use of the *verse* is the fruit of his creativity as well. St. Benedict was likewise the first to introduce the prayer at the beginning of the Hours with the versicle *O God, come to my assistance,* and he takes the appropriate versicle *O Lord, open my lips* from Psalm 50:17 to begin the Office of the Vigils. He places a variable verse after the hymns of Vespers and Lauds as a conclusion to the psalmody for the first nocturn of the ferial vigil and of the three nocturns of the Sunday vigil, and after the short reading of the little Hours and of Compline.

In what he refers to as the psalter, St. Benedict distributes the 150 psalms over the space of a week, insisting that this proportion never be reduced; even though he authorizes an alternate distribution of the psalms, he wants the number of 150 psalms to be recited each week (RB 18, 22). Besides eliminating the repetitions, he shortens the Roman Office of Vigils of his time by reducing the number of psalms prayed daily to twelve, the sacred number of the monastic tradition. However, in order to give greater development to the Sunday vigil, he adds three canticles from the prophets. Some psalms are repeated daily, such as the three psalms of Compline, which always remain the same. He reduces the number of psalms for Vespers from five to four. Those psalms which remain fixed in the selection and which are taken from the Roman basilica liturgy are the traditional Psalms 50 and 148–150 at the beginning and end of the morning psalmody; Psalms 3 and 94, which introduce the vigils; and Psalm 66, with which the morning psalmody opens. A personal option seems to have been the introduction of Psalm 94 as the invitatory. For the morning canticles, he adopts the Roman tradition.

It must be noted, as well, that it was St. Benedict who took the initiative of having read during the night Office "certain biblical commentaries from the Fathers, recognized as catholic and orthodox."[8] Among other elements we find the abbot's blessing before the readings of vigils, the Our Father recited at Vespers and Lauds, the litany of petitions at the principal Hours and the concluding prayer, which, in St. Benedict's monastery, were probably taken from the Roman prayers corresponding to the Gelasian series.[9]

St. Benedict does not limit himself to prescribing what monks ought to pray; he also speaks to the spiritual motivation with which the "divine service" ought to be rendered. One must remember, before all else, that although we are always in the presence of God, "we ought to believe that especially, and without the least doubt, when we are at the Divine Office" (RB 19, 1-2). Then he says that the psalmody ought to be recited with the attitudes already indicated in Sacred Scripture: "Serve the Lord with fear" (Ps 2:11); "sing the psalms wisely" (Ps 46:8); and "in the presence of the angels, I will praise you" (Ps 137:1). After all this St. Benedict concludes with the golden principle, "Let us sing the psalms in such manner that our minds can be in harmony with our voice" (RB 19, 3-7).

3. *The Concluding Prayers*

The Divine Office of the ancient Roman liturgy recognized euchological texts composed exclusively for the celebration of the Hours. The euchology proper to the Divine Office, written in the fifth to the seventh centuries, presupposes the existence of the euchology that was transmitted orally and scarcely ever recorded in the document.

[8] RB 9, 8. During this same period it was also the custom at St. Peter's in Rome; the first indications of the *capitula* are from the sixth century, the Codex 105 of the Capitular Library of St. Peter, and in the seventh century according to the *OR* XIV, 10: *Tractatus vero sancti Hieronimi, Ambrosi, ceterorum Patrum, prout ordo poscit, leguntur, OR* XIV, n.10, ed. V, Andrieu, *OR* III, p. 41, cf. pp. 29–30; in the eighth century, *OR* III A, nn.13–20, 22, Andrieu, *OR* II, pp. 486–488. In one of his sermons, St. Caesarius of Arles refers to the reading of patristic homilies, to the place of the homily which the bishop or priest was accustomed to give. Cf. Caesarius of Arles, *Sermo* I, 15, ed. M. J. Delage, SChr 175 (1971) 254–256.

[9] Cf. J. Pinell, *Anàmnesis* 5:81.

As witness to the previous period's burning creativity, we have the blessing of the lamp from the *Apostolic Tradition*, and the morning and evening prayers from the *Apostolic Constitutions*, which have already been presented.

Within the liturgical Roman sources one can recognize three series of prayer: the Veronese, the Gelasian, and the Gregorian. We will give a synthesis of the general themes of these three series. We will look at the contents of the prayer of praise as well as what the Church believed about its own Divine Office in the period of the ancient Roman liturgy.[10]

a) *The Veronese Series.* Together with the *libelli missarum,* the Veronese Sacramentary has transmitted to us a first nucleus of six Roman prayers for the morning and evening Offices: nn. 587–89 and 591–93. To these six prayers we need to add n. 1329, which was probably destined for the Office. Most of these prayers are ambivalent, but the dominant theme in all of them is principally proper to the evening song.

The thematic originality of this euchological set consists essentially in one anthropological vision of time—that man needs the night to rest from the fatigue of the day—but underlining as well the eschatological dimension of the same time: from the necessary changeability of time, one can reason to the immutability of God by means of the cultic service of the prayer.

b) *The Gelasian Series.* The Gelasian Sacramentary reproduces nineteen prayers—eleven morning and eight evening—which correspond to nn. 1576–1594; one of these, n. 1581, comes from the Veronese series (n. 587). The Gelasian is the Roman series that was the most popular of the series and the one that principally influenced the Latin euchological tradition. The basic appeal of this series is its theme of light. Starting with the only prayer from the Veronese which develops the theme of light (n. 587) and which the author of the Gelasian series has integrated into his series (n. 58), he then continues to multiply to the greatest extent, and with creativity and diverse literary forms, many derivations of this theme of light. The author of this series makes

[10] For these prayers, see the studies of J. Pinell, "Le orazioni composte per L'Ufficio Divino nell'ambito della tradizione eucologia latina. A. Rito romano antico. 1. La serie del Veronense. 2. La serie Gelasiana," *Not* 154 (1979) 250–265; 155 (1979) 310–340; idem, *Anàmnesis* 5:158–166.

evident a Christological interpretation of the image of sun and light. When he cites Psalm 73, he enriches verse 16 with an expression from Malachi 4:2 about the Sun of Justice whom he asks to remain in our hearts (n. 1590). The theme of "light as the gift of God," where the light of grace which God gives is identified with the very nature of God (n. 1579), can also be presented as a key to a Christological (n. 1587) or pneumatological (n. 1580) understanding. In opposing, antithetically, the themes of "light" and "darkness," the central argument of light is broken down into its elements and is seen as truth, faith, and virtue (nn. 1585, 1583, 1582). Many times the texts refer to the Johannine image of "walking in the light," with the concomitant meaning of "living in the light" (nn. 1582, 1577, 1584).[11] Visible light marks the course of time, but Christ, the Sun of Justice, the everlasting light, also demands our attention.

There are three prayers that are composed in the form of a little "eucharist" or expression of gratitude. The two morning prayers express gratitude for the grace of having come to the beginning of the day after having passed through the darkness of night (nn. 1576, 1548). The evening prayer expresses gratitude for having been protected during the day, but at the same time as it expresses gratitude, it includes an implicit sense of petition for protection during the approaching night (n. 1594). In one of the morning prayers there is the request that there be the grace to give thanks anew at the Vesper hour, and in the evening prayer a request to arrive unharmed through the night so as to be able to give praise in the morning.

c) *The Two Gregorian Series.* Compared with the Veronese and the Gelasian series, the series from the Gregorian Sacramentary carries little literary or doctrinal interest; these correspond to nn. 935–942 and 943–79. For the first series we refer the reader to the preceding euchological tradition. In the second series, which consists of a group of thirty-seven prayers, the Gregorian series is different from the euchological tradition of the Liturgy of the Hours. It transcribes and abbreviates texts that were composed for the Eucharistic celebration. In this way the Gregorian series prepared, but without success, the debatable formulary that the Roman liturgy would sustain for centuries with respect to the very euchology of the Divine Office. The ancient evening and morning prayers disappeared little by little, substituted as they

[11] Cf. John 8:12; 12:35; 1 John 1:6-7; 11:9-10.

were by the collect of the Mass, a practice that was in conflict with the style of the Roman rite. We will treat this issue later.

4. The Carolingian Reform and the "Roman-Benedictine" Office (8th–9th Centuries)

Around the eighth century the Benedictine Rule was disseminated in the West, and by the beginning of the second millennium, the Benedictine Office had been converted into the monastic Office par excellence within the Western Church. Its influence was felt even within the cathedral Office. Due to missionaries like St. Boniface who were closely linked to the Chair of Peter and to a spirit that looked to Rome as the model for all ecclesiastical life, and due to the efforts of the Holy See during this epoch in history, the Roman Office was assumed as a duty and affirmed as such in almost all the churches of Europe.

Within monastic gatherings, *consuetudines,* or customs, were being formed, and when, in the Carolingian movement, the synods and the legislation of Benedict of Aniane were to impose the Benedictine Rule, it is to this Rule of Benedict and these customs that he is referring.[12] So, therefore, the Benedictine Office, which takes effect at this time, is a hybrid Office, that is, it is infected with rites and added Offices or supplementary elements taken from a number of *consuetudines* or customs. For that reason it is essential to distinguish between the Office of the Rule of Benedict and the Office called "Benedictine," which in reality is a product of Carolingian and Aniane legislation from the eleventh century. Keeping these facts in mind, then, we can call that Office, which the Carolingian reform would impose on all the churches of Europe, the "Roman-Benedictine Office."

The Roman *cursus*, which the work of Amalarius was to make known and introduce into the churches of the Carolingian empire, was structured in the following manner:[13]

[12] The Synod of Aix-la-Chapelle of 817 says: *Tertio, ut omnes officium Sancti Benedicti faciant:* Mansi 14, coll. 349, 350. The same synod also published the *Capitulare monasticum* presented by Benedict of Aniane as the new letter from monasteries of the empire; cf. J. Semmler, *Corpus consuetudinum monasticarum* I (Siegburg, 1963) 503–536.

[13] The principal source is the work of Amalarius, edited by J. M. Hanssens, *Amalarii Episcopi opera liturgica omnia,* ST 138 (Vatican City, 1948), vol. I : *Introductio, Opera minora.* Vol. II (1948); *Liber officialis.* Vol. III (1950): *Liber de Ordine antiphonarii —Eclogae de Ordine romano—Appendix tomi I et II—Indices.*

a) Four types of nocturns can be identified: the Sunday vigil with eighteen psalms, nine readings, and nine responses; the ferial vigil with twelve psalms, three readings, and three responses; feastday vigils of saints with nine psalms, nine readings, and nine responses; the nocturns of Easter and Pentecost and their octaves with three psalms, three readings, and three responses.[14]

The three nocturns of the Sunday vigil began with the verse "O Lord, open my lips . . .," followed by the doxology in honor of the Trinity. Psalm 94 followed with an invitatory antiphon and the twelve psalms from the psalter, without antiphon, and divided into three groups of four psalms in each group; the doxology divided each group; all the psalms were sung while standing. After a sung versicle of transition from the psalmody to the reading, there were three readings, each one followed by a response. The other two nocturns had the same structure: the second with three psalms and an antiphon; the third with three psalms and an Alleluia instead of the antiphon. There were three readings and their responses for each nocturn. The nocturns concluded with the *Te Deum,* which, according to Amalarius, in Rome was only said on the feast of popes; on such occasions, the ninth response was omitted.

It is interesting to note that if the sun rose early, the nocturns were ended in order to begin the morning Hour of Lauds; if, however, the night Office ended before the rising sun, the choir would await the dawn before beginning Lauds.[15] This indicates the importance of time as symbol or of the pause that waits: one waited in order to emphasize Christ, the Light, in the celebration of Lauds. For Amalarius, the ritual sequence of the nocturns and of Sunday morning Lauds constitutes a vigil that flows into an encounter with the light that is the risen Lord; to celebrate a Sunday vigil, then, is to cross over symbolic time into the light.[16]

The Hour of Lauds is made up of seven psalms and one canticle from the Old Testament. The psalms are divided into two groups. The first group is composed of Psalm 92 (on ferial days, always Psalm 50),

[14] These four types of nocturns lasted until the reform of Pius X, at which time the number of nocturns was reduced to two.

[15] Cf. *OR* XVIII, 18, 19.

[16] Cf. *Adnotaciones de nocturnalibus officiis* I, 1; ibid., II, 1 in J. M. Hanssens, *Amalarii episcopi opera omnia* III, pp. 19–23.

Psalm 99 (on ferial days, the morning Psalms 5, 42, 64, 89, 142, and 91); Psalms 62 and 66 were sung as one psalm with a single *Gloria* and one antiphon; the canticle; the three *Laudate* psalms (148, 149, 150) were sung as a single psalm. The reading followed with its responsorial versicle, but not even the hymn was sung. The gospel canticle, the *Benedictus*, the prayers of petition, and the final collect, the sung *Benedicamus Domino* brought the Office of Lauds to a close.

c) All the daily Hours had the same structure. After the introduction, there was a section of Psalm 118, a brief reading, a short response, the prayers, the collect or oration, and the conclusion.

d) Vespers followed the same structure as Lauds, with five psalms and the gospel canticle, the *Magnificat*. However, unlike those of Lauds, the psalms were chosen according to the monastic system's biblical order.

e) Compline consisted of four unchanging psalms: 4, 30 (vv. 1-6), 90, and 133. This Office was colored by the versicle from Psalm 16:8 and the gospel canticle *Nunc dimittis*. There is no evidence of a penitential act, a hymn, or a final oration. The *Officium capituli* was proper only to monasteries or to some canonical environments.

II. FROM THE BREVIARY OF INNOCENT III TO THE LITURGY OF THE HOURS UNDER PAUL VI

The ideal prayer of the Hours was overshadowed in the course of centuries by two almost opposite tendencies. On the one hand, there was an overbearing multiplication of elements added to the schedule and to the content of the Office; and on the other hand, the natural rhythm of the Hours was abandoned. As a result, the complete celebration of the Divine Office, whether daily or on solemnities, and imposed by the Carolingian legislation upon all churches, became a heavy burden for the cleric dedicated to pastoral care.

1. The Breviary of the Roman Curia

From the historical point of view, it is necessary to remember that already in the eleventh century the Pope began to form around himself a kind of private or personal choral group, composed of closer coworkers and distinct from the Lateran canonical choir. They celebrated the Office together in the papal oratory dedicated to St. Lawrence. In 1215, Pope Innocent III (1198–1216), at the time of the Fourth Lateran Council, asked for a revision of the Office. Consequently, there was created the ordinal of Innocent III,[17] with a complete description of the total Office and of each part of the breviary. Out of the ordinal of Innocent III there arose the *Breviarium secundum usum Romanae Curiae,* with all its texts and rubrics. The ordinal and its breviary were revised by Honorius III. This latter breviary was the one adopted by the Friars Minor, according to the legislation given in the second Rule of St. Francis, 1223; in 1230 this version was copied and distributed. Later the superior of the Franciscans, General Minister Haymo of Faversham (d. 1224), used it to work out his ordinal.[18] With the work and prayer of the Friars Minor, the breviary was soon circulating everywhere.

We will briefly present the characteristics of the breviary of the Curia, designed by Innocent III and then adopted by the Franciscans.[19] Given the fact that the Roman Curia had endorsed the Carolingian Office described by Amalarius, we will limit ourselves to simply indicating that which is particular and innovative with respect to the Carolingian Office.

The first and most surprising new development can be found in the Hour of Prime on Sundays. From a body of three psalms there developed nine and, with the Athanasian Creed *(Quicumque),* the number came to be ten. While the structure of the Hours is in large part the one described by Amalarius, we find another innovation: the eighty-

[17] The ordinal of Innocent III is known thanks to the only copy made in Urbania in 1365. It starts from a model able to be dated about 1302 and done for Cardinal Egidio Albornoz. The manuscript (Paris BN, lat. 4162A) was studied by S. J. P. Van Diyk, *The Ordinal of the Papal Court from Innocent III to Boniface VIII and Related Documents,* SF 22 (Fribourg, 1975); this edition was completed by J. H. Walker, cf. *RL* 58 (1971) 432.

[18] In reality, the invention of a book intentionally meant to be an abbreviated form (from there comes the word "breviary") is attributed not to the secular clerics but to a monastic creation which came from the need to reduce the quantity of books used in choir in order to celebrate the Office in monasteries; cf. P. M. Gy, "Les premiers bréviaires de Saint-Gall (deuxième quart du XIe s.)," in *Liturgie, Gestalt und Vollzug* (Munich, 1963) 104–113. The combination of several books (those of the collects, the readings, and the antiphons), the shortened readings, and the reduction of antiphons and responses gave birth to a single large book, still choral but hardly a personal book. It was the increase in the number of monks capable of reading that led to the copying of shorter breviaries for personal use whether in the choir or while on a journey.

[19] V. Dijk, "An Authentic Copy of the Franciscan *Regula Breviary,*" *Scriptorium* 16 (1962) 68–76; ibid., "Some Manuscripts of the Earliest Franciscan Rules," *Franciscan Studies* 14 (1954) 253ff.; 16 (1956) 60ff.

one hymns used for all the Hours. In Prime and Compline there is the *Officium capituli;* and in Compline, there is a penitential act as well.

The series of readings and biblical pericopes was rigorously fixed to the least detail, thus greatly reducing the number of versicles to between eight and ten. On Easter Sunday and on the octave days of Easter, the Scriptures were not read. But the reading of hagiographic texts[20] grew, and in the Common Offices of the saints, only patristic, not biblical, texts were read.

A surprising norm governed the praying of the collect from the Sunday Mass as the concluding prayer to all the Hours of the Office prayed during the week.[21] Herein was interrupted the ancient Roman tradition of prayers proper to the Liturgy of the Hours; in this way the euchological patrimony with its rich theological and spiritual content was lost in the prayer of the Church.

With due respect to the celebration and conception of the breviary, it can be said that the celebration continued to be done in common, though not as solemnly: there was very little singing, and the ritual gestures were reduced to a minimum. It was appropriate to say that the Office was "said." In fact, the most common verb used in the ordinal of Innocent III is derived from the verb *dicere* ("it is said, we say, let it be said").

2. *The Breviary of Cardinal Quiñones*

If it is true that the breviary of Cardinal Quiñones, also called the Breviary of the Holy Cross, is not featured extensively within the rich evolutionary vein of the Roman Office, given the fact that it was suspended after only thirty-three years of vitality, its content is of great importance and for two reasons. First, because it reflects the aspirations of the generations that lived just before the Council of Trent. Secondly, because the new Liturgy of the Hours of Paul VI manifests aspects surprisingly common to both, as we will have an opportunity

[20] The hagiographic texts of the curial breviary are often taken from the *Liber Pontificalis* when it is a question of the lives of holy popes, and from the martyrology of Adone. This alone is sufficient to make one suspicious of the little guarantee offered by such readings, since they were abundantly full of legends and apocryphal material.

[21] In the Franciscan breviary, ms. 694 of the community library in Assisi, one can read the following rubric in folio 60: "ratio dicatur per totam hebdomadam de dominica ad omnes horas, nisi aliquod festum superveniat."

to see later. It was, without doubt, the most revolutionary reform in the history of the Divine Office because of its brevity and simplicity.

Cardinal Quiñones received the formal commission from Pope Clement VII (1523–1534) to reform the breviary.[22] The first edition, approved by Paul III in 1535, went through some eleven printings within the first year and a half. The revised edition appeared in 1536. Within its thirty-two years of usage, the Breviary of the Holy Cross went through over a hundred editions.[23] The criteria for the reform of the breviary are the following:

a) the annual reading of the Scriptures and the weekly prayer of the psalter;

b) the proposal to return to the sources. In the preface of his edition and directed to Paul III, Quiñones reaffirms this principle of citing authorities from the first centuries, such as the Councils of Laodicea and Toledo, St. Jerome, Pope Gelasius.[24] The same Paul III says in his letter that the breviary was reformed with consummate care and diligence, and according to the norms established by the ancient holy Fathers and councils;[25]

c) the simplification of rubrics. Ever since the breviary of the Curia, the rubrics had constituted a veritable labyrinth; they were so complicated and of such a nature that much time was lost on seeing and finding out what and how one ought to say one Office or the other;

[22] The same Pope Clement VII had previously assigned this work to Gian Pietro Carafa, who would later be Pope Paul IV, the pontiff who banned the breviary of Quiñones in 1588. The two men represented two distinct and opposite tendencies. Quiñones aspired toward making profound changes. Clement VII, indecisive, first opted for the current text of Carafa but afterward changed to that of Quiñones. Paul III (1534–1550) followed the same line. Paul IV, upon becoming pope, took up the current text again—which then had the full approbation of Pius V—thus withdrawing the approval that Paul III had previously given to the reformed breviary of Quiñones on February 5, 1535. The breviary of Quiñones, at first forbidden by Paul IV in 1558, then readmitted for use by Pius IV in 1559, would finally be abolished by Pius V in 1568 by means of the papal bull *Quod a nobis.*

[23] The breviary of Quiñones was studied and published (second edition) by J. Wickham Legg, *The Second Recension of the Quignon Breviary. Following an edition printed at Antwerp in 1537 and collated with twelve other editions to which is prefixed a handlist of editions of the first and second recension.* Vol 1: *Text*, HBS 35 (London, 1908); Vol. 2: *Liturgical Introduction with Life of Quignon. Appendices, Notes and Indices,* HBS 42 (London, 1912). We will continue to cite this work as Legg, volume, and page.

[24] Cf. Legg, 1:xxiii–xxx.

[25] Cf. Legg, 1:xxx.

d) general simplification and lightening of the Office.

Basically, the fundamental goal and criteria were to offer to those who had the obligation of "saying the breviary" a short book which was easily handled and which would really nourish the personal prayer and the spiritual life of the cleric dedicated to the care of souls. Quiñones's breviary was destined for private prayer and not for the choral Office. With those criteria in mind, the content and characteristics of the breviary were in harmony with the following principles:

a) Quiñones departed radically from the tradition of eight or nine centuries in the distribution of the psalms; for each of the Hours, he assigned only three psalms, which he distributed in such a way that the entire psalter was to be recited in one week. A quantitative criterion prevailed: the longest psalms were for the vigils, the others for the Hours. He also introduced "titles" for the psalms.

b) Quiñones gave particular importance to the lectionary, since he was convinced that the principal goal of the Office is to be didactic: to instruct the teachers of the Christian assembly through the Sacred Scriptures. For that reason, the nocturns would have three readings: the first from the Old Testament, the second from the New Testament (particularly the four Gospels and within one month), and the third from the Fathers of the Church. He quite completely purged the patristic lectionary of legendary texts about the saints.

c) The rubrics were to be very simple: there was to be no variety in the hymns of the Hours, in the prayers of Prime and Compline, nor in the psalms and antiphons for the Little Hours.

d) Short readings, responses, and prayers were abolished.

e) With reference to the structure of the Hours, strangely enough, he left the Our Father and the Hail Mary at the beginning of the Office; Lauds, without a hymn, forms a unity with the nocturns. He placed the hymns at the beginning of the Office and assigned only one antiphon for the group of three psalms in each Hour. He left the other Hours as they were but reduced the number of days on which they were obligatory. He also left the Athanasian Creed *(Quicumque)* in Sunday Prime, introducing the Apostles' Creed for the other days of the week as well as prior to the praying of Compline as part of the prayers, a feature that was subsequently suppressed.

The work was a success because Quiñones understood the situation and the exigencies of the clerics of his time, so different from those of the Carolingian epoch. Upon the clerics alone rested the obligation of praying the Office. Therefore, he wanted to hand over to them a suitable instrument to enhance their personal prayer life.

But this breviary was destined to fail, for various reasons.[26] The enthusiastic acceptance of the new breviary stirred up violent opposition in conservative circles. The Council of Trent, which at first seemed favorably inclined toward the breviary of Quiñones, elaborated on a working document that tended to abolish that breviary and resulted in the breviary of Pius V (1568), which basically eliminated anything new. In fact, the Council of Trent was alarmed by one of its consultants, the Spanish theologian Juan de Arze, who in 1551 handed the council fathers a memorandum of eighteen chapters[27] in which, after presenting a totally negative criticism of the Quiñones breviary, asked that it be abolished because, according to Arze, in addition to going against the ancient tradition, the arrangement of the Office is of divine right or at least is based on it.[28]

3. The Breviary of St. Pius V

The Tridentine breviary of St. Pius V (1568), promulgated by the papal bull *Quod a nobis* represented a return to the principles of Cardinal Carafa, who, during his brief pontificate as Paul IV, had suspended the breviary of Quiñones. The turnabout took place in spite of the fact that the approval of Quiñones's breviary had been renewed by Paul IV's successor, Pope Pius IV. The new breviary had to now constitute a restoration of the Roman Office and not be a new creation. For that reason, the reform of the Council of Trent, compared with that of Quiñones, is no more than a correction of the books of the Roman breviary that circulated in the middle of the sixteenth century. Those responsible for this restoration, and especially Cardinal Sirleto, who was its soul, affirmed the objective of not creating a new breviary but only of correcting the old one. It was principally the thirteenth-century breviary of the Roman Curia under Innocent III, which was disseminated by the Franciscans. The following brief synthesis can be made concerning the simplifications and innovations centering around the

[26] Cf. J. Jungmann, "Perché la riforma del Breviario del Card. Quignonez è fallita?" *Eredità liturgica e attualita pastorale,* Biblioteca di cultura religiosa 23 (Rome, 1962) 310–320. ET: *Pastoral Liturgy* (New York, 1962).

[27] Entitled *De novo Breviario Romano tollendo consultatio,* published in its entirety in Legg, 2:276–282.

[28] Cf. Legg, 2:163.

corrections and new ordering of the breviary of the Curia undertaken by Pius V:

a) The Hour of Prime on Sundays changed from ten psalms to five. Additional Offices were less frequently added, although the Office of *Sanctae Mariae in sabbato* was introduced for the temporal cycle. Also, the Office of the Dead was limited to certain days, as were the fifteen gradual psalms and the penitential psalms with the litany of the saints. The biblical readings were notably abbreviated, three times more brief than those of the Curial breviary. The same happened with the hagiographic texts; following the example of Quiñones, Pius V intended to abandon all legendary texts. But the great merit of Pius V, and perhaps the principal innovation, was that he again introduced the Sacred Scripture, albeit in rather short pericopes, for most days of the year. As for the patristic texts, the material taken from Carafa was used for the revision of the breviary of the Curia.

b) The corrective reforms of St. Pius V took into account only the clerics and the religious. The bull *Quod a nobis* addressed the topic of the recitation of the Office as the duty of clergymen and churches, of monasteries and convents, of religious and military orders, and finally, of places, men, or women that were exempt or dispensed from the jurisdiction of the bishop. There was only one reference made about the faithful; this concerned the Little Office of the Virgin Mary, the Office of the Dead, the penitential and gradual psalms, as carried out especially in confraternities. From this it seems that the participation of lay people in the Office was not taken into account by the post-Tridentine commission as a significant criterion for reform.

c) The theological conception enunciated by St. Pius V and by the papal bull *Quod a nobis* was that the Divine Office was for "the glorification of God and the fulfillment of the mission proper to ecclesiastics," and that they had to pray *for the Church.* For reasons of priestly spirituality, the Office came to be the prayer of and for the priest. It consisted of "prayers of praise and thanks to God." The Office, above all, was a communal act; but individual recitation of the Office was not only allowed but obligatory when not celebrated in choir. The bull of Pius V, for the first time, would consider individual recitation of the Office on the same level as its communal celebration.

With the appearance of the breviary, the Liturgy of the Hours slowly began to lose its character of being a communal celebration. When the practice of private, individual recitation was affirmed, soon the need to pray according to the natural rhythm of the hours of the day was also lost. In order to fulfill one's obligation, it was not only necessary to pray the entire breviary, at whatever hour of the day or night. The Divine Office continued being prayer, but not a prayer *of the hours.*

d) The Council of Trent also got bogged down in the dilemma between one Office or several Offices adapted for the churches and monasteries in the West. The multiplicity of Offices also offered great deficiencies. The task of the reform had been entrusted to the Roman See, which had opted for uniformity. It is noteworthy that the bull *Quod a nobis,* allowing arrangements of the Office to demonstrate its two hundred years of antiquity, diverse in nature, would implicitly admit the existence of legitimate diverse traditions, not only in the area of the religious orders and institutes but also in the local Churches. The new Office was, practically speaking, imposed upon the West; thus, unity in the prayer of the Western Church was achieved during the seventeenth and following centuries.

4. The Reform of St. Pius X

During the eighteenth and nineteenth centuries in France and Germany, there emerged a variety of diverse and reformed breviaries.[29] This was a sign that, at least in some circles, the Roman breviary was not appreciated. At first Benedict XIV had thought of initiating a radical reform. During Vatican Council I, there arose voices asking for a revision of the breviary, but because of the premature closing of the council, these voices were not heard. Meanwhile the Liturgical Movement occurred. It was in this climate that St. Pius X, in July 1911, appointed a nine-member commission to revise the breviary. Within four months they finished their work, and on November 1, 1911, the apostolic constitution *Divino afflatu* was published.

The disproportionate growth of the sanctoral cycle and the excessive weight of apostolic work among the clergy had begged for a less extensive breviary, especially for Sundays. The reform of St. Pius X basically consisted of a new distribution of the psalms, a diminution of the psalmody in some of the Hours but maintaining the weekly recitation of the psalter and its Roman-Benedictine distribution, insofar as that was compatible with the designated reduction of psalms. It is regrettable that in this reform the traditional group of *Laudate*

[29] Cf. M. Righetti, *Il Breviario: La storia liturgica* (Milan, 1969) 680–685.

psalms (148, 149, 150) would be lost to the Office of Lauds, traditionally part of all the Churches, both in the East and the West.[30] It eliminated almost all the additional Offices as well as Psalms 50 and 129. Some new norms were introduced in order to safeguard the dignity of the Sunday, of the Scriptures and the current psalter, and, in general, of the temporal cycle.

Pius X focused on the psalter as central to the Office. The psalms are the sacrifice of praise offered to God, the mirror of the reactions of human beings before their Creator, and lastly the voice of the whole Christ which "sings, groans, hopes and longs for union with God" as indicated in all the psalms.[31] The psalter, then, carries theological, anthropological, and Christological meaning for the one praying.

III. VATICAN COUNCIL II AND THE LITURGY OF THE HOURS UNDER POPE PAUL VI

Vatican Council II, unlike any other council in history, brought forth a constitution on the liturgy as its first solemn document: *Sacrosanctum Concilium.* In this document Vatican Council II laid the foundation for a true and profound general reform of the liturgy, and within that, the Liturgy of the Hours. All of chapter four is dedicated to the renewal of the prayer of the Church: the theology of the prayer of the Hours, pastoral aspects, the norms for effective reform, its spiritual value, the obligation and communal celebration, etc. The journey toward renewal of the Divine Office was long and eventful for the reform commission, the Consilium, which worked with the following four conciliar principles close at hand. They had to be faithful to the past; likewise, there was a strong call to be sensitive to the actual reality of the cleric; the persons praying the Office, whether clerics or laity, were to be able to live spiritually from its texts and be able to participate actively and fruitfully; finally, the Hours of the Office were to be prayed competently and at a reliable time. Some basic questions with respect to the structure of the Office were placed before the Synod of Bishops in October 1967.[32] A specimen of the new Office, with extracts from the

[30] A. Baumstark strongly censured this occurrence, and with reason, given the fact that according to him, besides their universal and secular use, these psalms were already found in the synagogal liturgy; cf. *Comparative Liturgy,* rev. B. Botte, trans. F. L. Cross (Westminster, Md., 1958) 38.

[31] Cf. *Divino afflatu: AAS* 3 (1999) 633–635.

[32] A. Bugnini, *The Reform of the Liturgy 1948–1975,* Trans. M. J. O'Connell (Collegeville, Minn., 1990) 507ff.

Institutio generalis, was sent to all the bishops of the world, the prelates, and general superiors in 1969.[33]

The new Liturgy of the Hours was announced publicly with the apostolic constitution of Pope Paul VI, *Laudis canticum,* on November 1, 1970, and published on April 11, 1971.[34] Previously, on February 2, 1970, it had been published as the *Institutio generalis de Liturgia Horarum,* and it accompanied the first volume of the Liturgy of the Hours. It was perhaps the most successful of all the documents on liturgical reform introduced by Vatican Council II. A second edition of this document was made on April 7, 1985, to coincide with the typical second edition of the Liturgy of the Hours.[35]

[33] What had been done up to this point was used in the French-speaking countries as experimental. It was a matter of dealing with the Divine Office at that urgent time: *Prière du temps présent. Nouvel Office,* approved on July 4, 1969.

[34] Officium Divinum ex decreto sacrosancti oecumenici Concilii Vaticani II, instauratum auctoritate Pauli PP. VI promulgatum. *Liturgia Horarum iuxta Ritum Romanum,* editio typica (Vatican City, 1971); editio typica altera (Vatican City, 1985). The Liturgy of the Hours, by its very nature, is destined to be celebrated at definite hours of the day and this cadence constitutes one of its principal characteristics. For that reason, it is preferable to call it the "Liturgy of the Hours." The expression "the Divine Office" is very generic and can refer to whatever liturgical celebration; the term "breviary" means simply "the compendium" and is the least adequate of the terms. The felicitous renaming, which indicates a renewed conception demanding a new mentality, appears for the first time in 1959 as the title of a book attributed to V. Raffa, *La Liturgia delle Ore* (Brescia, 1959).

[35] The most important innovation of the second typical edition of the Latin *Liturgia Horarum* consisted in biblical texts of both longer and shorter readings, of psalms, canticles, and some other biblical formulas, corresponding now to the revised New Vulgate, edited in accord with the apostolic constitution *Scripturarum thesaurus* of Pope John Paul II on April 25, 1979. According to that constitution, this new typical version ought to be the official one used for the liturgy. The other innovation consisted in introducing the Hebrew numbering for the psalms as the second number and noted within parenthesis, and the corresponding numbering of versicles from the long biblical readings, the psalms, and the canticles. The number of antiphons for the *Benedictus* and the *Magnificat* was increased to three for cycles ABC and for almost all the Sundays of the year, with reference to the gospel of the day. This second edition of the Liturgy of the Hours also included, besides the general index, ten indices: celebrations, hymns, antiphons, psalms, canticles, long and short readings, patristic readings, long and short responses.

Cf. *CIC,* can. 276, 2, 3°. For a detailed description of this edition, cf. V. Raffa, *Not* 22 (1968) 65–97; ibid., *RPL* 26 (1988) 79–86; A. Lessi, *Not* 23 (1987) 145–166; 24 (1988) 178–206; 290–326.

1. The General Instruction of the Liturgy of the Hours

The General Instruction of the Liturgy of the Hours (GILH) is a document that assumes the form of an instructive directory that is theological, liturgical, spiritual, and pastoral. The fundamental characteristic of this document is that it contains a renewed theological understanding of the Divine Office. Monsignor Bugnini said of it that it is "truly a theological, pastoral, ascetical, and liturgical treatise on the prayer of the Hours, on the importance of this liturgy, and on its component parts. It is a directory that serves not only for the celebration of the liturgy but for meditation on it."[36] We now present this renewed Liturgy of the Hours with the following reading on its diverse aspects.

a) The nature of the Liturgy of the Hours

1) The Liturgy of the Hours is defined in the General Instruction as the "public and common prayer by the people of God" (n. 1). It is primarily *prayer.* And insofar as it is *liturgy,* it ritualizes humanity's dialogue with God. The subject of this public and communal prayer is "the people of God," "the Christian community" (n. 270), or "the body of the Church" (n. 20).

2) It is a *prayer of praise,* the principal and ultimate end of the public-ecclesial prayer of the Liturgy of the Hours. It is the eternal praise introduced by Christ on earth (n. 1; *SC* 83). Praise is the fruit of contemplation of God; it is expressed in adoration and thanksgiving; it is the knowledge of the glory of God and a remembrance of the history of salvation (n. 185). This praise constitutes the gift of spiritual sacrifice offered to God in union with the Church triumphant (nn. 15 and 16).

3) It is *daily* prayer. The Liturgy of the Hours, by its very nature, is to be celebrated at definite hours of the day and of the night. Because of its remembrance factor, it has a clearly chronological reference to the distinct mysteries of salvation in relationship to the mystery of Christ and of the Church. And again, by its very nature, this prayer is destined to sanctify the entire course of day and night (n. 10), as well as of all human activity (n. 11). Herein the Church is allowed to resound with eternal praise and can carry out the teaching of Jesus and the apostles to pray constantly and without interruption.

[36] A. Bugnini, *Reform of the Liturgy 1948–1975,* 522.

b) The theology of the Liturgy of the Hours

The principal goal in studying the theology of the Liturgy of the Hours ought to consist in bringing into bold relief how that prayer is part of the mystery of Christ, and, at the same time, a reflection of the Trinitarian mystery. That particular aspect of the mystery of Christ finds its expression in the mystery of the Church celebrated in the mystery of the liturgy.

1) *The Liturgy of the Hours and the Trinitarian mystery:* The origin of the prayer of praise, its prototype, example, and model are all contained in the life of the Trinity and in the eternal praise exchanged between the Father, the Son, and the Holy Spirit. The Liturgy of the Hours is the earthly expression of that praise. In addition, the Trinity itself, particularly the Father, is the recipient of the worship offered in the Liturgy of the Hours (nn. 3, 8, 17, 27, 109).

2) *The Liturgy of the Hours and the mystery of Christ:* The Word of God, in becoming flesh, brought to earth the eternal Trinitarian praise, which is particularly echoed in the Liturgy of the Hours. "From then on in Christ's heart the praise of God assumes a human sound in words of adoration, expiation, and intercession . . ." (n. 3). This prayer of Christ is the source and model of the prayer of the Church (n. 4) and a particular realization of the priesthood of Christ in the Church (*SC* 83); it is "the very prayer that Christ himself, together with his Body, addresses to the Father" (n.15); it is prayer directed to the Father through Christ and in the name of Christ (n. 17). It is in this way that the Liturgy of the Hours becomes the special presence of Christ (n. 13; *SC* 7). It is also "the prayer of the Church with Christ and to Christ" (n. 2). From the point of view of the relationship between the Liturgy of the Hours and the mystery of Christ, the ecclesial prayer is *the memorial of the mystery of Christ,* of all that God has done for the salvation of humanity, particularly through the paschal mystery of Christ. If the entire liturgy is the actualization and the "making present" of the work of our redemption (*SC* 10) and if, in every liturgical celebration, the mystery of Christ is always present and operative for us (*SC* 2), then this is true also for the Liturgy of the Hours: it is the continuation in the Church of the prayer of Christ, and it makes present and ritualizes, really and effectively, in the Church of today but also with an eye to the future, the paschal mystery of Christ, considered in its universal character and in its diverse phases.

3) *The Liturgy of the Hours and the mystery of the Church:* Intimately united to the mystery of Christ and to its soteriological dimension, the Liturgy of the Hours becomes part of the mystery of the Church, viz., its particular expression and manifestation. The Church, inasmuch as it is the "universal sacrament of salvation" (*LG* 48), is called to continue the work of Christ in being a praying community, identified with the praying Christ, who in the Church and through her continues exercising his priestly office (*SC* 83).

The ecclesial dimension of the Liturgy of the Hours is also intimately linked to the baptismal dignity of Christians: baptism constitutes the theological and ecclesial basis for the command to pray as the work of the priesthood. It is baptism that introduces us into the priesthood of Christ and incorporates us into the Church, making it possible for us to fully enter into the ecclesial *ministry of prayer.*

In order to guarantee the fulfillment of this duty to pray publicly in the Church, in a continuous and certain manner, and to assure this sacramental actualization of the prayer of Christ, the command to celebrate the Liturgy of the Hours has remained firmly in place for those who are called to live out their baptismal call, in a particular way, through priesthood and religious life (nn. 28, 29). The ecclesial nature of the Liturgy of the Hours is manifested most clearly when it is celebrated in community, which is its privileged and proper form (nn. 33, 20, 21, 24).

Furthermore, the ecclesial dimension of the Liturgy of the Hours is in close relationship with the action and the economic-salvific dynamic of the Holy Spirit in the Church. The praying Church, and its unity, depends upon the Holy Spirit, who is the actor, the one who indwells and inspires Christian prayer.

Finally, the ecclesial character of the prayer of the Church is defined within the context of the close union that exists between the pilgrim Church on earth and the glorious Church in heaven: "When the Church offers praise to God in the liturgy of the hours, it unites itself with that hymn of praise sung throughout all ages in the halls of heaven" (n. 16; cf. *SC* 83). Likewise, it is from that combined song that the pilgrim Church, while still on earth, receives a foretaste of the eschatological prayer in heaven (n. 16).

c) The spirituality of the Liturgy of the Hours

The ascetic value of the Liturgy of the Hours depends basically on the fact that in the complexity of its prayers and readings, it is "a wellspring of the Christian life" (n. 18), "a means of gaining God's manifold grace, a deepening of personal prayer, and an incentive to the work of the apostolate," where through prayer one seeks Christ and enters into his mystery (n. 19). As the source for the sanctification of humanity, through that humanity, then, the Liturgy of the Hours becomes the sanctification of chronological, cosmic, and existential time (n. 14). The Liturgy of the Hours is called to become a particular encounter of humanity with God and with Christ the Savior, and to make of time a sign and instrument of salvation.

The ascetic value of ecclesial prayer is rooted also in the fact that it is "a deepening of personal prayer" (nn. 19, 28). This does not mean that there exists an opposition between the prayer of the Church and personal prayer. Each of the Hours is a strong moment in that continuous life of prayer to which all Christians are called and which makes of their lives a kind of *liturgy* when the faithful offer their lives in loving service of God and of others in and with Christ (cf. *Laudis canticum* 8).

The Liturgy of the Hours also constitutes an optimal guarantee of spiritual unity between the workday and the Christian life, given the fact that in the liturgical hourly prayer, humans find the point of union, the spiritual unfolding of all their actions, the basis for the spiritual unity of work, of life, and of existence—all placed in relationship to the center of that unity in Christ and in the mystery of salvation.

The Liturgy of the Hours is also nourishment for, and the expression of, apostolic activity (n. 19), and those who celebrate the liturgy "bring growth to God's people in a hidden but fruitful apostolate" (n. 18), thus carrying out their real function of leading people to Christ (cf. n. 17). Those who exercise the sacerdotal ministry by their ecclesial prayer "fulfill the ministry of the Good Shepherd, who prays for his sheep that they may have life and so be brought into perfect unity" (n. 28).

d) Elements of the Liturgy of the Hours[37]

Before presenting the elements and their meaning, it would be convenient to see the simple and symmetric structure of the two principal hours—Lauds and Vespers—which incorporate most of these elements.

[37] P. Fernández, "Elementos verbales de la Liturgia de las Horas," *La celebración en la Iglesia*. Vol. 3: *Ritmos y tiempos de la celebración* (Salamanca, 1994) 449–512.

Lauds		*Vespers*
	Opening versicle	
(Invitatory Psalm 94)		
	Hymn	
	Psalmody	
Morning psalm		Two psalms
Canticle from OT		Canticle from NT
Psalm of praise		
	Short reading	
	Short responsory	
	Gospel canticle	
Benedictus	*Prayers*	*Magnificat*
Invocations	Our Father	Intercessions
	Collect	
	Closing formula	

1) *Psalms and canticles.* The Liturgy of the Hours of Paul VI introduced a new distribution of the psalter, in conformity with *SC* 89 and 91, whose essential orientations refer to the distribution of the psalter in a longer space of time than the traditional space of one week. The post-conciliar reform opted for the psalter to be prayed within the space of four weeks. The so-called cursing psalms were omitted, as well as individual verses of the same type in other psalms.[38]

Together with the psalms in the liturgical psalter, we also find thirty-five biblical canticles, of which twenty-six are from the Old Testament and nine from the New Testament. To these we need to add the Gospel canticles: *Benedictus, Magnificat,* and *Nunc dimittis.* It must be noted that, historically, the introduction of a canticle from the New Testament into the psalmody of the Vesper hour was an innovation.

The psalms are religious compositions and religious works, prayer texts that accompanied and nourished the faith of the people of Israel. Christ himself prayed the psalms. The Church, people of the new

[38] Cf. N. Füglister, "Vom Mut zur ganzen Schrift: Zur vorgesehenen Eliminierung der sogenannten Fluchpsalmen aus dem neuen römischen Brevier," *Stimen der Zeit* 184 (1969) 186–187; AA.VV., "Pour au contre les psaumes d'imprécation," *ViSpi* 122 (1970) 291–336; E. Bianchi, "I salmi imprecatori," in collective work *Dinanzi a te la benedizione e la maledizione* = Parola spirito e vita. Quaderni di lettura biblica 21 (Bologna, 1990) 83–100; M. Augé, "I salmi imprecatori nella *lectio divina* dell'antico monachesimo," *Psallendum: Miscellanea di studi in onore del Prof. Jordi Pinell I Pons, O.S.B.*, SA 105, AL 15 (Rome, 1992) 47–58.

covenant, has never ceased singing them in the liturgy, particularly the Liturgy of the Hours. The Liturgy of the Hours, with its desire to teach as well as theologize, tries to have the Christian meaning emerge in the singing of the psalms and canticles. For that reason, there is placed at the beginning of each psalm an antiphon that guides the prayer of the psalm in one or the other sense. We can also see that each psalm has a *title*, which gives a summary of the literal sense of that psalm; likewise, we find a *sentence* from the New Testament or from one of the Fathers that helps us pray in a Christological or ecclesial way. The prayer of each psalm concludes with the "Glory be to the Father" in order to situate it within the frame of Trinitarian praise. Finally, after each psalm, the psalm-prayer (n. 112) can be prayed. It is a prayer inspired by the psalm itself and one that expresses both the interior resonance of the psalm and the experience of the one praying it.[39]

As to the forms of making the psalms a prayer, it is best to recite or sing them in harmony with the literary genre that is appropriate to each. From this viewpoint, the Church then adopts definite and characteristic forms that give a certain variety to the celebration, such as the read proclamation, recitation or song in two choirs, the dialogue between soloist and assembly, hymnic or unison chant.

2) *Readings.* The objective of the reform for what is referred to as the biblical readings was that they offer, in the Divine Office, the fundamental process of the history of salvation (cf. *SC* 92). In the aforementioned apostolic constitution *Laudis canticum* (n. 5), Paul VI affirmed: "In the new cycle of readings from holy Scripture there is a more ample selection from the treasury of God's word, so planned as to harmonize with the cycle of readings at Mass. The passages provide in general a certain unity of theme and have been chosen to present, in the course of the year, the principal stages in the history of salvation" (cf. GILH 143, 146).

The patristic and hagiographic readings, as established in *SC* 92, ought to be selected in such a way so as to read, primarily, the Fathers, Doctors, and other writers of the Church and, secondarily, the histori-

[39] According to an ancient tradition, in both the cathedral and the monastic Offices, after each psalm there was a moment of silence and a psalm-like collective prayer. Three series of that ancient repertoire from the fifth to the sixth century were published by P. Verbraken, *Oraisons sur les 150 psaumes*, LO 42 (Paris, 1967); cf. J. Pinell, "Le collette salmiche," in *Liturgia delle Ore: Documenti ufficiali e Studi*, Quaderni di Rivista Liturgica 14 (Turin-Leumann, 1972) 269–286.

cally true lives and passions of the saints. For all these readings, the General Instruction states that the ultimate goal should be meditation on the Word of God and love of that Word, such as the tradition of the Church has always fostered (nn. 163–64). The second goal is to help the people of God understand the true meaning of the times and liturgical feasts (n. 165); and the third goal is to offer access to the rich, spiritual patrimony of the Church (n. 165).

3) *Versicles and responses.* These prayers can be considered as appendices to the readings, their echo and conceptual prolongation. They are a help for meditation on the text previously read, but especially lend themselves as a response to the Word proclaimed, a liturgical need given the fact that the liturgy is a celebratory process and dialogue in prayer. At the same time the versicles and responses contribute a new light to the text proclaimed, inserting that text into the story of salvation, where the fullness of its meaning and its poetic and musical dimensions are revealed. The short responses can be substituted by other songs, a homily, or silence (n. 202).

4) *Hymns.* Placed at the beginning of each Hour, the hymns are liturgical compositions which dispose us and lead us into the mystery which is being celebrated at that Hour, feast or liturgical cycle. Vatican Council II ordered a revision and enrichment of the hymns of the Divine Office: "Hymns are to be restored to their original form, as far as may be desirable. They are to be purged of whatever smacks of mythology or accords ill with Christian piety. Also, as occasion may warrant, other selections are to be made from the treasury of hymns" (*SC* 93).[40] In addition to the classical hymns, "the conferences of bishops may adapt the Latin hymns to suit the character of their own language and introduce fresh compositions, provided these are in complete harmony with the spirit of the hour, season, or feast. Great care must be taken not to allow popular songs that have no artistic merit and are not in keeping with the dignity of the liturgy" (n. 178).

5) *Petitions.* These supplications, in their four elements, represent a balance between fact and prayer pedagogy: an invocation to God, the anamnetic reference to salvation history, evoking a situation either of the community or of the Church, and the common formula for intercessory prayer. There are different kinds of petitions: the *offering prayer*

[40] A. Lentini, *Hymni instaurandi Breviarii Romani, Not* 4 (1968) 99–113; idem, ed., *Te decet hymnus: L'Innario della "Liturgia Horarum,"* Vatican Polyglot Press, 1984.

of Lauds, which refers to the day that has just begun (praise of God; thanksgiving for creation and life; the sacredness of work; diverse petitions), and the *intercessory prayers* of Vespers, in which the intentions of the Church, of humanity, and the memory of the deceased are brought before the assembly (nn. 51, 181–182). "The conferences of bishops have the right to adapt the formularies given in the book of the liturgy of the hours and also to approve new ones" (n. 184).

The restoration of some 1269 petitions to the Hours of Lauds and Vespers represents one of the great riches of the restored Liturgy of the Hours; it implies the retrieval of an ancient element of the Office that developed from or was adopted from the Jewish prayers of intercession, attested to by Clement of Rome and St. Justin.[41] The petitions are concluded with the Our Father and the final oration.

6) *Orations.* With the Liturgy of the Hours of Paul VI there was a restoration, according to the ancient Roman tradition, of the use of morning and evening prayers, of the Little Hours, and of Compline for ferial days during the Church year. These prayers express the characteristic proper to each Hour (cf. nn. 199–200). The combined number of texts used exclusively for the Divine Office is seventy prayers. More than half of the prayers are new; the rest are taken, in whole or in part, from ancient Roman, Ambrosian, and Gallican-French sources. The mind of the Church concerning the Liturgy of the Hours is precisely and explicitly reflected in these texts. At the same time, they constitute the basis for a theology on liturgical prayer in its double dimension of being for the glorification of God and for the sanctification of humanity.[42]

Lauds, prayed daily at dawn with the return of light, suggests a spiritual ambience of joy, confidence, and enthusiasm; at the beginning of human activity, this Hour invites one to offer the day's work for service and mission. The traditional theological theme is that of the resurrection of Christ and his presence in the world as "the sun born on high" for the salvation and liberation of all humankind.

[41] Cf. A. Baumstark, *Comparative Liturgy,* 74–75.

[42] Cf. A. Dumas, "Le orazioni dell'Ufficio feriale nel Tempo *per annum,*" *Liturgia delle Ore: Documenti ufficiali e Studi,* Quaderni di Rivista Liturgica 14 (Turin-Leumann, 1972) 251–268; J. Pinell, *Las oraciones del salterio "per annum" en el nuevo libro de la Liturgia de las Horas,* (Rome, 1974); D. Sartore, *Introduzione alla Liturgia delle Ore* (Rome, 1971); idem, "Una serie di orazioni *ad matutinas* e *ad vespertinas* di origine gallico-franca," *Psallendum,* op. cit., 247–266.

Vespers, sung while the light is declining, invites one to take a look at the work accomplished. It suggests that, together with the consciousness of a certain fatigue and tiredness, there may also be weakness and culpability. But it also suggests confidence in God like the confidence Christ expressed in his death. Themes such as gratitude for the blessings of God and the offering of a spiritual sacrifice of praise recur, as do the themes of time as a salvific sign and the mutability of time as compared with the immutability of God. The remembrance of the passion of Christ is present every Friday, and all the prayers make reference to the Easter experience of Emmaus. The Church, lifting her suppliant voice, defines herself as a suppliant people.

The middle Hours (Terce, Sext, None), which are meant to sanctify the daily activity of Christians through a brief moment of prayer, makes reference to the meaning of human work, to its heaviness, duration, and reward. We find clear and spontaneous biblical references to the paschal happenings narrated in the Gospel, to the example of the apostles and to the Pentecost event narrated in the Acts of the Apostles: Pentecost at Terce; the prayer of Peter at Sext; his encounter with Cornelius and the prayer of Peter and John at the temple at the Hour of None. At the Hour of Terce, when remembrance is made of the Pentecost happenings, prayer is offered for a renewed outpouring of the Spirit on the Church of today. A third series of allusions proceeds from the events surrounding the redemptive passion of Jesus: the road to Calvary at Terce, the crucifixion at Sext, and the death of Christ and the salvation of the repentant thief at None. At the Hour of None on Saturdays there is reference to the Virgin Mary.

Compline, which immediately precedes the evening rest, necessarily brings with it the allusion to the sleep of death and awakening to the resurrection of Christ, particularly on Saturday evenings into Sunday, whether the historical-symbolic aspect or the ascetical. Other themes are those of the presence of God, of protection against the insidious Evil One, of peace and restorative sleep that will permit us to return faithfully and joyfully to divine service.

7) *Silence.* Responding to *SC* 30, holy silence has been happily restored to the Liturgy of the Hours and has taken its proper place there. This does not consist in a mere simple ritual pause or a lack of words and gestures, but in a liturgical action carrying a strong sense of mystery, pneumatology, and ecclesiology; that is to say, the silence is observed "in order to receive in our hearts the full sound of the voice of

the Holy Spirit and to unite our personal prayer more closely with the word of God and the public voice of the Church" (n. 202). What establishes a typology of liturgical silence is the nature and the goal of silence insofar as it is the *pneumatological place*, totally related to the presence and the action of the Holy Spirit, without whom there is no Christian prayer (n. 8). In order that dialogue with God, which is the proper measure of the celebration of daily prayer, may be efficacious, the *liturgies of silence* are envisaged after each psalm according to the ancient tradition, after the readings (nn. 202, 112, 124), after the homily (n. 48), and during the intercessory prayers (n. 193).[43]

8) *Song*. Of all the liturgical books coming out of the postconciliar reform, the Liturgy of the Hours, in its Praenotanda, is the one that dedicates most numbers to song—eighteen in all—and in these the raison d'etre of song as part of the liturgical celebration is best defined. The use of song or chant in the celebration of the Liturgy of the Hours must be seen as that which responds best to the nature of this prayer; song is an indication of greater solemnity and of the most profound union of hearts (n. 268). The other elements of the lyric genre, such as psalms, canticles, hymns, and responses, reach their fullest meaning only through song (n. 269). Priceless are the words of n. 270: "In celebrating the liturgy singing is not to be regarded as an embellishment superimposed on prayer; rather, it wells up from the depths of a soul intent on prayer and praise of God and reveals in a full and complete way the community nature of Christian worship." Song is enthusiastically recommended for Sundays and feast days (n. 271). With song, Lauds and Vespers should be brought into relief as the axes about which the entire Office rotates (n. 272).

The principle of progressive solemnity, that is, one that admits several intermediate stages between the completely sung Office and the recitation of all its parts, allows for a necessary variety, governed by the tonality of the day or the Hour that is being celebrated, by the nature of the elements of the Office, by the numbers or character of the community, and by the number of cantors available (n. 273). A clear

[43] The concept "liturgies of silence" has been inserted into n. 5 of the *Directorium de Opere Dei persolvendo* in the Benedictine monastic Liturgy of the Hours, cf. R. Leikam, "Liturgias del silencio: Un concepto a profundizar en el *Directorium de Opere Dei persolvendo* del *Thesaurus Liturgiae Horarum monasticae*," *EO* 12 (1995) 253–278.

reference is also made to the adaptation that must be made to the times and circumstances, for example finding new forms of song for our times, a frame of mind and action that has always been present in the life of the Church (n. 273).

2. *The Nature and Spirit of the Different Hours*

The daily structure of the Liturgy of the Hours is not only the result of the fact that each one of the Offices comes during and at determinate moments of the day but also because of the thematic content referred to in the Hours and to the mysteries of salvation historically tied to those hours of the day. Since what follows is but a summary and introduction, we suggest that the reader go to the Liturgy of the Hours itself and, more concretely, to the concluding prayers of the different Hours. Their theological and spiritual content are of great value, in addition to their ability to give us the sense of each moment of prayer that we are celebrating.

a) *Lauds and Vespers.* These two Hours constitute the nucleus and double axis of the daily Office (cf. nn. 37 and 40). The day and the night have a close relationship with human life and express the fundamental rhythm of every living being. The ecclesial tradition has been to bless this cosmic rhythm with the prayer of Lauds and Vespers.

In the celebration of Lauds, many of the texts refer to morning, dawn, light, the sunrise, and the beginning of the day. They deal with the gifts of God given for the service of humankind, which in turn are converted into the praise and glory of the Creator. Traditionally, Psalms 62 and 50 belong to this category. On the other hand, this cosmic theme also evokes the resurrection of Christ, the light which illumines the world and which "comes to visit us from on high" and to guide us in our daily life (cf. n. 38).

With the evening prayer we come to offer the Lord the work of our day and the praise transformed into a spiritual sacrifice of thanks, as expressed in Psalm 140:2. Also, this Hour clarifies the relationship between cosmic themes and the mysteries of salvation: the Last Supper of the Lord was celebrated at dusk (Matt 26:20; Mark 14:17); nightfall reminds us of the darkness, of the passion and death of Christ, through which the most perfect sacrifice was offered. Evening is also a reminder of the transitory nature of all created things and the definitive awaiting for the kingdom of God that will take place on the final cosmic day (cf. n. 39).

b) *The Office of Readings.* This celebration, as now proposed in the Roman liturgy, is a space of time dedicated to the reflective and contemplative listening to the Word of God. It can be a way of deepening one's self in *lectio divina* with biblical and patristic texts as a basis.

The Office of Readings is celebrated at a moment in the day that is most appropriate for tranquil and serene reflection. In particular circumstances, it can also be celebrated in the silence of the night, for example in the vigils of some important feast of the liturgical year (cf. nn. 55–73).

c) *Terce, Sext, None, or the Little Hours.* Outside of choir, in order to preserve the tradition of praying during the course of one's work, one could choose one of the three Little Hours, the one that best fits the given moment of the day. The Fathers of the Church set these Hours in relationship with other happenings in the story of redemption in the persons of Christ or the Holy Spirit. The concluding orations of these Offices make special mention of this relationship (cf. nn. 74–83).

d) *Compline.* This prayer is recited before the nocturnal rest, even if that is after midnight. When the day is about to end, we confidently put ourselves into the hand of God. Psalms 4, 90, and 133 were traditionally prayed. The high point of this Hour is the Canticle of Simeon (Luke 2:29-32), which expresses joy and gratitude to God for having permitted us to find Christ our Savior. At the end of this Hour, the medieval tradition introduced the singing of a Marian antiphon in the form of a prayer, which, in addition to its devotional character, was meant to lift our last thoughts of the day to the Mother of God, so intimately associated with the work of redemption (cf. n. 92).

3. The Pastoral Aspects of the Liturgy of the Hours

I will summarize here the most outstanding points of the *Institutio generalis de Liturgia Horarum* with a view to the pastoral aspects of the Liturgy of the Hours.

The celebration of the Liturgy of the Hours is an important goal of pastoral action; those who take part in it, therefore, contribute to the growth of the people of God, and their prayer is converted into a wellspring or fountain of Christian life (n. 18).

The community celebration of the Liturgy of the Hours, on whatever level—diocesan, parochial, or other—makes visible the Church of Christ (nn. 20–22). For this reason, the role of the ministers for the Liturgy of the Hours, that is, those who have received the sacred command or given a particular order to celebrate it, consists in calling together the community and directing its prayer, providing the necessary catechesis for the common celebration, and teaching the people how to participate (n. 23; cf. *SC* 84; *PO* 5). All this ought to enter into the pastoral and evangelistic objective of a pastor: to form praying communities. Another consequence of the communitarian ideal of prayer within the Liturgy of the Hours is the recommendation that there be a common celebration made up of priests, religious, laity, and even families (nn. 24–27), especially at Lauds and Vespers.[44]

In order to facilitate the participation of the faithful within the basic structure of the Liturgy of the Hours (cf. n. 33), necessary adaptions can be made: longer or more adequate readings (nn. 46, 248, 250); a homily (n. 47); holy silence (n. 48); appropriate songs instead of the response (n. 49); a selection of psalms that might facilitate a gradual or better understanding of the same (nn. 247, 252); the substitution of a ritual (n. 246); and the celebration of votive Offices (n. 245).

The General Instruction (nn. 93–99) deals with the joining of an Hour of the Office with the celebration of the Mass. "In particular cases, if circumstances require, it is possible to link an hour more closely with the Mass when there is a celebration of the liturgy of the hours in public or in common" (n. 93). However, this possibility ought to be used with discretion and sound pastoral criteria, given the fact that both liturgical celebrations, even if they are not opposed to each other, are distinct in their goal and structure, and ought to be celebrated as such at separate times.

Pastorally speaking, by means of an adequate catechesis, one could more conveniently deepen one's understanding of the relationship between the Liturgy of the Hours and the celebration of the Eucharist in the light of what is expressed in n. 12 of our document: the Liturgy of the Hours is the *extension of* and the *preparation for* the Eucharist. The Eucharist is the source and culmination of all cultic and sanctifying action as well as of the Christian life itself. From the Eucharist as *source,* the Liturgy of the Hours prolongs the presence of Christ, though in a different manner. Christ is the extension of the salvific power of the paschal mystery. In many of the psalms, the one praying is invited to

[44] J. M. Bernal, "De la celebración de las horas al rezo privado del oficio (siglos XI–XVI)," *Liturgia de las Horas: Veinte siglos de historia,* Dossiers CPL 36 (Barcelona, 1988) 85.

renew the covenant between God and humankind by offering a worthy sacrifice, the sacrifice of praise, adoration, intercession, and thus be given a taste of eternal glory. This idea of Eucharist as source of our sanctification is completed in the idea of Eucharist as the *culmination* of all celebrational and prayerful worship. Through the fruitful celebration of the Liturgy of the Hours, the one praying becomes prepared and matured to again enter into the dynamism of the Eucharistic memorial.

Of great importance in the pastoral care of the Liturgy of the Hours is that the celebration be structured and developed so as to give attention to all the ministries of the liturgical assembly and not only to the achievement of correct gestures and postures (nn. 253ff). Special attention must be given to the chant or song when preparing for the celebration of, and participation in, festive prayer (nn. 267–284).

One of the characteristics of the Liturgy of the Hours of Paul VI is its flexibility. Imagination is required, starting with the spirit of the renewed form and understanding of the Liturgy of the Hours, so that the liturgy will be celebrated with gestures and symbols that are both eloquent and meaningful. The ancient tradition of popular celebrations of the Church's prayer, especially during the fourth and fifth centuries, is a model for us today as well. There is nothing to impede actual communities from developing popular forms of morning and evening prayer for community-wide parish celebrations. As an example, a parish or community might use a *lucernarium* as an opening ritual for Sunday Vespers or other great feasts of the liturgical year.

IV. THE MONASTIC-BENEDICTINE LITURGY OF THE HOURS

The Renewed Liturgy

Within the range of liturgical renewal promoted by Vatican Council II, we find ourselves dealing not only with the renewal of the Roman Liturgy of the Hours but also with the typically monastic-Benedictine Office. The document that testifies to this is the *Thesaurus Liturgiae Horarum Monasticae* and its *Directorium de Opere Dei persolvendo* of 1977.[45] The principles and objectives of the Council, together with the liturgical renewal that followed it, could not but provoke a profound

[45] *Thesaurus Liturgiae Horarum Monasticae,* ed. Secretariat of the Abbot Primate O.S.B., Badia Primaziale Sant' Anselmo (Rome, 1977); *Not* 13 (1977) 157–191.

need for renewal within the heart of the Benedictine Confederation. The steps toward the renewal of the monastic Liturgy of the Hours were at first insecure ones. It was seen from the start that discretion would be needed so as not to lose the great values of the monastic tradition and yet reach out to the new needs of the Church and of the monastic communities of our time. It was a matter of achieving a balanced harmony between *nova et vetera.*

The change from a *Breviarium Monasticum,* promulgated by Paul V in 1612, to a *Thesaurus Liturgiae Horarum Monasticae* is justified not only because of and within the context of the conciliar renewal—where the *Thesaurus* was prepared—but also because of the requests of Benedictine monastics in the Church of our time. A *Breviarium Monasticum* was not a desirable choice for monastics, given the monolithic nature and uniformity of the breviary. Rather, what was needed was the preparation of a *Thesaurus* as a kind of resource book with materials and suggestions easily adapted by a concrete community to its Liturgy of the Hours. This option constitutes a typical example of legitimate diversity and liturgical adaptation, according to the rich and varied monastic tradition as well as to the principles contained in the Benedictine Rule.[46] Within a legitimate pluralism of celebration, a pluralism both dynamic and enriching, the *Thesaurus* allows and urges each monastic community to express sincerely and authentically its condition and call, celebrated in proper form and in harmony with the rhythm of the monastic life that characterizes it in its present reality, making use of the material and various possibilities which the *Thesaurus* and the *Directorium* contain and suggest.[47]

[46] Following the *Ordo* of the Office as given in the Rule, chapters 18, 22–23, St. Benedict establishes the following: ". . . if perhaps someone is not pleased with this arrangement of the Psalter, another arrangement can be made which seems better, provided that in any case there be retained the rule of reciting the entire Psalter of 150 psalms during the course of each week so that at the vigil of each Sunday, the Office will begin with the same psalm." So it is that the *Thesaurus Liturgiae Horarum Monasticae* presents four schemata for the psalter, distinguished by the capital letters A, B, C, and D. Plan A corresponds to the *cursus* of the Benedictine Rule; plan B responds to the principle of freedom, which we have just cited and which is offered by the same Rule. In both of these plans the hebdomadary may be used for both weeks. Plans C and D present an arrangement of psalms to extend over two weeks. Cf. *Thesaurus, Schemati Psalterii,* 38–57.

[47] For the renewal of the Benedictine monastic Liturgy of the Hours, its history and principles, its theological and liturgical value and content, cf. R. Leikam,

The *Directorium de Opere Dei persolvendo* does not pretend to repeat or summarize what was provided in the Roman *Institutio generalis de Liturgia Horarum* but publicizes norms that had directed the monastic tradition in the light of the principles of renewal proposed in the latter. Among the goals of this document, indicated in its *Prooemium* and which we now cite, is that "the monastic tradition, in the area of prayer, be in touch with the spiritual tendencies present in the world and culture of today, according to that legitimate pluralism by which the Church recognizes those elements which are valid for the building up of the Body of Christ." A second goal of the *Directorium* consists in "presenting simple reflections which will throw light on the diverse aspects of liturgical prayer which carry such great importance for the monastic life," and "through which reflections all the sons and daughters of St. Benedict may discover their own thought about the celebration of the *Opus Dei*, the spiritual crown of the monastic life."

CONCLUSION

1. *Before Vatican Council II:* From the simplicity of the ancient Roman Liturgy of the Hours, continuing on through the constitution of a solemn Divine Office, and arriving at the beginning of the Breviary and its reforms of the current Liturgy of the Hours, we must say that the road covered has had its great stages or phases. It may be appropriate to present a synthesis and the characteristic of each stage. In these are found some models that have been called "historic models of reform" in the Divine Office.

The first epoch was a period of enrichment and creativity. It was the epoch during which time, prayer, and celebration were harmoniously

---

La Liturgia de las Horas Monástica en el Directorio del Thesaurus Liturgiae Horarum Monasticae. *Historia y teologia* (Buenos Aires, 1990); ibid., "El *Thesaurus Liturgiae Horarum Monasticae* de 1977 y la renovación del Opus Dei benedictino," *Cuadernos Monásticos* 86 (1988) 299–330; H. Ashworth, "The Renewal of the Benedictine Office," *Not* 13 (1977) 192–196; R. Gantoy, "Les chantiers de la prière: A propos d'un récent Directoire pour l'Office," *CL* 60/1 (1978) 45–55; T. Schnitker, "Der Thesaurus Liturgiae Horarum Monasticae und seine Bedeutung für die Liturgiewissenschaft," *LJ* 28 (1978) 45–56; P. Visentin, "Un Direttorio modello della Liturgia delle Ore," *Mysterion. Nella celebrazione del Mistero di Cristo la vita della Chiesa,* Miscellanea in occasione dei 70 anni dell'Abate Salvatore Marsili, Quaderni di Rivista Liturgica, n.s., 5 (Turin, 1981) 525–539; O. Lang, "Welche Anregungen bieten die 'Allgemeine Einfuhrung' und die 'Rechtlinien für das Monastische Stundengebet' für unser Chorgebet?" *Erbe und Auftrag* 57 (1981) 405–15; 58 (1982) 22–32.

joined and where the two great traditions—the cathedral and monastic traditions—met and enriched each other. The Divine Office was considered the daily prayer celebrated by Christian communities with a certain solemnity.

The next stage of the journey was characterized by a tendency toward synthesis. There was a tendency to unite in one book and in one unique structure all the constitutive elements of the Office. During this stage the common dimension of celebrating the Office was minimized in order to make room for the prayer of the Church understood as a private matter and proper to only one segment of the people of God, namely, the clerics. The freedom with which texts were chosen was replaced by a certain rigidity and obligation.

The meaning attributed to the element of "prayer" evolved, given the fact that from a conception of prayer as predominantly the praise of the Trinity, it evolved into a pedagogical tool. In the last analysis it became a matter of evaluating or justifying the burdensomeness of the Office against the obligation to pray it, thus converting the Office into a formative moment.

The ecclesial factor played its role in the evolution of the prayer of the Church. The Divine Office and its diverse forms appear very narrowly linked to the Church and to its own self-knowledge. The development and stabilization of a clerical Church would make of the Office "the prayer of the cleric." The very structure of common prayer made it burdensome and impractical, reason enough to convert it into a rational and formative instrument with a view to individual praxis. On all this the ecclesial factor played a role of imposing liturgical uniformity.

A further determining element was that of spirituality, that is, the variety of ways in which one's relationship with God assumes a cultural understanding of the human person, the world, history, and interpersonal relationships. Historically it is clear that no one community experience of prayer and relationship with God could express every other community's culture and spirituality. Choices became centered in the individual and thus promoted an emphasis on individualism. The result was that, having one's own book of prayer—the breviary—the cleric performed his prayer, reading, and meditation as a private experience oriented to spiritual fruitfulness.

2. *After Vatican Council II:* With a new Liturgy of the Hours there was a reversal from the secular tendency of considering the Divine

Office as a clerical and private affair to one of giving to each Christian the possibility of having first-hand contact with an experience of prayer that is proper to the whole Church in all times and in the entire Body of Christ.

The reform and renewal of the Divine Office promoted by Vatican Council II has been and continues to be the most profound renewal in history. Its objective was not only to reform the book itself—called, at that time, the breviary—but also to renew and enlarge the prayer of the people of God, the Body of Christ, the Church. The Church's teaching on communion and participation, also promoted by the same Vatican Council, could not but give a profoundly ecclesial impression to the Liturgy of the Hours, adaptable to the specific exigencies of people and communities of diverse arrangement, condition, and vocation within the Church. The very intimate nature of these groups calls them to manifest that particularity by means of and through the daily and hourly celebration of prayer.

The simplicity of the celebrational structure, the new and more functional distribution of the psalter, the abundant use of the Word of God, the variety of patristic texts, the rich collection of prayers and collects—all form a renewed Liturgy of the Hours, capable of deepening, enlivening, and profoundly orienting all Christian prayer to the nourishment of the spiritual life of the people of God. The suggestions offered by the Liturgy of the Hours represent a model of prayer, rich in content, open and universal, thus allowing us to make our own, day after day, the very prayer of Christ to the Father in and through the rhythm of prayer offered by the Church in its entirety. The community celebration of prayer in the Church represents a moment during which the community is mindful of its call to "pray always."

The reclaiming and the reevaluation of the liturgical celebration of prayer within the true and natural hours of the day and night make it possible for the praise of the salvific mystery to accomplish its function of sanctifying time and the entire lives of the faithful. This is done in a kind of *liturgia* which the faithful offer in service of God and for the love of brothers and sisters in communion with the action and gift of Christ.

"The canticle of praise which resounds eternally throughout the heavenly mansions and which Jesus Christ, the great high priest, introduced into this desert land, has been carried out faithfully and constantly by the Church, through a marvelous variety of forms."

These words, together with those of Paul VI in initiating the apostolic constitution *Laudis canticum*, can very well serve as a conclusion to this chapter on the Liturgy of the Hours in the Roman West. Through this history and theology of ecclesial prayer, together with the experiences of the Christian East, we can certainly see, on the one hand, the variety of forms that the Church has given to the song of praise of Christ, and, on the other hand, how the same Church has sought ways to continue, faithfully and continuously, that canticle to Jesus Christ. In summary, the Church has not only developed all its capacity for liturgical prayer through the celebration of the Liturgy of the Hours but has also actualized or made present the saving power of God.

Bibliography

AA.VV. *Liturgia delle Ore: Documenti ufficiale e studi.* Quaderni di Rivista Liturgica 14. Turin, 1972.

AA.VV. *Liturgia de las Horas: La celebración en la Iglesia.* Vol. 3: *Ritmos y tiempos de la celebración*, 283–524. Salamanca, 1990.

AA.VV. *Liturgia de las Horas: Veinte siglos de historia.* Dossiers CPL 36. 2nd ed. Barcelona, 1994.

Baümer, S., and R. Biron. *Histoire du bréviaire.* 2 vols. Paris, 1905.

Campbell, S. *From Breviary to Liturgy of the Hours: The Structural Reform of the Roman Office, 1964–1971.* Collegeville, Minn., 1995.

Guiver, G. *La compagnia delle voci: Liturgia delle Ore e popolo di Dio nell'esperienza storica dell'ecumen cristiana.* Milan, 1991.

Klöckner, M., and H. Rennings, eds. *Lebendiges Stundengebet: Vertiefung und Hilfe.* Freiburg im Breisgau, 1989.

Lopez Martin, J. *La Oración de las Horas: Historia, teología y pastoral del oficio divino.* 3rd ed. Salamanca, 1994.

Martimort, A. G. "La oración de las horas." In *La Iglesia en oración: Introducción a la liturgia*, 1047–1173. Barcelona, 1992.

Pinell, J. "Le orazioni composte per l'Ufficio Divino nell'ambito della tradizione eucologia latina. A. Rito romano antico. 1. La serie del Veronense. 2. La serie Gelasiana." *Not* 154 (1979) 250–265; *Not* 155 (1979) 310–340.

____. *La liturgia delle ore. Anàmnesis* 5.

____. "La liturgia de las horas, alabaanza del misterio." In *Vida religiosa* 35 (1974) 23–38.

____. "El número sagrado de las horas del oficio." In *Miscellanea liturgica in onore di S. E. Card. Lercaro,* 2:887–934. Rome, 1967.

Raffa, V. "Liturgia de las Horas." *NDL* 1164–1191.

____. *La Liturgia delle Ore: Presentazione storica, teologica e pastorale.* 3rd ed. Milan, 1990.

____. "L'Ufficio divino del tempo dei carolingi e il Breviario di Innocenzo III confrontati con la Liturgia delle Ore di Paolo VI." *EphLit* 85 (1971) 206–259.

____. "Dal Breviario del Quignonez alla Liturgia delle Ore di Paolo VI." In *Liturgia delle Ore: Documenti ufficiali e studi,* 289–363. Quaderni di Rivista Liturgica 14. Turin-Leumann, 1972.

Reynal D. *Théologie de la liturgie des heures.* Paris, 1978.

Sartore, D. *Introduzione alla Liturgia delle Ore.* Rome, 1971.

Rubén M. Leikam, O.S.B.

4

The Liturgy of the Hours in the Non-Roman West

I. THE LITURGY OF THE HOURS OF NORTH AFRICA

1. Monastic Office

We know very little about the Divine Office of North Africa. Some information has been found in the *Ordo monasterii,* which refers to a Western monastic *cursus* that probably is the oldest of the West. This is a primitive monastic rule book from around the year 395 that was written in Latin and has been attributed to Alypius of Tagaste in North Africa.[1] The *Ordo* was taken on by St. Augustine in his Rule and was also used by St. Caesarius of Arles in his Rules for monks. According to chapter 2 of the *Ordo,* the *cursus* of the Hours was the following:

a) *Matins:* Psalms 62, 5, 89.

b) *Terce, Sext, None:* one responsorial psalm, two antiphonal psalms, reading, conclusion.

c) *Lucernarium:* one responsorial psalm, four antiphonal psalms, one responsorial psalm, reading, conclusion.

d) *Nocturns:* in the months of November, December, January, and February: twelve antiphonal psalms, six responsorial psalms, three

In this chapter we follow the valuable and well-documented study of R. Taft, *The Liturgy of the Hours in East and West: The Origins of the Divine Office and Its Meaning for Today,* published by The Liturgical Press, 2nd rev. ed. (Collegeville, Minn., 1993).

[1] See the critical text in L. Verheijen, *La Règle de Saint Augustin* (Paris, 1967) 1:148–152; commentary in 2:205–213. G. P. Lawless, "*Ordo monasterii:* Structure, Style and Rhetoric," *Augustinianum* 22 (1982) 469–491. Idem, "*Ordo monasterii:* A Double or Single Hand?" *Studia Patristica* 17/2 (Oxford, 1982) 511–518.

readings; in the months of March, April, September, and October: ten antiphonal psalms, five responsorial psalms, three readings; in the months of May, June, July, and August: eight antiphonal psalms, four responsorial psalms, two readings.

2. *Cathedral Office*

In his *Confessions* (V, 9), St. Augustine says that his holy mother Monica "went to church two times a day, in the morning and in the evening, with fidelity . . . to listen to you and to your words, and you were able to listen to her through her prayers." In his commentary on Psalm 49:23, Augustine seems to indicate the existence of a cathedral prayer for Matins and Vespers in his description of the attitude of those who view religious practice as a kind of business deal with God when they say: "I will get up each day, I will go to church, I will unite myself to the chant of a Matins hymn, to a second Vespers hymn, to a third or a fourth at home; every day I will offer a sacrifice of praise, and I will make an offering to my God." Augustine's love for chanting, psalmody, and the hymns is also evident, demonstrating the importance that all these elements had in the cathedral prayer of his church.[2]

The *Vita Fulgentii,* attributed to the Carthaginian deacon Ferrandus, tells that Fulgentius, bishop of Ruspe in North Africa, must have taught the clergy to sing and pronounce the psalmody well, decreeing that "each week all the clergy and the widows and the lay people who were capable should fast every Wednesday and Friday, ordering everyone to be present at the daily vigils, fasts, and morning and evening prayers."[3] In reference to the cathedral vigils, Augustine speaks of vigils celebrated before Easter, Pentecost, and the feast of St. Cyprian, as was usual before the big feasts and anniversaries of the principal martyrs of the local churches.

II. THE LITURGY OF THE HOURS OF THE GALLICAN RITE

1. *The Monastic and Cathedral Office*

The oldest monastic *cursus* of Gaul is that of Cassian, established for his monastery of St. Victor in Marseilles, as well as for the monastery

[2] See F. van der Meer, *Augustine the Bishop* (London, 1978) 325–337.

[3] PL 65:147.

of Lerins, which was founded by his disciple Honoratus. Famous bishops like St. Caesarius of Arles came from Lerins and spread the Office through all of France. In the *Institutes* of Cassian, written about 417 to 425, the practice of the urban monastic Office of Bethlehem is mentioned. Through this description of the Offices of Egypt and Palestine, we indirectly learn more about the Gallican Office of Lerins.

a) In the Gallican Office each psalm, and not just a unit of psalms as in Egypt and Palestine, concluded with the "Glory to the Father" (*Institutes,* II, 8). This is a difference that still exists today, distinguishing the Eastern monastic psalmody from the Western.

b) The nocturnal Office began at cockcrow and lasted until the sun set, as in Bethlehem (*Institutes,* II, 1). It consisted of a continuous psalmody and was followed by readings, as was done in Egypt. Contrary to the practice in Bethlehem, in Gaul Lauds was separate from Nocturns (see *Institutes,* III, 6).

c) The morning Office at sunrise in Gaul did not include Psalms 50, 62, and 89 as in Bethlehem but rather Psalms 62, 119:147–148, and Psalms 148–150 (*Institutes,* III, 3-6).

d) The Hours of Terce, Sext, and None included three psalms as in the East (*Institutes,* III, 2-3).

e) The *undecima* (eleventh) hour, or Vespers, as in Bethlehem, had a continuous psalmody similar to that sung in Egypt, with readings preceded, perhaps, by elements of the cathedral Office, such as Psalm 140 and a *lucernarium,* or "light service" (*Institutes,* III, 8-11).

f) On Friday night a vigil was celebrated, as in Bethlehem (*Institutes,* III, 1-2).

The system of Cassian was later transformed into the monastic rules of St. Caesarius and St. Aurelian of Arles. Although the Offices of these two authors maintain the fundamental structure of Cassian, there is an increase in the psalms and in the manner of singing them. New elements such as hymns and verses of intercession taken from the psalms are added, and the *cursus* is extended to include other more common and developed Hours and vigils. As Caesarius and Aurelian describe in the Office schedule of Arles that follows below, Matins and the *lucernarium* come from the cathedral Office and were added to an already complete monastic schedule, where the nocturnal Office and the *duodecima* represent the exact parallel of the celebrations that open and close the monastic day of Cassian.

Nocturns
 (Vigils)
Matins
 (Saturdays, Sundays, Feasts: Prime)[4]
Terce–Sext–None[5]
Lucernarium
Duodecima[6]
 (Vigils)

In the most important Hours, the Nocturns and the *duodecima,* the psalmody opens with a fixed invitatory psalm. Aurelian also adds a triple *Kyrie eleison* at the beginning and end of each Office and after the monastic psalmody. Although Caesarius does not make a reference to this in his Rules, canon 3 of the Second Council of Vaison, held under his leadership in 529, ordered that the *Kyrie eleison* be introduced in the cathedral Offices of the morning, at Vespers, and in the Mass.[7]

In the two Hours of cathedral Matins and the *lucernarium* there are no readings, but the ordinary monastic Hours have between one and three biblical readings. The vigils, however, have a collection of readings and psalmody, referred to as *missae.* Each *missa* included three *orationes* (three readings, each followed by a prayer) and then three psalms. The core of the Gallican monastic vigils was not established by the continuous psalmody but rather by the readings. This demon-

[4] Historically, this is the oldest clear reference to Prime, a celebration that is justified by Aurelian in chapter 28 of his Rule for monks in the same way that Cassian had already done: prohibit the monks from returning to sleep after Matins. According to St. Caesarius, Prime is celebrated only on Saturdays, Sundays, and feast days.

[5] The festal Hour of Terce functioned in the same way as the τυπικά in the monastic Byzantine tradition: originally it was a presanctified monastic communion rite that took place on days on which there was no Eucharistic celebration. Aurelian, in his Rule for monks (57, 11-17), says that on Sundays and feast days Terce is followed by the Our Father, and all receive communion while singing a psalm, because the Mass is celebrated when the abbot considers it useful.

[6] The *duodecima* was an Office that followed the *lucernarium,* with twelve psalms and three antiphonal psalms (Caesarius), or eighteen psalms and one antiphon (Aurelian). Between the two authors the *duodecima* of the week of Easter included eighteen psalms, three antiphonal psalms, two readings that were taken from the Apostle, and a gospel reading of the resurrection. This Office opened with Psalm 103:19b-24a as a welcoming.

[7] Mansi, 8, 727.

strates the enormous importance that biblical readings had in the Office of Arles.

The hymns represent a new element in the Western monastic tradition, making their first appearance in the Rules of Arles. While the lesser Hours have the same hymn for the whole year, the greater Hours have two specific hymns on alternating days, except for feast days, Sunday Matins, and during Easter week. All these days have their own hymns.

Another important source in knowing more about the Gallican Divine Office is the sermons of St. Caesarius of Arles.[8] In them we find not only information that corresponds to the monastic Rules of Caesarius but also a rich spiritual doctrine that gives testimony to the meaning of that ecclesial prayer with psalms, readings, silence, and collects.

III. THE LITURGY OF THE HOURS OF THE AMBROSIAN RITE

1. *The Offices of Milan in the Time of St. Ambrose*

St. Ambrose (339–397) documents the existence of cathedral Offices in his see of Milan, where he was bishop from 374 to 397, the year of his death. He writes of the psalmody at the beginning and the end of the day and during the night.[9] In reference to the Hour of Matins, Ambrose mentions a daily synaxis that the Christians had to participate in. He writes of this in his commentary on Psalm 118, where he also explains the traditional symbolism of the prayer at sunrise: Christ, the Sun of justice.[10]

For Ambrose, the evening prayers are the "Vespers sacrifice," citing the classic Psalm 140:2 used in Vespers of the Milanese cathedral.[11] In his *Confessions* (X, 12), St. Augustine reminds us that Ambrose composed the Vespers hymn *Deus, creator omnium,* which probably was sung during the Vespers celebrations. The public and solemn vigils were celebrated at the times of the great solemnities, among them Easter and the feast of the apostles Peter and Paul.

[8] See R. Leikam, "*Psallentes et orantes:* La doctrina espiritual sobre la oración de la Iglesia en los Sermones de s. Cesáreo de Arlés," *EO* 11 (1994) 153–180.

[9] *Explan. ps.* 1, 9; CSEL 64, 7.

[10] *Expositio ps.* 118, 19, 22, 30, 32; CSEL 62, 433, 437–439.

[11] *Expositio ps.* 118, 8, 48; CSEL 62, 180.

According to the testimony of the *Life of Ambrose,* written by Paulinus in 420, the first time that the church of Milan began to celebrate with antiphons, hymns, and vigils was during the conflict with Empress Justina during Holy Week of 385. Justina wanted to give a basilica to the Arians but faced the rejection of Ambrose. As a result, the imperial troops surrounded the church, keeping Ambrose and his followers under siege for three days. They took advantage of this time to sing hymns and psalms with antiphons in a responsorial manner.[12] St. Augustine also writes of this event in his *Confessions* (IX, 7).

2. From the Old Ambrosian Office to the Ambrosian Breviary

The scarce documentation that we have about the Ambrosian Office does not allow us to know its exact structure before the monastic-Carolingian influence. The manuscripts of the eleventh and twelfth centuries, above all the *Manuale* of Valtravaglia[13] and the *Ordo et caeremoniae* of Beroldus,[14] offer a detailed description of the Ambrosian Office. These manuscripts allow us to integrate earlier fragmented documents and verify that, despite widespread reforms, the original notation has been conserved up to the twentieth century. In the basic structure of even the most evolved form of the Office, elements and criteria remain that must have come from a much older period. Examples of this include the union of the vigil Office with the Matins Office in one unique celebration, the Sunday vigil psalmody composed of Old Testament canticles instead of psalms, and the criteria that direct the distribution of the canticles, hymns, and prayers.

Comparing the Ambrosian Office with other liturgies, we come to the conclusion that the monastic-Carolingian influence consisted primarily in the introduction of a psalmody cycle similar to the Roman and Benedictine cycle. In a basic outline of Vespers, we see that along with the psalmody derived from Roman-Benedictine influence, traces remain of an old, original psalmody: the *lucernarium,* reduced to an antiphon; a psalmic verse, the *responsorium in choro;* and the *antiphona*

[12] See Ambrose, *Epist.* 20, 24–25; PL 16:1001–1002; also *Explan. ps.* 1, 9 in CSEL 64, 8.

[13] M. Magistretti, ed., *Manuale ambrosianum ex Codice saec. XI olim in usum Canonicae Vallis Travalliae,* 2 vols., Monumenta veteris liturgiae ambrosianae 2 (Milan, 1905).

[14] M. Magistretti, ed., *Beroldus sive ecclesiae Ambrosianae Mediolanensis kalendarium et ordines saec. XII* (Milan, 1894).

in choro, exclusive of Sundays and feast days. While the Roman rite had only one euchological text, which was like a final prayer for each Hour, the Ambrosian rite of older times had multiple prayers for one and the same celebration.

The Ambrosian Office underwent widespread reforms after the fifteenth century with the purpose of going back to the old tradition. Below we can see the structure of Vespers and Matins of the medieval rite until 1983:

a) VESPERS

I *Lucernarium*
(Sundays: "Antiphona in choro")
Hymn *(Deus creator omnium)*
Responsory

II	*Sundays and weekdays*	*Feasts*
	Five psalms*[15]	Proper psalm
		Psalms 133 and 116*
		(Feasts of saints: Proper psalm*)

*Magnificat**
(sometimes twelve *Kyries*)

III *Baptismal commemoration:*
Responsory*
Psallendae (processional antiphons) with a station in the baptistry*
Blessing

b) MATINS
VIGILS Hymn *(Aetene rerum conditor)*
Responsory (invitatory song)
Canticle of the Three Young Men (Daniel 3:52-56)

Weekdays	*Saturdays*	*Sundays—Feasts*
Psalm 1 to 108 (in groups of ten = decurias five groups each week)*	Exodus 15:1-9*	Isaiah 26:9-20*
	Psalm 118 (half each Saturday)*	1 Samuel 2:1-10*
		Habakkuk 3:2-19 (summer: Jonah 2:2-9)*
Reading and responsory		
Reading and responsory		
Reading (without responsory)		

[15] * = accompanied by a prayer, before or after.

Te Deum
BENEDICTUS
(Sundays and feast days: "Antiphon to the Cross" and Exodus 15:1-19*)

LAUDS

Weekdays	*Saturdays*	*Sundays-Feasts*
Psalm 50*	Psalm 117*	*Benedicite**

Psalms 148–150 and 116*
"Direct" psalm
(*Laus angelorum magna,*
according to the old structure)
Hymn *(Splendor paternae gloriae)*
Twelve *Kyries*

STATION *Baptismal commemoration:*
Responsory
Procession to the baptistry (with *Psallendae* on Sundays)
Strophes of a psalm*
Blessing

3. The New Ambrosian Liturgy of the Hours

The reform of the Ambrosian Office in the spirit of Vatican II began to come into practice in 1981 with the publication of a diurnal for the faithful: *Diurna laus* (this publication anticipated the complete edition of the Ambrosian Office).[16] On June 11, 1981, the Congregation for the Sacraments and Divine Worship approved the *Institutio generalis Liturgiae Horarum iuxta ritum sanctae Mediolanensis Ecclesiae.* This is the collection of norms and principles that govern the Ambrosian organization of the Divine Office.[17] Since 1983 five volumes of the new Ambrosian Liturgy of the Hours were published.[18] Above all, it tries to improve the Office by better distributing the psalms, reevaluating the baptismal commemoration and intercessions, and revising the eucho-

[16] *Diurna Laus: Salterio a uso delle Comunità di Rito ambrosiano* (Casale Monferrato, 1981).

[17] Congregation for the Sacraments and Divine Worship, *La Liturgia ambrosiana delle Ore. Institutio generalis: Testo e commento,* Sussidi di Pastorale Liturgica 3 (Milan, 1983).

[18] *Liturgia delle Ore secondo il rito della Santa Chiesa Ambrosiana: Riformata a norma dei decreti del Concilio vaticano II e promulgata dal Cardinale Maria Martini,* 5 vols. (Milan, 1983–1984).

logical repertoire. Although the new Ambrosian Liturgy of the Hours also includes prayers for the midday Hours (with Terce, Sext, and None as alternates) as well as the complete Hours, here we will give only the structure of the principal Offices.

a) OFFICE OF READINGS

O God, come to my aid . . . Gloria . . .
Hymn *(Aeternae rerum Conditor)*
Responsory (Invitatory Psalm 94) on solemnities, feast days, and Sundays of the major liturgical seasons. *Or:* Canticle of the Three Young Men (Daniel 3:52-56) in the weekday Offices
Psalmody (Saturdays and Sundays: canticles of the Old Testament)
Biblical reading and responsory
Patristic reading (without responsory)
Laus angelorum magna[19] (Sundays and feasts *Te Deum)*
Prayer
We bless the Lord . . .

b) LAUDS

O God, come to my aid . . . Gloria . . .
Benedictus
First prayer
(On some solemnities and feast days: *Antiphona ad crucem*)[20]

[19] For more about the Ambrosian *Laus angelorum magna,* see the long article of E. T. Moneta Caglio, "Lo jubilus e le origini della salmodia responsoriale," *Jucunda laudatio* 15 (Venice, 1976–1977) 134–183. The *Laus angelorum* is still the Matins hymn of many Eastern liturgies today. For the Byzantine liturgy it can be found in the ὁρολόγιον, and for the Armenian liturgy in the *Brevarium Armenium sive Dispositio Communium Armenicae Ecclesiae Precum* (Venice, 1908) 111–112. We also must note that in the Byzantine liturgy as well as in the Armenian, the *Laus angelorum* is found at the end of Lauds, after the psalms called *In laudate* (Psalms 148–150), as in the old structure of Ambrosian Lauds.

[20] The antiphon *Ad crucem,* a characteristic element of the Sunday Matins Office, was sung repeatedly around three crosses with lighted candles during the procession from the cathedral to the altar, a glorious and illuminating symbol of the Paschal Christ. The stational rite of the antiphon *Ad crucem,* which in earlier times acted as a bridge between Matins and Lauds, was formed as a weekly commemoration of the resurrection on Sunday. The old procession having disappeared, the antiphon remains and is chanted only on Sundays during the major liturgical seasons and on some solemnities and feasts.

Psalmody: Canticle of the Old Testament
Lauds psalms (chosen from the psalter, ending with Psalm 116)[21]
Direct psalm
Second prayer[22]
Hymn *(Splendor paternae gloriae)*
Acclamation to Christ the Lord[23]
Our Father[24]
Blessing

c) VESPERS

I Initial greeting: The Lord be with you . . .
Rite of the light *(lucernarium)* with a responsory[25]
Hymn *(Deus Creator omnium)*
(On some solemnities and feast days: Responsory *In choro)*
(Here a reading can be done, possibly followed by a homily)

[21] A typical characteristic of the Ambrosian rite is to conclude the series of the three psalms of praise *In laudate* (148–150) with the very short Psalm 116, employed with a doxological function, as it seemed to have been used in the Hebrew liturgy. It also was spread among the Eastern Churches of Semitic languages, where the three psalms *In laudate* are followed by Psalm 116, as in the Chaldean, Maronite, and Syriac rites.

[22] This prayer is like a psalm. For the psalm prayers of the Ambrosian Liturgy, see the study of I. Biffi, "Le Orazioni Salmiche nella Diurna Laus Ambrosiana," *A* 59 (1983) 261–277, with the appendix, pp. 278–303, where the Latin and Italian texts of each psalm collect are published, with more information on the sources.

[23] The *Acclamations to Christ the Lord* today consist of six acclamations to Christ the Lord, almost all of them coming from Sacred Scripture. Two *Kyrie eleisons* follow each acclamation. This structure is in place of the twelve *Kyries* that in earlier times concluded the Office of Lauds and were the remains of the litanic prayer. A prayer of strong Christological character and a catechism about Jesus Christ have come from this. See also the study of I. Biffi, "Le acclamazioni a Cristo Signore nelle Lodi," *A* 58 (1982) 75–81.

[24] In the Ambrosian tradition the Our Father is considered a truly conclusive prayer, placed at the culminating point of the Office. A prayer of ecclesiastical composition never follows it.

[25] The *lucernarium,* or rite of the light, is retained as an older and more primitive element of the Vespers tradition in the Western and Eastern liturgies. It also has roots in the Jewish Vespers sacrifice. The first Christian formula is written about in the *Apostolic Tradition* 25 and is attributed to Hippolytus of Rome. The purpose of the rite is to give thanks for the gift of the material light and the gift of the divine Light. From this formula texts of acclaiming praise to Christ as the Light of the world came about, such as the celebrated hymn φως ἱλαρόν, which was sung at

II Psalmody:

Sundays, memorials and weekdays	*Solemnities and Feasts*
Two psalms	One proper psalm
	Psalms 113 and 116

First prayer
Magnificat
Second prayer

III Commemoration of baptism, possibly with a procession (in the celebration of saints: *Psallenda* and a prayer referring to the saint)[26]
Canticle of the New Testament (I and II Vespers on Sundays) or responsory (weekdays)
Prayer
Intercessions
Our Father
Blessing

IV. THE LITURGY OF THE HOURS OF THE HISPANIC RITE

The basic structures of the Hispanic Office, relatively similar to those of the Ambrosian liturgy, have the double advantage of not having been contaminated by the Romano-Benedictine *ordo*, as the Milanese rite was, and of not having undergone reforms and adaptations.

Vespers in the Byzantine Church. The Armenian Liturgy uses this hymn in Saturday Vespers, followed by a prayer in which the theme of light predominates as a symbol of the revelation of God to humankind. Around this initial nucleus other elements developed: beginning monitions and final blessings, litanic prayers, and above all the use of the lucernal psalms, among which Psalm 140 stands out. Beginning in the fifth century, the Vespers Office began to lose its exclusively lucernal character in order to convert itself into an Office that was more adaptable to the diverse liturgical days. Only an antiphon or responsory remains from the *lucernarium,* as the Ambrosian and Hispanic rites show. The important thing is that according to the historical information, the *lucernarium is* not considered a part of Vespers, but rather Vespers is a transformation of the *lucernarium.*

[26] The third and last part of the Ambrosian Vespers is called the "stational" part, which is normally formed as the commemoration of baptism. In the old Ambrosian Office, at the end of Lauds or Vespers there was a procession to the two baptistries of Milan while chanting the *Psallendae* (antiphons and responsories). The origin of this stational part is found in the processions from the basilica of the Anastasis to the chapel of the Holy Cross, which followed the Matins and Vespers celebration in Jerusalem of the fourth and fifth centuries, as Egeria attests in her *Diary of a Pilgrimage,* 24:4-7. In the new Ambrosian Liturgy of the Hours the baptismal commemoration was restored as a conclusion to Vespers.

Although it has some principles and elements in common with the Ambrosian liturgy, such as the fixed Sunday hymn *Aeterne rerum Conditor* and the plurality of the euchological texts, the Hispanic liturgy has undergone its own evolution in an autonomous and original form. The Office was formed between the fifth and the seventh century and was used throughout the Spanish Church until the end of the eleventh century, when the Roman rite began to be imposed. The old rite, however, continued to be celebrated here and there in some chapels. The first printed Mozarabic breviary was the *Breviarium Gothicum* of A. Ortiz in 1502.[27]

In the Hispanic rite two clearly different Offices existed: a cathedral Office and a monastic Office. They differed in the number of Hours and in the abundance or scarcity of different formularies.

1. Cathedral Office

The cathedral Office has only two official Hours: Vespers and a vigil Matins Office. Only on the penitential weekdays—Lent and days of litanies or solemn fasting—are Terce, Sext, and None also included. For this celebration, in addition to an abundant collection of chants, hymns, and prayers, the following are also necessary: (a) the *Liber Psalmorum;* (b) the *Liber Canticorum;* (c) the *Liber Hymnorum;* (d) the *Liber Orationum Psalmographus;* (e) the *Liber Orationum Festivus;* (f) the *Antiphonarium.* These unite the chants of the feast day and Sunday Office, as well as the chants of the Mass.

One of the characteristics of this Office is the greater importance of the antiphon than the psalter, and of the feast prayer than the psalmographus. This entailed the reduction of the psalms to one or two verses for each antiphon, with the exception of the ordinary weekday Office. As a consequence, the antiphons, responsories, and prayers came to make up practically the body of the cathedral Office. From its establishment as a local Office in the last decades of the sixth century until the work of its codification by St. Julian of Toledo, the Hispanic cathedral Office transformed itself progressively, passing through various evolutionary phases. Three kinds of Offices can be identified: ordinary weekdays, Sundays, and feasts. This is a distinction that is

[27] F. A. de Lorenzana, *Breviarium gothicum secundum beatissimi Isidori,* corrected edition of the *Breviarium* of A. Ortiz, published in Toledo in 1502 (Madrid, 1775); reproduced in PL 88.

founded in the structure that the *ordo* assumes in each one of these three forms, as well as in the genres of texts that each uses.

a) VESPERS

Weekday	*Sunday-Feast Day*
Offering of light[28]	Offering of light
Vespertinum,[29] *Lucernarium* psalm	*Vespertinum.* Verse
	(Prayer)
	Sonum[30]
Antiphon. Psalm	Antiphon. Verse
Antiphon. Psalm	*Alleluiaticum.*[31] Verse
Hymn	Hymn
(Verse)	(Verse)
(Supplication)[32]	(Supplication)
Completuria[33]	*Completuria*
Our Father[34]	Our Father
(Petition)[35]	(Petition)
Blessing	Blessing
	Psallendum.[36] Prayer

[28] This was a beginning rite. The deacon lit the lamp and elevated it before the altar, saying: *In nomine Domini nostri Iesu Christi lumen cum pace.* The congregation responded: *Deo gratias.*

[29] This corresponds to the Ambrosian *lucernarium.*

[30] This is a very ornate melodic song, formed from verses of psalms. It is possible that during the *Sonum* incense was offered on the altar and in the church.

[31] Antiphon with alleluias.

[32] The diaconal monition that invites all to prayer.

[33] The principal and concluding prayer with themes of the Office: time, day and night, light, the life of humankind, work and rest, the sun and the lamp, nature as a creation of God, Christ the true and eternal Light. In the feast-day Office the theme will be the objective of the feast or the liturgical time that corresponds to it. The congregation does not respond "Amen" to this prayer, given that the *completuria* connects with the Our Father without any change, giving it a special character.

[34] This conserves the dignity of all prayer, essential and complete. It is recited by the president of the celebration. The congregation responds "Amen" to each of the petitions.

[35] A brief intercalation of the Our Father.

[36] An additional devotional that consists of an antiphon, a psalm, and a prayer to accompany the processions to chapels or sepulchers of martyrs. This is similar to the procession to the baptistries of the Ambrosian Office.

The weekday Matins Office, which is the oldest form, and the feast-day Matins are almost identical. For this reason we will only present outlines of the weekday and Sunday Matins. But to understand some details, it is necessary to examine first the nocturnal Office, which is the official vigil Hour of the monastic *ordo:*

b) NOCTURNAL WEEKDAY OFFICE

Antiphon: *Venite, adoremus* and Psalm 94
Versicle: *Domine, labia mea aperies*
Canonical psalms: 3, 50, 56
Recapitulatio with *Gloria.*[37] Prayer
Three *missae*[38] of three psalms each, followed by a responsory
Responsorial
One *missa* of three canticles with a responsorial
Two readings: one from the Old Testament and one from the New, with a verse called *laudes*
Hymn
Blessings (= three versicles of the canticle from Daniel 3)
Clamores[39]
Supplication
Three *Kyries*
Completuria
Our Father
Petition
Blessing
Miserationes[40]
Prayer

[37] The *recapitulatio* or *subpsalmatio,* exclusively of Hispanic monastic use, is formed by integrating the first versicle of each one of the three cited psalms into the only doxology that closes the group of the canonical psalms.

[38] The psalms and antiphons are arranged in groups of three called *missa.* In the monastic Office, the *missa* consisted of a group of three psalms, without antiphons or prayers, and a responsory. A first level of evolution from the primitive *missa* is completed in the ordinary weekday Office of the cathedral *ordo.* The *missa* will continue evolving into the feast-day Office: multiple *missae* according to the level of solemnity of the feast.

[39] This is made up of a mosaic of versicles of psalms, chosen in order to give the whole composition a strong penitential feeling.

[40] Chants in which the *Deus miserere* is repeated without stopping, with a concluding prayer of petition for forgiveness and the intercalation of prayers for the needs of all.

c) MATINS

Weekday	*Sunday*
Antiphon. Psalm 3	Hymn *Aeterne rerum Conditor*
Prayer	Prayer of *Aeterne*
	Canonical psalms: 3, 50, 56 with antiphons *concordes*[41]
	Prayer *de psalmis canonici*
Antiphon. Psalm. Prayer	Antiphon. Psalm verse. Prayer
Antiphon. Psalm. Prayer	Antiphon. Psalm verse. Prayer
Antiphon. Psalm. Prayer	*Alleluiaticum*. Psalm verse. Prayer
Responsory	Responsory
Antiphon. Psalm 50. Prayer	
Antiphon. Old Testament canticle (Prayer)	Antiphon. Old Testament canticle (Prayer)
	Antiphon. *Benedictiones*. (Prayer)
Antiphon. Matins psalm	*Sonum*
Antiphon. Psalms 148, 149, 150	Antiphon. Psalms 148, 149, 150
(Reading)	(Reading)
Hymn	Hymn
(Verse)	
(Supplication)	(Supplication)
Completuria	*Completuria*
Our Father	Our Father
(Petition)	(Petition)
(Benedictio)	*(Benedictio)*
	Psallendum
	Prayer

In this outline of Matins two parts are clearly recognized: one that is from Psalm 3 to the responsory and another that is from Psalm 50 until the end. The first part represents a reduced form of the monastic vigil, designated as the "little cathedral vigil," referring to two similar cases: the Byzantine ὄρθρος and the old Matins of the Ambrosian rite.

[41] These are antiphons composed of selected psalm phrases. They are the same in extension and succession of sounds, so that the three can be sung with the same melody.

2. *The Monastic Office*

The monastic Office, in addition to the Offices of Vespers and Matins, includes another five official Hours—*ad completam, ad nocturnos, ad tertiam, ad sextam, ad nonam*—and eleven unofficial (or private) Hours, during which the monks recited prayers in their own cells before or after the official Hours. The overwhelming overload of Hours represents the monks' intention to try to sanctify time, materially occupying it with prayer. The entire monastic Office with its very old characteristics is written about in a book, the *Liber Horarum.*[42] The monastic *ordo* also had conserved its own basic structures for the two main Hours, not only in the Rule for the monks of St. Isidore of Seville (ca. 560–636) but also in the Rule of St. Fructuosus of Braga († 665).

The rich formularies of the cathedral Office contrast with the sobriety of the monastic, with the psalms always making up the immutable body of the Office. The fundamental theme of the few euchological texts that accompany the psalms is the action of prayer: ascesis and union with God at the same time, a source of illumination for all monastic spirituality. But the Eleventh Council of Toledo (675) imposed on monasteries the observance of the cathedral *ordo* for the Offices of the two main Hours. For these Hours the monks adopted the same liturgical books of the respective metropolitan churches.

V. THE CELTIC LITURGY OF THE HOURS

1. *The Monastic* Cursus *of St. Columban*

St. Columban, who arrived in Ireland from Gaul around 590, gives us a brief description of the Irish monastic *cursus* of his time in chapter 7 of his *Regula monachorum.*[43] The main characteristic was the very long and continuous nocturnal psalmody, especially during the winter nights.

St. Columban divides the Office into six Hours—three daytime Hours and three nocturnal Hours. Each daytime Hour has the traditional psalms, which we find in almost all areas for the lesser Hours. But the nocturnal Hours at the beginning of the night *(initium noctis)* and at midnight *(medium noctis)* are composed of twelve psalms each.

[42] J. Pinell, *Liber Orationum Psalmographus,* Monumenta Hispaniae Sacra, serie litúrgica 9 (Barcelona-Madrid, 1972).

[43] G. S. Walker, *Sancti Columbani opera,* Scriptores latini Hiberniae 11 (Dublin, 1957) 128–132.

Matins, divided into two parts *(matutinum,* also called *vigilia)* includes 36 psalms during the days of the week (24 in the summer), increasing to a maximum of 75 psalms on the Saturdays and Sundays of winter (36 psalms in the summer). This adds up to 99 psalms during weekend winter nights, and 108 psalms during the complete winter *cursus* of Saturday-Sunday, if we add on the nine psalms of the daytime Hours. The psalms of the nocturnal Hours are grouped into units of three called *chora.* Of the three psalms of each unit, only the last one has an antiphon. The monks prayed up to 25 *chorae* (= 75 psalms) at Matins of Saturday and Sunday (= 150 psalms, or the whole psalter). In chapter 9 of his other Rule, the *Regula coenobialis,* St. Columban explains that after each psalm the monks kneel and pray, except on Sundays and during the Easter season, when they only bow their heads and each one repeats to himself three times: "Save me, O God, for the waters threaten my life" (Ps 69:2).[44]

2. *The Antiphonary of Bangor*

In order to reconstruct the *ordo* of the Celtic monastic Office of the sixth and seventh centuries, we must also look at other important documents of the Irish rite. This means looking at the only liturgical source of the Office that has survived to our time, the Antiphonary of Bangor,[45] written around the years 680 to 691. In this Antiphonary (henceforth AB), which proposes a structure of the monastic Office that is practically the same as the Ambrosian cathedral Office, we find the exact number of the daytime Hours: second, third, sixth, ninth, Vespers. The general structure of the Hours included:

1. Three psalms[46]
2. *Gloria in excelsis* (AB 116) *Ad matutinum et ad vespertinurn*
3. Collect
4. *Oratio communis*

The structure of the nocturnal Hours was the following: the Office *ad initium noctis,* also called *duodecima* by St. Columban in the *Regula coenobialis* (III), with twelve psalms (distributed in *chorae)* followed by

[44] Ibid., 158.

[45] Milan, Bib. Ambrosiana, ms. C 5 inf.; ed. F. E. Warren, *The Antiphonary of Bangor,* 2 vols., HBS 4, 10 (London, 1893–1895). M. Curran, *The Antiphonary of Bangor and the Early Monastic Liturgy* (Dublin, 1984).

[46] Columban, *Regula monachorum,* 7.

silent prayer, two readings, and the collect. This Office ended with an additional devotion called *Ad pacem celebrandam* (AB 34), which was made up of psalm verses and prayers of intercession for peace and reconciliation. The Apostles' Creed followed (AB 35), and the Our Father (AB 36), and with this the Office ended.

The Office of midnight *(medium noctis)* had twelve psalms, the hymn *Mediae noctis tempus est*, and the collect. The Office of Matins included two parts. The first was a continuation of the psalmody of the vigil (called *matutinum* or *vigilia*) and concluded with a collect. The second part, which is also mentioned in other sources, was called *matutini, laudes, sollemnitas matutina* and came from the cathedral Office. This second part included:

1. Canticle *Cantemus Domino* and *Collectio post canticum*
2. Canticle *Benedicite* and *Collectio post benedictionem*
3. Psalms 148–150 and Collectio *post laudate*
4. Gospel (on Sundays) and *Collectio post evangelium*
5. *Gloria in excelsis* (*AB* 116: every day)
   Te Deum (AB 7: on Sundays)
6. Hymn (Sunday *Spiritus divinae lucis;* weekdays *Hymnum dicat,* Saturday *Sacratissimi martyres*) and *Collectio post hymnum*
7. *Oratio communis fratrum* and commemoration of the martyrs[47]
8. Our Father

In spite of the different elements of the Celtic Office, we are able to note some of its common characteristics:

a) The *hymns:* In the field of liturgical poetry, the Irish authors are noted for their ability to express the contents of the Christian faith, applying the canons of the ancestral lyric and the rich patrimony of the Celtic culture. The Antiphonary of Bangor contains a considerable repertoire.[48]

[47] The *Oratio communis fratrum* (*AB* 40-56). It consists of a particular Irish form of prayers composed of verses taken from the psalms, which are always followed by a very short prayer. The second part or last section of the *oratio communis* (*AB* 52-56), which we call "double conclusion," consists of a commemoration *ad libitum* of the martyrs, with a collect *ad martyres de martyribus,* or the more common conclusion: a psalm followed by a collect.

[48] For the Celtic hymnody see C. Blume, *Hymnodia Hibero-Celtica saeculi V–IX,* in *Analecta Hymnica Medii Aevi* 51 (Leipzig, 1908) 259–364. A study of this has also been done by M. Curran, *The Antiphonary of Bangor,* 17–85.

b) The *collects:* Given that many texts come from or are inspired by Gallican, Hispanic, or Ambrosian texts, the collects do not make up an original euchological body. It is for this reason that we come across subjects in common with or differing from the Divine Office of the Western liturgies of the Continent, imported in the comings and goings of the monks of St. Columban. The structure of the texts is in general very simple, a mediocre Latin that prefers poetic allusions and the association of psalm verses in the complicated development of theological subjects. But we are able to identify one structural and literal kind of characteristic that is original to the Celtic euchology: the rhythmic composition of many of its prayers, which can be observed in some of the antiphons.[49]

[49] To give an example of the series of rhythmic collects that are found in the Antiphonary of Bangor, we have transcribed the following lines.

AB 26 *Ad matutinum.*

Deus qui pulsis tenebris / diei lucem tribuis,
adventum veri luminis / tuis effunde famulis,
qui regnas.

Bibliography

Borella, P. *Il Rito Ambrosiano.* Biblioteca di Scienze Religiose, Session III: La liturgia, no. 10. Brescia, 1964.

____. "Il Breviario Ambrosiano." Excursus III. In M. Righetti, *Manuale di Storia Liturgica,* 2:675–715. Milan², 1955.

Cattaneo, E. *Il Breviario Ambrosiano: Note storiche ed illustrative.* Milan, 1943.

Curran, M. *The Antiphonary of Bangor and the Early Irish Monastic Liturgy.* Dublin, 1984.

Heiming, O. "Zum monastischen Offizium von Kassianus bis Kolumbanus." *ALW* 7 (1961) 89–156.

Magistretti, M. *La Liturgia della Chiesa Milanese nel secolo IV.* Milan, 1899.

Magnoli, C. "Un Direttorio non solo per la celebrazione ma anche per la meditazione. Confronto tra la *Institutio* Ambrosiana delle Ore e quella Romana." *ScC* 114 (1986) 325–351.

Navoni, M. "La nova Liturgia Ambrosiana delle Ore: Lettura storico-comparativa." *ScC* 114 (1986) 235–324.

Pinell, J. *Liturgia delle Ore. Anàmnesis* 5.

____. "El oficio catedral hispinico." *Ph* 175 (1990) 9–37.

Taft, R. *The Liturgy of the Hours in East and West: The Origins of the Divine Office and Its Meaning for Today.* 2nd rev. ed. Collegeville, Minn., 1993.

Robert F. Taft, S.J.

5

The Theology of the Liturgy of the Hours

The New Testament kerygma teaches that Christ died for our sins and rose for our salvation so that we might die to sin and rise to new life in him. Since Christian liturgy is but a means of entering and celebrating this movement of salvation, any theology of Christian liturgical prayer must be rooted in the developing tradition evolving out of Christian reflection on that kerygma.[1]

WORSHIP IN THE NEW TESTAMENT

A fundamental principle of this kerygma is that everything in Sacred History—every sacred event, object, place, theophany, cult—has been recapitulated and "personalized" and assumed into the person of the Incarnate Christ. He is God's eternal Word (John 1:1, 14); his new creation (2 Cor 5:17; Gal 6:15; Rom 8:19ff.; Rev 21–22); the new Adam (1 Cor 15:45; Rom 5:14); the new Pasch and its lamb (1 Cor 5:7; John 1:29, 36; 19:36; 1 Pet 1:19; Rev 5ff.); the new covenant (Matt 26:28; Mark 14:24; Luke 22:20; Heb 8–13); the new circumcision (Col 2:11-12); the new heavenly manna (John 6:30-58; Rev 2:17); the new temple (John 2:19-27); the new sacrifice and its priest (Eph 5:2; Heb 2:17–3:2; 4:14–10:14); the fulfillment of the sabbath rest (Col 2:16-17; Matt 11:28–12:8; Heb 3:7–4:11) and the messianic age that was to come (Luke 4:16-21; Acts 2:14-36). All that went before is fulfilled in him,

[1] See chap. 21 of R. Taft, *The Liturgy of the Hours in East and West: The Origins of the Divine Office and Its Meaning for Today,* 2nd rev. ed. (Collegeville, Minn., 1993) = *La Liturgia delle Ore in Oriente e in Occidente: Le origini dell'Ufficio divino e il suo significato oggi,* Testi di teologia 4 (Milan, 1988) = *La Liturgie des Heures en Orient et en Occident: Origine et sens de l'Office divin,* Mysteria 2 (Turnhout, 1991).

and that includes cultic realities: "Do not let anyone condemn you in matters of food and drink or of observing festivals, new moons, or sabbaths. These are only a shadow of what is to come, but the substance belongs to Christ" (Col 2:16-17; cf. Heb 10:1). The Old Testament temple and altar with their rituals and sacrifices are replaced, not by a new set of rituals and shrines, but by the self-giving of the very Son of God.[2] Henceforth, true worship pleasing to the Father is the saving life, death, and resurrection of Christ.

LITURGY AND CHRISTIAN LIFE

Since through baptism we too are Christ, our worship is this same sacrificial existence in us. "Living is Christ," Paul tells us (Phil 1:21), and to be saved is to be conformed to Christ by dying to self and rising to new life in him (2 Cor 4:10ff.; 13:4; Rom 6:3ff.; Col 2:12-13, 20; 3:1-3; Gal 2:20; Eph 2:1ff.; Phil 2:5ff.; 3:10-11, 18, 21). For we know "the power of his resurrection" only by the "sharing of his sufferings, becoming like him in his death (Phil 3:10).

For St. Paul, therefore, liturgy is Christian life. Never once does he use cultic nomenclature (liturgy, sacrifice, priest, offering) for anything but a life of self-giving, lived after the pattern of Christ.[3] This life, according to the several New Testament metaphors for it, is a process of conversion into Christ. His life is the story of entering sinful humanity and returning it to the Father through the cross, a return that was accepted and crowned in Christ's deliverance and exaltation (Phil 2:5ff.). And this same story the New Testament presents as the story of everyone, the archetype of our experience of returning to God through a life of death to self, lived after the pattern Christ showed us: "He died for all, so that those who live might live no longer for themselves, but for him who died and was raised for them" (2 Cor 5:15).

Liturgy, therefore, has the same purpose as the gospel: to present this saving message in anamnesis as a continual sign to us not of a past history but of the present reality of our lives in him. What we celebrate is the fact that Jesus lived, died, and rose for our salvation, and that we have died to sin and risen to new life in him, in expectation of the final fulfillment. Baptized into the mystery of his death and

[2] The personalizing and spiritualizing of cult as an interior reality had been adumbrated in the Old Testament: see, for example, Psalms 40/41:6-8; 49/50:8-13; 50/51:16-19; Amos 5:21-24; Hos 6:6; Mic 6:6-8.

[3] See, for example, Rom 1:9; 12:1; 15:6; Phil 2:17; 4:18; 2 Tim 4:6; also Heb 13:11-16.

resurrection, we rise in him, having "put on Christ" (Gal 3:27), so that, as St. Paul says, "I have been crucified with Christ, and it is no longer I who live, but it is Christ who lives in me" (Gal 2:19-20). Henceforth he dwells in us, prays in us, proclaims to us the word of his new covenant, seals it with his sacrifice, feeds us with his body and blood, draws us to penance and conversion, glorifies the Father in us. In proclamation and preaching he communicates to us his mystery; in rite and song he celebrates it with us; in sacramental grace he gives us the strength to live it. The purpose of the liturgy is to generate in our lives what the Church realizes for us in its public worship.

LITURGY: A WORK OF THE CHURCH

Liturgy is one of the ways in which the Church responds in praise, surrender, thanksgiving, to the call of God's revealing, saving word and deed. This eternal doxology is a response to something, and it is important to note that this divine action itself is an integral part of liturgy, which comprises both God's unending saving activity and our prayerful response to it in faith and commitment throughout the ages.

Liturgy, then, is the common work of Christ and his Church. Far from being extrinsic to our liturgy, Christ is its chief protagonist. This is what makes possible the extraordinary claims the Church has made about the nature of Christian worship. Our prayers are worthless, but in the liturgy Christ himself prays in us. For the liturgy is the efficacious sign of Christ's saving presence in his Church. His saving offering is eternally active and present before the throne of the Father. By our celebration of the divine mysteries, we are drawn into the saving action of Christ and our personal self-offering is transformed into an act of the Body of Christ through the worship of the Body with its Head.

This is what our true liturgy, Christian life, is all about. Our common worship is but a living metaphor of this saving reality, not only representing and re-presenting it to us constantly in symbol to evoke our response in faith and deed, but actively effecting it in us through the work of the Holy Spirit, in order to build up the Body of Christ into a new temple and liturgy and priesthood in which offerer and offered are one.

This is how all liturgy is dynamic anamnesis: not just a psychological reminiscence, not mere remembering, but an active and self-fulfilling prophecy in which, by the power of God's indwelling Spirit, we become what we celebrate, while at the same time thanking and glorifying him for that great gift. Liturgy reminds us of the powerful deeds of God in Christ. And being reminded we remember, and remembering we celebrate, and celebrating we become what we do.

THE DIVINE OFFICE AS LITURGY

In the New Testament dispensation, therefore, liturgy is simply a celebration of the Christian life, and the same is true of the Liturgy of the Hours. It is no more, no less than a common celebration of what we are, or rather of what we have become and are ever becoming in Christ. If what we are as a group is the Body of Christ, and if the eternally present Christ is an everlasting hymn of praise and glory before the throne of the Father, it is our vocation to enter and to live that very same Christ-life of priestly praise and glory. And so the Church, as his Mystical Body, associates itself with the eternal priestly prayer of its Head. In so doing, the Church truly participates in the salvific praise of Christ, according to the theology of *Mediator Dei* (see nos. 142–144) and the Constitution on the Sacred Liturgy (see nos. 83–85).

NEW TESTAMENT CONTEXT FOR THE PRAYER OF THE HOURS

It is only within this New Testament context of worship that a theology of the prayer of Hours can be articulated. Indeed, elements that will enter the ultimate synthesis are already present in the New Testament instructions on how to pray (Matt 6:5-15; 7:7-11; 18:19; 21:22; Luke 11:1-13; 18:1-14; Mark 11:24-25; John 14:13-14; 15:7; Jas 1:5-8; 1 John 5:14-16)—alone or in common, insistently, asking for what we need with faith and confidence, yet humbly and with few words—plus the testimony of the prayer of Jesus (e.g., Matt 26:36-44; Mark 1:35; Luke 3:21; 5:16; 6:12; 9:18, 28; 11:1; 22:41-46; John 17) and his followers (e.g., Luke 24:53; Acts 2:46; 3:1; 10:9, 46; 12:5, 12; 13:14-16; 1 Thess 1:2, etc.).

This New Testament witness comprises several elements especially significant for the development of the Liturgy of the Hours:

1. *Anamnetic prayer.* Based on models inherited from Israel (e.g., Isa 6:10; 63:7), biblical memorial or anamnesis informs not only the Eucharist—"Do this in my remembrance [ἀνάμνησις]" (Luke 22:19; 1 Cor 11:25-26)—but provides the dynamic of all Christian prayer. We first recall God's saving action, then respond in thankful praise and glorification for his mighty deeds.

2. *Incessant prayer.* The command to "pray always" is one of the New Testament's most frequently repeated imperatives (Luke 18: 1; 21:36; Eph 6:18; Col 4:2; 1 Thess 5:16-18).

3. *Watching prayer.* Keeping vigil, informed by the example of Jesus' night prayer (Luke 6:12), acquires its eschatological dimension from the exhortations to watch and pray (Matt 26:40-41; Luke 21:36; Col 4:2) and to keep vigil for the coming of the Lord (Matt 24:43-44; Mark 13:32-37; Luke 12:35-46; 1 Thess 5:2, 6; Rev 3:3; 16:15; cf. 2 Thess 2).[4]

4. *Prayer at set times.* The Jewish heritage of prayer at set times, continued by Jesus' first disciples (Acts 2:1, 15; 3:1; 10:3, 9, 30), was later adapted by the Church. Especially important in the developing tradition of Christian cathedral and monastic prayer will be the Christian application of the Old Testament prescription to pray morning and evening, and, especially in the Latin tradition, of the psalmist's reference to prayer seven times a day (Ps 118/119:164).

5. "God is light." Sun and light, basic symbols for God and salvation in pagan and Jewish antiquity, continue to provide a fundamental theme for the same realities in the New Testament, especially in the Johannine literature and later in the patristic theology of the Hours.

THEOLOGY OF THE CATHEDRAL HOURS

Initially, Morning Praise and Evensong, with Eucharist, were the principal ways in which the Church exercised in common its λειτουργία of remembrance, thankful praise, and insistent prayer. The original impulse for these prayer times may have derived from the Jewish tradition, but it was not long before the monastic emphasis on the New Testament imperative of constant prayer would induce urban monastics to synthesize the monastic day Hours with the morning and evening services of the cathedral churches, thus filling out the *cursus* of canonical Hours as we know them today.

Morning and evening, the beginning and end of the day, were but "symbolic moments" in which to express what ought to be the quality of the whole day. By the beginning of the fifth century the cathedral

[4] Add, too, the parable of the virgins and the bridegroom (Matt 25:1-13; Luke 12:35-46)—the bridegroom is obviously Jesus (Matt 9:14-15; Mark 2:18-20; Luke 5:33-35)—which is interpreted as a Christian Passover Haggadah. See A. Strobel, *Ursprung und Geschichte des frühchristlichen Osterkalendars*, TU 121 (Berlin, 1977) 29–45.

Offices had fleshed out the bare bones of psalmody and prayer with rites and symbols that revealed the morning and evening Hours as sacraments of the mystery of Christ.

The basic natural symbol from which this ritual elaboration springs is light, a theme that can be traced back to the Old Testament and beyond, to the prominent use of sun imagery in the paganism of the Mediterranean world. Christians were quick to apply this symbolism to Christ; it is a constant New Testament theme, especially in the Johannine literature:

In him was life, and the life was the light of all people. The light shines in the darkness, and the darkness did not overcome it. . . . The true light, which enlightens everyone, was coming into the world (John 1:4-5, 9).

I am the light of the world. Whoever follows me will never walk in darkness but will have the light of life (John 8:12; cf. 9:5).

I have come as light into the world, so that everyone who believes in me should not remain in the darkness (John 12:45-46; cf. 12:35-36).

In Christ, this illumination has already been accomplished:

[Give] thanks to the Father, who has enabled you to share in the inheritance of the saints in the light. He has rescued us from the power of darkness and transferred us into the kingdom of his beloved Son, in whom we have redemption, the forgiveness of sins (Col 1:12-13; cf. 1 Thess 5:5; Heb 6:4; 10:32).

Ephesians 5 and 1 John 1:5-7; 2:8-11 stress that this illumination has a moral and communitarian dimension, and a pregnantly beautiful passage concludes the Apocalypse with the vision of the light of the Lamb in the City of God, the New Jerusalem, the Heavenly City. The passage is a deliberate fulfillment of the prophecy of Isaiah (60:1-3, 11, 19-20) in the prophet's vision of the same heavenly abode:

I saw no temple in the city, for its temple is the Lord God the Almighty and the Lamb. And the city has no need of sun or moon to shine on it, for the glory of God is its light, and its lamp is the Lamb. The nations will walk by its light, and the kings of the earth will bring their glory into it. Its gates shall never be shut by day—and there will be no night there (Rev 21:22-25).

This light that Christ gives is salvation, and it is received in baptism (Heb 6:4-6), which is why the early Church called baptism φωτισμός or φώτισμα ("illumination"), and those to be baptized were the *illuminandi* or φωτιζόμενοι.

So Christians prayed facing east, seeing in the rising sun a symbol of the risen Christ, Light of the world. Malachi 4:2 had prophesied that "the sun of righteousness shall rise, with healing in its wings," and Zechariah proclaimed that in Jesus "the dawn from on high will break upon us, to give light to those who sit in darkness and the shadow of death, to guide our feet into the way of peace" (Luke 1:78-79). Already in the last decade of the first century, *1 Clement* 24:1-3 relates the natural succession of light and darkness to the resurrection of the just at the parousia: "We see, beloved, that the resurrection was accomplished according to the time. Day and night make visible to us a resurrection. Night goes to sleep, the day rises." And in their evening prayer, at the setting of the sun and the onset of darkness, the hour of lamplighting, Christians were drawn to see the evening lamp as a symbol of Christ the Light of the world, the lamp of the Heavenly City, where there is no darkness or night but only day, and to render thanks to God for it.

Cyprian's treatise *On the Lord's Prayer* 35–36 (ca. 250) first applies this theme to early Christian prayer times:

> One must also pray in the morning, that the resurrection of the Lord may be celebrated by morning prayer. . . . Likewise at sunset and the passing of the day it is necessary to pray. For since Christ is the true sun and the true day, when we pray and ask, as the sun and the day of the world recede, that the light may come upon us again, we pray for the coming of Christ, which provides us with the grace of eternal light.

MORNING PRAISE

By the beginning of the Golden Age of the Fathers at the end of the fourth century, this vision has become integral to the fabric of Christian daily prayer. Basil's *Longer Rules* (37:3), Chrysostom's *Commentary on Psalm 140* and *Baptismal Catecheses* (VIII, 17), and the *Apostolic Constitutions* (VIII, 38–39) all make it clear that Morning Praise served to consecrate the day to the works of God, to thank him for benefits received, especially the benefit of redemption in the rising of his Son, to rekindle our desire for him as a remedy against sin at the beginning of the day, and to ask for continued help.

And so at the start of the day we do as Jesus did (Mark 1:35): we begin the day with prayer. In Morning Praise we renew our commitment to Christ by consecrating the day through thanks and praise. And the Hour provides our symbols. The rising sun, one of the ongoing marvels of God's creation, a source of life and food, warmth and light, leads spontaneously to praise and thanks and to prayer for protection throughout the day. And since we celebrate what we are, and our core reality is that we have been saved by the saving death and resurrection of Jesus, the rising sun calls to mind the true Sun of Justice, in whose rising we receive the light of salvation. Integral to the celebration is the exercise of our priestly intercession for the whole world, for as Christ's Body we share in his responsibilities too.

EVENSONG

In the evening, after the day's work is done, we turn once more to God in prayer. A basic element of the rite of Vespers in the early tradition is thanksgiving for the light. The Church used the lamplighting at sunset to remind us of the Johannine vision of the Lamb who is the eternal lamp of the Heavenly Jerusalem, the sun that never sets. We see this already at the beginning of the second century, in the domestic rite alluded to by Tertullian in his *Apology* (39:18) and described in the *Apostolic Tradition* (25), with its thanksgiving prayer at the bringing in of the evening lamp:

We give you thanks, Lord, through your Son Jesus Christ our Lord, through whom you have shone upon us and revealed to us the inextinguishable light. So when we have come to the beginning of the night, and have satisfied ourselves with the light of day which you created for our satisfying, and since now through your grace we do not lack the light of evening, we praise and glorify you through your Son Jesus Christ our Lord, through whom be glory and power and honor to you with the Holy Spirit, both now and always and to the ages of ages. Amen.

The passing of day reminds us of the darkness of Christ's passion and death and of the passing nature of all earthly creation. But the gift of light reminds us again of Christ the Light of the world. With Vespers we close the day, much as Compline does in the later urban monastic Offices. And as in Morning Prayer, the service of Evensong closes with intercessions for the needs of all humankind, and then in the collect and final blessing we thank God for the graces of the day, above all for the grace of the risen Christ. We ask pardon for the sins of the day and request protection during the coming night.

Another basic theme, repentance for the sins of the day gone by, is why the Fathers chose Psalm 140 for Vespers, according to Chrysostom's *Commentary on Psalm 140*, 1:

They ordered it to be said as a salutary medicine and forgiveness of sins, so that whatever has dirtied us throughout the whole length of the day . . . we get rid of it in the evening through this spiritual song. For it is indeed a medicine that destroys all those things.[5]

In his *Longer Rules* (37:4), Basil also emphasizes thanksgiving and confession of the faults of the day as the purpose of the evening Hour. The collect that concludes Evensong in the *Apostolic Constitutions* (VIII, 37) expresses a like spirit:

O God . . . who has made the day for the works of light and the night for the refreshment of our infirmity . . . mercifully accept now this, our evening thanksgiving. You who have brought us through the length of the day and to the beginning of the night, preserve us by your Christ. Grant us a peaceful evening and a night free from sin, and give us everlasting life by your Christ.

The request for protection during the darkness of night has eschatological overtones. We know not the day nor the hour (Matt 24:36; 25:13); death comes like a thief in the night (1 Thess 5:2; 2 Pet 3:10; Rev 3:3; 16:15); the bridegroom comes at night and we must be found waiting, lamps in hand (Matt 25:1-13). This is a standard theme of night prayer, like the cosmic theme of those at vigil joining their voices to those of the angels and all creation in praise of God, as in the *Benedicite* of Daniel, while the world sleeps.

Canon 27 of the *Canons of Hippolytus* from Egypt around 336 to 340 expresses this eschatological theme, showing how it forms the bridge uniting evening and morning prayer, which, once again, like all liturgy, are simply moments expressive of the ceaseless hymn of praise that is Christian life:

Let each one take care to pray with great vigilance in the middle of the night, for our fathers have said that at that hour all creation is assiduous

[5] PG 55:427; also *Baptismal Catecheses*, VIII, 17–18, ed. A. Wenger, SCh 50:256–257.

in the service of praising God, all the angelic hosts and the souls of the just bless God. For the Lord testifies to this saying, "In the middle of the night there was a cry: Behold, the bridegroom has come, go out to meet him" (Matt 25:6). At cockcrow, again, is a time when there are prayers in the churches, for the Lord says, "Watch, for you do not know at what time the Master will come, in the evening, or in the middle of the night, or at cockcrow, or in the morning" (Mark 13:35), which means we must praise God at every hour. And when a man sleeps on his bed, he must pray to God in his heart.[6]

THE HOURS: AN ESCHATOLOGICAL PRAYER

It should be clear from these texts that the early cathedral Office can be called a "sanctification of time" only in the sense that time is "sacramentalized" into a symbol of the time that transcends time. In the liturgical mystery, time becomes transformed into event, an epiphany of the kingdom of God. All creation is a cosmic sacrament of our saving God, and the Church's use of nature's symbols in the Office is but a step in the restoration of all things in Christ (Eph 1:10). For the Christian, everything, including the morning and evening, the day and the night, the sun and its setting, can be a means of communication with God: "The heavens are telling the glory of God; and the firmament proclaims his handiwork" (Ps 19:1).

But the earliest tradition of non-Eucharistic public prayer affirms nothing that would sustain later theories of the Hours as a "sanctification of time" with an ethos and theology different from, even opposed to, the "eschatological" orientation of the Eucharist. Morning Praise and Evensong, like all prayer in both the Old and the New Testament, are a glorification of God that wells up from the joyful proclamation of his saving deeds: "The Mighty One has done great things for me, and holy is his name" (Luke 1:49). This is the core of biblical prayer: remembrance, praise, and thanksgiving. For celebrations are celebrations *of* something: through symbol and gesture and text we proclaim and render present once again the reality we feast. In the early liturgical tradition this reality is one unique event, the paschal mystery in its totality, the mystery of Christ and of our salvation in him. This is the meaning of baptism; it is the meaning of Eucharist; it is the meaning of the Hours as well. The anamnesis of the Christ-event is the wellspring of all Christian prayer.

[6] *PatOr* 31:397.

Hence the Liturgy of the Hours, like all Christian liturgy, is an eschatological proclamation of the salvation received in Christ, and a glorification and thanksgiving to God for that gift. In this original and primitive sense, the Liturgy of the Hours, indeed all liturgy, is beyond time. For the Christian, there is really no sacred space, no sacred persons or times; all are redeemed in Christ, for whom only God is holy and those to whom he has given his sanctification, his saints, that is, his people.

THE HOURS: A CLERICAL MINISTRY?

The *Apostolic Constitutions* (II, 59) exhorts the congregation to be present regularly at the Offices of Morning Prayer and Evensong, as well as at the Sunday vigil and Eucharist:

> When you teach, bishop, command and exhort the people to frequent the church regularly, morning and evening every day, and not to forsake it at all, but to assemble continually, and not diminish the Church by absenting themselves and making the Body of Christ lack a member. For it is not only said for the benefit of the priests, but let each of the laity hear what was said by the Lord as spoken to himself: "He who is not with me is against me, and he who does not gather with me scatters" (Matt 12:30). Do not scatter yourselves by not gathering together, you who are members of Christ. . . . Do not be neglectful of yourselves, nor rob the Savior of his members, nor divide his body, nor scatter his members, nor prefer the needs of this life to the Word of God, but assemble each morning and evening, singing psalms and praying in the Lord's houses, in the morning saying Psalm 62 and in the evening Psalm 140.

Note that this exhortation is directed not just to the clergy but to the laity as well. This is important to counteract a common misconception in interpreting the fact that certain categories and groups in the Church may be commissioned to pray the Office in the Church's name. One can and must pray *for* everyone, including the Church and its needs and intentions, and the Church can depute ministers and religious to do so. But no one can pray *in place of* anyone else, like some living prayer wheel that spins on vicariously while the world goes about its business. Some can be called to assume freely the obligations of a life more totally dedicated to prayer in common—but not in the sense that they are "official pray-ers" for others, who thereby can consider themselves freed from the evangelical command to watch and pray. The burden of common prayer is incumbent on all.

THE SPIRIT OF THE MONASTIC OFFICE

But what of the monastic obligation of choir? Surely the monastic orders are deputed to offer the official cult in the name of the whole Church, are they not? According to Dom Adalbert de Vogüé in his classic commentary on the Rule of St. Benedict, no early monk at his prayers had any idea of "performing an act in the name of the Church."[7] This purely Latin notion is largely the result of urban monasticism in the West from the fifth/sixth centuries, when monastic communities served major city sanctuaries such as the great Roman basilicas and were responsible for the public cult. This eventually resulted in the Cluniac *monachus propter chorum* ideology and passed into the Benedictine revival literature of modern times.

But the earliest monks had no such "liturgical mystique." For them, life was one continual prayer, with no compartmentalization of life into "liturgical" prayer and other kinds of prayer and work. The one rule was the absolute primacy of the spiritual in the everyday lives of these ascetics. "Single-mindedness" is the characteristic of the monk, and the aim of this unilateral existence was the life with God.

As far as the prayer of Hours was concerned, such a life was lived by taking literally the New Testament imperative of unceasing prayer. So the monks prayed while they worked and worked while they prayed. What they sought ultimately was what modern spiritual writers would call a "state of prayer," a degree of spiritual perfection in which one's every breath, one's very existence, is a continuous prayer not subject to fragmentation into successive acts nor to interruption by external activities. Necessary activities such as eating forced the early monk to interrupt his *offices,* but he *never* interrupted his *prayer!* So the rule was not, as today, to fix a *minimum* number of hours for prayer and give the rest of the time to other occupations, but to fix a *maximum* amount of time to be grudgingly accorded to such physical necessities as sleep and give the rest to prayer.

Only later does the monastic Office get detached from the rest of life and become an "obligation," a *pensum* to be gotten through whenever

[7] *La Règle de s. Benoît,* VII: *Commentaire doctrinal et spirituel,* SCh hors série (Paris, 1977) 193ff. = *The Rule of St. Benedict: A Doctrinal and Spiritual Commentary,* Cistercian Studies 54 (Kalamazoo, Mich., 1983) 139.

one can. Later, too, is the notion of the monastic Office as a "public cult." Originally monastic psalmody was God's word to us. The monks' psalms were not chants of praise in the mouth of the Church, as in cathedral prayer, but God's word on which to meditate before turning to him with prayerful response. But eventually the monastic psalmody comes to be seen as the Church's prayer to God, our message to him, thus approaching the cultic notion of cathedral psalmody that is simply not found in the earliest monastic texts. Of course, the two ideas are not opposed, for God is indeed glorified in the liturgy by us—but only insofar as we are sanctified by his grace, for our glorification of him is his gift to us, not ours to him.

So there is originally a slightly different orientation in the cathedral and monastic spiritualities of the prayer of Hours. But they eventually come together in urban monasticism, so today I think it is legitimate to say that the differences are more in style than in substance, more in the structure and aim of the Offices than in their theologies. The vocation of all Christians, not just monks, is to be a living prayer, and long-standing tradition has also taught monks that their praise of God is part of the official λειτουργία of the Church. By vocation they are privileged to give more frequent common symbolic expression to what, ideally, must be the rhythm of the whole of every Christian life: a prayerful, continuous communion with the living God and with one another in him. This is the theology of the monastic Office expressed in the Preface of the post-Vatican II *Thesaurus Liturgiae Horarum Monasticae* issued by the Benedictine Confederation in 1977.

CONCLUSION: THE HOURS—A CELEBRATION OF LIFE IN CHRIST

The Liturgy of the Hours, then, is a sanctification of life by turning to God at the beginning and end of each of its days, and whenever one is able in between, to do what all liturgy always does: to celebrate and manifest in ritual moments what is and must be the constant stance of our every minute of the day, namely, our unceasing priestly offering, in Christ, of self, to the praise and glory of the Father in thanks for his saving gift in Christ.

All true Christian liturgy is a celebration of that reality. Thus the Offices at the beginning and end of the day are but ritual moments symbolic of the whole of time. As such, they are a proclamation of faith to the world and partake of our mission to witness to Christ and his salvation. They are also a praise and thanksgiving for this gift of salvation in Christ. Lastly, they are our priestly prayer, as God's priestly people, for our needs and those of the entire world.

Bibliography

Cuva, A. *La Liturgia delle Ore: Note teologiche e spirituali.* BELS 4. Rome, 1975.

De Reynal, D. *Théologie de la Liturgie des heures.* Paris, 1978.

De Vogüé, A. "Le sens de l'office divin." In *La Règle de s. Benoît,* VII: *Commentaire doctrinal et spirituel,* 184–248. Paris, 1977. English translation: *The Rule of St. Benedict: A Doctrinal and Spiritual Commentary,* 127–172. Cistercian Studies 54. Kalamazoo, Mich., 1983.

Fischer, B. *Dienst des Lobes—Dienst der Fürbitten: Zur Spiritualität des Stundengebetes.* Kölner Beiträge 23. Cologne, 1977.

Lebendiges Stundengebet: Vertiefung und Hilfe. Ed. M. Klöckener and H. Rennings. Freiburg-Basel-Vienna, 1989, esp. pp. 121–216; 409–430; 442–461.

Liturgia delle Ore: Documenti ufficiali e studi. Quaderni di Rivista Liturgica 14. Turin-Leumann, 1972.

Magrassi, M. "La spiritualità dell'Ufficio divino." In *Liturgia delle Ore: Documenti ufficiali e studi,* 365–404. Quademi di Rivista Liturgica 14. Turin-Leumann, 1972.

Martimort, A.-G. "The Liturgy of the Hours." *CP* 4:151–275. Collegeville, Minn., 1986.

Roguet, A.-M. *The Liturgy of the Hours: The General Introduction with Commentary,* 81–101. Collegeville, Minn., 1971.

Taft, R. *The Liturgy of the Hours in East and West: The Origins of the Divine Office and Its Meaning for Today.* Collegeville, Minn., 1986. Chap. 21: "Toward a Theology of the Liturgy of the Hours," pp. 331–365.

____. "'Thanksgiving for the Light': Towards a Theology of Vespers." *Diakonia* 13 (1978) 27–50. Revised ed. in his *Beyond East and West: Problems in Liturgical Understanding,* 127–149. Washington, 1984.

Visentin, P. "Dimensione orante della chiesa e Liturgia delle Ore." In *Liturgia delle Ore: Documenti ufficiali e studi,* 131–159. Quaderni di Rivista Liturgica 14. Turin-Leumann, 1972.

Part II

The Liturgical Year

Matias Augé, C.M.F.

6

The Liturgical Year in the First Four Centuries

The general notion of what we now call the liturgical year is relatively recent. Even if in the thirteenth century some authors sketched the outline of a system of annual liturgical celebration and inspired the idea of the liturgical year, it was only in the sixteenth century that the celebrations of the annual cycle came to be understood as a unity, with the name "the year of the Church" *(Kirchenjahr)* or later "the Christian year." In the nineteenth century, Prosper Guéranger used the expression (which has become familiar in the meantime) "the liturgical year" in his famous work *L'année liturgique.* At any rate, the current structure of the liturgical year was fixed in the sixth century and is the fruit of a process which began in apostolic times with the celebration of Sunday and which was followed by the annual celebration of Easter.

I. THE CELEBRATION OF SUNDAY

1. The Origin of Sunday as a Day of Worship

In the New Testament there are references to Sunday which, taken together with the first patristic texts that treat of this issue, indicate in a fairly certain fashion that the observance of Sunday as a day of worship began with the apostles.

1 Corinthians 16:1-2: St. Paul had promised the Council of Jerusalem to remember the poor members of that church (cf. Gal 2:10). Now he is writing to the faithful in Corinth so that they can prepare their alms for this purpose. The importance of this passage for our discussion right now is that Paul asks that the collection be taken "on the first day of every week," that is, the day after the Sabbath, or Sunday. The Apostle chooses this day in order to guarantee that the collection for the poor will be taken up regularly. This shows that the Christian community at Corinth follows the rhythm of the Jewish seven-day week and that the first day after the Sabbath has a particular significance. In this regard we should also note that a bit later, in the middle of the second century, according to the witness of St. Justin, the collection for the needy in Rome took place at the end of the Sunday Eucharistic assembly.[1]

Acts 20:7-12: St. Paul is at Troas, a guest of the Christian community that he had founded there. The last day of his stay is "the first day of the week," and all the members of the community are gathered for "the breaking of the bread," a term that refers to the celebration of the Eucharist (cf. Luke 24:35; Acts 2:46; 1 Cor 10:16). The reference to "large room upstairs" (cf. Mark 14:15) and to the "many lamps" that light the room constitutes a veiled hint at the nature of the meeting as one for worship. Therefore, what is being referred to is a Eucharistic celebration held on a certain day. Everything about the account makes one think of a regularly scheduled meeting. The community is not meeting in order to send the Apostle on his way, given that, according to the account, it is the Apostle who is given time in the meeting. The meeting is not called for his sake.

Therefore, what this account refers to is a Eucharistic assembly that took place on the first day of the week. However, there is a disagreement in the literature about which day is being referred to here. Some say that Luke fixed the dates and the calendar in Acts with a faithful adherence to the Jewish system. In this case, the meeting would have taken place on the evening of the Sabbath, when, according to Jewish computation, the new day began. Others insist, rather, that the author of Acts would be able to refer to the Greek or Roman reckoning, in which case this evening meeting on "the first day of the week," would have taken place on Sunday evening.[2]

Revelation 1:9-10: The importance of the text is rooted in the fact that it is the only passage in the New Testament in which the first day of the week is called "the Lord's day." [The original Greek uses the adjective κυριακή. In Latin this became *dominica dies,* which gave rise in

[1] Justin, *First Apology,* 67, 6.

[2] The various opinions can be found in W. Rordorf, "Origine et signification de la célébration du dimanche dans le christianisme primitif: État actuel de la recherche," *MD* 148 (1981) 103–122. See also T. J. Talley, *The Origins of the Liturgical Year,* 2nd ed. (Collegeville, Minn., 1991) 13–17.

some European languages to names for the first day of week that contained a remnant of the Latin word for "Lord," for example, *domenica* (Italian) or *dimanche* (French).] This phrase calls to mind a parallel one in 1 Corinthians 11:20, "the Lord's supper."[3] The adjective κυριακή refers to κύριος, the Lord risen as Messiah and Son of God (cf. Acts 2:36; 1 Cor 12:3; Phil 2:9-11, etc.). The context of the passage in Revelation is not directly connected with worship. Some authors, however, refer to a document of Syriac origin that is almost contemporary, the *Didache,* where the day of the Lord is the regular day for the community to gather to celebrate the Eucharist: "On the day of the Lord come together, break bread and hold Eucharist, after confessing your transgressions that your offering may be pure."[4]

Note that the expression "day of the Lord" also refers to the "day of YHWH," an Old Testament term with a largely eschatological sense that can refer to, among other things, the definitive intervention of God in the messianic times.[5] We might also say that, in its ambiguity, this name for Sunday proclaims the entire paschal mystery of Jesus Christ and does not refer only to his resurrection as an isolated event.

These New Testament texts, while not giving an absolute and final answer to the question about the origin of Sunday as a day of worship, contribute to the general impression that "the day of the Lord" is a genuinely Christian creation. The immediate cause of the institution of Sunday as a day for worship seems to be its connection with the appearances of the Risen One to the apostles.[6] The Synoptic Gospels indicate the precise day of the Lord's resurrection and the appearances

[3] Rordorf believes that the Christian name for Sunday, κυριακή, is derived from κυριακόν; and that that day was chosen for the celebration of the Eucharist because of the resurrection (*Sabbat und Sonntag in der Alten Kirche,* Traditio Christiana 2 (Zürich, 1972) xiv–xxi.

[4] "The Teaching of the Apostles (Didache)," in *The Apostolic Fathers,* trans. Kirsopp Lake (Cambridge, Mass, 1945) 14, 1.

[5] P. Auvray and X. Léon-Dufour, "Giorno del Signore," *Dizionario di Teologia Biblica* (Turin, 1972) 473–480.

[6] This is the thesis of Rordorf, *Sunday: The History of the Day of Rest and Worship in the Earliest Centuries of the Christian Church* (Philadelphia, 1968) 177–237. This thesis is taken up by, among others, S. Marsili, *I segni del mistero di Cristo: Teologia liturgica dei sacramenti,* BELS 42 (Rome, 1987) 377. Others think instead that the foundation and cause for Sunday was the resurrection of the Lord. See C. S. Mosna, *Storia della domenica dalle origini fino agli inizi del V secolo: Problema delle origini e sviluppo, culto e riposo, aspetti pastorali e liturgici,* AGreg 170 (Rome, 1969) 42–60.

to the apostles: the first day of the week or the first day after the Sabbath (Matt 28:1; Mark 16:2; Luke 24:1). John also tells that on the first day after the Sabbath the holy women went to the tomb (John 20:1), which they found to be empty, and that on the evening of the same day Jesus appeared to the apostles (John 20:19). Eight days later, again on a Sunday, Christ appeared to them a second time, when Thomas was also present (John 20:26). The appearance of the Risen One to the disciples at Emmaus also took place on the same day as the resurrection (Luke 24:13). The precision with which the tradition dates the appearances is worthy of note. Just as noteworthy are the allusions found in some of these stories to meals that the Risen One shared with the disciples (Luke 24:30, 42; Mark 16:14; see also Acts 1:4; 10:41). The Eucharist, which has since the very beginning formed the nucleus of Sunday worship, is connected with these meals.[7]

In sum, we can argue that Sunday was born in the Eucharistic and spiritual climate (pneumatological and eschatological) of the appearances of the Risen One in the vicinity of Jerusalem. Even if the only New Testament witness that explicitly mentions a Sunday celebration (Acts 20:7-12) refers to a Pauline community, outside of Palestine, the available data lead to a fundamental agreement with those who connect Sunday worship with the appearances of the Risen One.[8]

2. *The Connection Between the Sabbath and Sunday*[9]

The Sabbath, the holy day that belongs to the Lord, is also the only day of the week that has a name in Hebrew. The others are simply called (in relation to the Sabbath) the first, the second, the third, etc. *Shabbath* is derived from a root which means "to stop," "to rest." The primary characteristic of the Sabbath is exactly this: abstention from work. But in the long tradition of Israel, the celebration of the Sabbath has carried with it a beautiful and meaningful theology of the cove-

[7] F. X. Durwell, *The Resurrection: A Biblical Study* (New York, 1960) 320–323.

[8] Hypotheses that connect Sunday to a non-Christian origin, whether in the worship of the sun, in practices of the Mandeans, or in those of the Qumran community are considered inconsistent by the majority of scholars. See Mosna, *Storia,* 30–42; Rordorf, "Origine," 111–113; J. López-Martin, "El origen del domingo: Estado actual de la cuestión," *Salmanticensis* 38 (1991) 285–293.

[9] N. Negretti, *Il settimo giorno: Indagine critico-teologica delle tradizioni presacredotali e sacredotali circa il sabato biblico* (Rome, 1973); J. Latorre, "Del sábado al domingo en la Escritura," *Ph* 32 (1992) 453–474; M. Sales, "L'osservanza del sabato: Dal Settimo Giorno al riposo di Dio in Dio," *Communio* 133 (1994) 9–27.

nant. It is a sign, at the same time communal and familial, of the messianic promises given by God. It allowed each individual member of the people to experience the fundamental unity of the faith. It was fundamentally a memorial of God the Creator, who "rested the seventh day" (Exod 20:11; cf. Gen 2:1-3), and God the Liberator from Egyptian slavery (cf. Deut 5:12-15). In the postexilic period, the Sabbath became the object of minute ritual specifications (cf. Jer 17:19-27; Neh 13:15-22) and scrupulous legal codification. All this, even though its origin was in a tremendous reverence for the Sabbath, ended by making this day a burden for people, no longer a joyous feast but a burdensome law.

The problem of the relationship between the Jewish Sabbath and the Christian Sunday at the very beginning of Christianity is extremely complex. The polemic regarding the Sabbath seems to come from the time of Jesus' public ministry (cf. Matt 12:1-8; Mark 3:1-6; Luke 14:1-6). These are texts that reflect a precise historical situation in which Jesus was to be found in a Jewish environment. However, they probably also contain traces of a polemic that arose after Jesus, between Jews and Christians, as well, perhaps, as recalling disputes among various groups of Christians, some of whom still observed the Sabbath.[10]

Jesus' claim to be "lord of the Sabbath," one that places that day at the service of human beings (cf. Mark 2:27-28), clarifies his messianic nature. It is, however, true that Jesus did not abolish the Sabbath. What is more, what he said about the old Law in general can just as well be applied to the Sabbath: "I have come not to abolish, but to fulfill" (Matt 5:17). Jesus did not abolish the Sabbath, but he enriched it by associating it with messianic notions.

Apparently there was no problem with Sabbath observance for the first Christians who were of Jewish origin. They continued to observe the Law, went to the temple, and attended synagogue (cf. Acts 13:14, 44; 17:2; 18:4). At Philippi, where, in all likelihood, there was no synagogue, Christian missionaries gathered on the Sabbath at a place of prayer near a river in front of the city gate (cf. Acts 16:13). The first Christians did not take the step of transferring the legal day of rest from the Sabbath to Sunday. We have seen that Sunday was a day for worship, not for rest. At any rate, what Jesus had to say about the Sabbath

[10] A full view of the various positions can be found in H. Weiss, "The Shabbath in the Synoptic Gospels," *Journal for the Study of the New Testament* 38 (1990) 13–16.

and the Law, as well as the way he acted in its regard, could not have been a matter of indifference to the first Christians. The apostolic letter sent from Jerusalem to the Churches of Syria and Asia did not mention Sabbath observance among the obligations they asked Christians of a pagan origin to take on (cf. Acts 15:28-29), and Paul was opposed to judaizing tendencies that showed themselves in the communities of Galatia and Colossae (cf. Gal 4:8-10; Col 2:16-17).

Primitive Christianity developed a theology of the Sabbath very quickly, which shows that late Jewish ideas were intentionally brought into a Christian environment. The Letter to the Hebrews, after a long midrashic development on the theme of rest and the Sabbath that takes its start with Psalm 95:8-11 and Genesis 2:2, eventually speaks of Sabbath rest (cf. Heb 4:4) with a future, eschatological dimension. It is the perfect Sabbath, the rest that will fulfill the promises of God, which are still in effect (cf. Heb 4:1). From this perspective, the Sabbath and its rest are a heavenly, future good toward which the people of God are now on the way, a future time of salvation, which will be accompanied by the absence of evil and the doing of good, the summation of all good in Christ. This theme is taken up again by the Apostolic Fathers and other writers during the first three centuries.[11]

Judaizing tendencies, which would have been favorable to Sabbath observance, were also to be found in the part of the Christian Church that was of Gentile origin. Willy Rordorf examines the relevant data according to a threefold scheme: the maintenance of Sabbath festivals in a Jewish Christian environment, the complete abandonment of its observance in the parts of the Christian world that had a pagan origin, and the Eastern Churches' attempt to reintroduce a modified version, in which it was spiritualized and not subject to legal prescriptions, in the fourth century.[12]

3. *The Names for Sunday: A Theological Approach*

Sunday is the ancient nucleus of the entire liturgical year. This can be understood by looking at the different names that the day received in the first centuries of the Church. The Fathers of the Church showed what Sunday meant by emphasizing a variety of aspects of the paschal mystery, which the Sunday celebration was intended to memorialize, in their writings on the subject.

[11] The texts can be found in Rordorf, *Sabbat,* n. 11.

[12] Ibid., xiv.

The first day after the Sabbath: This is the oldest name given to Sunday and is really a Jewish term. In the Gospel account (cf. Mark 16:2 and parallels), this day evokes the resurrection of Jesus, which took place on the first day after the Sabbath. This name came to be used by Christians because of its symbolism. As the "first day" it called to mind Genesis 1 especially, the beginning of creation, and more precisely, the creation of light (Gen 1:3-5). In this context the Christian day of worship is also given a name of pagan origin, the day of the sun. Justin was the first Christian author to use this symbolism, making an explicit connection between the beginning of creation and the Lord's resurrection. "But we hold this common gathering on Sunday, since it is the first day, on which God transforming darkness and matter made the Universe, and Jesus Christ our Savior on the same day rose from the dead."[13]

Later many of the Fathers would take up the biblical symbolism of light and interpret the "first" creation as a type and figure of the "second" creation.[14] This gives more prominence to the resurrection of the Lord. The prophets had already considered the future salvation to be a new creation (cf. Isa 41:20; 45:8; 48:7). Sunday is connected with the very beginning and is called the "first day" for this reason, which was itself a sign of the beginnings of a salvation that would culminate with Easter. The mystery of Christ the Lord embraces all of the past, beginning with creation itself. So Sunday, the Lord's Day, memorializes the first and the new creation. It is a memorial of Easter, but an Easter that is the center of a grand plan of God for salvation. The expression "first day of the week," referring to Sunday, gives the Easter theme a weekly expression, as a passage from darkness to light, as a victory over death, as resurrection and the newness of life. For these reasons Christians spent the day in joy.[15]

The day of the Lord: This expression is found in Revelation 1:10. We have seen that it appears in the *Didache* in a context that is clearly connected to worship. The "day of the Lord" calls to mind, especially, the day of resurrection, because the Lord (κύριος) is a title of Jesus as

[13] Justin, "First Apology" in *St. Justin Martyr: The First and Second Apologies*, trans. L. W. Barnard (New York, 1997) chap. 67.

[14] Cf. Eusebius of Caesarea, Athanasius of Alexandria, and Jerome in Rordorf, *Sabbat*, n. 44; n. 117, n. 129. In the text, the Latin word *dominicum* refers both to the day of the Lord and the Eucharist that was celebrated on it.

[15] *Didascalia*, 5, 20 in Rordorf, *Sabbat*, n. 129.

raised by the Father (cf. Rom 1:4; 10:9; Phil 2:11). On the day of Pentecost, Peter proclaimed that Christ was risen from the dead and had sent the Holy Spirit. He ended by saying, "Therefore let the entire house of Israel know with certainty that God has made him both Lord and Messiah, this Jesus whom you crucified." (Acts 2:36). St. Jerome, when speaking of Easter, says: "The Lord's day, however, the day of the resurrection, the day of Christians, is our day. It is called the Lord's day because on this day the Lord ascended to the Father as Victor."[16]

With the resurrection Jesus enters into the divine joy, which was his by right until his birth. In this way Sunday comes to be understood as the day that showed the power of the triumph and victory of Christ, who, in the resurrection, has become the source of life, of grace, and of strength.

The "day of the Lord" was also the day on which the first Christian communities met in order to remember the Lord with the Eucharist, or the "Lord's supper": "We (the faithful) of the new covenant celebrate on that day of the Lord which is our Passover; we are always sated with the body of the Savior and we always take part in the blood of the Lamb. . . ."[17]

During the uproar caused by the persecution of Diocletian at the beginning of the fourth century, some Christians in Abyssinia, in Proconsular Africa, were surprised during a Sunday celebration of the Eucharist and taken away as prisoners to the proconsul of the city. Accused of unlawful assembly, they replied, "We cannot exist without the Lord's supper."[18]

While Sunday reminded Christians of Easter, it was also the day on which the Church revitalized itself in the Eucharistic assembly. In the Sunday celebration of the Eucharist, the Church was conscious of being the σύναξις, that is, the community called together for the purpose of the celebration, in which it was built up in unity as the Body of Christ:

Now when thou teachest, command and warn the people to be constant in assembling in the Church, and not to withdraw themselves

[16] Jerome, "Homily on Easter Sunday," in *The Homilies of Saint Jerome,* trans. Marie Liguori Ewald (Washington, 1966) n. 94.

[17] Eusebius of Caesarea, "De solemnitate paschali" in Rordorf, *Sabbat,* n. 114.

[18] "Acta ss. Saturnini, Datiui, et aliorum plurimorum martyrum in Africa" in Rordorf, *Sabbat,* n. 109. In the Latin text, the word "dominicum" refers both to the Lord's day and to the Eucharist celebrated on it.

but always to assemble, lest any man diminish the Church by not assembling, and cause the body of Christ to be short a member. For let not a man take thought of others only, but of himself as well, hearkening to that which our Lord said: *Every one that gathereth not with me scattereth.* Since therefore you are the members of Christ, do not scatter yourselves from the Church by not assembling. Seeing that you have Christ for your head, as He promised—for you are partakers with us—be not then neglectful of yourselves, and deprive not our Savior of His members, and do not rend and scatter His body. And make not your worldly affairs of more account than the word of God; but on the Lord's day leave every thing and run eagerly to your Church; for she is your glory. Otherwise, what excuse have they before God who do not assemble on the Lord's day to hear the word of life and be nourished with the divine food which abides for ever?[19]

In conclusion, the day of the Lord was the memory and the very presence of the Risen Lord among those gathered in his name. Christians, reconciled, met in a festive and joyous assembly in order to proclaim the historical, salvific, and sacramental presence of the Lord.

The eighth day: Among the expressions that the ancient Christians used to name Sunday, the "eighth day" has a particularly intense significance. The name seems to be found in the New Testament. It might come, in fact, from the account of the appearances of the Risen One in John 20:26: "Eight days later. . . ."

To say that Sunday is the eighth day (of the week) may seem paradoxical, given that the eighth day, that is, the one that follows the seventh, is also the first. So the eighth day is the first day. But if one thinks in a diachronic fashion, and even more in an eschatological fashion, the eighth day becomes an allusion to a new reality, an announcement of eternal beatitude, the definitive encounter with the Lord. Starting with this idea, the Fathers of both East and West, albeit in different ways, worked out a theology of history in which the Greek cyclical notion of history came together with the Hebrew notion, in which history moves forward and derives its meeting and its final goal in the Lord. The first mention of Sunday as the "eighth day" is found around the year 135 in the *Epistle of Barnabas.* The author, in the context of an anti-Jewish polemic, says:

[19] *Didascalia,* 2, 59, 2-3, in Rordorf, *Sabbat,* n. 102, p. 103. Translation in R. H. Connolly, *Didascalia Apostolorum* (Oxford, 1929; reprint Norwich, 1969) 124.

Do you see what he means? The present Sabbaths are not acceptable to me, but that which I have made, in which I will give rest to all things and make the beginning of an eighth day, that is the beginning of another world. Wherefore we also celebrate with gladness the eighth day in which Jesus also rose from the dead, and was made manifest, and ascended into Heaven.[20]

The Sabbath remains the seventh day, the close of the Old Testament, whereas the day of Christ's resurrection, Sunday, is the "eighth day," the beginning of the new age.

The symbolism of Sunday as the eighth day was later enriched by typological interpretations of circumcision, which took place on the eighth day, relating it to baptism (cf. Col 2:11-13) and to the eight people saved from the flood: Noah, his wife, the three sons, and the three daughters-in-law (cf. 1 Pet 3:18-21; 2 Pet 2:5). This was the approach of Justin, Origen,[21] and others. The celebration of baptism became a figure or type of the arrival of the ultimate eighth day, the day of final salvation.

All these considerations of Sunday as the eighth day call to mind that in waiting for the future age, one is waiting for the Easter Christ, who will come to consummate our salvation. The eighth day, therefore, becomes a sign of our full participation in the paschal mystery. The gift of the Holy Spirit at Pentecost also enters into this discussion. The day of Pentecost is an eighth day that will come after a week of seven weeks, the fiftieth day after Easter (7 x 7 = 49 + 1).[22] Sunday is the memorial of the eschatological gift of the Holy Spirit, which anticipates the parousia. The significance of Sunday for history and salvation extends, just as the mystery of salvation itself does, from Genesis to Pentecost and the outpouring of the Holy Spirit, finally to the return of the Lord at the end of time. "All that which concerns the salvation of humanity had its beginning and completion on the day of the Lord."[23]

4. *Later Developments Concerning Sunday in the Fourth Century*

On March 3, 321 (eight years after the emperor Constantine granted freedom of worship to Christians) the same emperor made a law that

[20] *The Epistle of Barnabas*, in *The Apostolic Fathers*, 15, 8-9.

[21] Rordorf, *Sabbat*, nn. 81, 82, 98.

[22] Ambrosiaster, "Liber quaestionum ueteris et noui testamentum," ibid., n. 118.

[23] Ibid.

established that on the "day of the sun" all judges, urban dwellers, and artisans (with the exception of peasants) were to rest. In July 321, another imperial law was made prohibiting any judicial act that had a contentious character from being carried out on Sunday, but was explicit in allowing those acts that led to joy and peace, such as the liberation of slaves. Later, in 337, new laws relating to Sunday appeared that were more specifically religious in their motivations and made specific mention of worship.[24]

From the fourth century on, several provincial synods issued disciplinary norms that focused on the obligation to participate in the Sunday Eucharist, even as they demonstrated at the same time great tolerance. A good example is the Council of Elvira in Spain (300–302 and 306–313), which was the first of this type and was repeated later by a number of others: "If someone stays for some time in a certain place and does not go to church on three Sundays, he should be excluded for a brief time so that he might know that he is being punished."[25]

Beginning in the fourth century, the nature of Sunday as a day for worship became fixed, and there developed an Office for prayer on Sunday. At the end of this century, we find at Jerusalem and in other Eastern Churches the practice of a vigil of Sunday in which the entire community took part. We are especially familiar with the vigil as it was practiced in Jerusalem because of the account of the pilgrim Egeria.[26] She describes an Office with psalms and prayers. The climax of the celebration was the reading of the resurrection account from the Gospels, which only the bishop could do. This was done as though by the angel, before the empty tomb. It was an extremely solemn popular Office, which exalted Sunday as a weekly memorial of the mystery of Easter.[27]

As we have seen, this period saw the transformation of Sunday into a Christian Sabbath. St. Ephraem the Syrian was the first who, in connection with the Sunday rest, made a connection with the law for the Sabbath.[28]

[24] The laws of Emperor Constantine relating to Sunday may be found in Rordorf, *Sabbat*, nn. 111–113. On the issue of resting on Sunday, see H. Huber, *Geist und Buchstabe: Der Sonntagsruhe* (Salzburg, 1958).

[25] "Concilium Illiberritanum, can. 21" in Rordorf, *Sabbat*, n. 110.

[26] Aetheria, "Peregrinatio ad loca sancta," in Rordorf, *Sabbat*, n. 123.

[27] R. Taft, *The Liturgy of the Hours: The Origins of the Divine Office and Its Meaning for Today* (Collegeville, Minn., 1986) 28–29 et passim.

[28] Ephraem the Syrian, "Sermo ad nocturnam dominicae resurrectionis 4," in Rordorf, *Sabbat*, n. 116.

II. THE ANNUAL CELEBRATION OF EASTER

Some authorities assume that an annual celebration of Easter was already known in the Apostolic Church.[29] We note, however, that there are no direct witnesses in favor of such a celebration. Two texts from Acts (Acts 12:3-4; 20:6) do speak of an annual recurrence of what was probably the Jewish Passover. It is important that the Synoptic Gospels describe the Last Supper as a Passover meal. Jesus commanded his disciples to prepare a room for the Passover (Mark 14:14; Matt 26:18; Luke 22:8). Paul, following John's chronology, interpreted the death of Jesus as the real Passover sacrifice (1 Cor 5:7). Finally, we must note that some authorities have argued that 1 Peter was built on the literary platform of a preexisting paschal catechesis, one intended for the newly baptized.[30] Even if the current discussion is less insistent on this hypothesis, one can say that 1 Peter and other New Testament texts cited above witness to the origin of the Christian paschal celebration and its separation from its Jewish matrix. This was a process that began in apostolic times. Christians celebrated a Passover "in spirit and in truth" in the hearts of the disciples of Jesus, before there was even a rite or a festival as such.[31]

1. Data Regarding the Celebration

The first explicit witnesses to the annual celebration of Easter come from Asia Minor and date from the second half of the second century. These Churches celebrated Easter on the fourteenth of Nisan, the day on which the Jewish people were commanded to sacrifice lambs. These Christians, called "Quartodecimans," were convinced that the death of Christ had been substituted for the Jewish Passover, the *Pesach.* They celebrated Easter by fasting on the fourteenth of Nisan, ending the fast with the celebration of the Eucharist at the conclusion of a nocturnal vigil between the fourteenth and fifteenth of Nisan. The other Churches, taking the lead from Rome, celebrated Easter on the Sunday after the fourteenth of Nisan.

[29] H. Auf der Maur, *Feiern im Rhythmus der Zeit* I: *Herrenfeste in Woche und Jahr,* Gottesdienst der Kirche: Handbuch der Liturgiewissenschaft, Teil 5 (Regensburg, 1983) 65–66. T. J. Talley, *Origins of the Liturgical Year,* 4.

[30] F. L. Cross, *1 Peter: A Paschal Liturgy* (London, 1954).

[31] R. Cantalamessa, *La Pasqua della nostra salvezza: Le tradizioni pasquali della Bibbia e della primitiva Chiesa* (Turin, 1971) 109–115; S. Marsili, *I segni del mistero di Cristo,* 382–383.

In the first half of the fourth century, Eusebius of Caesarea, in his *Ecclesiastical History* (5:23-25) tells us about a controversy that arose in this regard at the end of the second century. Around the year 190 the climax of this controversy was reached, and Pope Victor threatened to excommunicate the Christian communities that accepted the Quartodeciman formula. Eusebius tells us that Irenaeus of Lyons tried to bring peace between the two sides. The bishop of Lyons recalled for the Pope that forty years earlier St. Polycarp of Smyrna was in Rome in order to deal with the same question with Pope Anicetus. At that time the two arrived at an agreement that respected the respective traditions. The vast majority of contemporary scholars assign priority to the Quartodeciman Easter formula.

The controversy was not over whether Easter recalls the death or the resurrection of Christ, but rather whether Easter should be celebrated on the day of Christ's death or on the day of his resurrection. The former would stress the continuity between the Christian Easter and the Jewish Passover, while the latter would stress its novelty. Tradition has, rightly, connected the Quartodeciman Easter tradition to John. The tradition from Peter and Paul that connects Easter with Sunday is considered doubtful. Sunday became fixed as the day for the celebration of Easter in the third century.

The decree concerning Easter that was issued by the Council of Nicea in 325[32] was no longer directed at the controversy with the Quartodecimans, who had already disappeared, but at the diversity of principles that had been adopted by the various Churches for the computation of the date for Easter. Some of these followed the new and rather inadequate method of calculation that had recently been adopted by Jewish communities.

2. *The Structure of the Celebration*

In the oldest documents from the second and third centuries, Easter appears essentially as a rigorous fast, which had a different length, of one or more days,[33] in various Churches. It was followed by an

[32] R. Cantalamessa, ed., *Easter in the Early Church: An Anthology of Jewish and Early Christian Texts,* trans. J. M. Quigley and J. T. Lienhard (Collegeville, Minn., 1993) n. 53.

[33] On the question of this paschal fast, see P. Jounel, "Le jeûne pascal," *MD* 45 (1956) 87–92 and M. Augé, "La revalorización del *ieiunium paschale*," *EO* 9 (1992) 277–286.

assembly during the night consisting of prayers and readings and ending with a celebration of the Eucharist. Already in the second century, Easter was a feast that continued for fifty days. In fact, for ancient Christians Pentecost referred to the entire fifty-day period, with an emphasis on the fiftieth day because it formed the conclusion to the entire period. For example, Tertullian refers to it as a "feast day"[34] that deserves the same "solemnity and joy" that characterizes Easter day.[35]

The oldest witnesses to the annual celebration of Easter are mostly from Asia Minor: *The Epistle of the Apostles,* an apocryphal text written about the year 150; the homily *On Easter* by Melito of Sardis, from around the year 165; and the homily *Holy Easter* by an anonymous Quartodeciman from the end of the second century. There are a number of other less important texts.

In chapter 15 of *The Epistle of the Apostles,* there is a reference to Acts 12. In the form of a prophetic prediction, Christ says:

After I have gone to the Father. You are to remember my death (cf. 1 Cor 11:24-26). Now when the Pascha comes, then one of you will be thrown into prison *for my name's sake* (cf. John 15:21; Luke 21:12; Rev 2:3), and he [will be] in grief and anxiety that you celebrate Pascha while he is in prison and [away] from you; for he will grieve that he does not celebrate the Pascha [with] you. Thereupon I will send my power in the [form] of the angel Gabriel, and the gates of the prison will open, and he will come out and come to you (cf. Acts 12:3-11); until the cock crows. But when you have completed the memorial that is for me, and my Agape, he will again be thrown into prison *for a testimony* (cf. Mark 13:9), until he comes out of that place and preaches what I have delivered to you. . . ."[36]

In this instance, Easter is the commemoration of the death of Jesus in a vigil that ends with a celebration of the Eucharist.

From the homily of Melito of Sardis we know that the Passover account from the Book of Exodus played an important role in this vigil. Aside from this reference to the reading of Exodus 12, Melito's homily *On Easter* does not tell us anything about the celebration of the vigil. The homily by the anonymous Quartodeciman is also focused on a

[34] Cantalamessa, *Easter,* n. 93.
[35] Ibid., n. 92.
[36] Ibid., n. 14.

typological exegesis of Exodus 12. This last text, however, makes clear that the Eucharist was part of the full development of the celebration of the paschal mystery.

From Syria, during the first half of the third century, the *Didascalia* gives us a description of the paschal vigil that is a bit more detailed. Having prescribed a total fast for the preceding Friday and Saturday as a sign of mourning for the passion and death of the Lord, the text says: "You shall come together and watch and keep vigil all the night with prayers and intercessions, and with reading of the prophets, and with the gospel and with psalms, with fear and trembling and with earnest supplication, until the third hour of the night. . . ."[37]

During the first part of the third century, Tertullian, in a text (which is not very clear) from his work *De baptismo* (19:1), and Hippolytus, in the commentary *In Danielem* (1:16), present Easter as a day that is appropriate for baptism. Witnesses to this practice became more numerous after the beginning of the fourth century.

3. *The Theological Framework*

In the two Easter homilies from the second century mentioned above, Easter is viewed as a celebration of the redeeming death of Christ. This is part of a theological framework characterized by global concerns, that is, one in which the paschal mystery of Christ is considered to be the culminating moment that gathers into itself all the great events of salvation history.

The central concern of the homily *On Easter* is the passion of Christ. Melito first highlights the saving value of Easter. He then shows how the divine work of salvation is for the benefit of sinful humanity. Finally, he explains how the people of Israel, to whom the rites that prefigured the Christian Pasch had been entrusted, were punished by God and how the ancient symbols no longer functioned. The real Pasch was perfectly completed by Jesus Christ, who was victorious over sin and death. The content of the paschal celebration is, therefore, the victorious death of Christ as the culminating moment in the entire work of redemption. In the apotheosis of the Redeemer with which the homily ends, we read:

"Who (is there) that contradicts me?
102. I (am the one)," says the Christ.

[37] Ibid., n. 86.

"I am the one that destroyed death
and triumphed over the enemy
and trod down Hades
and bound *the strong one*
and carried off mortals to the heights of heaven;
I (am the one)," says the Christ.
103. "Come then, all you families of men
who are permeated with sins,
and get *forgiveness of sins* (cf. Acts 10:43; 26:18).
For I am your forgiveness,
I (am) the Pascha of salvation. . . ."[38]

The homily *Holy Easter* by the anonymous Quartodeciman is very similar in content. The text opens with a hymn to Christ, Life and Light. There follows a section on the Jewish Passover and then a section on the Christian Easter. It ends with a lyrical praise of Christ, Pascha.

In these homilies there is an extension of the connection between Easter and the sacrifice of the paschal lamb (cf. 1 Cor 5:7). The phrase "mystery of Easter," which first appears in these authors, is made to cover the entire saving plan of God and to be synonymous with the "mystery of Christ" of which St. Paul had spoken (cf. Col 4:3; Eph 3:4). The celebration of Easter commemorates the entire mystery of Christ, which culminated in the saving event of the cross. This global importance of the mystery celebrated at Easter had a different nuance in different Churches. Although they work from different perspectives, Christine Mohrmann[39] and Raniero Cantalamessa[40] have shown the various dimensions of the ancient theology of Easter.

a) From an Easter centered on Passion to an Easter centered on passage

The connection of Easter "Pascha" with "passion" is a result of a popular etymology that connects the word πάσχα with the Greek πάσχειν, πάθος, and with the Latin *pati, passio.* This was the approach of Melito of Sardis, the anonymous Quartodeciman, and others who followed after them. According to this tradition, Easter was the celebration of the totality of our redemption but was first of all a commemoration of

[38] Ibid., n. 24.

[39] C. Mohrmann, "Pascha, Passio, Transitus," *Études sur le latin des chrétiens,* 1 (Rome, 1961) 205–222.

[40] Cantalamessa, *Pasqua,* 157–218, and *Easter,* xiii–xxx.

the victorious passion of Christ, connected, typologically, with the sacrifice of the paschal lamb (cf. 1 Cor 5:7). The central rite of Easter, seen in this way, was the Eucharist that announces "the death of the Lord until he comes" (1 Cor 11:26).

At the beginning of the third century, Clement of Alexandria and Origen were the first Christian authors who, although still thinking of Easter as a commemoration of the passion, affirm that the term *Pascha* does not come from the Greek πάσχειν but from the Hebrew *phas*, meaning "passage" or "transition" (in Greek: διάβασις).[41] Clement draws a moral conclusion from this: Easter is "the passage from all trouble and from all objects of sense."[42] Similarly, Origen spiritualized and universalized Easter, which, according to him, the Church and all believers celebrated unceasingly in the sacraments (of baptism and the Eucharist), because "he is always passing over in thought and in every word and every deed from the affairs of this life to God and hastening toward his city."[43]

St. Jerome, like many others, spoke of Easter as a passage *(transitus)* but emphasized that, according to Exodus, the passage is the Lord's.[44] St. Augustine accepts this correction of meaning and creates a synthesis of the two approaches, Easter as passion and Easter as passage, in this way: "For by suffering the Lord made the passage from death to life and opened a way for us who believe in his resurrection by which we too might pass from death to life.[45]

For Augustine, the Easter of the Church is essentially realized in the (daily) celebration of the Eucharist. However, this does not render the annual celebration of Easter less important and significant.[46] For St. Ambrose, however, the paschal sacrament that is even more perfect is baptism and Eucharist: "a passing from sin to life, from guilt to grace, from defilement to sanctification."[47]

These developments tended to shift the most important moment, in terms of typology, from the sacrifice of the lamb (Exodus 12) to the passing through the Red Sea (Exodus 13–14). As a result, as has been

[41] Cantalamessa, *Easter*, n. 37; n. 33.

[42] Ibid., n. 33.

[43] Ibid., n. 43, n. 39.

[44] Ibid., n. 114.

[45] Ibid., n. 126.

[46] Ibid., n. 130.

[47] Ibid., n. 109.

said already, baptism comes to be seen as the sacrament proper to Easter.

b) Easter as a recapitulation

The conception of Easter as a recapitulation, taking up an idea of St. Paul (Eph 1:10), was intended to show the unity, from creation to redemption, in the saving plan of God. The term appears frequently in paschal catechesis, emphasizing the mystery of the resurrection. As a single example, we will cite here a text by Gaudentius of Brescia: "The Son of God, 'through' whom 'all things were made' (John 1:3), by his resurrection raises up the fallen world on the same day, and at the same time, as he himself had earlier created it out of nothing. 'All things' were to be restored 'in Christ . . .'" (Eph 1:10).[48]

St. Paul spoke of baptism in terms of a new creation (cf. 1 Cor 5:17; Gal 6:15). In this context, Easter is the baptism of the world and the regeneration of all creation.

c) Easter as parousia

According to a Jewish tradition, the messiah was to arrive during Passover. Starting from this point, some Christian authors spoke of waiting for the parousia during the night of Easter. St. Jerome took up this tradition again and affirmed that Christians celebrate the paschal vigil as an expectation of the coming of Christ.[49] Lactantius, for his part, was convinced that Christ would return on that night and "would receive the kingship over the world."[50] St. Augustine, however, saw the paschal vigil as a sign or figure of the ongoing expectation of the final appearance of the Lord. In a text that brings together in a perfect equilibrium the three essential elements of the paschal celebration (remembrance, presence, and waiting), the bishop of Hippo says:

> And so, in this vigil of ours, we do not await the Lord as if he were still about to rise; rather, our yearly feast renews the memory of his resurrection. But still, when we celebrate this feast we recall past events in such a way that, by this same vigil, we create a sign of something we do by living in faith. For this whole time, in which this world

[48] Ibid., n. 118; n. 76.
[49] Ibid., n. 113.
[50] Ibid., n. 103.

passes as if in one night, the Church keeps vigil, gazing with the eyes of faith upon the holy Scriptures as if they were lamps in the night, until the Lord comes.[51]

This eschatological dimension is also present in the paschal texts from Asia, at least in *The Epistle of the Apostles.*[52]

4. The process of the expansion of Easter in the course of the fourth century

At the end of the fourth century, due especially to the influence of the community at Jerusalem,[53] the process began by which the events of Easter were historicized, with the various events of the paschal mystery distributed to separate celebrations. This process was not uniform in the various Churches and was slower in the West than in the East.

The process of the expansion of Easter took place in concentric circles that grew ever larger. The original Easter Vigil, preceded by one or more days of fast, spread out, as indicated earlier, into fifty days lived as one joyous and festive day. From the vigil, then, there came the celebration of the Easter Triduum—Friday, Saturday, and Sunday, which were interpreted as a memorial of the death, burial, and resurrection of the Lord respectively. This led to the development of Holy (or Great) Week. Then the fast was lengthened to forty days, and so became Lent, for which we have a clear testimony in the *Epistola festalis* of St. Athanasius in 334. Within the period known as Pentecost there emerged, still in the fourth century, the fiftieth and fortieth days. There also developed an octave of Easter, during which the bishops finished the mystagogy of the neophytes.

In Chapter 8 below we will study the history of these and other developments that little by little gave a structure to the liturgical year within the framework of the Roman liturgy.

[51] Ibid., n. 129.

[52] Ibid., n. 14.

[53] Fundamental in this regard is the witness of the *Itinerarium Egeriae.* See Cantalamessa, *Easter,* nn. 116–116b.

Bibliography

I. THE CELEBRATION OF SUNDAY

AA.VV. *Der Sonntag: Anspruch-Wirklichkeit-Gestalt.* Würzburg-Freiburg/Schweiz, 1986.

AA.VV. *Domenica, il giorno dei giorni.* Atti della XXVIII Settimana Liturgica Nazionale. Rome, 1980.

AA.VV. *La domenica oggi: Problemi e proposte pastorali.* Ed. R. Falsini. Nuova Collana Liturgica, 2nd ser. 9. Milan, 1991.

AA.VV. *Il giorno del Signore.* Assisi, 1988.

Auf der Maur, H. *Feiern im Rhythmus der Zeit* I: *Herrenfeste in Woche und Jahr.* Gottesdienst der Kirche: Handbuch der Liturgiewissenschaft, Teil 5. Regensburg, 1983.

Augé, M. *La domenica festa primordiale dei cristiani.* Universo Teologia 34. Cinisello Balsamo, 1995.

Bianchi, E. *Giorno del Signore, Giorno dell'uomo: Per un rinnovamento della domenica.* Casale Monferrato, 1994.

Brandolini, L. "Domenica," *NDL* 352–368.

Dianich, S. "Per una teologia della domenica." *Vita Monastica* 124–125 (1976) 97–116.

García, J. "Contributions and Challenges to the Theology of Sunday." *Wor* 52 (1978) 369–374.

Jounel, P. *Le dimanche.* Paris, 1990.

Lemmens, L. "Le dimanche à la lumiere des apparitions pascales." *QL* 72 (1991) 177–190.

López Martin, J. "El origen del domingo: Estado actual de la cuestión." *Salmanticensis* 38 (1991) 269–297.

Massi, P. *La domenica nella storia della salvezza: Saggio teologico pastorale.* Historia salutis 4. Naples, 1967.

Mosna, C. S. *Storia della domenica dalle origini fino agli inizi del V secolo: Problema delle origini e sviluppo, culto e riposo, aspetti pastorali e liturgici.* AGreg 170. Rome, 1969.

Rooney, M. "La domenica." *Anàmnesis* 6:67–91.

Rordorf, W. "Origine et signification de la célébration du dimanche dans le christianisme primitif: État actuel de la recherche." *MD* 148 (1981) 103–122.

____. *Sunday: The History of the Day of Rest and Worship in the Earliest Centuries of the Christian Church.* Trans. A.A.K. Graham. Philadelphia, 1968.

____, ed. *Sabbat und Sonntag in der Alten Kirche.* Traditio Christiana 2. Zürich, 1972.

Tillard, J.-M. R. "Le dimanche, jour d'alliance." *Sciences Religieuses* 16 (1964) 225–250.

II. THE ANNUAL CELEBRATION OF EASTER

Auf der Maur, H. *Feiern im Rhythmus der Zeit* I: *Herrenfeste in Woche und Jahr.* Gottesdienst der Kirche: Handbuch der Liturgiewissenschaft, Teil 5. Regensburg, 1983.

Botte, B. "La question pascale: Pâque du vendredi ou Pâque du dimanche?" *MD* 41 (1955) 84–95.

Cabié, R. "A propos de la 'Question Pascale': Quelle pratique opposait-on a celle des Quartodecimans?" *EO* 11 (1994) 101–106.

______. *La Pentecôte: L'évolution de la Cinquantaine pascale au cours des cinq premiers siècles. Bibliotheque de liturgie.* Tournai, 1965.

Cantalamessa, R. *La Pasqua della nostra salvezza: Le tradizioni pasquali della Bibbia e della primitiva Chiesa.* Turin, 1971.

____. *Easter in the Early Church.* Trans. J. Quigley and J. Lienhard. Collegeville, Minn., 1993.

____. *I più antichi testi pasquali della Chiesa: Le omelie di Melitone di Sardi e dell'Anonimo Quartodecimano e altri testi del II secolo.* BEL, Sectio Historica 33. Rome, 1972.

Casel, O. "Art und Sinn der ältesten christlichen Osterfeier." *JLw* 14 (1938) 1–78.

Chupungco, A. *Shaping the Easter Feast.* Washington, 1992.

Haag, H. *Vom alten zum neuen Pascha: Geschichte und Theologie des Osterfestes.* Stuttgarter Bibelstudien 49. Stuttgart, 1971.

Jounel, P. "The Year." In *CP* 4:31–76.

Lemoine, B. "La controverse pascale du deuxième siècle: désacords autour d'une date." *QL* 73 (1992) 223–231.

Mohrmann, C. "Pascha, Passio, Transitus." *Études sur le latin des chrétiens.* Vol. 1, *Le latin des chrétiens,* 205–222. Rome, 1961².

Nocent, A. "Il triduo pasquale e la settimana santa: Il tempo pasquale." *Anàmnesis* 6:93–145.

Talley, J. *The Origins of the Liturgical Year.* 2nd ed. Collegeville, Minn., 1991.

Elena Velkova Velkovska

7

The Liturgical Year in the East

In the ancient Byzantine tradition, as in the Roman one, the temporal organization of a specific liturgical year was assigned to a twofold calendar usually placed at the beginning or end of the biblical lectionaries, the *Praxapostolos* (pericopes from the Acts of the Apostles, the letters of Paul, and later the Catholic Epistles), and the Gospel. Rather than actual calendars, they are two series of tables with the simple list of the *incipit* and *desinit* of the readings for Sundays, feasts, and memorials, that is, of only the liturgical (Eucharistic) days. The table relative to the movable cycle (Easter to Holy Saturday) takes the name of κανωνάριον or συναξάριον, and that relative to the fixed cycle (September 1 to August 31) can be called μηνολόγιον or also συναξάριον. In order to distinguish this last table from the liturgical books of the same name, it has been suggested that they be indicated as menologies and "minor" synaxaria.[1] From the knowledge we have, the oldest copies of such tables do not go back beyond the ninth century.[2]

As the "New Rome," the Church of Byzantium is the only one that follows the Roman calendar of 12 months and 365 days, although the civic New Year, unlike that of Rome and Jerusalem, falls on September 1, the Day of the Indiction, instead of January 1. From here originates the widespread but unfounded opinion that September 1 marks the beginning of the Byzantine liturgical year, which is assigned, rather, to

[1] J. Noret, "Ménologes, Synaxaires, Ménées: Essai de clarification d'une terminologie," *AB* 86 (1968) 21–24.

[2] This is probably the date assigned to the tables of the *Vaticano gr. 2144* (see Μηνολόγιον . . . *sive Kalendarium Ecclesiae Constantinopolitanae* . . ., ed. S. A. Morcelli [Rome, 1788]) and of the *Mosca S. Sinodo gr. 85* (Sergij, *Polnoj mesjaceslov* [Vladimir, 1901] 409–412).

Easter. In accord with Genesis 1:5b, the liturgical day is computed from sunset to sunset.

1. In the Cathedral of Constantinople in the Ninth/Tenth Century

The liturgy of Constantinople, like that of Rome and Jerusalem, is essentially a stational liturgy, linked, that is, not only to the cathedral but to a network of churches, monasteries, and urban shrines connected processionally to each other, and of which, in the span of the year, the dedication or particular feasts and memorials are celebrated. This stational aspect has profoundly marked the make-up of the liturgy of the local Church of Constantinople, the history of its Eucharist, its Liturgy of the Hours, and, above all, its liturgical year.[3]

Given that for now specific studies on the genesis and formation of the liturgical year in Constantinople are not available, we will need to be satisfied with taking a summary view of it as it appears in two witnesses in the book commonly called the τυπικόν of the Great Church, the codices *Patmos 266* and *Jerusalem Hagios Stauros 40*. It is a matter in both cases of a synaxarion or of a compendium with eulogy of the saints arranged according to the order of the calendar. The model of the codex of Patmos would rise again to prominence between the end of the ninth and the beginning of the tenth century, while the codex of Jerusalem is privileged testimony of the edition of the συναξάριον patronized by Constantine VII Porphyrogenitus and appeared at the end of the sixties of the tenth century.[4] In addition to the hagiographic material for every day, the two witnesses of the synaxarion have preserved for us the relative rubric directives also for pre-Lent to the Sunday after Pentecost, and they carry, therefore, an exceptional importance for the study of every aspect of the Byzantine tradition of the cathedral in the tenth century.[5]

a) Pre-Lenten time

Between the series of Sundays after Pentecost and the beginning of Lent, the cathedral τυπικόν envisages a connection of two weeks with three Sundays (Sunday of the Prodigal Son, Meatfare, and Cheesefare).

[3] J. F. Baldovin, *The Urban Character of Christian Worship: The Origins, Development, and Meaning of Stational Liturgy*, OCA 228 (Rome, 1987) 167–226.

[4] For the dating see A. Luzzi, "Il semestre estivo della recensione H* del Sinassario di Costantinopoli," in *Studi sul Sinassario di Costantinopoli*, 5–7 and notes 1–3.

[5] A.Dmitr, 1:1–152, and J. Mateos, *Le Typicon de la Grande Église. Ms. Sainte-Croix N°. 40*, 2 vols., OCA 165–166 (Rome, 1962–1963).

By convention one can call it pre-Lenten time. The readings for the Saturday-Sunday Eucharistic Liturgy, in fact, introduce themes proper to the Lenten journey, such as the Christian meaning of food, examples of conversion (e.g., the prodigal son), and several times the eschatological discourse on Jerusalem (according to Matthew and Luke).[6]

With the following Monday begins the week of lighter fasting, Cheesefare (τοῦ τυροφάγου),[7] so called because consuming dairy products is still permitted. It seems that this distinct period of fast was introduced at the time of the Emperor Heraclius (610–641).[8] Wednesday and Friday are a true anticipation of the typical Lenten day. Let us note, however, that the Saturday-Sunday readings continue the customary pre-Lenten catechesis based on the Christian meaning of food, true prayer, and true fasting, probably because they were prior to the reform of Heraclius.[9] On the Saturday of Cheesefare, attention is drawn besides to a memorial "of the ascetics, of the bishops, and of the martyrs." On the Sunday following, in the stational Church of the Holy Apostles, the memorial "of Archbishop Flavian of Constantinople and Leo of Rome and of the emperor Marcianus and Pulcheria"[10] was celebrated.

b) Lent

The Byzantine legislation on Lent is summed up principally in canon 52 of the Council in Trullo (691/692), which prohibits the celebration of the Eucharistic Liturgy in Lent, except for Saturdays, Sundays, and the feast of the Annunciation. At the same time it reaffirms the daily celebration (Monday–Friday) of the Liturgy of the Presanctified Gifts (τῶν προηγιασμένων Δώρων) or, rather, the reserved Sacrament consecrated in the Eucharistic Liturgy of the preceding Sunday.[11] The "Great

[6] Mateos, *Typicon*, 2:2–3.

[7] Mateos, *Typicon*, 2:4–11.

[8] A. Rahlfs, "Die alttestamentlichen Lektionen der griechischen Kirche," *Mitteilungen des Septuaginta-Unternehmens der K. Gesellschaft der Wissenschaften zu Göttingen* (Berlin, 1909–1915) 1:202–205; cf. J. Herburt, *De ieiunio et abstinentia in ecclesia byzantina ab initiis usque ad saec. XI*, Corona Lateranensis 12 (Rome, 1968) 57–58; T. J. Talley, *The Liturgical Year* (Collegeville, Minn.) 181.

[9] Mateos, *Typicon*, 2: 5-11; the readings are Romans 14:19-23; 16:25-27; 13:11b–14:4; Matthew 6:1-13 and 14-21.

[10] Mateos, *Typicon*, 2:8–9.

[11] P.-P. Joannou, *Discipline generale antique*. Vol. 1, Part 1: *Les canons des conciles oecuméniques (IIe–IXe s.)*, Pontifical Commission for the Redaction of the Code of Eastern Canon Law (Grottaferrata, 1962) 230.

Church" was thus desirous to ensure daily communion in Lent as an integral part of the ascetic path together with fasting, prayers, and good works. If, then, one keeps in mind that at Hagia Sophia even in the Pentecostal period the Eucharistic celebration was not daily in the time under consideration, Lent appears rather as a strongly Eucharistic period.

The typical Lenten day (Monday–Friday) involved three daily synaxes: Matins; a *hora media,* Terce-Sext, celebrated between Terce and Sext (Τριτοέκτη) with a semi-continuous reading of Isaiah; and Vespers with a semi-continuous reading of Genesis and Proverbs joined to the Liturgy of the Presanctified Gifts and lengthened in a partial vigil (παννυχίς). On Saturdays and Sundays (considered as the final day of the week) the customary complete Eucharistic Liturgy was celebrated. The few scheduled hymnody texts insist in general on the value of fasting and penance. The two readings for the Eucharistic Liturgy use the Letter to the Hebrews and preferably the Gospel of Mark.

On the first Saturday of Lent the feast of St. Theodore was celebrated in the church of the same name in the district of Sphoràkios but not in the cathedral, which followed the feast-day cycle. In both places Mark 2:2–3:5, on the freedom to eat and to work even on the Sabbath, was read. It is to be noted that in the Byzantine tradition the Saturdays of Lent are considered holy days.[12] In the cathedral the first Sunday is dedicated to the memory of the prophets Moses, Aaron, and Samuel, the second commemorates St. Polycarp of Smyrna, while the third does not hold a specific commemoration.[13] On the other hand, that which characterizes the second and third Sunday is the invitation—an invitation merely formal at this period— addressed to parents so that they may conduct their children to the pre-baptismal catechesis that began the following Monday. The *Typikon* also informs us that from Tuesday to Friday a veneration of the cross took place, without furnishing further precise information.[14] Beginning with the fourth Sunday we note that the varying commemorations linked to determined shrines do not involve proper hymnody elements, while the readings are concentrated on the preparation of the catechumens for baptism.[15]

[12] Mateos, *Typicon,* 2:19–21.

[13] Mateos, *Typicon,* 2:21–23, 30–31, 38–39.

[14] Mateos, *Typicon,* 2:40–45.

[15] Mark 9:17-31 for the fourth Sunday and Mark 10:32-45 for the fifth Sunday (Mateos, *Typicon,* 2:46–47, 56–57).

One such item of interest gives probable evidence also for the Byzantine tradition of an older Lenten season of only three weeks.[16]

Characteristic of the fifth Saturday is the celebration that took place in the Marian shrine of Blachernai in thanksgiving for liberation from the invasion of the Persians and the Avars in 626. On that occasion the celebrated Akathist hymn was sung.[17] The last week of Lent, called "Palm Week," is concluded with the Sunday of the same name, introduced by the "Saturday of Lazarus," a type (τύπος) of the resurrection of Christ and for this reason assigned to the Christian initiation. Characteristic of Palm Sunday was the procession, conducted in an informal way and therefore without any special blessing of the branches.[18]

c) Holy Week

The κανωνάριον of the Byzantine cathedral did not know the Western technical term "Sacred Triduum" or "Easter Triduum" but spoke of a "holy and great" Monday, Tuesday, etc., until the "holy and great Sunday" of the Resurrection. Nevertheless, from the historical facts we see that the notion of "Triduum" is not altogether foreign to the older Byzantine tradition, for some lectionaries of the ninth century relate only the scriptural passages assigned to the celebrations of Thursday, Friday, and Saturday. Monday, Tuesday, and Wednesday do not differ in any way from an ordinary ferial day of Lent except for the presence of a Gospel passage read during the Liturgy of the Presanctified Gifts and the readings of Terce-Sext and Vespers.[19]

At sunset on Holy Thursday the vigil Liturgy introduced by Vespers takes place. This is followed by the washing of the feet with relevant readings (John 13:1[3]-11 and 12-17), the two Old Testament readings proper to Vespers of Lent, and the three readings of the Eucharistic Liturgy, in the course of which, as in the Roman Rite, the patriarch consecrates the oil of chrism (μύρον). The gospel narrates all the happenings of the day by creating a long passage composed of Matthew 26:1-20; John 13:1-17; Matthew 26:21-39; Luke 22:43-44; Matthew

[16] M. E. Johnson, "From Three Weeks to Forty Days: Baptismal Preparation and the Origins of Lent," M. E. Johnson, ed., *Living Water, Sealing Spirit: Readings on Christian Initiation* (Collegeville, Minn., 1995) 118–136 (already published in *SL* 20 [1990] 185–200).

[17] Mateos, *Typicon,* 2:52–55.

[18] Mateos, *Typicon,* 2:62–67.

[19] Ezekiel at the *hora media,* Exodus and Job at Vespers (Mateos, *Typicon,* 2:66–73).

26:40–27:2. In this composite there appears the narration, already read, of the washing of the feet, a sign that in the period prior to the ninth century the dramatic ritual of the washing had not yet been adopted.[20] It originates from Jerusalem, as do the twelve passages of the Passion read during the vigil following Vespers on Holy Thursday.[21]

Good Friday does not substantially differ from any other Friday of Lent, except for the veneration of the relic of the lance and the catechesis that the patriarch held for the candidates for baptism in the Church of Peace. As on Holy Thursday, a long composite passage (Matt 27:1-38; Luke 23:39-43; Matt 27:39-54; John 19:31-37; Matt 27:55-61) of the Passion that resumes the narration introduced on Thursday is read during Vespers.[22] At the end of the Matins of Saturday, a Liturgy of the Word, already of Easter intonation (Ezek 37:1-14; 1 Cor 5:6-8; Gal 3:13-14), presents the recounting of the burial (Matt 27:62-66), which is followed by the first shift of the baptized.[23]

The solemn Easter Vigil is not a nocturnal vigil in the Byzantine tradition but, as on Holy Thursday, a partial vigil that begins at sunset with Vespers, identical in the psalmody to any other Saturday of the year. A celebration of the Word follows with seven or more readings from the Old Testament, while in the baptistry the patriarch confers the Christian initiation on the candidates for baptism. At the end of this he solemnly enters the cathedral with the neophytes in white garments to preside at the Eucharistic vigil Liturgy.[24] The Matins, Liturgy, and Vespers of Easter do not differ in structure from their more common Sunday version during the year. So it can be said that on the celebrational plane Sunday was truly presented as a weekly Easter.[25]

d) The paschal Pentecost

Characteristic of the Pentecostal period is the daily celebration of the Eucharistic Liturgy with a semi-continuous reading of the Acts of the Apostles and the Gospel of John. The first week, a true and proper "octave"—the only one noted in the κανωνάριον of Constantinople—is

[20] Mateos, *Typicon*, 2:72–77.

[21] Mateos, *Typicon*, 2:76–79; S. Janeras, *Le Vendredi-saint dans la tradition liturgique byzantine: Structure et histoire de ses offices*, AL 13 = SA 99 (Rome, 1988) 109–113.

[22] Mateos, *Typicon*, 2:78–83; Janeras, *Vendredi-saint*, 290–291, 307–315, 374–379.

[23] Mateos, *Typicon*, 2:82–85.

[24] Mateos, *Typicon*, 2:84–91; G. Bertoniere, *The Historical Development of the Easter Vigil and Related Services in the Greek Church*, OCA 193 (Rome, 1972) 113–139.

[25] Mateos, *Typicon*, 2:92–97; Bertoniere, *Easter Vigil*, 140–153.

called "of the renewal" (τῆς διακαινησίμου)[26] and entails the stational celebration in the shrines dedicated to the apostles, to the Mother of God, to St. Stephen and St. John the Evangelist and his brother James, to SS. Peter and Paul, and to St. John the Baptist. The second Sunday of Easter that concludes the "octave" (Ἀντίπασχα) is dedicated, as in all Christian traditions, to the memory of the appearance to Thomas.[27]

The third Sunday commemorates the faithful Joseph of Arimathea, Mary Magdalen, and the other disciples of the Lord, who from the sadness of Holy Saturday are in this way linked to the joy of the resurrection. The Gospel passage (Mark 15:43–16:8) sets forth again the scene of the deposition from the cross to the empty tomb, that is to say, the entire paschal mystery. The following three Sundays present instead the episodes of the paralytic (John 5:1-15), of the Samaritan (John 4:5-42), and of the man born blind (John 9:1-38), traditionally used for the post-baptismal mystagogy.[28] Twenty-five days after Easter we have the exclusively Eastern feast of "Midpentecost," based on John 7:14-30,[29] and on the fortieth day the solemnity of the Ascension.[30] The seventh Sunday provides instead for the commemoration of the Fathers of the Council of Nicea, which the subsequent codex of Jerusalem extends to the first six councils.[31]

The eighth Sunday after Easter is the solemnity of Pentecost, with the vigil after Vespers and the conferring of baptism right after Matins. The narrative of the descent of the Holy Spirit is left to the epistle (Acts 2:1-11), and the gospel alludes to "the Spirit, which believers in [Jesus] were to receive" (John 7:37-53). No mention is made of the cathedral at the characteristic rite of the Genuflection (γονυκλισία) that took place during the second Vespers of Pentecost, when the use of the prayer while kneeling was taken up again on ferial days, a custom forbidden for all of paschal time.[32]

[26] Theodore the Studite, *Letters:* PG 99:1700c.

[27] Mateos, *Typicon,* 2:108–109. The term *Antipascha* was known to Abbot Leontius (ninth century), *Vita di Gregorio di Agrigento,* 15 (PG 98:576A) and 18 (PG 98:580C); John Damascene, *Carmen in dominicam Antipaschatis:* PG 96).

[28] Mateos, *Typicon,* 2:114–171, 118–119, 122–123, 124–125.

[29] H. R. Drobner, "Die Festpredigten der Mesopentecoste in der Alten Kirche," *Richerche patristiche in onore di Dom Basil Studer, O.S.B.,* Augustinianum 33 (Rome, 1993) 137–170.

[30] Mateos, *Typicon,* 2:120–121 and 126–129.

[31] Mateos, *Typicon,* 2:130–133 and Apparatus.

[32] Mateos, *Typicon,* 2:136–139.

e) Time after Pentecost

Originally there were two distinct periods: one from the Monday after Pentecost to the Sunday following the Exaltation of the Cross (September 14) close to the autumnal equinox and the ancient civic New Year, and a second period that extended from that date until the beginning of Lent. In the first period the Saturday-Sunday Gospel passages for the Eucharistic Liturgy were from Matthew and the second from Luke. In all, the time after Pentecost comprised thirty-four weeks—or even less depending on the date of Easter—up to the Saturday that precedes the Sunday of the Prodigal Son.[33] The first Sunday after Pentecost is the feast of All the Holy Martyrs. It should be noted that the same seasonal periods beginning from the feast of the Exaltation of the Cross are also present in the West Syrian tradition and are a sign of great antiquity.

f) Fixed cycle

The *Typikon* of the Great Church does not possess a terminology to indicate the rank of the feasts. The designation of the level of the feasts varies in the post-patristic period. John of Euboia (c. 744) considers some of them "highlighted" (εὔσημοι),[34] and before him Pseudo-Athanasius (seventh/eighth century) speaks of the feasts of the Lord (δεσποτικαὶ ἑοριααὶ),[35] a practice followed by Andrew of Crete († 740)[36] and Theodore the Studite.[37] Leo Tuscus of Pisa (a. 1173/1174) speaks instead of *magna festivitas*,[38] and a text published by Cardinal Pitra distinguishes between "great, little, and middle" feasts.[39]

As in the West, the fixed cycle begins with the civic New Year, which in ancient Byzantium was not on January 1, as for example in Jerusalem, but on September 1, and was inaugurated with a solemn propitiatory stational procession.[40] The *Typikon* of the cathedral did not

[33] Mateos, *Typicon*, 2:141–167.

[34] *Sermo in conceptionem s. Deiparae*, 10: PG 96:1473C–1476A and 1497B).

[35] PG 28:917B.

[36] *Homilia in s. Georgium:* PG 97:1172A.

[37] *Parvae Catecheseis*, 64, ed. G. Cozza Luzi, in *Nova Patrum Bibliotheca* 10, 1 (Rome, 1905) 52, and *Constitutio Monasterii Studii:* PG 99:1704D.

[38] A. Jacob, "La traduction de la Liturgie de saint Jean Chrysostome par Leon Toscan. Edition critique," OCP 32 (1966) 156; for the dating: M. Coll I Alentorn, "Un Català promotor de la traducció de la Litùrgia de sant Joan Crisòstom," *Miscellania liturgica catalana* (Barcelona, 1978) 49–52.

[39] *Spicilegium Solesmense* (Paris, 1858) 4:555.

[40] P. Schreiner, "Historisches und Liturgisches zum Byzantinischen Neujahr," *Rivista di Studi Bizantini e Slavi* 2 (1982) 13–23.

recognize a rigid system of classification of the feasts into particular categories, but from the data at our disposal we are at least able to determine an order of the principal feasts on the basis of the liturgical importance accorded to them.

In the first place are the feasts of the Exaltation of the Cross (September 14), Christmas (December 25), and the Theophany (January 6). These are preceded and followed by a Saturday and a Sunday dedicated to them and with proper passages for the Eucharistic Liturgy, without, however, the weeks included in them being understood as a period of preparation or an "octave." Of these three feasts, only Christmas and the Theophany had a solemn vigil with Vespers, seven or more biblical readings, an evening Eucharist and παννυχίς. For the Exaltation of the Cross a partial vigil of only three readings without the evening Eucharist was scheduled as it was for the feasts of the second type: the Birth of the Theotokos (September 8), the anniversary of the Dedication of the Churches of Chalkoprateia and Hagia Sophia (December 18 and 23), the feast of the Annunciation (March 25), the anniversary of the founding of Constantinople (May 11), the feast of the Apostles Peter and Paul (June 29), the remembrance of the Fathers of the Council of Chalcedon (July 16), the Transfiguration (August 6), and the μετάστασις of the Mother of God (August 15).[41]

For a third type of feast the vigil element is restricted to only three readings of Vespers. These feasts are the Entrance into the Temple of the Theotokos (November 21), the Apostle Andrew (November 30), and John the Baptist (June 24). One notices as in Constantinople in the ninth century that the feast of the Apostle Andrew did not yet have a particular liturgical relevance, and the Cathedral of Hagia Sophia does not present him either as a protector or founder of the episcopal see on the Bosporus.[42]

Some specific particularities of the Constantinople calendar merit mention. On different occasions certain memorials are transferred to the nearest Sunday,[43] and on the day following a feast is celebrated commemorating those figures associated with the transferred memorial. So on the day after the Birth of the Theotokos, the feast of St. Joachim and St. Ann is celebrated (September 9); in like manner, on

[41] Mateos, *Typicon*, 1.

[42] Mateos, *Typicon*, 1.

[43] For example: October 3, Dionysius the Areopagite; November 14, Justinian and Theodora.

December 26, the Mother of God; January 7, St. John the Baptist; February 3, Simeon; and March 26, the Archangel Gabriel.

A unique and extremely interesting aspect of the liturgical year in ancient Byzantium is the importance accorded to the commemoration of natural calamities and events of war, understanding them as a time for offering thanksgiving to God for their end or for having escaped danger.[44] Generally on such days a processional with a stational Liturgy took place, often with the participation of the patriarch or emperor.

2. In the Monastic Traditions Between the Ninth and Tenth centuries

It is well known that after the second period of iconoclasm (843) the cenobites of Studium organized in Constantinople a liturgical system blending the solemn Liturgy of the Hours of the cathedral with the more temperate hourly prayer of the monks of Palestine, their land of origin. The Studites developed the role of liturgical poetry and in particular the hymn canon. The vast production was then collected into special anthologies assigned to the same number of days/periods and liturgical cycles. Thus was born the ῾Οκτώηχος and the Μηνάια for the weekly and annual cycle, and the Τριώδιον and Πεντηκοστάριον for Lent and Eastertime.[45] We see now the principal differences that the Studite monastic rite involves in respect to that of the cathedral, basing ourselves principally on the τυπικά of the monastery of San Salvatore of Messina (after 1165) and of Theotokos Evergetis of Constantinople (twelfth century?).[46]

a) Pre-Lenten time

Pre-Lent comprises not three but four Sundays and begins with that called "the Sunday of the Pharisee and the Publican," from the scrip-

[44] For example: October 26, November 6, December 14, January 26, June 5 and 25, August 7 and 16, etc. See Baldovin, *The Urban Character of Christian Worship*, Appendix, p. 300.

[45] See R. F. Taft, *The Byzantine Rite: A Short History* (Collegeville, Minn., 1992) 52–66 (with bibliography).

[46] M. Arranz, ed., *Le Typicon du monastère du Saint-Sauveur à Messine. Codex Messinensis gr. 115, A.D. 1131*, OCA 185 (Rome, 1969) and A.Dmitr, 1:256–610. On the dating discussed, of both the sources, see respectively M. Re, *Il copista, la datazione e la genesi del* Messan. Gr. 115 (Typicon *di Messina*) Bollettino della Badia Greca di Grottaferrata, n.s. 44 (1990) 145–156, and P. Gautier, "Le Typikon de la Théotokos Evergétis," *REB* 40 (1982) 12–13.

tural passage of the day (Luke 18:10-14), which the hymn canon of Matins, composed by the Studite abbot George (eleventh century), exalts as a model of humility. Meatfare Saturday is dedicated to the commemoration of the deceased "fathers and brothers" (i.e., monks), and the memorial of "our holy ascetic fathers" is celebrated on Cheesefare Saturday. The monastic mark taken from the liturgical year is evident.[47]

b) Lent

For the first Saturday the Studite revision of the liturgical year retains the memorial of St. Theodore, which in its origin was tied to a particular stational church and was not celebrated in the cathedral. The following Sunday, the first of Lent, begins to be called "Sunday of Orthodoxy," a yearly commemoration of the reestablishment of the veneration of the icons.[48] The third Sunday is dedicated to the veneration of the cross, which in the cathedral ritual took place during the fourth week. Recently it has been suggested that this veneration would have referred to the return to Jerusalem of the relic of the Cross by Heraclius, which occurred in the first days of March in 630 during the fourth week of Lent.[49]

The second, fourth, and fifth Sundays do not involve special commemorations, but an examination of the hymnody assigned to them reveals a situation truly unique. While on the pre-Lenten Sundays the hymn canon of Matins comments lyrically on the Gospel passage of the day, on these three Sundays of Lent the hymn canons refer to Gospel excerpts different from those read during the Eucharistic Liturgy. To be precise, the theme of the hymnody for the second Sunday is the parable of the prodigal son (Luke 15:11-32); for the fourth Sunday, the parable of the Samaritan (Luke 10:30-37); and for the fifth Sunday, the parable of the rich man and Lazarus (Luke 16:19-31), while the respective gospels are Mark 2:1-12 for the second Sunday, Mark 9:17-31 for the fourth Sunday, and Mark 10:32-45 for the fifth Sunday. The thematic splitting finds an explanation from the fact that on these Sundays the hymnody canon comments on the Gospel passages assigned them in the lectionary of Jerusalem. Thus a sort of

[47] Arranz, *Le Typicon du Saint-Sauveur;* A.Dmitr, 1:499–512.

[48] J. Gouillard, *Le Synodikon de l'Orthodoxie: Edition et commentaire,* Travaux e memoires 2 (Paris, 1967).

[49] Janeras, *Vendredi-saint,* 298–299.

simultaneous bi-ritualism is set up in which the Eucharist remained bound to the lectionary of Constantinople, and the Liturgy of the Hours to themes suggested by the lectionary of Jerusalem.[50]

Proper to the Thursday of the fifth week is a very long penitential hymn canon attributed to Andrew of Crete (c. 660–740),[51] while the date assigned to the Akathist hymn varies according to place.[52] Lent concludes with the commemoration of the resurrection of Lazarus on the sixth Saturday.

c) Holy Week

As in the cathedral, Palm Sunday involves a commemorative procession, and the first three days of Holy Week completely follow the common Lenten model. On Holy Thursday occurs the ritual of the washing of the feet, which, according to local traditions, took place before or after the Liturgy or even after supper.[53] On Thursday night the twelve passages of the Passion originating from Jerusalem are read in the course of Matins. The Hours of Prime, Terce, Sext and None acquire then a particular importance from the monastic reinterpretation of ceremonies proper to Jerusalem.[54] Vespers of Good Friday lacks the Liturgy of the Presanctified Gifts as the Easter Vigil loses any tie with Christian initiation. The accent of the Easter celebration is moved thus to Matins, sung at the first light of dawn on Sunday. This new way of celebrating Easter expresses also a different theology of the feast. The remembrance perspective is clouded, and the celebration, being in hymnody, becomes almost an experience of a meeting with the Risen One.[55]

[50] See S. Janeras, "L'antico 'Ordo' agiopolita di Quaresima conservato nelle preghiere italo-greche del ambone," *EO* 5 (1988) 77–87, and G. Bertoniere, *The Sundays of Lent in the Triodion: The Sundays Without a Commemoration,* OCA 253 (Rome, 1997).

[51] Arranz, *Le Typicon du Saint-Sauveur,* 222–223; A.Dmitr, 1:535–536.

[52] It is set on the fifth Saturday in the *Typikon* of Evergetis (A.Dmitr, 1:537), on the Saturday before the Annunciation in the *Typikon* of Casole (Torino gr. C III 7, a. 1173, f. 114r), and on March 20 in that of Messina (Arranz, *Le Typicon du Saint-Sauveur,* 223–224).

[53] Arranz, *Le Typicon du Saint-Sauveur,* 234–235; A.Dmitr, 1:547–549 (before the Liturgy); Iena, Universitätsbibliothek, G. B. q. 6a (τυπικόν of the Patir of Rossano, 13th cent.) = *Grottaferrata G. a. 29,* f. 94v-95r (after the Liturgy); *Grottaferrata G. a. 1* (Typikòn of the Theotokos of Grottaferrata, a. 1299/1300), 127v–128v (after supper).

[54] Janeras, *Vendredi-saint,* passim.

[55] Janeras, *Vendredi-saint;* Bertoniere, *Easter Vigil;* and more generally, Taft, "In the Bridegroom's Absence: The Paschal Triduum in the Byzantine Church," in *La cele-*

d) The paschal Pentecost

In comparison with Lent, the Studite organization of the Pentecost period remains very close to the cathedral model: there is no splitting of themes on the Sundays, and the hymnody reflects the Gospel passages presented by the Byzantine lectionary. Nevertheless, some important modifications can be noted: (a) the Sunday hymn theme also dominates the following week, laying the basis for the creation of a series of "octaves" of a variable number of days, as if the Sundays were the same as thematic feasts (St. Thomas, the Ointment-Bearers, the Samaritan, etc.);[56] (b) the Ascension appears as a feast by now independent as much from Easter as from Pentecost, given that paschal time is understood to be concluded at the vigil of the Ascension and the Sunday of Pentecost acquires an octave.[57] Like Meatfare Saturday, the Saturday preceding Pentecost is tied to the commemoration of deceased brethren.

e) Weekly cycle

Beside the *proprium* hymnody for principal times, the Studites elaborated a ferial service of them structured around a cycle of daily commemorations in a weekly rhythm. In practice, each day resulted in being "dedicated" to one or more saints, rather like that which occurs today in the Roman Church, in which is preserved the medieval memorial, rendered optional however, of Sancta Maria in Sabbato. The elaboration of the cycle is rightly attributed to the hymnodists Joseph and Theophane (ninth century), but evidences of them are discernible in the Palestinian Sinai Book of Hours gr. 863, a manuscript dated to the ninth century but could go back to a more ancient period. Mondays and Tuesdays are considered penitential, Wednesdays and Fridays are dedicated to the Cross, Thursdays to the Mother of God, and Saturdays to the martyrs.[58] The later Syriac Book of Hours alternatively presents

brazione del Triduo Pasquale: Anamnesis e mimesis. Atti del III Congresso Internazionale di Liturgia, Rome, May 9–13, 1988, AL 14 = SA 102 (Rome, 1990) passim, and "A Tale of Two Cities: The Byzantine Holy Week Triduum as a Paradigm of Liturgical History," in J. Neil Alexander, ed., *Time and Community: In Honor of Thomas Julian Talley* (Washington, 1990) passim.

[56] For example, Arranz, *Le Typicon du Saint-Sauveur,* 258–260; A.Dmitr, 1:568–569.

[57] Arranz, *Le Typicon du Saint-Sauveur,* 283–284; A.Dmitr, 1:596–600.

[58] Mateos, "Un Horologion de Saint-Sabas: Le codex sinaitique grec 863 (IXe siècle)," *Mélanges Eugène Tisserant,* ST 233 (Vatican City, 1964) 3:49–54.

Tuesdays in honor of the Baptist, Thursdays of the apostles, and Saturdays honoring the dead as well as the martyrs.[59] The manuscript tradition of the hymn books registers other variants to this series that, however, in the tenth century appears stabilized, although not in details.[60] On the other hand, the hypothesis cannot be granted that the series of daily commemorations springs from the commentary to the *Hexameron* of Anastasius the Sinaite (seventh century) because the work is at least four centuries later than Anastasius.[61]

f) Fixed cycle

The fixed cycle is less touched by the reform. In practice, the calendar of Constantinople is maintained with some local memorials and is pruned by this time of any reference to, and implication of, the stational Liturgy proper to the cathedral. The principal feasts acquire a day of preparation (προεόρτιον) and a post-feast period (μεθέορτον) of three to eight days duration, on the last of which occurs the so-called "restitution" of the feast (ἀπόδοσις). But to say it as English-speaking people do, the liturgical year is made up not only of "feasts" but also of "fasts" that in the monastic calendar come to acquire liturgical importance, leaving a mark on the structure of the Office of the day.[62] Besides the Lenten fast itself there is a pre-Christmas fast also of forty days (November 15 to December 24), a movable one in preparation for the feast of the Apostles Peter and Paul (from the second Monday after Pentecost to June 28), and a fixed one (August 1 to 14) in preparation for the feast of the Dormition of the Theotokos. Then come the fasts considered penitential: on August 29 (the martyrdom of John the Baptist) and on September 14 (the Exaltation of the Cross), even if the latter falls on a Saturday or a Sunday. The vigils of Christmas and the Theophany acquire a solemn celebration of the Hours of Prime,

[59] M. Black, *A Christian Palestinian Syriac Horologion (Berlin MS.Or. Oct. 1019)*, Cambridge, 1954, 85–86 (Ordinary of Vespers) and 103–143 (hymnographic anthology).

[60] Ch. Hannick, *Le texte de l'Oktoechos*, in *Dimanche: Office selon les huit tons* 'Οκτώηξος, La Prière des Eglises de rite byzantin 3 (Chevetogne, 1972) 39–40 and 54.

[61] This was the hypothesis of A. Grabar, "L'iconographie du dimanche principalement à Byzance," in AA.VV., *Le Dimanche*, LO 39 (Paris, 1965) 169–184; however, see *CPG* 7770.

[62] The fasts are fixed in *Regesta*, 985 (a. 1107 ca.); see *Les Regestes des actes du Patriarcat de Constantinople*, fasc. 3: V. Grumel, *Les Regestes de 1043 à 1206* (Paris, 1947) 70–72.

Terce, Sext, and None in imitation of Good Friday, while between these two feasts is delineated a special liturgical period of twelve days (δωδεκαήμερος).[63]

In the Eastern ambience (Sinai and Palestine), where the liturgical Regulation of the lavra of St. Sabas is the custom, strong discrepancies with respect to the Studite Regulation are not noted in the calendar of feasts and commemorations. The tendency is underlined, however, of applying the most festive setting possible of the "octaves" not only to the feasts and fixed memorials but also in paschal time. The Sunday of the Paralytic is extended by three days, and the Office of Midpentecost is sung for another eight. The ἀκολουθία of the Samaritan is sung on Sunday and on the following Thursday, Friday, and Saturday, while on Monday, Tuesday, and Wednesday that of Midpentecost is sung. The ἀκολουθία of the man born blind is sung until Tuesday morning, and on the Saturday after Pentecost all the ἀκολουθία of the feast is repeated.[64] The singing of the Easter troparion is explicitly given up on Wednesday morning.[65]

The numerous post-feasts, octaves, and restitutions in concentric circles have practically destroyed the unity of the Easter-Pentecost time, broken by now into so many separate celebrations: Easter, the Sundays, Ascension, Pentecost. We are now far from the idea of Pentecost as the unitary feast of fifty days duration of seven weeks (7 x 7 + 1) and the symbolic season of the new times inaugurated by the paschal victory of Christ begun in the resurrection and continued in the mysteries of the ascension, the seating at the right hand of the Father, and the descent of the Holy Spirit. This unity, as we have seen, was still well expressed in the *Typikon* of the cathedral in the ninth and tenth centuries.

3. *From the Fourteenth Century to Our Time*

With the progressive dying out of the cathedral tradition after 1204, the Byzantine liturgical year came to correspond in fact to that expressed in the Jerusalem *Typikon* of St. Sabas. Its history, nevertheless, cannot yet be said to be concluded. In the course of the late Middle Ages the Sundays of Lent, remaining so to speak "free," have received many commemorations of monastic character. The fourth Sunday is linked

[63] For example, in the Apostolos *Gerusalemme, S. Saba 266* (11th/12th cent.), f. 132r.
[64] *Gerusalemme S. Saba 312* (a. 1201) *Typikon*, ff. 119r–123r.
[65] Ibid., f. 166r, *Sinai gr. 1095* (13th cent.), f. 142v and *Sinai gr. 1097* (a. 1214), f. 60r.

to the memory of St. John Climacus and the fifth to St. Mary the Egyptian. Meanwhile the feast of Orthodoxy, established on the first Sunday to commemorate the restoration of the cult of the icons, was transformed ever more, at least in the Greek ambience, into a sort of confessional celebration, becoming *de facto* the feast of the Orthodox Church and its faith. In 1368, on the second Sunday, almost as a prolongation of the themes of the first, is assigned the memory of St. Gregory Palamas, the strenuous defender of hesychast doctrine canonized by his disciple Philotheos Kokkinos. Only the surviving Byzantine churches of southern Italy and the monasteries called "Basilian" will continue to follow the more sober Studite liturgical year. In the monastery of Grottaferrata (Rome) this is the practice even in our time.[66]

The Easter Triduum always accents more the dramatic character of the celebrations, developing in a late period a series of mimetic rites such as the elevation of the cross from which Christ is unnailed and placed in the shroud, and a funeral procession with the winding sheet at the end of Matins of Holy Saturday. This is the ritual of Holy Week —actually of the entire liturgical year—which without doubt calls back to the Church the largest number of faithful. But the greatest modification to which the ritual of Holy Week has been subjected consists in the systematic inversion of the Hours for which today the ὄρθρος, or Matins (Vigil–Lauds), is on those days anticipated on the preceding evening, and all the Little Vesper and post–Little Vesper celebrations, included in the Easter Vigil, are celebrated in the morning.[67]

The feasts come to be thus organized: twelve great feasts, of which nine are of the Lord: Exaltation of the Cross (September 14), Christmas (December 25), the Theophany (January 6), the Encounter in the Temple (February 2), the Annunciation (March 25), Palm Sunday, the Ascension, Pentecost, and the Transfiguration (August 6); and three of the Theotokos: the Nativity (September 8), Entrance into the Temple (November 21), and the Dormition (August 15). Easter, inasmuch as it is the "feast of feasts," is considered separately. The remaining feasts and memorials are divided into:

[66] See Νέον Ἀνθολόγιον πληρέστατον τε καὶ ἀκριβέστατον, Rome, 1598 (tradition of Salento) and Ὡρολόγιον σὺν Θεῷ κατὰ τὴν ἔκπαλαι τάξιν οὐ μὴν ἀλλὰ καὶ Τυπικὸν τοῦ τῆς κρυπτοφέρρης μοναστηρίου, Rome, 1677 (monastic tradition).

[67] A good synthesis can be found in Taft, "In the Bridegroom's Absence," and "A Tale of Two Cities," passim.

a) ordinary feasts of the first category with nocturnal vigil (ἀγρυπνία—where it is the practice), feast psalmody, and Gospel passages in Matins. Belonging to this category are the feasts of St. John the Evangelist (September 26 and May 8), St. John Chrysostom (November 13), St. Nicholas (December 6), the Three Magi (January 30), St. George (April 23), SS. Peter and Paul (June 29), the birth and martyrdom of St. John the Baptist (June 24 and August 29), and the feast of the title of the church;

b) ordinary feasts of the second category (feasts of the Mother of God, of the angels, and of the apostles);

c) minor feasts of the first category (local saints);

d) minor feasts of the second category;

e) days of simple commemorations (Lenten days).

With the correction of the calendar promoted in 1580 by Pope Gregory XIII and its increasing adoption in all the countries of Western Europe, there exists today a difference with respect to the Julian calendar of thirteen days, a difference inexorably destined to increase. In the course of our century a number of Orthodox Churches have in turn adopted the Gregorian calendar, limited to the fixed cycle, while they use the Julian reckoning in order to calculate the date of Easter. The Julian calendar for the feasts of the fixed cycle is today followed by the Churches of Russia and Serbia and at Mount Athos as well as by the Ukrainian Catholic Church. The adoption in Greece of the Gregorian calendar (1924) provoked the schism of the "Old Calendarists."

Finally, in matters that concern the Eastern Catholic Churches, including themes of the liturgical year, we need to take into account a progressive departure from the common Byzantine calendar by means of the adoption of the solemnities, feasts, and memorials proper to the Roman calendar, such as Corpus Christi, the Sacred Heart (called "Christ the Philanthropist"), and Christ the King.[68] Therefore, those feasts that have actually been adopted celebrate an idea or a devotion which the Western Roman Church itself holds less liturgical and which in any case is totally extraneous to the whole of Byzantine spirituality.[69] In the same way, the veto imposed in the past by the Roman

[68] S. Parenti, "Una *Diataxis* italo-greca inedita del XIV secolo per la solennità del 'Corpus Domini,'" *EphLit* 108 (1994) 440–455.

[69] Congregation for the Eastern Churches, *Instruction for Applying the Liturgical Prescriptions of the Code of Canons of the Eastern Churches* (Vatican City, 1996).

authority to celebrate the memory of St. Gregory Palamas has caused some Churches to institute in its place a "feast of the holy relics."[70]

[70] *Liturgicon Missel byzantin a l'usage des fidéles* (Beirut, 1960) 93–97.

Bibliography

I. GENERAL

Janeras, S. *Bibliografia sulle Liturgie Orientali 1961–1967.* Rome, 1969.

Sauget, J.-M. *Bibliographie des Liturgies Orientales 1900–1960.* Rome, 1962.

II. TEXTS

A.Dmitr, 1 and 3.

Analecta hymnica Graeca e codicibus eruta Italiae inferioris, 1. *Schirò consilio et ductu edita,* 1–13. Rome, 1966–1983.

Arranz, M. *Le Typicon du monastère du Saint-Sauveur à Messine. Codex Messinensis gr. 115, A.D. 1131.* OCA 185. Rome, 1969.

Delehaye, H. *Synaxarium Ecclesiae Constantinopolitanae e codice Sirmondiano, adiectis synaxariis selectis.* Brussels, 1902. Propylaeum ad *Acta Sanctorum Novembris.*

Follieri, E. *I calendari in metro innografico di Cristoforo Mitilineo.* 2 vols. Subsidia hagiographica 63. Brussels, 1980.

Garitte, G. *Le calendrier palestino géorgien du Sinaiticus 34 (Xe s.).* Subsidia hagiographica 30. Brussels, 1958.

Mateos, J. *Le Typikon de la Grande Eglise. Ms. Sainte-Croix no. 40,* 1–2. OCA 165–166. Rome, 1962–1963.

Nilles, N. *Kalendarium Manuale utriusque Ecclesiae Orientalis et Occidentalis.* 2 vols. Oeniponte, 1896–1897.

Renoux, M. A. *Le codex arménien Jérusalem 121.* Vol. 2: *Edition comparée du texte et de deux autres manuscrits. PatOr* 36. Turnhout, 1971.

Tarchnisvili, M., ed. *Le grand lectionnaire de l'Eglise de Jérusalem (V^e–VIIIe siècle).* CSCO 188–189 and 204–205; Scriptores Iberici, 9–10 and 13–14. Louvain, 1959–1960.

III. STUDIES

AA.VV. *Le Dimanche.* LO 39. Paris, 1965.

Andronikov, C. *Il senso delle feste.* 2 vols. Rome, 1973.

____. *Il senso della Pasqua nella liturgia bizantina.* 2 vols. Liturgia e vita 6–7. Turin, 1986.

Arranz, M. *«Les fêtes théologiques» du calendrier byzantin.* In *La Liturgie expression de la foi,* 29–55. BELS 16. Rome, 1979.

Bertoniere, G. *The Historical Development of the Easter Vigil and Related Services in the Greek Church.* OCA 193. Rome, 1972.

Cabié, R. *La Pentecôte: L'évolution de la Cinquantaine pascale au cours des cinq premiers siècles.* Bibliothèque de liturgie. Tournai, 1965.

Dalmais, I.-H. "Le Dimanche dans la liturgie byzantine." *MD* 46 (1956) 60–66.

Donadeo, Sr. M. *L'anno liturgico bizantino.* Brescia, 1991.

Grumel, V. "Sur l'ancienneté de la fête de la Transfiguration." *REB* 14 (1956) 209–210.

____. "Le typicon de la Grande Eglise d'après le manuscrit de Saint Croix. Datation et origine." *AB* 85 (1967) 45–57.

Janeras, S. *Le Vendredi-saint dans la tradition liturgique byzantine: Structure et histoire de ses offices.* AL 13 = SA 99. Rome, 1988.

Kniazeff, A. "La lecture de l'Ancien et du Nouveau Testament dans le rite byzantin." In *La prière des Heures,* 201–251. LO 35. Paris, 1963.

Labate, A. *Cinque inni bizantini inediti per le solemnità della Pasqua.* Messina, 1980.

Luzzi, A. *Studi sul Sinassario di Costantinopoli.* Testi e studi bizantino-neoellenici 8. Rome, 1995.

Maxim, V. *De festis Conciliorum Oecumenicorum in Ecclesia Byzantina.* Grottaferrata, 1942.

Mosna, C. S. *Storia della domenica dalle origini fino agli inizi del V secolo.* Rome, 1969.

Regan, P. "The Fifty Days and the Fiftieth Day." *Wor* 55 (1981) 194–218.

Rordorf, W. *Sunday: The History of the Day of Rest and Worship in the Earliest Centuries of the Christian Church.* Trans. A.A.K. Graham. Philadelphia, 1968.

Salaville, S. "La fête du Concile de Nicée et les fêtes des Conciles dans le rite byzantin," *Echos d'Orient* 24 (1925) 445–470.

____. "La formation du calendrier liturgique byzantin d'après les recherches critiques de Mgr Ehrhard." *EphLit* 50 (1936) 312–323.

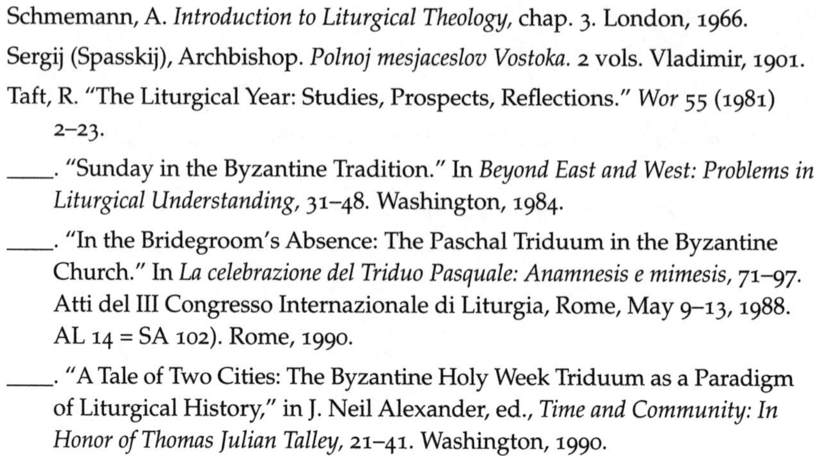

Schmemann, A. *Introduction to Liturgical Theology,* chap. 3. London, 1966.

Sergij (Spasskij), Archbishop. *Polnoj mesjaceslov Vostoka.* 2 vols. Vladimir, 1901.

Taft, R. "The Liturgical Year: Studies, Prospects, Reflections." *Wor* 55 (1981) 2–23.

____. "Sunday in the Byzantine Tradition." In *Beyond East and West: Problems in Liturgical Understanding,* 31–48. Washington, 1984.

____. "In the Bridegroom's Absence: The Paschal Triduum in the Byzantine Church." In *La celebrazione del Triduo Pasquale: Anamnesis e mimesis,* 71–97. Atti del III Congresso Internazionale di Liturgia, Rome, May 9–13, 1988. AL 14 = SA 102). Rome, 1990.

____. "A Tale of Two Cities: The Byzantine Holy Week Triduum as a Paradigm of Liturgical History," in J. Neil Alexander, ed., *Time and Community: In Honor of Thomas Julian Talley,* 21–41. Washington, 1990.

Talley, T. J. *The Origins of the Liturgical Year.* 2nd ed. Collegeville, Minn., 1991.

Tyciak, J. *Das Herrenmysterium im byzantinischen Kirchenjahr.* 2nd ed. Trier, 1976.

Matias Augé, C.M.F.

8

The Liturgical Year in the Roman Rite

We will examine the liturgical year of the Roman Rite by considering the Easter season first, for which Lent is the preparation. Then we will look at the Christmas season (and Epiphany), for which Advent is the preparation. We will finish the study by examining the season known as Ordinary Time, or *per annum*. Given the limitations of space available to us, we will not be able to undertake a detailed and complete treatment. After briefly sketching the origins and development of the various seasons, we will pause to consider the current arrangement of the liturgical year, a product of the reforms of Vatican II, at greater length. However, it may be necessary from time to time to return to a consideration of the historical background in order to clarify our understanding of the current situation.

I. DEVELOPMENTS IN THE CELEBRATION OF EASTER FROM THE FOURTH CENTURY TO THE SIXTEENTH CENTURY

There are very few witnesses to the celebrations of Easter in Rome in the first four centuries. However, the sources are rich with material from the fifth to the seventh century. Of special interest during this period are the *Sermons* of St. Leo the Great and the first Roman sacramentaries, with their corresponding *ordines* and lectionaries. From them we learn that by means of a process that we might refer to as increasing "historicization," one's attention is focused on the individual events of the redemption, while at the same time the global vision of the whole mystery seems to become obscured. This process, which began in the course of the fourth century, takes definite shape between the fifth and seventh centuries. So, from the ancient all-inclusive celebration of the night of Easter, there is a movement to the sacred

Triduum and finally to Holy Week. Pentecost, which had originally referred to the entire period of the fifty days after Easter, is no longer seen as one whole period of celebration; rather, Pentecost comes to refer to a single celebration, the fiftieth day after Easter. Finally, the preparation for Easter came to be organized and gave rise to Lent.

In the course of the second part of the seventh century and the first half of the eighth, a fusion of the Roman liturgy with the customs of Frankish Gaul took place. Then, with the definitive influence of the *PRG* in the tenth century, the now transformed Roman liturgical books returned to Rome, where they became the standards. The Roman Curia codified these books in the twelfth and thirteenth centuries in such fashion that they eventually became the books of the Tridentine reform of the sixteenth century. During the course of this long period of time, the celebration of the Easter cycle underwent new and definitive developments. Among the principal ones are Holy Thursday (originally the last day of Lent) becoming part of the sacred Triduum and the Easter Vigil being anticipated on Holy Saturday. In this way the sacred Triduum no longer referred to the passion, death, and resurrection of Christ but became the Triduum of the passion and death. The detachment of the passion and death of Christ from his resurrection is evident, in that there developed, after the "Triduum of the death" a second "Triduum of the resurrection" on the Sunday, Monday, and Tuesday of Easter.

1. The Sacred Triduum and Holy Week

At the end of the fourth century, St. Ambrose adopts the phrase *Triduum sacrum* to refer to the days on which Christ suffered, lay in the tomb, and rose.[1] A few years later St. Augustine uses the phrase *Sacratissimum triduum crucifixi, sepulti, suscitati.*[2] Concerning the celebration of the sacred Triduum in Rome, we have a letter from Innocent I to the bishop Decentius of Gubbio, around the year 416, in which he mentions a special celebration of the passion on Friday and of the resurrection on Sunday, with a fast on Friday and Saturday.[3]

The Friday before Easter did not originally have any special connection with the sacred Triduum. We know that at Rome, at the end of the fourth century, the reconciliation of penitents took place on that

[1] Ambrose, *Epist.* 23, 12–13: PL 16:1073–1074.

[2] Augustine, *Epist.* 55,14, 24; PL 33:215.

[3] Innocent I, *Epist.* 25, 4, 7; PL 20:555–556.

day.[4] Later, in the seventh century, the reconciliation of penitents took place during the course of a morning Mass celebrated at the *tituli* (see the three different and independent arrangements found in the *GeV,* nn. 352–359, 360–363, 364–367). The *GeV* also refers to a second Mass celebrated during the evening in the *tituli,* the principal theme of which was the double *traditio:* the betrayal of Judas and the institution, or better, the handing on *(traditio)* of the Eucharist to the disciples (*GeV,* nn. 391–394; cf. *GrH,* nn. 333–337). The *PRG* of the tenth century refers only to the chrism Mass and the evening Mass, anticipated at the third hour (*PRG* XCIX, 222 and 252), and places the reconciliation of penitents prior to the chrism Mass (*PRG* XCIX, 224). The liturgical books of the thirteenth century and the *MR1570* only have the formula that corresponds to the Mass that recalls the institution narrative. The confection of the chrism and the blessing of the oils took place in the cathedrals and is recounted in the pontificals (see *PR* 1596). In the sixteenth century, the only Mass on Holy Thursday was already anticipated in the morning.

The reservation and adoration of the Blessed Sacrament on Holy Thursday are first noted in the twelfth and thirteenth centuries. The feast of Corpus Christi was instituted in 1264. Reservation took place in the sacristy, which was solemnly decorated for the occasion. The liturgical books of the sixteenth century direct that the reservation take place within the church proper, on an altar or a place that has been appropriately prepared, and that the Sacrament be brought to the place of repose in procession. The popularity of the adoration of the Eucharist reserved in a pyx (which popular thought identified with the tomb of Christ) was the decisive element in causing Holy Thursday to become one of the days counted among the sacred Triduum. The washing of the feet became an element of the Holy Thursday liturgy with the arrival in Rome of the *PRG* (XCIX, 287–294), according to which the rite took place after Vespers.

We have a report of the celebration of Good Friday, according to the papal liturgy in Rome, from the middle of the seventh century, in the *GrH* (nn. 338–355), which records the *orationes sollemnes* from the liturgy of the Word celebrated in the Basilica of Santa Croce in Gerusalemme. From the same time period, the liturgy of the Word in the priestly

[4] Jerome, *Epist.* 77, 4: PL 22:692. See also the letter of Innocent I referred to previously.

celebrations in the *tituli* was connected with the adoration of the cross and the communion of the people (*GeV,* nn. 395–418). The adoration of the cross entered the papal liturgy in the eighth century, but the people and the clergy did not receive communion (*OR* XXIII). Later the liturgical books of the thirteenth century direct that only the pope is to receive communion. In this way there developed the custom that only the presider of the celebration would receive communion. This norm remained in force until the reforms of Pius XII in 1956.

Saturday was originally a day without any liturgy at all, dedicated to prayer, penance, and fasting.

The culminating moment of the sacred Triduum and all of Holy Week was the Easter Vigil, which celebrated *totum paschale sacramentum.* St. Leo the Great, in a sermon that was probably delivered during an Easter Vigil, said, "The reading of the gospel has set forth for us the entire mystery of Easter,"[5] indicating that the reading of the gospel done on that night contained both the passion and the resurrection of the Lord. Some years before this, in 385, Pope Siricius tells us that the Easter Vigil is the night for baptism,[6] and St. Leo the Great says that numerous candidates prepare during Lent.[7] In the seventh century we find a rich structure for the Easter Vigil, which is permeated by three fundamental elements: the celebration of the Word, baptism, and the Eucharist (for the papal liturgy: *GrH,* nn. 363–382; for the liturgy in the *tituli: GeV,* nn. 425–462). It should be noted, however, that the liturgy in the *tituli* begins with the lighting and blessing of the paschal candle, a rite that only enters the papal liturgy at a later time.

Already by the sixth century the Easter Vigil had begun to be anticipated in the evening hours of Saturday. This tendency became more pronounced in the following centuries. Finally, with Pius V's prohibition of the celebration of Mass after noon *(MR1570),* the vigil Mass was moved to the morning. There were other new developments in the Easter Vigil: in the course of the eighth century the papal liturgy adopted the blessing of the light, but without any accompanying

[5] St. Leo the Great, *Tractatus* 72 *(De passione Domini)* 1: CCL 138, 441. Note that, according to A. Chavasse, the editor of this edition, the sermon was delivered on Good Friday.

[6] Siricius, *Epist.* 1, 2: PL 13:1134–1135. The Pope speaks of Easter and Pentecost as traditional days for baptism. See also St. Leo the Great, *Epist.* 16, 6: PL 54:701; *Epist.* 168: PL 54:1210.

[7] St. Leo the Great, *Tractatus* 40 *(De ieiunio Quadragesimae)* 2: CCL 138, 225.

formulas. The *PR* XII (XXXII, 1-10) is the first document in which we find the blessing of the new fire, the procession with the acclamation *Lumen Christi,* the blessing of the paschal candle, and the text of the *Exsultet.* The solemn rite of the light began as a practical necessity for the illumination of the evening celebration.

The Mass for Easter Sunday did not appear early in Rome. St. Leo the Great was content simply to preach during the holy night. The celebration of Easter Sunday grew along with the tendency to anticipate the Easter Vigil earlier and earlier on Saturday evening. At the beginning of the sixth century, the Eucharist with which the Easter Vigil ended was thought by John the Deacon to be a celebration belonging to Saturday.[8] In the *GeV,* next to the *Orationes et praeces ad missam in nocte* (nn. 453–462), there is a second Mass for Easter *Dominicum Paschae* (nn. 465–467). Here the Mass during the night is part of Sunday. As we will see later, the octave of Easter is the following Sunday.

St. Leo the Great witnesses to the reading of the passion of the Lord on the Sunday, Wednesday, Friday, and Saturday before Easter in his sermons *De passione Domini.* The Sunday prior to Easter is called *Dominica in palmas de passione Christi* in the *GeV* (nn. 329–333). The reference to palms is absent, however, in all the Roman *Epistolari* and *Evangeliari* of the seventh and eighth centuries.[9] The original title probably did not mention palms, since this rite did not reach Rome until the end of the tenth century. The title "Passion Sunday" probably best expresses the content of the Gelasian Sacramentary for this day.[10] The procession with palms became a custom only after the appearance of the *Ordo de die palmarum* of the *PRG* (XCIX, 162–206), which had a decisive influence on the Roman liturgical books in the thirteenth century. From then on, the Palm Sunday liturgy would combine the ancient Roman celebration of the passion with the commemoration of the entrance of Jesus into Jerusalem.

These and other characteristic rituals encountered in the week prior to Easter show that what we call Holy Week today already had a

[8] John the Deacon, *Epistula ad Senarium,* 12: PL 59:405.

[9] A. Chavasse, *Le Sacramentaire gélasien (Vaticanus Reginensis 316). Sacramentaire presbytéral en usage dans les titres romains au VIIe siècle.* Bibliothèque de théologie 1. Série IV: Histoire de la théologie 1 (Tournai, 1958) 234.

[10] P. Jounel, "La liturgie du mystère pascal. 2: Le dimanche des Rameaux," *MD* 68 (1961) 52–57.

distinctive personality in the sixth and seventh centuries, the nucleus of which was the passion of the Lord.

2. *Pentecost—The Fifty Days of Easter*

The celebration of the fifty days of Easter as a festive unity precedes both the sacred Triduum and Holy Week. In the most ancient sources of the Roman liturgy there is already present the outline of an organization of the Sundays of the Easter season into a season of Pentecost, that is, a liturgical period of fifty days. However, this collapsed in favor of celebrations that were more narrowly connected to the particular events of the paschal mystery. Some Roman writers at the end of the fourth century and the first half of the fifth show that the word "Pentecost" was coming to be used more and more to designate the fiftieth day and not the entire fifty-day period after Easter.[11] For St. Leo the Great, the descent of the Holy Spirit upon the apostles was the principal content of the day of Pentecost.[12] He is also the first witness to a Roman celebration of the ascension on the fortieth day after Easter.[13]

The increasingly early celebration of the Easter Vigil on Saturday favored the development of an autonomous liturgy proper to Easter, the texts for which would emphasize the event of the resurrection as a partial aspect of the one paschal mystery. This can be seen in the formula *In dominica sancta ad missam* of the *GrH* (nn. 383–391), which was taken up in the *MR1570*. This celebration is clearly separate from that of the Easter Vigil. The octave day for Easter fell on the Saturday before the Sunday called *post albas* (*GrH*, nn. 429–434). In this way the octave lost its original meaning and reduced Easter Week to Sunday, Monday, and Tuesday. The first hint of this shortening is found in the seventh and eighth centuries with the *OR*, which provides for only three stational liturgies during this week, on Sunday, Monday, and Tuesday (*OR* I, nn. 15–18). In the *MR1570* (according to the edition of Urban VIII), the days of the octave from Wednesday on are lower in rank than Monday and Tuesday.

Mention should be made of the introduction of Vespers for Easter Sunday in the seventh century, because of its baptismal character. The *GrH* (nn. 389–391) contains the prayers, and the *OR* XXVII, from the

[11] Siricius, *Epist.* 1, 2: PL 13:1134–1135; Ambrosiaster, *Quaestiones veteris et novi Testamenti:* CSEL 50, 167–168.

[12] St. Leo the Great, *Tractatus de Pentecosten:* CCL 138, 465–505.

[13] St. Leo the Great, *Tractatus de Ascensione Domini:* CCL 138, 450–461.

eighth century, gives a detailed description. The celebration took place in three stages. It began inside the Lateran Basilica, moved to its culminating moment with a procession to and stop in the baptistry, and ended in the contiguous oratory of Santa Croce. It was here that Pope Hilarius deposited the Constantinian reliquary of the cross in the fifth century and where neophytes received the *consignatio* during the Easter Vigil. Amalarius commented on these Vespers.[14] While this would disappear in Rome during the thirteenth century, it was still very much alive in other Western Churches.

The octaves of Easter and Pentecost did not exist in the time of St. Leo. The texts for the octave of Easter appear between the sixth and eighth centuries. The *GeV* contains a formula for every day of the *totius albae* week (nn. 468–498) and a Mass for the following Sunday *Octabas Paschae die dominico* (nn. 499–503). Later this first week of Pentecost seems to lose its particular character as a prolongation of the feast to the entire Easter season. The Sundays that follow the octave of Easter in the *GeV* are called second, third, etc., *post clausum Paschae.* In the *GeV* we also find formulas for the vigil of Pentecost (nn. 624–636) and *Orationes ad vesperos infra octabas Pentecosten* (nn. 646–651) and the formula *In dominica octavarum Pentecosten* (nn. 676–682). With the introduction of the octave, Pentecost Sunday becomes an autonomous feast and definitively loses its character as the end of the Easter season. At the same time, however, Pentecost Sunday becomes a sort of replica of the solemnity of Easter with the celebration of the sacraments of Christian initiation.

3. *Lent*

Even though its origins are not clear, Lent appears as a time of preparation prior to the paschal fast of the Friday and Saturday before Easter. In a letter to Marcella from around 384, St. Jerome is the first witness in Rome to the existence of Lent (Quadragesima), which was characterized by fasting.[15] The Lenten sermons of St. Leo the Great also have a clear ascetical and moral content, with a focus on fasting and the practice of virtue. Lent became the framework for the final

[14] Amalarius, *Liber de ordine Antiphonarii,* 52; *De glorioso officio quod fit circa vespertinales terminos in paschali hebdomada in Romana Ecclesia:* PL 105:1295–1296.

[15] Jerome, *Epist.* 24, 4: PL 22:428. Some refer to the witness of the historian Socrates († after 439) in Rome, who speaks of a three-week period of fasting as a time of preparation for Easter (see Socrates, *Historia ecclestiastica,* 5, 22: PG 67:633).

preparation of catechumens or *illuminandi* for baptism on Easter night. It is clear, then, that the Lenten liturgy witnessed to by the *GeV* is strongly influenced by baptismal themes. This will gradually lessen as the Church lacked a real catechumenate.

Lent is also the time for penance for those who submitted to the practice of public penance. The beginning of Lent, fixed at the sixth Sunday before Easter, was anticipated on the Wednesday immediately prior (already called *Caput Quadragesimae* in the *GeV*, n. 83), probably in order to achieve a total number of forty days of fasting. On this Wednesday the public sinners, having donned penitential garb and ashes, were sent out of the assembly and obliged to undergo public penance. At the beginning of the fifth century, according to Innocent I, the penitents at Rome were reconciled on the Thursday prior to Easter.[16] This is later confirmed by the *GeV* (nn. 349–363).

In the sixth and seventh centuries, this season is lengthened with the introduction of Septuagesima, Sexagesima, and Quinquagesima Sundays. The formulas present in the *GeV* (nn. 69–72, 73–77, 84–88) are more recent interpolations. This lengthening was probably done to stress the penitential nature of Lent and Easter during a time when repeated Gothic and Lombard invasions caused people to be predisposed to supplementary practices of prayer and penance. In the eighth century, with Pope Gregory II (715–731), the Thursdays of Lent were given their own formulas for the celebration of the Eucharist, where there had previously been none.[17]

It is clear that with the passing of time, the whole Christian community became identified with the groups of catechumens and penitents in the preparation for Easter. This occasioned more frequent listening to the Word of God, more intense and lengthy prayer, and the constant practice of penance, especially fasting, in the liturgical framework of a Lent that was becoming ever more well organized. Scholars, working after the research of A. Chavasse, are trying to delineate the various stages of development of the Lenten liturgy.[18]

[16] Innocent I, *Epist.* 25, 7, 19: PL 20:559.

[17] L. Duchesne, *Le Liber Pontificalis: Texte, introduction et commentaire* (Paris, 1886) 1:402.

[18] See the synthesis of A. Nocent, "La quaresima," *Anàmnesis* 6:152–155; H. Auf der Maur, *Feiern im Rhythmus der Zeit* I: *Herrenfeste in Woche und Jahr,* Gottesdienst der Kirche: Handbuch der Liturgiewissenschaft, Teil 5 (Regensburg, 1983) 143–153. See his bibliography on pp. 143–144.

Only toward the end of the eleventh century, by which time the institution of public penance had completely disappeared, is there a documentary witness to the distribution of ashes to all the faithful on the Wednesday before the first Sunday of Lent. The Synod of Benevento (1091), which was presided over by Urban II, prescribed this rite for both the clergy and laity in the course of a penitential liturgy with a procession.[19] The *MR1570* takes up this practice and places it before the celebration of the Eucharist. However, the name Ash Wednesday *(Feria IV Cinerum)* does not appear in the Roman Missal prior to the second half of the sixteenth century.

II. THE CELEBRATION OF EASTER AFTER THE REFORMS OF THE SECOND VATICAN COUNCIL

From the publication of the *MR1570* until the twentieth century, indeed, right up until the recent reforms of Vatican II, there were no important changes in the structure of the celebration of Easter. The most important novelty during this period was the restoration of the Easter Vigil by Pius XII in 1951,[20] followed by the new order for Holy Week, the *Ordo Hebdomadae Sanctae instauratus* of 1956.[21] The *Ordo* was inserted into the *MR1962*. These reforms were later reworked and perfected by Vatican II. For this reason we will concern ourselves here only with the current liturgy, the product of Vatican II.

The fundamental reasons underlying the current arrangement of the Easter celebrations are set out in the *General Norms for the Liturgical Year and the Calendar* (nn. 18–31; *DOL* 442). The height of the Easter celebrations and of the entire liturgical year is the Easter Triduum "of the passion and resurrection of Christ" (n. 18). Within the Triduum, the Easter Vigil is considered to be the "mother of all vigils" (n. 21; St. Augustine, *Sermo* 219; PL 38:1088). The season of Easter and the following fifty days are to be celebrated as "one feast day, or better as one 'great Sunday'" (n. 22). The season of Lent is a time of preparation for Easter. It disposes the faithful to celebrate the paschal mystery "through reminders of their own baptism and through penitential

[19] Mansi, 20, 739.

[20] This reform was promulgated by a decree of the Sacred Congregation for Rites on February 9, 1951, *ad experimentum* for one year (*AAS* 43 [1951] 128–137) and was renewed for an additional three years in 1952 (*AAS* 44 [1952] 48–63).

[21] A decree and instruction from the Sacred Congregation for Rites on November 11, 1955 (*AAS* 47 [1955] 838–847).

practices" (n. 27). Holy Week is "the remembrance of Christ's passion, beginning with his messianic entry into Jerusalem" (n. 31). The reforms of the twentieth century, in particular those that stem from Vatican II, represent a recovery of the best elements of the ancient Roman traditions and are inspired by a unitary vision of the celebration of Easter.

1. The Easter Triduum

Current liturgical books use the modern expression *Sacrum Triduum Paschale* to indicate the period that begins with the evening Mass of the Lord's Supper on Holy Thursday, reaches its high point at the Easter Vigil, and ends with Vespers on Easter Sunday, of the Lord's Resurrection (cf. *General Norms*, n. 19: *MR1970*). The Easter Triduum, taken as a whole, commemorates the mystery of the death and resurrection of Christ, both in its unity and in its successive phases. The following schema shows the essential moments of the Easter Triduum:

Proem (on the evening of Holy Thursday)

The supper	The paschal ritual	Mass of the Lord's Supper

The Easter Triduum proper (Friday, Saturday, and Sunday)

The cross	Christ's sacrifice	Celebration of the passion
The tomb	Christ's repose	The office of prayer
The empty tomb	Christ's resurrection	Easter Vigil

In this way the ancient Triduum of Christ dead, buried, and risen has been recovered. The evening celebration on Holy Thursday, but not the whole day, has come to be counted among the days of the Triduum as a sort of "sacramental" prologue; the Triduum really consists of the entire day on Friday, Saturday, and Sunday. One might say that while the Triduum displays for us the reality of the paschal mystery in its historical dimension, the evening celebration of Holy Thursday does the same in its ritual dimension.[22] It is the "sacramental" moment of the one paschal mystery.

The Mass of the Lord's Supper has a festal character and celebrates the institution of the Eucharist, which looks toward the cross and

[22] S. Marsili, "Il Triduo sacro" e il Giovedi santo," *RL* 55 (1968) 37.

resurrection. At the Last Supper, Jesus anticipated his sacrifice and its ultimate victory. The fundamental moments of the evening celebration of Holy Thursday are: the liturgy of the Word (Exod 12:1-8, 11-14; 1 Cor 11:23-26; John 13:1-15), the washing of the feet, the liturgy of the Eucharist, the reservation of the Blessed Sacrament, and the stripping of the altars (done in silence after the celebration). In comparison with the reforms of 1956, the most important innovation is the proclamation of Exodus 12, which reports the prescriptions for the Jewish paschal meal, as the first reading, and the use of selections from Psalm 115 as the responsorial psalm. This stresses the way in which the Lord's Supper is a memorial of the Passover. Christ gave us his Passover in the Eucharist, which demands that we, for our part, serve one another in charity (in this way a connection is made with the washing of the feet).

Given the multiplicity of elements that come together in this celebration, it is important to consider it as a unitary whole. A rubric for the Mass prescribes that the homily explain to the faithful the principal mysteries commemorated in this Mass, the institution of the Eucharist and the priestly ministry, as well as the Lord's commandment of mutual love. It is also to be noted that the priestly ministry and mutual love are the irreducible elements for the celebration of the Eucharist. The institution of the Eucharist should be seen, in the light of ancient Roman tradition, as a giving or handing on *(traditio)* to the disciples of these mysteries of his body and blood by the Lord so that they might celebrate them (see the prayer *Hanc igitur* in the *MR1970: tradidit discipulis suis*).

The celebration in honor of the Lord's passion on Good Friday afternoon is divided into three parts: the liturgy of the Word (Isa 52:13–53:12; Heb 4:14-16; 5:7-9; John 18:1–19:42), the adoration of the cross, communion. The reform of 1956 reintroduced the communion of the faithful, which has been retained but not without creating some problems, as we will see. Some have seen in the structure of the current celebration, which was a synthesis of various traditions, a linear movement: the passion proclaimed (the liturgy of the Word), the passion invoked (the solemn intercessions), the passion venerated (the adoration of the cross), the passion communicated (communion).[23] The

[23] J. Castellano Cervera, *L'anno liturgico: Memoriale di Cristo e mistagogia delle Chiesa con Maria Madre di Gesù. Corso di spiritualità liturgica,* Serie di Pastorale e di Studio 5 (Rome, 1987) 91.

problem is not in the harmony or the structure of the celebration in itself as much as with the relationship of this celebration to the other celebrations of the Easter Triduum, all of which are oriented toward the celebration of the Eucharist at the Easter Vigil.[24] Since Friday and Saturday "celebrate the paschal fast" (see *General Norms,* n. 28),[25] the problematic nature of the reception of communion on Good Friday becomes clear. We have already made mention of the complex history of the reception of communion on Good Friday. However, the problem is not fundamentally historical but theological. It is helpful to recall that Christ is really present not only in the Eucharist (see *SC* 7) but in other ways as well. It should also be noted that what is central to Good Friday is the glorious cross and that that reality is not limited to the time of its liturgical celebration.[26]

In comparison with the reform of 1956, the most important novelty in the liturgy of the Word on Good Friday is the selections for the first two readings. In particular, it has been noted that in the light of the first reading, taken from the Servant Songs of Second Isaiah, the image of the suffering Christ is brought into focus. However, according to the reading from the Gospel of John, which has been retained, the death of Jesus is not a failure but a triumph, a lifting up in two senses: on the cross and into glory.[27] Moreover, numerous euchological texts show that the entire celebration is a memorial of the paschal sacrifice of Christ.

Holy Saturday is the day of Christ in the tomb and does not have a proper liturgy. The Church recommends that one fast and spend time at the Lord's tomb while awaiting his resurrection. The significance of this day is expressed by texts for the Liturgy of the Hours.

[24] On January 16, 1988, the Congregation for Divine Worship in Vatican City published the *Circular Letter Concerning the Preparation and Celebration of the Easter Feasts (De festis paschalibus praeparandis et celebrandis).* Paragraphs 91–92 of this letter refer to the reception of communion at the vigil as "the moment of full participation in the mystery that is being celebrated" and state the desire that it express the fullness of the Eucharistic sign, that is, that communion be given under both species.

[25] The circular letter referred to in the preceding note speaks of the paschal fast of the two previous days as preparation for the joy of the Sunday of the resurrection (n. 39).

[26] The problem is well treated by S. Maggiani, "Per una più viva partecipazione al mistero. 1, *'Ecce lignum Crucis':* la Croce gloriosa," *RL* 77 (1990) 57–66. See also the circular letter (n. 71) to which reference is made in note 24 above.

[27] H. van den Bussche, *Giovanni, Commento del Vangelo spirituale* (Assisi, 1971) 543–544.

At the Easter Vigil "the Church awaits Christ's resurrection and celebrates it in the sacraments" (*General Norms*, n. 21). In the *MR1970* the vigil is related to Easter Sunday of the Lord's Resurrection by both celebrations being given a common title: "Easter Sunday *in Resurrectione Domini*." The basic structure of the celebration is identical to that which it had in *MR1570* as well as the reforms of 1951. We may distinguish four parts: the *lucernarium*, or celebration of light; the liturgy of the Word (Gen 1:1–2:2; Gen 22:1-18; Exod 14:15–15:1; Isa 54:5-14; Isa 55:1-11; Bar 3:9-15, 31–4:4; Ezek 36:16-28; Rom 6:3-11; Matt 28:1-10 [A]; Mark 6:1-8 [B]; Luke 24:1-12 [C]; celebration of baptism (if there are no baptisms, there is a blessing of water and the renewal of baptismal promises); the celebration of the Eucharist. By means of the "sacramental" signs of light, water, bread and wine, explained and made efficacious by the Word of God, the reality of the Lord's Passover is symbolized and made present so that it may become ours and that we may express it with our lives.[28] The basic symbolism of the Easter Vigil is the "illuminated night," or the "night over which day has triumphed," showing by means of ritual signs that the life of grace flows from the death of Christ. The vigil, given its relation to Passover, is nocturnal. Waiting, a characteristic of the vigil, points to the final coming of the Lord. This is explicitly noted in the rubrics of the *MR* at the beginning of the celebration.

The liturgy of the Word has been changed in a way that requires that some mention be made of it. The whole complex of readings invites us to consider the stages of the history of salvation, which is founded on the Passover of the Lord. The Lord's Passover becomes the Church's Passover, as Romans 6:3-11 proclaims (by means of baptism we participate in the death and resurrection of Christ). Easter is, therefore, an invitation to choose to live out one's own baptism.

The liturgy of Easter Sunday of the Lord's Resurrection celebrates the event of Easter as "the day of Christ the Lord." The biblical readings contain the Easter kerygma and the call to the tasks that the new life in the Risen Christ entails. As the opening prayer says, to celebrate Easter means to "renew our lives by the Spirit that is within us." The GILH (n. 213) directs that the custom of baptismal Vespers be retained

[28] The vigil may be schematized in this way: *Mysterium Lucis, Mysterium Verbi, Mysterium Aquae, Mysterium Agni, Mysterium Ecclesiae.* (Cf. P. Rainoldi, "Mistero, 3. 'Vegliare per il Signore,'" *RL* 77 [1990] 72–85).

where it still exists. The *Circular Letter Concerning the Preparation and Celebration of the Easter Feasts* (n. 98) asks that it eventually be restored.

2. The Season of Easter

This is once again the season of the fifty days after Easter. In recognition of this, the Sundays are called Sundays of Easter, and the octave of Pentecost has been suppressed. The current missal has also suppressed *Tempus Ascensionis,* which is still present in the *MR1962* beginning with the feast of the same name. The Ascension of the Lord is celebrated on the fortieth day but may be moved to the following Sunday. The paschal candle is no longer extinguished after the gospel of the Ascension, but after Compline on the day of Pentecost, which is the end of the season of Easter. The opening prayer of the evening Mass of the vigil of Pentecost Sunday states that "fifty days have celebrated the fullness of the mystery" of Easter, and the preface of the Mass for the day of Pentecost says explicitly that this day brought "the paschal mystery to its completion." The octave of Easter is retained because of its historical connection with the "mystagogical" week, or the initiation of the baptized, to the sacraments at the Easter Vigil. The eight days form a unity with Easter Sunday and are celebrated "as solemnities of the Lord." (*General Norms,* n. 24). Desiring to stress the unity of the mystery of Christ and of the Spirit, the euchological texts emphasize that the entire season of Easter is always the season of the Spirit.

To summarize, the paschal mystery is celebrated as one entire whole (death, resurrection, and ascension of the Lord, the descent of the Spirit). It might be a minor detail, but it would probably be more meaningful if on Pentecost Sunday, the end of the Easter season, the liturgical color were not red but the same white that was used on the other days of the fifty-day season of Easter.

In accord with both Western and Eastern traditions, the readings during the fifty days of Easter are taken from the following books of the New Testament: the Acts of the Apostles (which takes the place of readings from the Old Testament), the First Letter of Peter, the Letters of John, the Book of Revelation, and the Gospel of John. On the Sundays the readings are almost always harmonized with the gospel. The organization of the readings, however, has been profoundly renewed when compared with the *MR1570.* The principal themes of the readings may be synthesized in this fashion: the events of Easter are for us, so that we may participate, this is a work of the Spirit, especially in the celebration of the Eucharist, which is our Easter. In this way the ecclesial-sacramental meaning of the Easter celebrations is accentuated. The euchology of the Easter season has been renewed in a particular fashion in order to augment the pneumatological theme. This is especially true in the last week, when there is a strong emphasis on the Easter life as a "life according to the Spirit," while awaiting the eschatological Easter.

3. The Season of Lent

According to the second prayer for the blessing of the ashes on Ash Wednesday in the *MR1970*, the celebration of Easter means that as a result of the discipline of Lent, one has achieved "newness of life in the image of your Risen Son." Lent, therefore, is a time for preparation for Easter. This is confirmed by various documents: "The Lenten liturgy disposes both catechumens and the faithful to celebrate the paschal mystery: catechumens, through the several stages of Christian initiation; the faithful, through reminders of their own baptism and through penitential practices liturgy prepares the catechumens for the celebration of the paschal mystery by the several stages of Christian initiation: it also prepares the faithful, who recall their baptism and do penance in preparation for Easter" (*General Norms*, n. 27; cf. *SC* 109).

Lent runs from Ash Wednesday to the Mass *in Cena Domini* on Holy Thursday exclusive (cf. *General Norms*, n. 28). In this fashion, the season of Lent is clearly distinguished from the Easter Triduum. Given this clear distinction between the seasons, Septuagesima, Sexagesima, and Quinquagesima Sundays have been eliminated.

The rite for the blessing and distribution of ashes, with which the season of Easter penance begins, has been simplified and no longer takes place at the beginning of Mass, as it still did in *MR1962;* rather, it has been inserted at the end of the liturgy of the Word. A new formula for the imposition of ashes has been suggested (an invitation to conversion taken from Mark 1:15), along with the option of using the ancient formula taken from Genesis 3:19. The rite for the blessing and distribution of ashes can take place as a liturgy of the Word outside of Mass.

Aside from the euchological texts, notably enriched in comparison with *MR1570*, the current formulas for Lent provide for an ample selection of biblical texts. We will consider the formulas for Sunday, in particular the gospels, since the liturgy and the themes that are developed therein stress Sunday. In all the three years of the liturgical cycle (A, B, C), the first two Sundays recount the temptation of Jesus in the desert and the transfiguration on the mountain, taking the gospels from Matthew, Mark, and Luke respectively. In these two episodes we find the two faces of our participation in the paschal mystery. On the other three Sundays that precede Palm Sunday, the Sunday *de Passione Domini*, the *OLM* offers the possibility of three different but complementary itineraries that lead us toward the celebration of Easter.

The sacramental or baptismal itinerary: Cycle A introduces us to the mysterious reality of our Christian initiation. On the three Sundays passages from the Gospel of John which have been connected since ancient times with the baptismal scrutinies (exorcisms) are proclaimed: the Samaritan woman (John 4:5-42), the healing of the man born blind (John 9:1-41), the resurrection of Lazarus (John 11:1-45). In the *MR1570* these texts were read on weekdays. In these passages the personal revelation of Jesus to humanity is heard once again ("living water," "light of the world," "resurrection and life") and the reality of baptism is prefigured. Cycle A may be followed every year given the pastoral needs of a particular community. Specific prefaces are provided for these Sundays, which take up the theme of the gospel pericope of the day.

The Christocentric-paschal itinerary: Cycle B draws our attention to the Pasch of Jesus. The three Sundays present several passages from John in which we may contemplate, in an anticipatory way, the paschal mystery: Jesus is the real temple that will be destroyed—at his death—and rebuilt in his resurrection (John 2:13-25); in his sorrowful yet glorious exaltation, Christ is the fulfillment of what was prefigured by the serpent raised up by Moses in the desert (John 3:14-21); Christ is the seed which by dying and being sown in the ground gives life (John 12:20-33).

The penitential itinerary: Cycle C is constructed so as to be a catechesis on reconciliation as well as an invitation to conversion. On the three Sundays with which we are concerned, texts from Luke that exalt the mercy of God are proclaimed: the parable of the fig tree that bears no fruit (Luke 13:1-9); the parable of the prodigal son (Luke 15:1-3, 11-32); the story of the woman taken in adultery (John 8:1-11). Some scholars are convinced that this last passage is actually part of the Lucan tradition.

In this itinerary, baptism and penance appear as the two constants on which the whole Lenten path to full reconciliation between God and humanity rests. The collect for the first Sunday of Lent speaks of the celebration of Lent as the period of time "through which we may enter more deeply into the mystery of Christ."[29] The Latin text, taken from the *GeV* (n. 104), uses the expression Lenten *sacramentum.*[30] The weekdays of the five weeks of Lent, although autonomous, take up some of the themes of the Sundays.

Holy Week begins with Palm Sunday, which commemorates the entry of the Lord into Jerusalem with the rite of the blessing of palms and the proclamation of the passion of the Lord during the Mass. The *MR1970* substantially adopts the *Ordo* of 1956. The texts of the Liturgy of the Hours make frequent reference to the passion and the resurrection. For example, the hymn used at Vespers (which is also used on the weekdays before the Triduum) begins by proclaiming:

The standard of the King appears,
The mystery of the Cross shines forth
On which Life endured death
And from death brought forth life,[31]

and the second antiphon of Lauds invites one to acclaim Christ "the conqueror of death." This theme is also found in the *Magnificat* antiphon for second Vespers.

[29] Translator's note: The ICEL translation renders the Latin texts of the collect: *Concede nobis, omnipotens Deus, ut, per annua quadragesimalis exercitia sacramenti, et ad intellegendum Christi proficiamus arcanum, et effectus eius digna conversatione sectemur. Per Dominum.*

as:

Grant us, almighty God, that through this yearly observance of Lent we may enter more deeply into the mystery of Christ and draw upon its power in our lives. We ask this through . . .

See Mary Pierre Ellebracht: "In general we may say that in the orations, as frequently in other Christian Latin works, the word *sacramentum* is almost synonymous with *mysterium,*" *Remarks on the Vocabulary of the Ancient Orations in the Missale Romanum* (Nijmegen-Utrecht, 1963) 72.

[30] M. Augé, "Il 'sacramento della Quaresima: Orazioni e prefazi del Messale romano," *RPL* 14 (1977) 28–33.

[31] Venantius Fortunatus, *Vexilla regis prodeunt,* in *Cantate et Iubilate Deo: A Devotional and Liturgical Hymnal* (Chicago, 1999) 150.

The chrism Mass on the morning of Holy Thursday marks the end of Lent. This is a celebration with a value very particular to itself. Pope Paul VI made it a celebration of the ministerial priesthood, in which the priests renew, in the presence of their bishop, the tasks they took up at the time of the ordination. There is no consensus among scholars on the meaning and place of this celebration.[32]

III. THE SEASON OF THE MANIFESTATION OF THE LORD

Alongside the expansion of the annual celebrations of Easter, of which we have spoken above, other feasts also developed in the course of the fourth century that followed the solar calendar and therefore had a fixed date. Initially these celebrations were independent of one another and had no direct relationship to Easter. In the Western Churches they later came together to form the season of Christmas (Epiphany) and later the season of Advent, and constitute the second pole of the liturgical year. In the current arrangement of the liturgical year, the season of Christmas begins with the first Vespers of Christmas and ends with the Sunday after Epiphany (cf. *General Norms,* nn. 33–38). Therefore, there is no longer a season of Epiphany, as we find in the *MR1962,* which had the title *Tempus Epiphaniae* beginning with the feast of January 6. Guided by the liturgical reforms of Vatican II, the seasons of Advent, Christmas, and Epiphany are now grouped together under the title "The Manifestation of the Lord" (cf. *General Norms,* n. 32).

Here we are concerned only with the feasts of the Manifestation of the Lord in the Roman liturgy. We will study these feasts separately according to the order in which they came to be, because of the characteristics of those origins. Before proceeding further, we should note that their origins and later developments in this early period of the evolution of the liturgical year are complex and still, at least in some respects, not entirely well defined.

1. The Origins of Christmas

The oldest documentary witness to the celebration of Christmas on December 25 is Roman in origin. The document in question, from the year 354, is called the *Chronograph,* and is a sort of elaborate almanac that contains numerous references to the secular order of the year and

[32] A. Rose, "La signification de la Messe chrismale," *QL* 69 (1988) 22–66; R. Russo, "La Misa crismal. Un Proprio que exige grandes cambios," *EO* 10 (1993) 201–229.

two lists of burial dates, one for Roman bishops and the other for martyrs with, in both cases, a listing of the appropriate cemeteries.[33] Both burial lists are arranged according to the order of the calendar, not in their historical order, and the first date assigned to the *Depositio Martyrum* is December 25: *VIII Kal. Ian. Natus Christus in Betleem Iudeae.* In the *Depositio Episcoporum* the first date is December 27, the date of the burial of Pope Dionysius. The list then continues along through the various months of the year up to the notice of the burial of Eutichian on December 8. This is followed by the notices of the death of two popes who were not martyrs: Marcus († 336) and Julius († 352). The two burials are noted according to their historical order, not according to the order of the dates of the calendar. This makes it certain that the oldest date in the calendar is 336, given that in Rome the birth of Christ on December 25 marked the beginning of the liturgical calendar.[34]

How was December 25 chosen for the celebration of Christmas? There are various hypotheses. The feast marked the anniversary of the birth of Christ. Even if the actual date of the birth of Jesus is unknown, December 25 is indicated by an ancient tradition which held that Jesus was conceived on the same day and in the same month on which he died, March 25.[35] However, this tradition does not explain how the feast came to be celebrated but is rather an explanation for it. In fact, there were many different attempts, not all of which agreed, to date the birth of Christ in the ancient Church.

A second hypothesis, inspired by apologetics and the history of religions, states that the Roman Church would have been opposing the pagan feast called *Natalis (Solis) Invicti* (which was established in 275

[33] For those who are interested, the text may be found in C. Kirch and L. Ueding, eds., *Enchiridion fontium historiae ecclesiasticae antiquae* (Freiburg in Breisgau, 1941) nn. 543–544.

[34] Some have argued that the celebration of Christmas may be dated to around the year 300 or even earlier and that the feast originated in North Africa, not Rome. See T. Talley, *The Origins of the Liturgical Year,* 2nd ed. (Collegeville, Minn., 1991) 85.

[35] The principal authors in favor of this hypothesis are L. Duchesne, *Origines du culte chrétien: Étude sur la liturgie latine avant Charlemagne,* 5th ed. (Paris, 1920) 271–281. More recently this has been taken up again by Talley, *Origins of the Liturgical Year,* 88. A. Ammassari argues in his article "Alle origini del calendario natalizio," *Euntes Docete* 45 (1992) 11–16, that the birth of Jesus in the ninth month and the date of December 25 may even be said to derive from a Jewish-Christian tradition that is implicitly found in the Gospel of Luke.

by the emperor Aurelian on the winter solstice) with the birth of Christ, the true "sun of justice" (cf. Mal 3:20; Luke 1:78).[36] It must be noted that the institution of such a feast would have been harmonious with the idea of Constantine, who decreed in 321 that the day of the Lord, or Sunday, would become a civil day of rest. In support of this thesis, one should mention a Christian mosaic from the mausoleum of Julius in the Vatican cemetery, which dates from the middle of the third century. It represents Christ as Helios in his triumphal chariot. Mohrmann has made the same argument with philological arguments, noting that the Latin word *natalis* had long been used by Christians to refer to the anniversary of the "day of death." Fresh contact with the secular use of the word might cause there to be created a *natalis* that was a day of birth alongside a *natalis* that was a day of death.[37]

A third hypothesis does not so much explain the origin of Christmas as it does the extraordinary speed with which this feast, with its origin in Rome, spread throughout the entire Christian world. The struggle with Arianism caused a strong emphasis to be placed on the person of the God-Man. A feast for the birth of Christ would give a convenient liturgical expression to the profession of faith from Nicea that condemned Arianism in 325. Later, in the middle of the fifth century, this was confirmed by the ten Christmas sermons of St. Leo the Great, the best witness for the original meaning of Christmas in the Roman liturgy as well as author of some of the Christmas texts from *Ve.*

2. *Developments in the Celebration of Christmas up to the Present*

At the beginning of the fifth century, St. Augustine asserted that Christmas was a simple anniversary, a memorial. Easter, however, was held by him to be a *sacramentum.* He wrote:

But there is a sacrament in any celebration when the commemoration of the event is so made that it is understood to indicate something which must be reverently received. In that manner, therefore, we celebrate Easter, so as not only to call to mind what happened—that

[36] Bernard Botte argued this thesis in a decisive fashion in *Les origines de la noël et de l'épiphanie: Étude historique,* Textes et études liturgiques 1 (Louvain, 1932) 61–67. See, however, the recent study of S. Roll, "Botte Revisited: A Turning Point in the Research on the Origins of Christmas and Epiphany," *QL* 74 (1993) 153–170.

[37] C. Mohrmann, "Epiphania" *Études sur le latin des chrétiens.* Vol. 1, *Le latin des chrétiens,* 2nd ed. (Rome, 1961) 267.

Christ died and rose again—but we do not pass over the other things about him which bear witness to the significance of sacraments.[38]

Concentrating on the single mystery of Easter that effects, by means of the Easter sacraments, our passage from death to life, Augustine does not say that the mystery of Christmas contains the elements that make up a *sacramentum*. However, one must also refer to St. Leo the Great, for whom Christmas is a *sacramentum*.[39] It is not distinct from and independent of Easter but is its beginning, the dawn of salvation. In the annual celebration of the mystery of salvation, the fullness and height of which is Easter, the celebration of Christmas demonstrates the aspect of new birth of which redemption consists.[40]

The oldest texts for the celebration of Christmas are found in the *Ve*, at the end of the collection (nn. 1239–1272). There are nine Mass formulas—one or two for the vigil and the others for the feast. The texts resound with the doctrine of St. Leo the Great, one of their probable authors. The community renews the mystery of Bethlehem, where Christ, the Light of the world, came down into the darkness. In this mystery there takes place a wonderful renewal of the human person, who recovers his image in Christ, is recreated and reborn in the Word. Some of these formulas make up an important part of the Christmas euchology in *MR1970*. There is an early witness to the custom of the three Christmas Masses in the *GrH* (nn. 36–40, 41–48, 49–53), where they are assigned to three papal station churches: St. Mary Major (at midnight), St. Anastasia (at dawn), and St. Peter (during the day). Later the *GeV* (nn. 5–23) takes up the custom of the three Masses, but they are no longer celebrated at three different stations. The *MR1970* retains the option for every priest to celebrate three Masses, not, however, one immediately after another but according to the sequence of midnight, dawn, and day.

The *GeV* has a proper formula for the octave: *In octabas Domini* (nn. 48–53). In the *GrH* (nn. 82–84) the station for the octave is *ad Sanctam Mariam ad Martyres*, and the collect of the Mass is Marian in its content. Here we find the traces of the first Marian feast of the Roman liturgy on January 1 or the *Natale sanctae Mariae*, which later disappeared

[38] Augustine, *Epist.* 55, 1: PL 33:205. Cf. Augustine, *Letters*, vol. 1 (1–82), trans. Sr. W. Parson (New York, 1951) 261.

[39] St. Leo the Great, *Tractatus* 28 *(De Natale Domini)* 1: CCL 138, 139.

[40] J. Gaillard, "Noël, memoria ou mystère?" *MD* 59 (1959) 37–59.

with the emergence of other Marian feasts.[41] In any case, there was a Marian stamp on the feast of New Year's Day during the Middle Ages.[42] In the *MR1570* the festival was called *In circumcisione Domini et octava Nativitatis.* The reform of Vatican II has renewed the Marian character of this day, which is called *In octava Nativitatis Domini, Sollemnitas Sanctae Dei Genetricis Mariae* in the *MR1970.* The Roman Calendar (*General Norms,* n. 35) records that on this day the giving of the Most Holy Name of Jesus is also recalled.

Between Christmas Day and the celebration of its octave, we find a series of feasts of saints, which are connected with the celebrations of Christmas in such a way as to form a sort of unity with them. As early as the *Ve* there are, immediately after the Christmas Masses, two formulas for *In Natale Sancti Johannis Evangelistae* (nn. 1273–1283) and an additional two *In Natale Innocentum* (nn. 1284–1293). The Würzburg Lectionary makes note of the feasts of St. Stephen, St. John the Evangelist, St. Innocent, and St. Sylvester. The same is true of the *GrH* (nn. 62–66, 67–74, 75–78, 79–81). There is no feast of St. Sylvester in the *GeV.*[43] Later books also contained a formula for the Sunday after Christmas. The *MR1570* had celebrations for St. Stephen, St. John the Evangelist, the Holy Innocents, the Sunday *infra octavam,* St. Thomas of Canterbury, the sixth day *infra octavam,* and St. Sylvester. The *MR1970* retains the same feasts, but the memorials of the saints are placed in the Proper of the Saints. The Sunday within the octave is called the Feast of the Holy Family of Jesus, Mary, and Joseph. The weekdays of December 29, 30, and 31 have proper Masses.

The *OLM* offers a greater richness and variety of biblical readings for Christmas and the octave than was the case in the past. All these texts, euchological and biblical, show that Christmas is celebrated as a feast of redemption. This is in accord with the most ancient Roman tradition, stemming from Pope St. Leo the Great. This is immediately apparent in the collect for the vigil Mass (a text that was in the *GrH,* n. 33, and the *MR1570,* as well as the sacramentary currently in use):

[41] B. Botte, "La première fête mariale de la liturgie romaine," *EphLit* 47 (1933) 425–430. Chavasse, *Sacramentaire,* 381–388, 651–656.

[42] *Micrologus:* PL 151:1007.

[43] The Middle Ages saw in these saints the court of honor for the Christ Child and called them "Comites Christi" (cf. G. Durandus in his work of mysticism, allegory, and morality *Rationale divinorum officiorum,* I, 7, c. 41).

Deus, qui nos redemptionis nostrae annua exspectatione laetificas, praesta, ut Unigenitum tuum, quem laeti suscipimus Redemptorem, venientem quoque Iudicem securi videre mereamur.

3. *The Origin of Epiphany*

The feast of the Epiphany of the Lord, as the name suggests (ἐπιφάνεια = "manifestation" or "apparition") originated in the East. The oldest traces of the feast are found in Alexandria in Egypt. In the second century the gnostic sects were already celebrating this feast there as a commemoration of the Baptism of Jesus, which was also, in their opinion, his birth as Son of God.[44] It is not clear either when or how this gnostic celebration of the Baptism became the feast of the Epiphany in the Church of Egypt. It is known that, by the end of the fourth century, there was a feast of the Epiphany (celebrated on January 6) in various Eastern and Western Churches. These feasts differed greatly in their content: the baptism of Jesus, his birth, the adoration of the Magi, the miracle of Cana, and others. After the introduction of Christmas into the East, Epiphany was generally a celebration of the Baptism of Christ in these Churches. The first certain notice of its celebration in Rome is in the middle of the fifth century, when we find a series of Epiphany homilies given by St. Leo the Great. The object of the feast, according to these homilies, was the adoration of the Magi, the theme that would prevail in most of the Western Churches.

The development of Epiphany in the Eastern Churches was similar to that of Christmas in the West. In Egypt there was a pagan celebration of the light in honor of the birth of the sun god Aion from the virgin Kore. This happened at the time of the winter solstice, about two weeks after December 25, on the night of January 5 or 6. On this occasion water was drawn from the Nile and reserved.[45] This is probably the origin of the Eastern feast of the Epiphany, which focused, as has been said above, on the Baptism of Jesus.

4. *Developments in the Celebration of Epiphany up to the Present Day*

The oldest Mass formulas are found in *GeV* (nn. 61–68), where the feast is called *Theophania*. Later, in the *GrH* (nn. 87–91), we have the

[44] Clement of Alexandria, *Stromata* 1, 21: PG 8:887.

[45] Epiphanius of Salamis, *Adversus haereses*, 51, 22–30: PG 41:927–943. See also the study of R. G. Coquin, "Les origines de l'Epiphanie en Egypte," *Nöel-Epiphanie-Retour du Christ*. Semaine liturgique de l'Institut St.-Serge, *LO* 47 (1967) 139–170.

formula *Epiphania ad Sanctum Petrum.* In the most recent stratum of the *GeV,* there is also a vigil Mass for the feast (nn. 57–60). A formula for the octave is found only in the Gelasian from the eighth century. The liturgical books of the Roman Curia of the thirteenth century and, later, the *MR1570* took up these developments and, for the feast, used the formula of the *GrH.* The *Codex Rubricarum* of 1960 definitively eliminated the vigil and the octave. The *MR1970* maintained the formula for the Mass on the day of Epiphany that had been used in *MR1570.*

Adrien Nocent has made a synopsis of the biblical texts proclaimed on the day of Epiphany. One sees that there has been a fairly constant tradition in the choice of passages up to and including the current *OLM.*[46] According to the oldest *Antiphonari,* all the chants are derived from Psalm 71 [72], which is still used today as the responsorial psalm. We may conclude, therefore, that both the euchological texts and the biblical texts for the feast of the Epiphany have remained practically unchanged in the Roman liturgy. This allows us to reflect on the entire contents of the feast.

The Magi who come to visit Jesus (Matt 2:1-12) are considered to be the "first fruits of the nations" to whom he manifests himself because he is Lord of all the peoples of the earth. Based on this theme, the embolism of the preface in the *MR1570,* which we find in all of the textual traditions, from the vigil Mass in the *GeV* on, expresses the mystery celebrated in these words.

Quia ipsum in Christo salutis nostrae mysterium hodie ad lumen gentium revelasti, et, cum in substantia nostrae mortalitatis apparuit, nova nos immortalitatis eius gloria reparasti.

The thought behind this text is our renewal in the strength of the light of Christ, which drives away human darkness. The Epiphany celebrates the same mystery as Christmas, but it does so by focusing on the manifestation of the infinite glory of the only-begotten Son of the Father and the universal call to all people to find salvation in Christ.

The antiphons for the *Benedictus* at Lauds and the *Magnificat* at Vespers speak of the three great works celebrated on this day: the Magi, the Baptism of Jesus, and Cana. However, the Roman liturgy celebrates the feast of the Baptism of Jesus and remembers the miracle

[46] A. Nocent, "Il Tempo della Manifestazione," *Anàmnesis* 6:187.

of Cana on the first two Sundays of Ordinary Time respectively (the gospel reading from Year C).

5. The Season of Advent

According to its usage in the language of pagan worship, the Latin word *adventus* (a translation of the Greek παρουσία or ἐπιφάνεια) referred to the annual visit of the god to his temple in order to visit his people. The Roman *Chronograph* of 354 used the formula *Adventus Divi* to refer to the anniversary of Constantine's ascension. In the Christian authors of the third and fourth centuries, *adventus* is, among other things, one of the classic ways to refer to the coming of the Son of God among humanity, his manifestation in time and in the flesh.[47] In the ancient Roman sacramentaries, the term is used both for the coming of the Son of God in the flesh, the *Adventus secundum carnem*, and his coming at the end of time (cf. *GrH*, n. 813).

At the end of the fourth century, we find the first hints of a season of preparation for Epiphany in Gaul and in Spain. The oldest witness is a text attributed to St. Hilary of Poitiers († 367), where he speaks of three weeks of preparation for Epiphany.[48] The fourth canon of the Council of Saragossa, celebrated in the year 380, invited the faithful to attend the assembly during the three weeks that preceded the feast of the Epiphany.[49] It is a period that has a vaguely ascetical character without any specifically liturgical expression. It seems to be a season of preparation for baptism, which, according to the Eastern custom, was conferred on the day of Epiphany. In the fifth century we have more information for Gaul, the most important reference being that of Perpetuus of Tours on the arrangement of the fast. This referred to a thrice-weekly fast during the season that extended from the feast of St. Martin of Tours (November 11) until Christmas. J. A. Jungmann believed that this arrangement had its origin in a "Lent of St. Martin."[50] At Rome, where baptism on Epiphany was not the custom, there is no mention of a preparation for Christmas before the second half of the

[47] Cyprian, *Testimoniorum adversus Judaeos*, 2, 13: PL 4:735; Hilary of Poitiers, *Tractatus super psalmos* 118, 16, 15: PL 9:612.

[48] Concerning this text and its authenticity, see A. Wilmart, "Le prétendu *Liber Officiorum* de St. Hilaire et l'Avent liturgique," *RBén* 27 (1910) 500–513.

[49] J. Vives, ed., *Concilios visigóticos e hispano-romanos* (Barcelona, 1963) 17.

[50] J. A. Jungmann, *Advent und Voradvent: Überreste des gallischen Advents in der römischen Liturgie.* Gewordene Liturgie. Studien und Durchblicke (Innsbruck, 1941) 237–49.

sixth century. However, in this case it was a specifically liturgical institution from its beginning. The oldest documents in this regard are the liturgical texts of the *GeV* and, later, those of the *GrH*. The *tempora* of the month of December had a meaning independent of preparation for Christmas.

6. Developments in the Celebration of Advent up to the Present Day

In the *GeV* (nn. 1120–56) and in the *GrH* (nn. 778–813) we find a series of formulas that have been collected toward the end of the book under the title *Orationes de Adventu Domini*. These formulas do not seem to have been connected to Christmas, the texts for which are found at the beginning of the book, as we said earlier. Later, the proximity of Christmas caused its content to become part of these texts. The biblical passages indicated in the first Roman lectionaries show that the ancient Roman Advent referred both to the coming of the Lord in the flesh and at the end of time.[51]

A. Chavasse has distinguished two original textual traditions in the ancient formulas for Advent.[52] The older form, the presbyteral form contained in *GeV*, consisted of the six weeks prior to Christmas, whereas the second, that of the papal liturgy of St. Gregory the Great in the *GrH*, was only four weeks in duration. For a while both traditions coexisted in Rome. It is only in the liturgical books of the twelfth and thirteenth centuries that the custom of four weeks for Advent is definitively imposed.

After the Roman liturgy came into contact with that of Gaul, during the Carolingian era or even later, ascetical and penitential elements proper to the Gallican tradition were introduced into the Roman Advent. However, this did not change the structure of the Roman Advent.

A look at the gospel reading selected for the First Sunday of Advent in the ancient lectionaries will show how Advent was understood during the high Middle Ages. The passage used was the entry of Jesus into Jerusalem (Matt 21:1-9),[53] a choice that was not adopted by the *MR1570*. The pericope, also used at the beginning of Holy Week, shows the Lord "who comes" in humility and glory, as servant and as

[51] See the table in Nocent, "Il Tempo della Manifestazione," *Anàmnesis* 6:195.

[52] Chavasse, *Sacramentaire*, 412–426.

[53] This was true in the second phase of the *Evangeliarius* of Würzburg. See the table in Nocent, *Anàmnesis*, 6:195.

king, as a man and God. This episode was presented by the liturgy as an image of the whole mystery of the Advent of the Lord from his first coming, in which he fulfilled the messianic hopes of the ancient Chosen People, until his return in glory, when he will fulfill the hope of the Church.

Despite the complexity of the origins of Advent, this liturgical season eventually formed a unity with Christmas (Epiphany), for which it is the preparation. The reform realized after Vatican II has tried to make clearer the sense in which it is the preparation for Christmas and, at the same time, a time of expectation for the final coming of Christ: "Advent has a twofold character: as a season to prepare for Christmas when Christ's first coming to us is remembered, as a season when that remembrance directs the mind and hearts to await Christ's Second Coming at the end of time" (*General Norms,* n. 39).

Advent is therefore not a penitential time that looks forward to the return of the Lord for judgment but rather a celebration of the Incarnation, and only in that light a time of waiting for the parousia. The celebration of the birth of Jesus prepares us for the definitive encounter with him (see collect for December 21). The first coming of Christ began that which the second and final coming will bring to completion. The presence of both these aspects of the mystery of Christ explains why the two comings of Christ are interwoven in the texts. On the other hand, in every celebration, each of which occurs in time and space and yet is eschatological as well, there emerges the entire paschal mystery, which began at the Incarnation but which will be fulfilled at the parousia.

In the current arrangement, Advent begins with first Vespers of the Sunday that falls on November 30 or is nearest to that date and ends with first Vespers of Christmas (see *General Norms,* n. 40). In the *MR1970* each of the weekdays from December 17 to December 24 has a proper Mass, which was not the case previously. Until December 16 the weekdays only have a proper collect and biblical readings. The tone of eschatological expectation is stronger in the biblical and euchological texts of the first two weeks, whereas there is special attention to preparation for Christmas in the remaining weeks, especially after December 17.[54]

[54] Concerning the new arrangement of biblical readings, see A. Carideo, "Il Lezionario del Tempo di Avvento: Nell'attesa della tua venuta," *Il Messale Romano*

IV. THE SEASON OF ORDINARY TIME

The beginnings of Ordinary Time may be found simply by looking at Sunday celebrations that lacked additional liturgical specification. The number of ordinary Sundays (and weeks) was gradually reduced in the first centuries as the liturgical year began to be organized. In the earliest documents these Sundays had no specific title. So, for example, the *GeV* contains sixteen formulas for Masses with the generic title . . . *pro dominicis diebus* (nn. 1178–1241). Later, in the Gelasian of the eighth century and in other sources close to it, we find six Sundays *post Theophaniam* and between twenty-two and twenty-seven Sundays *post Pentecosten.* In the *MR1570* there are from four to six Sundays *post Epiphaniam* and twenty-four Sundays *post Pentecosten.* These few historical data suffice to give one an idea of the profound rearrangement accomplished by Vatican II in this part of the liturgical year. Indeed, one might well speak of this as a liturgical season that is completely new, both in name and in content. These Sundays, and their respective weeks, are no longer referred to as being *after* Epiphany or *after* Pentecost; they have been given a unity, a continuity, and an internal cohesion, thus creating the season now known as Ordinary Time. It begins on the Monday that follows the Sunday after January 6 and lasts until the Tuesday before Lent, inclusive. It begins again with the Monday after Pentecost and ends before first Vespers of the first Sunday of Advent (see *General Norms*, n. 44).

The Sundays and the weekdays of Ordinary Time derive their character especially from the biblical readings assigned by the *OLM.* Whereas the readings chosen for the seasons that have a particular liturgical character are chosen so as to be in harmony with those seasons, the readings of Ordinary Time work according to a principle of semi-continuity; that is to say, an entire book is read in a sequence, with some sections being omitted for pastoral reasons. At this point

del Vaticano II: Orazionale e Lezionario, Quaderni di Rivista Liturgica 6 (Turin-Leumann, 1984) 1:39–70. For the euchology see M. Augé, "Le collette di Avvento-Natale-Epiphania nel Messale Romano, " *RL* 59 (1972) 614–627; B. Baroffio, "Le orazioni dopo la comunione del Tempo di Avvento," *RL* 59 (1972) 649–662; G. Francesconi, "Per una lettura teologico-liturgica dei prefazi di Avvento- Natale-Epiphania del Messale Romano," *RL* 59 (1972) 628–648; F. Brovelli, "Le orazioni del Tempo di Avvento e di Natale," Il Messale Romano del Vaticano II: Orazionale e Lezionario, 1:97–136.

we will summarize the criteria by which the readings are distributed (for more details, see *OLM* 1981, *Praenotanda*, nn. 103–110).

Sunday has three readings: the first from the Old Testament, the second from an apostle (a letter or the Book of Revelation), and Gospel. Beginning with the third Sunday there is a semi-continuous reading of the synoptic Gospels: Matthew (Year A), Mark (Year B), and Luke (Year C). In Year B, given the brevity of Mark's Gospel, five readings from John 6 are inserted after the sixteenth Sunday. The Old Testament readings are thematically harmonized with the Gospels. The apostolic readings, also semi-continuous, are taken from the letters of Paul, James, and Hebrews. The readings for the thirty-fourth Sunday, the last in Ordinary Time, "celebrate Christ the universal King. He was prefigured by David and proclaimed as king amid the humiliations of his Passion and Cross; he reigns in the Church and will come again at the end of time" (*OLM* 1981, *Praenotanda*, n. 108).

The weekdays do not have a proper euchology for Mass but do have a proper arrangement of biblical readings. This arrangement is divided into two years, but the gospel is the same in both years. The first reading is taken either from the Old Testament or from an apostle (a letter, the Acts of the Apostles, or the Book of Revelation). These alternate in periods of irregular length, since the various books differ in length. For the gospels, the arrangement that has been adopted provides that Mark is read first (weeks 1–9), then Matthew (weeks 10–21), and finally Luke (weeks 22–34). It should be noted that the weekday lectionary for Ordinary Time is an absolute novelty in the Roman liturgy.

The contents of the euchology for the Sunday Masses of this liturgical period consider the mystery of Christ in an extremely varied fashion. Some national missals have added prefaces, a series of alternative collects for the Sundays that are thematically harmonized with the biblical readings, and additional collects that may be chosen for use on weekdays.

During Ordinary Time, the Liturgy of the Hours uses a four-week division of the psalter with readings, responses, antiphons, and invocations. The only proper texts are the biblical and patristic readings for each day, the antiphons for the *Benedictus* and *Magnificat*, and the Sunday collects recited at Lauds and Vespers.

The Sundays of Ordinary Time may be thought of as Sundays in a pure state. They express, without any secondary specification, the mystery of Sunday as a weekly celebration of Easter. Ordinary Time celebrates the mystery of Christ (and the Church) in their totality every week, especially on Sunday (see *General Norms,* n. 43). The key to understanding this season is always the mystery of Christ. The semi-continuous reading of the Gospels is at the center of Christian spirituality because it presents us with the life and words of Jesus, what he did and what he taught. To understand the mystery of Christ in Ordinary Time means that one must take one's vocation as a disciple seriously. This means that one endeavors to hear and follow the Teacher in daily life, that one does not bracket off ordinary life but sees it as a saving moment. The semi-continuous reading of the other books of the Old and New Testaments gives the Christian community a chance to measure its own perseverance in faithfully awaiting the coming of the Lord against the examples of the Chosen People of God and the primitive Christian community. Ordinary Time is a time for growth and maturation, a time in which the mystery of Christ is called to penetrate ever more deeply into history until all things are finally caught up in Christ. The goal, toward which all of history is directed, is represented by the solemnity of Christ the King.

The paschal cycle divides Ordinary Time into two sections. This does not hinder the progressive celebration of the mystery of Christ. In fact, the paschal cycle offers a wonderful continuity in the evocation of the life of Christ. We recall that Lent begins with the accounts of the temptations and the transfiguration, moments in which Jesus stepped decisively onto the road that would lead him to Easter. This was the goal and culmination of his life and, therefore, that which sheds light on all of the events and words of his entire existence.

The current Roman liturgical books append a series of solemnities of the Lord to the end of Ordinary Time: Trinity Sunday, Corpus Christi, the Sacred Heart, and Christ the King. These solemnities, which have arisen in the second millennium of the Christian era, are not intended to celebrate a particular aspect of the mystery of Christ or to provide some new and specific content that is not to be found in the other celebrations of the liturgical year. In any case, they are festivals that may be easily understood in the theological context of Ordinary Time that we have already outlined.

Bibliography

AA.VV. *L'anno liturgico.* Atti della XI Settimana di studio dell'Associazione Professori di Liturgia, Brescia, August 23–27, 1982. Studi di liturgia, n.s. 11. Casale Monferrato, 1983.

AA.VV. *L'Anno liturgico: Storia, teologia e celebrazione. Anàmnesis* 6. Genoa, 1988.

AA.VV. *Ritmos y tiempos de la celebración.* La celebración en la Iglesia 3. Salamanca, 1990.

Adam, A. *The Liturgical Year: Its History and Its Meaning after the Reform of the Liturgy.* Trans. M. O'Connell. New York, 1981; Collegeville, Minn., 1990.

Auf der Maur, H. *Feiern im Rhythmus der Zeit* I: *Herrenfeste in Woche und Jahr.* Gottesdienst der Kirche: Handbuch der Liturgiewissenschaft, Teil 5. Regensburg, 1983.

Beckhauser, A. *Viver em Cristo: Espiritualidade do Ano Litúrgico.* Petrópolis, 1992.

Bergamini, A. *Cristo festa della Chiesa: Storia-teologia-spiritualità-pastorale dell'anno liturgico.* Parola e Liturgia 10. Rome, 1982.

Bernal, J. M. *Iniciación al Año litúrgico.* Academia Christiana 24. Madrid, 1984.

Castellano Cervera, J. *L'anno liturgico: Memoriale di Cristo e mistagogia della Chiesa con Maria Madre di Gesù. Corso di spiritualità liturgica.* Serie di Pastorale e di Studio 5. Rome, 1987.

Dalmais, I. H., P. Jounel, A.-G. Martimort. *The Liturgy and Time. CP* 4.

López Martin, J. *El año liturgico: Historia y teología de los tiempos festivos cristianos.* Biblioteca di autores cristianos, Popular 62. Madrid, 1984.

Marsili, S. "Anno liturgico." In *I segni del Mistero di Cristo: Teologia liturgica dei sacramenti.* Ed. M. Alberta. BELS 42. Rome, 1987.

Righetti, M. *Manuale di storia liturgica.* Vol. 2, *L'anno liturgico.* 3rd ed. Milan, 1969.

Sodi, M., and G. Morante. *Anno liturgico: Itinerario di fede e di vita. Orientamenti e proposte catechetico-pastorali.* Studi e ricerche di catechetica 11. Turin-Leumann, 1988.

Taft, R. "The Liturgical Year: Studies, Prospects, Reflections." *Wor* 55 (1981) 2–23.

Talley, T. *The Origins of the Liturgical Year.* 2nd ed. Collegeville, Minn., 1991.

I. DEVELOPMENTS IN THE CELEBRATION OF EASTER FROM THE FOURTH CENTURY TO THE SIXTEENTH CENTURY

Beatrice, P. F. *La lavanda dei piedi: Contributo alla storia delle antiche liturgie cristiane.* BELS 28. Rome, 1983.

Bergamini, A. "Quaresima." *NDL* 1080–1083.

____. "Triduo pasquale." *NDL* 1431–1435.

Cabié, R. *La Pentecôte: L'évolution de la Cinquantaine pascale au cours des cinq premiers siècles.* Bibliotheque de liturgie. Tournai, 1965.

Chavasse, A. *Le Sacramentaire gélasien (Vaticanus Reginensis 316). Sacramentaire presbytéral en usage dans les titres romains au VIIe siècle.* Bibliothèque de théologie. Série IV. Histoire de la théologie l. Tournai, 1958.

Fuchs, G., and H. M. Weikmann. *Das Exsultet: Geschichte Theologie und Gestaltung der österlichen Lichtdanksagung.* Regensburg, 1992.

Jounel, P. "Le dimanche et le Temps de Paques. 2: La tradition de l'Église." *MD* 67 (1961) 163–182.

____. "La liturgie du mystère pascal. 2: Le dimanche des Rameaux." *MD* 8 (1961) 45–63.

____. "La nuit pascal. 2: La tradition de l'Église." *MD* 67 (1961) 123–44.

____. "Les vêpres de Pâques." *MD* 49 (1957) 96–111.

Marsili, S. "Il 'Triduo sacro' e il 'Giovedi santo.'" *RL* 55 (1968) 21–37.

Pinell, J. "La benedicció del ciri pasqual i els seus textos." *Liturgica* 2:1–119. Scripta et Documenta 10. Montserrat, 1958.

Schmidt, H. A. P. *Hebdomada Sancta.* Vol. 2, *Fontes historici, commentarius historicus.* Rome, 1957.

Stevenson, K. "The Ceremonies of Light: Their Shape and Function in the Paschal Vigil Liturgy." *EphLit* 99 (1985) 170–185.

Van Dijk, S. J. P. "The Medieval Easter Vesper of the Roman Clergy." *SE* 19 (1969/1970) 261–363.

II. THE CELEBRATION OF EASTER AFTER THE REFORMS OF THE SECOND VATICAN COUNCIL

AA.VV. *Il Messale Romano del Vaticano II: Orazionale e Lezionario.* Vol. l, *La celebrazione del Mistero di Cristo nell'anno liturgico,* 177–484. Quaderni di Rivista Liturgica, n.s. 6. Turin-Leumann, 1984.

Bellavista, J. "La actual Cincuentena pascual." *Ph* 11 (1971) 223–231.

____. "Los temas mayores de la Cincuentena pascual." *Ph* 19 (1979) 125–135.

Bugnini, A., and C. Braga. "Ordo Hebdomadae Sanctae instauratus: Commentarium." *EphLit* 70 (1957) 81–228.

Catella, A., and G. Remondi, eds. *Celebrare l'unità del Triduo pasquale.* Vol. 1, *Il Triduo oggi e il Prologo del Giovedì santo.* Quaderni di Rivista Liturgica, n.s. 9/1. Turin-Leumann, 1994.

____. *Celebrare l'unità del Triduo pasquale.* Vol. 2, *Venerdì santo: La luce del Traffito e il perdono del Messia.* Quaderni di Rivista Liturgica, n.s. 9/2. Turin-Leumann, 1995.

Cavagnoli, G. "La celebrazione pasquale nella rinnovata liturgia romana: Analisi della struttura rituale." *RL* 77 (1990) 18–36.

Heinz, A. "Die Sonntagsformulare der Osterzeit im Missale Romanum Pius V und Paulus VI." *LJ* 28 (1978) 86–111.

Mosso, D. "Per celebrare il Triduo pasquale: La proposta del Messale Romano." *RL* 61 (1974) 222–235.

Vorgrimler, H. "Zum theologischen Gehalt der neuen Osternmachtfeier." *LJ* 21 (1971) 32–37.

III. THE SEASON OF THE MANIFESTATION OF THE LORD

AA.VV. "Avent, Noël, Épiphanie." *MD* 59 (1959).

AA.VV. "Avvento-Natale-Epifania: Celebrazione della Manifestazione del Signore." *RL* 59 (1972) fascicle 5.

AA.VV. *Il Messale Romano del Vaticano II: Orazionale e Lezionario.* Vol. 1, *La celebrazione del Mistero di Cristo nell'anno liturgico,* 37–175. Quaderni di Rivista Liturgica, n.s. 6. Turin-Leumann, 1984.

AA.VV. *Noël, Épiphanie, Retour du Christ.* Semaine liturgique de l'Institut Saint-Serge. LO 40. Paris, 1967.

Bergamini, A. "Avvento." *NDL* 127–130.

____. "Natale/Epifania." *NDL* 857–860.

B. Botte. *Les origines de la Noël et de l'Épiphanie: Étude historique.* Textes et études liturgiques 1. Louvain, 1932.

Chavasse, A. "L'Avent romain, du VIe au VIIIe siècle." *EphLit* 67 (1953) 297–308.

Croce, W. "Die Adventsliturgie im Licht ihrer geschichtlichen Entwicklung." *ZKTh* 76 (1954) 257–296.

Cullmann, O. *Der Ursprung des Weihnachtsfestes.* Zürich/Stuttgart, 1960^{2}.

Engberding, H. "Der 25. Dezember als Tag der Feier der Gehurt des Herrn." *ALW* 2 (1952) 25–43.

Frank, H. "Frühgeschichte und Ursprung des römischen Weihnachlfestes im Lichte neuerer Forschung." *ALW* (1952) 1–24.

Jungmann, J. A. *Advent und Voradvent: Überreste des gallischen Advents in der römischen Liturgie,* 237–294. Gewordene Liturgie. Studien und Durchblicke. Innsbruck, 1941.

Lemarié, J. *La manifestation du Seignor: La liturgie de Noël et de l'Épiphanie.* LO 23. Paris, 1957.

Mohrmann, C. "Epiphania." *Études sur le latin des chrétiens.* Vol. 1, *Le latin des chrétiens.* 2nd ed., 245–275. Rome, 1961.

Raffin, P. "La fête de Noël, fête de l'évenement ou fête d'idée?" In *Le Christ dans la liturgie.* Conférences de Saint-Serge, XXVIIe Semaine d'Études Liturgiques, 169–178. BELS 20. Rome, 1981.

IV. THE SEASON OF ORDINARY TIME

AA.VV. "El 'Tiempo Ordinario' del año litúrgico." *Ph* 32 (1992) 179–254.

AA.VV. *Il Messale Romano del Vaticano II: Orazionale e Lezionario.* Vol. l, *La celebrazione del Mistero di Cristo nell'anno liturgico,* 485–587. Quaderni di Rivista Liturgica, n.s. 6. Turin-Leumann, 1984.

AA.VV. "Il Tempo Ordinario."*RPL* 4 (1995) 3–62.

AA.VV. "Les dimanches verts." *MD* 46 (1956).

Damian Gaitan, J. *La celebración del Tiempo Ordinario.* Biblioteca Liturgica 2. Barcelona, 1994.

López Martin, J. "Tiempo Ordinario." *NDL* 1967–1972.

Nocent, A. *The Liturgical Year.* Vol. 4, *Sundays Nine to Thirty-Four in Ordinary Time.* Collegeville, Minn., 1977.

Scicolone, I. "Il Tempo 'per annum.'"*Anàmnesis* 6:207–220.

Gabriel Ramis

9

The Liturgical Year in the Non-Roman West

There is no doubt that the annual Easter celebration is the nucleus from which the liturgical year has evolved and developed in all the liturgies. This evolution and development are verified in the liturgical books, through which we are able to follow the path of such development. We are also able to follow the evolution indirectly, above all in the sermons of the Fathers, since they were preached on Sundays and holy days of the liturgical year.

THE AFRICAN LITURGY

We do not have any liturgical books of the African liturgy that would allow us to follow the development and evolution of the liturgical year, but we are able to do this by using indirect testimonies. We know that at the beginning of the third century the celebration of Easter and Pentecost formed a single feast of fifty days, as if it were the celebration of only one Sunday. This cycle will later develop into the celebration of the Easter Triduum, Holy Week, and Lent. The Christmas cycle is made up of the feast of the Epiphany and the fast at the beginning of the year. These two cycles are already very well defined in the post-Nicene period.

THE AMBROSIAN LITURGY

At the end of the fourth century at Milan, Saturday was considered one with Sunday, and for this reason Saturday was not a day of fasting. Saturday and Sunday formed a weekly unit in which the mystery of the risen Lord was celebrated. At this same time in Milan the two cycles of Christmas and Easter already existed.

1. Lent and Easter

The celebration of Easter Sunday is preceded by the celebration of the Easter Triduum. The latter, which is included within Holy Week, begins with Palm Sunday. The days of Holy Week are called weekdays *in authentica.*

After Lent we come to the celebration of Easter and the Easter Triduum. Lent begins with the first Sunday, called *In capite ieiunii.* This first Sunday is followed by four more, and these four Sundays are followed by Palm Sunday, the beginning of Holy Week. Since neither Saturday nor Sunday was a day of fasting at Milan, two weeks of fasting were established before beginning Lent in order to complete the forty days of fasting. These were the Sundays of Sexagesima (sixty days) and Quinquagesima (fifty days).

The fifty days of Easter continue and prolong the celebration of Easter. These fifty days are celebrated as if they were only a single feast, and for these days the Alleluia song is reserved. Later the feast of the Ascension and the Rogation Days were added.

2. Advent and Christmas

In the Ambrosian liturgy, Advent is parallel to Lent: there are six weeks of Advent, with their respective Sundays. Advent begins on the eve of the first Sunday; the sixth Sunday is dedicated to the Virgin Mary.

In the week that precedes Christmas, the Office of Matins has its own psalmody, different from that used on other days. After the sixth century this week was called *de exceptato.*

The feasts of St. Stephen, St. James, the Holy Innocents, and the Mass of St. James all follow Christmas; on the first day of the year the octave of Christmas and the Circumcision of the Lord are celebrated. On the day of the Epiphany the feast of Easter is announced, and the catechumens are invited to enroll for baptism.

At Milan the Christmas feast comes after the feast of Epiphany, the latter being celebrated earlier at Milan than at Rome. To calculate the feast of Epiphany at Milan, the Eastern computation, which was based on the phase of the moon, was used. Thus the celebration of the feast of Easter at Milan did not coincide with the celebration at Rome.

3. Ordinary Time

The Sundays that fell outside the cycles mentioned above were distributed in the Missal of 1751 in the following way: fifteen Sundays after Pentecost; five Sundays after the feast of the Beheading of St. John the Baptist; the first Sunday of October; the Sunday before the dedication of the church; three Sundays after the dedication. We also must note that the Milanese liturgical year begins after the feast of St. Martin.

THE GALLICAN LITURGY

Although the Gallican sources did not evolve completely and are therefore quite faulty, we nevertheless are able to discover a fairly complete structure of the liturgical year.

1. *Advent*

The sources do not agree on the length of Advent. According to the Bobbio Missal, Advent has three Sundays; however, according to the lectionary of Schettstadt, it has six. The Trier lectionary includes four Sundays with these titles: (a) *ante una hebdomada de natale Domini;* (b) *ante una dominica de natale Domini;* (c) *ante natale Domini;* (d) *ante Nativitate Domini.*

2. *Christmas-Epiphany*

The Bobbio Missal and the *Missale Gothicum,* together with all the lectionaries, reproduce the feasts of this cycle, which include the Vigil of Christmas (except the lectionaries of Trier and Schettstadt); Christmas; the Circumcision of the Lord (except the lectionary of Schettstadt); the Vigil of Epiphany (except the Bobbio Missal and the lectionary of Schettstadt); and the Epiphany of the Lord.

Between the feasts of Christmas and the Epiphany of the Lord, the missals celebrate the following saints: Stephen, the Apostles James and John, and the Holy Innocents. The Luxeuil lectionary only celebrates the feast of the Apostle James, but after the Circumcision the feast of St. Genevieve is celebrated.

3. *Lent*

The Schettstadt and the Trier lectionaries include five Sundays in Lent. The Trier lectionary proposes a special Sunday before the beginning of Lent, and each of the Lenten Sundays is given a particular title.

The sacramentaries do not follow the ordered development of Lent; after the formulary of the beginning of Lent, other formularies of Lent or fasting are proposed, without being assigned a concrete day of celebration. Following these formularies and before the celebration of Holy Week, the Mass for the "handing over" of the Symbol (Creed) is celebrated.

4. Holy Week

Holy Week opens with Palm Sunday. In the lectionary of Luxeuil it is called *Dominica in authentica.* In the lectionary of Trier there is a Mass called *Ante una die coena Domini.*

The sacramentaries do not have the formulary of the Palm Sunday Mass; omitting these days of Holy Week, they skip directly to the celebration of the Easter Triduum, which begins with the celebration of Holy Thursday and ends with the Easter Vigil.

5. Easter Season

This season begins with Easter Sunday and ends with the feast of Pentecost. The sacramentaries only offer us the Masses of Easter and of the octave of Easter, ending with the Sunday of the octave, the *Dominica clausum Pascha.* The Bobbio Missal only proposes, in addition to the Easter Sunday Mass, three Easter Masses, whereas the *Missale Gallicanum Vetus* gives Mass formularies for two Sundays of Easter.

The lectionaries are more explicit. The Luxeuil lectionary includes five Sundays after Easter, as does the lectionary of Trier, while that of Schettstadt includes only three Sundays of Easter. All the sources agree on the feast of the Ascension, the Rogation Days, and the feast of Pentecost.

6. Ordinary Time

Among the sources there exist great differences about Ordinary Time. Whereas the sacramentaries barely offer Mass formularies, the lectionaries of Trier and of Schettstadt offer a great number of readings for this time.

THE HISPANIC LITURGY

Sunday was recognized all through the liturgical year as the Lord's Day, and for this reason it had special features. This is demonstrated in the peculiar structure of the cathedral Office and in the celebration of the Mass, in which the *Gloria* and the *Benedictiones* were sung, and after which a list of martyrs was recited.

But there is no doubt that the liturgical year is planned around the annual celebration of Easter. This celebration is lengthened by the Easter season, the fifty days between Easter and Pentecost. Lent and Holy Week were organized as a preparation for this period.

1. Lent

Lent begins with the first Sunday, called *Ad carnes tollendas*. This Sunday did not have a penitential character. During Vespers on this Sunday, the Alleluia was sung joyfully. The fast began on Monday.

The structure of Lent consisted of five Sundays, on which the catechumens were reminded of the great catechetical themes: the temptations of Jesus, the Samaritan woman, the man born blind, and the raising of Lazarus from the dead. The third Sunday, the Sunday after the account of the Samaritan woman, is called *De mediante*, because it divides Lent into two parts. The second part of Lent, after the *De mediante* Sunday, is called *De Traditione*, because in this second half of Lent the emphasis is placed upon the passion of Christ, above all in the hymns and prayers of the Office.

Before the celebration of Mass on Palm Sunday, the olive branches and palms are blessed, and in the Mass of this Sunday the chrism is blessed. Holy Week begins on this Sunday. The Easter Triduum begins on Holy Thursday and ends with the Easter Vigil. On Holy Thursday the Mass is celebrated in the afternoon *(ad nonam)*. There is another Mass *(per titulos)* for those who could not attend the afternoon Mass in the principal church; the same thing occurs on Holy Saturday.

On Good Friday there are two celebrations: the first is at midmorning, at the hour of Terce, in which the solemn adoration of the cross is celebrated in the church of that name; later in the afternoon, at the hour of None, there is the Office called *De indulgentia*. This is a penitential Office for the purification of the whole Church, which takes place exactly at the time of Jesus' death. During this Office, reconciliation of the penitents is also celebrated. Participation in this celebration is a necessary condition for sharing later in the Easter communion.

On Holy Saturday the Easter Vigil was celebrated at night. The vigil was made up of the *lucernarium*, or light ceremony; twelve readings, with the prayers of the faithful interspersed among them; the celebration of Christian initiation; and finally the Mass. The Easter Triduum concluded with the celebration of the Easter Vigil.

2. Easter and the Easter Season

On Easter Sunday the Mass of the Lord's resurrection was celebrated. This Sunday was the only feast that had an octave, which concluded on the following Sunday. Then followed the Sundays of Easter, until fifty days were completed—seven Sundays, counting the Sunday of the octave. After forty days, that is to say, the Thursday after the sixth Sunday, the feast of the Lord's Ascension was celebrated. From Ascension to Pentecost, the canonical litanies were celebrated. These were penitential days in preparation for the feast of Pentecost.

3. Advent-Christmas-Epiphany

In the fourth canon of the Council of Saragossa, a time of preparation is prescribed for the feast of Epiphany. This time of preparation is the first indication of the formation of Advent. The declaration of the council leads us to affirm that the Christmas celebration came after Epiphany.

Later, Advent developed into six weeks (five in tradition A), beginning after the feast of St. Martin and ending with the feast of Christmas. During Advent, specifically on December 18, a feast in honor of the Virgin Mary was observed.

After Christmas the feasts of St. Stephen, St. James, the "brother of the Lord" (Matt 13:55; Mark 6:3), and St. John were celebrated.

The beginning of the year was marked by the feast of the Circumcision of the Lord and by the feast *In caput anni,* which had a penitential character.

The feast of Epiphany was celebrated on January 6. After this the feast of the Holy Innocents was celebrated in order to conform to the Gospel chronology, since the slaughter of the children of Bethlehem did not take place before the Magi had gone to adore Christ but rather after.

4. Penitential Days

In addition to Lent, penitential days were established throughout the whole liturgical year. At the beginning of the year, the feast called *In caput anni,* three days of penitence were observed between January 1 and Epiphany. Before Pentecost three days of canonical litanies, also penitential days, were celebrated. Before the feast of St. Cyprian in September and before the feast of St. Martin in November, three days of fasting were observed.

5. Ordinary Time

The Sundays of the rest of the liturgical year were called *De quotidiano.* These Sundays are understood as independent celebrations, and there is no coherent cycle among them. The number of Sundays changes, depending on the different manuscripts.

6. The Sanctoral Cycle

In the calendar, the celebrations of the apostles Peter and Paul, Andrew, John the Evangelist, James the Less, Simon, Judas, and James the Great occupy the first part. After them come the Hispanic martyrs and also the martyrs of the universal Church. For John the Baptist, the feasts of his birth and martyrdom are celebrated. Also celebrated are the feasts of the Exaltation of Cross, the Chair of St. Peter, and St. Michael.

There are very few feasts of the confessors—only those of St. Martin, St. Jerome, and St. Augustine. St. Emilian is the only Hispanic confessor who appears in the calendar.

During Lent there are no celebrations of the feasts of any saints. The feasts of saints that are celebrated during the Easter or Advent seasons take on characteristics proper to these periods of the liturgical year.

CONCLUSION

After considering all the things we have just explained, we are able to come up with the following conclusions about the liturgical year in the non-Roman Western rites:

—the obvious centrality of the Easter celebration: the Easter Triduum, which comprises Thursday, Friday, and Saturday; and Sunday, which is the great feast of the resurrection of the Lord and which is followed by an octave;

—the celebration of the fifty days of Easter, with the feast of the Ascension forty days after Easter, and the celebration of the Rogation Days between this feast and Pentecost;

—the parallelism between Lent and Advent, with six weeks dedicated to each of these seasons;

—the Marian aspects of the last days of Advent, not only in the celebration of the sixth Sunday in the Ambrosian liturgy but also in the feast of the Virgin Mary on December 18 in the Hispanic liturgy.

Bibliography

THE AFRICAN LITURGY

Rousseau, O. "Saint Agustin et les homélies de Carême," *Rev Lit et Monastique* (1930) 105–119.

THE AMBROSIAN LITURGY

Callewaert, C. "La quaresima a Milano al tempo di S. Ambrogio." *A* 8 (1932) 273–282.

Cattaneo, E. "Appunti sull'ottava di Natale." *A* 14 (1938) 305–307.

Heiming, O. "La vigilia dei Santi nell'antico rito milanese." *A* 19 (1943) 112–118.

____. "Altliturgische Fastenferien in Mailand." *ALW* 2 (1952) 44–66.

Magistretti, M. "L'anno liturgico." *A* 13–14 (1937–1938) 241–245; 265–268; 19–21; 29–32; 85–89.

THE HISPANIC LITURGY

Aliaga, E. *Victoria de Cristo sobre la muerte en los textos eucarísticos de la octava pascual.* IEHE = Monografías 19. Rome, 1973.

Altes, F.-X. "L'evolució de les festes de Cap d'Any en l'antic Ritu Hispànic." *RCT* 6 (1981) 359–378.

Callewaert, C. "Le carême primitif dans la liturgie mozarabe." *RHE* 15 (1914).

Ferro Calvo, M. *La celebración de la venida del Señor en el oficio hispánico: Estudio histórico doctrinal de los formularios del Oficio para el ciclo natalicio en las dos tradiciones del rito hispánico.* Madrid, 1972.

Gibert, J. *Festum Resurrectionis: Estudio de las lecturas bíblicas y de los cantos de la liturgia de la Palabra de la misa hispánica durante la cincuentena pascual.* BELS 10. Rome, 1977.

Janini, J. "Cuaresma visigótica y carnes tollendas." *Antologica Annua* 9 (1961) 54–70.

Rovalo, P. "Temporal y santoral en el adviento visigodo: Su relación a través del oficio." *HS* 19 (1966) 243–320.

Sotillo, L. "El culto de la Virgen santísima en la liturgia hispano-visigótica-mozárabe." *Miscelanea Comillas* 22 (1954) 89–192.

Vives, J. "Santoral visigodo en calendarios e inscripciones." *AST* 14. Barcelona, 1941.

Ignazio M. Calabuig, O.S.M.

10

The Liturgical Cult of Mary in the East and West

I. THE PRESENCE OF THE VIRGIN IN THE LITURGY

Before tracing the history of liturgical devotion to the Virgin Mary and the reasons for its development, it seems useful, from a methodological point of view, to remind ourselves of what is apparent to all: the Mother of the Lord Jesus occupies a place of considerable importance in the Church's liturgy in both the East and the West. This is a liturgical fact of great importance because it places her at the very heart of the liturgy, the ritual celebration of the salvation accomplished in Christ.

The commemoration of the Virgin involves aspects of Christian worship that are not marginal but rather are integral to its very structures: the calendar, because the Church dedicates many feasts to the one who is blessed among women (Luke 1:42); the celebration of the Eucharist, the memorial of Easter, in which the Mother of Jesus is always recalled with loving reverence; the sacramental rites, signs that communicate grace, in which the mention of holy Mary, sometimes subtle and sometimes bold, has various meanings; the Liturgy of the Hours, which is almost a catalogue of the various expressions—veneration, praise, supplication, etc.—of Marian devotion; churches that are dedicated to the Blessed Virgin. In its structure and iconology, especially in the East, devotion to Mary provides an illustration of the cooperation of the new Eve in the saving work of the Redeemer.

In liturgical art—music, painting, sculpture, etc.—the image of the Virgin plays a great part. This is extremely significant for its frequency, the great value of the artistry involved, and the light that these works shed on the celebration of the saving mystery.

The Constitution on the Sacred Liturgy of Vatican II, *Sacrosanctum Concilium*, synthesizes, in an authoritative way, what the Church teaches about the place of the holy Theotokos in the liturgy: "In celebrating this annual cycle of the mysteries of Christ, Holy Church honors the Blessed Mary, Mother of God, with a special love. She is inseparably linked with her son's saving work."[1]

Liturgical devotion to holy Mary encompasses a vast area. It is necessary, however, to interpret it correctly both in order to dispel doubts about the legitimacy of such devotion in a liturgical setting and also to make evident how valuable it is in the liturgy, which has as its ultimate aim nothing other than the perfect glorification of God and the sanctification of humanity.[2]

II. HISTORICAL PROFILE

When one tries to present a historical scheme that deals at one and the same time with both East and West, some disjunction will inevitably result. Nevertheless, it seems to me that the history of Marian devotion can be divided into these periods: 1. The first century: The biblical witness; 2. The period before the Council of Nicea; 3. The period from the Council of Nicea (325) to the death of Gregory the Great († 604); 4. The seventh century: A decisive time; 5. The eighth and ninth centuries both in the Byzantine East and in the West; 6. The period from the tenth century to the beginning of the Council of Trent (1545); 7. The period from the end of the Council of Trent (1563) to the Second Vatican Council (1962–1965); 8. The period of postconciliar liturgical renewal.

1. The First Century: The Biblical Witness

The importance of the biblical witness is evident to all. The New Testament, a document of the liturgical praxis of the primitive Church, provides the literary foundation for devotion to the Blessed Virgin in the liturgy. Of course, it is not possible to claim that one can find a fully developed form of Marian devotion in the New Testament. However, current research finds in Matthew 1–2 and Luke 1–2 (the so-called "infancy narratives"), in John 2:1-12 and 19:25-27, as well as in Revelation 12, not insignificant signs of a high esteem or feeling of reverence for the "mother of the Lord" (Luke 1:43), derived from the

[1] *SC* 103.
[2] *SC* 7.

awareness that the Matthean and especially the Lukan and Johannine communities had of the role of Mary in the history of salvation.

The Marian texts in the New Testament were written with both a Christological intention and awareness: to define Christ's identity in a full and complete fashion. The disconcerting event of the resurrection, by which he was reborn from the womb of the earth, made manifest that Jesus was Messiah and Savior, Lord of glory and Son of God (cf. Acts 2:36; 4:12; 5:31). The resurrection, therefore, revealed Jesus' divine origin. But, quite justifiably, the community of disciples wondered what his human origins had been. In what woman's womb and in what fashion had the Word been made flesh (cf. John 1:14)? Christian reflection on the birth of Jesus in history was stimulated by consideration of the event of Easter. In the Gospel accounts, the light of Easter illumines the birth of Christ.[3]

Contemporary exegesis highlights two facts: (1) A considerable number of the "Marian texts" in the infancy narratives have a liturgical character. "The narratives of Luke," observes O. Battaglia, "are not mere chronicles of historical events. They are *liturgical narratives* rich with allusions to and citations of the Old Testament."[4] A. Valentini, in turn, writes, in reference to the Visitation (Luke 1:39-56): "The entire passage is presented with a liturgical character: in the *structure,* by means of which it presents the announcement of salvation, to which the joyous profession of faith is a response; in the *canticles* that are placed on the lips of Elizabeth (1:42-45) and Mary (1:46-55); and by the special *vocabulary* used in the pericope."[5]

(2) The second fact highlighted is that the evangelists are witnesses to the beginnings of the early Christian community's veneration for Mary of Nazareth. H. Schürmann, making a connection between Luke 1:28 ("full of grace") and Luke 1:42 ("Blessed are you among women"), comments: "As Mother of the Messiah, Mary is the most blessed of all women. . . . In this way the exaltation of Mary, to which the angel has referred in 1:28, also begins in the midst of humanity. The veneration

[3] See the stimulating work of A. Serra, *Dimensioni mariane del Mistero Pasquale. Con Maria, dalla Pasqua all'Assunta* (Milan, 1995).

[4] *La Madre del mio Signore: Maria nei vangeli di Luca e di Giovanni* (Assisi, 1994) 23.

[5] "Lc 1, 39-45: Primi indizi di venerazione della Madre del Signore," *Marianum* 58 (1996) 337. G. Aranda Pérez shows himself sensitive to the liturgical nature of the Visitation in his fine study "La Visitación: el Arca nuevamente en camino," in A. Aparicio, ed., *Maria del Evangelio* (Madrid, 1994) 177–207.

of Mary by the early Christian community and by Luke, handed down in this account, is expressed in these words. It is important to note that this appears in the New Testament as a doxology before it becomes a dogmatic assertion."[6] In other words, Luke 1:39-45, before it was a biblical text, was a text of liturgical piety.

a) Liturgical narratives and titles of veneration

The New Testament, then, not only contains the foundations for a liturgical piety focused on the Mother of the Lord but also serves as a witness to the beginnings of Marian devotion itself. This is expressed especially in narratives which have a profound importance on the level of symbol and liturgy and in which one encounters titles that express various aspects of the role played by the Virgin in salvation history. This is a role that, in a variety of ways, draws together all of revelation—from Genesis (3:15, 20) to Revelation (12:1-6)—and concerns all the "actors" on whom salvation depends: Christ, the incarnate Word and, in him and through him, the Father and the Holy Spirit, Israel, the Church, and humanity.

Marian titles are not simply *epitheta ornantia* but are rather liturgical-doctrinal expressions that derive from the Church's faith in Christ and his saving work. Concerning these titles, A. Valentini writes: "One is impressed, in the narrative concerning the Visitation, by the remarkable series of titles and praises which, under the influence of the Spirit, come to be applied to the Virgin. She is proclaimed as more 'blessed' than all women (v. 42), 'the mother of my Lord' (v. 43), 'blessed' (v. 45; cf. v. 48b), 'faithful one' (v. 45). She herself, with her inspired voice, prophesies that 'all generations will call me blessed' (v. 48b)."[7]

Because of its importance, it will be useful to present a synthesis here of the New Testament's doctrinal-liturgical witness concerning the Virgin of Nazareth, because it will shed light on later developments in Marian piety.

The Gospel of Matthew. In the first Gospel, Mary is the virgin mother of Jesus, and therefore mother of the Messiah, the Davidic king, the Son of God. Her motherhood is the work of the Holy Spirit (1:18), and in her the prophecy of Emmanuel, "God with us," who was to be born of a virgin, was fulfilled. Mary was the wife of Joseph, and since he was of the house of David, Jesus became "son of David, son of Abra-

[6] *Il vangelo di Luca* (Brescia, 1983) 1:168.

[7] "Lc 1, 39-45: Primi indizi," n. 5, pp. 333–334.

ham" (1:1). Two traditions seem to come together in Mary: that of the *gebirah,* the queen-mother, to whom pertains a certain dignity in the court and who enjoys special powers, and that of *Jerusalem-the mother of all,* to whom all people come (Isa 49:23; 60:1-6). Into these two positions comes Mary; she is "the *queen-mother* of the newborn *king-messiah.* Her knees become the natural throne for the child's royal majesty."[8] Before her those who come from afar, representing all the nations, prostrate themselves. In Matthew's Gospel the "justice" of Mary is that of the poor of the Lord, that is, it is found in love for the law of God and in faithful submission to his will and to the decisions of her spouse.

The Gospel of Luke. The third Gospel offers a penetrating and different portrait of Mary:

—In her, a poor Galilean woman, spouse of Joseph of Nazareth (1:26), the figure of the *servant of the Lord* (1:38) is perfectly fulfilled. She nourishes her piety with the Bible, realizes that in her the messianic prophecies will be fulfilled, connects the apparently humble events of her life with the great events of salvation history, observes the law of the Lord with care (Luke 2:22, 23, 24, 27, 39) and places her trust in him (1:38).

—By agreeing to be part of God's plan, she is the *faithful one* (1:45) par excellence, in the line of "Abraham, our father" (1:55). However, she surpasses him in the strength and purity of her faith.[9] She is a woman who accepts the mysterious plan of God, according to which her Son will be a "sign of contradiction" (2:34) and her own soul will be pierced by a sword (2:35). She is a mother who will ponder her Son's deeds, the meaning of some of which she will not understand (2:51b).

—She is the *daughter of Zion,* spouse of Yahweh, the personification of Israel faithful to its covenant. In writing about Mary, Luke introduces Eve, the mother of the living (Gen 3:20) as an antithesis. Anna, the mother of the prophet Samuel (1 Sam 1–2) is introduced as an analogue, and Mary surpasses Judith, the heroine of Bethulia (Jdt 13:18). She is the fulfillment of the "virgin who will conceive and bear a son"

[8] "Regina," in *Nuovo Dizionario di Mariologia* (Cinisello Balsamo [Milan], 1985) 1192. In what follows, this will be abbreviated *NDM.*

[9] Cf. G. Ravasi, "Beata colei che ha creduto! (Lc 1, 45)," *Marianum* 50 (1988) 159–175; S. Muñoz Iglesias, "La fe de Maria y la fe de Abraham," *Marianum* 50 (1988) 176–192.

(Isa 7:14). She is also presented as the image of the wise woman (2:19, 51b) of the new times.

—She is the *mother of the messianic King* (1:32-33), the Son of God (1:35), whose conception took place not by human means but through the Holy Spirit and the power of the Most High. The evangelist draws together in Mary, who has become the abode of God, some important Old Testament symbols, such as the primordial earth (Gen 2:7), the temple (1 Kgs 8:10-13), the cloud (Exod 13:22), and the ark (2 Sam 6:2-11).

—She is the *holy, spiritual woman,* "full of grace" (1:28), the object of divine favor (1:30), who is moved by the Holy Spirit. Her heart is the treasury of the Lord's infancy (2:19, 51b). Her song is a glorification of God "for the great things" (1:49) he has done in her and a prophetic warning of God's intended action, for he will cast the mighty from their thrones and raise up the humble (1:52). Her vocation and mission as "mother of Jesus" are a factor in the growth of the new people of God (Acts 1:14).

The Gospel of John. In the fourth Gospel the figure of Mary is drawn with markedly theological traits. Located at both the beginning (2:1-12) and the end (19:25-27) of Jesus' public life, in a sort of grand inclusion, she relates at one and the same time to Christ and to the Church.

The wedding at Cana (2:1-12). By means of the chronological note "the third day" (2:1), a connection is made both to the revelation at Sinai (Exod 19–24) and to the resurrection of Christ (John 2:19-21; 1 Cor 15:3-4). In this regard, A. Serra says, "Just as at Sinai Yahweh revealed his glory by giving the law to Moses, so too at Cana Jesus revealed his glory by giving the better wine, a symbol of the new law which is his gospel."[10] Later he adds, "In the theological structure of the fourth Gospel, a thread runs between the 'third day' of Sinai, the 'third day' of Cana, and the 'third day' of Christ's glorifying passion. These are three milestones along the one route of salvation."[11] In the episode concerning the wedding at Cana, the mother who points out the lack of wine appears as:

—"a *representative* of humanity in trouble and *Judaism* with its messianic hope: She is the image of humanity and of Israel awaiting a liberation, mysterious for humanity, messianic but still too human for Israel."[12]

[10] "Bibbia," in *NDM,* 276.

[11] Ibid.

[12] M. Thurian, *Maria madre del Signore, immagine della Chiesa* (Brescia, 1965) 150.

—*the servant of redemption,* who directs members of the new messianic community toward Christ and his commandments: "Do what he tells you" (2:5), words that echo those of the Sinai covenant: "Everything which the Lord has spoken we will do" (Exod 19:8; 24:3, 7).

—*the true spouse of the messianic wedding:* "In their deeds and in their words, the Virgin and Christ move beyond the merely human level of local festivities, surpassing the young spouses of Cana in order to become the spiritual husband and wife of the messianic banquet."[13]

—*the fulfillment of the Synagogue and the beginning of the Church:* "As a 'woman' (v.4)," writes A. Serra, "she brings together the old Israel, which had heretofore been connected to the Temple, to its final salvation. Insofar as she was the 'mother of Jesus' (vv. 1, 3, 5, 12), she represents the beginning of the Church, which finds its first members among the disciples present at the banquet."[14]

—*Calvary* (19:25-27). At the cross, when the time was accomplished (12:23; 13:1), when Jesus was raised up from the earth in order to draw all to himself (12:32), immediately before he said "It is finished," his creative word transformed the *woman* into a *mother*. "*Woman,* here is your son" (19:26); "Here is your *mother*" (19:27). Jesus declares that his mother (19:25, 26), called "woman" in a clear allusion to the symbolism of the new Eve (Gen 3:15, 20), "from this moment on should consider the beloved disciple, standing next to her, not only as a son but as her son, her very own son, because she is *the Mother,* the Mother of all, the new Eve who bears the brothers and sisters of Jesus."[15] "From that hour the disciple took her into his own home" (19:27). A. Serra writes that "he accommodated her as part of his acceptance of Christ."[16]

In this acceptance of the mother of Jesus as his own mother, as one of the great spiritual benefits of the faith that connects the Master and his friends,[17] we see one of the oldest expressions of the veneration-love-filial piety of the beloved disciple for the mother of Jesus, who has become his mother. The expression "beloved disciple" refers to all disciples who, because of their faith and their observance of the commandments, love Jesus and are loved by him (14:21). In conclusion,

[13] J. P. Charlier, *Le signe de Cana* (Paris, 1959) 77.

[14] "Bibbia," in *NDM*, n. 10, p. 281.

[15] P. Guilbert, *Marie des Écritures* (Montrouge, 1995) 245.

[16] "Bibbia" in *NDM*, n. 10, p. 292.

[17] See I. de la Potterie, "La parole de Jésus «Voici ta mère» e l'accueil du Disciple (Jn 19, 27b)," *Marianum* 42 (1980) 84–125.

"The liturgical acceptance of the gift of God constitutes an early and fundamental expression of the cult of the Blessed Virgin."[18]

b) "From now on all generations will call me blessed" (Luke 1:48b)
All discourse about the legitimacy of the veneration of the Mother of the Lord makes use of an especially probative argument based on the words of the Virgin herself: "From now on all generations will call me blessed" (1:48b). Exegetes are all in agreement that Luke 1:48b is a Lukan redaction, which the evangelist has inserted, not without leaving traces of his activity, into the text of a Jewish Christian hymn—the *Magnificat*—which was certainly used in the liturgy. But "this expression," according to A. Valentini, "although it comes from the pen of the evangelist, presupposes the existence of a devotion to Mary within the Lukan community."[19] G. Ghiberti, after having studied the problems connected with the passage and its prophetic character, and the question whether "prophecy arises from the liturgy" or "liturgy from prophecy," holds that "at the moment of redemption both exist together. Prophecy recalls that which happened in the past . . . and is verified in the events of the present. Without an incipient form of praise . . . for Mary, I think that this expression in the Lukan redaction would be difficult to explain."[20]

The *Magnificat* is a liturgical hymn composed, under the influence of the Holy Spirit, in a Jewish Christian community. The hymn was placed, also under the influence of the Holy Spirit, on the lips of Mary, the purest voice of the old Israel and the best-known member of the nascent Church. The *Magnificat* is both praise of God and thanksgiving for his power and mercy, for the "great things" (1:49) he has done in the humble woman Mary—the gift of being the mother of the Messiah —for the good of all the people. Into this praise of God, powerful and merciful, is inserted verse 48b, prophetic in origin and the only verse in the hymn that has a verb in the future tense: "Surely from now on all generations will call me blessed." On the one hand, this is an asser-

[18] I. M. Calabuig, "Il culto alla beata Vergine: fondamenti teologici e collocazione nell'ambito del culto cristiano," in E. Peretto, ed., *Aspetti della presenza di Maria nella Chiesa in cammino verso il Duemila* (Rome-Bologna, 1989) 308.

[19] "Lc 1, 39–45: Primi indizi," n. 5, p. 351. Valentini cites F. Mussner, "Lk 1:48f.; 11:27f. und die Anfänge der Marienverehrung in der Urkirche," in *De primordiis cultus mariani.* Acta Congressus Mariologici-Mariani in Lusitania anno 1967 celebrati (Rome, 1970) 2:25–34.

[20] "Lc 1:48b: anche genere agiografico?" *Rivista Biblica* 39 (1991) 140.

tion that the proto-Christian community already testifies to Mary's blessedness. It is also a prediction that this "blessedness" will be proclaimed in all times and by "all generations," because all people will benefit from the gift that God gave to the Virgin of Nazareth.

In the narrative block extending from Luke 1:26-38 (the Annunciation) to Luke 1:39-56 (the Visitation and the *Magnificat*), the praise of the Virgin in Luke 1:48b ("will call me *blessed*") appears to be of a piece with the reverent greeting of the angel (1:28) and that of Elizabeth, which is full of admiration and blessing (1:42, 43, 45). These greetings, which had been private, will now be proclaimed in all times and places. The object of this praise is the fullness of grace given by God to the Virgin (1:28), her extraordinary faith (1:45) and adherence without any reserve to God's plan, and, more than anything else, the great gift of her motherhood of the one who is God and Messiah. In other words, Luke 1:48b works on a variety of levels to turn us to her who is blessed (1:28), to her who is the faithful servant and disciple (1:38, 45), to the Virgin Mother of the Messiah and Lord (1:42).

c) Conclusion

The liturgical veneration of the Mother of the Lord has value and meaning only if rooted in the Word of God and only if it fits harmoniously into the celebration of the history of salvation. As we have seen, this is exactly what Scripture testifies to. In so doing, it reflects the experience of the early Christian communities, especially those of Luke and John, where there were the beginnings of veneration for the Mother of Jesus. In taking stock of this scriptural witness, it cannot be forgotten that it is relative to the "Christ event," from which it derives its meaning, and that it is a work of the Spirit. According to A. Valentini, ". . . the Spirit who causes Elizabeth and her son to rejoice before the Mother of the Lord is the same Spirit *who has shaped the heart of the Virgin,* which *has roused up in her the yes of faith and made her the Mother of the Son of God.* The Spirit, the author of these marvels, is at the origin of the Church's devotion to her who is *blessed* for her motherhood and *blessed* for her faith."[21]

2. *The Pre-nicene Era*

The period between the postapostolic era (the beginning of the second century) and the Council of Nicea (325) is particularly important for

[21] "Lc 1, 39–45: Primi indizi," 335.

the formation of the Christian liturgy and, of special interest for us, for the formulation of the expression of liturgical piety concerning the Mother of the Lord.

a) A mistake that needs to be dispelled

Opinions on the antiquity of the first manifestations of liturgical devotion to the Blessed Virgin vary, for the simple reason that the idea of "Marian devotion" is not ambiguous. Most scholars, for example, hold that the liturgical cult of the Mother of the Lord is later than the cult of the martyrs. This is an acceptable opinion if one allows that for a "liturgical cult" there must be a fixed *date* (that of the martyrdom) and a fixed *place* (the martyr's tomb) at which the community gathers to celebrate the memory with a sacred rite—the Eucharistic synaxis. This is not the case for Mary: the date of her death is not known, and no community claims to possess her body. But the cult of the martyrs was originally exclusively *local*. For example, the community of Smyrna gathered each year to celebrate the memory of the holy bishop Polycarp on February 23, the day of his martyrdom. If, however, one understands "liturgical cult" to refer to an act of veneration that arises out of the celebration of the liturgy, of which it forms a harmonious part, the liturgical cult of the Virgin is older than those of the martyrs. Moreover, it is *universal*. It arises in all the regions into which Christianity spread in the era before Nicea.

Relative to this era, when our speaking of distinctions between a "liturgical cult" and a cult that is "non-liturgical" constitutes a glaring anachronism, there exist texts that have their origin in preaching, hymnody, or sacraments, all surely liturgical, and contain expressions that are doubtless expressions of veneration for the Mother of the Lord. To them one must add the writings that had a great influence on the liturgy and some archeological evidence that helps us to reconstruct the Church's worship.

b) The homily "On the Pasch" of Melito of Sardis

The only "annual feast" of the pre-Nicene era was Easter. During an Easter Vigil celebrated according to the Asian tradition on 14 Nisan sometime between 160 and 170, Melito of Sardis preached a homily entitled *Perì Pascha* ("On the Pasch"). During the vigil Exodus 12 was read, the story of the institution of Passover. In the course of the homily, Melito mentions the Mother of Jesus four times (nn. 66, 70, 71, 104) and calls her "the lovely ewe-lamb" (n. 71). The affirmation that

Christ "became incarnate in a virgin" (n. 70) is for doctrinal purposes; it was necessary to state in a precise fashion, contrary to recurrent misinterpretations, that the incarnation of the Word took place in Mary's womb without human intervention.

But in the second half of the second century, after the controversies that Ignatius of Antioch († ca. 110), Aristides of Athens († after 117), Justin of Rome († ca. 165) and Irenaeus of Lyons († ca. 202) had confronted, the term "virgin," especially the expression "the Virgin," referred, in specific contexts, clearly and simply to the Mother of the Lord and had taken on a liturgical nuance. It is used with a sense of veneration and awe, stemming from wonder at the divine and virginal motherhood of Mary. But the attention of historians of Marian devotion is especially directed to the sentence "He is the one born from Mary, the lovely ewe-lamb" (n. 71). In the context of his comment on Exodus 12, the bishop of Sardis attributes to the Virgin the characteristics of the "paschal lamb" which are proper to the Son, "the spotless, unblemished lamb" (1 Pet 1:19; cf. Exod 12:5). Mary is seen as the "lovely ewe-lamb"—the adjective used in the original *(kalós)* carries the two meanings of "good" and "lovely"—pure and without any stain. In the heart of the Easter Vigil the Mother of Jesus is called to mind in a way which implies veneration and which applies paschal terminology (the lamb) to her.

c) Hymnody

In the second and third centuries, hymns were composed which, like those in the New Testament[22] on which they were modeled, had both their origin and their destination in the liturgy.

The *Odes of Solomon,* a collection of hymns from the first half of the second century, contains forty-two hymns, composed in Greek and modeled on the psalms of the Old Testament. *Ode* 19:6-11 celebrates the virginal motherhood of Mary in cryptic language. The pain of "giving birth" bequeathed to Eve (cf. Gen 3:16) is contrasted with the Virgin's painless delivery; it praises her active participation in the incarnation of the Word. The history of Marian piety cannot ignore that in a worshiping assembly of the first decades of the second century, the celebration of the salvation effected by God in Christ included a

[22] Luke 1:46-55 *(Magnificat);* 1:68-79 *(Benedictus);* 2:14 *(Gloria in excelsis);* 2:29-32 *(Nunc dimittis);* Phil 2:6-11; Col 1:13-20; 1 Tim 2:21-25; 1 Pet 2:21-25; Rev 5:9-10; 12-13; 11:17-18; 15:3-4; 19:1-2, 5, 6-8.

mention of Mary of Nazareth that was full of respect and admiration, of real, even if incipient, veneration.

Less certain is the liturgical use of the *Sybilline Oracles*, composed before 180 (1:323 abcde; 8:357-358, 456-479). Section 8:456-479 is a free and gentle paraphrase of the annunciation of Gabriel to Mary (Luke 1:26-38), written with an undeniable sympathy and with a clear sense of veneration for the Mother of Jesus, the woman favored by divine grace (v. 461), pure and modest, able to awe and to cause wonder, to smile and to blush (vv. 463-468) but, more than anything else, able to decide with courage, for whom "the Word came down with speed into her body" (v. 469).

d) The Eucharistic anaphora and the rite of baptism

In the so-called *Apostolic Tradition*, an undoubtedly ancient document of uncertain origin (Alexandrian? Roman?), once attributed to Hippolytus of Rome, there appears the oldest Eucharistic anaphora that we currently know. In its "Thanksgiving," short and essentially Christological, the Virgin is mentioned twice: "We thank you, O God, by means of your beloved Son Jesus Christ, who in these latter days you have sent to us as Savior, Redeemer, and Messenger of your will . . . whom you have sent from heaven into the womb of a *virgin;* and he was conceived, was incarnate and shown to be your Son, born of the Spirit and of the *Virgin*" (n. 4). The reason for this assertion is not Mariological—the veneration of the Mother of the Lord—but theological and Christological: to glorify God for the gift of Jesus, his Son, born of the Virgin. But the mention, in a context that is clearly liturgical, highlights Mary's essential function in salvation history. She is the Virgin Mother of Christ, the Word of God, Savior of humankind. This ancient mention of the Virgin does not disappear from the anaphora but remains an element of all Eucharistic Prayers, and is destined to be increasingly highlighted in further liturgical developments.

The Virgin is called to mind again in another section of the *Apostolic Tradition* that gives the rite of baptism on Easter night. In this rite the second immersion of the catechumen is preceded by a series of questions on faith in Christ: "Do you believe in Jesus Christ, Son of God, who was born by means of the Holy Spirit of the *Virgin Mary* . . . died and rose on the third day?" (n. 21). Then the catechumen, having confessed that Christ was born of the Virgin by means of the Holy Spirit, is himself born unto a life with God by water and the Spirit (cf. Gen 3:5).

The liturgical rite contains the kernel of a parallelism between the birth of Christ and the birth of the Christian, which in the following centuries will develop both in doctrine and in the liturgy.

If one ponders "the importance of the Eucharistic Prayer and the rite of baptism for the liturgical life of the Church, one would have to conclude that the anaphora of the *Traditio* and its rite for Christian initiation, in both of which the Virgin is named—when there is no mention of the angels, the patriarchs, the prophets, the apostles, or the martyrs—offers a precious sign: the Sunday Eucharist and the sacrament of baptism offer an ancient and natural place of the Virgin. Her memory is recalled in a context that is strictly Christological and ecclesial, with special reference to the saving event of the incarnation."[23] This veneration of the Mother of the Lord takes place in a paschal context, at the altar and the baptismal font. From a liturgical point of view, this is important.

e) Churches

The dedication of a church to the Virgin is an important expression of Marian piety, of a sort that is especially liturgical. In the era before the Council of Nicea, the patriarch Theonas († 307) built a church in Alexandria that very soon came to be called "The Church of Saint Mary"; in so doing, the Virgin came to be identified with the church building named in her honor.[24]

Prior to the church in Alexandria there were two "buildings" in the area of Palestine dedicated, respectively, to the mystery of the incarnation and the *transitus* of the Virgin. The first is at Nazareth, the place of the annunciation of Gabriel to Mary, where excavations done in 1955 and later have brought to light a real Judeo-Christian church, the Marian character of which is attested to by two graffiti dating from the second or third century. These provide moving testimony of pilgrims traveling to Nazareth to venerate the Virgin and to seek her protection.[25] The second is in Jerusalem, where archeological researches done since 1972 and the study of material taken from the *Transitus Virginis* lead one to conclude that the sacred kiosk called the "Tomb of Mary" witnesses to the existence of a Jewish Christian worship site, certainly

[23] Calabuig, "Il culto," n. 18, p. 296.

[24] Cf. G. Giamberardini, *Il culto mariano in Egitto* (Jerusalem, 1975) 1:105.

[25] B. Bagatti, *Gli scavi di Nazaret*, Vol. 1: *Dalle origini al secolo XII* (Jerusalem, 1967) 146–152; E. Testa, *Nazaret Giudeo-Cristiana* (Jerusalem, 1969) passim.

dating from the era prior to Nicea, which had a Marian character and was connected to the memory of the end of the earthly life of the mother of Jesus.[26]

In the fourth century, after long-standing rivalry, that part of the Church which was Gentile in origin overtook that which was of Jewish origin, and the latter disappeared almost completely. This fact made certain that the texts with a Jewish Christian origin would be viewed with suspicion. Among these were important documents about the earthly life of Mary. Thus expressions of piety that came from her own family circle were neglected, although "they evinced a profound esteem for her, in a way that was really familial."[27]

f) The Sub tuum praesidium

The famous troparion *Sub tuum praesidium,* with its origin in an Alexandrian context, was "found"at the beginning of the twentieth century in an Egyptian papyrus dating from the end of the third century.[28] Because of its great antiquity, it is noteworthy for a number of reasons: from the perspective of *worship* because it is a collective invocation, liturgical in origin, that shows us the custom on the part of the Christian community of turning directly to Mary to seek her aid in the hour of trouble ("Despise not our petitions in our necessities, but deliver us always from all dangers"); from the perspective of *doctrine* because it recognizes the divine (*Theotokos,* "God-bearer") and virginal ("O pure one") motherhood of Mary, who was specially chosen by God ("O blessed one"), and her merciful and powerful intercession ("We fly to thy patronage . . . deliver us").

The *Sub tuum praesidium,* because of its great antiquity, its dense content, and its grief-stricken supplication, has become a part of nearly all liturgies and is considered to be "the oldest prayer to the Virgin."[29]

[26] B. Bagatti, "Nuove scoperte alla tomba della Vergine a Getsemani," *Studi Biblici Francescani Liber Annuus* 22 (1972) 236–290; idem,"Ricerche sulle tradizioni della morte della Vergine," *Sacra Doctrina* 18 (1973) 185–214.

[27] B. Bagatti, "Maria nella prima espansione missionaria della Chiesa in Palestina," in D. Bertetto, ed., *Maria Ausiliatrice e le missioni* (Rome, 1977) 122.

[28] Giamberardini, *Il culto mariano in Egitto,* n. 24, p. 96.

[29] R. Iacoangeli, "'Sub tuum praesidium.' La più antica preghiera mariana: filologia e fede," in S. Felici, ed., *La mariologia nella catechesi dei Padri: età prenicena* (Rome, 1989) 207–240; A. M. Triacca, "'Sub tuum praesidium': nella 'lex orandi' un'anticipata presenza della 'lex credendi,'" ibid., 183–205.

g) Literature that inspired the liturgical veneration of the Mother of Jesus
In this discussion of pre-Nicene materials, we cannot forget two texts that had a noteworthy influence on the liturgical veneration of the Mother of the Lord: the *Nativity of Mary* and the *Transitus of Mary.*

The *Nativity of Mary,* or the *Protoevangelium of James,* is an apocryphal work of the second half of the second century, probably composed in a Jewish Christian community in the Diaspora, and "catholic" in both feeling and doctrine.[30] It comes from a source that is both apologetic and hagiographic. The anonymous author demonstrates that he possesses a lively awareness of the eminent dignity of Mary, the chosen creature of God and one whom he has favored with singular graces, that she is the Mother of the incarnate Word and faithful servant of the Lord. This awareness finds expression, at least in the realm of personal piety, in a sense of profound *veneration,* stemming from devout *love* and manifested in frequent *praise.*

From the liturgical viewpoint, the *Protoevangelium* marks an important stage in the history of Marian devotion: (a) a number of Marian feasts have their origin and inspiration in it (the memorial of SS. Joachim and Anna, the parents of the Blessed Virgin, on July 26; the Nativity of Mary on September 8; the Presentation of Mary in the Temple on November 21; the Immaculate Conception on December 8); (b) it became one of the most important sources of Marian iconography and, for some, of Marian hymnody; (c) it served as the source for a good deal of liturgical material of different types (antiphons, responsories, etc.);[31]

[30] For information on editions of the *Nativity of Mary,* or the *Protoevangelium of James,* and bibliography concerning them, see L. Moraldi, ed., *Apocrifi del Nuovo Testamento* (Turin, 1994) 1:37–81. The translation, according to the Bodmer papyrus, is on pp. 83–112. The translation of the *Protoevangelium* is on pp.123–139. For a study that deals specifically with Marian doctrine and devotion, see L. M. Peretto, *La mariologia del Protovangelo di Giacomo* (Rome, 1955); G. M. Roschini, "I fondamenti dogmatici del culto mariano nel 'Protovangelo di Giacomo,'" in *De primordiis cultus mariani,* 4:253–271.

[31] An interesting text that demonstrates both the diffusion of the *Protoevangelium of James* and its influence on the liturgy is the *Psalmus responsorius.* It appears in a papyrus of the first half of the fourth century, and one may reasonably hold that the original appeared at the end of the third century. The *Psalmus* is essentially a rhythmic paraphrase, intended for liturgical use, of the *Nativity of Mary.* See R. Roca Puig, *Himne à la Vierge Marie.* "Psalmus responsorius." Papir llatí del segle IV (Barcelona, 1965); L. M. Peretto, "*Psalmus responsorius.* Un inno alla Vergine Maria di un papiro del IV secolo," *Marianum* 29 (1967) 255–265.

the numerous blessings that the priests of the Jerusalem Temple imparted to Mary (cf. VI, 2; VII, 2; XII, 1) became, after the "New Testament blessings" (cf. Luke 1:28, 30, 42–43, 45, 48–49; 11:27), the most immediate source of the "liturgical blessings" of holy Mary. In addition, the blessings that were placed on the lips of the Jerusalem priests express what were actually the sentiments of the author of the *Protoevangelium* and his community concerning the Blessed Virgin.

The *Transitus Mariae,* or the *Dormitio Virginis,* is another document that has had an influence on the development of Marian liturgical piety. It exists in various versions, none of which, at least in the form in which they have come down to us, dates from the era before Nicea.[32] Be that as it may, some scholars—B. Bagatti, E. Testa, F. Manns—have identified in them an ancient nucleus which dates from the second or third century and which is characterized by a vocabulary typical of the Jewish Christian theology of that time.[33]

This *Transitus* literature has contributed, in large measure, to giving a specific character to the feast celebrated on August 15, the inspiration for much Marian iconography as well as abundant material for use in the liturgy. The *Transitus* is a story in liturgical shape, a sort of liturgy of preparation for death and a burial ritual. In this context, itself rich with interesting hints about Jewish Christian doctrine—Christological, ecclesiological, Mariological, eschatological—are numerous Marian symbols (dove, temple, ark, gate of heaven, palm tree), titles, and "liturgical greetings" directed to Mary by the apostles, singly and as a group. "The apostles went into the house of Mary and said with one voice: Mary, our sister, mother of all those who are saved, may the grace of the Lord be with you!"[34] Since the symbols, titles, and liturgi-

[32] For a careful study of the various versions of the *Transitus Mariae,* see G. Aranda Pérez, *Dormición de la Virgen. Relatos de la tradición copta* (Madrid, 1995), especially pp. 15–41. For the history of the traditions about the Assumption, see S. C. Mimouni, *Dormition et assomption de Marie. Histoire des traditions anciennes* (Paris, 1995). On the history of the research into these traditions, see the same author's article "Histoire de la recherche relative aux traditions littéraires et topologiques sur le sort final de Marie," *Marianum* 58 (1996) 111–182.

[33] Bagatti, "Nuove scoperte," n. 26, p. 239.

[34] *Transitus Romanus* (cod. Vat. gr. 1982, pp. 181–189) 28. A critical edition of the *Transitus Romanus* was done by A. Wenger, *L'assomption de la T. S. Vierge dans la tradition byzantine du VIe au Xe siècle. Études et documents* (Paris, 1955) 209–241. It was translated into Italian by L. Moraldi in *Apocrifi del Nuovo Testamento* (Turin, 1994) 3:189. The *Transitus Romanus* was the object of a particular study by F. Manns, *Le récit*

cal greetings, all expressions of great reverence for the "Mother of the twelve branches,"[35] are found in the sections that are held to be oldest, it is very probable that they too belong to the original nucleus and therefore are evidence of Marian liturgical piety of the pre-Nicene period.

h) The contribution of archaeology to the history of Marian piety

In section (e) above, wherein church buildings are discussed, mention was made of the graffiti discovered in Nazareth, in the place where it is thought that the Virgin received the angel's message, and of the signs of Marian devotion found in Jerusalem in connection with the so-called Tomb of Mary. But there are other pieces of evidence from the pre-Nicene era that must be mentioned; in reference to these items, there remains some doubt either about their Marian interpretation or their liturgical use. These pieces of evidence come from various countries in the Middle East or the area surrounding the Mediterranean, but are mostly to be found either in Palestine[36] or Rome.

Some inscriptions must be mentioned. Among them is the epitaph of Abercius, bishop of Hierapolis in Phrigia, written sometime between 170 and 200, in which mention is made of the Virgin Mary, using exalted language full of liturgical symbolism, in combination with the Eucharist.[37] There are a number of early Christian inscriptions in Rome, one of which, in rather cryptic language, is a unique acclamation of the victory of Christ, Mary, and Peter.[38] Others, like the Vatican graffito *Florenti vivas cum Maria in Christo*,[39] show that even in the era

---

de la Dormition de Mariae (Vat. Grec 1982). Contribution à l'étude des origines de l'exégèse chrétienne (Jerusalem, 1989). See also A. M. Serra, "Alle origini della letteratura assunzionista. Uno studio di Frédéric Manns," *Marianum* 56 (1994) 291–309. Manns holds that the *Transitus* predates the Council of Nicea.

[35] *Transitus Romanus*, 16. According to the translation of L. Moraldi, *Apocrifi*, 3, n. 33, p. 186.

[36] C. Vidal Manzanares, "María en la arqueología judeo-cristiana de los tres primeros siglos," *Ephemerides Mariologica* 41 (1991) 353–364.

[37] B. Emmi, "La testimonianza mariana dell'epitaffio di Abercio," *Angelicum* 46 (1969) 232–302.

[38] M. Guarducci, "Maria nelle epigrafi paleocristiane di Roma," *Marianum* 25 (1963) 248–261, especially 249–252; F. de P. Solá, "La santísima Virgen en las inscripciones, principalmente sepulcrales, en los primeros siglos del cristianismo," in *De primordiis cultus mariani*, 63–77.

[39] Ibid., 72.

before Nicea the Virgin "was considered to be the protector of the dead and their benevolent mediator before Christ."[40]

The paintings in the catacombs, objects of many authoritative studies,[41] also offer important testimony. Because of its antiquity and recognized importance, particular mention must be made of the "Marian iconography" of the Priscilla catacombs on Via Salaria nuova in Rome. The following are especially well known:

a) *The adoration of the magi,* in the central arch of the "Greek Chapel," from the middle of the third century.[42] The Virgin appears in a majestic pose, seated on a throne, in the act of presenting her divine Son to the magi for their adoration.

b) *The Virgin with the Infant,* the very well-known painting found in the so-called crypt of the Madonna, one of the oldest sections of the catacombs, which can be dated to the first decade of the third century.[43] The Virgin is presented with the Infant in her arms. On her right is the figure of a philosopher pointing at a star that is shining on the head of the divine Child. At a little distance is the scene of a shepherd carrying a lamb on his shoulders, in surroundings that seem like Paradise. The figure of the philosopher has been variously identified with Isaiah, because of his prophecy of the virgin who will conceive and bear a son (Isa 7:14); with Balaam, because of the prediction "A star shall advance from Jacob" (Num 24:17); and with David, because of the oracle saying "From the womb, before the morning star, I have begotten you" (Ps 110:3). Probably, however, the picture is intended to portray "a generic allusion to messianic prophecy without referring to any precise individual."[44]

c) The so-called *Annunciation,* which appears in a funeral chamber from the end of the second century. It shows a woman seated on a throne, before whom a figure in tunic and pallium raises his arm as though in conversation. Authoritative studies argue that this repre-

[40] Guarducci, "Maria nelle epigrafi paleocristiane di Roma," n. 38, p. 261.

[41] J.-M. Salgado, "Le culte rendu à la très sainte Vierge Marie durant les premiers siècles à la lumière des fresques de la catacombe de Priscille," in *De primordiis cultus mariani,* 5, n. 38, pp. 43–62. This study has a useful bibliography.

[42] F. Tolotti, *Il cimitero di Priscilla. Studio di topografia e architettura* (Vatican City, 1970) 258–275.

[43] P. Testini, *Le catacombe e gli antichi cimiteri cristiani in Roma* (Bologna, 1966) 288.

[44] F. Bisconti, "L'iconologia mariana antenicena," in S. Felici, *Mariologia,* n. 29, pp. 252–253.

sents the annunciation of Gabriel to Mary (cf. Luke 1:26-38). Others hold that it is an undetermined messianic prophecy. In any case, Mary appears as the woman who is predestined to become the Mother of the Messiah-Redeemer, the incarnate Word.

It is not obvious that these and other images of the Virgin[45] were objects of devotion on the part of the faithful; rather they were part of a ritual complex, fruit of a feeling of devotion and expressions of the community's faith in the Virgin's role in salvation history. She was seen as the virgin mother of the Savior, the new Eve, that place where the two New Testament economies met and became one. This was a mystery that was actualized in the mystery of worship, the full manifestation of which—the resurrection of the body and the final judgment—the dead buried in the catacombs were awaiting.

3. *From the Council of Nicea (325) to the Death of Gregory the Great († 604)*

The period extending from the Council of Nicea (325) to the end of the sixth century, which coincides with the golden age of patristics, is particularly important for the history of liturgical devotion to the Mother of the Lord. It was during this time, in fact, that a number of Christological-Marian feasts took definite shape.

The Council of Nicea, which put an end, at least doctrinally, to the grave crisis of Arianism, was a decisive moment for the dogmatic proclamation of the faith of the Church in the divinity of Christ. Following the dogmatic affirmation that the Logos is true God, not created but eternally begotten of the Father, with whom he is coeternal and consubstantial, the faithful understood more clearly the dignity of Mary of Nazareth. Of Jesus, the Word incarnate and very God, she was the real virgin mother according to the flesh.

For a clearer treatment of the material, it will be useful to consider the development of liturgical piety in the West and East separately.

[45] That images in the catacombs are to be understood as referring to Mary is not always certain. For example, C. Dagens argues, with good reason, in "A propos du cubiculum de la Velatio," *Rivista di archeologia cristiana* 47 (1971) 119–129, that what other scholars see as a *velatio virginis* (a scene to the right of the figure in the position of prayer), and *Mary as the model of consecrated virgins* (the scene to the left, which depicts a woman seated with an infant baby in her arms), is to be interpreted rather as a scene taken from family life—a wedding (*velatio nuptialis*) and motherhood.

a) In the West

The development of Marian piety in the East often preceded that in the West. In this case, however, it is better to start with the West because of the liturgical fact of the institution of the feast of December 25, itself closely connected with the Council of Nicea.

THE INSTITUTION OF THE FEAST OF CHRISTMAS

One might well argue that the institution of the feast of Christmas at Rome, around the year 336, translates the Christological definition of Nicea into liturgy.[46] Scholars are not in total agreement about the original character of this feast or why it was fixed on December 25. Some hold that it is apologetic in character, instituted to form a contrast between the pagan feast of *Natalis solis invicti* (December 25) and the celebration of the Lord's nativity, he who is the true Sun of justice (Mal 3:20). Others think that December 25 was chosen because of its relation to March 25. This latter was considered to be, since the end of the third century, a day of mystery on which various of the events connected with our salvation took place, among them the *conception* and *death* of Jesus.[47] If Jesus was conceived on March 25, he would have to have been born on December 25.

In any case, the feast of December 25 focused on the mystery of the incarnation and birth of the Savior from the virginal womb of Mary. This would have many beneficial effects for the development of Marian liturgical piety, because it is impossible to celebrate the birth of the divine Son without remembering the virginal Mother.

[46] On the origins of the feast of Christmas, see B. Botte, *Les origines de la Noël et de l'Épiphanie. Étude historique* (Louvain, 1932); J. Lemarié, *La manifestation du Seigneur. La liturgie de Noël et de l'Épiphanie* (Paris, 1953); J. Mossay, *Les fêtes de Noël et de l'Épiphanie d'après les sources littéraires cappadociennes du IVe siècle* (Louvain, 1965); A. Bergamini, "Natale/Epifania," *NDL* 919–922; A. Nocent, "Natale e Epifania," in *L'anno liturgico. Storia, teologia e celebrazione* (Genoa, 1988) 177–191; T. Talley, *The Origins of the Liturgical Year* 2nd ed. (Collegeville, Minn., 1991) 85–108.

[47] On the saving events that occurred on March 25, see V. Loi "Il 25 marzo data pasquale e la cronologia giovannea della passione in età patristica," *EphLit* 85 (1971) 48–69; A. H. Scheer, "Aux origines de la fête de l'Annonciation," *QL* 58 (1977) 97–169. St. Augustine is one of the witnesses to the tradition that Christ was conceived and died on March 25: "Octavo enim Kalendas apriles *conceptus* creditur quo et *passus*"(*De Trinitate,* IV, 5; CCL 50, 172; and ". . . octavo calendas Aprilis, quo die *conceptus* Dominus creditur, quia eodem die etiam *passus* est" *(De diversis quaestionibus,* 56; CCL 44A, 96.

The lectionary and antiphonal—In the course of the fourth to the sixth century, the feast of Christmas developed at Rome to the point where, in the second half of the sixth century, there was a vigil Mass and three stational Masses. One took place during the night at St. Mary Major. Another took place at dawn at St. Anastasia, and the third and oldest took place at St. Peter's Basilica. There was also a progressive development of a body of readings and chants for the celebration of the Eucharist and the Divine Office. In these readings and songs, which celebrated the birth of the Son, there was naturally mention of the Mother.

In the time of Gregory the Great († 604), the readings, as witnessed by the Würzburg Lectionary, consisted of pericopes taken from Matthew 1:18-21 (". . . she was found with child through the power of the Holy Spirit") for the vigil Mass; Luke 2:1-14 ("She gave birth to her firstborn son . . .") for the Mass during the night; Luke 2:15-20 ("Mary treasured all these things and reflected on them in her heart") for the Mass at dawn.[48]

The *Antiphonale Missarum* contains texts with a clearly Mariological tone, such as the offertory antiphon *Ave Maria, gratia plena* (Fourth Sunday of Advent) and the communion antiphon *Exulta filia Sion, lauda filia Hierusalem* (December 25, Mass at dawn),[49] both of which were understood to be Marian texts.

Still richer was the collection of Marian texts in the *Antiphonale Divini Officii* for the celebration of Christmas. In it there are responsories and antiphons that are of great value liturgically and artistically, and give profound witness to a deep devotion to the Mother of Jesus. Among the responsories, mention must be made of *Beata Dei Genitrix Maria, sancta et immaculata virginitas* and *Beata viscera Mariae Virginis.*[50] The first two of these are directed immediately to the Virgin. Among the antiphons are *Genuit puerpera Regem, Virgo verbo concepit, Beata Mater et innupta Virgo, Hodie intacta Virgo Deum nobis genuit.*[51] These and similar texts exalt Mary's motherhood, emphasizing particularly the notions of divinity, messianism, salvation, its uniqueness, and her virginity.

[48] Nocent, "Natale e Epifania," n. 46, pp. 180–182.

[49] R.-J. Hesbert, *Antiphonale Missarum septuplex,* according to the Gradual of Monza and the Antiphonaries of Rheinau, Mont-Blandin, Compiègne, Corbie, and Senlis (Brussels, 1935), n. 7 bis (p. 11) and n. 10 (p. 14).

[50] *CAO,* 4, nn. 6162, 7569, 6171.

[51] Ibid., 3, nn. 2938, 5456, 1570, 3104.

Homilies—The homily is an integral part of the celebration of the liturgy. On December 25 the homily is necessarily related to the birth of the Messiah as it was announced by the prophets and told by the evangelists, the wonderful mystery of the God-Man born of the Virgin Mother. This has given rise to excellent homilies that also shed light on the saving role of Mary of Nazareth. Here it will have to suffice to make mention of St. Zeno of Verona († 382), St. Maximus of Turin († 430), St. Peter Chrysologus († 450), and St. Leo the Great († 461).[52] The result is that a not inconsiderable part of the literature on Mary from the patristic era comprises fragments of Christmas homilies. Some texts, because of the gravity and solemn beauty of the discourse, show how aware their authors were of the unique dignity of the Mother of God. There is, for example, this Christmas passage from St. Leo the Great:

Virgo regia davidicae stirpis eligitur,
quae sacro gravidanda fetu
divinam humanamque prolem
prius conciperet mente quam corpore.
Et ne superni ignara consilii
ad inusitatos paveret effectus,
quod in ea operando erat a Spiritu sancto,
conloquio discit angelico.
Nec damnum credit pudoris
Dei genetrix mox futura.[53]

Other texts contain expressions of spontaneous bursts of ardor, like this touching passage from St. Augustine:

Lacta, mater, cibum nostrum;
lacta panem de caelo venientem
et in praesepi positum

[52] Zeno of Verona, *Tract.* 1, 54: CCL 22, pp. 128–129; *Tract.* 2, 8: CCL 22, pp. 176–178; Maximus of Turin, *Sermo* 61b: CCL 23, pp. 253–255; *Sermo* 61c: CCL 23, pp. 257–259; *Sermo* 62: CCL 23, pp. 261–264; Augustine of Hippo, *Sermones* 185–196: NBA 32/1, pp. 2–77; *Sermones* 369–372: NBA 34, pp. 476–499; Peter Chrysologus, *Sermones* 140–149: CCL 24A, pp. 846–930 (these should be considered with caution because not all of them are genuine works of Peter Chrysologus); Leo the Great, *Tract.* 21–30: CCL 138, pp. 85–159.

[53] *Tract.* 21, 1: CCL 138, p. 86.

veluti piorum cibaria iumentorum. [. . .]
Lacta eum qui talem fecit te,
ut ipse fieret in te,
qui tibi et munus fecunditatis attulit conceptus
et decus virginitatis non abstulit natus.[54]

There is no doubt that these Christmas homilies were also liturgical expressions of devotion to the Virgin and that they made an important contribution to the diffusion of love for holy Mary among the Christian people.

Euchology—In Rome, between the fourth and sixth centuries, the euchology connected to Christmas was especially rich theologically. In Section XL of the Verona Sacramentary there are nine formularies, divided into two groups, for the feast of Christmas: I–IV (the vigil Mass and three formularies) and V–IX (the vigil Mass and four formularies). Of these, the second comes, in all probability, from the pontificate of Gelasius I (492–496).[55]

In Section XL the Virgin is mentioned in formulas 1244, 1245, 1252, 1257, 1270. These are brief mentions, to the point, whose theological foundation is mostly from the doctrine of Leo the Great († 461) and the Council of Chalcedon (451) on the two natures—divine and human—subsisting in the one divine Person of the incarnate Word in the womb of Mary. She is seen as the holy and sacred Virgin, object of Old Testament prophecies, the place where the two economies meet. Her virginal birth, an entirely new thing, is the sign that the new economy of grace has begun *(novus ordo, novitas creaturae),* freeing humanity from its ancient slavery to sin *(vetustas antiqua).* It is also a sign that the generative principle of the new humanity is the Holy Spirit, not fleshly concupiscence. In a word, the *Virgo-Mater* brings to birth the *Deus-Homo* and reveals the mystery.

The euchology of the so-called *Rotulus* of Ravenna stands out.[56] Dating from the second half of the fifth century, it was composed for the ferial days before the feast of Christmas—a sort of Advent *ante*

[54] *Sermo* 369, 1: NBA 34, p. 476.

[55] I. M. Calabuig, *Los formularios V–IX de la sección XL del Sacramentario de Verona* (Rome, 1964).

[56] S. Benz, *Der Rotulus von Ravenna nach seiner Herkunft und seiner Bedeutung für Liturgiegeschichte kritisch Untersucht* (Münster, 1967). The text appears on pp. 5–16. The *Rotulus* has also been edited along with the Verona Sacramentary, pp. 173–178.

litteram—and contained many important references to the Virgin. These attracted the attention of liturgists during the postconciliar liturgical reforms.[57]

The *Rotulus* shares the doctrinal foundation of the *Veronense*. In the *Rotulus* the figure of the Virgin is drawn using robust theology and refined language; frequent recourse is made to language about light *(claritas, splendor, fulgeo, corusco, lumen, illumino)*, metaphors from the Psalter (because the Word found a dwelling place in her, Mary is the *tabernaculum* and the *domus* of the King, the *thalamus* and the *cubiculum* of the Spouse, the *templum* and *domicilium* of God). There is a preference for abstract nouns that define the nature of being. Christ, true God, is *deitas* itself. Mary is the essence of *virginitas*.

In conclusion, the institution of the feast of Christmas at Rome was the principal cause for the development of a euchology that was both Marian and Christological and at the same time well-balanced and of high theological quality.

Other feasts—The institution of the feast of Christmas, which became the second pole of the liturgical year, already had, by the sixth century, important consequences for the development of other feasts.

—*The season of Advent*: Before achieving a fixed form in Rome in the second half of the sixth century, various versions of Advent had been tried in Spain. The Council of Saragossa (381–383) had prescribed a period of three weeks (from December 17 to January 6) for preparation for baptism, which, according to the Oriental custom, had been conferred on the feast of the Epiphany.

In Gaul, St. Gregory of Tours († 594) makes mention of a penitential period extending from November 11 until Christmas.

Ravenna, as well, as is indicated by the orations in the *Rotulus*, knew a period of preparation for Christmas, the purpose of which was "more for the contemplation of the mystery than asceticism, more theological than penitential."[58]

At Rome, in the second half of the sixth century, Advent lasted for six weeks, and was reduced to four by St. Gregory the Great († 604).

[57] A. Rose, "Les oraisons du Rotulus de Ravenne dans le nouveau Missel Romain," *QL* 52 (1971) 271–294; A. Ward, "'*Sancti Spiritus luce repleta.*' The Blessed Virgin of the Rotulus of Ravenna in Recent Latin Missals," *Marianum* 53 (1991) 221–252.

[58] J. Castellano Cervera, *L'anno liturgico memoriale di Cristo e mistagogia della Chiesa con Maria Madre di Gesù* (Rome, 1991) 147.

From the beginning it had the dual character of preparation for Christmas, that is, for the celebration of the coming of the Lord in the flesh and expectation of his final coming in glory. Insofar as it was a preparation for Christmas, the liturgy of Advent took on a Marian tone, especially on the Wednesdays and Fridays of this winter season. On Wednesday the Würzburg Lectionary assigned Isaiah 7:10-15 *(Pete tibi signum . . . Ecce virgo concipiet)* as the epistle and Luke 1:26-38 *(Missus est angelus Gabriel)* as the gospel. This resulted in a Mass that was both a powerful and intelligent commemoration of the mystery of the incarnation. On Friday the epistle was Isaiah 11:1-5 *(Egredietur virga de radice Iesse)* and the gospel was Luke 1:39-47 *(Exsurgens autem Maria).* Thus, this was another Mass with an explicitly Marian subject matter.

—*The institution of the first Western Marian feast*. The first Western Marian feast came about in a way that shows a close dependence on December 25. According to B. Botte, many scholars are of the opinion that a memorial of the Virgin—*Natale sanctae Mariae*—was instituted in Rome during the second half of the sixth century and placed on January 1, the octave of Christmas.[59] A formulary was composed for the new feast between 560 and 590. In the antiphonal sections, use was made of the Common of Virgins, applying those texts to the *Virgo virginum:*

Introit: *Vultum tuum*
Gradual: *Diffusa est gratia*
Offertory: *Offeruntur regi*
Communion: *Simile est regnum caelorum . . . homini negotiatori.*[60]

The readings were probably also taken from the Common of Virgins:

Epistle: Sirach 24:11ff.
Gospel: Matthew 13:44ff.

The euchological texts, however, as shown by B. Botte and A. Chavasse,[61] were original, markedly Marian, extremely well written, witnesses to a liturgical devotion to holy Mary that was highly refined

[59] B. Botte, "La première fête mariale de la liturgie romaine," *EphLit* 47 (1933) 425–430.

[60] Hesbert, *Antiphonale Missarum septuplex,* n. 16 bis (pp. 22–23).

[61] A. Chavasse, *Le Sacramentaire Gélasien (Vaticanus Reginensis 316)* (Tournai, 1958) 651–656; G. Frénaud, "Le culte de Notre Dame dans l'ancienne liturgie latine," in H. du Manoir, ed., *Maria: Études sur la sainte Vierge* (Paris, 1961) 6:159–167.

and theologically rich. Among them, the collect *Deus, qui salutis aeternae*[62] was especially fine and is still in use in the liturgy for January 1. Apparently the feast did not last long. In the course of the seventh century it was moved aside under the influence of the Gallican feast *In circumcisione Domini.*[63] It took the name, substituted the gospel of the Mass with the pericope of the circumcision (Luke 2:21-32), and introduced other changes, but on the whole it retained the Marian character of the feast.

The dogmatic definition of Ephesus (431)

Countering Nestorius, the Council of Ephesus (431) sanctioned the legitimacy of the title *Theotokos* or *Dei Genetrix,* with which the Church has, ever since, venerated the Blessed Virgin: "If someone does not confess that Emmanuel is God in the true sense of the word, and that therefore the holy virgin is the Mother of God because she begot according to the flesh the Word who is God, let him be anathema" (canon 1).[64]

The canons of Ephesus were directly Christological both in scope and in intent. Nevertheless, scholars recognize that the declarations of Ephesus are extremely important in Mariology and see in them one of the most important factors in the development of Marian piety. Vatican II said: "Accordingly, following the Council of Ephesus, there was a remarkable growth in the cult of the People of God towards Mary, in veneration and love, in invocation and imitation."[65] Without desiring in any way to diminish the importance of this statement, we would argue that the establishment of the feast of Christmas a hundred years earlier had, from a liturgical point of view, a greater influence than did the definition of Ephesus.

Following the Council of Ephesus, Sixtus III († 440) restored and expanded the basilica erected by Pope Liberius († 366) on the Esquiline hill, dedicating it to the Mother of God and decorating it with awe-inspiring mosaics, which still exist in part. It was the intention of Sixtus III that the Basilica of St. Mary Major would perpetuate the memory of

[62] *GrH,* n. 82.

[63] *GaG* "VIII" = *Missale Gothicum (Vat. Reg. lat. 317),* ed. L. Mohlberg, RED, Series maior, Fontes V (Rome, 1961): *Ordo missae in circumcisione Domini nostri Jesu Christi,* nn. 51–63.

[64] DS 252.

[65] *LG* 66.

the Council of Ephesus and glorify the Mother of Jesus as Mother of God. Especially interesting is the dedicatory inscription, which was, at one time, in the façade of the basilica:

Virgo Maria, tibi Xystus nova tecta dicavi
digna salutifero munera ventre tuo.
Tu genitrix ignara viri, te denique foeta
visceribus salvis edita nostra salus.
Ecce tui testes uteri tibi praemia portant
sub pedibusque iacet passio quaeque sua,
ferrum, flamma, ferae, fluvius, saevumque venenum;
tot tamen has mortes una corona manet.[66]

The last two lines allude to the procession of martyrs depicted in the mosaics, which have since disappeared from the sides of the basilica. Each of the martyrs, witnesses of Christ *(tui testes uteri),* were praising the Virgin Mother with the device with which he was tortured beneath his feet.

What St. Mary Major is to sacred architecture, the *Communicantes* of the Roman Canon is to Eucharistic euchology. The text, solemn and harmonious, is a remarkable synthesis of the faith and piety of the Church:

Communicantes,
et memoriam venerantes,
in primis gloriosae semper Virginis Mariae,
Genetricis Dei et Domini nostri Iesu Christi.

Scholars do not agree about the origin and date of the *Communicantes.* In any case, its definitive formulation was at the end of the fifth century or, at the latest, the beginning of the sixth,[67] during a period that

[66] E. Diehl, *Inscriptiones latinae christianae veteres* (Berlin, 1925) 1:182–183.

[67] See, in chronological order: C. Callewaert, "S. Léon, le 'Communicantes' et le 'Nobis quoque peccatoribus,' *SE* 1 (1948) 123–126. This was a study published after the death of its author in 1943; P. Borella, "S. Leone Magno e il 'Communicantes,'" *EphLit* 60 (1946) 93–101; H. Frank, "Beobachtungen zur Geschichte des Messkanons," *ALW* 1 (1950) 107–119; B. Capelle, "Problèmes du 'Communicantes' de la Messe," *RL* 40 (1953) 187–195; S. M. Meo, "La formula mariana 'gloriosa semper virgo Maria genetrix Dei et Domini nostri Ieus Christi' nel Canone romano e presso due pontefici del VI secolo," in *De primordiis cultus mariani,* 2:439–458; R. Falsini, "In comunione con . . . La presenza di Maria nella prece eucaristica" in

was very powerfully and rapidly influenced by the Christological doctrine of Ephesus (431) and Chalcedon (451), as well as the magisterial teaching of St. Leo the Great († 461). Every word of the venerable formula is dense with meaning: *communicantes,* because the Church that celebrates the sacred mysteries on earth is in full and profound communion with the Church already enjoying the glory of heaven; *memoriam venerantes,* a delightful expression with which the worshiping assembly expresses its attachment made with reverent love *(veneratio)* for the blessed in heaven; *in primis,* in the long list of saints the Virgin is mentioned in the first place because of her unique dignity and her unique mission in salvation history; *gloriosae,* because she is caught up in the glory of God; *semper Virginis,* an explicit affirmation of the faith of the Church in the perfect and perpetual virginity of Mary; *Genetricis Dei,* the first and most essential title of the Virgin of Nazareth, which describes her role in the economy of salvation, solemnly recognized by the Council of Ephesus; *Domini nostri Iesu Christi,* because the Savior *(Iesus),* born of Mary, is the Lord *(Dominus)* and the Messiah anointed by God *(Christus).*

Hymnody

The hymn is an important expression of liturgical worship. St. Paul was already exhorting the Christians at Ephesus to teach and admonish one another, saying, "as you sing psalms and hymns and spiritual songs among yourselves, singing and making melody to the Lord in your hearts" (Eph 5:19; cf. Col 3:16).

In the West, during the fourth to sixth centuries, beginning with St. Hilary of Poitiers († 367), there was important development in Christian hymnody that was strictly liturgical in character and largely literary. From the point of view of Mary and the liturgy, it is important to make mention of the hymn *Veni, redemptor gentium,* composed by St. Ambrose († 397) for Christmas Eve and still in use in the Roman liturgy. In this hymn Ambrose, with exalted language tempered with biblical and patristic metaphors, expresses the intense desire for the coming of the Savior and considers with delicacy and awe the mystery of the conception of Christ: the virginal womb of Mary in which the divine Word became present:

R. Falsini, ed., *Maria nel culto della Chiesa. Tra liturgia e pietà popolare* (Milan, 1988) 117–131.

Veni, redemptor gentium,
ostende partum Virginis;
miretur omne saeculum:
talis decet partus Deum.

Non ex virili semine,
sed mystico spiramine
Verbum Dei factum est caro
fructusque ventris floruit.

Alvus tumescit Virginis,
claustrum pudoris permanet.
Vexilla virtutum micant,
versatur in templo Deus.

Procedat e thalamo suo,
pudoris aula regia,
geminae gigas substantiae
alacris ut currat viam.[68]

Given this text, there is no need to highlight any further the reverent attention with which Ambrose contemplated the Virgin, who became, in virtue of the mystery of the incarnation, *templum, thalamus,* and *aula regia* of the Word.

Aurelius Prudentius († 405), a contemporary of St. Ambrose, was the greatest Christian poet of the West during this era. Unlike the bishop of Milan, Prudentius did not compose his hymns for liturgical use but drew inspiration and subject matter from the liturgy. The situation with his hymnody is sort of paradoxical: without being, strictly speaking, liturgical, these hymns show a profound understanding of worship, nourished both by his frequent attendance at liturgical celebrations and the attention he paid to the liturgical seasons. In the course of its history, the liturgy has recognized Prudentius's importance by adopting a number of his hymns for important celebrations of the liturgical year.

Some examples follow. For Vespers of the Solemnity of the Mother of God (January 1), the liturgy suggests a hymn composed from several selections taken from Cathemerinon IX *(Hymnus omnis horae).* The wonderful strophe that follows is among them:

[68] *In nocte Natalis Domini,* 5–20: Bibliotheca Patrum 13, pp. 39–40.

O beatus ortus ille, Virgo cum puerpera
edidit nostram salutem feta Sancto Spiritu
et puer redemptor orbis nos sacratum protulit.[69]

The hymn for the Office of Readings on the Solemnity of March 25 is also taken from the *Cathemerinon XI,* a hymn for Christmas. The sixth strophe is worthy of special mention. With breadth of vision and real ardor the poet sees the virginal womb of Mary as the place where the world's joy is concentrated; from it will come humanity's new age, from it will come the light of dawn—Christ:

O quanta rerum gaudia
alvus pudica continet,
ex qua novellum saeculum
procedit et lux aurea.[70]

Very attentive to the figure of the Virgin, Prudentius always considers her in a Christological perspective: as the new Eve in association with the new Adam and in relation to the ineffable mystery of the incarnation, by which, through the gift of the Father and the work of the Holy Spirit, she became the Virgin Mother of the incarnate Word.[71] In his personal life Prudentius was deeply devoted to the Virgin, and through the centuries his influence on the liturgy helped many others to become so devoted as well.

Paulinus of Nola († 431) was a poet of delicate and refined tastes. In *Carmen* VI *(Laus sancti Iohannis),* he placed on Elizabeth's lips a reverent and joyful greeting, a poetic expansion of the one with which she had greeted the Mother of the Lord:

Salve, o mater, ait, domini, salve pia virgo,
immunis thalami coitusque ignara virilis,
sed paritura deum; tanti fuit esse pudicam;
intactae ut ferres titulos et praemia nuptae.[72]

[69] *Cathemerinon* IX, 18–21: CCL 126, p. 48.

[70] *Cathemerinon* XI, 57–60: CCL 126, p. 62.

[71] I. Rodríguez, "La mariología en Prudencio," *Estudios Marianos* 5 (1946) 347–358; E. del S. do Corazón (Llamas), "Aurelio Prudencio y el culto mariano en la España primitiva," in *De primordiis cultus mariani,* 5:145–178; J. Pascual Torró, *Intemerata puella. Estudios de mariología prudenciana* (Valencia, 1992).

[72] *Carm.* VI, 151–154: CSEL 30, p. 12.

But if Paulinus had not dared to address the Virgin directly, Sedulius († ca. 450) did not share the same reserve. In the *Carmen paschale,* probably composed before 431, at the end of the poetic paraphrase of Gabriel's annunciation to Mary and of the birth of Jesus, he directs a greeting to the Virgin that has been widely used in the Roman liturgy:

Salve, sancta parens, enixa puerpera regem,
Qui coelum terramque tenet per saecula, cuius
Nomen et aeterno complectens omnia gyro
Imperium sine fine manet; quae ventre beato
Gaudia matris habens cum virginitatis honore
Nec primam similem visa es nec habere sequentem:
Sola sine exemplo placuisti femina Christo.[73]

The Roman liturgy is indebted to Sedulius for the Lauds hymn on December 25 as well. This is composed of the first seven strophes of the *Hymnus abecedarius,* a Christological poem that has some excellent strophes dedicated to the Virgin. There is a poetic contemplation of the marvelous nature of Mary's divine and virginal motherhood. This is a standard theme which, in Sedulius's verses, is not at all trite or stale but able to arouse genuine religious feeling even in someone of our own day who is praying it:

Clausae parentis viscera
caelestis intrat gratia;
venter puellae baiulat
secreta quae non noverat.

Domus pudici pectoris
templum repente fit Dei;
intacta nesciens virum
verbo concepit Filium

Enixa est puerpera
quem Gabriel praedixerat,
quem matris alvo gestiens
clausus Ioannes senserat.[74]

[73] *Carmen paschale* II, 63–69: CSEL 10, pp. 48–49.
[74] *Hymnus* II, 9–16: CSEL 10, pp. 163–164.

The review of the Christological-Marian hymnody of this period—the fourth to sixth centuries—should end with the name of Venantius Fortunatus († 601), an elegant and subtle poet who took his inspiration from classical forms but whose content was deeply Christian. He wrote some hymns for liturgical use, among which the famous *Vexilla regis prodeunt* and *Pange, lingua, gloriosi* have become part of the Office for Holy Week.[75] In honor of the Virgin, Venantius composed a long poem *(In laudem sanctae Mariae)* in which there are sincere expressions of Marian piety—reverence, praise, supplication—but which does not lend itself to liturgical use.[76] On the other hand, the hymn *Quem terra, pontus, aethera* works extremely well in the liturgy and is used in the Office of the Blessed Virgin, but its attribution to Venantius is not certain. This hymn is another awestruck meditation on the motherhood of Mary of Nazareth, in whose womb there is enclosed he who rules the universe and to whom heaven, earth, and sea render praise:

Quem terra, pontus, aethera
colunt, adorant, praedicant
trinam regentem machinam,
claustrum Mariae baiulat.

Cui luna, sol et omnia
deserviunt per tempora,
perfusa caeli gratia
gestant puellae viscera.

Beata mater munere,
cuius, supernus artifex,
mundum pugillo continens,
ventris sub arca clausus est.

Beata caeli nuntio,
fecunda Sancto Spiritu,

[75] In the current Liturgy of the Hours, *Vexilla Regis prodeunt* is used as the Vespers hymn for Holy Week and for the feast of the Triumph of the Cross (September 14). *Pange, lingua, gloriosi,* divided into two sections, is used at the Office of Readings and Lauds for the days of Holy Week.

[76] The text of the poem is in S. Alvares Campos, *Corpus marianum patristicum* (Burgos, 1970) 6:378–388.

desideratus gentibus
cuius per alvum fusus est.[77]

During the fourth to sixth centuries, Marian hymnody in the West, with its thematic foundation in the mystery of the Lord's manifestation—incarnation, birth, epiphany—yields some examples of excellent compositions. For the most part they are the fruit of personal piety but reflect themes and use language proper to the liturgy, and they have frequently been incorporated into the liturgy. However, while not downplaying their character as works of literature, the authors of these hymns had aims that were sometimes catechetical, which motivated them to tell about the story, and sometimes related to liturgy, which motivated them to speak of the Virgin. At any rate, the principal attitudes of liturgical piety for holy Mary—praise, love, invocation, invitation to imitation—are already present in these hymns, which in two and a half centuries had taken on both an artistic maturity and a firm place in the Church's worship.

b) In the East

Since the feast of Christmas, which was destined to have such a strong influence on the development of Marian piety, was established in Rome, about 336, it seemed useful to begin this study with a consideration of liturgical evidence from the West. However, the Churches in the East gave rise to many manifestations of liturgical devotion to the *Theotokos*. There is, in particular, the phenomenon of the Marian feast.

The Church in Jerusalem

In the period under consideration (325–604), various feasts of a Christological-Marian character, or even a purely Marian character, came out of Jerusalem. It is to be expected that this would happen in Jerusalem, where various incidents in the childhood of Jesus (e.g., the presentation in the Temple, Luke 2:22-38; the twelve-year-old Jesus being found in the Temple, Luke 2:41-50) took place, as well as the saving mysteries of Easter. To the biblical data can be added a number of traditions that locate both the "house of Mary" and the place of her burial in Jerusalem. All this led the community of Jerusalem to celebrate in ritual what had taken place right where they were.

[77] AH 50, pp. 86–87.

—The *presentation of Jesus in the Temple.* Egeria, the famous pilgrim who visited the holy places between the years 381 and 384, says that in Jerusalem "the fortieth day after Epiphany . . . was celebrated with great solemnity . . . like Easter."[78] According to Egeria's narrative, the object of the feast is mentioned in the gospel passage, which said that "Joseph and Mary . . . took the Lord to the Temple and that Simeon and the prophetess Anna . . . saw him, and they recalled the words they had said when they saw the Lord and offerings the parents made."[79]

In the first half of the fifth century, three homilies by Hesychius of Jerusalem († 451) attest to the importance that the feast had taken on in the Holy City.[80] Hesychius called it "the feast of the purification," but, he adds, "it would not be a mistake to call it the feast of feasts . . . because in it is recapitulated the entire mystery of Christ's incarnation. . . . In this feast Christ is carried as a newborn yet is recognized as God."[81]

In the fifth century the Jerusalemite synaxis was not familiar with the rite of light. In it, according to the famous Armenian lectionary of that century, the *canon* "All the ends of the earth have seen the salvation of our God" is carried out, and Galatians 3:24-29, which focuses on the genuine descent of Abraham and the real divine sonship, which is now to be had only "by faith in Christ Jesus," is read, along with Luke 2:22-40, the Gospel story that recounts the presentation in the Temple.[82]

Around 534 the feast was introduced into the liturgy of Byzantium.[83] Here the aspect of encounter *(ypapanté)* of Jesus with Simeon and Anna, representing the people, was stressed to such an extent that it became the characteristic element of the celebration and even gave it its name.

[78] *Itinerarium,* 26: SCh 296, pp. 254–256. Counting the forty days beginning with Epiphany (January 6), which was also originally the memorial of the birth of Jesus, the celebration of his presentation would have taken place on February 14.

[79] Ibid.

[80] A critical edition of the two Greek homilies has been prepared by M. Aubineau, *Les homélies festales d'Hésychius de Jerusalem* (Brussels, 1978) 1:1–76. The third, which has come down to us in Georgian, was published by G. Garitte, "L'homélie géorgienne d'Hésychius de Jérusalem sur l'Hypapante," *Le Muséon* 84 (1971) 353–372.

[81] Omelia I, 1, p. 24.

[82] A. Renoux, *Le codex arménien Jérusalem 121:* PatOr 36, p. 229.

[83] Theophane, *Chronograph,* A.C. 534: PG 108, 488.

—*The feast of August 15.* According to the Armenian lectionary, in a place located three miles from Jerusalem on the road to Bethlehem, a Marian feast was celebrated even before the Council of Ephesus. There were three readings: Isaiah 7:10-16a, the famous prophecy about the virgin mother of Emmanuel; Galatians 3:29–4:7, with its famous verse 4:4 ("born of woman, born under the law"); and Luke 2:1-7, the story of Jesus' birth. This was, then, a celebration of the divine, virginal, and saving motherhood of Mary.[84] There is nothing that would allow us to think that this was a commemoration of her death or assumption or that it was a feast for the dedication of a church.

According to some scholars, certain local elements were inserted into this global feast of Mary's motherhood: the *rest* of the pregnant Virgin at Kathisma, three miles from Jerusalem, while she was traveling toward Bethlehem.[85] The *canon* of the feast alludes to this rest: "Arise, Lord, and go to the place of your rest, / you and the ark of your strength" (Ps 132:8). In the liturgical interpretation, the *ark* was holy Mary, who bore the Son of God in her womb; the *rest* was the stop that the Virgin made prior to entering Jerusalem, but, even more, the fact that the Word deigned to dwell—to rest—in her womb.[86]

Historical research up to now has not clarified the reason for the choice of August 15 for this feast, nor has it clarified the process by which it became the global memorial of the divine motherhood or, more specifically, why it became the celebration of the Virgin's passing away (*koimesis* in Greek, *dormitio* in Latin), that is, her real *dies natalis.* It was probably because of the influence of a tradition rooted in Jerusalem, which was supported by a vast apocryphal literature on the *transitus* of Mary.[87] In any case, toward the end of the fifth century, the Church of Jerusalem celebrated the dormition of Mary in the basilica of Gethsemani, where the "tomb of Mary" was venerated.[88]

[84] B. Capelle, "La fête de la Vierge a Jérusalem au V siècle," *Le Muséon* 56 (1943) 1–33.

[85] The *Protoevangelium of James* (17:2) alludes to the Virgin's rest at the third mile. Moraldi, *Apocrifi del Nuovo Testamento,* 1:134–135.

[86] Chrysippus of Jerusalem († 479), in his *Homily on the Mother of God,* delivered on August 15, commented on Psalm 132:8: "Lord . . . your *peace* is the Virgin, whose womb is your *rest,* because she has become your bed and your dwelling" (PatOr 19, p. 338).

[87] On the traditions concerning the Assumption, see note 32 above.

[88] M. Jugie, *La mort et l'assomption de la sainte Vierge. Étude historico-doctrinale* (Vatican City, 1944) 172–212; B. Capelle, "L'Assunzione e la liturgia," *Marianum* 15 (1953) 241–276; Bagatti, "Nuove scoperte," 236–244.

At the end of the sixth century, the emperor Maurice (582–602) made the feast of August 15, understood as the *dormitio* of the Holy Mother of God, obligatory throughout the empire.[89]

—*The Nativity of Mary*. The feast of September 8 also has its origin in Jerusalem. According to the *Protoevangelium of James* (chapters 1–5), the Virgin Mary was born in the Holy City, in the house of Anna, which tradition says was located near the Sheep Pool, the famous healing shrine where Jesus, the greatest of healers, cured a paralyzed man (John 5:1-17). The relationship between the birth of Mary and the pool of Bethesda might merely be a matter of geography (the house of Anna being near to the healing shrine), or, as E. Testa argues, it might have a medical origin. Anna, seeking to be healed from her infertility, used the healing waters of the shrine. Testa, in fact, sees in chapters 1–4 of the *Protoevangelium of James* traces of the "healing ritual" used in the pool.[90]

In any case, toward the end of the fifth century a church dedicated to Holy Mary was erected next to the pool. The pilgrim Theodosius, who visited Jerusalem in the first half of the sixth century, says that he saw it: "Iuxta piscinam probaticam ibi est ecclesia domnae Mariae."[91] September 8 may well have been the date of the church's dedication, the annual memorial of which gave rise to the feast of the Nativity of Mary.

Under the emperor Justinian († 565) the feast moved from Jerusalem to Constantinople, where, at the same time, the famous hymn writer named Romanus the Melodist († 560) was active. He composed a *Hymn for the Nativity of Mary*[92] for the feast, drawing its inspiration almost entirely from the *Protoevangelium of James* (chapters 1–4). In the hymn he uses the themes of light, joy, and life, which would become characteristic of the feast of September 8.

—*The Presentation of Mary.* This feast also has its origins in Jerusalem. It seems to derive from the dedication of the new church that had been built with the financial assistance of the emperor Justinian I to honor Mary—the so-called Nea Church (November 21, 543). Built on

[89] This was handed down by the historian Nicephorus Callistus, *Historia ecclesiastica* 17, 28: PG 147, 292.

[90] *Maria terra vergine,* II: *Il culto mariano palestinese (secc. I–IX),* Studium Biblicum Franciscanum 30 (Jerusalem, 1985) 6–7, 17–20.

[91] *De situ terrae sanctae,* 8: CCL 175, p. 119.

[92] P. Maas and A. Trypanis, *Sancti Romani Melodi cantica* (Oxford, 1963) 276–280.

the ruins of the Temple, the church was called "new" in order to distinguish it from the earlier church, also dedicated to Mary, that had been built near the Sheep Pool opposite the Temple. The new church was splendid. The historian Procopius said of it: "In Jerusalem, the emperor Justinian consecrated a sanctuary to the Virgin which has no equal and which the local people call the New Church."[93]

The feast stems from the legend found in the *Protoevangelium of James* (7:2-3), according to which Mary, a three-year-old child, was brought by Joachim and Anna to the Temple so that she could be brought up near the Holy of Holies. But more than this fantastic story, what the Church of Jerusalem wanted to celebrate was the profound dedication of Mary, the real Temple of God, to the Lord's service.

The feast for November 21 was, apparently, mostly local in character. Only toward the end of the seventh century was it taken up into the Byzantine liturgy and, much later, into the Roman liturgy.[94]

The Church of Constantinople

From the fourth to the sixth century Constantinople became a second moving force behind the development of liturgical Marian piety. From this city, not infrequently because of imperial decrees, a number of feasts of the Virgin were disseminated throughout the Christian world.

—*The Christmas cycle*. In all probability, the Roman feast of Christmas was introduced to Constantinople at the beginning of the reign of Theodosius I (379–395). On December 25, 380, St. Gregory Nazianzen, who had only recently become patriarch of the imperial city (379–381), gave a homily on the birth of Christ.[95] The result was that a liturgical space developed around December 25 wherein the memory of the Mother of God enjoyed particular attention. In this space the most important dates were the *Sunday before Christmas* and *December 26,* both of which dates focused specifically on the divine motherhood.

The Marian character of the Sunday before Christmas, on which, it seems, the prophecy of the virgin mother of Emmanuel (Isa 7:10-14)

[93] The [original Italian] of the quotation is taken from D. M. Sartor, *Le feste della Madonna. Note storiche e liturgiche per una celebrazione partecipata* (Bologna, 1988) 118.

[94] There is evidence that the feast was celebrated at Constantinople in the time of Patriarch Germanus (715–730), who dedicated two homilies to it (cf. PG 98, 292–309; 309–320). It was officially adopted in the Roman liturgy only in 1371, during the pontificate of Gregory IX.

[95] *Oratio 38*: SCh 358, pp. 104–149.

and the gospel of the Annunciation (Luke 1:26-38) were read, is clear in the homily given by Proclus of Constantinople between 428 and 430.[96]

It is more difficult to determine exactly when December 26 became fixed as the feast of the glorious *Theotokos.* This must have happened during the sixth century, according to the principle that on the day after a solemnity one celebrated the "secondary" person in the mystery that had been celebrated.

—*The feast of the Annunciation.* Since the third century, March 25, which had marked the beginning of spring prior to the Gregorian calendar reform, had been considered a "day of mystery"; it was thought that, among other things, the incarnation of the Word in the womb of Mary had taken place on March 25.[97]

By a process, the dynamics of which are still not at all clear, of prayerful contemplation on the incarnation of the Word, the feast of the Annunciation evolved. The documentary evidence that has come down to us does not allow us to determine where this happened. In a letter written in 561, the emperor Justinian affirms that the feast was introduced eleven years earlier, in 550, at the time of the reorganization of the liturgy in Constantinople.[98] In the same year Romanus the Melodist composed his well-known *Hymn for the Annunciation.*[99] After the period of Justinian, because of the prestige of the Church of Constantinople and the growing acceptance of the Byzantine rite, the feast of the Annunciation spread to the other patriarchates.

—*The Akathist hymn.* The composition of the *Akathist,* the most famous hymn of the Byzantine Church, took place between the second half of the fifth century and the first years of the sixth. It has been called "the privileged expression of the correct doctrine concerning,

[96] *Oratio 1*: PG 65, 680–692. According to the witness of Theophane, the homily was given on a Sunday (cf. *Chronograph,* A.C. 423: PG 108, 236; see also D. M. Montanga "La liturgia mariana primitiva," *Marianum* 24 (1962) 84–128. R. Caro, "Proclo de Constantinopla orador mariano del siglo V," *Marianum* 29 (1967) 377–492; J. A. de Aldama, "La primera fiesta litúrgica de Nuestra Señora," *Estudios ecclesiásticos* 40 (1965) 46–48.

[97] For a complete history of the solemnity of the Annunciation, see C. Maggioni, *Annunciazione. Storia, eucologia, teologia liturgica* (Rome, 1991) 30–73; A. H. Scheer, "Aux origines de la fête de l'Annonciation," n. 47.

[98] M. van Esbroeck, "La lettre de l'empereur Justinien sur l'Annonciation et la Noël en 561," *AB* 86 (1968) 351–371.

[99] In SCh 110, pp. 20–41.

and piety toward, the Mother of God,"[100] and is a masterpiece of liturgy and of great importance for the Church.

The *Akathist* hymn consists of twenty-four strophes divided into two parts. The first (1–12) is narrative and follows the biblical drama of the birth of Christ—annunciation, visitation, shepherds, magi, the flight to Egypt, the presentation in the Temple—and "responds better to the formulary of the ancient feast of the incarnation, Christmas, than to that of the Annunciation, only instituted in the sixth century."[101] The second part (13–24) is dogmatic, a short *summa* on Mariology: the virginal life of Mary, the virginal conception, the divine motherhood, the virgin birth, Mary as the defender and model of virgins, Mary as source of the sacred mysteries of baptism, Mary as the protector of the Christian empire.

The *Akathist* hymn, which is still surprisingly fresh after fifteen centuries, has its own date and is a proper feast in the Byzantine and Slavic traditions. The fifth Saturday of Lent, known as *Akathist* Saturday, has had a noteworthy influence on a number of liturgies, even those of the West.

The Church of Syria

In the Syrian liturgy, strongly Marian in tone, the memory of the Virgin is first of all found on the Sundays that precede Christmas and especially on December 25. For the Syrians, the birth of the Son, the God-Man, is really a feast of the Mother. In fact, the greater part of the so-called *Hymns for the Virgin* of St. Ephrem († 373), who is, for all time, one of the greatest of those who have sung of the Virgin, was composed expressly for the Christmas liturgy.[102] James of Sarug († 521), also a great poet, witnesses to the progressive formation of a calendar in which the figure of the Virgin assumes ever greater importance. The eight *Mariological Homilies* of the bishop of Sarug were delivered on Christmas (three), on the Sunday immediately before Christmas

[100] E. M. Toniolo, "Akáthistos," *NDM*, 17.

[101] E. M. Toniolo, "L'inno Acatisto, monumento di teologia e di culto mariano nella Chiesa bizantina," in *De cultu mariano saeculis VI–XI*, Acta Congressus Mariologici-Mariani in Croatia anno 1971 celebrati (Rome, 1972) 24.

[102] An edition of the Syriac, with a German translation, has been done by E. Beck, *Des heiligen Ephraem des Syrers Hymnen de Nativitate*, Corpus scriptorum Christianorum Orientalium 186–187. There is an English translation by K. E. McVey, *Ephrem the Syrian: Hymns* (New York, 1989).

(four), and focused on episodes connected to the Lord's birth—the annunciation, the visitation, etc.—or August 14 (one homily) in the context of the celebration of the *transitus* of Mary.[103]

In addition, there are hymns and homilies by Severus, patriarch of Antioch († 538).[104] There is also the homily of Antipatrus of Bostra († ca. 557), *In Annuntiationem*,[105] delivered on the Sunday before Christmas.

Characteristic of the Syriac liturgy, especially the East Syriac, from which the Maronite and Chaldean liturgies arose, is the interpretation of feasts that were originally agricultural in a Eucharistic-Marian fashion—the Virgin who had charge of fields of wheat and vineyards, because from her came the bread and wine of the Eucharist.[106] Among these one might notice especially the feast of the Virgin of the Sprouts or the Ears (of wheat) celebrated on May 15. However, it is difficult to tell whether this arose in the sixth century.

The Church of Alexandria

In the period under consideration (325–604), the Church of Alexandria, from which both the Coptic and Ethiopian Churches descended, remained one of the most prominent centers of Marian piety.

Since the end of the fourth century, the bishops of Alexandria, continuing the custom begun by Patriarch Theonas († ca. 300) dedicated churches to the Blessed Virgin[107] and remembered her in an especially intense fashion in the Eucharistic anaphora in use since the fourth century:

[103] Edited by C. Vona, *Omelie mariologiche di s. Giacomo di Sarug* (Rome, 1953).

[104] For the hymns see the English-language edition edited by E. W. Brooks: Inni 3 (PatOr 6, p. 47; 7, p. 50; 8, p. 50; 9, pp. 51–52; 10, p. 52; 11, pp. 53–54; 14, pp. 56–57). Three of the famous cathedral homilies of Severus, Marian in content, are connected to Christmas, in particular the Sunday before Christmas. They are II (*On the Annunciation*: PatOr 38, pp. 272–279; XIV (*The Memorial of the Holy Mother of God*, PatOr, pp. 400–415); and LXVII (*Mary, the Ever-Virgin Holy Mother of God*, PatOr, pp. 349–367).

[105] PG 85, 1175–1792.

[106] M. Doumith, "Marie dans la liturgie syro-maronite," in H. du Manoir, *Maria. Études sur la sainte Vierge* (Paris, 1949) 1:327–340; A.-M. Massonnat, "Marie dans la liturgie chaldéenne," ibid., 341–351.

[107] Giamberardini, *Il culto mariano in Egitto*, 1:97–105, 133–134, 153–154, 189–190.

Praecipue vero Virginis in omi tempore
sanctae et gloriosae Mariae
Dei Genitricis
Et miserere nostrum omnium
precibus eius.[108]

The Alexandrian Church remembered, ritually, the divine motherhood of Mary, her perpetual virginity, her sanctity and glory, and her intercession on behalf of humanity.

The feast of Christmas, celebrated on Koiak 29 (= December 25), also became a feast of the Mother because of the singular cooperation of the Virgin in the incarnation and birth of the Son, Jesus. As a result, the homilies delivered at Christmas are full of Marian doctrine and piety. Among these homilies, one should mention those of St. Anastasius († 373), Proclus († 446), who was bishop of Cizicus before becoming patriarch of Constantinople (434–46), and St. Cyril of Alexandria († 444).[109]

As far as the development of feasts is concerned, the Coptic tradition presents, quite certainly since the sixth century, a characteristic proper. It had two feasts for the commemoration of the end of the Virgin's life. Tûbah 21 (January 16) celebrated the *death* or *dormition*, and 206 days later, Misrî 16 (August 22) saw the commemoration of her *assumption* into heaven.[110]

In the sixth century, as is documented by the famous calendar of Oxyrhyncus, which was assembled for the liturgical year 535–536,[111] the Egyptian Church celebrated three feasts of the Virgin: the first commemorated the divine motherhood, the second the dormition, and the third the glorious assumption. The collection of homilies that has resulted is very rich. Beginning with a consideration of the divine motherhood, the incomparable dignity of Mary is also important, as is her perpetual virginity, her exemplary life, her role as mediatrix, her role as protector of the Church, her heavenly glory and royal mercy.

The Alexandrian liturgy delights in focusing on the role of Mary in salvation history. There is special delight in the Coptic practice of greeting Mary as the "Mother of Emmanuel," because in her womb

[108] Ibid., 134–138.

[109] Ibid., 139–149, 162–169, 203–204.

[110] Ibid., 169–177.

[111] H. Delahaye, "Le Calendrier d'Oxyrhynque pour l'année 535–536," *AB* 42 (1924) 83–99.

the Word became "God with us," (Isa 7:14; Matt 1:22). Especially in the Ethiopian tradition, Old Testament symbolism is used for the celebration of the Mother of God.

The Armenian Church

In its reverence for the Mother of God, the Armenian Church is not at all inferior to the other Eastern liturgies. Indeed, it may be said to surpass them in the mystical depth of some of its texts.

The liturgy of the Armenian Church is rooted in that of Jerusalem.[112] This explains why, for example, the Armenian feast of August 15 was originally, like that of the Holy City, a celebration of the divine and virginal motherhood, and used the same psalms and readings.[113] Only in the eighth century did it begin to be a celebration of the Assumption when it took on elements of the *Transitus Mariae*.[114] The same Jerusalem roots are to be found in the Armenian feasts of February 2, September 8, and November 21.

On the feast day of the Jerusalem saints Simeon and Anna (February 15), the *Armenian Synassary of Ter Israel,* the oldest parts of which come from the fifth century, enunciates the principle that guides commemoration of the Virgin in the Armenian liturgy. ". . . on the occasion of all the feasts and blessings of the redemptive acts of Christ, the Holy Church causes the Mother of the Lord to be part of the feasts and blessings, lauding and praising her with her only Son, with the Father and with the Holy Spirit, now and forever."[115]

The liturgical Marian piety of the Armenian Church is evident also in the many churches that are dedicated, beginning in the fifth century, to the Mother of the Lord and in the many monastic communities under her protection.[116]

The Armenian liturgy has a predilection for the theme of light: God is light and lives in inaccessible light (1 Tim 6:16); Jesus is light (John 8:12), and the glory of God shines on his face (2 Cor 4:6); the disciples

[112] Ch. Renoux, "Liturgie arménienne et liturgie hiérosolymitaine," in *Liturgie de l'Église particulière et liturgie de l'Église universelle* (Rome, 1976) 275–288.

[113] Ch. Renoux, "La fête de l'Assomption dans le rite arménien," in *La Mère de Jésus-Christ et la Communion des Saints dans la liturgie* (Rome, 1986) 235–253.

[114] Ibid., 241–246.

[115] PatOr 21, p. 52.

[116] M. Tallon, "Le culte de la Vierge Marie en Asie Mineur du Ier au XVe siècle," in H. du Manoir, *Maria. Études dur la sainte Vierge* (Paris, 1956) 4:909–911.

are sons of the light (John 12:36; Luke 16:8). As part of this theological complex, the Armenian liturgy greets with joy and delight the Blessed Virgin, Mother of the Light.

4. A Decisive Century: The Seventh Century

At the time of Pope Gregory the Great (590–604), the great organizer of the Roman liturgy, the only Marian feast celebrated in Rome was January 1. But in the course of the seventh century, under the influence of the East, other feasts that were either Christological, however with strong Marian overtones or explicitly Marian, were introduced into the calendar of the City. In particular, one must mention February 2, March 25, August 15, and September 8.

a) In the Church of Rome

It would be best to begin with what happened in Rome in the seventh century, because the choices made then had a decisive influence both in time and space. We feel the effects up until our own day, and all of Europe was affected.

The feast of February 2

With its origins in Jerusalem in the fourth century, the feast of February 2 was probably introduced in Rome during the pontificate of Theodorus I (642–649), who was born of Greek parents in Jerusalem.[117]

The title of the feast in the Gregorian tradition *(Hypapanti),* the readings (Mal 3:1-4 and Luke 2:28-40), and the euchological texts (*GrH* 124–127) show that the celebration, focused as it was on the meeting between Jesus and Simeon in the Temple, had a predominantly Christological character. But the station at St. Mary Major and the chants (among which were *Ave gratia plena Dei genetrix Virgo* and *Adorna thalamum tuum Sion*[118]) which accompanied the procession from the Church of St. Hadrian at the Forum to the basilica on the Esquiline show that the focus of the feast was shifting to the figure of the Virgin. So much so was this case that in the Gelasian tradition it already appears under the title *In purificatione sanctae Mariae,* despite the fact that there had been no change in the euchology (*GeV* 829–831).[119] This title remained in the Roman liturgy until 1969.

[117] *Liber pontificalis,* 1:331.

[118] Hesbert, *Antiphonale Missarum septuplex,* 29a, pp. 37–38.

[119] A. Chavasse, *Le sacramentaire gélasien (Vaticanus Reginensis 316)* (Tournai, 1958) 401–402.

The procession of February 2 was probably a Christian version of an old pagan procession with a character of purification and expiation that took place in Rome every five years at the beginning of February (the *Amburbale*). The Roman procession was both penitential and festive in nature, as is indicated by the violet color of the vestments and the lighting of candles in honor of Christ, "the light to illumine the nations" (Luke 2:32).

The feast of August 15

Around the year 650 Rome took up the feast of August 15, which already had the end of the earthly life of the Virgin as its object. The biblical texts for the Mass (the epistle: *Mulierem fortem,* Proverbs 31:10-31; or *Ego quasi vitis,* Sirach 24:23-31; or *Sapientia vincit malitiam,* Wisdom 7:30–8:4 ; the gospel: Luke 10:38-42, the episode with Mary and Martha); and the antiphons (introit: *Vultum tuum;* gradual: *Propter veritatem;* alleluia: *Specie tua;* offertory: *Offerentur;* communion: *Dilexisti*) are taken in large part from the Common of Virgins.[120]

The orations of the Gregorian formulary (*GrH* 661–664) present a theology that is still not certain about the bodily nature of the assumption of the Virgin. The collect and the postcommunion make no mention of it. The prayer over the gifts (*GrH* 663) strongly affirms the fact of Mary's death *(pro conditione carnis migrasse cognoscimus)* and her role as intercessor in heavenly glory *(in caelesti gloria apud te pro nobis intercedere sentiamus).* The collect for the station, however, the famous prayer *Veneranda* (*GrH* 661), offers some excellent ideas on the glorification of the Virgin's body. She underwent death *(sancta Dei genetrix mortem subiit temporalem),* but she could not be vanquished by death *(nec tamen mortis nexibus deprimi potuit).*[121] It is probable, however, that the oration *Veneranda* was inserted into the formulary only at a later time, under the pontificate of Sergius I (687–701).

In the Gelasian formulary (*GeV* 993–996) the motif of the bodily assumption is absent, but there is an indefinite reference to it in the prayer over the gifts (*GeV* 995). At Rome the doctrine of the bodily

[120] Ibid., 383–397; G. Frénaud, "Le culte du Notre Dame dans l'ancienne liturgie latine," in H. du Manoir, *Maria. Études sur la sainte Vierge,* 6:173–179.

[121] See the excellent study of B. Capelle, "L'oraison 'Veneranda' à la messe de l'Assomption,"*Ephemerides Theologicae Lovanienses* 26 (1950) 354–364, and "Mort et assomption de la Vierge Marie dans l'oraison 'Veneranda,'" *EphLit* 66 (1952) 241–251.

assumption of Mary made slow progress. From the second century there were circumspect mentions of it in various *Transitus Mariae*. They are reserved, but they are there. However, this was far from the liturgical expression of the faith.

The feast of March 25

Around 660 the feast of the Annunciation was introduced into the papal liturgy at Rome. Nearly ten years had passed since the letter of Justinian I (561) on the adoption of the *Evangelismos* in Byzantium.

In *GrH* (140–143) the feast does not appear with the ancient title of *Annuntiatio Domini* but with a title that has a more Marian flavor, *Annuntiatio sanctae Mariae*. The biblical readings are those one might expect: Isaiah 7:11-15, the prophecy of the virgin who will bear a child, was the epistle, while the gospel was Luke 1:26-38, the annunciation of Gabriel to Mary.

The antiphons for the feast take up texts from the Common of Virgins for the introit *(Vultum tuum)* and the gradual *(Diffusa est)*. However, for the offertory *(Ave Maria)* and communion *(Ecce virgo concipiet)*, the texts are of a Marian nature and fit perfectly into the celebration.[122]

The euchological foundation of *GrH* is found in four beautifully constructed orations. One, probably inserted into the formulary toward the end of the century, was for the stational procession (*GrH* 140). Three others were for the Mass (*GrH* 141–143). As a group, these prayers profess a strong Christological faith. Christ is true God and true man born of the virginal womb of Mary. The postcommunion prayer, the famous *Gratiam tuam,* brings together, in a wonderful way, the entire mystery of Christ, from the incarnation to the resurrection, in conformity with the character of March 25:

Pour out your grace into our spirit, O Lord,
you, who by the annunciation of an angel
have revealed to us the *incarnation* of your Son;
by his *passion* and cross
guide us to the glory of the *resurrection* (*GrH* 143).

In the Gelasian tradition (*GeV* 847–853), most of which derives from the same period as the *Gregorianum,* the feast of March 25 appears to

[122] Hesbert, *Antiphonale Missarum Septuplex*, 33a–33b, pp. 43–44.

be an intentionally Marian celebration: "In annuntiatione sanctae Mariae matris Domini nostri Iesu Christi." In the secret prayer there is the explicit statement that the gifts are offered on March 25 "in honor of the blessed and glorious ever Virgin Mary, Mother of God" (*GeV* 849).

Even if they do so with differing degrees of intensity, the traditions of the Gelasian and the Gregorianum accentuate the Marian elements of the mystery of the incarnation of the Word. In this way the feast of March 25 became a Marian feast and remained one until 1969.

The feast of September 8

Toward the end of the century, between 680 and 695, a fourth Marian feast was introduced in Rome: the Nativity of Mary (September 8). The first reading in the formulary for the Mass was Sirach 24:11-13, 15-20, *In omnibus requiem quaesivi;* the gospel was Luke 1:37-39, *Exsurgens Maria,* the story of the Visitation. Later the genealogy of Jesus, *Liber genereationis Iesu Christi* (Matthew 1:1-16), was substituted as the gospel.

A neat solution was found for the antiphonal chants: they were taken from the chants for August 15.[123] More effort seems to have been put into the euchological texts: the collect and the prayer over the gifts are excellent examples both of form and content and remain in use for September 8 in the Roman Missal until today.

The collect (*GrH* 681) rightly directs the celebration of the Nativity of Mary toward the mystery of the birth of Christ, in whom is the mystery of our salvation: "beatae Virginis partus exstitit salutis exordium." The prayer over the gifts (*GrH* 682) affirms in a very delicate manner the perpetual virginity of Mary, even in giving birth: "qui natus de Virgine matris integritatem non minuit sed sacravit." This text was honored by being directly cited by the Second Vatican Council.[124]

The euchological texts of the Gelasian tradition (*GeV* 1016–1019) were mostly taken from the preexisting formulas, which, except for the collect (*GeV* 1016), remain somewhat removed from the specific event being celebrated.

The instruction of Sergius I (687–701)

From 687 to 701, Sergius I, a native of Antioch in Syria, was bishop of Rome. Like Theodorus I (642–649), another Eastern pope, he favored

[123] See above, p. 262.

[124] *LG* 57.

the development of liturgical Marian piety. The *Liber Pontificialis* records this notice: "Constituit autem ut diebus Adnuntiationis Domini, Dormitionis et Nativitatis sanctae Dei genetricis semperque virginis Mariae ac sancti Symeonis, quod Ypapanti Greci appellant, letania exeat a sancto Hadriano et ad sanctam Mariam populus occurrat."[125]

In the light of what has already been said, the notice can be understood in this way: Sergius I ordered that on the feasts of the Annunciation, the Assumption, and the Nativity of Mary, the papal Mass was to be preceded by a stational procession from St. Hadrian at the Forum to St. Mary Major. This was modeled on the already existing procession on February 2.

Conclusion

At the end of the seventh century, a series of positive factors worked together for the four Marian feasts: the participation of the bishop of Rome at the Eucharistic synaxis; the place chosen for the celebration—the splendid Basilica of St. Mary Major; the stational procession; and the beauty of the Gregorian melodies.

The four feasts were of Eastern origin but found a warm welcome in Rome. This was aided by the election of priests of Eastern origin to the Chair of Peter and by the presence of Eastern monastic communities that had come to Rome as refugees from heretical movements and, beginning in 622, from the Muslim occupation of many territories in the Middle East.

In the seventh century there were not popes of the stature of a St. Leo the Great († 461) or St. Gregory the Great († 604), but the prestige of the See of Peter was not really in decline. In the liturgical field, along with the reuse and adaptation of already existing texts, there were flashes of real creativity in the development of Marian euchology.

Later the extraordinary diffusion of the Roman rite made sure that the four feasts, around which liturgical Marian piety would be arranged throughout the Middle Ages, were celebrated in the most remote areas.

b) In the Gallican and Spanish liturgies

We will treat the Gallican and Spanish liturgies together because they are both products of the same "historical phenomenon."[126] In the

[125] *Liber pontificalis*, 1:376.

[126] J. Pinell, "La liturgia gallicana," *Anàmnesis* 2:63.

Churches of Gaul and Spain there was "a patrimony of liturgical traditions, coming from the East, from Italy, but especially from Latin Africa."[127] In these Churches, in imitation of the liturgical creativity of Rome, there developed the first schools of euchology which developed texts for the celebration of the Eucharist, the sacraments, and the liturgical Offices for morning and evening.

These schools, although they developed under the influence of the liturgical creativity of Rome, did not allow themselves to be dazzled either by the literary style of the Roman euchology or by the structure of the Roman Mass. They remained faithful to their own traditions for both the structuring of rituals and for the style of euchological compositions.

In the Gallican liturgy

Since the end of the sixth century, according to St. Gregory of Tours († 594), a *festivitas sacra* in honor of Holy Mary was celebrated in Gaul on January 18.[128] Without doubt the object of this feast, placed after the celebrations of Christmas and the Epiphany, was the divine motherhood of the Virgin. However, already by the seventh century the object of the feast had shifted and it became a feast of the Assumption of Mary, a celebration of the transfer *(translatio)* of her virginal body and her most pure soul from earth to the glory of heaven. This is attested by the *Missale Gothicum* (*GaG* 94–105),[129] the most important source of the liturgy of Gaul, in the middle of the seventh century.

In the *contestatio* (*GaG* 98), which corresponds to our preface, the author makes mention of the joy of the Church for the threefold event of Mary's *birth*, her *motherhood*, and her glorious *transitus*. He suggests a theological justification for the last:

Cuius [Mariae] sicut gratulati sumus *ortu*,
trepudiamus *partu*,
ita glorificamur in *transitu*.
Parum fortasse fuerat,
si te Christus solo sanctificasset introitu,

[127] Ibid.

[128] *Liber in gloria martyrum*, 8: MGH *Scrip. rerum merovingiarum*, I/2, p. 43.

[129] B. Capelle, "La messe gallicane de l'assomption: son rayonnement, ses sources," in *Miscellanea liturgica in honorem L. Cuniberti Mohlberg* (Rome, 1949) 2:33–59.

nisi etiam talem matrem adornasset egressu.
Recte ab eo suscepta es in assumptione feliciter,
quem pie suscepisti conceptura per fidem.
Ut quae terrae non eras conscia,
non teneret rupes inclusam.

In the *praefatio* (*GaG* 94), the introduction to the Mass, it is made clear that it was Jesus himself who, with the help of the apostles, took his Mother to heavenly glory: "[Rdemptor noster] beatam matrem Mariam, famulantibus apostolis, transtulit ad honorem." Without doubt, the Church of Gaul did not share the reluctance of the Church of Rome regarding the *transitus Mariae*.

In the Spanish liturgy

The seventh century was the golden age of ecclesiastical literature and liturgy on the Iberian peninsula. In this century there were eminent bishops like St. Leander († 600) and his brother St. Isidore († 636) of Seville; St. Ildephonsus († 667), the author of the well-known *Libellus de virginitate sanctae Mariae,* Eugene († 657), and Julian († 690) at Toledo; and, at Saragossa, St. Braulius († ca. 651).

Liturgical activity was intense and was expressed in proper ritual structures with an unmistakable style. But this creativity was directed toward unity. In fact, after the Arian crisis was overcome by the conversion of King Recaredus at the Third Council of Toledo (589), an impulse toward unity—political, religious, and social—pervaded the entire peninsula. In the area of ritual and worship, the Fourth Council of Toledo vigorously promoted the principle of the unification of the liturgy in the Visigothic kingdom:

. . . placuit ut omnes sacerdotes,
qui catholicae fidei unitate complectimur,
nihil ultra diversum,
aut dissonum in ecclesiasticis sacramentis agamus [. . .].
Unus igitur *ordo* orandi atque Galliam conservetur,
unus modus in missarum solemnitatibus,
unus in vespertinis matutinisque officiis,
nec diversa sit ultra in nobis ecclesiastica consuetudo.[130]

[130] Cap. II: Mansi, X, 616.

The memory of the Virgin during Advent and Christmas—From the very beginning, the Spanish liturgy developed Marian themes during Advent and Christmas. On the Sundays before Christmas the gospels of the Annunciation (Luke 1:26-38) and the Visitation (Luke 1:39-47) were read. These were taken up in the euchological texts, resulting in compositions of great theological depth.

The *illatio* of the Second Sunday of Advent showed the wonderful harmony between the angel who promised, the Virgin who believed, and the Spirit who acted":

quem [Christum] inter homines et propter homines nasciturum
calestis nuntius enarravit,
virgo terrena dum salutaretur audivit,
Spiritus Sanctus in utero dum veniret creavit;
ut Gabriele *pollicente,*
Maria *credente,*
Dei vero Spiritu *cooperante,*
sequeretur salutationem angelicam securitas,
promissionem perficeret veritas,
et Altissimi obumbrante virtute
didicisset se esse fecunda virginitatis.[131]

The consideration of Mary as *the Believer* (Luke 1:45) leads one to a deeper understanding of her role in the economy of salvation as Mother of the Son of God, the Savior, and image of the Church. The Virgin's divine motherhood, fruit of her faith and of the grace of the Spirit, becomes a model for the motherhood of the Virgin Church:

. . . Deum suum prius mente,
dehinc ventre concepit.
Salutem mundi *prima* suscepit
virgo plena gratia Dei,
et ideo vera mater Filii Dei.[132]

But it was not only during Advent that the memory of the Virgin was frequently mentioned. It was also prominent during the celebration of Christmas. The *illatio* of December 25 is one of the most beautiful texts that has ever been written on the relationship between Mary

[131] *MoS* 14. Edited by J. Janini, *Liber missarum de Toledo y libros místicos* (Toledo, 1982) 6.
[132] Ibid., 6–7.

and the Church. The author of the *illatio,* in order to exalt the Church, shows how much it is like Mary, the glorious mother of the Savior:

Unigenitus tuus factus est ancillae suae filius,
dominus matris suae,
partus Mariae
fructus Ecclesiae;
qui ab illa editur,
ab ista suscipitur;
qui per illam pusillus egreditur,
per istam mirificus dilatatur.
Illa salutem populi creavit;
haec populos.
Illa utero vitam portavit;
haec lavacro.
In illius membris Christus infusus est;
in istius aquis Christus indutus est.
Per illam qui erat nascitur;
per istam qui perierat invenitur.
In illa redemptor gentium vivificatur;
in ista gentes vivificantur.[133]

The likeness between Mary and the Church is found, above all, in the birth to supernatural life and takes place in the sacraments, especially baptism. The mystery of the birth of Christ the head, which took place in Mary's womb, is continued in the birth of the members, which takes place in the baptismal font, the womb of the Church.

The feast of Holy Mary—Since the second half of the sixth century there has been a feast of Holy Mary in Spain, focusing on her divine and virginal motherhood but celebrated on different dates in different areas. The bishops of the Tenth Council of Toledo (656) made two important decisions in this regard:[134]

—they forbade the feast of March 25, because it seemed unacceptable to them to celebrate the mystery of the incarnation of the Word in the middle of Lent, both because festivals were strictly forbidden during this period and, especially, because the celebration of the mystery of the death and resurrection of Christ was so near;

[133] Ibid., 114, p. 40.
[134] Cap. I: Mansi, XI, 33–34.

—they fixed a common date for the feast of the Virgin. For the entire Visigothic kingdom it was to be celebrated on December 18, eight days before the solemnity of Christmas: "sollemnitas dominicae Matris die decimo quinto Kalendarum Ianuariarum celebretur."[135]

A single feast of the Virgin was celebrated on the same date. But it was a feast celebrated with great solemnity. This was the solution adopted by the Spanish Church for the memorial of Holy Mary.

The Marian themes of the Spanish liturgy are numerous and well developed: the divine motherhood and perpetual virginity; the cooperation of Mary, the new Eve, in the work of salvation; her holiness and fullness of grace; the woman of faith, servant of the Lord, the image of the Church; her regal mercy and uninterrupted intercession.[136] These themes developed by means of the language of ritual that is always trying to reflect Scripture, with a spirit full of reverence. Sometimes the connection between the two was close and sometimes rather loose.

5. The Seventh–Eighth and Ninth Centuries in the Byzantine East and in the West

In the eighth century two events took place which, in the realm of politics, had great importance: the loss of Greece and the Balkans, which had been occupied since 580 by Slavic tribes from across the Danube, and the definitive separation of Syria, Palestine, and Egypt from the Roman Empire and the Christian world because of the growth, since 622, of Muslim power. To these must be added the constant threat of Persian invasion on the far eastern flank of the empire.

In this situation the Byzantine Church turned in on itself and tried to gather its strength in, for example, the Council "in Trullo" (692) near Constantinople. But very soon the Byzantine Church would have to face two crises that had internal origins. One was the iconoclast movement, which was hostile to all use of images in Christian worship and disturbed the empire from about 725 to about 843. The second was the controversy regarding jurisdiction over the Bulgars. This caused a serious division, the schism of Photius (867), and a gradual distancing from Rome.

[135] Ibid., 34.

[136] G. Gironés, *La Virgen María en la liturgia mozárabe* (Valencia, 1964); J. Ibánez and F. Mendoza, *María en la liturgia hispana* (Pamplona, 1975).

a) The liturgical situation

In the area of liturgy, during the eighth and ninth centuries, the Byzantine Church adopted a stance of continuity and consolidation of the remarkable developments of its so-called "imperial phase," i.e., the period of Justinian († 565) and his immediate successors.

According to R. F. Taft, "In the ninth century, the Great Church of Constantinople had thoroughly worked out its liturgical system and codified it in the Typicon of the Great Church."[137] This was a well-organized liturgy, with a well-defined calendar and books. The influence of monasticism in it was very strong and growing, as was the imprint of the imperial court. To a certain extent, in fact, the liturgical celebrations of the cathedral of Hagia Sophia were part of the ceremonial of the court. But it was also a liturgy that was capable of renewing itself, especially from a hermeneutic perspective. To the cosmic vision of the liturgy, in which, according to St. Maximus the Confessor († 662), the liturgy directs us to heaven, one could add a "more literal and symbolic" interpretation of the "history of the liturgy."[138] This latter stemmed from St. Germanus of Constantinople († 793), according to whom the liturgy is a "real symbol" of the history of salvation in Jesus.

At the end of the ninth century the Byzantine calendar contained the following feasts that were either Marian in character or made some strong reference to the Blessed Virgin:

September 1	The beginning of the liturgical year. The synaxis of the Mother of God of Miasene (Armenia)
September 8	The Nativity of the Mother of God. It was preceded by a vigil and followed by four days of post-festival liturgies.
September 9	SS. Joachim and Anna, the parents of the *Theotokos*
November 21	The entry of the mother of God into the Temple. It was preceded by a vigil and followed by four days of post-festival liturgies.

[137] *Le rite byzantin: Bref historique* (Paris, 1996) 52.
[138] Ibid., 56.

December 9	The conception of Anna, the mother of the Mother of God
December 26	The synaxis of the Mother of God or the divine motherhood of Mary
The Sunday after Christmas	St. Joseph, the husband of the Mother of God
February 2	The feast of the *Hypapanti,* or Meeting. It was preceded by a vigil and followed by seven days of post-festival liturgies.
March 25	*Evangelismos,* or the Annunciation. It was preceded by a vigil.
The Fifth Sunday of Lent	Feast of the *Akathistos*
Friday after Easter	Feast of the Source of Life, which receives and gives life
May 11	The dedication of Constantinople to Mary
July 2	Deposition of the Clothing of the Mother of God, or *Maphorion,* in the church of Blacherne
July 25	The Dormition of Anna, the mother of the Mother of God
August 15	The Dormition of the Mother of God. This feast was preceded by a fast of fourteen days and a vigil and was followed by an octave.
August 31	The Deposition of the Virgin's Cincture in the Marian sanctuary at Chalcoprateia

But when considering Marian theology, one cannot consider only the explicitly Marian feasts. More than a few Christological feasts shed light on the role that the Mother of the Lord had in the mystery being celebrated. So, for example, the Byzantine liturgy, unlike any other, gave great attention to the participation of Mary in the mystery of the passion and resurrection of the Son. In the Offices of Great Friday and Great Saturday, her voice, that of the Lamb without stain, Mother of the immolated Lamb, is heard clearly above all the other actors in the paschal event.

b) In the West

The renowned medievalist and historian Dom J. Leclerq holds that the West, during the eighth and ninth centuries, and so coinciding with the "Carolingian renaissance," was dominated by a certain "Marian apathy." This gave rise to a certain "Marian decline."[139] This position has been tempered by the meticulous research of L. Scheffczyk[140] and H. Barré.[141] They demonstrate the real progress that has been made in Mariology, not so much in the area of doctrine as in our understanding of the development of Marian piety in the liturgy. In these centuries there were theologians like Ambrosius Autpertus († 781), who did pioneering work concerning some problems in Mariology. It is to them that we owe the institution of the weekly memorial of the Blessed Virgin on Saturday and texts like the hymn *Ave, Maris stella,* which would be important parts of liturgical Marian piety in the West.

Hymns, responsories, and antiphons

In the eighth and ninth centuries the fine hymnographic tradition of the Latin West continued. Here we will mention only some Marian hymns that are still in use in the Roman liturgy:

—The *Ave, maris stella* (Common the Blessed Virgin, 2nd Vespers). The author of this ninth-century hymn is unknown, but it has become the hymn par excellence of Marian feasts. What is especially winning about it is the way that it treats, in a manner both simple and doctrinally profound, the themes of divine motherhood *(Dei mater alma)* and perpetual virginity *(semper virgo, virgo singularis);* the mission of Mary as the new Eve and her cooperation in the salvation of humanity *(sumens illud "Ave," mutans Evae nomen);* her liberating mercy *(solve vincla reis);* and her efficacious intercession *(sumat per te precem),* which guides one surely on the way to Christ *(iter para tutum).*[142]

—The hymn *Refulsit almae dies lucis candidus* (Presentation of the Lord, Office of Readings). Composed by Paulinus II of Aquileia († 802), strophes 2, 4, 10 and 12 are actually used in the hymn for the Office of Readings for February 2. The Virgin appears in a most solemn and

[139] "Grandeur et misère de la dévotion mariale au Moyen-Age," *MD* 38 (1954) 122–135, especially 124–126.

[140] *Das Mariengeheimnis in Frömmigkeit und Lehre der Karolingerzeit* (Leipzig, 1959).

[141] *Prières anciennes de l'Occident à la Mère du Sauveur* (Paris, 1963).

[142] A. Lentini, ed., *Te decet hymnus. L'innario della "Liturgia Horarum"* (Rome, 1984) 255; AH 51, p. 140.

human light as she, obedient to the Law, brings her Son to the Temple. She is aware of the mystery of the Infant she carries in her arms—that he is God himself hidden beneath the veil of flesh that he took from her—and is full of maternal love for the little Child, whose face she kisses with affection:

Mater beata carnis sub velamine
Deum ferebat umeris castissimis,
dulcia strictis oscula sub labiis
Deique veri hominisque impresserat
ori, iubente quo sunt cuncta condita.[143]

—the hymn *Quod chorus vatum venerandus olim* (Presentation of the Lord, Vespers). Attributed to Hrabanus Maurus († 856),[144] this text has a serious tone and a classical feel to its movement. It is an important example of the way the role of Mary was highlighted in the feast of February 2, which had become the feast *In purificatione b. Mariae Virginis*. Divine motherhood, perpetual virginity, powerful intercession, and mercy are the Marian themes that the hymn gives voice to. The themes are not original, but the hymn is composed with fine literary taste and the touching participation of the soul.

—The hymn *Conditor alme siderum* (Advent Season, Vespers), composed for Advent by an unknown author of the ninth century. The following strophe works especially well:

Vergente mundi vespere,
uti sponsus de thalamo,
egressus honestissima,
Virginis matris clausula.[145]

—The hymn *Fit porta Christi pervia* (Mary, Mother of God, Lauds) was written by an unknown author in the ninth century.[146] It is a good example of the way in which Christological, Mariological, and ecclesiological themes can be brought together, while at the same time making use of biblical symbols—the east door of the Temple (Ezek 44:1-2), the stone hewn from the mountain (Dan 2:34), the sun coming forth like a bridegroom (Ps 19:6).

[143] Lentini, *Te decet hymnus,* 150; AH 50, p. 132.
[144] Lentini, *Te decet hymnus,* 152; AH 50, p. 206.
[145] Lentini, *Te decet hymnus,* 73; AH 51, p. 46.
[146] Lentini, *Te decet hymnus,* 87; AH 27, p. 118.

—The hymn *O quam glorifica luce coruscas* (the Assumption, Lauds) was composed in the ninth century by an anonymous author for the feast of August 15.[147] It proclaims with awe the Church's faith in the assumption of the Virgin, who, with her soul and the body from which Christ was born *(natus hinc Deus est corpore Christus)*, now "dwells" in heaven, exalted above all the citizens of the heavenly city:

sublimis *residens*, virgo Maria,
supra caeligenas aeteris omnes.

To the hymns one might add the *tituli*, dedicatory poems for churches and altars dedicated to the Blessed Virgin. This is an important and relevant liturgical fact, but the *tituli* often became supplications to the Mother of the Lord. For example, one might make reference to this *titulus* of Alcuin († 704), which is important in the history of Marian piety:

Haec tibi sancta domus sancta est, sanctissima virgo,
Virgo Maria dei ac genitrix intacta tonantis.
Perpetuam mundo genuisti, virgo, salutem,
Quapropter mundus totus te laudat ubique.
En ego, quippe tuus famulus, te laudo camenis.
Tu mihi dulcis amor, decus, et spes magna salutis,
Auxiliare tuum servum, clarissima virgo.
Necnon cunctorum precibus hic annue fratrum,
Ad te qui clamant: "Virgo tu gratia plena,
Per te conservet semper non gratia Christi."[148]

The publication of the *Antiphonale Missarum septuplex* (1935) and the *Corpus Antiphonalium Officii* (six volumes published between 1963 and 1979), edited by R.-J. Hesbert, and the appearance of editions of many votive Offices prior to the eleventh century have allowed H. Barré to put together a preliminary *corpus* of Marian antiphons and responsories ranging from the sixth to the ninth century,[149] and to which he was able to apply a systematic treatment from the viewpoints of music and liturgy. Antiphons and responsories, often valuable both

[147] Lentini, *Te decet hymnus*, 203; AH 51, p. 146.

[148] MGH *Poëtae* 1, p. 313.

[149] "Antiennes et répons de la Vierge," *Marianum* 29 (1967) 153–245; J. M. Canal, "Elementos marianos en la antigua liturgia romana," *Ephemerides mariologicae* 16 (1966) 289–317.

liturgically and literarily, were the fruit of ongoing "rumination" over Scripture by monks or were well-made adaptations of homiletic texts.

The following responsory belongs to the Office of December 25 and shows how much this is truly both the celebration of the birth of the Son of God and the first feast of the Virgin Mother:

Nesciens Mater Virgo virum,
peperit sine dolore Salvatorem saeculorum,
ipsum Regem angelorum;
sola Virgo lactabat, ubere de coelo pleno.
Vers. Ave Maria, gratia plena, Dominus tecum.—Sola.
Vers. Beata viscera Mariae Virginis,
quae portaverunt aeterni Patris Filium.—Sola.[150]

The lovely antiphon which follows also has to do with Christmas:

Virgo Dei Genetrix, quem totus non capit orbis
In tua se clausit viscera factus homo:
Vera fides Geniti purgavit crimina mundi,
Et tibi virginitas inviolata manet.[151]

This is an awe-inspiring contemplation both of the condescension of the Word, who, although God, became a man and who, although infinite, enclosed himself within a woman's womb, and of the divine and virginal motherhood of Mary. It is also a nice affirmation of the necessity of true faith in Christ, both his divinity and his humanity, as the only way in which the world may be forgiven of its sin.

The famous antiphon that follows is taken from a sermon entitled *In Natali sanctae Mariae* from the end of the seventh century:

Sancta Maria, succurre miseris,
iuva pusillanimes, refove flebiles,
ora pro populo, interveni pro clero,
intercede pro devoto femineo sexu.[152]

This sorrowful prayer to the Virgin uses six imperatives relating to supplication *(succurre, iuva, refove, ora, interveni, intercede)* on behalf of a number of different categories of the faithful, ranging from the poor

[150] *CAO*, IV, n. 7212.

[151] *CAO*, III, n. 5448.

[152] *CAO*, III, n. 4702; H. Barré, *Prières anciennes de l'occident à la Mère du Sauveur: des origines à saint Anselme* (Paris, 1963) 38–42.

and needy *(miseri)* to virgins consecrated to the service of God *(devotus femineus sexus)*. The reasons for the long-lasting success and popularity of this antiphon may be found in its attention to persons and the mournful tone of its supplication, which in turn presupposes the faithful recognition of the Virgin's merciful intercession.

The memorial of the Blessed Virgin "in sabbato"

One of the most characteristic institutions of liturgical Marian piety during the Carolingian era was the dedication of Saturday to the Blessed Virgin.[153]

Between 784 and 791 a copy of the Gregorian Sacramentary "inmixtum" was sent to the court of Charlemagne by Pope Adrian. Alcuin realized immediately that the papal sacramentary *(GrH)* would not be completely suitable either for the needs of the Franco-German populace or for the needs of the monasteries in which the monks were already mostly priests. For Ordinary Time, *GrH* contained only Masses for the Sundays. For Eucharistic celebrations on the weekdays it would be necessary to repeat the Sunday formulary over and over. In order to avoid this inconvenience, Alcuin compiled a double series of Masses for the seven days of the week.

Sunday	*de S. Trinitate*	*de gratia S. Spiritu postulanda*
Monday	*pro peccatis*	*pro petitione lacrimarum*
Tuesday	*ad postulanda Angelica suffragia*	*pro tentationibus cogitationum*
Wednesday	*de s. sapientia*	*ad postulandam humilitatem*
Thursday	*de caritate*	*contra tentationes carnis*
Friday	*de S. Cruce*	*de tribulatione*
Saturday	*de S. Maria*	*in commemoratione S. Mariae*[154]

Alcuin's initiative worked out well. It was practical, even if, from a liturgical view, some of what he did was debatable, especially as

[153] For more on the commemoration of the Blessed Virgin on Saturday, see the synthesis of S. Rosso, "Sabato," in *NDM* 1216–1228, with appropriate bibliography on 1228.

[154] Cf. "Il ciclo liturgico settimanale," in J. A. Jungmann, *Eredità liturgica e attualità pastorale* (Rome, 1962) 392. ET: "The Weekly Cycle in the Liturgy," in *Pastoral Liturgy* (New York, 1962) 255. The texts for the two series of Masses appears in PL 101, 455–456.

concerns the formularies of the second series. The formulary for Sunday sought grace from the Holy Spirit, but those for the other days of the week, with the exception of Saturday, were marked by a strongly individualistic or private character.

In comparing the two series, one interesting fact is immediately apparent. The "intentions" of the two series are different for each day, with the exception of Saturday, which in both cases is Marian in orientation. We do not know the reason for this or why Alcuin wanted Saturday to be devoted to the Blessed Virgin. In later centuries, that is, after Alcuin's work, theologians and liturgists came up with seven "reasons," which, however much they reveal about the feelings of the authors, do not tell us what was on Alcuin's mind.[155]

The readings for the first Mass for the Virgin were Sirach 24:14-16 *(Ab initio et ante saecula)* and Luke 10:38-42 *(Intravit Iesus in quoddam*

[155] In the thirteenth century the following "reasons" were given (we report them here without citing individual sources): 1. Saturday is the day God *blessed* (cf. Gen 2:3) and Mary is the one who is "*blessed* among women" (Luke 1:42). The blessed day is therefore appropriate for her who is the Blessed of the Most High. 2. In the same way, Saturday is the day *sanctified* by God, and Mary is "full of grace" (Luke 1:28). Therefore it is right to dedicate the holy day to her who is All Holy. 3. Saturday is the day on which God rested after creation (cf. Gen 2:2), but the true "rest" of God is Mary, to whom the liturgy applies the words of Sirach 24:8: "The one who created me *rested* inside my tent." 4. Just as Saturday is the *gateway* to Sunday, so too Mary is the *gateway* through which Christ came into the world. 5. Saturday is the *dies media* between Friday (sorrowful) and Sunday (joyous). It is not possible to pass from pain to glory without crossing over it. So too is Mary the *media* between us, living in this land of exile, and Christ, who is already in heavenly glory. 6. On the Saturday on which Christ lay in the tomb and the apostles in their unbelief were in hiding "for fear of the Jews" (John 20:19), the *faith* of the Church was to be found in Mary. For this reason the Church, each Saturday, recalls the *memory of the Virgin who believed* and awaited the resurrection of the Son. 7. The same Mother of Jesus has shown her special love for this day. Every Friday evening in the church of Blacherne, in Constantinople, without any human intervention, the veil that covered the icon of the *Theotokos* was removed. The icon then remained suspended in the air until the ninth hour of Saturday, visible to the faithful. At that time, again apparently without human intervention, it was once again covered and returned to its usual place.

As is evident, these "reasons" are either fantastic or mere coincidences. Nonetheless, they provide explanations for a liturgical fact. However insufficient they might otherwise be, two of them are still meaningful for a person of our times, since they show Saturday to be the day of preparation for *Dies Domini.* Saturday is the day of Mary's *faith.*

castellum), both still in use for Marian commemorations, and there were four well-constructed orations: *Concede nobis famulis tuis; Tua, Domine, propitiatione; Sumptis, Domine, salutis nostrae;* and *Omnipotens Deus, famulos.*[156] Thematically, the formulary contrasts the dangers of the present life and its essential *sadness* with the assurance of receiving, by means of the intercession of the Virgin, the security, ease, and peace of the life to come.

No readings are indicated for the second Mass. The orations *Famulorum tuorum; Oblationibus nostris; Quaesumus, Domine Deus noster;* and *Fideles tuos, quaesumus*[157] are also well made but do not always possess the same linearity as the first set. Thematically, they reflect the medieval person's awareness of the mystery of sin and of the fact that the human person is radically incapable, acting solely on the basis of nature, to act in a way pleasing to God. For this reason faithful recourse is made to the Mother of the Lord:

Famulorum tuorum, quaesumus, delictis ignosce,
et qui *placere de actibus nostris non valemus,*
Genetricis Filii tui Domini nostri Iesu Christi intercessione,
quae tibi sunt placita semper meditantes,
mundo corde iugiter *et dictis exsequamur et factis.*

Alcuin was proud of his undertaking and sent copies of his collection to his friends. As a result, the Mass for Saturday was diffused little by little throughout Charlemagne's empire, first in the monasteries, then in the cathedrals and parishes. Berthold of Constance wrote: "Almost everywhere, every week, the votive Mass of the Holy Cross is said on Friday and that of the Mother of God on Saturday, not because it is commended but because of devotion."[158]

Marian piety in the collections of homilies

By the end of its evolution, the homiliary, or collection of homilies of the holy Fathers along with selections of their biblical commentaries, was no longer simply a handbook to aid preachers in the fulfillment of their task but had become a real liturgical book. The patristic readings proclaimed at the Divine Office were taken from it.

[156] *Liber sacramentorum,* Cap. VII, *Sabbato missa de sancta Maria:* PL 101, 455.
[157] Ibid. *Item missa in commemoratione sanctae Mariae:* PL 101, 455–456.
[158] *Micrologus de ecclesiasticis observationibus,* 59: PL 151, 1020.

Insofar as liturgical Marian piety is concerned, these collections have a fundamental importance. They show that "Marian homilies" diverged from Christmas homilies, as was shown by H. Barré,[159] to become a sort of anthology of Marian texts. They promoted contemplation of the mystery of the Virgin and gave rise to a new direction for homilies.

During the Carolingian era two famous collections of homilies were made:

—The *Homiliary* of Alan of Farfa († ca. 779), which contained three homilies for the feast "in natali sanctae Mariae."[160] These were not sermons for the celebration of the Nativity of Mary (September 8) but for the feast of the Assumption (August 15), so the term *natalis* is used in the sense of the *dies natalis* of the apostles and martyrs, i.e., of their entrance into heaven. These sermons, full of Augustinian allusions, show how Marian preaching, which began with the mystery of the birth of the Savior, evolved toward the mystery of the Assumption and focused more and more on the role of the Virgin in the history of salvation and the life of the Church.[161]

—The *Homiliary* of Paul the Deacon († 799) was composed at the request of Charlemagne, who wanted to supply the monks and clerics of his kingdom with a volume that would not only provide properly systematized readings for the night Office but would also serve as a manual on preaching.[162] Aside from various homilies for specifically Marian feasts, *In Purificatione sanctae Mariae* (February 2),[163] *In Adsumptione sanctae Mariae* (August 15),[164] and *In Nativitate sanctae Mariae*

[159] "Sermons marials inédits 'in Natali Domini,'" *Marianum* 25 (1963) 39–93.

[160] R. Grégoire, *Les homéliaires du Moyen Âge. Inventaire et analyse des manuscrits* (Rome, 1966) 60–61. The three sermons are: 1. (II, 64) *Celebritatis hodiernae diei admonet* (PL 57, 867–868; *CPL* 223); 2. (II, 65) *Adest nobis, dilectissimi, optatus dies* (PL 39, 2104–2107; *CPL* 368); 3. (II, 66) *Scientes, fratres dilectissimi, auctori nostro* (PL 57, 865–868; *CPL* 368).

[161] A. Hamman, La dévotion mariale d'après les premiers homéliaires," in *De cultu mariano saeculis VI–XI*, 4:217–225, especially 223–224.

[162] See the description of the Homiliary in R. Grégoire, *Les homéliaires du Moyen Âge*, n. 360, pp. 71–114.

[163] Three homilies are suggested for this feast: 1. (I, 65) *Exultent virgines virgo peperit Christum*, incorrectly attributed to Augustine (PL 39, 1657–1658; *CPL* 285); 2. (I, 66) *Non solum ab angelis et prophetis* by Ambrose of Milan (CCL 14, pp. 56–57); 3. (I, 67) *Sollemnitatem nobis hodiernae celebratis* by the Venerable Bede (CCL 122, pp. 128–133.

[164] For the feast of August 15, a selection from St. Bede is suggested: (II, 70): *Haec lectio, fratres carissimi, pulcherrima ratione* (CCL 120, pp. 225–226).

(September 8),[165] this homiliary presents quite a few additional Marian texts, especially for the seasons of Advent and Christmas-Epiphany. Liturgical Marian piety was nourished by these texts for centuries.[166] They not only passed on a remarkable patristic inheritance of Mariology but also furnished material used in the composition of texts used in liturgical Marian devotion.

But Paul the Deacon was not only an intelligent collector of homilies. He also composed a number of them, among which are two for the feast of the Assumption;[167] these were liturgical homilies, in which the themes of Mary's divine motherhood, her unique holiness, her role as an efficacious exemplar, and her glorious assumption come together and lead to an affirmation of the Virgin's universal intercession:[168]

. . . quae [Maria] toto mundo protulit languenti salutem,
pro universis suum Natum et Dominum pietate solita intercedit.[169]

Although small, the homiletic output of Ambrosius Autpertus († 781) is also significant. His homily *In purificatione sanctae Mariae*[170] joins together an attachment to the Church's traditions and original insights about the role of the Virgin; the meaning of the offering and sacrificial gesture of Mary in taking the Son to the Temple; the meaning of her behavior in relation to the *Ecclesia ex Iudaeis;* the connection between her divine motherhood and her spiritual motherhood.[171]

The liturgical influence of a pseudepigraphic letter

In the history of liturgical Marian piety, the letter *Cogitis me,* which was written by Paschasius Radbertus, abbot of Corbie († ca. 865) but

[165] For the feast of the September 8, a passage from St. Ambrose is suggested: (II, 77): *Morale est omnibus ut qui fidem exigunt fidem astruant* (CCL 14, pp. 39–43).

[166] T. Gallus, "De cultu mariano apud Paulum Winfridum († 799),"in *De cultu mariano saeculis VI–XI,* 3:319–328.

[167] *Hom. I in Assumptione b. Mariae Virginis* (PL 95, 1565–1569) and *Hom. II in Evangelium "Intravit Iesus in quoddam castellum"* (PL 95, 1569–1574).

[168] C. Pozo, "El culto de María en las homilías de Pablo Diácono sobre la Asunción," in *De cultu mariano saeculis VI–XI,* 3:329–338.

[169] *Hom. I:* PL 95, 1569.

[170] CCCM 27B, pp. 985–1002.

[171] T. Koehler, "Les origines d'un thème devotionnel: la maternité de Marie dans la piété occidentale entre 750–1110. Étude historique et culturelle," in *De cultu mariano saeculis VI–XI,* 4:347–379, especially 347–358; D. Iogna-Prat, "Le culte de la Vierge sous le règne del Charles le Chauve," in *Le culte de la Vierge Marie dans la société médiéval* (Paris, 1996) 65–68, 84–89.

which was presented by him as a work of St. Jerome entitled *Epistola beati Hieronymi ad Paulam et Eustochium de assumptione sanctae Mariae Virginis,*[172] has been especially important. The letter is, more than anything else, an essay in which Paschasius justifies and illustrates the veneration rendered by the Church to the Mother of the Lord.[173] Since it was distributed with the authority of St. Jerome, the letter contributed to the consolidation of the feast of the Assumption in the West, which Paschasius wanted to free from any trace of the merely legendary —such as the fantastic tales of the Eastern *transitus* traditions—and which also made sense, even without the glorification of the body.[174] From a liturgical point of view, the letter is worthy of attention because some passages in it have been used for centuries as "patristic readings" in the Office of August 15 and also because of the importance accorded the liturgy as a *locus theologicus,* where, especially in antiphons and responsories, one encounters a constant repetition of liturgical texts.

Amalarius of Metz: A liturgist sensitive to the person of Mary

Amalarius of Metz († 850), archbishop of Trier and later administrator of the diocese of Lyons, is regarded as one of the most important liturgists of the ninth century. His best-known work, the *Liber de ecclesiasticis officiis* or *Liber officialis,* went through three editions during his

[172] A critical edition was prepared by A. Ripberger, *Der Pseudo-Hieronymus-Brief IX "Cogitis me." Ein erster marianischer Traktat des Mittelalters von Paschasius Radbert* (Freiburg, 1962) 57–113.

[173] R. Rosini, "Il culto della b. Vergine nella lettera "De assumptione sanctae Mariae Virginis" ('Cogitis me') dello Pseudo-Girolamo," *De cultu mariano saeculis VI–XI,* 3:433–459.

[174] Haec idcirco dixerim, quia multi nostrorum dubitant, utrum assumpta fuerit simul cum corpore, an abierit relicto corpore. Quomodo autem vel quo tempore, aut a quibus personis sanctissimum corpus eius inde ablatum fuerit vel ubi transpositum, utrum vere surrexerit, nescitur, quamvis nonnulli astruere velint eam iam resuscitatam et beata cum Christo inmortalitate in caelestibus vestiri. [. . .] Verumtamen quid horum verius censeatur, ambigimus; melius tamen Deo totum, cui nihil impossibile est, committimus, quam aliud temere definire velimus auctoritate nostra, quod non probamus. [. . .] Quod, quia Deo nihil est impossibile, nec nos de beata Maria factum abnuimus, quamquam propter cautelam, salva fide, pio magis desiderio opinari oporteat quam inconsulte definire, quod sine periculo nescitur (nn. 9, 10, 12: ed. A. Ripberger, *Der Pseudo-Hieronymus-Brief IX "Cogitis me,"* 61–63.

lifetime, the last appearing in 835.[175] The work of Amalarius gives us precious liturgical information, but his excessive tendency to allegorize in interpreting the rites does not much lend itself to genuine liturgical spirituality.

Amalarius shows that he is quite aware of the presence of the Virgin in the liturgy. His language is sober, his motive is Christological, but at the same time his touching devotion to the Mother of the Lord comes through. See how he comments, from a perspective, on the mention of the Virgin in the *Communicantes* in the Roman Canon:

Communicantes et memoriam venerantes . . . Communicare, hoc est participare; memoriam venerare, hoc est in *memoria honorabiliter tenere* quod sancta Maria virgo per adventum Spiritus Sancti genetrix facta est Filii Dei Iesu Christi Domini nostri, qui Deus et homo est, per quem Patrem supplicamus, et fidem communicare debemus, et credere quod, Spiritu Sancto veniente, Filius Dei natus est ex ea, et virginitas eius non est violata.[176]

In commenting on the embolism of the Our Father, Amalarius recalls the intercession of the Virgin, seen here in prayerful communion with the apostles:

Intercedente pro nobis beata et gloriosa semper virgine Dei genetrice Maria et beatis apostolis tuis Petro et Paulo atque Andrea. Invocamus nobis in adiutorium genetricem Dei quae virgo fuit ante partum, virgo in partu, virgo post partum, et beatos apostolos, qui nobis haec mysteria celebranda tradiderunt, ritis ac praesentibus veniam promereri, nec de futuris cautelam, nisi nobis eorum oratione donetur.[177]

Let us also look at the way in which Amalarius, with powerful patristic allusions, comments on the famous Advent antiphon taken from Isaiah 45:3:

Rorate, caeli, desuper, et nubes pluant iustum; aperiatur terra, et germinet salvatorem [. . .] Aperta est terra, uterus scilicet sanctae Mariae virginis

[175] A critical edition was done by I. M. Hanssens, *Amalarii episcopi opera liturgica omnia,* vols. 1–3, ST 138–140 (Vatican City, 1948–1950). The *Liber officialis* was published in vol. 2, pp. 13–543.

[176] *Canonis missae interpretatio,* 35: Hanssens, *Amalarii episcopi opera liturgica omnia,* 1:312.

[177] Ibid., 66: Hanssens, *Amalarii episcopi opera liturgica omnia,* 1:334.

sine damno virginitatis, et protulit germen totius mundi odoris; qui bonus odor redolet per universum mundum.[178]

There are many other examples of the attention Amalarius gave to the person of the Mother of the Lord. They show how, beyond his tendency to allegorize, he understood very well the meaning of the presence of the Virgin in the celebration of the Divine Office, because the Virgin was present, in a perspective that was Trinitarian, Christological, and ecclesial, in the saving events celebrated in the liturgy.

6. From the Tenth Century to the beginning of the Council of Trent (1545)

The lengthy period to be considered here, from the tenth century to the eve of the Council of Trent (1545), begins and ends with moments of deep crisis, which the Church managed to survive. It begins with the papacy's dark "iron century," but the second half of the century sees a renewal of the empire of Charlemagne in the person of Otto the Great († 973), crowned emperor by Gregory XII in 962. It ends just before the beginning of the Council of Trent, called to deal with the profound crisis that had gripped the Church since 1517 because of the Reform of Martin Luther. During this time as well there were many important events in the history of Marian piety that must be pointed out, even if we must do so with rather large strokes.

a) New feasts of the Virgin

Because of the many repercussions that result from the institution of a new feast, we will begin with a consideration of the development of new feasts commemorating the Virgin.

The feast of the Conception

Since the end of the eighth century the Byzantine Church celebrated, on December 9, the feast of the Conception of St. Anna, mother of the *Theotokos.* Evidence for this is a *canon* or hymn composed by Andrew of Crete († 740) for the opening of the celebration[179] and a homily delivered by John of Eubea († 750): ". . . one must celebrate ten events in a solemn fashion. And the first [. . .] is when Joachim and Anna received the joyful announcement of the wholly immaculate and Mother

[178] *Liber officialis,* IV, 30, 9: Hanssens, *Amalarii episcopi opera liturgica omnia,* 2:503.

[179] C. A. Bouman, "The Immaculate Conception in the Liturgy," in E. D. O'Connor, ed., *The Dogma of the Immaculate Conception: History and Significance* (Notre Dame, Ind., 1958) 114–115.

of God, Mary. The second is the most august birth of Mary; *in the first,* I say, *we celebrate the conception;* in the second, however, we celebrate the birth."[180]

The feast of the Presentation never had as much prominence as the Nativity or the Annunciation, but it steadily gained importance. In 883 it is mentioned in the *Nomocanon* of Patriarch Photius.[181] The emperor Leo the Wise († 912) and George, the metropolitan of Nicomedia, who lived during the second half of the ninth century, delivered sermons which show that the feast was celebrated throughout the empire during their time.[182] In 1166 Manuel Comenus decreed that the feast of December 9 would be included among those days on which abstention from work was prescribed.[183]

The object of the feast was, therefore, the conception on the part of the infertile Anna (an active conception) of the future Mother of God, as told in the *Protoevangelium of James;*[184] but by means of this apocryphal-traditional material, it is intended to celebrate a particular intervention of God that places the Blessed Virgin, from the very first instant of her existence, under the protection of the Most High and removes her from the influence of the Evil One.

From the East the feast passed into the West, according to the path already noted, among which were the settling of Eastern monks in Italy and the frequent contacts between Byzantium and southern Italy. In fact, the feast of December 9 appears on the famous marble calendar in Naples, sculpted between 840 and 850: "Conceptio sanctae Mariae Virg."[185] But beyond southern Italy, the feast was also celebrated in England in the eleventh century. A number of liturgical documents witness to this: a number of calendars predating 1100, which read, for December 8: "Conceptio sanctae Dei genetricis Mariae";[186] the *Benedictio*

[180] *Sermo in Conceptionem sanctae Deiparae,* 10: PG 96, 1474–1475. Toward the end of the homily (23: PG 96, 1499), John of Eubea notes that the feast of December 9 "is not known by all."

[181] Tit. VII, cap. I: PG 104, 1069.

[182] Bouman, "The Immaculate Conception in the Liturgy," 115. For the history of the feast in the West, see A. M. Cecchin, "La concezione della Vergine nella liturgia della Chiesa occidentale anteriore al secolo XIII," *Marianum* 5 (1943) 58–114.

[183] C. Passaglia, *De immaculato Deipare semper virginis conceptu* (Naples, 1855) 3:1106–1107.

[184] Cf. 1–4: Moraldi, *Apocrifi del Nuovo Testamento,* 1:123–126.

[185] The calendar is reproduced in DACL 11/2:1591–1592.

[186] F. Wormald, *English Calendars before* A.D. *1100* (London, 1934) 126, 167, 223.

in Conceptione sanctae Mariae of the Exeter Pontifical;[187] the Canterbury Pontifical;[188] and the three orations of the formulary for December 8 in the Missal of Leofric.[189]

It is evident from these texts that the object of this feast was shifting from the one who conceived—Anna, by means of an active conception—to the one who was being conceived—Mary. The liturgical texts, following the line of the *Protoevangelium of James,* point out that the conception of Mary was announced by the message of an angel (*beatam Dei genitricem angelico concipiendam praeconavit oraculo*—Canterbury Pontifical), that the Virgin was chosen by the Holy Spirit long before she conceived the Word (Exeter Pontifical) and sanctified prior to birth (Canterbury Pontifical). God intervened with his grace in the conception of Mary because his only-begotten Son would be conceived by her (*ex qua [Maria] eius [Dei] conciperetur Unigenitus*—Exeter Pontifical). The unique conception of Mary, in which she became a participant in God's plan of salvation, is worthy of veneration (*veneranda conceptio*—Canterbury Pontifical and the Missal of Leofric). The English liturgy discerned a unique intervention on the part of God in the conception of Mary and felt obliged to celebrate it with adequate solemnity (*cuius [Mariae] conceptionis sacra solemnia congrua frequentatione celebratur*—the Missal of Leofric).

This was the situation for the feast of December 8 in England prior to the Norman occupation. It was swept aside along with other liturgical usages.[190] But the feast was restored at the beginning of the twelfth century by the action of Anselm the Younger († 1148), bishop of London and nephew of the great Anselm of Canterbury († 1109) and some of his collaborators and friends, among whom were Osbert of Clare and the Benedictine monk Eadmer, the former disciple and secretary of Anselm. His *Tractatus de conceptione sanctae Mariae* had a

[187] The text of the blessing, which follows the tripartite structure typical of the Spanish and Gaulish liturgies, is reproduced in Bouman, "The Immaculate Conception in the Liturgy," 131.

[188] R. M. Wooley, ed., *The Canterbury Pontifical* (London, 1917) 118–119.

[189] F. E. Warren, ed., *The Leofric Missal as Used in the Cathedral of Exeter (1059–1072)* (Oxford, 1883) 268.

[190] See the well-documented study by G. Gagov, "L'ambiente liturgico e culturale inglese a favore dell'Immacolata e Giovanni Duns Scotus," in *Virgo Immaculata. Acta Congressus Mariologici-Mariani Romae anno MCMLIV celebrati* (Rome, 1955) 4:74–89.

decisive influence on the history of the dogma of the Immaculate Conception.[191]

The object of the restored feast seems to have changed. The attention was no longer on the body of Mary in which the divine Word would be made incarnate but on her soul: "The children of holy Church," wrote Eadmer, "ought to venerate the first moments of her creation *(primordia creationis tuae venerari)*, which they believe to have been holy, pure, free from the taint of sin and corruption *(a corruptionis vel peccati ruga discreta)*."[192]

The restored feast of December 8 passed from England to France, first to Normandy and then to the diocese of Lyons. This provoked a reaction from Bernard († 1153), who, in his famous letter *Ad canonicos Lugdunenses*, expressed his amazement that in the oldest and most illustrious Church in France there had been introduced "a new festival, a rite of which the Church knows nothing, of which reason cannot approve and for which there is no authority in tradition."[193] The abbot of Clairvaux, an heir of the Augustinian doctrine on original sin, held that the conception of Mary occurred in a normal fashion and was not holy because the marital embrace was, due to fallen nature, weakened by sinful concupiscence:

"[. . .] If, therefore, it was quite impossible for her to have been sanctified prior to the conception, because she did not then exist, nor in the act of her conception, because of the presence of sin, it remains that she was sanctified after her conception, when she was already in the womb, and that this sanctification excluded sin and rendered her birth, but not her conception, holy. [. . .] This being so, what reasons can there be for a feast of the Conception? How, I ask, can a conception be holy which was not of the Holy Spirit, not to say that it was of sin; and how can a feast be kept in honor of what was not holy?"[194]

[191] G. Geenen, "Eadmer, le premier théologien de l'Immaculée Conception," in *Virgo Immaculata*, 90–136 (see note 190).

[192] *Tractatus de conceptione sanctae Mariae*, 19: critical edition by H. Thurston and T. Slater (Freiburg im Br., 1904) 24.

[193] *Epistola* 174, 1: *Opere di san Bernardo*, VI/1, ed. F. Gastadelli (Milan, 1986) 6/1:729. ET: *The Letters of Saint Bernard of Clairvaux*, trans. B. James (Chicago, 1953), Letter 215, section 1.

[194] Ibid., sections 7, 9. For a balanced treatment of St. Bernard's opposition to this new feast, see F. Gastadelli, "San Bernardo e l'Immacolata Concezione. Significato storico e teologico della lettera *Ad canonicos Lugdunenses*," *Marianum* 54 (1992) 111–124.

The position taken by Bernard made it more difficult for the feast to spread, but, on the other hand, it gave rise to a flourishing of studies that led to a deeper understanding of the doctrine of Mary's Immaculate Conception. Theologians like Thomas Aquinas († 1274) and Bonaventure († 1274) took Bernard's side. Opposed to them were, aside from Eadmer, theologians like the English Benedictine Nicholas of St. Albans, who admired Bernard but was firmly opposed to him in this theological debate. He wrote *De celebranda Conceptione beatae Mariae contra beatum Bernardum.*[195]

The Franciscan John Duns Scotus († 1308), another theologian from the British Isles, deepened the ideas of Eadmer and furnished the key for a resolution of the principal objections to the doctrine of Mary's Immaculate Conception; it does not oppose, but rather affirms, the dogmatic truth of universal redemption because the Virgin too was redeemed, but in a unique manner. She was *preserved* from sin in expectation of the merits of the death of Christ, the one and universal Redeemer, the perfect Mediator.[196] In the following centuries the dispute between the so-called maculists and immaculists became very vigorous, dividing nations, religious orders, and universities into opposing factions. However, little by little the immaculist cause won out.

During the thirteenth to the fifteenth century the feast spread, and one notices something new. During the period of Avignon (1309–1376), the popes participated in the Mass that was celebrated in the Carmelite church on December 8. When they returned to Rome, they allowed its celebration in the Roman Curia and in the City. In this period the liturgy for September 8 provided a prudent choice, a sure point of reference. It provided the readings (the epistle: Proverbs 8:22-35, *Dominus possedit me;* the gospel: Matthew 1:1-16, *Liber generationis Iesu Christi*), and in more than one instance one need only replace the word *nativitas* with the word *conceptio* in order to arrive at the "proper" for December 8:

[195] Published by C. H. Talbot, "Nicholas of St. Albans and Saint Bernard," *RBén* 64 (1954) 83–117. The text appears on pp. 92–117.

[196] The writings of Duns Scotus on the Immaculate Conception have been collected by C. Balic, *Ioannes Duns Scotus Doctor Immaculatae Conceptionis,* vol. 1, Textus Auctoris (Rome, 1954).

Magnificat Antiphon: September 8	Magnificat Antiphon: December 8
Gloriosae Virginis Mariae *Nativitatem* dignissimam recolamus. Sentiant omnes tuum iuvamen quicumque celebrant tuam sanctam *Nativitatem*.	Gloriosae Virginis Mariae *Conceptionem* dignissimam recolamus. Sentiant omnes tuum iuvamen quicumque celebrant tuam sanctam *Conceptionem*.

In general, the liturgical texts focus on the soteriological nature of the feast, developing an antithesis between Eve and Mary as a foreshadowing of the immaculate conception of the future Mother of the Savior and the way in which this conception is intrinsically part of the divine plan both for the divine motherhood and for the salvation of the human race. This collect and the postcommunion in the Missal of Fécam show how this was done:

Deus ineffabilis misericordiae,
qui primae piacula mulieris per virginem expianda sanxisti,
da nobis quaesumus *conceptionis eius*
digne sollemnia venerari,
quae *Unigenitum tuum* virgo *concepit* et virgo peperit
Dominum nostrum.
Caelesti alimoniae vegetati libamine,
quaesumus, Domine Deus noster,
ut nos gloriosae semper virginis Mariae continua foveat protectio.
cuius nostrae causa salutis extitit *hodierna conceptio*.[197]

In the fifteenth century two events had a profound impact on both the history of the dogma and on the liturgy of the Immaculate Conception: the celebration of the Council of Basel (1431–1437) and election to the Chair of Peter (1471) of Cardinal Francesco della Rovere as Sixtus IV.

The question of the feast of the Conception of Mary was on the agenda of the Council, but when it was treated (September 17, 1438), the Council had already been closed by Eugene IV (September 18, 1437), for whom its decisions had no canonical standing. The Council had formally declared that:

[197] Texts taken from Bouman, "The Immaculate Conception in the Liturgy," 142.

doctrinam illam disserentem gloriosam Virginem Dei Genitricem Mariam, praeveniente et operante divini numinis gratia singulari, *numquam actualiter subjacuisse originali peccato; sed immunem semper fuisse ab omni originali et actuali culpa*, sanctamque et immaculatam; tamquam piam et consonam culto ecclesiastico, fidei catholicae, rectae rationi, et sacrae scripturae, ab omnibus catholicis approbandam fore, tenendam et amplectendam.[198]

Despite the fact that the decree was promulgated while the Council was in schism, it had a great influence and showed the future direction that the Magisterium would take.

The pontificate of Sixtus IV (1471–1484), a Franciscan friar and a well-educated theologian, marked an important stage in the history of the feast of the Immaculate Conception. In his decisions in favor of the immaculist doctrine there can be seen an intelligent response to the excesses of the maculist opposition. In 1475 Vincenzo Baldelli, a Dominican friar and a fiery preacher, became the leader of those opposed to the doctrine and lost no opportunity to agitate against the doctrine of the Mary's immaculate conception, holding it to be a "dogma pestiferum, diabolicum." In 1477 Sixtus IV answered with the bull *Cum praecelsa*,[199] in which hc approved the Mass and the Office of the Immaculate Conception composed by Leonardo Nogarolo, a famous cleric from Verona who was the protonotary of the papal chancery. With the bull *Cum praecelsa*, Sixtus IV did not make the feast of December 8 obligatory and universal, nor did he order the new formularies to be inserted into the Roman liturgical books. However, by authorizing the general use of these formularies on the feast of the Immaculate Conception and during the octave, he took an important step in favor of the immaculist doctrine and the diffusion of the feast. This was the first time that a pope had officially intervened, calling on his *auctoritas apostolica*, in favor of the feast of December 8 and so, implicitly, also in favor of the doctrine associated with it.

For the readings of the new Mass, Nogarolo kept Proverbs 8:22-35 *(Dominus possedit me)* as the epistle, but changed the gospel, substitut-

[198] Session XXXVI: Mansi, XXIX, 183. For the positions of the theologians at the time of the Council of Basel, see H. Ameri, *Doctrina theologorum de Immaculata B.V. Mariae Conceptione tempore Concilii Basileensis* (Rome, 1954).

[199] A critical edition of the bull appears in C. Sericoli, *Immaculata B. M. Virginis Conceptio iuxta Xysti IV constitutiones* (Sibenici-Roma, 1945) 153–154.

ing Luke 11:27-28 *(Loquente Iesu ad turbas)* for Matthew 1:1-16 *(Liber generationis Iesu Christi)*. This is, at one and the same time, a praise of the divine motherhood and of her faith. For the antiphons and the gradual, he returned again and again to the Song of Songs, which gives the formulary a lovely tone, as is clear from the introit.

Egredimini et odete, filiae Sion, Reginam vestram,
quam laudant astra matutina,
cuius pulchritudinem sol et luna mirantur
et iubilant omnes filii Dei.[200]

The collect is interesting because one can see in it hints of the 1854 definition and also because it is still in use for the Mass of December 8:

Deus, qui per immaculatam Virginis conceptionem
dignum Filio tuo habitaculum praeparasti:
quaesumus, ut qui ex morte eiusdem Filii tui praevisa
eam ab omni labe praeservasti,
nos quoque mundos eius intercessione ad te pervenire concedas.[201]

Because of a Christological necessity—providing a home for the Son that is fitting for his holiness and divinity—and because the eventual saving death of the same Christ is foreseen, God the Father preserved the Virgin from original sin in her conception.

This was not the only intervention of Sixtus IV in favor of the liturgy of the Immaculate Conception. Three years later, on October 4, 1480, he issued the brief *Libenter*,[202] with which he approved the Office and Mass composed by Bernardine of Bustis († 1513), a Franciscan friar who was the author of a famous *Mariale* and was well known for his apostolic zeal, his doctrine, and the sanctity of his life. The approbation was a sort of gesture of friendship. Sixtus IV allowed Friar Bernardine, and to any others who desired, the right to say "pro devotione sua [. . .] libere et licite" the new liturgical formularies, which were full of unction and openly confessed Mary's privilege of conception without sin. The Mass, with a proper sequence and preface, was distinguished for the richness of its metaphors—temple, sanctuary,

[200] The formulary is reproduced in Bouman, "The Immaculate Conception in the Liturgy," 151–152.

[201] Ibid., 151.

[202] A critical edition is available in Sericoli, *Immaculata B. M. Virginis Conceptio iuxta Xysti IV constitutiones*, 155.

palace, sun, star, rose, lily, fountain—with which it alluded in a symbolic manner to the Immaculate, and for the variety of perspectives from which it described her: Spouse, Lady, Mother, Mistress, Daughter. The formulary ends up being rather exuberant, far from the balance of Nogarolo's.

The feast of the Visitation

During the period under consideration here—from the tenth century to the beginning of the Council of Trent (1545)—the Roman liturgy was enriched by another feast, which commemorated the episode in salvation history when Mary of Nazareth visited her cousin Elizabeth, as recounted in Luke 1:39-56. In the Roman liturgy, since the sixth century, when the season of Advent became fixed, the episode was celebrated on Friday of the *tempora* of Advent, on which the first reading was Isaiah 11:1-5 *(Egredietur virga de radice Iesse)* and the gospel was Luke 1:39-47 *(Exsurgens autem Maria).*

Only beginning in the thirteenth century was there a feast explicitly for the Visitation (July 2). This reflected, once again, the influence of the East. On this date, in Constantinople, there was a feast that celebrated "the memorial of the deposition of the burial urn in which the mortal remains of the Mother of Christ rested in the church called Blacherne, given by the bishop Juvenal of Jerusalem to Pulcheria, consort of the emperor Marcian (450–457)."[203] According to another tradition, the object of the feast was, rather, the deposition of Mary's clothing, which had been brought to the imperial city in 473, during the reign of Leo I, the Thracian.[204]

During the period of the Crusades, the Latins came to know the Eastern feast of July 2 and took the date but profoundly changed the object of the feast. They reoriented it, as the gospel reading of the Byzantine *typikon* suggested (Luke 1:39-49, 56), to the Visitation. Among the first witnesses to the celebration of the feast in the West is a *constitutio* of the Council of Mans in 1247. The feast of the Visitation was included among the days listed as *dies feriandi,* or days on which one abstained from work.[205]

[203] P. Sorci, "La Visitazione nella Liturgia," *Theotokos* 5 (1997) 54.

[204] A. Kniazeff, "Les fêtes byzantines d'intercession de la Théotokos des 2 juillet et 31 août," in *La Mère de Jésus-Christ et la Communion des Saints dans la liturgie* [Conf. St. Serge, 1985] (Rome, 1986) 134–148.

[205] "Nova constitutio. [. . .] Sequuntur dies feriandi per annum in dioecesi Cenomanensi [. . .] *Julius.* Visitatio B. Mariae Virginis" (Mansi, XXIII, 764). Some scholars

It is universally recognized today that John Jenstein († 1400), the archbishop of Prague (1378–1396), had an important role in the institution of the feast of the Visitation.[206] In a synod celebrated on June 16, 1386, he introduced it into his diocese, placing it on April 28 and composing, according to the taste of the time, an Office in rhyme[207] and the Mass.

During the consistory of April 8, 1389, under the influence of the same Cardinal Jenstein, Urban VI instituted the feast of the Visitation, fixing it on July 2. By instituting this new feast, the Pope hoped, by the intercession of the Virgin, to bring peace to the Church by ending the Great Schism, in which he was opposed by the Avignon anti-pope Clement VII. But death took Urban VI on October 15 of this same year, before he was able to sign the document that would effect the institution of the feast. It would be his successor, Benedict IX, who would formalize the feast with the promulgation of the bull *Superni benignitas Conditoris* on November 9, 1389.[208] However, the new pope did not like the Office *Exsurgens Maria abiit in montana,* composed by Cardinal Jenstein, and commissioned another by the Benedictine cardinal Adam Easton, bishop of London. But the new Office *(Accedunt laudes Virginis)*[209] was also unacceptable to Boniface IX, who ordered the adoption of "the [Office] of the Nativity of Mary with the Mass *Salve sancta parens* and the gospel *Exsurgens,* which is read on Friday of Ember Week in Advent."[210]

hold that the *nova constitutio* was added after 1247. According to L. Wadding, the famous Franciscan historian, something similar may be said of the decree of the Franciscan General Chapter of 1263, which was held in Pisa and presided over by St. Bonaventure. Supposedly it was decreed that the feast of the Visitation be introduced into the liturgy of the Order ("Jussum item ut novae hae festivitates admitterentur in Ordine, videlicet Conceptionis beatae Virginis Mariae, *Visitationis* eiusdem . . .," *Annales Minorum,* IV [Florence, 1931] 244). This is, however, imprecise, because it traces "the notice from a copy of the text of the statutes that is late, dating from 1263, and seems to have been 'updated,' which means that elements were added to it after the date." J. V. Polc, "Visitatio beatae Mariae Virginis": da seicento anni nell'Occidente liturgico," *EphLit* 103 (1989) 270.

[206] For the history of the feast, the study by J. V. Polc, *De origine festi Visitationis B.M.V.* (Rome, 1967) is fundamental.

[207] The Office has been partially published in AH 48, nn. 399 (pp. 427–429), 402–404 (pp. 432–433).

[208] *Bullarium Romanum* (Lyons, 1655) 3:293–294.

[209] The Office is partially reproduced in AH 24, n. 29, pp. 89–92 (the antiphons and the responsories) and in AH 52, nn. 42–44, pp. 47–50 (the hymns).

[210] P. Sorci, "La Visitazione nella Liturgia," 61.

The apostolic constitution of November 9, 1389 established that "festum [. . .] Visitationis B. Mariae Virginis [. . .] sexto nonas Iulii annis singulis in Dei Ecclesia cum laudum cantico sub duplici officio per Orbem universum solemniter celebraretur."[211]

The reception of the feast was not uniform, however. In the troubled context of the Great Schism, the feast of the Visitation seemed like a badge of loyalty for the nations that adhered to the pope in Rome. For this reason the nations that adhered to the anti-pope in Avignon—Spain, France, and parts of Germany—did not accept it immediately. Rather, its acceptance was gradual and came as a result of decisions by local Churches and the religious orders as well as new interventions of the Magisterium, such as the Council of Basel, on July 1, 1441, after it had been rejected by Eugene IV, which promulgated a decree that "per singulas christianorum Ecclesias, quolibet anno, sexto nonas Iulii festum [. . .] Visitationis gloriosae Virginis celebretur";[212] and Nicholas V, who ordered that "all the local Churches accept the feast for which he issued the bull *Romanorum gesta pontificum* on March 26, 1451, in which he republished the bull of Boniface IX in its entirety";[213] and Sixtus IV, who allowed the Augustinian hermits to maintain the Office of the Visitation which appeared in the Appendix of the breviaries of the Roman Curia.[214]

During the time of Sixtus IV many Offices of the Visitation were in use, among them the one composed by John Jenstein *(Exsurgens Maria abiit in montana),* another by Adam Easton *(Accedunt laudes Virginis),* and one by the Dominican Raymond of Capua († 1399) *(Collaetentur corda fidelium).*[215] To these might be added the Office *Candida plebs fidelium,* which was widely used among the Franciscans,[216] and the Office *In splendoribus sanctorum,* composed by Thomas of Corcellis after the decree of the Council of Basel.[217]

With the proliferation of these formularies, the need was felt for a more sober style of Office, more in keeping with the style of the

[211] *Bullarium Romanum,* n. 208, p. 294.

[212] Sessio XLIII: Mansi, XXIX, 213.

[213] Sorci, *La Visitazione nella Liturgia,* n. 203, p. 63.

[214] S. Bäumer, *Histoire du Bréviaire* (Paris, 1905) 2:217.

[215] This Office is partially reproduced in AH 24, n. 30, pp. 94–97 (the antiphon and responsories) and AH 52, nn. 45–47, pp. 51–53 (the hymns).

[216] AH 24, n. 31, pp. 98–101.

[217] P. Sorci, "La Visitazione nella Liturgia," n. 203, p. 62.

Roman liturgy. Cardinal Francis Quiñones moved in this direction, but not always with the needed discernment. In the first edition of his famous *Breviarium sanctae Crucis* (1535), mention of the feast of the Visitation is minimized: the hymn *Ave Maris Stella,* the Common of Virgins, the gospel passage Luke 1:39-56, the oration *Omnipotens sempiterne Deus,* "generic and moralizing."[218]

In the *editio princeps* of the *Missale Romanum,* printed at Milan in 1474 during the pontificate of Sixtus IV, the Mass of the Visitation[219] calls for the antiphons *Transite ad me omnes qui concupiscitis me* (cf. Sir 24:24, 25, 26) for the introit; *Unde hoc mihi* (cf. Luke 1:43-47) for the offertory; *Mansit autem Maria* (cf. Luke 1:56) for the communion; *Ego quasi terebintus* (Sir 24:22-29) for the epistle; *Ego effudi flumina. Rigabo horum planatationum* (cf. Sir 24:40-42) for the gradual; *Ut facta est vox salutationis* (cf. Luke 1:44) for the alleluia; and *Exsurgens autem Maria* (Luke 1:39-47) for the gospel. The euchological texts were *Deus, cuius Unigenitus* for the collect; *Suscipe, quaesumus, Domine* for the prayer over the gifts; and *Sacra libantes mysteria* for the postcommunion prayer.

On the whole, the formulary draws out the saving nature of the events celebrated. Just as the Savior, already within the womb of Mary, sanctifies John within the womb of his mother Elizabeth with an outpouring of the Holy Spirit, so too baptism, by means of water and the Spirit, sanctifies the children of adoption in the baptismal font, the womb of mother Church.

The feast of the Presentation of Mary

The feast of the Presentation of Mary in the Temple appeared in Jerusalem in the sixth century and was originally purely local in nature.[220] The feast made a late appearance in the West. There are hints that it was celebrated in the monasteries of southern Italy in the ninth century. From there, helped by the Normans, it passed to England, where it is found in the calendar of Winchester before 1100 and is described in these terms: "Oblationis s. Mariae in templo Domini cum esset trium annorum."[221]

The decisive force behind the diffusion of the feast in the West was Philip de Mézières († 1405), a French Crusader, and chancellor of Peter

[218] Ibid., 66.

[219] Ibid., 65–66.

[220] See "The Presentation of Mary," above, pp. 254–255.

[221] P. Radò, *Enchiridion Liturgicum* (Rome, 1966) 2:1357.

I Lesignan, the titular king of Jerusalem, who lived in Cyprus. De Mézières was attracted by the splendor with which the feast of November 21 was celebrated in the city and promoted its celebration in the West. In 1372 he was at Avignon because Gregory XI had introduced the feast to the Latin Church and approved an Office and Mass for it, on which he had worked with de Mézières. The Pope examined the liturgical texts, and having received a favorable response from the theologians and cardinals he had consulted, he gave permission that on November 21 the feast of the Presentation of Mary be celebrated in the church of the Friars Minor at Avignon. The celebration, in which many cardinals from the Curia took part, was a sort of "additional approval."[222] In the following year, Charles V of France arranged for the feast to be celebrated in the Palatine Chapel in Paris. Thus, little by little the feast of the Presentation spread throughout western Europe. On July 12, 1472, Sixtus IV allowed the churches and religious orders that so desired to celebrate it as a facultative feast.[223] One might say that the feast became "general" from this time on.

In the second half of the fifteenth century, no fewer than seven Offices were circulating in the West, of which the one prepared by Philip de Mézières and Gregory XI was the most successful. It was a poetic Office with readings from good sources: Fulbert of Chartres, Bernard of Clairvaux, Ambrose of Milan, and Peter Damian.

The idea behind the formulary was the preparation of the Virgin for her role as Mother of God. Mary is in the Temple, Israel's holiest place, because, having conceived the Son of God within her womb, she is herself the holy temple of the Most High:

[222] The same de Mézières, in *Epistola de solemnitate Presentationis beatae Mariae* directed to all the faithful ("Universis in Domino fidelibus"), explains how the papal approval took place: "8. Factaque relatione de omnibus ad Sanctitatem Domini nostri Papae, idem vicarius [. . .] illius qui non cessat matrem honorare in terris [. . .] *celebrandi deinceps* publice solemnitatem Praesentationis beatae Mariae in templo a fidelibus pie, sancte, et digne *tollerantiam seu permissionem misericorditer concessit.* Et facta est solemnitas Praesentationis beatae Mariae cum officio suo proprio sepetacto in Curia Romana, beatissimo *Papa Gregorio tollerante* [. . .] in ecclesia Fratrum Minorum, videlicet die Dominica xxj. die mensis Novembris, a natitvitate Domini m.ccc.lxxj."—W. E. Coleman, *Philippe de Mézières' Campaign for the Feast of Mary's Presentation* (Toronto, 1981) 47.

[223] Bäumer, *Histoire du Bréviaire,* 2:110.

Virgo sancta templo data
post facta est Dei templum,
templum est plebs Deo grata
Mariae sequens exemplum.[224]

The formulary of the Mass[225] provides antiphons for three classic texts: *Gaudeamus omnes in Domino* as the introit; *Felix namque es, sancta Virgo Maria* as the offertory; and *Beata viscera Mariae Virginis* as the communion. The readings—Sirach 24:23-31 *(Ego quasi vitis fructificavi)* for the epistle and Matthew 1:1-16 *(Liber generationis Iesu Christi)* for the gospel—were probably chosen to underline the essential vocation of the Virgin: to be the mother of Jesus (v. 16). The Mass contains a long *prosa*, which is a paraphrase of the Ps-Matthew *De nativitate Mariae* but lacks genuine poetic inspiration. The collect *(Deus, qui beatam Virginem)*, the prayer over the gifts *(Haec munera)*, and the post-communion prayer *(Sacramenta quae sumpsimus)* are well done and full of useful ideas, such as "the temple of the heart," "spiritual sacrifice," "listening to the voice of the Spirit," "growth in heavenly discipline," "the ritual offering," and "the sacrifice of life."

[224] *Officium Praesentationis*, vers.: Coleman, *Philippe de Mézières Campaign*, 69.
[225] Ibid., 79–83.

Philippe Rouillard, O.S.B.

11

The Cult of Saints in the East and the West

The cult and the invocation of saints have held and still hold today, although in varying degrees, a considerable place in the life of Christians and the liturgy of the Church. In the beginning the martyrs, bishops, and other saintly persons were held in veneration in the local church where they lived. Later on some of them gained universal renown and found a place in the calendars of all churches. Finally, for reasons not always clear, a small number of saints—for instance, St. Anthony of Padua and St. Rita of Cascia—became the objects of extraordinary popular devotion throughout the world, although their place in the Church's liturgy is modest or even nonexistent. In this last case, we observe the many modalities of the relationship that arises more or less spontaneously between an exceptional figure and a community that welcomes it, canonizes it, and gives it a role to play or acknowledges the role that it does have in the life of its time.

We shall present first the history of the cult of saints from the origins of Christianity down to our own time. Until the sixth century, there was one tradition for both East and West, but subsequently there was a divergence between East and West. Next we shall try to show the significance of the liturgical cult of saints in the contemporary Church.

I. HISTORY OF THE CULT OF SAINTS

In the East as well as in the West, the liturgy of the saints has a twofold source: the cult of martyrs, whose anniversary was celebrated by the community gathered around their tombs, and the cult of bishops, whose memory was kept with devotion by the churches they used to head. Each church possessed its own calendar, which was gradually enlarged in two ways: it welcomed martyrs from other churches and also illustrious figures, like the apostles, who played a fundamental role in the universal Church. Thus one passed from the "memory" of martyrs and bishops to the "feasts" of saints.

The tracing of this evolution is no mere historical task. The latter is the means of recapturing the values and the functions pertaining to each category of saints, whom we tend to celebrate in too uniform a manner nowadays; it is also the means of understanding what sort of sanctity, as the centuries roll along, the Church judges to be deserving of a cult.

1. *From the Origins to the Sixth Century*

a) The cult of the martyrs

In the beginning this was only one of the forms of the cult rendered to the dead: it was a cult of memory, a way of ensuring that the dead person lived on in the memory of the living; for the living, it was a way of being nourished by the example and courage of those who gave their lives to attest to their faith (the word *martyr* comes from the Greek and means "witness").

What distinguished the cult of martyrs from the cult of the ordinary dead was the fact that the anniversary gatherings did not concern only the family but the entire local community, and that those gatherings continued not for a few years but indefinitely. The Christian memory of the martyr is lasting.

Obviously, our documentation regarding the cult of the martyrs during the first centuries is fragmentary. The East preceded the West. The earliest testimony concerns Polycarp, bishop of Smyrna, who was martyred in 155 or 156. In a letter written less than a year after his death, the Christians of Smyrna wrote, "We later took up his bones . . . and laid them away in a suitable place. There the Lord will permit us, so far as possible, to gather together in joy and gladness to celebrate the day of his martyrdom as a birthday, in memory of those athletes who have gone before us, and to train and make ready those who are to come hereafter."[1] In all probability, this meeting included the celebration of the Eucharist.

In the West, we find the earliest documents in Carthage, at the time of St. Cyprian and the persecution of Decius (250). In a letter to his

[1] *Martyrdom of Polycarp,* in *Early Christian Fathers,* ed. and trans. C. C. Richardson and others, Library of Christian Classics 1 (Philadelphia, 1953) 17–18.

clergy, Cyprian gives this recommendation concerning the confessors of the faith: "You should keep note of the days on which they depart this life; we will then be able to include the celebration of their memories in our commemorations of the martyrs."[2] In another letter, speaking of three martyrs of Carthage, he adds, "We never fail to offer sacrifices on their behalf every time we celebrate in commemoration the anniversary dates of the sufferings of these martyrs."[3] These two texts show us that the celebration of the martyrs' anniversaries was already customary at Carthage at the time of Cyprian and that it included the Eucharistic sacrifice.

In contrast, it seems that at Rome no special cult was rendered to martyrs before the middle of the third century. It was Valerian's bloody persecution, during the summer of 258, that caused a change: on August 6, Pope Sixtus II and six of his deacons were put to death; on August 10, it was the deacon Lawrence's turn. In June of the same year, the remains of St. Peter and St. Paul were placed in safety. The Church of Rome wanted to keep the memory of a summer that brought so grievous a trial.[4]

The veneration of the martyrs included a Eucharistic synaxis at their grave on the anniversary day of their death (*dies natalis,* that is, "birthday [in heaven]"). It also expressed itself in inscriptions written by Christians near the martyrs' tombs in order to implore their prayer. Only after the Peace of the Church, following Constantine's Edict of Toleration in 313, did people begin to erect over the martyrs' graves small edifices marking their presence and sheltering their cult; such an edifice was called a *memoria* or *martyrium.*

b) The cult of confessors and bishops

The risk, but also the opportunity, of martyrdom ceased with the end of the persecutions. Thus impoverished, the Church sought new forms that would substitute for martyrdom.

Already in the third century, the custom had been to venerate the persons (bishops usually) who had suffered either prison or exile for their faithfulness to Christ but had not been put to death. These

[2] St. Cyprian of Carthage, *Letter* 12, *The Letters of St. Cyprian of Carthage,* 4 vols., trans. G. W. Clarke, Ancient Christian Writers 43, 44, 45, 46 (New York, 1984–1986) 1:82.

[3] *Letter* 39, ibid., 2:55.

[4] See P. Jounel, "L'été 258 dans le calendrier romain," *MD* 52 (1957) 44–58.

courageous witnesses were called *confessores*, because they confessed their faith; occasionally they were given the title "martyrs." Such was the case with Pope Pontian († 235) and Pope Cornelius († 253), who died after having been deported. Such was also the case, after the Peace of the Church, with bishops like Paulinus of Trier († 358), Dionysius of Milan († 359), and Athanasius of Alexandria († 373), who were sent into exile for resisting Arianism.

In the second half of the fourth century, the most illustrious monks were compared to martyrs. Since persecutions had ended, one could no longer be a martyr by shedding one's blood, but one could be a martyr by practicing asceticism. Monks succeeded martyrs in their renunciation of the world, their resolve to follow Christ, and their battle against the powers of evil. They also succeeded martyrs in popular devotion. At the time of his death, St. Antony of Egypt ordered his disciples to hide his burial place to prevent the construction of a *martyrium*. A few bishops who had spent long years in monastic life were also part of this group; they owed their renown more to their asceticism than to their episcopal function. Such was the case with St. Basil of Caesarea († 375) and his brother St. Peter of Sebaste († 391), both venerated before 395, and in the West, St. Martin of Tours († ca. 397), who became the object of cult immediately after his death.

This cult rendered to confessors remained exceptional at the end of the fourth century. The panegyrists explained that these monks and bishops were true martyrs, even though they did not shed their blood for Christ. The term "confessor" persisted through the centuries, and in the Missal of Pius V, in use until 1970, all male saints bear the title of martyr or confessor. The Missal of Paul VI abandoned this ancient term, which by then had become ambiguous.

The systematic veneration of bishops arose from another view. Every church was anxious to know how it was descended from the apostles, and so it kept the list of its bishops, with their names, their dates of death, and sometimes their burial places. These lists, which had a historical value, soon took on a liturgical character, because they were read during Mass to manifest the communion of the present Church with its successive bishops; they were called *depositiones episcoporum* (burial dates of bishops).

In the fifth and sixth centuries, the lists of local bishops were blended with those of local martyrs; the community rendered a liturgical cult to both groups by celebrating their anniversaries every year.

This liturgical evolution went hand in hand with a theological rationale: it is legitimate and beneficial to keep and venerate the memory not only of martyrs but also of bishops, who in another way contributed to the growth of the local church. The community remembered them, holding the firm belief that for their part they would remember their community and come to its help.

c) The twofold enlargement of the calendar

Up to this point, the calendar of each community had remained purely local, containing only its own martyrs and its own bishops. And indeed, this custom is easily understood because the cult was celebrated on the tomb of the saint and because the tomb was inviolable.

However, already in the second half of the fourth century, we see some exceptions. For instance, the *Chronograph of 354*[5] lists three martyrs from Carthage: St. Perpetua, St. Felicity, and St. Cyprian, along with several martyrs from towns close to Rome—Ostia, Albano, Porto. These early cases of adoption are explained by the close bonds that united these churches to that of Rome. More surprising is the fact that, about 380, Constantinople celebrated St. Athanasius of Alexandria and St. Cyprian of Carthage.[6] Similarly, the anniversary of the deacon and martyr Vincent of Saragossa († 304) was celebrated in the whole world.[7]

The spread of the cult of martyrs and other saints, regarded as indispensable protectors, was providentially fostered by the discovery and the transfer of the holy bodies. The phenomenon was most noticeable in Constantinople, which by then had become the imperial residence. The emperors wanted the second Rome to be as rich as the first in relics and other treasures, and they had all the illustrious bodies they could acquire transported to Constantinople. In 356 the relics of St. Timothy were brought to the city; in 357, those of St. Andrew and St. Luke, and so on. The same thing happened in many churches of Asia Minor, which followed the example of the capital. These saints of

[5] L. Duchesne, *Le Liber pontificalis: Texte, introduction. et commentaire* (Paris, 1886) 1:10–12; 2nd ed. by C. Vogel, 3 vols. (Paris, 1955–1957); also in K. Kirch, "Chronographus Anni 354," in *Enchiridion fontium historiae ecclesiasticae antiquae*, 7th ed. (Freiburg, 1941) nos. 543–544.

[6] See their panegyric by Gregory of Nazianzus in PG 35:1082–1128; 1160–1193.

[7] St. Augustine, *Sermon* 276, *The Works of Saint Augustine*, trans. E. Hill, ed. J. Rotelle (Brooklyn, 1994) 8:31.

foreign origin were the adoptive children, or rather the adoptive fathers or mothers and patron saints, of their new cities.

The second enlargement of the calendars and the cult of saints was due to the addition of saints who did not belong to a local community but to the whole Church. Quite often the date of their death was unknown, and what was celebrated was not their anniversary but their memory or their feast. We have here a shift of importance for the history of the cult of the saints: it detached and distanced itself from the cult of the dead. By pondering the honors due their martyrs and bishops, Christians came to understand that they may and must render similar veneration to those who, in the beginning, were witnesses and shepherds to the whole Church, and all their successors, who, by their teaching and their deeds, had built up the universal Church. This evolution of the cult reveals a maturation of the notion of sanctity and a growing awareness of the unity of the Church in time and space.

A first group of saints entered the calendar following in the wake of the feast of Christmas, established in many churches in the fourth century. Thus, in Caesarea of Cappadocia, about 380, St. Stephen, the first martyr, was commemorated on December 26, St. Peter, St. James, and St. John on December 27, and St. Paul on December 28. In a calendar of Carthage dating from 506,[8] the feast of Christmas on December 25 was followed by the feast of St. Stephen on December 26, St. John and St. James on December 27, and the Holy Innocents on December 28. This group of Christ's witnesses remained almost unchanged until the liturgy of our day.

In this way, a first sketch of a universal calendar takes shape: it was accepted that any given church may and must celebrate the feasts of saints with whom it had no particular connection. The principle is set, even though in the beginning it was applied with a cautiousness that would disappear in subsequent times. This cult, rendered to martyrs, some apostles, and one evangelist, was directed to Christians held in high regard less for their personal holiness than for the eminent role they played in the building of the Church, and therefore in God's work among humans. Viewed in this manner, the cult of saints belongs essentially with the celebration of the mysteries of salvation, and, correctly understood, the sanctoral cycle joins and completes the temporal cycle.

[8] DACL, VIII–1, 644–645.

2. *In the East, from the Sixth Century to Our Day*

The liturgical calendars of the different Eastern churches present both common points and variable developments. In all these churches, veneration was directed first to their martyrs: those who spent their lives in that community itself and those to whom a sanctuary was dedicated. Some monks and nuns whose ascetical life was comparable to martyrdom, as well as bishops and doctors who defended the faith, were also the objects of cult. The holy patriarchs and prophets of the Old Testament, who played a primary role in the revelation of God and the leadership of God's people, had a more specific place: Abraham, Moses, David, and the great prophets were venerated often in connection with a church built and dedicated in their honor. After the sixth century the majority of churches added to their calendars only the champions of the anti-iconoclastic battle of the ninth century and St. Gregory Palamas († 1359), the last defender of the Orthodox faith against the Latin theologians.

The Coptic Church honors especially Egyptian saints. The Chaldean Church has only twenty-five feasts of saints, all celebrated on Friday, in union with the passion of Christ. The calendars of the Byzantine churches were augmented from the tenth century on by the addition of the most celebrated saints from all regions of the empire, and even of great Western saints. It is possible to sense that such a universal openness was hiding a political agenda. Finally, the Russian Church has continued to our day to list new saints in its calendar. In June 1988, on the occasion of the thousandth anniversary of the conversion of Russia, a council of the Orthodox Church held in Zagorsk canonized nine saints of the Russian Church, among whom the more recent is Theophane the Recluse, a bishop who died in 1894.[9]

Most saints are commemorated only in the prayer of the Hours, in hymns, troparia, and other pieces. The main collections are the Byzantine *Menaia,* which contains one volume per month,[10] and the Syriac *Menologies.*[11] Among the Western Syrians, the Eucharistic anaphora contains a "canon of the Doctors," which names fifteen defenders of the Orthodox faith.

[9] See *Documentation Catholique* 85 (1988) 740–749.

[10] *The Festal Menaion,* trans. Mother Mary and Archimandrite Kallistos Ware (London, 1977).

[11] Published by F. Nau in *PatOr* 10, 1.

In summary, in the Eastern churches, besides the martyrs, witnesses to the faith in times of persecution, and bishops and doctors, witnesses to the faith threatened by heresies, are venerated in a special way.

3. *In the West, from the Sixth Century to Vatican II*

The earliest and richest documentation is found in Rome, in the three great sacramentaries of the sixth and seventh centuries. The Verona Sacramentary opens with some forty Masses of martyrs (1–168), all of which have a rather short proper preface. During the year only twenty-two saints have a feast, in general Roman martyrs, often with several formularies (twenty-eight for St. Peter and St. Paul on June 29; fourteen for St. Lawrence on August 10). The Old Gelasian Sacramentary, in use in Roman parishes, contains in Book 2 formularies for some fifty feasts of saints: Roman martyrs, but also those apostles who have a church in Rome; furthermore, it contains a Common of Saints with eight formularies.[12] The Gregorian Sacramentary *(Hadrianum)* is the papal sacramentary, in which are found eighty-three formularies for the temporal and seventy-nine for the sanctoral cycle.[13]

When, shortly before the year 800, Charlemagne received from Rome a copy of this Gregorian Sacramentary, which he intended to impose on the entire Western Empire, the calendar of saints appeared to him too limited, too exclusively Roman. Consequently, the Frankish liturgists added to it feasts of universal saints that had entered Gaul in various ways. These were chiefly feasts of apostles or saints placed on the same footing as apostles: the Conversion of St. Paul on January 25, St. Matthias on February 24, St. Mark on April 25, St. Bartholomew on August 24, the Beheading of John the Baptist on August 29, St. Matthew on September 21, St. Luke on October 18, St. Simon and St. Jude on October 28, and St. Thomas on December 21. The feast of All Saints on November 1 was also added.

The intention of universalization is obvious, especially since Gallic and Frankish saints venerated in many churches, such as St. Genevieve, St. Denis, St. Germain, St. Rémy, and St. Hilary, are not placed in the official calendar; these local saints remain venerated only at the local level.

[12] See A. Chavasse, *Le sacramentaire gélasien* (Tournai, 1958).

[13] See A. Chavasse, "Le sanctoral et le temporal grégoriens: Distribution et origine des pièces utilisées," *EO* 3 (1986) 263–288.

At the end of the tenth century, the liturgical books, revised and enriched by Frankish and Germanic liturgists, found their way back to Rome, and Rome kept all the transalpine additions. So the basic calendar that can be called the universal calendar of the Roman Church was established. From the tenth to the twentieth century, this Roman calendar became the reference for many Western churches and grew richer and heavier because of deliberate additions or simply because of the vagaries of current trends. The increasing number of saints led to eliminatory reforms.

In the eleventh century Pope Gregory VII decided that all martyr popes would have a feast. This decision, in conformity with his politics—enhancement of the pontifical power—brought into the calendar some thirty popes, most of whom were practically unknown; they would remain there until 1969.

Another thrust came from the monastic orders that flourished in the twelfth century. They obtained the inclusion into the Roman calendar of St. Maurus on January 15, St. Antony on January 17, St. Scholastica on February 10, St. Benedict on March 21, St. Hilarion on October 10, and St. Sabbas on December 5.

In this same twelfth century, the cult of saints underwent still another shift. Whereas in the preceding centuries liturgical honors had been granted to all the persons of the past who seemed qualified for such honors, from now on the Church recognized and venerated as saints contemporary men and women. The first modern saint admitted into the calendar was St. Thomas Becket, archbishop of Canterbury, who was murdered in his cathedral on December 29, 1170, immediately venerated as a martyr, and canonized in 1173. This martyr of modern times opened the doors of the sanctoral, and in the following century Franciscans and Dominicans entered them. Very rapidly St. Francis of Assisi, St. Clare, St. Anthony of Padua, St. Peter of Verona, and St. Dominic became objects of cult. So the calendar became the mirror of the current life of the Church.

The number of feasts of saints jumped from 90 in the twelfth century to 220 on the eve of the Council of Trent. Upon request of the council, Pius V in 1568 ordered a selection that brought the number of feasts of saints down to 130. All the same, the feasts of saints, ancient but mostly recent, resumed their invasion of the calendar: 12 feasts were added in the sixteenth century, 50 in the seventeenth, 31 in the eighteenth, 23 in the nineteenth, and 25 from 1900 to 1960. These 140 saints written into the calendar between the Councils of Trent and Vatican II belong to five main groups: monks in the eleventh and twelfth centuries, whose cause was promoted by the orders they founded; princes and kings in the countries of northern Europe to encourage the Catholics of those regions in their battle against the Reformation; popes and bishops who played some important role; male religious and some female religious who founded or reformed an order or a congregation; finally, the group of doctors of the Church, both Eastern and Western, introduced by Leo XIII to foster ecumenism.

On the eve of the Second Vatican Council, the Roman calendar contained about 270 feasts of saints (without counting the Marian feasts). Besides, there were numerous feasts proper to dioceses and religious orders. A revision was in order.

4. *The Cult of Saints after Vatican II*

In its Constitution on the Liturgy (nos. 104 and 111), the Second Vatican Council gave the general directions for the reform of the sanctoral: the feasts of saints proclaim the wonderful works of Christ, but they must not take precedence over the Lord's feasts, and particularly over Sundays; many among them must regain their local or particular character; only feasts of saints who have a universal importance will be extended to the whole Church.

A new calendar, *Calendarium Romanum generale* (General Roman Calendar), was published in 1969. About one hundred feasts of saints were eliminated. There were four solemnities (St. Joseph, St. John the Baptist, St. Peter and St. Paul, All Saints), 23 feasts, 63 obligatory memorials, and 95 optional memorials. In all, there were only 90 obligatory celebrations, the same number as in the twelfth century.

What were the criteria used in this reform? Through a concern for historical accuracy, 27 feasts of saints whose existence or cult was uncertain were rejected. Seventy saints who were practically unknown —many Roman martyrs among them, particularly martyr-popes introduced as a group by Gregory VII—were removed. On the other hand, in order to manifest the universality of holiness in time and space, it was decided to represent every continent and to feature at least one saint from every century. Finally, it was prescribed that each saint be commemorated on the anniversary of his or her death *(dies natalis).* The only exceptions to this rule concerned a few saints whose feast occurred either during Lent or just before Christmas. Thus, St. Gregory the Great's feast was moved from March 12 to September 3, the anniversary of his episcopal ordination, and St. Thomas the Apostle's feast was moved from December 21 to July 3, the anniversary of the translation of his body to Edessa.

An excellent decision established the principle that the celebration of many "memorials" could be optional. Even saints listed in the calendar of the universal Church are not necessarily venerated in all countries, by all communities, or every year. It is a good thing that 95 memorials remain optional.

Is this calendar perfect? The idea of representing every continent and every century is somewhat artificial; overnight, Christians of the whole world were face to face with saints who were and remained completely unknown to them, for instance, St. Turibius of Mongrovejo, archbishop of Lima, on March 23; St. Martin de Porres, also from Lima, on November 3; St. Josaphat, of the Ruthenian Church, on November 12, with an obligatory memorial. A genuine liturgical cult presupposes a relationship between the saint and the Christian people, and such a relationship cannot be brought into existence by decree. One is also surprised that historically uncertain saints like St. Scholastica on February 10 and St. Elizabeth of Hungary on November 17 are among obligatory memorials.

On balance, the calendar of 1969 deserves a favorable appraisal because it reestablishes a just equilibrium between Sundays, ferial days, and feasts of saints. It projects a better image of the Church, which recognizes its saints and celebrates their memorials without being smothered by them.

II. THE SIGNIFICANCE OF SAINTS TODAY

Having recounted the history of the cult of saints, we must now ask what the significance of this cult within the whole of the Christian liturgy is today. In this research we shall rely primarily on the Roman Missal of Paul VI and secondarily on the Liturgy of the Hours.

1. *A Celebration of the Mystery of the Church*

Without a doubt, the cult of the saints is first of all a celebration of a benevolent God who attracts human beings and calls some of them to a particular mission. Every saint is a manifestation of God; as the first preface for the Common of Holy Men and Women proclaims, "You are glorified in your saints, for their glory is the crowning of your gifts."

But the sanctoral is also a vast feast of the Church, spread out over the whole year. More explicitly than the Missal of Pius V, that of Paul VI celebrates saints in connection with the ministry they discharged in the Church: in the first place come the apostles, upon whom God established the Church and who to this day guide the people of believers; then the martyrs, whether from the past or contemporary; then the pastors, with special formularies for a pope or a bishop, for the bishop who founded a church, for a missionary; then the doctors of the Church, men and women, who fulfilled the ministry of the intellect at the service of faith; then the virgins, and eventually the foundresses of female congregations; then the saints of every category, with special formularies for religious, for the persons who devoted themselves to works of charity or to teaching; finally for the holy women "whose home is built on faithful love."

In this classification of saints according to the role they played in the Church, the Missal of Paul VI shows major progress in comparison with that of Pius V, which, in a surprising way, categorized saints by negative qualifications: Common of a Confessor Not a Bishop, of a Virgin Not a Martyr, of a Martyr Not a Virgin, and finally of a woman neither a virgin nor a martyr.

The new classification emphasizes the function fulfilled by the saints in God's Church. In the best sense of the term, saints appear as the "civil servants" of the Church, as the ministers of God's people, on a par with the faithful and wise stewards of whom the Lord speaks.

2. *Intercessors and Models*

Throughout the centuries, Christian communities have had recourse to the saints' protection, to their intercession with God, and, in certain cases, to their examples. Several approaches are possible in our dialogue with saints. The first one consists in addressing praises and prayers to God with the saints, as we do by singing the *Sanctus* of the Mass "with the angels and all the saints." A second approach, the most frequent in the liturgy, consists in praying to God, relying on the saints' intercession; innumerable collects for the feasts of saints ask for this intercession. A third approach is a direct address to saints; the Middle Ages and modern times have very often followed this method. Still today there are many sanctuaries and chapels that propose to devotees a prayer to St. Joseph, St. Anthony, St. Rita, or St. Thérèse of Lisieux. It seems that this type of prayer never entered the liturgy but remained on the margins, in the domain of devotion and private piety, a domain always in flux. The Church has not wanted to encourage an attitude that would tend to lead to a sort of divinization of the saints and to a deviation of liturgical worship.

The question of the role of saints as examples to be imitated is more delicate. Obviously, many saints illustrate for Christians a life inspired by the gospel. The abstract counsel of the gospel finds a living application in the saint's life, St. Francis of Assisi being one of the best examples of this. But beyond this relationship between the gospel and the saint's life, there is the question of the saints as models to be followed or imitated. Numerous collects of the missal ask that we might imitate the saints. But how are Christians to imitate persons as exceptional as St. Thomas Aquinas or St. John Vianney? At least in certain cases, the word "example" seems to us a literal but inaccurate translation of the Latin *exemplum* or *exemplar,* which means not "example" but "something exemplary," an "exemplar." Many saints are rare and precious samples, but practically inimitable, of the power and imagination of God who raised them for a unique mission.

Anyhow, it is striking to observe that popular devotion turns to favorite saints as to efficient intercessors without worrying about whether they should be imitated. The faithful who invoke St. Anthony of Padua have no ambition to resemble him. One could say that to present too many saints as examples or models for today's Christians would be to forget the specific character of their vocation and of the role they played in the Church.

3. Truly Christian Saints?

The Constitution on the Liturgy (nos. 104 and 111) states that by celebrating the anniversaries of saints, "the Church proclaims achievement of the paschal mystery in the saints who have suffered and have been glorified with Christ. . . . The feasts of the saints proclaim the wonderful works of Christ in his servants."

But, when perusing the collects of the saints in the missal and the Liturgy of the Hours, one must recognize that the wonderful works of Christ, and especially the paschal mystery, appear very rarely in the prayers for feasts of saints. These collects show the saints in their relationship to God (a unique God), to the Church, to each Christian, but Christ is rarely named and the proclamation of the paschal mystery is almost totally absent. Out of some 175 collects for feasts of saints in the missal, only 50 have an explicitly Christological character, and 7 mention the paschal mystery. This strange absence of Christ affects both the proper collects and those of the Commons of Saints. Out of 17 collects offered for the Common of Pastors, only 3 mention Christ. Some vernacular missals, notably the Italian missal, have made a praiseworthy effort to give the prayer material of the feasts of saints a more definite Christian character. One must wish that a more extensive work be devoted to the liturgical cult of saints, and particularly to the prayer texts, so that the person of Christ the Savior, his paschal mystery, and also the presence of the Holy Spirit may appear more clearly.

4. *Liturgical Cult and Popular Devotion*

The liturgical celebration of saints is not sufficient to answer the desires and the needs of the Christian people in their relation to those God has chosen and who can and must continue to intercede in favor of human beings. Some male and female saints are the objects of popular devotion either in the whole world or in a particular community; this devotion is expressed in extra-liturgical forms that the Church cannot ignore.

It is often difficult to understand why saints who did not play a role of first importance in their own time have become protectors and intercessors in great demand. It is at once arduous and fascinating to research the process by which the historical saint has become the saint of popular piety.[14]

Besides saints with a worldwide renown, there are others who remain the objects of local devotion. First, this devotion corresponds to the legitimate need for *particularity*. While the best-known saints have a worldwide responsibility, another more modest figure is the patron of a village, a parish, a brotherhood or sisterhood. Such a saint is a specialist and is specialized. Relationships of reciprocal kinship and service are established. The people trust and celebrate the saint, but their saint must reciprocate by protecting them and obtaining for them the graces which they request and which commemorative plaques will attest to.

[14] Thus this "phenomenon," as exemplified by St. Anthony of Padua, has been remarkably well studied in *San Antonio di Padova fra storia e pietà: Colloquio interdisciplinare su "il fenomeno antoniano"* (Padua, 1977).

This devotion corresponds also to a profoundly human need for closeness. Whereas God dwells in an inaccessible abode, our saint dwells among us. On the saint's feast day, his or her statue is carried in procession through the village; little statues kept in the homes, medals, and images ensure that the saint is within reach. Not only close but tangible, the saint is reassuring; he or she listens to the devotees' prayers, whether recited collectively or individually. However, the traditional rites must be exactly observed because they are the conditions of the covenant between saint and people.

This popular devotion risks entailing deviations and abuses. But rather than opposing it, the Church must endeavor to evangelize and Christianize it by showing that a given saint has exemplified such and such an aspect of the gospel, and by reminding the people that the saint, sent by God, must lead the people under his or her protection to God.

CONCLUSION

The liturgical cult of saints and devotion to the saints are alive and well in our time. The reform of 1969 has restored a healthy balance by placing a good number of saints back in the local calendars. This reform has recaptured for the saints a better image by stressing their ecclesial function. This is not to say that its task is completed. In order to put into practice the instructions of Vatican II, the liturgists' work must improve many collects whose tenor is too moralizing, and show more forcefully that the saints "proclaim the wonderful works of Christ." It must also show that, at least for certain saints, they have lived the paschal mystery.

Lastly, the cult of saints must remain ambivalent. It expresses the life of the Church under its different aspects, from the evangelizing mission to the life of silence and solitude or the performance of works of charity. The cult of saints unceasingly nourishes the Church with its own history, viewed under the angle of holiness, and it gives thanks to God for God's love of humankind. At the same time, it encourages Christians in their personal lives. Far from competing with the celebration of the Lord's mysteries, the cult of saints demonstrates how wondrously these mysteries find their application in the adventure of humankind.

Bibliography

Auf der Maur, H. "Feste und Gedenktage der Heiligen." In *Feiern im Rhythmus der Zeit* II/1. Gottesdienst der Kirche: Handbuch der Liturgiewissenschaft, 6/1:65–357. Regensburg, 1994.

Augé, M. "I santi nella celebrazione del mistero cristiano." *Anàmnesis* 6:247–259.

Beinert, W. *Die Heiligen heute ehren.* Freiburg, 1983.

Bibliotheca Sanctorum. 12 vols. Rome, 1961–1970.

Brown, P. *The Cult of the Saints.* London, 1981.

"Fede in Cristo e culto dei santi." *RL* 65 (1978) 291–346.

Jounel, P. "Santi (Culto dei)." *NDL* 1338–1355. Rome, 1984.

____. "The Veneration of the Saints." *CP* 4:109–129. Collegeville, Minn., 1986.

Moioli, G. "La santità e il 'santo' cristiano: Il problema teologico." *ScC* 109 (1981) 353–374.

"Saints. *DSp* 14:196–230. Paris, 1990.

Saints et sainteté dans la liturgie. Conférence Saint-Serge, 1986. Rome, 1987.

Wilson, S., ed. *Saints and Their Cults.* Cambridge, 1983.

I. HISTORY OF THE CULT OF SAINTS

1. From the Origins to the Sixth Century

Delehaye, H. *Les origines du culte des martyrs.* Subsidia hagiographica 20. 2nd rev. ed. Brussels, 1933.

____. *Sanctus: Essai sur le culte des saints dans l'antiquité.* Subsidia hagiographica 17. Brussels, 1927.

Duval, Y. *Auprès des saints corps et âmes: L'inhumation "Ad Sanctos" dans la chrétienté d'Orient et d'Occident du IIIe au VIe siècle.* Paris, 1988.

Gaiffier, B. de. "Réflexions sur les origines du culte des martyrs." *MD* 52 (1957) 19–43.

Saxer, V. *Morts, martyrs, reliques en Afrique chrétienne aux premiers siècles.* Théologie historique 55. Paris, 1980.

Stern, H. *Le calendrier de 354: Etude sur son texte et ses illustrations.* Bibliothèque archéologique et historique 55. Paris, 1953.

Visentin, P. "Formazione e sviluppo del Santorale nell'anno liturgico." *RL* 65 (1978) 279–319.

2. In the East, from the Sixth Century to Our Day

AA.VV. *The Byzantine Saints.* London, 1981.

Dalmais, I. H. "Les commémorations des saints dans l'office quotidien et hebdomadaire des liturgies orientales." *MD* 52 (1957) 98–108.

____. "Mémoire et vénération des saints dans les églises de traditions syriennes." In *Saints et sainteté dans la liturgie,* 79–91. Conférence Saint-Serge, 1986. Rome, 1987.

Evdokimov, P. "La sainteté dans la tradition de l'Eglise Orthodoxe." In *La nouveauté de l'Esprit,* 108–136. Spiritualité orientale 20. Bellefontaine, 1977.

Renoux, C. "Les premières manifestations liturgiques du culte des saints en Arménie." In *Saints et sainteté dans la liturgie,* 291–303. Conférence Saint-Serge, 1986. Rome, 1987.

Spidlik, T. "Saints dans les Eglises byzantine et russe." *DSp* 14:197–202. Paris, 1990.

3. In the West, from the Sixth Century to Vatican II

Jounel, P. *Le culte des saints dans les basiliques du Latran et du Vatican au XIIe siècle.* Ecole Française de Rome 26. Rome, 1977.

____. "Le sanctoral du sacramentaire de la collection Phillips." In *Rituels: Mélanges P.-M. Gy,* 347–366. Paris, 1990.

____. "Le sanctoral. romain du VIIIe au XIIe siècle." *MD* 52 (1957) 59–88.

Moreton, B. "The Mass-Sets of the Sanctoral" In *The Eighth-Century Gelasian Sacramentary: A Study in Tradition,* 102–159. Oxford, 1976.

Triacca, A. M. "Le sanctoral de la liturgie ambrosienne: Des données à la théologie liturgique." In *Saints et sainteté dans la liturgie,* 325–356. Conférence Saint-Serge, 1986. Rome, 1987.

4. The Cult of Saints after Vatican II

Dubois, J. "Les saints du nouveau calendrier: Tradition et critique historique." *MD* 100 (1969) 157–178.

Jounel, P. *Le renouveau du culte des saints dans la liturgie romaine.* Rome, 1986.

Paternoster, M. "Il culto dei santi nei nuovi libri liturgici." *RL* 65 (1978) 320–333.

Peloso, F. *Santi e santità dopo il Concilio Vaticano II: Studio teologico-liturgico delle orazioni proprie dei nuovi Beati e Santi.* Rome, 1991.

Sustaeta, J. M. "Presencia de los santos en el Calendario y su celebracion en el Misal." *Ph* 26 (1986) 211–231.

II. THE SIGNIFICANCE OF SAINTS TODAY

Auf der Maur, H. "Theologie der Heiligenfeiern." In *Feiern im Rhythmus der Zeit,* II/1. Gottesdienst der Kirche: Handbuch der Liturgiewissenschaft, 6/1:264–279. Regensburg, 1994.

Chavasse, A. "Sanctoral et année liturgique." *MD* 52 (1957) 89–97.

Cunningham, L. *The Meaning of Saints.* San Francisco, 1980.

Donghi, A. "La memoria dei santi nel messale romano." In *Il Messale romano del Vaticano II,* 2:211–245. Turin, 1981.

____. "Dall'eucologia del santorale, una tipologia della santità." In *Il Messale romano del Vaticano II,* 2:246–278. Turin, 1981.

"Liturgie et sainteté." *MD* 201 (1995).

Lodi, E. "La sainteté dans les textes eucologiques romains." In *Saints et sainteté dans la liturgie,* 211–39. Conférence Saint-Serge, 1986. Rome, 1987.

Peyrous, B. "La sainteté dans l'Eglise depuis Vatican II." *NRT* 107 (1985) 641–657.

Wegman, H. A. "Successio Sanctorum." In *Time and Community,* in honor of T. J. Talley, 219–241. Washington, 1990.

Whalen, M. "Saints and Their Feasts: An Ecumenical Exploration." *Wor* 63 (1989) 194–209.

Matias Augé, C.M.F.

12

A Theology of the Liturgical Year

The need to provide a theological framework and understanding for the liturgical year was already a concern for the pioneers of the liturgical movement but has become an even greater concern for liturgists working and writing after Vatican II. This theology would move beyond the merely organizational value that is built into the concept and, at the same time, provide some elements of the liturgical and pastoral catechesis that is essential if the liturgical year is to have a significant meaning in the spiritual life of Christians. The liturgical year is organized as an annual celebration of the mystery and the mysteries of Christ and of the saints, who are the concrete realization of this mystery. Celebrated by the Church, the liturgical year is a support for the growth of Christian communities and for individual members of the faithful, who are all called to achieve perfect stature in Christ.

1. Toward a Theology of the Liturgical Year

In the *Missale Romanum* of 1570, like its predecessors, the Proper of Seasons *(Temporale)* began with Advent and ended with the Twenty-Fourth Sunday after Pentecost. This indicates that the annual cycle of liturgical celebrations was considered to be a unity and was also thought to be clearly distinct from the civil year. But nothing much was made of this until the liturgical movement provided a deeper reflection on the liturgical year. Those involved with this movement sought to develop a spiritual theology, one which would move beyond a mere catechesis and that would allow the Christian people to live the mysteries celebrated in the course of the annual cycle more fully. Here we will limit ourselves to a consideration of two scholars whom we consider to be representative of the period prior to Vatican II.

The Benedictine Père Guéranger (1805–1875) published the nine volumes of his work *L'année liturgique* between 1841 and 1866. It has been frequently reprinted and translated.[1] In it the author stresses the power of the celebration(s) of the liturgical year, which re-present salvation. ". . . [T]he ecclesiastical year . . . is neither more nor less than the manifestation of Jesus Christ and His Mysteries, in the Church and in the faithful soul."[2] Later, taking up an expression of Paul (Gal 4:19), he asserts that the result of the communion with the various mysteries—joyous, sorrowful, and glorious—celebrated in the liturgical year is the "formation of Christ within us."[3] This work had a noteworthy influence on the formation of liturgical spirituality. Nonetheless, Guéranger, despite his formulation of the premises for a correct theological vision, still had an understanding of the liturgical year that was fundamentally pedagogical.

For a vision of the liturgical year that was substantially theological, we must turn to another Benedictine, Odo Casel (1886–1948), and his "doctrine of the mysteries" *(Mysterienlehre)*. In his work *Das christliche Kultmysterium*, the first edition of which was published in 1932, Casel argues that the content of the liturgical year moves beyond history as the "great deed of God upon mankind, the redeeming work of Christ which wills to lead mankind out of the narrow bounds of time into the broad spaces of eternity."[4] The liturgical year follows step by step the progressive development of the mystery of Christ and re-presents it, but "it is the entire saving mystery which is before the eyes of the church and the Christian, more concretely on every occasion."[5] This is possible because "it is the whole mystery which takes place in the Mass; the mysterium is always whole."[6] This doctrine of Casel, in its substance, has been accepted both by Vatican II in its Constitution on the Sacred Liturgy and by the author of this article.

[1] F. Brovelle, "Per uno studio de *L'année liturgique* di P. Guéranger. Contributo alla storia del movimento liturgico," *EphLit* 95 (1981) 145–219.

[2] Abbot Guéranger, O.S.B., *Advent*, vol. 2 of *The Liturgical Year*, trans. L. Shepherd, O.S.B., 4th ed. (Westminster, Md.: Newman Press, 1948) 9.

[3] Ibid., 17.

[4] O. Casel, *The Mystery of Christian Worship*, Milestones in Catholic Theology, trans. B. Neunheuser, 4th ed. (New York: Crossroads, 1999) 67.

[5] Ibid.

[6] Ibid., 68.

2. *Methodological Premises*[7]

Almost all scholars who study the liturgical year begin with a historical summary and move on to analyze the various liturgical texts, euchological and biblical, from the different seasons of the year. Generally speaking, this method respects the historical evolution of the liturgical year, a necessity if one hopes to understand the precise object of the various celebrations of which the year consists, as well as the doctrinal and spiritual content of the various seasons and feasts. However, almost all these authors preface their work with a short treatment of the understanding of time and festivals according to the biblical tradition.

Some scholars add yet another chapter introducing the theology of the *entire* liturgical year, a chapter in which one finds treatments of the most varied topics (the nature of time, festivals, the mystery and/or mysteries of Christ, the Trinitarian dimension of the liturgy, as well as its ecclesial and anthropological dimensions, etc.). From a strictly methodological point of view, it seems self-evident that it is only after achieving a global vision of the liturgical year and of all its parts in their historical, liturgical and celebrative, theological and pastoral aspects that one is able to suggest some ideas for a synthetic understanding of the liturgical year in its wholeness. However, most monographs on the liturgical year lack such a theological chapter, which would take up and consider systematically all the salient theological elements that had emerged from the analysis of the various seasons of the liturgical year. The result is that works of this type do not arrive at a *single* theology of the liturgical year but at *several*, each corresponding to one or another of the various seasons and festivals.

The liturgical year is presented to us with a multiple, but nonetheless organic, variety of elements that celebrate and elaborate upon the one mystery of Christ in all its aspects. Faithful to this idea, derived from the liturgical year itself, we will first offer a short theological synthesis focusing on the centrality of the mystery of Christ in the liturgical year, of whose memory it is the cyclical celebration. Then we will provide a summary of the various readings that make up the different seasons of the annual cycle that recalls this mystery.

[7] A. M. Triacca, "Anno liturgico: verso una sua organica trattazione teologica," *Salesianum* 38 (1976) 613–621; G. Cavagnoli, "Rassegna bibliografica sull'Anno liturgico," *RL* 75 (1988) 443–459.

3. The Liturgical Year Is a Cyclical Memorial of the Mystery of Christ

The liturgical year consists, before all else, of the weekly "Lord's Day," which commemorates the resurrection of the Lord (cf. *SC* 102; 106), and of the annual solemnity of Easter and the other feasts that form the celebration of the "annual cycle of the mysteries of Christ" (*SC* 103). What is special about the seasons of celebration in the context of the liturgy is not, therefore, only that they take up the holiness of all created things, and the significance and historical meaning of the feasts of the Bible but, especially, that they point to the mystery of Christ as the central event and essential object of all feasts and celebrations. The Second Vatican Council taught:

"Holy Mother Church believes that it is for her to celebrate the saving work of her divine Spouse in a sacred commemoration on certain days throughout the course of the year. Once each week, on the day which she has called the Lord's Day, she keeps the memory of the Lord's resurrection. She also celebrates it once every year, together with his blessed passion, at Easter, that most solemn of all feasts.

"In the course of the year, moreover, she unfolds the whole mystery of Christ from the incarnation and nativity to the ascension, to Pentecost and the expectation of the blessed hope of the coming of the Lord" (*SC* 102).

The liturgy, seen in this way as the action of God who continues to save by means of ritual signs, sustains and makes real in time, by means of celebrations, the saving riches of the Lord. We may argue, therefore, with Marsili,[8] that the liturgical year is the moment in which the totality of the history of salvation, that is to say, Christ in all the ways he is manifest in the past, the present, and the future, is actualized at a specific moment in time in a concrete ecclesial assembly at a particular time of the year. Fleeting time is fragile, so the time of liturgical celebration takes on the character of καιρός, that moment in which salvation is offered and made real: "After Christ's glorious ascension, the work of salvation is carried on above all through the celebration of the liturgy, which, with good reason, may be called the final age in the history of salvation."[9]

[8] S. Marsili, "Anno liturgico," *I segni del mistero di Cristo: Teologia liturgica dei sacramenti*, BELS 42, ed. M. Alberta (Rome, 1987) 439.

[9] *Collection of Masses of the Blessed Virgin Mary—Sacramentary* (Collegeville, Minn., 1992), Preface, n. 11.

So the liturgical year is neither a series of ideas nor a sequence of festivals that are of greater or lesser importance, but a Person, "Christ himself, who is ever living in his Church."[10] Salvation, which has been accomplished by him "principally by the paschal mystery of his blessed passion, resurrection from the dead, and glorious ascension" (*SC* 5), is offered in the various sacramental actions that characterize the dynamism of the liturgical calendar. In this way the Church affirms that the Pasch of Christ, and the redemption it accomplishes, is at the center of the history of salvation and of the liturgy and is also, therefore, at the center of the celebrations of the liturgical year. The same reality that the liturgical year celebrates each Sunday ("the weekly Easter") is commemorated on Easter Day ("the annual Easter"). It is also the fundamental content of the other celebrations of the annual cycle.

The liturgy of the Church, while it celebrates the mystery that is eternally present in Christ, historicizes its various moments and recalls them at particular points during the course of the year. As we have said above, to argue the centrality of the mystery of Christ to the liturgical year does not require that its cosmic symbolism be denied. In fact, certain elements and cosmic phenomena have played an important role in many of the feasts, the development of their themes, and their rituals. Such cosmic elements and phenomena serve as vehicles for the mystery that is celebrated.[11]

The titles in the ancient Roman sacramentaries express very clearly the "circular" or "cyclical" nature of the celebrations of the liturgical year. The annual celebration of the mystery and mysteries of Christ returns in the *anni circulus*.[12] Liturgical time, characterized by the "circularity" proper to the cosmic year, creates a synthesis of the history of salvation, but does not enclose it within the circle. The "circularity" of the liturgical year causes one to consider that the year is to be understood as a succession of points along the timeline of the history of salvation, a moment of the great jubilee year (cf. Luke 25) or "the year of the Lord's grace" begun by Christ (Luke 4:19, 21).

[10] Pius XII, *Mediator Dei,* no. 165.

[11] A. Chupungco, "Feste liturgiche e stagioni dell'anno," *Concilium* 17 (1981) 249–260.

[12] *Liber sacramentorum romanae ecclesiae ordinis anni circuli* (the Gelasian Sacramentary, seventh century); *Incipit sacramentorum de circulo anni expositum* (Gregorian Sacramentary *[Hadrianum],* eighth century).

The liturgical year is not, therefore, to be confused with the fatalistic idea of the eternal return of the seasons. It is instead a time that repeats itself like a spiral progressing toward the parousia. The repetition of the celebrations, year after year, offers the Church an opportunity to have continuous and uninterrupted contact with the mysteries of the Lord. "Like a path that goes around and up a mountain, slowly making the ascent to the height, we are to climb the same road at a higher level, and go on until we reach the end, Christ himself."[13]

The Christ-event, which reaches its apex at Easter, gives fullness to time but is not ended in time. Every person who lives in history is called to become involved in the saving event. In this fashion the liturgy makes real the history of salvation filling all time with the mystery of Christ.

4. Word and Sacrament in the Liturgical Year

The liturgical year has, therefore, a sacramental character and is a sign that manifests and makes present in an efficacious fashion the saving power of Easter for the faithful, because it provides a framework of meaning within which the Church proclaims the Word and celebrates the sacraments, in particular the Eucharist. This is the saving event that reaches its apex in the paschal mystery of Christ, an event which is unique and which occurred only once (ἅπαξ: cf. Heb 9:26-28; 1 Pet 3:18) for all (ἐφάπαξ: cf. Rom 6:10; Heb 7:27; 9:12; 10:10), and which continues to be present and efficacious for all people of all times in the community where the goods of salvation have been deposited, the Church of Christ (cf. Acts 2:42-46; 4:32ff., etc.). In the dynamic of the economy of salvation, this is possible by the work of the Holy Spirit.[14] After Easter, Christ and his mysteries are spiritualized. From this moment on, Casel asserts, "the Spirit of God is encountered by means of the mysteries of Christ."[15] However, the Spirit hands on the mysteries of Christ as they are celebrated in the course of the annual cycle.

[13] Casel, *Mystery of Christian Worship,* 63.

[14] "In this sacramental dispensation of Christ's mystery the Holy Spirit acts in the same way as at other times in the economy of salvation: he prepares the Church to encounter her Lord; he recalls and makes Christ manifest to the faith of the assembly. By his transforming power, he makes the mystery of Christ present here and now. Finally the Spirit of communion unites the Church to the life and mission of the Church" (*CCC,* no. 1092).

[15] O. Casel, *Die Liturgie als Mysterienfeier, EO* 9 (Freiburg im Breisgau, 1922) 102.

What the Bible tells from the Book of Genesis to the Book of Revelation the liturgy re-presents along its annual path from the First Sunday of Advent to the Last Sunday of Ordinary Time: the sole plan of salvation. In the Bible this happens "by deeds and words, which are intrinsically bound up with each other. As a result, the works performed by God in the history of salvation show forth and bear out the doctrine and realities signified by the words; the words, for their part, proclaim the works, and bring to light the mystery they contain" (*DV* 2). In the fashion appropriate to it, the liturgy tells this story once again, interprets it, announces that it has been realized in the mystery of Christ, "who is himself both the mediator and the sum total of Revelation" (*DV* 2). The liturgy confers a certain reality on the Word of God insofar as it announces that the Word is accomplished in our day: ". . . the Church, especially during Advent and Lent and above all at the Easter Vigil, re-reads and re-lives the great events of salvation history in the 'today' of her liturgy."[16]

In the celebration of the liturgy, Jesus' statement becomes true once again: "Today this scripture has been fulfilled in your hearing" (Luke 4:21, NRSV). We may affirm, however, that the liturgy accomplishes a still greater actualization, in that Christ himself "is present in his word since it is he himself who speaks when the holy scriptures are read in the Church" (*SC* 7).

In every case the fullness of the mystery of Christ is celebrated *per verbum et sacramentum.* That which is proclaimed in the Word is brought to its culmination in the sacramental act. Word leads to sacrament in the celebration, in the most profound of realities which assures that there may always be contact with the saving reality of Christ, who is always alive and active in the Spirit and in his community.[17] The liturgy "is the locus where the Word of God is brought to fullness once again, being made real by means of the memorial that celebrates it."[18]

[16] *CCC*, no. 1095.

[17] P. Visentin, "Celebrazione ecclesiale e dinamismo della Parola: Prospettiva teologiche," *Dall'esegesi all'ermeneutica attraverso la celebrazione, Bibbia e Liturgia* 1, Caro Salutis Cardo, Contributi 6 (Padua, 1991) 183–191.

[18] A. M. Triacca, "La Parola celebrata: Teologia della Celebrazione della Parola," *Dall'esegesi all'ermeneutica attraverso la celebrazione, Bibbia e Liturgia* 1, Caro Salutis Cardo, Contributi 6 (Padua, 1991) 46.

The sacramental presence of the glorious Christ in the liturgical year is none other than the paschal mystery of Christ made real in the actualization of the salvation accomplished by God in Christ for us. This is possible because "with God 'Today' is an abiding presence."[19] The mystery of Christ is made manifest by means of the "mysteries," which are the "actions" by means of which Christ reveals the saving plan of God. However, the Church can proclaim at all its feasts that that day is the "today" of the mystery commemorated on that particular day.[20] The faith of the Church sees that all the events of the life of its Savior are "mysteries" that bring salvation. Thus, the liturgical year is the celebration of the whole complex of the saving actions of Christ throughout the history of salvation from the beginning of its revelation in creation up unto its final realization.

Pius XII recognized, in the encyclical *Mediator Dei,* that the mysteries of the life of Christ are always present and working and that "each mystery brings its own special grace for our salvation."[21] While it is true that the encyclical speaks of the mysteries of Christ mostly as examples of virtue, thinking of them more in terms of exemplary morality than of ontology, the doctrine of Pius XII is extremely important in reinforcing what we said above and will repeat here, in the words of Burkhard Neunheuser: "The causality of the individual mysteries of Christ works when we celebrate the corresponding feast, in the proclamation of the Word of God, in the celebration of the sacrament and all of the corresponding symbolic actions."[22]

In reality, the liturgical year is not a mirror of the earthly life of the Lord but of his "mystery," that is, the saving plan of God as it was revealed in Christ. Since it was Christ who carried out these deeds by which salvation was obtained, all the saving events that the Church celebrates, make present, by virtue of the Spirit, the mystery who is Christ. The purpose of all of this is not, as it may sometimes seem, to effect a dramatic reproduction of the life of Christ. The ultimate reality of all these celebrations is always the totality of the one mystery of Christ. In all the celebrations that seem in themselves to be partial, the

[19] Casel, *Mystery of Christian Worship,* 142.

[20] See, for instance *MR1970,* where the *Exsultet* of the Easter Vigil says: *Haec nox est, in qua, destructis vinculis mortis, Christus ab inferis victor ascendit.* See also the preface for Pentecost Sunday and the various texts of the Masses for Christmas.

[21] Pius XII, *Mediator Dei,* no. 165.

[22] B. Neunheuser, "L'année liturgique selon Dom Casel," *QLP* 38 (1957) 290.

Eucharist is celebrated in which the mystery is complete. "It is the entire saving mystery that is before the eyes of the Church. . . ."[23] The liturgical year may be understood as a single Easter Eucharist divided into many parts, each celebrating a different aspect of the redemptive mystery, throughout the course of the year.

The liturgical year takes up and develops during the annual cycle the mysteries of the Lord that the Eucharistic anamnesis commemorates.[24] In the celebrations of the Eucharist according to the ancient Mozarabic liturgy of Spain, there is a rite that is especially important in this regard. After the institution narrative, using the words of 1 Corinthians 11:24-25, with its twofold command to repeat the actions of Jesus, the priest, when he comes to the breaking of the bread, breaks the host into nine parts and arranges them in the form of a cross on the paten. Each piece stands for a mystery of the life of Jesus: incarnation, birth, circumcision, epiphany, passion, death, resurrection, glory (ascension), and kingdom (second coming).[25] One might say that it is not only the Body of the Lord, the Eucharist, which is on the altar in this case; rather, it is an image of the entire liturgical year. The prayer over the gifts for Holy Thursday *(MR1970)* says:

". . . quoties huius hostiae commemoratio celebratur, opus nostrae redemptionis exercetur."

The liturgical year has, therefore, a mystagogical dimension, that is, it introduces the faithful to the mystery of Christ.[26] The presence of Christ in the annual cycle is not static but dynamic, a communion-communication with the ecclesial assembly and each of its members. Participation in the mystery of worship nourishes faith, increases hope, strengthens charity (cf. the prayer after communion of the First Sunday of Lent in *MR1970*). It is especially the collects (i.e., the opening prayers) and the prayers after communion that express this aspect of the celebration. Two examples follow:

[23] Casel, *Mystery of Christian Worship*, 67.

[24] O. Casel, *Faites ceci en mémoire de moi*, LO 34 (Paris, 1962) 41–44. The author compares the development of the anamnesis of the Eucharistic Prayer with the development of the liturgical year beginning with the nucleus of the paschal mystery.

[25] See the *Missale Hispano-Mozarabicum*, nos. 124–130 (*Praenotanda), Not* 24 (1988) 712–714.

[26] See *CCC*, no. 1075.

Tribue nobis, quaesumus, Domine, mysteriis paschalibus convenienter aptari, ut quae laetanter exsequimur perpetua virutute nos tueantur et salvent (*MR1970*, collect for Friday of the Fifth Week of Easter).

Quos tuis, Domine, reficis sacramentis, continuis attolle benignus auxiliis, ut redemptionis effectum et mysteriis capiamus et moribus (*MR1970*, prayer after communion for the Twenty-Fifth Sunday in Ordinary Time).

"To conform our life" to the paschal mystery or to be "transformed" by the mysteries that are celebrated is not to be understood merely on the psychological, emotional, intellectual, or ethical levels but on the level of one's very being. From one's participation in the mysteries of Christ one should derive evidence of a life:

. . . *Domine, supplices deprecamur, ut, quod in nobis mysterio geritur, opere impleatur* (prayer after communion for the Third Sunday of Lent).

The saving time of the liturgical year is for the Church. The mystery of Christ becomes the source of life for the Church (cf. *MR1970*, prayer after communion for the Saturday after Ash Wednesday), and the Church, in its turn, completes the mystery of Christ. The *today* of the liturgical festivals reveals at one and the same time the time-bound and eternal nature of the mysteries they celebrate as well as their meaning for the life of the faithful.

5. In the Various Mysteries of the Annual Cycle, We Celebrate the One Mystery of Christ

"In the liturgical year the various aspects of the one Paschal mystery unfold."[27] In fact, although the various phases of the annual cycle pause for a while to contemplate certain saving events, they do so in view of the one saving design carried out by Christ that culminated in the mystery of Easter. This cyclical memorial of Christ follows an itinerary of three seasons: Advent-Christmas-Epiphany, Lent-Easter, Ordinary Time. We will show its essential contents not by following a chronological-liturgical order but rather one that is theological-liturgical.

a) During Lent-Easter the Church proclaims the paschal events of the passion, death, resurrection, and ascension of Christ, which lead up to the gift of the Spirit. These events are celebrated as the central moment and fulfillment of the saving plan of God for humanity. So these events have a meaning "for us," insofar as we have become par-

[27] Ibid., no. 1171.

takers of the new life of the Risen Lord. This is what the Church celebrates in a particular fashion, with a variety of symbols, at the Easter Vigil, the heart both of the paschal celebrations and the entire liturgical year. But Lent, which is the preparation for it, and the fifty days of the season of Pentecost, which prolong it, celebrate the same reality.

Lent is structured as a real spiritual journey, according to three modalities that are different from each other but form a complementary whole. It allows us to retrace, guided by the pages of the Old and New Testaments, the principal stages of the history of salvation that culminates in the Pasch of Jesus. We relive this history knowing that we too are its real protagonists. In this way the liturgy invites us to true faith and conversion so that we might accept the gift of God.

The Easter season celebrates the same events of the Pasch of Jesus, illustrating, however, the fruits that we derive from the Church by means of the sacraments of initiation (baptism, confirmation, and Eucharist) and the grace of the action of the Holy Spirit. The preface for the Mass of Pentecost Sunday says that the gift of the Holy Spirit "brought the paschal mystery to its completion." By its participation in the paschal sacraments, the Church is constituted, in the Spirit, as one reality with the Lord Jesus, the Body of Christ. The entire mystery of the Church takes its origin in Easter and finds there its eternal strength. The paschal event is lived as an ecclesial-sacramental event, as a force for renewal and witness, as the source of growth and mission for the Church, as an anticipation of new life and an expectation of final fulfillment in Christ. This is all suggested by the reading at Mass of the Book of Revelation during this season.

b) The content of the season of Advent-Christmas-Epiphany is contemplated at the liturgy in the framework of salvation history. In particular, the birth of Jesus is seen in the context of God's saving design, brought to its completion by Christ at Easter. Jesus who was "descended from David according to the flesh" is the same who was "declared to be Son of God with power according to the spirit of holiness by resurrection from the dead." (cf. Rom 1:1-7, NRSV).[28] The birth of Jesus is celebrated as the birth of the Redeemer who comes to save us. The prayer over the gifts at the evening Mass of the Vigil of Christmas expresses this idea in the following words:

[28] This passage from the writings of St. Paul is the second reading on the Second Sunday of Advent (Year A).

Tanto nos, Domine, quaesumus, promptiore servitio haec praecurrere concede sollemnia, quanto in his constare principium nostrae redemptionis ostendis.

The liturgy knows that Christmas is always present in the Church in the light and reality of the paschal mystery.

The second coming of Christ, a recurrent theme especially in the first weeks of Advent, is closely connected with the first coming. The certainty of the coming of Christ in the flesh encourages us as we wait for his glorious final appearance, when the messianic promises will be finally and completely fulfilled. In fact, in the birth of Jesus the ancient promises are fulfilled, and the way to eternal salvation is opened. This is a salvation which, although it has already been accomplished at Easter, will be definitively fulfilled when the Lord returns. This idea is developed in the first preface for Advent:

Qui, primo adventu in humilitate carnis assumptae, dispositionis antiquae munus implevit, nobisque salutis perpetuae tramitem reseravit: ut, cum secundo venerit in suae gloria maiestatis, manifesto demum munere capiamus, quod vigilantes nunc audemus exspectare promissum.

The Church awaits him who is already present in its midst but who will reveal himself anew at the glorious final manifestation. The hope that Advent proclaims is an invitation to accept the gradual nature of the way in which salvation is finalized in us and in the world.

During this season of the annual cycle, the liturgical texts ask of us a certain vigilance that is made manifest in our good works, honesty, and conversion in view of communion with God. It brings to birth within us a joy that stems from the experience of salvation. The theme of joy is present, especially in the texts for the Third Sunday of Advent. The entrance antiphon in the Missal invites us to rejoice always in the Lord. The same theme shows up again in the opening prayer, in a number of antiphons in the Liturgy of the Hours, and in some of the biblical readings heard at Mass.

c) Ordinary Time, beginning with Sunday, its fundamental nucleus, presents a global reading of the mystery of Christ. On Sunday the reality of the paschal mystery of the Lord's death, resurrection, and ascension is perpetuated. On this day, the way of prayer, the acceptance of the gift of the salvation, and our waiting for the final Sunday that will never end are all brought together. The semi-continuous reading of the Gospel is the proclamation of the Risen Christ, whose earthly life among people is contemplated, episode by episode. In the daily contemplation of the words and deeds of Jesus, we are helped to assume the attitude that guided Christ in his life, a total giving over to the will of the Father, even to the giving of self. To understand the mystery of Christ as it is presented during Ordinary Time means that we have to take the nature of discipleship seriously. This means we must listen and follow the Master in daily life, not putting it into parentheses but seeing it as a saving moment. The semi-continuous reading of the other books of the Old and New Testaments offers us the chance to measure our following or imitation of Christ against that of the People of God and the faithful perseverance of the primitive Christian community. Ordinary Time is a time for continual confrontation with the life of Christ, with which the Christian's life becomes ever more deeply joined.

The strong presence in the calendar of the memorials of the martyrs and the saints during this season of the liturgical year must be considered in light of this deepening of the mystery of Christ in us. The saints, in particular the martyrs, fully participated in the paschal mystery of the Lord, and their sanctity consists in that participation. The saints are holy insofar as they identify with Christ, insofar as they live in the full communion with the Easter Christ. It is in this context that the saints are presented as models of the Christian life and valid intercessors for the People of God (cf. *SC* 104).

6. Conclusion

The liturgical year does not take up the events of Jesus' earthly life in order to consider them either from a merely historical or chronological point of view, or even as models to be imitated. The liturgical year celebrates the mystery of Christ made present for us in time in the hearing of the Word and in participation in the sacraments. The liturgical year has, therefore, a sacramental character. It is more a *memoria* than an *imitatio*, more an ἀνάμνεσις than a μίμησις. Consequently, the spirituality of the liturgical year is a process of progressive transformation in Christ. In the course of the annual cycle, the community is called to rediscover, to celebrate, and to live the gift of salvation.

In concluding, we argue that the theology of the liturgical year presupposes what we might call the fundamental theology of the liturgy. If the liturgical year is the ecclesial celebration of the mystery of Christ in the passage of time, its theology is the same as that of the liturgy itself. What is specific to the theology of the liturgical year is simply to be found in the cyclical celebration of the mystery of Christ in the time and space of the solar year. The passage of the liturgical seasons and the feasts creates a particular reading of the mystery of Christ. This emerges from the biblical and euchological texts used by the Church in the celebration of the mystery and the mysteries of Christ.

Bibliography

Auf der Maur, H. *Feiern im Rhythmus der Zeit* I: *Herrenfeste in Woche und Jahr.* Gottesdienst der Kirche: Handbuch der Liturgiewissenschaft, Teil 5, 223–228. Regensburg, 1983.

Augé, M. "Teologia dell'Anno liturgico." *Anàmnesis* 6:9–34.

Barsotti, D. *Il mistero cristiano nell'anno liturgico.* 2nd ed. Florence, 1956.

Bergamini, A. "Anno liturgico." *NDL* 60–66.

Casel, O. *The Mystery of Christian Worship.* Westminster, Md., 1962.

Marsili, S. "Anno liturgico." In *I segni del mistero di Cristo: Teologia liturgica dei sacramenti,* 408–411. BELS 42. Rome, 1987.

Triacca, A. M. "Anno liturgico: Verso una sua organica trattazione teologica." *Salesianum* 38 (1976) 613–621.

Vagaggini, C. *Theological Dimensions of the Liturgy.* Trans. L. Doyle and W. Jurgens. Collegeville, Minn., 1976.

Verheul, A. "L'Année liturgique: De l'histoire à la théologie." *QL* 74 (1993) 5–16.

Part III

Liturgical Space

Ignazio M. Calabuig, O.S.M.

13

The Rite of the Dedication of a Church

When the assembly *(ecclesia)* of the Lord's disciples gathers to celebrate the divine mysteries, it creates a "holy space," and there a building for worship is usually erected, provided the assembly continues to meet there. But the relationship between the community and the place where it meets is such that, by a happy ambiguity, the name of the assembly itself becomes the name of the building: Church/church.

Once the habitual place of meeting becomes a "building for worship," the community feels the necessity, and the joy, of reserving it exclusively for worship of God by means of an action that expresses this decision and, more importantly, calls down God's favor upon it. So it is today, so it was in antiquity. This eminently liturgical action is the rite of dedication of a church.

As the assembly gave its name to the building, so too it has impressed on the actions and texts of the rite of dedication its own face and its consciousness of its nature, its relationship with Christ and, through him, with the Father and the Holy Spirit, its mission, and its journey toward the eschaton.

The rite of dedication of a church is not used frequently; it is inevitably something extraordinary, even though, as today, it has become accessible to the majority of the ecclesial communities. It is extraordinary because churches are not built every day and because, too, many local communities have already had their churches for centuries.

In any case, the liturgy of dedication gives the Lord's disciples a favorable occasion for reflecting on their own identity, the authenticity of their worship, the seriousness of their commitment to the Church, and the genuineness of their following of Christ.

But the rite of dedication is also the result of a long and complex process; it is therefore necessary to trace its history, even though this is sometimes lacking in interest. This history runs from the pre-Constantinian period to our day. It will enable us to discern the line of development, to single out the constant ritual sequences and the most characteristic elements, and to grasp the features the rite has gradually taken on due to events in the history of the Church and of the various cultural periods.

THE PRE-CONSTANTINIAN PERIOD

We must not expect to find a ritual for the dedication of church in the first three centuries of Christianity. Churches did not exist, for at least two reasons. First, historical conditions did not permit the construction of buildings of worship for the Christian communities, lacking as they did a juridical personality and subject as they were to recurring persecutions. In addition, the communities with their basis in the teaching of Christ and the apostles were reluctant to provide themselves with a building for worship. They could boast that, in contrast to paganism, they had neither temples nor altars nor images nor victims. Toward the end of the first or beginning of the second century, Minucius Felix, an apologist, wrote:

"You think that because we have neither temples nor altars, we are hiding the object of our worship. But what image can you imagine to honor God, when, if you think carefully about it, human beings themselves are his images? What temple can you build for him when the entire universe which he created cannot contain him? . . . Is it not better to dedicate to him a sanctuary in our souls? . . . The victim that pleases him is a right spirit, a pure heart, a sincere soul. To practice virtue, then, is to call upon God; to practice justice is to offer sacrifices to God; to abstain from cheating is to render God favorable; to snatch a human being from danger is to sacrifice to God the best kind of victim. There you have our sacrifice, there you have the worship due to God."[1]

For this worship they did not need buildings of stone. This passage from Minucius Felix and other contemporary texts[2] show how deeply the disciples had imbibed the Pauline idea of "spiritual worship" (Rom 12:1), which was derived from the teaching of the Lord.

[1] Minucius Felix, *Octavius* 32 (CSEL 2, 45–46).

[2] See Origen, *Contra Celsum* VIII, 17 (SCh 150, 210–212).

1. The Teaching of the New Testament

By his actions and his words Jesus had brought about a profound change in the attitude of the disciples toward the Jerusalem temple and Levitical worship. At the very moment of his death, "the curtain of the temple was torn in two, from top to bottom" (Matt 27:51) to signify the end of a worship that was bound up with the temple and, more generally, the end of Judaism as part of the economy of salvation. Moreover, at the beginning of his ministry, Jesus performed a very meaningful "purification" of the temple (John 2:13-22) and announced its replacement by his own risen body (John 2:18-22) as the center of a new worship in spirit and in truth (John 4:20-24), the place in which "the whole fullness of deity dwells bodily" (Col 2:9), the sacred enclosure from which, more than from the temple of Ezekiel's vision (Ezek 47:1-12), water gushes "from the spring of the water of life" (Rev 21:6; see John 4:13-14; 7:37-39; 19:34).[3]

When the Apostle Peter speaks of the communion of life that the sacraments of initiation establish between Christians and Christ, the "living stone," he instructs them: "Like living stones, let yourselves be built into a spiritual house, to be a holy priesthood, to offer spiritual sacrifices acceptable to God through Jesus Christ" (1 Pet 2:5).

In the letters of Paul "the transference to the community and to the faithful of the attributes of the Temple—the house of God, of the living God, sanctity—is made quite naturally by St. Paul as he writes. He presupposes that this is an established and self-evident fact . . .:"[4] "Do you not know that you are God's temple and that God's Spirit dwells in you? If anyone destroys God's temple, God will destroy that person. For God's temple is holy, and you are that temple" (1 Cor 3:16-17; see 6:19); "We are the temple of the living God" (2 Cor 6:16). The Church is the "temple of God," because by reason of faith and baptism the Spirit of God dwells in Christians.

[3] Still valuable is Y. Congar, *The Mystery of the Temple,* trans. R. F. Trevett (Westminster, Md., 1962). On the idea of worship in the New Testament and the cultic experience of the Church see: O. Casel, *The Mystery of Christian Worship and Other Writings,* ed. B. Neunheuser (Westminster, Md., 1962); S. Lyonnet, "La nature du culte dans le NT," in *La liturgie après Vatican II,* ed. J. P. Jossua and Y. Congar (Paris, 1967) 357–384; O. Cullmann, *La fede e il culto della Chiesa primitiva* (Rome, 1974); S. Marsili, "La liturgia, momento storico della salvezza," in *Anàmnesis* 1:33–156.

[4] Congar, *The Mystery of the Temple,* 151.

2. *Toward the House Church* (Domus Ecclesiae)

After Pentecost the disciples of Christ continued to go to the temple (see Acts 2:46; 5:42), but soon, especially for the memorial they were to celebrate according to the command of the Lord (see 1 Cor 11:23-26), they turned their homes into special places of Christian worship: "Day by day, as they spent much time together in the temple, they broke bread at home and ate their food with glad and generous hearts, praising God and having the goodwill of all the people" (Acts 2:46-47). The eucharistic meaning of the phrase "they broke bread" is commonly accepted by the exegetes. In any case, the celebration of the Eucharist, insofar as it is a celebration of the new Passover, came to be held in the same domestic setting as the old Passover (see Exod 12:1-14).

Some of these houses are explicitly mentioned: first of all, the "room upstairs" (Acts 1:13) where the disciples met, "together with certain women, including Mary the mother of Jesus, as well as his brothers" (Acts 1:14), while awaiting the gift of the Spirit. It was probably this same house in which the risen Jesus appeared to his disciples on Easter Sunday (Luke 24:33) and to which Peter went after being set free: "the house of Mary, the mother of John whose other name was Mark, where many had gathered and were praying" (Acts 12:12). Then there was the house of Aquila and Priscilla, both in Ephesus (see 1 Cor 16:19) and in Rome (see Rom 16:5), where the Christian community (ἐκκλησία) gathered; the house of Philemon, in which the community at Colossae gathered (Phlm 2); the house in Troas where Paul celebrated a nocturnal Sunday Eucharist in a well-lit room on the third floor (see Acts 20:7-12).

The repetition, in the same house, of the eucharistic celebration and of meetings for prayer, in an atmosphere of faith and fellowship, turned it into a fixed place of Christian worship, with consequent architectural adaptations. We have two important examples of such houses: the *domus Ecclesiae* of Dura Europos (Syria), a type of house common in the Middle East, dating back to around 250 and used permanently, perhaps exclusively, for the community's liturgical celebrations: a room with paintings on its walls—the Good Shepherd, Adam and Eve, Peter saved from shipwreck on Lake Tiberias, etc.—and a pool that served as a baptistery; two adjoining rooms which suggest a "distinction between prayer-room and supper-room."[5] The second

[5] B. Bagatti, "Dura Europos," *Encyclopedia of the Early Church* 1 (New York, 1992) 255.

example is the house of Peter at Capernaum, sanctified by the frequent presence of the Lord, which "very quickly became a place of religious meetings for the Christian community of Jewish origin."[6]

The supreme expression of Christian worship—the celebration of the Eucharist—came into being in a house, in "a large room upstairs, already furnished" (Luke 22:12). It could therefore continue to be celebrated and experienced in a house.

FOURTH TO SEVENTH CENTURIES

The edict of Licinius and Constantine (313) granted the Christian community not only religious freedom but the right to own places of public worship.[7] Eusebius (d. ca. 339) wrote: "The next stage was the spectacle prayed and longed for by us all—dedication festivals in the cities and consecrations of the newly built places of worship."[8] The Christian communities were now faced with a very important problem: the choice of an architectural model for their places of worship. Since neither the Jerusalem temple nor the synagogue nor, a fortiori, the pagan temple could be an acceptable point of reference, they chose as a model the *basilica forense,* a civic building that had plenty of room for meetings, which was after all an essential requirement of the Christian liturgy.

Eusebius speaks explicitly of "dedication festivals," to be understood as meaning, not a celebration according to an already existing ritual *(ordo),* but a sacred ceremony that combined deeply rooted anthropological elements (the inauguration of a building has always been a festive and popular event), others of a generically religious kind, familiar to pagans (processions, sprinkling with purifying water, the offering of sacrifices), and still others clearly derived from the Bible. The Scriptures were, after all, familiar with dedications of pillars (see Gen 28:18), altars (see Num 7:10-11, 84, 88), and, above all, the several dedications of the temple in Jerusalem.[9]

[6] S. Loffreda, *Cafarnao: La città di Gesù* (Jerusalem, 1978) 30.

[7] Lactantius, *De morte persecutorum* 48, 5-10 (SCh 39, 133–134).

[8] Eusebius of Caesarea, *Historia ecclesiastica* 10, 3, 1 (SCh 55, 80); ET: *The History of the Church,* trans. G. A. Williamson (Baltimore, 1965) 382.

[9] See 1 Kgs 8 (dedication of Solomon's temple); Ezra 6:13-18 (dedication of the temple of Zerubbabel); 1 Mac 4:36-61 (dedication of the temple in the time of Judas Maccabeus, after its profanation by Antiochus).

1. The First Historical Testimony

The cathedral of Tyre was solemnly dedicated between 316 and 319. Eusebius, who gave the address at the dedication, tells us of it.[10] The ritual of the celebration, which was attended by a great throng of people and in which a large number of bishops participated, must have consisted essentially of the eucharistic synaxis, with the proclamation of suitable readings and the singing of appropriate psalms.[11]

Eusebius shows himself clear about the idea that the "living temple of the living God"[12] is the community of the faithful, but as an orator and a bishop of the court, he feels the fascination of great buildings[13] and the pomp of the Jerusalem temple, which he evokes several times in his address. The building of splendid basilicas throughout the empire and a widespread sense of "victory" lead to a dangerous change: the return to the vocabulary of the Old Testament and the mentality at work in Levitical worship, from which the New Testament had deliberately distanced itself:

"Due to influences exerted by the external environment, both religious and of the court, on the basilical celebration, the basilica was given the name 'temple' and was gradually understood to be the sumptuous dwelling of God. The eucharistic liturgy was again associated with the idea of a 'sacrifice' carried out by a specialized personnel (the clergy); the table became a sacred stand, untouchable by the laity, lit by candelabra, clothed in precious hangings, and hidden by veils *(tetravela)* that concealed the course of the sacred mysteries from the eyes of the profane."[14]

[10] The discourse, addressed to Paulinus, bishop of Tyre, is certainly by Eusebius. It is reproduced in the latter's *Historia ecclesiastica* 10, 4, 2–72 (SCh 55, 81–104).

[11] In his address Eusebius cites various psalms. It may be thought that some of these which were especially appropriate were actually sung during the rite of dedication: Psalm 86(87):3 ("Glorious things are said of thee, O city of God"); Psalm 117(118):22 ("The stone which the builders rejected has become the head of the corner"); Psalm 121(122):1 ("I rejoiced at the things that were said to me: 'We shall go into the house of the Lord'").

[12] *Historia ecclesiastica* 10, 4, 22 (SCh 55, 88); ET, 388.

[13] In his eulogy of Bishop Paulinus (*Historia ecclesiastica* 10, 4, 37–45: SCh 55, 93–96), Eusebius extols the grandeur and splendor of the cathedral of Tyre, which Paulinus had built.

[14] G. Genero, "Una dimora per celebrare i santi misteri: Tappe storiche dell'architettura liturgica," in *La dimora di Dio tra gli uomini: Tempio e assemblea* (Acts of the 43rd National Liturgical Week, Rome, 1993) 23.

The Fathers did not fail to criticize this deviation, even as early as the fourth century, but especially in the fifth.[15]

2. Elements Making Up the Dedication of a Church

In the period from the first half of the fifth century to the seventh century inclusive, we already find most of the ritual sequences that would be more or less successfully combined and give rise to the spacious rite of the dedication of a church.

a) Celebration of the Eucharist

In both East and West the essential act in the dedication of a church is the celebration of the Eucharist. When Eusebius notes with satisfaction the building of churches everywhere, the "description" he gives of a dedication makes of it a celebration of the Eucharist with a lengthy liturgy of the Word:

"Our leaders performed ceremonies with full pomp, and ordained priests [celebrated] the sacraments and majestic rites of the Church, here with the singing of psalms and intoning of the prayers given us from God, there with the carrying out of divine and mystical ministrations; while over all were the ineffable symbols of the Saviour's Passion. And together, people of every age, male and female alike, with all their powers of mind, rejoicing in heart and soul, gave glory through prayers and thanksgiving to the Author of their happiness, God Himself. Every one of the dignitaries of the Church present delivered a public oration according to his ability, inspiring the great audience."[16]

In Rome, for a long period, the rite of dedication of a church included only the celebration of the Eucharist. Pope Vigilius explained Roman practice in 538, in a reply to Bishop Profuturus of Braga: "If a basilica of the saints has been renovated from the foundation up, then, beyond

[15] A typical example is this passage from St. Jerome (d. 420): "The true temple of Christ is the soul of the believer; adorn it, clothe it, offer it gifts, receive Christ into it. Of what value is it to make walls gleam with jewels while Christ dies of hunger in the poor?" (*Epistula* 58, 8; CSEL 54, 536–537).

[16] *Historia ecclesiastica* 10, 3, 3–4 (SCh 55, 80–81); ET, 383. Eusebius is not, strictly speaking, describing the rite of the dedication of a church but is enthusiastically conveying the immensity of the whole affair. Scholars see in the phrase "divine and mystical ministrations" (θειαῖς καὶ μυστικαῖς . . . διακονίαις) clear reference to the eucharistic celebration.

any doubt, the sanctification attendant upon a consecration will be completely accomplished when the rite of Mass is celebrated in it."[17] Pope Vigilius knows of the practice of placing relics of the martyrs under the altar, but he does not regard this as necessary, "for we know that the consecration of any church in which no shrine [= relics of the martyrs] is included, is accomplished simply by the celebration of Masses."[18]

b) Depositing of martyrs' relics

In the second half of the fourth century and in certain places (northern Italy, the East, etc.), the placing of martyrs' relics beneath the altar became an integral part of the rite of dedication of a church. Various factors played a part in the introduction of this element.

The first was a fact of the *history of worship,* namely, the very ancient veneration of the martyrs. This found expression in the practice of adorning their tombs with decorative components: ornamental friezes, paintings, arched niches *(arcosolia),* lamps, inscriptions, and so on; in the building of monuments or small sacred shrines *(aedicula)* over the tombs; in the celebration of the Eucharist on the anniversary of their martyrdom; in the jealous safeguarding of literary memorials and the quasi-liturgical reading of the *Acta martyrum;* in pilgrimages to their tombs in order to obtain protection and help; and in the desire of each community to possess their own relics of the great heroes of the faith, which were regarded as "more precious than very costly gems."[19]

Other factors were *theological:* the assimilation of the martyrs, regarded as true and perfect disciples,[20] to Jesus crucified, whose attitude of self-surrender and forgiveness the martyrs made their own (see Acts 7:55-60); the relationship between the death of the martyrs, which is the sacrifice of their own lives, and the eucharistic celebration, which is the ritual sacrifice of Christ's death; the eschatological thrust of the death of the martyrs, who sacrifice the present life for the

[17] Vigilius, *Epistula ad Profuturum episcopum Bracarensem* 4 (PL 69:18).

[18] Ibid.

[19] *Martyrdom of Polycarp* 18, 2 (SCh 10, 268).

[20] A text of Ignatius of Antioch, himself a martyr, that expresses this idea is rightly famous: "Incite the wild beasts to become my sepulcher and leave nothing of my body behind, so that when I am dead I shall burden no one. I shall be *truly a disciple of Christ* when the world shall see my body no more" (*Letter to the Romans* 4, 2: SCh 10, 130).

sake of the future, eternal life, and the eschatological character of the Eucharist, which the Church celebrates in expectation of the glorious coming of Christ (see 1 Cor 11:26); the bond established within the communion of saints between the martyrs, who live in God, and the community that preserves their mortal remains; the relationship between "martyr and altar," attested in Revelation 6:9, where, at the opening of the "fifth seal," the seer discovers "under the altar the souls of those who had been slaughtered for the word of God and for the testimony they had given," which is a graphic expression of the association of the martyrs, witnesses to the Word, with the sacrifice of Christ.

Still other factors were *liturgical* and *architectural:* the central place given to the altar within the basilica reflects the centrality of Christ in the liturgical assembly, of which the martyrs are the most eminent "members"; the transformation of the altar from movable wooden table to fixed structure of stone. From these considerations it follows, on the one hand, that the greatest honor that can be given to witnesses of Christ is to bury them beneath the altar, where the sacrificial offering of their Lord is perpetuated; and, on the other, that the relics of the martyrs are regarded as gems more precious than even splendid basilicas.

The placing of the relics of the martyrs is not intended to "sanctify" the new space for worship or, much less, the altar.[21] It has its place in the ongoing rite of dedication: the "presence" of the relics of the martyrs increases the joy of the community, which is already gladdened by the inauguration of a new church building; the altar with the relics, that is, Christ with his most outstanding witnesses, brings to completion the symbolic meaning of the church as building.

Ambrose of Milan (d. 397) is an important witness to the practice of depositing martyrs' relics in its connection with the dedication of a church. The saint, who in this matter follows the usage of the East, is aware that the depositing of the relics is not an essential element, but he regards it as having pastoral value. From the viewpoint of a theology of the liturgy, his thinking has an exemplary correctness:

[21] The 1977 rite of the dedication of a church nicely sums up the ecclesial tradition: "It is not . . . the bodies of the martyrs that render the altar glorious; it is the altar that renders the burial place of the martyrs glorious," *ODEA* IV, 5; ET in *The Rites of the Catholic Church* (New York, 1980; Collegeville, Minn., 1991) 2:407.

"Let these triumphant victims approach the place where Christ is the offered victim. But he who suffered for all is upon the altar; those who have been redeemed by his suffering are beneath the altar."[22]

But the depositing of the relics was attended with a difficulty: relics of martyrs were not always available in a particular place. Various solutions of the difficulty were adopted: the fragmenting of the martyrs' bones in order to multiply relics; the transfer of relics from one place to another; the use of "substitute relics" *(sanctuaria, brandea),* that is, objects, usually pieces of cloth, that had been touched to the martyrs' bodies or at least to their tombs.

Rome would for a long time be opposed to the fragmentation of the bodies of the martyrs.[23] The Christian East, however, did not scruple to divide the bones of the martyrs and to transfer them from one city to another.

c) Anointing with chrism

As early as the patristic age, the Church's reflection on Christ led it to see in the altar of Hebrews 13:10 a reference to Christ: "We have an altar (θυσιαστήριον; = Christ) from which those who officiate in the tent [or: tabernacle] have no right to eat,"[24] and to coin the formula according to which Christ is victim, priest, and altar of his own sacrifice.[25]

The Fathers had also reached this identification between Christ and altar—*altare Christus est*—from the Pauline allegory according to

[22] Ambrose of Milan, *Epistula* 77 (22), 13 (CSEL 82/3, 134).

[23] Usually cited on this point is Gregory the Great's answer to Empress Constantina, who had asked him for "the head of St. Paul or some part of his body": "Let the Most Serene Lady know that when Romans give relics of the saints, it is not their custom to dare take something from the body. They only send a box containing a piece of cloth that has been placed on the most sacred bodies of the saints. This is placed with due veneration in the church to be dedicated; so great are the works of power accomplished by this relic, that it is as if the saints' bodies had been brought to that particular place" (*Registrum* IV, Epist. 30, in *MGH, Epistulae,* ed. P. Ewald and L. M. Hartmann, 1:264–265).

[24] According to C. Spicq, who is followed by many exegetes, the altar in Hebrews 13:10, which is contrasted with the tabernacle or tent, "can only signify the center of the new worship, Jesus Christ, and, more precisely, Christ sacrificed" (C. Spicq, *L'Epître aux Hébreux* II: *Commentaire* [Paris, 1953] 425).

[25] See *Rites of the Catholic Church* 2, IV, 1. Let me cite, from among many patristic texts, this one from St. Epiphanius of Salamis (d. 403): "In which [the sacrifice of the cross] one and the same [Christ] was victim, sacrifice, priest, altar, God, man, king, high priest, sheep, lamb" (*Panarion* II, 1: *Haeresis* 55; PG 41:479).

which "the rock was Christ" (1 Cor 10:4). But the name "Christ" means "Anointed." How, then, could the altar be a complete symbol of the "Lord's Anointed" unless it too were anointed? It was doubtless some such considerations that suggested the rite of anointing the altar, but the rite was intended, above all, to repeat the gesture of Jacob, who "took the stone that he had put under his head and set it up for a pillar and poured oil on the top of it" (Gen 28:18).

This rite certainly originated in the East. Ephraem the Syrian (d. 373) is the first witness to it; in singing his praise of oil he writes: "Oil . . . provides anointing for altars, because they bear the sacrifice of reconciliation."[26] In the second half of the fifth century Pseudo-Dionysius attests that the anointing of altars was a rite regularly prescribed both canonically and liturgically: "The rubrics for the most holy sacraments lay down that the divine altar must be consecrated with sacred outpourings of the ointment."[27]

From the East the rite passed to Gaul, where it became increasingly important. The Council of Agde (506), celebrated with Caesarius of Arles as president, decreed that a "priestly blessing" be added to the anointing,[28] and the Council of Epaona that only altars of stone could be anointed with sacred chrism.[29]

In Spain, Council II of Seville (619), with St. Isidore presiding, while energetically confirming that bishops alone had authority to set up, bless, and anoint altars, let it be understood that the practice of anointing altars was of long standing.[30]

[26] *Hymnus de oleo* I, 3, in *S. Ephraem Syri, hymni et sermones,* ed. Th. J. Lamy (Malines, 1886) 2:788. The idea is seen again in *Testamentum Domini* (fifth century): "Oil . . . provides anointing for altars, so that they may bear our sacrifice" (*Testamentum Domini nostri Iesu Christi,* ed. I. E. Rahmani [Mainz, 1889] 156).

[27] Pseudo-Dionysius the Areopagite, *Ecclesiastica hierarchia* IV, 12; ET: *Pseudo-Dionysius: The Complete Works,* trans. C. Luibheid, The Classics of Western Spirituality (New York, 1987) 232.

[28] "It has been decided that altars should be consecrated not only by anointing with chrism but also by a priestly blessing" (Concilium Agathense, 14; CCL 148, 200).

[29] "Altars are not to be consecrated by anointing with chrism unless they are made of stone" (Concilium Epaonense 26; CCL 148A, 30).

[30] "Let presbyters . . . not dare arrogate to themselves . . . what is permitted only to high priests . . . such actions as the ordination of presbyters and deacons and the consecration of virgins; or the erection and blessing or anointing of an altar; nor may they licitly consecrate a church or an altar" (Concilium Hispalense II, n. VIII; Mansi 10:559).

Rome does not seem to have been attracted by this rite with its evident Old Testament origin. The rite would be introduced there only in the eighth century.

d) Washing with water

The washing with blessed *(exorcizata)* water is another element that goes back to the period we are examining here (fourth to seventh centuries). The use of ritual washings had been frequent in both Jewish and pagan worship. Their use in the dedication of churches is attested in the East, Gaul, and Rome. In his already mentioned letter to Profuturus of Braga (538), Pope Vigilius says that the washings are not necessary in the dedication of a restored church,[31] thereby letting it be understood that they were customary in other dedications. Gregory the Great (d. 604), in a letter to the missionary monks in England, decided, with great pastoral tact, that pagan temples *(fana idolorum)* were not to be destroyed but were to be changed into places of worship of the true God, having first been sprinkled with blessed water.[32]

Washing with water and anointing with chrism: two ritual elements that liken the dedication of a church to Christian initiation. But, in my opinion, this parallelism was not deliberately sought by the authors of the ancient *ordines*; nevertheless, the parallelism did become both a key for interpreting the entire rite and a guide to its structure.[33]

[31] See *Epistula ad Profuturum Bracarensem* 4 (PL 69:18).

[32] "The shrines of idols belonging to that people [the Angles] should by no means be destroyed; rather, let the idols in them be destroyed. Water should be blessed, it should be sprinkled in these shrines; altars should be built and relics placed in them, for, provided the shrines are well built, they ought to be shifted from the worship of demons to the service of the true God" (*Registrum* XI, *Epistula* 56; *MGH, Epistulae* II, 331).

[33] In the eleventh century, Ivo of Chartres (d. 1115), in his *Sermo* 4: *De sacramentis dedicationis* (PL 162:527–535), gives an allegorical reading of the entire rite of dedication of a church. In it the various sprinklings and anointings are interpreted in light of the liturgy of the sacraments of Christian initiation. In our own century, the authors of the *Ordo ad ecclesiam dedicandam et consecrandam (PR1961)* took the outline of Christian initiation—baptism, confirmation, Eucharist—as their guiding idea in structuring the ritual of dedication. On the question see S. Marsili, "Dedicazione senza consacrazione. Ossia: teologia liturgica in una storia rituale," *RL* 66 (1979) 578–601, especially 582–586.

e) The opening of the door

The *aperitio ianuae* harks back, at least for its inspiration, to the rite celebrated in Constantinople by Patriarch Eutychius on December 24, 567, on occasion of the completion of the basilica of Hagia Sophia. The rite was a kind of dedication: the patriarch, surrounded by the people and carrying the book of Gospels, entered the basilica as the versicle *Attollite portas* (Ps 24:7, 9) was being sung. It was a simple, solemn, and meaningful rite: Christ, the true king of glory (Ps 24:8, 10), represented by the book of Gospels, enters the sanctuary of the new people of God, thereby fulfilling, even if only symbolically, the ancient liturgy of entrance into the temple.[34]

f) The sign of the cross

The rite of the *consignatio ecclesiae* goes back probably to the seventh century. The bishop, on entering a new church, traces a large cross, in the form of an X, on the floor. The rite was later expanded by adding the writing of the alphabet, in Greek and Latin, on a double layer of ashes strewn on the ground. Whatever its origin, the rite certainly signifies a taking possession.

g) First signs of regression

The grant of religious freedom, to begin with, and then the conversion of the barbarian peoples to Christianity led to the building of many places of worship, from the second half of the fourth century down through the seventh. There were, therefore, many "churches to be dedicated."

The faithful knew that only Christ, the community, and the individual faithful are the true temple of God; they knew, therefore, that the buildings they constructed were meant, not to "provide God with lodging," but to make available a place in which to fittingly celebrate the divine mysteries.[35] A "law of development" was at work that can be seen in any group when it becomes numerous. Communities everywhere were happy to build their own places of worship; they regarded

[34] The rite is described succinctly by John Malalas, *Chronographia,* Book 18 (PG 97:716).

[35] In this regard, there is a very illuminating text of St. Augustine: "The house of God is the city. For the house of God is the people of God, since the house of God is the temple of God. What does the Apostle say? 'The temple of God is holy, which you are (1 Cor 3:17)'" (*Enarrationes in Psalmos* 126, 3; CCL 40, 1858).

these as signs of their presence and identity in society. They felt that these buildings somehow reflected them, and so they did not hesitate to transfer their own name, *ecclesia*/church, to these buildings.[36]

As early as the period from the fifth to seventh centuries, however, there were signs of regression from the New Testament ideal:

—The sacralizing tendency became increasingly strong; for example, previously people were fully aware that a church became "sacred" due to the celebration in it of the divine mysteries; now, at least in some cases, they held it necessary first to "consecrate" the building in order that the divine mysteries might be celebrated in it.

—The altar, made now of stone and consecrated by anointing, came to be thought of not as the eucharistic *table* but as the *altar* of sacrifice, reserved to the sacred ministers alone, untouchable by the laity, inaccessible to women.

—Old Testament models became dominant. In many cases the magnificence of Solomon's temple, the grandiose rites of its dedication, the priesthood of Aaron, and Levitical worship exerted a powerful influence, but wrongly so, since people did not take into account that Old Testament worship was only a foreshadowing *(umbra)* of the truth, which belongs to the worship "in spirit and in truth" (John 4:24) that Christ willed.

—A tendency emerged, in part because of undertakings promoted by emperors and the wealthy, to erect buildings remarkable for their size, their architectural beauty, and the sumptuousness of their furnishings. This led to a strident contrast between the splendor of the church of stone and the wretchedness, in many cases, of the interior temple.

—Once the necessity of avoiding confusion with pagan rites had become a thing of the past, the practice grew of using terms that had previously been carefully avoided (*ara, templum,* etc.). But along with the words ideas crept in that were somewhat incompatible with the uniqueness of the *domus Ecclesiae* and the Christian sacrifice.

RITUALS OF THE EIGHTH CENTURY

In the eighth century we already find fairly well-structured rituals for the dedication of churches. Three of these have great historical importance: the Byzantine, the Roman, and the Gallican.

[36] On this philological development see the basic study by Ch. Mohrmann, "Les dénominations de l'église en tant qu'édifice en grec et en latin au cours des premiers siècles chrétiens," *RSR* 36 (1962) 155–174.

1. The Byzantine Ritual

The well-known *Codex Barberini* (Biblioteca Vaticana, ms. grec. 336), of the eighth century, contains the ritual for the dedication of a church according to the Byzantine rite.[37] The rite unfolds over two days: on the first, the bishop consecrates the altar in the presence only of the clergy; on the second, in the presence of the entire people, he inaugurates the new building for worship and dedicates it to the Lord. There is thus a clear distinction between "consecration" (καθιέρωσις) and "dedication" or inauguration (ἐγκαίνια).

The consecration of the altar has five parts:

—*litanic prayer and diaconal intercession,* in which, after recalling the great "dedications" of the Old Testament, the deacon asks the gift of the Spirit for the bishop and his ministers, that they may correctly accomplish the consecration of the altar and the dedication of the new church building;

—*purification with water:* the bishop washes the altar with baptismal water, pouring this on the table and pillars; after repeated and abundant washings, the bishop himself dries the table and pillars of the altar, while intoning first Psalm 83 *(Quam dilecta tabernacula tua),* then Psalm 131 *(Memento, Domine, David);*

—*anointing of the altar:* using holy μύρον, the bishop traces three crosses on the altar table, at the center and the two sides, and then with his thumb anoints with oil the entire surface of the table and its pillars, to the accompaniment of Psalm 132 *(Ecce quam bonum et quam iucundum)*. Then, as Psalm 92 is sung *(Dominus regnavit, decorem indutus est),* he spreads a cloth over the table;

—*incensation of the altar and anointing of the church:* after the anointing of the altar, which is the heart of the celebration, the bishop incenses the altar, the presbyterium, and the nave of the church, while reciting Psalm 25 *(Iudica me, Domine)* one or more times. Meanwhile, one of the concelebrating bishops anoints all the pillars of the church with μύρον, tracing a cross on each;

—*prayer of dedication:* the bishop concludes the rite with the prayer of dedication, in which he asks the "Lord of heaven and earth" that the new altar may become a "true holy of holies," before which the

[37] *BAR*, nn. 150–156, pp. 159–173. There is useful information on the Byzantine rite of dedication in S. Salaville, *Cérémonial de la consécration d'une église selon le rite byzantin avec introduction et notes explicatives* (Vatican Polyglot Press, 1937).

priests may stand as before the throne of God's glory and offer the unbloody sacrifice for the forgiveness of sins and the completion of all sanctification. The inauguration of the church takes place on the next day. The rite includes essentially two actions: the transfer of the relics and the celebration of the Eucharist;

—after a nocturnal vigil kept in a nearby church where the relics are displayed, the bishop at dawn ends the office with the acclamation: "Glory to you, O Christ, God, pride of all, joy of the martyrs." The procession follows immediately, with a bishop carrying the relics. When the procession reaches the new church, there, in front of the main door, the cantors intone the troparion: "Gates, lift up your portals," inspired by Psalm 24. The doors are opened and the bishop enters, carrying the relics, these *pignora* of holy Church, and followed by all the people; he puts the relics in the place prepared for them and, after the singing of the τρισάγιον, ends the translation with a prayer;

—the celebration of the "divine liturgy" follows, in which two readings are proclaimed: Hebrews 3:1-4 (the honor of the builder, Christ, surpasses that of the house, the Church) and Matthew 16:13-18 ("You are Peter, and on this rock I will build my Church").

2. *The Roman Ritual*

Ordo XLII: *Quomodo in sancta romana ecclesia reliquiae conduntur* is the ritual for the dedication of a church in eighth-century Rome.[38] The *Ordo* distinguishes several steps:

—*the procession with the relics* (nn. 1–3): as litanies are sung, the bishop betakes himself to the church where the relics are kept that are to be placed beneath the altar; at the end of the litanies, he says the prayer *Aufer a nobis,* places the relics on a paten, and gives this to a presbyter; the procession then returns, to the singing of the antiphon *Cum iucunditate exhibiti;*

—*preparatory rites* (nn. 4–6): on reaching the new church, the bishop enters, closes the door, and, with the help of the ministers, performs some preliminary rites: he blesses the water *(aqua exorcizata),* prepares the cement (a mixture of water, chrism, and lime) for sealing the sepulcher *(confessio),* and washes the altar *(baptizat altare);*

—*entrance of the relics, and their deposition* (nn. 7–12): meanwhile the choir sings a second litany; at the end of it the bishop leaves the

[38] See M. Andrieu, ed., *Les Ordines Romani du haut moyen âge* (Louvain, 1956) 4:351–413.

church and says the prayer *Deus, qui in omni loco*; he takes the relics and, as a third litany is sung, carries them in procession to the altar and places them on it; he anoints the four corners of the *concession* with chrism and places the relics in it, along with three particles of the Lord's body and three grains of incense, while the antiphon *Sub altare Domini* is being sung;

—*anointing of the altar and sprinkling of the church* (nn. 13–18): after the sepulcher has been closed, the bishop says the prayer *Deus, qui ex omni cooptatione,* seals the sepulcher with the cement, and anoints it with chrism; he also anoints the four corners of the altar. He then covers the altar by spreading a cloth over it, and says the prayer *Descendat, quaesumus,* which has an epileptic character. He then walks down the nave of the church and sprinkles it with blessed water, using a sprig of hyssop (see Ps 51:9);

—*celebration of the Eucharist* (nn. 19–20): after the sprinkling of the church, the choir intones the entrance antiphon, and the celebration of the Eucharist begins and continues in the usual manner. In keeping with a biblical model (see 1 Mac 5:56), the feast of dedication lasts for eight days during which Mass is celebrated daily.

The Roman setting of *Ordo* XLII is confirmed by two facts: its prayer texts are found in genuinely Roman sacramentaries,[39] and its antiphons are attested in the Roman strata of the ancient antiphonaries.

3. *The Gallican Ritual*

The testimonies of St. Gregory of Tours (d. 594),[40] the Angoulême Sacramentary,[41] the *Missals Francorum,*[42] and, above all, *Ordo* XLII (end of the eighth century),[43] in which the influence of the Byzantine and Roman rituals can be seen, tell of the Gallican way of dedicating a church.

[39] The prayers *Aufer a nobis* (*Ordo* XLII, 1), *Deus, qui ad salutem* (ibid., 4), *Deus, qui ex omni cooptatione* (ibid., 13), and *Descendat, quaesumus* (ibid., 16) occur in *GrH* (ed. J. Deshusses) in nn. 814, 986, 819, and 816 respectively.

[40] *De gloria beatorum confessorum* 20 (PL 71:842–844); *Vitae Patrum* VIII, 8, 11 (PL 71:1047–1048, 1049–1050); XV, 1 (PL 71:1071–1072); *Historia Francorum* IX, 40 (PL 71:518–519).

[41] See P. Saint-Roch, ed., *Liber Sacramentorum Engolismensis* (Le Sacramentaire Gélasien d'Angoulême [= *GeA*]); CCL 159C (Turnhout, 1987), nn. 2019–2026, 2029–2052.

[42] See L. C. Mohlberg, ed., *Missale Francorum* (= *GaF*) (Rome, 1957), nn. 56–58.

[43] M. Andrieu, ed., *Les Ordines Romani du haut moyen âge,* 4:339–347.

Beyond the Roman and Byzantine influence, the Gallican ritual has some original traits; above all, it reveals a theological background that sets it apart. In this background we see a strong allegorizing tendency; an accentuated clericalism, due to which the people are marginalized at climactic moments of the rite; the use of almost exclusively Old Testament models for the many exorcisms, sprinklings, and purifications; a deeply rooted theology according to which the whole of creation is subject to the Evil One, so that before anything can be dedicated to divine worship, it must be purified and removed from all demonic influence.

The dedication includes the following steps:

—*preparatory rites and taking possession* (nn. 1–5): the lighting of twelve candles on the interior walls of the church (n. 1), a rite destined for lasting success; the procession, which reaches the entrance to the church, where the bishop strikes the sill three times with his staff and orders the door to be opened: *Tollite portas principes vestras,* this being followed by the singing of the entire Psalm 24 (n. 2); the entrance of the procession, which, to the singing of the litanies of the saints, makes its way to the altar, before which the bishop and ministers prostrate themselves (n. 3); the writing of the alphabet on the floor (n. 4);

—*purification of the altar and body of the church* (nn. 6–17), a set of ceremonies in which, after preparing the "water of exorcism" (a mixture of water, salt, ashes, and wine (nn. 7–8), the bishop sprinkles "water with his fingers" on the four corners of the altar (n. 11); then, using a sprig of hyssop, he sprinkles the altar, circling it seven times, while the antiphon *Asperges me hysopo et mundabor* and Psalm 51 are sung. He then passes through the body of the church, sprinkling the walls and floor to the singing of the antiphon *Exsurgat Deus* together with Psalm 68 and the antiphon *Qui habitat in adjutorio Altissimi* together with Psalm 91 (n. 12). Meanwhile, two or three ministers go and sprinkle the outside walls (n. 13). When the bishop has completed the sprinkling, he returns to the altar as the antiphon *Introibo ad altare Dei* is sung, together with Psalm 43 (n. 17);

—*anointing of the altar and the body of the church* (nn. 18–26): the great rite of purification is followed, quite consistently in the theological perspective of the Gallican rite, by the rite of consecration. This begins with the offering of incense (n. 18) and the anointing of the altar with the oil of catechumens: the bishop twice anoints the four corners and entire surface of the table; during the first anointing the antiphon *Erexit*

Iacob lapidem in titulum is sung, with Psalm 84; during the second, the antiphon *Sanctificavit Dominus tabernaculum suum* with Psalm 46 (nn. 18–20). The altar and church are then anointed with sacred chrism, while the antiphon *Ecce odor filii mei* and Psalm 87 are sung. When the anointings are completed, the bishop returns to the altar and, using some grains of incense, forms a cross on the altar (n. 24) and says the prayer for the blessing of the altar, *Deus omnipotens in cuius honorem* (n. 25). This part of the rite fittingly ends with the singing of the antiphon *Confirma hoc, Deus* (n. 26);

—*blessing of the cloths and liturgical furnishings* (n. 27): with appropriate prayers, the cloths and everything intended for use in the new church are blessed; the chalice and paten are consecrated by an anointing with chrism and the accompanying prayer;[44]

—*transfer of the relics* (nn. 28–29): once the church has been consecrated, the congregation goes in procession to the place where the relics are being kept; the transfer is done in festive procession, with acclamations, incensations, and many lighted candles (n. 28). When the procession reaches the altar, a curtain is closed between the people and the bishop, who places the relics in the *sepulchrum* of the altar, while the antiphon *Exsultabunt sancti in gloria* and Psalm 149 are sung (n. 29);

—*celebration of the Eucharist* (nn. 30–31): the bishop returns to the sacristy and dons festive vestments; the altar is covered with a cloth and the lamps are lit (n. 30); the choir intones the entrance antiphon and Mass begins.

In the perspective adopted in the Gallican rite, the celebration of the Eucharist has ceased to be the real rite of consecration of the new church and has become instead a kind of "inaugural Mass" for the new sacred building. Even the *depositio reliquarum* has lost some of its original character; the shifting of it from the beginning of the rite (Rome) to the end (Gaul) and the performance of it in secret have altered its meaning.

4. Ambrosian Ritual

The *Ordo ambrosianus ad consecrandam œclesiam et altaria*, which is handed down in codex 605 of the Biblioteca Capitulare of Lucca and

[44] See L. C. Mohlberg, ed., *Liber Sacramentorum Romanae Æcclesiae ordinis anni circuli* (= *GeV*) (Rome, 1960), nn. 695–702; A. Dumas, ed., *Liber Sacramentorum Gellonensis* (= *GeG*), CCL 159 (Turnhout, 1981), nn. 2429–2450.

published in 1902,[45] is a coherent, simple *ordo* containing some valuable euchological texts. The dedication is divided into two main phases, which have parallel ritual sequences. The first takes place outside the church, the doors of which are still closed, and includes the washing of the building to the singing of Psalm 51 *(Miserere mei)* and the antiphon *Asperges me;* the tracing of the sign of the cross on the door with the bishop's staff; the anointing of the outside walls with chrism; the writing of the alphabet on them; the traditional dialogue between the bishop and a deacon, which takes place within the new building to the accompaniment of verses 7-10 of Psalm 24 *(Domini est terra);* the opening of the door, which is accomplished symbolically with the bishop's staff; and the entrance into the church to the singing of the antiphon *Intrate portas eius in confessione.*

The second phase takes place within the new church and includes the washing of the pavement and the interior walls; the writing of the alphabet on a cruciform layer of ashes, accompanied by the singing of Psalm 119 *(Beati immaculati in via)* and the antiphon *Quam metuendus est locus iste*; the anointing of the interior walls with chrism and the lighting of twelve candles. The properly dedicatory element takes the form of euchological texts uttered successively at the head of the nave *(Omnipotens sempiterne Deus, qui caelestia),* in the middle of it *(Omnipotens sempiterne Deus, qui ubique),* and at the altar *(Domine sancte pater et clemens).* The *ordo* of Lucca, which is beyond doubt Ambrosian, raises some questions that have not yet received a complete answer: Why is there no reference to the placing of saints' relics beneath the altar, a ritual especially dear to St. Ambrose (d. 397)? Why is no anointing of the altar provided, but only a washing accompanied by the singing of Psalm 85 *(Quam dilecta tabernacula tua)* with the antiphon *Altaria tua, Domine*? Did the *Oratio ad fontem benedicendum,* which follows without a break upon the prayer dedicating the altar, mean perhaps that the dedication also included the inauguration of the baptistery?

5. The Ritual of Ravenna

The *ordo* preserved in ms. lat. 2292 of the Bibliothèque Nationale of Paris, which comes from the abbey of Nonantola (Modena), seems to

[45] G. Mercati, *Antiche reliquie liturgiche ambrosiane e romane* (Rome, 1902) 1–27. The Lucca codex is from the eleventh century, but the majority of its ritual sequences go back to the eighth and ninth centuries.

give the rite of the dedication used in the Church of Ravenna.[46] The course of the ritual has many points of contact with the Ambrosian rite of dedication, but the euchological texts are proper to this ms. Outstanding among them is the prayer for the consecration of the altar with its pronounced epiclesis *(Descendat to de caelo super hoc altare Spiritus Sanctus et tuae gratiam benedictionis infundat).*

6. The Spanish Ritual

The *Ordo ecclesiae consecrandae* in the Pontifical of Narbonne is a hybrid rite resulting from the fusion of elements from *Ordo* XLI and *Ordo* XLII, on the one hand, and from the Spanish *ordo* for the dedication of churches, on the other.[47] In all probability the Narbonne *ordo* was composed in the second half of the ninth century, that is, at the time when the Church of Narbonne moved from the Spanish rite to the Franco-Roman rite, a passage promoted by the Carolingian liturgical reform. But the compiler did not hide his sympathy for the old Spanish rite, whose prayers and more important chants he retains, preferring them to the Franco-Roman. To be noted among the euchological texts is the combined blessing of church and altar, which can be regarded as a characteristic of the Narbonne *ordo.*

THE RITE OF DEDICATION FROM THE TENTH TO THE FIFTEENTH CENTURY

From these centuries four *ordines* in particular call for attention, since they played a considerable part in the historical genesis of the rite of dedication of a church: the Romano-Germanic Pontifical of the Tenth Century *(PRG),* the Pontifical of the Twelfth Century *(PR XII),* the Pontifical of the Roman Curia *(PR XIII),* and the Pontifical of William Durandus *(PGD).*

1. The Romano-Germanic Pontifical of the Tenth Century[48]

During the ninth century a process of amalgamation involving the Roman ritual and the Frankish ritual gave rise to a series of "mixed

[46] Edition of text with commentary: M. S. Gros, "L'ordo pour la dédicace des églises dans le Sacramentaire de Nonantola," *RBén* 79 (1969) 386–374. According to Gros, the *ordo* is to be dated between the sixth century *(terminus a quo)* and the eighth *(terminus ad quem);* see ibid., 374.

[47] See M. S. Gros, "El ordo romano-hispánico de Narbona para la consagración de iglesias," *HS* 19 (1966) 321–401.

[48] See C. Vogel and R. Elze, eds., *Le Pontifical romano-germanique du Xe siècle* (= *PRG*). I: *Le texte* (Nn. I–XCVIII) (Vatican City, 1963).

rituals." Two in particular are important: *Ordo* XLVIII,[49] derived from a fusion of *Ordo* XLI with *Ordo* XLII, and the Sacramentary of Drogo of Metz,[50] in which allegories and dramatizations abound.

But the main work to be examined is the *PRG,* since this represents a decisive point in the formation of the rite of dedication. The *PRG* saw the light between 953 and 960 in the scriptorium of St. Alban's Abbey, which was under the patronage of the archbishop of Mainz, in the time of William, son of Emperor Otto I. The political importance of the see of Mainz, the cultural prestige of St. Alban's Abbey, and the contemporary decline of Roman liturgical activity favored the success of the *PRG.*

The *PRG* contains three documents on the rite of dedication: XXXV: *Quid significent duodecim candelae* (pp. 99–121), which is a detailed commentary on *Ordo* XLII and important for understanding the criteria used in the liturgical hermeneutics of the time; XXXII: *Ordo romanus ad dedicandam ecclesiam* (pp. 82–89), a balanced combination of *Ordo* XLI and *Ordo* XLII; and *Ordo* XL: *Ordo ad benedicendam ecclesiam* (pp. 124–173), which is like the preceding in structure but is distinguished from it by a superabundant, disproportionate ritual complexity and by a dramatic and sacralizing mentality carried to extremes. For example, the bishop three times walks around the outside walls of the church and sprinkles them (nn. 12, 15, and 18); he three times strikes the threshold of the door with his staff and three times, using verses of Psalm 23, tells the deacon, who is inside the church, to open the door (nn. 14, 17, and 20); on entering the church he three times utters the greeting *Pax huic domui* (n. 21) and, three times again, circles the entire space of the church in order to sprinkle the walls (n. 44). To the anointing of the altar and the walls is added an anointing of the door-jambs (n. 124); to the writing of the Latin alphabet is added that of the Greek alphabet (n. 26). Surprising, too, are the double exorcisms, which each time requires a lengthy set of prayers (nn. 5–9, 27–41), the extensive series of blessings of objects making up the furnishings dedicated to divine worship (nn. 73–122), and the rite of enclosing in the "sepulcher" of the altar not only the relics of the saints but also three particles of the eucharistic bread *(tres portiones corporis Domini)* and three grains of incense (nn. 136–137).

[49] M. Andrieu, ed., *Les Ordines Romani du haut moyen âge* IV, 403–413.

[50] J. B. Pelt, ed., "Le Sacramentaire de Drogon," *Etudes sur la Cathédrale de Metz* I: *La liturgie,* n. 508.

It is easy to grasp the spirit of the rite: from the theological viewpoint, it takes the form of a grandiose liturgical action aimed at expelling the Evil One from the building to be dedicated and rendering everything sacred, including even the liturgical furnishings. From the ritual point of view, the rite stands out for its exuberance, the gusto expressed in its repetitions, the tendency to dramatization, the profusion of lights, the abundance of sprinklings, incensations, and anointings, and the almost exclusive recourse to Old Testament models (see Exod 40:9-11; Lev 8:10-11). The *ordo* is marked, on the other hand, by felicitous choices of antiphons and psalms, and there are not lacking some fine texts, such as the prayer for the dedication of the church (n. 48).

2. *The Pontifical of the Twelfth Century*[51]

A little more than a century later there appeared in Rome *PR XII*, which is, as it were, a first "Romanization" of *PRG*. As far as the rite of dedication is concerned, *PR XII* substantially follows the structure of *PRG* and repeats its texts; at the same time, however, it is a revision of *PRG*, although not a radical one. Above all, it simplifies some ritual sequences: the seven sprinklings of the altar (*PRG* n. 43) become three (n. 33) in *PR XII*; the threefold greeting to the church (*PRG* n. 21) is reduced to one (n. 16); the prescription that "three portions of the Lord's body" (*PRG* n. 136) are to be placed in the "sepulcher" of the altar is wisely removed; there remains only the prescription regarding the three grains of incense (n. 52). Some structures are revised: for example, the transfer of the relics, which in *PRG* seems divided, as it were, into two truncated parts, (nn. 10, 123–134), becomes a unified action in *PR XII* (nn. 41–49).

PR XII is also an expression of a strongly revitalized liturgical activity in Rome, which began in the time of Gregory VII (1073–1085) and was continued by his successors. Once again, "Roman" liturgical books spread throughout all of Europe by way of the papal legates.

3. *The Pontifical of the Roman Curia*[52]

PR XII was not strictly speaking a "papal pontifical," since it was also used by, for example, the bishops of the suburbicarian sees. In the time

[51] See M. Andrieu, ed., *Le Pontifical romain au moyen âge* I: *Le Pontifical romain du XIIe siècle* (= *PR XII*) (Vatican City, 1938), n. XVII, pp. 176–195.

[52] See M. Andrieu, ed. *Le Pontifical romain au moyen âge* II: *Le Pontifical de la Curie romaine au XIIIe siècle* (= *PR XIII*) (Vatican City, 1940), n. XXIII, pp. 421–440.

of Innocent III (1198–1216), the masters of ceremonies at the Lateran Basilica, using *PR XII* as a basis, composed a pontifical intended specifically for celebrations at which the pope presided. This was *PR XIII,* the Pontifical of the Roman Curia in the thirteenth century.

In the rite for the dedication of a church, *PR XIII* follows the structure given in *PR XII* and ratifies the simplification that the latter effected in relation to *PRG*. On the other hand, it carries further the process of sacralization seen in *PRG*. Thus *PR XIII* prescribes a triple sign of the cross in many formulas: *per Deum ✠ verum, per Deum ✠ vivum, per Deum ✠ sanctum* (n. 5), *in nomine Patris ✠ et Filii ✠ et Spiritus ✠ Sancti* (n. 9). Finally, *PR XIII* has a taste for rubrical precision, which helps to a cohesive and linear unfolding of the celebration.

Because of its origin in the papal scriptorium, its intrinsic merits, and its spread beyond the Alps during the Avignon years of the papacy (1309–1367), *PR XIII* gradually replaced *PR XII.*

4. The Pontifical of William Durandus[53]

William Durandus, a canonist and bishop of Mende, using *PR XIII* as a basis, composed for his personal use a pontifical *(PGD)* that was destined to have great success and to replace *PR XIII,* even in Rome itself.

PGD introduces various elements into the rite for the dedication: the sign of the cross, which the bishop makes with his staff while uttering the formula *Ecce crucis signum, fugiant fantasmata cuncta* (n. 37); the singing of the *Veni, creator Spiritus* immediately after the bishop enters the church (n. 41); in the litany of the saints, a threefold appeal for the consecration: *Ut hanc ecclesiam . . . bene ✠ dicere . . . ; bene ✠ dicere et sancti ✠ ficare; bene ✠ dicere, sancti ✠ ficare et conse ✠ crare digneris* (n. 44); the singing of the *Veni, creator Spiritus* while the incense is burning on the altar, an impressive ritual moment this, but one that carried with it the danger of being overvalued in comparison with other strictly consecratory actions: the anointings, the prayer of dedication, the eucharistic celebration itself (III, no. 64).

In the text we see a tendency to expand the formulas: the greeting *Pax huic domui* becomes *Pax huic domui et omnibus habitantibus in ea* (n. 39), accompanied by the singing of an antiphon that makes the Trinity the source of this peace: *Pax aeterna ab aeterno Patri huic domui; pax perennis, Verbum Patris, sit pax huic domui; pacem pius Consolator huic*

[53] See M. Andrieu, ed., *Le Pontifical Romain au Moyen Age* III: *Le Pontifical de Guillaume Durand* (= *PGD*) (Vatican City, 1940), n. II, pp. 455–478.

praestet domui (n. 40); the concise formula accompanying the sign of the cross over the altar table (*Sanctificetur hoc altare, in nomine Patris et Filii et Spiritus Sancti: PR XIII*, n. 39) is expanded, but as a result the direction of it is changed: *Sanctificetur hoc altare in honore omnipotentis Dei et gloriosae virginis Mariae et omnium sanctorum et ad nomen et memoriae sancti talis* (n. 68). Unfortunately, *PGD* turns into a set rite what was envisaged simply as a hypothesis in *PR XIII*, namely, the consecration of an altar without any dedication of the church (III, nn. 1–93). This is a "concession" inspired by practical reasons, but, with an essential part removed, the rite does not fully convey the symbolism of the church building as a sign of the mystery of Christ (the altar) and of the Church (the nave).

As in the Gallican rituals of the eighth century, so in the *PGD* the celebration of the Eucharist is seen no longer as the decisive consecratory rite but simply as a suitable complement: *Omnibus expeditis, revertitur pontifex in sacrarium et . . . induit se ad missam* (no. 100).[54]

5. Later Pontificals Down to Vatican II

The Pontifical of William Durandus was thus successful: the *Liber Pontificalis*—the first printed edition of the Roman Pontifical, published in 1485 by order of Innocent VIII and edited by Agostino Patrizzi Piccolomini, bishop of Pienza and former secretary of Pius II, and by John Burchard, the famous pontifical master of ceremonies—simply reproduced the *PGD* or, more accurately, was a kind of "critical edition" of it. This was because the new book eliminated the added parts, restored omissions, and corrected errors of various kinds; it noted that in the copies of the *PGD* then in circulation there were *multa addita, pleraque intermissa, plurima vero vitiata*. In the *Ordo dedicationis* the changes were almost exclusively stylistic.

In 1595 Clement III promulgated the edition we might call "Tridentine" because of its reference to the great conciliar event of the sixteenth century, at which the title *Pontificale Romanum* was used for the first time. This was in substance a reprint of the *Pontificale secundum ritum Romanae Ecclesiae*, which had been edited and published by Alberto Castellari, O.P. (Venice, 1520); the latter had been in its turn a revision of the *editio princeps* of 1485. In the *Ordo dedicationis* the variants

[54] In the case of a consecration of an altar without a dedication of the church, the celebration of the Eucharist even becomes optional: *Quibus expeditis, pontifex ingreditur sacrarium et parat se, si velit, ad missam* (III, n. 81, p. 496).

were minimal: it prescribed that after the address of the bishop on the respect the faithful should show to places dedicated to God and on their duty to pay tithes to the clergy, two decrees of the Council of Trent were to be read: the first (session XXII, chap. XI of the Decree on Reform) on the punishments to be inflicted on those who dared usurp ecclesiastical possessions; the second (session XXV, chap. XII of the Decree on General Reform) on the excommunication awaiting those who "refuse to pay tithes or hinder their payment."

Neither the *editio princeps* of 1485 nor the "Tridentine" edition of Clement VIII (1595) had pruned the very full ritual in *PGD*, in which, however, it is difficult to make out a clear line of development. The ritual, though spacious and impressive, was also inaccessible to the people and wearying for the bishop. In fact, some bishops, to avoid the fatigue caused by the rite, omitted the dedication of new churches, including even the cathedral.

6. The Dedication of a Church in the Pontifical of 1961

On January 25, 1959, Pope John XXIII announced the celebration of Vatican Council II, which was formally convoked on December 25, 1961, and opened on October 11, 1962. On the agenda of the coming council was a discussion of the liturgical situation. Despite this, the Congregation of Rites engaged in an especially intense activity during these three transitional years: it promulgated some documents that laid the foundations for a general and systematic reform of the liturgy (the *Codex rubricarum* of July 25, 1960), and it published some very important liturgical books, such as the *Breviarium Romanum*, which appeared in a new *editio typica* on April 15, 1962, and a revised *Missale Romanum* (June 23, 1962). Also published was the new typical edition of the second book of the *Pontificale Romanum (PR1961)*, which was promulgated on April 13, 1961,[55] and contained the rite of the dedication of a church.

Some have seen in this intense activity an attempt of the Roman Curia to hold back or channel the conciliar debate on liturgical reform by confronting Vatican II with a fait accompli; others, however, probably with greater accuracy, saw in it only the continuation of the extensive liturgical revision that had been going on since the first years of

[55] *Pontificale Romanum*. Pars Secunda. Editio typica emendata (Vatican Polyglot Press).

the pontificate of Pius XII (1939–1958).[56] In any case, the promulgation of these liturgical books just before the opening of Vatican II inevitably made them stopgaps: it was unthinkable that an ecumenical council which intended to discuss the state of the liturgy should feel its path blocked by the diligent work of a Roman congregation.

The motivations at work and the criteria followed in the editing of *PR1961* are carefully laid out in the document (*positio,* dated December 20, 1959) in which Fathers A. Bugnini and C. Braga, who were assigned to the historical section of the Congregation of Rites (where Msgr. A. P. Frutaz and Father J. Löw served as reporters *[relatores]*) explained their commission's work:

"The rite of the dedication of a church that is found in the Roman Pontifical is very fine and rich, but it no longer meets modern needs and situations. First of all, it is too long; the rhythm of modern life does not allow for rites that are so protracted; people weary of them; the fatigue caused by such long and complex rites becomes excessive for consecrating bishops, especially if these are elderly and if there are many such consecrations. Moreover, the general liturgical and pastoral awakening has led to a reassessment of what is essential; if the sacred rites are to be brought closer to the people they must be simplified, made almost transparently intelligible by means of easy, almost natural symbols, and carried out in such a way that the people can comfortably take part in them. In the present rite, however, the people remain completely excluded from a considerable part of the sacred function."[57]

The changed times, simplification, quest for the essential, participation of the faithful, and transparent symbolism—these are the motifs and themes that would be seen again in the constitution *Sacrosanctum*

[56] See F. Dell'Oro, "Il rinnovamento della liturgia sotto il pontificato di Pio XII e Giovanni XXIII," in the collective work *Assisi 1956–1986: Il movimento liturgico tra riforma conciliare e attese del popolo di Dio* (Assisi, 1987) 189–278, especially 273–277.

[57] Passage reprinted by F. Dell'Oro, ibid., 268. These norms are partly to be found also in the decree of promulgation: "Since our age . . . has changed so much in comparison with earlier times and since the origin and meaning of the individual rites are better known, there is a legitimate desire of suitably revising the more important sacred actions described in this second part of the Roman Pontifical and of simplifying their form so that the faithful may more easily take part in them and grasp their deeper meaning" (*PR1961*, p. 2).

Concilium (December 4, 1963) as the criteria that inspired the liturgical reform.

As a matter of fact, the ritual in *PR1961*, titled *Ordo ad ecclesiam dedicandam et consecrandam*, was considerably simplified and clearly divided into four parts: (1) washing and dedication of the church; (2) depositing of the relics; (3) consecration of the church and the altar; (4) Mass.

The first part has the rites of the *lustratio*, to be performed by the bishop and ministers, robed in violet vestments. It is subdivided into five sections and is a kind of "baptism" of the new building for worship:

—the sprinkling of the walls (nn. 9–12), which the bishop performs while walking around the church only once instead of the three times prescribed by *PR1596*; meanwhile the choir sings Psalm 87 *(Fundamenta eius in montibus sanctis)* with the antiphon *Bene fundata est;*

—entrance into the new church (nn.13–15), which includes the traditional rite of knocking on the door and commanding that it be opened *(Attollite portas)*, the greeting of the new building (*Pax huic domui*, which has been restored to its original tenor), and the singing of the litany of the saints;

—the washing of the interior of the church (nn. 16–18); this includes, first, the sprinkling of the walls with "Gregorian" water, while the choir sings Psalm 122 *(Laetatus sum)* and the antiphon *Haec est domus Domini;* then the sprinkling of the pavement, lengthwise (from altar to door) and crosswise (from left to right), which is accompanied by the singing of Psalm 84 *(Quam dilecta tabernacula tua)* and the antiphon *Non est hic aliud;*

—the washing of the altar (nn. 19–23), which is performed separately in order to bring out the special and unique part the altar plays in the cultic edifice: the bishop sprinkles the altar as he circles it, and then with his thumb, which he dips in "Gregorian" water, he traces five crosses, at the center and the four corners, as the choir sings Psalm 43 *(Iudica me, Deus)* and the antiphon *Introibo ad altare Dei;*

—the taking possession of the church and the dedication of it (nos. 24–25): the former is symbolized by the traditional writing of the Greek and Latin alphabets, while Psalm 48 *(Magnus Dominus)* is sung with the antiphon *O quam metuendus est;* the second is given expression in the "preface" *Vere dignum . . . Teque suppliciter exorare*, which raises some questions as to the meaning of the word *dedicatio* in the title of this section.

The second section, the depositing of the relics, which renews a traditional sequence of rites that is characteristic of the Roman dedication, is of considerable importance, although it has undergone some changes. The bishop and ministers lay aside their violet vestments and don white vestments. This part has two sections:

—*transfer of the relics* (nn. 26–30), which entails two processions: one to collect the relics from the place outside the church where they have been kept since the vigil; the other to bring them to the altar where they are to be enclosed in the "sepulcher." The bishop, the ministers, and at least some of the people take part in both processions. During the first procession, the antiphons *O quam gloriosum est regnum, Movete, Sancti Dei, Ecce populus custodiens iudicium,* and *Via sanctorum* are sung, but for pastoral reasons these may be replaced by popular hymns; during the second, Psalm 149 *(Cantate Domino)* is sung with the antiphon *Istorum est enim* and, at the point when the procession enters the church, the beautiful antiphon *Ingredimini, Sancti Dei;*

—*depositing of the relics* (nn. 31–35): after the relics have been placed in a "coffin" near the altar, the bishop incenses them and then places them in the "sepulcher" while the choir sings the antiphons *Sub altare Dei sedes accepistis, Sub altare Dei audivi voces occisorum,* and *Corpora Sanctorum;* then he blesses the cement that has been made with "Gregorian" water, and a mason closes the "sepulcher." The ritual sequence ends with the prayer *Deus, qui ex omni cooptatione Sanctorum,* which comes from *GeV* 710.

In the intention of the editors, the third part, the consecration of the church and the altar, is intended specifically for consecrations. It consists of an extensive anointing of the new church, a "strengthening" as it were, and has two sections:

—*consecration of the church* (nn. 36–41): the bishop circles the walls, tracing with thumb dipped in chrism twelve crosses at the points marked by twelve painted crosses; he anoints, incenses, and lights a candle at each of these points, while the choir sings Psalm 147 *(Lauda, Ierusalem, Dominum)* with the antiphon *Lapides pretiosi;* among the chants for use as the occasion requires are the fine hymn *Caelestis urbs Ierusalem* and the responsories *Haec est Ierusalem civitas magna* and *Plateae tuae, Ierusalem;*

—*consecration of the altar:* this is the climactic part of the rite: the bishop traces five crosses on the altar table (at the center and the four corners) and five others, of which one is made on the *frons altaris* and four at points where the table and its supports meet; meanwhile the choir sings Psalm 45 *(Eructavit cor meum),* a royal epithalamium that has been given a christological meaning since antiquity, and the antiphon *Unxit te Deus,* which recalls the royal and priestly anointing of Christ. The incensation of the altar follows, to the accompaniment of one or more antiphons, among them *Stetit Angelus, Data sunt ei incensa multa,* and *Ascendit fumus aromatum,* and ending with the prayer *Dirigatur,* which recalls the symbolism of incense as given in Psalm 140. This is followed by the impressive rite of the invocation of the Spirit: on the altar table are burning crosses made with grains of incense, while the bishop kneels before the altar and the choir sings the *Veni, Sancte Spiritus.* After a usual introductory sequence, consisting of an exhortation *(Dei Patris omnipotentis),* a diaconal call (*Flectamus genua,* silent prayer, and a collect *(Deus omnipotens, in cuius honore),* the bishop chants the consecratory preface *(Vere dignum . . . Et ut propensiori cura),* which goes back to *PR XII.*

With the climactic moment now past, the following ritual sequences of the third part (blessing of the altar cloths and other furnishings for worship;[58] "clothing" of the altar for the celebration of the Eucharist[59]) appear to be, and in fact are, complementary.

The third part ends with the diaconal call *Benedicamus Domino—Deo gratias,* which is a dismissal formula and is therefore out of place because premature. The bishop and ministers withdraw to the sacristy.

While the altar is being prepared, the choir sings Psalm 95 *(Cantate Domino canticum novum)* with the antiphon *Confirma hoc, Deus, quod operatus es in nobis,* which also suggests that the consecration of the church is now complete.

Despite some progress as compared with *PR1596,* the editors have not succeeded in the fourth part, the Mass, in bringing out the consecratory value of the eucharistic celebration for the dedication of the church. All things considered, in *PR1961* the celebration of the Eucha-

[58] In order to render the rite less onerous, a rubric says that this blessing can be given before the rite (see n. 49, p. 43); some commentaries found this solution attractive.

[59] The "clothing" of the altar corresponds to the giving of a white garment to the newly baptized; for this reason, those who favor an allegorical assimilation of the dedication of an altar to Christian initiation would have liked this "clothing" to be done by the bishop and not, as the rubric states, by ministers or servers (see n. 50, p. 43).

rist appears to be a part of the entire rite of consecration but not the principal consecratory action. It is recommended that the bishop himself celebrate the Eucharist and that this be a solemn rite, but it is explicitly allowed that the bishop may delegate a presbyter, and the Mass may be simply a "read Mass," to use the terminology of the time.

PR1961 showed noteworthy progress in the desired simplification of the rite of dedication. To its credit were the introduction of co-consecrating bishops, which made the rite a true concelebration and made it possible to perform simultaneously the ritual sequences (depositing of relics, anointings, etc.) at the main altar and the side altars, which were often numerous at that time; the pastoral intention that guided the reform and the care taken to elicit an active participation of the people; the always clear, even if at times debatable, structural line; the intelligent suppression of formulas and gestures that were simply duplications; the recovery of the original tenor of various texts.

Despite these merits, *PR1961*, which came out on the eve of the opening of Vatican II, was not received with enthusiasm. Above and beyond some matters of detail and some less felicitous structural choices, *PR1961* was challenged chiefly for two "innovations": the distinction made between *dedicatio* (first part) and *consecratio* (third part), which is not justifiable either in the light of history or in virtue of the texts themselves;[60] and the structuring of the rite of dedication of a church on the model of the sacraments of Christian initiations (baptism, chrismation, Eucharist), which is to be regarded as erroneous and the result of an unacceptable allegorism.[61]

[60] In the liturgical tradition the terms *dedicatio* and *consecratio*, when used in the *Ordo dedicationis*, were essentially synonymous and interchangeable. This was reflected in the title of the rite in *PR1596*: *De ecclesiae dedicatione seu consecratione*, whereas in *PR1961* it was *Ordo ad ecclesiam dedicandam et consecrandam*. The fact was noted by S. Marsili in his article "Dedicazione senza consacrazione" (note 33, above). In addition to being artificial, the distinction is not even respected within the two parts: the first or "dedicatory" part contains the most explicitly consecratory formula in the entire rite (*Descendat quoque in hanc ecclesiam tuam, quam . . . nos indigni consecramus, Spiritus Sanctus tuus septiformis, gratiae ubertate redundans*, n. 25, pp. 23–24); on the other hand, in the third or "consecratory" part, we find the verb *dedicare*, while the "consecratory" formula is certainly a weaker one: *templum istud . . . benedicere et sanctificare digneris, per cuius sacram reverentiam et honorem sanctissimo nomini tuo hoc altare dedicamus. Huius igitur, Domine, efflagitis precibus, dignare hoc altare caelesti sanctificatione perfundere et benedicere* (n. 40, pp. 40–41).

[61] See Marsili, "Dedicazione senza consacrazione," 582–586. But L. Chengalikavil sees a positive aspect in "this kind of liturgical hermeneutics": "The reform

7. The Dedication of a Church in the Pontifical of 1977

On May 29, 1977, a decree of Cardinal G. R. Knox promulgated the *Ordo dedicationis ecclesiae et altaris*, which is part of the *Pontificale Romanum ex decreto sacrosancti oecumenici Concilii Vatican II instauratum, auctoritate Pauli Pp. VI promulgatum.*[62] From December 4, 1963, date of the promulgation of the constitution *Sacrosanctum Concilium,* to that day in 1977 the Roman liturgy had been the subject of a far-reaching, enthusiastic, and radical renewal. The *Ordo dedicationis* was one of the last fruits of this effort at renewal and advancement. When it was published, some of the principal workers during that period of work had died or had been called to other tasks.

The redaction of the new *Ordo* had been entrusted to *Coetus a studiis XXI bis,* which had been established for the work in May, 1970. In March 1972 a plenary meeting of the Sacred Congregation for Divine Worship approved the plan of the new *Ordo,* which was printed in a volume *pro manuscripto* in the spring of 1973 and sent to the episcopal conferences, the centers for liturgical studies, and a considerable number of experts for their suggestions and remarks. It was in light of these that the typical edition of 1977 was prepared.

The *Ordo* contains seven chapters: placing of the first stone of a church (I); dedication of a church (II); dedication of a church in which the sacred mysteries are already being celebrated (III); dedication of an altar (IV); blessing of a church (V); blessing of an altar (VI); blessing of a chalice and a paten (VII).

a) Editorial criteria

The editorial criteria followed in the *Ordo* were essentially the same as those that directed the entire liturgical reform of Vatican II, but with some emphases and adaptations suggested or required by the specific character of this rite. The following may be mentioned as among the criteria certainly followed in developing the *Ordo*: the *simplification* of the rite, which was not to mean, however, a reduction of its symbolic and expressive power but, following the course begun in *PR1961,* was

indirectly and implicitly recognizes that the liturgy of dedication must deal with the living temple. The sacraments that make Christians and the Christian community ought to be somehow recalled and celebrated" ("La dedicazione della chiesa e dell'altare," in *Anàmnesis* 7:78).

[62] *Ordo dedicationis ecclesiae et altaris,* Editio typica (Vatican Polyglot Press, 1977) (= *PR1977*).

to apply the principle of *nobilis simplicitas* set down in the constitution *Sacrosanctum Concilium* (n. 34); the *active participation of the faithful,* in keeping with a universal requirement of the liturgical reform and with a characteristic of the early rituals that had gradually been obscured to the point where the dedication of a church took place with the nave empty of the faithful (only *PR1961* had "readmitted" the people to take part in the rite); the *retrieval,* in the measure possible, of the original structure of the Roman dedication, something that called for fidelity to the liturgical tradition of Rome but also for attention to authentic ritual developments down the centuries; the *truthfulness and eloquence of the signs.* "Truthfulness" would require, for example, that so characteristic a rite as the deposition of relics not be made obligatory in every case. Should the dedication of a church be omitted because the body of a saint is lacking (the breaking up of relics being rightly excluded)? "Eloquence" would require a return to the full splendor of signs; thus the five anointings of the altar table were to be replaced by a gesture of superabundance: the bishop "*pours chrism* on the middle of the altar and on each of its four corners, and it is recommended *(laudabiliter)* that he *anoint the entire table of the altar* with this."[63]

From the theological viewpoint, the felt need was that the *Ordo* should faithfully mirror the *ecclesiology of Vatican II,* a more than simply legitimate requirement for a rite that by its nature should bring out the relationship of the church-as-sign (the building of stone) to the Church-as-mystery (the community which is the ecclesial body of Christ, the *communio Sanctorum*). But this requirement led in turn to an accentuation of the *christological element* of the liturgical action, since the Church-as-mystery exists and is what it is solely in relation to the mystery of Christ, with which it is inseparably connected.

b) The directing principle

While it is important thus to identify the editorial criteria at work in the *Ordo* in *PR1977,* it is even more important to call attention to the principle that directed the entire elaboration of the work: the celebration of the Eucharist is the fundamental consecratory action. Thus the introduction to this section of the *Ordo* says: "The celebration of the Eucharist is the most important rite, and the only necessary one, for

[63] *PR1977,* II, n. 64; ET: *The Rites of the Catholic Church* (Collegeville, Minn., 1991) 2:225.

the dedication of a church."[64] This principle clearly distinguishes the rite in *PR1977* from the preconciliar *Ordo*. But, when strictly applied, the principle was to have important consequences in regard to the meaning to be given to some "consecratory structures" that had been authoritatively introduced into the *Ordo* since antiquity and were not lacking in attractiveness. What meaning was to be given, for example, to the anointing of the altar with sacred chrism, which is attested in the West since the sixth century? What meaning was to be assigned to the *prex dedicationis*, which has been traditional in the East and the West? Other questions, too, arose: If the edifice for worship is dedicated by the celebration of the Eucharist, does it not follow that all churches and chapels are already dedicated? What is the special character of the"Mass of dedication"? What meaning is to be given to the distinction between dedicating a church (ch. II) and blessing it (ch. V)? How justify the dedication of a church in which the sacred mysteries have already been celebrated?

PR1977 did not give a complete answer to these and other questions. The liturgy is an expression of the *mysterium*, and this does not always admit of answers that satisfy the Cartesian rational mind. On the other hand, *PR1977* does give excellent solutions of some problems and has successfully harmonized elements of diverse origin.

According to *PR1977*, the special character of the Mass of dedication consists in this: at this first eucharistic celebration the ecclesial community, represented in all its parts, manifests its intention of dedicating the new building exclusively and perpetually to divine worship. To this end it performs some traditionally consecratory actions (anointing of altar and walls), prays the Lord in his kindness to protect this place and the community that gathers in it, and celebrates the Eucharist, which, as it sanctifies the hearts of the faithful who receive the sacred mysteries, so in a way it sanctifies the altar and the church in which the body and blood of the Lord have been given a place.

According to *PR1977*, the entire eucharistic celebration, from the entrance into the new building until the dismissal, is, in varying ways and degrees for the various parts, a rite of dedication, and every ritual sequence seeks to bring out an aspect of the "mystery of communion" of Christ and the Church.

[64] Ibid., n. 15 (ET: 362).

S. Marsili has with keen insight pointed out the principle that directs the new *Ordo* and its "true and proper novelty [which] consists in *shifting the emphasis* to the rite in its entirety, so that all the elements of it, even those that are traditional, are given a new role: that precisely of giving back . . . its true identity to the church as place of worship."[65] In support of his claim he cites a passage from the decree of promulgation:

"A church is the *place* where the Christian community is gathered to hear the word of God, to offer intercession and praise to him, and above all to celebrate the holy mysteries; and it is the place where the holy sacrament of the Eucharist is kept. Thus it stands as a special *[peculiaris]* kind of *image of the Church itself,* which is God's temple built from living stones. And the *altar* of a church, around which the holy people of God gather to take part in the Lord's sacrifice and to be refreshed at the heavenly meal, stands as *a sign of Christ himself,* who is the priest, the victim, and the altar of his own sacrifice."[66]

c) The celebration of the rite

The dedication of a church is in four parts: (1) introductory rites (nn. 28–52); (2) liturgy of the Word (nn. 53–56); (3) prayer of dedication and anointings (nn. 55–71); (4) eucharistic liturgy (nn. 72–85).

The *introductory rites* are made up essentially of four ritual sequences:

—the *assembly* of the community at another church, preferably the church of the mother community, where the martyrs' or saints' relics are stored that are to be kept under the altar of the new church. This assembly is an expression of three liturgical and ecclesial realities: the fact that the hierarchically structured community is the true agent and celebrant of the rite of dedication; that it is from the faith of the mother community, symbolized by its church, that a new community of Christ's disciples emerges, with the new cultic edifice being its sign and point of reference; that, ideally, the local Church assembles with its outstanding children who have given to Christ the witness of martyrdom or of a life lived heroically according to the gospel, thus giving rise to an important manifestation of the communion of saints. The bishop's words to the people already voice some themes that will be developed throughout the celebration: the importance of the eucharistic

[65] Marsili, "Dedicazione senza consecrazione," 594–595.

[66] Decree of publication, in ET: 346 (emphases added).

celebration in the dedication of a church *(convenimus ad novam ecclesiam sacrificii dominici celebratione dedicandam)*; the reference to the celebration of the liturgy of the Word *(Verbum Dei audientes cum fide)*; the recall of the baptismal font as the place where the Christian community is born *(communitas nostra ex uno baptismatis fonte renata)*; the directedness of the entire sacramental life to the growth of the community, which is the true spiritual temple *(in templum spirituale crescat)*;

—the *procession* to the new church (n. 32): after the bishop's address, the people of God moves out on a real journey to the new church that is, however, also a symbol of the journey of ascent of the pilgrim Church on earth toward the heavenly temple (see Rev 21:22). The *Ordo* suggests as a processional song Psalm 122, one of the "psalms of ascent," which is effectively introduced by the antiphon *In domum Domini laetantes ibimus;*

—the *"station"* at the threshold of the church (n. 33): having reached the new church, the faithful halt before the still closed door. Here is where the bishop meets the delegates of the community and in particular those who have played an active part in the construction of the new meeting place. In the history of the various *ordines* for dedicating a church, this meeting is a new ritual sequence, the purpose of which is to appreciate in a liturgical way an ancient, profoundly human and Christian reality: the work done by human beings in building a church;

—the *opening of the door* (nn. 34–35), a classic element in the rite of dedication: the door is closed because the church has not yet been inaugurated or "opened" for the celebration of the divine mysteries, and it is now opened in order that, by entering through it, the local Church may take possession of the new building. Every theatrical element (the dialogue between the bishop outside the church and a deacon inside it) has been removed from the rite in order to have a liturgical structure in which the natural movements of entrance are already an adequate expressive support for a typically liturgical act. The short rite includes the opening of the door, the invitation to the faithful to enter the church, and the entrance of the assembly to the accompaniment of Psalm 24 (23), a characteristic entrance song for such an occasion. In light of the antiphon *(Elevamini portae aeternales, et introibit rex gloriae)*, the entrance is also seen as the enthronement of Christ, the true king of glory, in his royal dwelling, namely, the community of the faithful, which acknowledges his lordship and welcomes him into its midst;

—the *blessing and sprinkling of water* (nn. 48–50), which is a very ancient but not original ritual sequence. *PR1977* has taken a balanced approach to it: it has changed the emphasis within the rite, shifting it from the walls of the church building to the faithful who make up the Church as community; it has thereby turned the sprinkling into a sign of conversion *(poenitentiae signum)* and a reminder of baptism *(baptismi memoria);* it has not, however, thought it appropriate to eliminate every reference to the ancient *lustratio,* which reminds the faithful of the mysterious influence of the Evil One even on material structures, which are subject to transiency and corruption (see Rom 8:20-21). In any case, the *lustratio* is geared, as to its true object, to the purification of the spiritual temple, the community of the faithful: *Spiritus Sancti gratia / templum purificet habitationis suae, / quod nos sumus* (no. 50).

The second part, the *liturgy of the Word* (nn. 53–56), is simply an appropriate "set of readings" for the Mass of dedication. But the liturgical legislator has paid particular attention to this ritual sequence, which can be called "new," since the historical rites of dedication did not have it. *PR1977* intends to emphasize the fact that the community is born of the word of God, is nourished by it, and grows and develops by means of it.

The liturgy of the Word takes the form of a *dedicatio ambonis,* a dedication of the place that is a sign of the Word of God; but this dedication is marked by a deliberate liturgical simplicity. It has two stages:

—the *showing of the book:* the bishop at his throne shows the lectionary to the people, saying meanwhile: "May the word of God always be heard in this place, as it unfolds the mystery of Christ before you and achieves your salvation within the Church" (n. 53). There is then a little procession from throne to ambo, during which the readers and the psalmist show the lectionary to the entire congregation *(omnibus aspiciendum);*

—the *opening of the book:* even during the Easter season, the obligatory first reading is Nehemiah 8:2-4, 5-6, 8-10, because in the intention of the liturgical legislator it describes the *liturgy of the Word* as unmistakably a *dedicatio ambonis* ("The scribe Ezra stood on a *wooden platform* . . . and Ezra *opened the book* in the sight of all the people": vv. 4-5) and emphasizes the irreplaceable role of the Word in the formation of the community. Thus an episode focused on the proclamation and reception of the Law, which exegetes regard as the "moment of birth" of the postexilic community, becomes a symbol of the rite by which the community, gathered around the gospel of Christ, celebrates the *natalis ecclesiae*.

The third part—*prayer of dedication and the anointings* (nn. 57–71)—consists of the ritual sequences especially characteristic of the rite of dedication, but each of them is aimed, not at "sanctifying" the walls and altar of the new edifice for worship, but at revitalizing the awareness that Christians are themselves the true temple of God and at recalling the sacraments through which they have become the holy dwelling place of the Father and the Son and the Spirit.

At the ritual level of this third part, the altar is rightly given special prominence. But this is accomplished more by the ritual actions than by the words: the relics of the martyrs are placed under the altar (n. 61) to signify that the sacrifice of Christ is continued in the suffering of his members; the anointing of the altar is followed by the anointing of the walls (nn. 63–65), just as the anointing of Christ is the source of the anointing of Christians; it is at the altar that the offering of incense begins, followed by the incensation of the walls (nn. 66–68), just as it is from the sacrifice of Christ that the "good fragrance" of Christians comes; from the altar the light spreads outward (nn. 69–71), just as from Jesus the light radiates that enlightens every human being.

The third part contains six ritual sequences:

—the singing of the *litany of the saints* (nn. 57–60): this traditional element in the rite of dedication has endured various changes of place down the centuries. In *PR1977* the litany is given a place comparable to that which it has in other dedicatory rites of the Roman Pontifical, that is, it is a very prayerful preparation for the climactic moment of the rite. In any case, the closeness of the singing of the litany to the depositing of the relics of the saints gives rise to a harmonious ritual and thematic unity that has these outstanding members of the body of Christ at its center;

—the *depositing of the relics* (n. 61): this ancient ritual sequence, to be performed only when the *veritas rerum* allows, preserves its lofty symbolic value. It involves a *vigil of prayer* before the relics on the previous day (n. 10); the solemn *transfer* of the relics, which is accomplished in the procession to the new church (n. 31); the *depositing* of the relics beneath the altar by the bishop himself, as Psalm 15 *(Domine, quis habitabit in tabernaculo tuo?)* is sung, along with one of the two classic antiphons, *Sub altari Dei* and *Corpora Sanctorum;*

—the *prayer of dedication* (n. 62) is a new composition that replaces the two earlier consecratory "prefaces" (one for the church, the other for the altar), thereby emphasizing the unbreakable connection between church and altar. The commentators have brought out the classic structure of the prayer, its poetic power, its doctrinal richness, its biblical and patristic inspiration. The function of this *prex* is to express with clarity the will of the local community to dedicate the new building perpetually and exclusively to the worship of God and to ask for God's favor so that the place may be a sign of the celebration of the divine mysteries and a reminder of the ecclesial responsibilities that the disciples of Christ accept: prayer, mercy, justice, a life according to the gospel;

—the *anointing of the altar and the walls* (nn. 63–65): just as the Eucharist is the center of Christian worship, so the altar is the ideal center of a church: everything leads toward the altar and everything leads away from the altar. For this reason *PR1977,* in reaction against the inversion introduced into *PR1961,* has restored the proper order of the anointings: first that of the altar, then those of the walls. The reason: just as *in reality* it is from the anointing of Christ that the anointing of the members derives and takes its meaning, so too in the order of *signs* the anointing begins with the stone of the altar, which is the symbol of Christ, and moves on then to the stones of the walls, which symbolize Christians, the stones that make up the Church (see 1 Pet 2:4).

The anointing of the altar is done as follows: first of all, the bishop utters a formula that expresses the meaning and purpose of the anointing, namely, that the altar may become a "visible *sign* of the mystery of Christ and his Church" (n. 64); he then anoints the altar table, for which *PR1977* has restored, without rendering it obligatory, the ancient solemn gesture of anointing the entire altar table with sacred chrism (*quo laudabiliter totam mensam linit*—n. 64). The anointing of the walls follows; this task the bishop may entrust to presbyters, thus making possible a kind of dedicatory concelebration; in keeping with tradition there are twelve anointings, but only four if the church is small in size (n. 64). During the anointing of the walls Psalm 84 is sung *(Quam dilecta tabernacula tua),* accompanied by the antiphon *Ecce tabernaculum Dei cum hominibus* or the antiphon *Templum Domini sanctum est.*

—the *incensation of the altar and the church* (nn. 66–68); the impressive rite of the *benedictio incensi,* which was already present in *PR XII* and was enriched by *PGD* with the singing of the *Veni, Sancte Spiritus,* has been reduced in size in *PR1977,* as truthfulness to the situation requires. The reason: from the ritual point of view, this rite had exceeded proper bounds, to the point where it led the faithful to the erroneous persuasion that it was the climax of the entire celebration. *PR1977* has kept the rite of burning incense at the altar, but this is now accompanied by the singing, not of the *Veni, Sancte Spiritus,* but of Psalm 138 *(Confitebor tibi, Domine),* along with one of the two traditional antiphons, *Stetit angelus iuxta aram templi* or *Ascendit fumus aromatum.* The words of the bishop explain the meaning of the rite in terms of worship (incense as symbol of the pleasing fragrance of sacrifice and of prayer ascending to God) as well as in christological and ecclesial terms: "May our prayer ascend as incense in your sight. As this building is filled with fragrance so may your Church fill the world with the fragrance of Christ" (n. 66);

—the *illumination of the altar and the church* (nn. 69–71): until this point, light as a ritual element has not been part of the *Ordo;* the rubrics repeatedly advise that lights are not to be used in the processions, either in the entrance procession or in the procession leading to the proclamation of the gospel (n. 54b), the reason being that the use of light as a sign is deliberately reserved to the present ritual sequence, which is intended to be a moment of fervent praise of Christ the Light. The rubric prescribes: "Then the festive lighting takes place: all the candles, including those at the places where the anointings were made, and the other lamps are lit as a sign of rejoicing" (n. 71). Meanwhile, some verses of the splendid song of Tobit are sung (Tob 13:10, 13-14ab, 14c-15, 17), accompanied by one of two antiphons: *Venit lumen tuum, Ierusalem* or *Ierusalem, civitas Dei.* The theological meaning of the rite is both profound and clear: it is a reminder that Christ is the "light of the world" (John 8:12), "a light for revelation to the Gentiles" (Luke 2:32), the only true light of the Church. The chants send a clear missionary message: "All *nations* will walk in your light"; "*all people on earth* will pay you homage"; "*nations* will come from afar."

The fourth part is the *eucharistic liturgy* (nn. 72–85), which is not, however, to be understood in the usual sense of "celebration of Mass," since it has begun at the very beginning of the dedication. It is to be understood, rather, as in *MR1970,* as the ritual space that stretches from the presentation of the gifts to communion. In this part the following are to be noted: the fine preface *V. D. Qui templum gloriae tuae*

(n. 75), which comes from the Ambrosian tradition and in which, understandably, some ideas already expressed in the prayer of dedication reappear; the intercessions used in Eucharistic Prayer III (n. 77), which turn into a lyrical prayer that the new building for worship may be a *domus salutis et aula caelestium sacramentorum,* a place where the gospel of peace is proclaimed and the community celebrates the divine mysteries with joy; Psalm 128 *(Beatus omnis qui timet Dominum),* which is set down as the song for communion, being a psalm to which the tradition has given a eucharistic interpretation (the table in the home, as interpreted by the liturgy, is "the table of the Lord"—1 Cor 10:20) and an ecclesiological interpretation as well (the children of the just person are "the children of the Church"), as is suggested by the antiphon: *Sicut novellae olivarum, Ecclesiae filii sint in circuitu mensae Domini.*

The *Ordo* also provides a ritual sequence for the "Inauguration of the Chapel of the Most Blessed Sacrament" (nn. 80–82). This sequence, which can be called "new" in relation to the ancient *ordines* in which it did not have a place, is to be read in the light of a healthy realism, as a response to a need of the ecclesial community: since, according to ancient tradition, the sacred species are to be kept in the church so that they may be brought to the sick and may also be the object of prayer of silent adoration, they are carried in procession to the place prepared for them, to the singing of Psalm 147 *(Lauda, Ierusalem, Dominum),* which is often used in eucharistic settings.

In all this, the *veritas rerum* is respected: as the bishop inaugurates the *cathedra* by occupying it and as the ambo is inaugurated by reading the Word of God from it, so too the chapel of the Most Blessed Sacrament is inaugurated by placing the sacred species in the tabernacle.

d) The reception of PR1977

Experts on the liturgy gave a favorable reception to *PR1977*. While the new *Ordo* was found puzzling or met with reservations at one or another point,[67] it was regarded, on the whole, as "one of the best

[67] Among the observations made to me the following seem worthy of attention: the proposal that the rite of the blessing of water (nn. 48–50) be done in the baptistery of the new building; the suitability of giving greater importance to the inauguration of the ambo (n. 53), even though the present arrangement does not lack a foundation; the suggestion that the lectionary be further enriched; the request that the summary of the "theology of the altar," now found in the *Praenotanda* of the

things produced by the liturgical reform of Vatican II."[68] Its essential merit was that it had restored "the true identity of the church as place of worship."[69]

The good points commonly singled out are: the main theological idea, which is to show that the church building is a sign of the Church as community and to make the people aware that the "holiness" of the building depends not on the "blessed stones" but on the saving words proclaimed in it, the holy sacrifice offered there, the sacraments of salvation celebrated there, and the Spirit who dwells in the hearts of the faithful gathered in holy assembly; the active role of the celebrating community; the clear linear structure of the *Ordo* and of the individual ritual sequences; the criteria followed in the simplification of the rite, which, while needed, has not taken away its wealth of meaning but has made this accessible and usable in most cases; the balance between attention to the classical line (the "pure" Roman liturgy) and the preservation of impressive ritual sequences added down the centuries, a balance that has not been achieved, however, without sometimes adopting compromise solutions.

5) Conclusion

This history of the development of the *Ordo dedicationis*, like that of every other rite, reflects the ups and downs of the Church's own history with its cultural changes, its political and social situations, and the theological emphases that have succeeded one another through the centuries. But it reflects also, and above all, the Church's idea of itself and its fidelity to Christ.

The history of the *Ordo* is the wide-ranging and varied story of a tension that is both inevitable and takes many forms. I am referring to the tension

"Dedication of an Altar," be shifted to the *Praenotanda* of the "Dedication of a Church." In other cases, the remarks were dictated by the personal tastes of the critic, who proposed various ritual sequences that are perhaps acceptable but lack any foundation in the tradition, or were due to obvious oversights in reading the *Ordo*, such as that of the critic who bemoaned the loss of the ancient order followed in the anointing (first the altar, then the walls of the church), without realizing that this is the order followed in *PR1977* (see nn. 63–65).

[68] M. Paternoster, "Analisi rituale e contenuti teologici dell 'Ordo dedicationis ecclesiae et altaris,'" *RL* 66 (1979) 615.

[69] Marsili, "Dedicazione senza consacrazione," 594.

—between the gospel call for a worship "in spirit and in truth" (John 4:23) that is not conditioned by this place or that and the pragmatic need for the Lord's disciples to gather under a roof and around a table in order to celebrate the divine mysteries;

—between a nostalgia for the sumptuous Old Testament models of dedication and the deliberate simplicity of the first dedicatory rites of Christian worship;

—between the stone walls of the cultic building and the living stones that are the faithful (see 1 Pet 2:5);

—between the numerous washings aimed at freeing the new church from every influence of the Evil One and the grateful memory of baptism;

—between the repeated anointings seen as the power that consecrates a temple and the celebration of the Eucharist as alone consecrating the altar, the church, and everything in it;

—between wood, which is a reminder of the domestic table, and stone, a powerful symbol of Christ (see 1 Cor 10:4) that requires an altar of stone;

—between an ecclesiology dominated by an awareness of the *communio sanctorum* and an ecclesiology dominated by the idea of hierarchy;

—between the rejection of everything deriving from the pagan conception of temples and the acceptance of everything about temples that is an expression of authentic worship;

—between the search for simple liturgical signs and the adoption of complex ritual sequences in which transparent allusion is replaced by annoying allegorism;

—between the sacred and the holy, simplicity and pomp, unlimited time and the need of limiting the time of the celebration;

—between the joyous participation of the faithful in the rite and their exclusion at its most important moments, so as to open the doors of the new cultic building only when the building has already been consecrated.

Some of these tensions are cultural in character, others are of a liturgical nature, and still others are of the theological order. But these tensions have not rarely been fruitful and, when incorporated into a higher synthesis, have gradually led to the postconciliar *Ordo dedicationis*. Every "cultural era" has made its contribution to the development of the *Ordo*, which shows visible traces of Oriental, Gallican, and Germanic influences.

In the age-long process by which the rite has been formed, the sense of continuity and the consciousness of the radical originality of the Christian cultic building have won out over the tensions between diverse attractions and ideas.

Even in periods when the sacral vision of the temple was in the ascendant or when people strayed from the right path and sought inspiration in Old Testament models of dedication or turned their gaze to the pomp of the imperial court, some theological ideas remained firm, even if they were not always sufficiently visible. Some of these are:

—the awareness that from the viewpoint of the New Testament, the true temple of God is the risen Christ (see John 2:21) and that the Christian community and the individual faithful are also a temple (see 1 Cor 3:16-17; 6:19);

—the conviction that the cultic edifice is a multivalent sign, full of meaning and, from some points of view, paradoxical, since, though tied to the earth, it is a sign of the people of God on their journey to the glorious revelation of their Lord;

—it is a sign of the heavenly sanctuary into which Christ has entered in order "to appear in the presence of God on our behalf" (Heb 9:24);

—it is a sign of and place for the many-sided activity of the Church: latreutic, sacramental, caritative, and so on;

—it is a sign of the communion of saints and the place of meeting between the liturgy of heaven and the liturgy of earth, between the inhabitants of "the Jerusalem above" (Gal 4:26) and human beings who are exiles journeying to their fatherland.

The *Ordo dedicationis,* whether Ambrosian or Roman, Byzantine or Coptic, is a "liturgical structure" in which the Church engages itself wholly as the people of God that is hierarchically structured and diversified by its multiplicity of charisms, and in which, too, without economizing, the Church makes use of the richest and most expressive "liturgical signs." The *Ordo* is a book that summarizes fundamental aspects of ecclesiology, profound exegetical insights, and bursts of real poetry about the mystery of the Church. The rite is rich in symbolism, being a kind of gallery of images of the Church:

—the holy *city* (see Matt 5:14; Rev 21:23; *PR1977,* nn. 62, 71, 75) that is illumined by the light of the Lamb;

—the *tent* that travels with the people of God on their groping pilgrimage through the wilderness (see Exod 33:7-11; 2 Sam 7:6; *PR1977,* nn. 62, 74);

—the *temple* of Jerusalem, a potent sign of God's presence in the midst of his people, a presence that is fulfilled in Christ and the ecclesial community (see *PR1977*, nn. 48, 50, 57, 62, 64, 75, 79, 84);

—the *vine*, planted by the heavenly vintner and the object of his special love (see Isa 5:1-7; Matt 21:33-43; *PR1977*, n. 62);

—the chaste *virgin* who keeps herself for Christ (see 2 Cor 11:2; *PR1977*, n. 62);

—the *bride* resplendent in glorious beauty (see Eph 5:26-27; Rev 19:7; 21:2, 9; 22:17; *PR1977*, n. 62);

—the fruitful *mother* of children (see Gal 4:26; Rev 12:17; *PR1977*, n. 62).

Bibliography

SOURCES AND DOCUMENTS

BAR 159–173.

Ordo Romanus XLII. In M. Andrieu, ed. *Les Ordines Romani du haut moyen âge*, 4:309–349.

Ordo Romanus XLII, ibid., 351–402.

Pontificale Romano-Germanicum saeculi decimi. XXXIII: *Ordo Romanus ad dedicandam ecclesiam;* XXXIV: *Item benedictio basilicae novae;* XXXV: *Quid significent duodecim candelae;* XL: *Ordo ad benedicendam ecclesiam.* In C. Vogel and R. Elze, *Le romano-germanique du Xe siècle*, 82–88, 89, 90–121, 124–173. Vatican City, 1963.

Pontificale Romanum saeculi XII. XVII: *Incipit ordo ad benedicendam ecclesiam.* In M. Andrieu, ed., *Le Pontifical romain au moyen âge* I: *Le Pontifical romain du XIIe siècle*, 176–195. Vatican City, 1938.

Pontificale secundum consuetudinem et usum Romanae Curiae. XXIII: *Ordo ad benedicendam ecclesiam.* In M. Andrieu, ed., *Le Pontifical romain au moyen âge* II: *Le Pontifical de la Curie romaine au XIIIe siècle*, 421–440. Vatican City, 1940.

Pontificale G. Durandi. II: *De ecclesiae dedicatione.* In M. Andrieu, ed., *Pontifical romain au moyen âge* III: *Le Pontifical de Guillaume Durand*, 455–478. Vatican City, 1940.

Pontificale Romanum. Editio typica emendata II. Vatican Polyglot Press, 1961.

Ordo dedicationis ecclesiae et altaris deque aliis locis et rebus sacrandis. Editio typica [in fact: *ad experimentum*]. Vatican Polyglot Press, 1973.

Ordo dedicationis ecclesiae et altaris necnon benedictionis aliorum locorum et rerum. Editio typica [in fact: *ad experimentum*]. Vatican Polyglot Press, 1974.

Ordo dedicationis ecclesiae et altaris. Editio typica. Vatican Polyglot Press, 1977. ET: "Dedication of a Church and an Altar." In *The Rites of the Catholic Church,* 2:339–428. New York, 1980; Collegeville, Minn., 1991.

STUDIES

AA.VV. *Gli spazi della celebrazione rituale.* Milan, 1984.

AA.VV. *Il tempio.* Acts of the 18th National Liturgical Week, Monreale, Aug. 28–Sept. 1, 1967. Rome, 1968.

AA.VV. *La dimora di Dio tra gli uomini: Tempio e assemblea.* Acts of the 43rd National Liturgical Week, Rome, 1993.

AA.VV. *Spazio e rito.* Acts of the 23rd National Liturgical Week, Rome, 1996.

Benz, S. "Zur Geschichte der Römischen Kirchweihe nach den Texten des 7. bis 9. Jahrhunderts." In AA.VV., *Enkainia,* 62–109. Gesammelte Arbeiten zum achthundertjährigen Weihegedächtnis der Abteikirche Maria Laach, am 24 August 1956. Düsseldorf, 1956.

Braga, C. "In secundam partem Pontificalis Romani." *EphLit* 76 (1962) 201–280.

Calabuig, I. M. "L'Ordo dedicationis ecclesiae et altaris. Appunti di una lettura." *Not* 13 (1977) 391–450.

Chengalikavil, L. "La dedicazione della chiesa e dell'altare." *Anàmnesis* 7:54–109.

Congar, Y. *Le mystère du Temple.* Paris, 1957. ET: *The Mystery of the Temple.* Trans. R. F. Trevett. Westminster, Md., 1962.

Emminghaus, J. H. "Der Gottesdienstliche Raum und seine Gestaltung." In *Gottesdienst der Kirche: Handbuch der Liturgiewissenschaft,* 3:347–416. Regensburg, 1987.

Evenou, J. "Le nouveau rituel de la dédicace." *MD* 134 (1978) 85–105.

Gelineau, J. "Le lieu de l'assemblée." In *Dans vos assemblées,* 1:107–124. Paris, 1971.

Iñiguez, J. A. *El altar cristiano.* Vol. 1: *De los orígenes a Carlomagno.* Vol. 2: *De Carlomagno al siglo XIII.* Pamplona, 1978, 1991.

Jounel, P. "Dedicazione delle chiese e degli altari." *NDL* 352–367.

Jounel, P., and A. M. Roguet. *Dédicace d'une église.* Tournai, 1962.

Martimort, A. G. "Le rituel de la consécration des églises." *MD* 63 (1960) 86–95.

Mazzarello, S. "Il nuovo rito della dedicazione di una chiesa." In *Cristo ieri oggi e sempre,* 173–192. Acts of the 29th National Liturgical Week, Rome, 1979.

Righetti, M. *Manuale di storia liturgica,* 1:416–553. 3rd ed. Milan, 1964.

Salaville, S. *Cérémonial de la consécration d'une église selon le rite byzantin.* Vatican City, 1937.

Valentini, G., and G. Caronia. *Domus Ecclesiae: L'edificio sacro cristiano.* Bologna, 1969.

MONOGRAPHS

MD 70 (1962): *La dédicace des églises.*

MD 136 (1978): *Des lieux pour célébrer.*

MD 197: *L'espace liturgique.*

Phase 111 (1979): *Las casas de la Iglesia.*

RL 1979/4: *La chiesa spazio liturgico per la communità cristiana.*

RPL 88 (1978): *Il nuovo "Rito della dedicazione della Chiesa."*

Vita Monastica 145 (1981): *La communità tempio del Signore.*

Crispino Valenziano

14

Liturgical Architecture

Space and time, the coordinates that define human existence in the world, emerge from their formless chaos and produce the formed world; they become "here" and "now" and thus acquire a "meaning" for humanity. In our worship we neither sacralize them (in the pagan manner) nor sanctify them (in the Hebrew manner), but we do give them a new form in the liturgy. For Christians, it is by becoming elements of a liturgical celebration that space and time become the here and now of the paschal mystery, of the historical events of salvation, even while not being cut off in any way from ordinary times and places.

Liturgically, then, the specific character of the church as cultic edifice has, neither more nor less, the same relationship to space that the specific character of the Christian feast has to amorphous time. Our problem, therefore, is one of architecture, of shaping space in an orderly and beautiful way by turning it into a place through the liturgical meaning imposed on it.

This meaning is mediated along the two lines of function and structure, and this in a permanent parallelism and correspondence that preserves the built-up place from both the mechanical functionalism and the abstract structuralism to which it would be reduced were it to be constructed solely in function of the rites to be celebrated or solely with a structure based on identifying signs (functionalism and structuralism are two dangers to which all twentieth-century architecture has largely succumbed). A ritual function requires a purpose to be achieved, and a structure based on signs requires a cause that produces it. My exposition will therefore explain the two components in such a way as to bring out the essential organization of a liturgical building. Such a building is, at one and the same time, a cultic edifice for ritual functions and for the celebration of the sacraments, and a church by reason of its sign-structure, having its cause in the figurative metonymy of the Church as a kingdom assembly of priests.

Both components, then, exist in a similar way as far as the essential elements of the liturgy are concerned, but they also show many varieties as far as the many rites to be celebrated and the many ecclesial Rites that exist are concerned. In relation, however, to the diversity of architectural styles that concretize the components, it has to be said that while in certain cultural phases or places the styles are supported by typologies that are, in addition, univocal, yet no style is inherently alien to the cultural transversality of the liturgy, which is analogous to the transversality of the Christian message and Christian salvation. Eastern churches and western churches are therefore different, and so are the churches of different periods and the churches built by one or other architect.

My essay will follow the trajectories already mentioned. Meanwhile, my wish is for greater inculturation (that there be churches in every culture by which the Churches show forth their identity) and for a finer poetic quality (that there be churches representing every kind of esthetic creativity, with the aid of which the Holy Spirit will express and effect the marriage of the Church and the Word of God in human time and space).

It is evident that I shall be mixing together theological and historical aspects with canonical regulations that I take from the fundamental prescriptions of the liturgical books and from the great ecclesial tradition, while distinguishing this tradition from possible distortions and accidental regressions, but without embalming it in meaningless typologies. At the same time, I shall be proceeding architectonically and shall not venture into other aspects, except insofar as necessary. Clients, consultors, and brokers are jointly involved.

I. IDENTIFYING QUALIFICATIONS

It is customary to tell an architect who asks for advice as he begins to plan: "Design the altar, ambo, and baptistery we want; locate them and cover them." That is: Do not try to cover a containing space where different things will be successively located (a good general principle!), because you will not succeed either in identifying the "containing space" or in specifying the "things." The planning of a liturgical building depends on the description of the altar, the ambo, and the baptistery, and on their unified interrelationship as prescribed by logic and theology.

1. Altar

An altar by its structure symbolizes the table both of the last evening and of Calvary on the last day of Jesus' self-emptying life. The reason: the altar is the place of remembrance of the Supper and of the sacrifice of Christ the Savior: of the whole Christ, head and members, Bridegroom and Bride (this aspect of remembrance is sometimes signified also by the relics of the martyrs that are placed in the altar). The function of the altar is to receive the specifically Christian bread and wine of the supper-sacrifice. Any other use would in small or great measure betray the nature of the altar; it is for this sole use that ministers gather at the altar.

Meaningful and unequivocal forms of the altar have emerged and have become so normal that other forms, rightly or wrongly used by exception, are easily reducible to them. Ever since the Christian altar has come into use, it has been of stone or is as solid as stone, for "the rock is Christ." There is but one altar, for "Christ is one," his table is one, his Calvary is one. It is square or tends to be square, for it is a table open "to the four winds" of the world. It is elevated, for it is a Calvary to which all "shall lift their eyes." It is small or tends to be small, for it does not receive a "mass of bloody victims."

The location is determined by the synaxis. It stands at the end of the main axis of the church, as the focal point and goal of the Church. It stands (preferably) under the "ciborium" [baldachin], the place of christological remembrance under the invocation of the Spirit.

An iconography follows that derives from the altar's own iconology. It is signed by the cross, it is named from the Chi-Rho, it is "of gold" like the altar of the eschatological apocalypse, it bears the image of Christ the Lamb; and the ciborium, if there is one, bears the image of the Spirit as dove.

From the Church of Jerusalem, the womb of mimetic memory in every respect for liturgical architecture since the very beginning, since Emperor Constantine, there has come the imitation of the elevation on which the altar is based, the "bema," which recalls the "upper room" of the Cenacle. The iconography of the bema, with its "historical" and/or "typological" and/or "theological" images, always reflects the eucharistic celebration that takes place there. But in the various cultures the platform has taken on a variety of characteristics, these even being integrated each with the next. Thus the basilica of the Roman Empire included an apse; the temple usages of the Persian Empire turned the bema into a sanctuary enclosed by a high wall, after the manner of the Hebrew "holy of holies"; the churches of the Malabarese would replace the wall with a "curtain" in the Hebrew manner, and the Armenians would do the same. Meanwhile, the churches of the Byzantines and the Slavs would provide the bema with iconastases of varying degrees of transparency, with the intention that these were to be revealing veils or else iconastases describing the mysteries that lie beyond time and beyond the celebration of them in time.

In the East the altar is located in the center of the sanctuary; the Copts in particular, however, have pushed back, toward the apse, altars of ansate shape that repeat the form of the embracing apse; the Syro-Chaldeans place the altar directly against the back wall. The West has created analogous situations by placing the altar at the center of the bema, sometimes between transennas or openwork screens, but also more or less toward the front or toward the back. The exception was the baroque form that made the altar the base for devices on the wall and brought to completion in the post-Tridentine period the reductive process, begun by the Gothic, of multiplying altars in the nave or in chapels not cut off from the nave.

In the West after Vatican II a type of altar not previously known in such a universal form is the altar facing the people. In fact, it is not so much the altar as it is the celebration that faces the people. But this successful pastoral solution, which is the direct opposite of having an enclosing wall or curtain (this was in any case a move in the direction of Judaism), needs to be further defined in order to avoid distorted projections and unforeseen consequences. An example: the full-blown platform that absorbs everyone and everything and transforms the bema into an inappropriate stage, a widespread practice that reduces liturgical participation.

2. *Ambo*

By its structure the ambo symbolizes the empty tomb on Easter morning, for it is the place at which the proclamation that founds the faith is repeated. Moreover, in Christian eyes the liturgical proclamation of the Scriptures, of both the Old and the New Testaments, is by its very nature a proclamation of Easter; otherwise, it would bring neither message nor salvation through Christ in thc Spirit. It is the function of the ambo to bring the voice of the reader to the gathered assembly, just as it was the function of the wooden platform erected for reading the Scriptures on the festive days of the rebuilding of Jerusalem. While mechanical means of amplifying the voice may seem to render the ambo useless, there is still a need of gathering the assembly around it. For the Christian assembly is brought together by the Spirit through the Word, and through the Word the assembly is united and given direction in the Spirit.

From this function very meaningful and eloquent forms derive. The ambo is built to be a "monument"; the Gospels use that term of the tomb on Easter. It is exclusively one, even when it has two or three stories; so too the tomb of the risen Jesus was one. It is elevated, even higher than the altar, for the proclamation of salvation comes from on high.

From its function it also derives its location as catalyst of the celebration. Originally, for structural reasons, it stood at the center of the nave, and then, for practical reasons, at the side, but always in the nave, not on the other side of the threshold dividing the nave from the bema on which the altar stands.

From its function its specific iconography is also derived. It is signed with the tombstone rolled back and (sometimes) covered like the Anastasis in Jerusalem, and it bears the image of the angel-deacon who tells the good news to the "myrrh-bearing" women or tells of the risen Jesus appearing to Mary Magdalene, the "apostle to the apostles."

It is only the rotunda of the Anastasis in Jerusalem that never had an ambo, for there the proclamation of Easter (whether during the celebration or apart from an actual celebration) is accomplished by the open door to the physically present empty tomb, in the presence of which any symbolization of the event would be superfluous. All other churches have "imitated" the Anastasis by symbolizing the event in various ways, depending on the culture. The Chaldeans place the ambo at the center of the nave and connect it with the sanctuary by means of a narrow walkway called *beth seqaqone,* which symbolizes the narrow path followed by truth from earth to heaven. In like manner, Emperor Justinian installed the covered ambo at the center of Hagia Sophia, linking it to the sanctuary by a similar "isthmus." A notable case is that of the Syrians, who likewise place the ambo at the center of the nave but up on a bema; as we Latins have transformed the bema of the altar into a presbyterium, the Syrians have made a comparable use of the bema beneath the ambo—and done so with greater reasonableness than we have shown and with a better eye to the assembly.

The growing incomprehensibility of the liturgical languages has in time led to a gradual omission of the ambo; this was a common occurrence. But the phenomenon reached the lowest level of tolerability with the omission of the "monument" in the baroque West, for this omission conspired with the incomprehensibility of Latin to effect the loss of paschal spirituality and of sacramental symbolic values. The recovery has been marked by the same slowness that has marked the recovery of the liturgical use of vernaculars. The two, working together, have effected a recovery of the rich mystery aspect of Easter with its iconic elements. Think of the temporal iconization of Sunday as the weekly paschal feast, with the spatial iconization taking the form of the ambo as the Easter feast of the nave. Provided always that this recovery is not further delayed by an excessive emphasis on the function of the structure. Think of how our liturgical reform has been blocked in this respect (as I said) for the purpose of reducing a kind of purely visual liturgical participation. This reduction has led to the placement on the usual full platform of so-called ambos—I mean the lecterns that are set up facing the assembly and are all the less meaningful as they are more pretentious.

The ambo, then, attracts to itself the whole range of problems affecting the nave, of which it is the focal point.

The structure of the nave symbolizes the "church" as the part does the whole; in other words, the figurative metonymy of the church, the entire liturgical building, describes the nave by identifying it in an emblematic way. This is to say that the nave defines the church as a place. And not without reason, since the function of the ambo is to welcome the synaxis.

The assembly is the Church acting liturgically. More or less sporadic practices of separating the ministers of the altar by placing them on the bema prove to be striking statements about ecclesiologies in crisis. In such cases the result is to play (inside and outside the building) with architectonic symbolizations of the church, as well as with anthropomorphic, cosmomorphic, and other allegorizations, that are alien and derivative and are not potentially constitutive "ecclesial" symbols but substitutes for these.

The iconography of the hall shows its "ecclesiality" (if it does not, it is spurious). In varying ways but with a sure touch, it represents the history of the ecclesial people from the ancient assembly to the new assembly or, in other words, its unity, holiness, catholicity, and apostolicity or, in still other words, its mirroring celebration of the faith (the ecumenical councils in the hall of Bethlehem . . .) or of the liturgy. When the main door is centered in the façade of the church, it represents Christ as "door to the sheepfold," and the gaze travels to the central window in the back wall where Christ is the "sun of justice," like Alpha looking toward Omega. And where the hall is connected with the sanctuary by a cupola, the cupola depicts the glorious Christ over the "omphalos," with the linked four evangelists at the four pendentives on the large load-bearing pillars around the symbolic center of the building, marking as it were the center of the earth under the center of the heaven that opens above: for it is at the omphalos that every sacramental *admirabile commercium* is celebrated. It is not by chance that the Constantinian basilica in Bethlehem did not mark the omphalos on the pavement (as was customary in other churches lacking a cupola) but opened up the pavement over the grotto where the divine Word had his human birth.

In the nave the assembly gathers in a dynamic, not a static, way: not so much arranged stagnantly (a condition emphasized by the lateral naves, if there are any) as ready for the processional movement (toward the altar or baptistery) and in the right posture (toward the altar or ambo or baptistery). Paradoxically, there is a blatant contrast with the static arrangement of the ministers of altar in churches where, unduly separated from the body of the assembly, they are drawn up near the altar even when not serving at it, so that they manage to cancel out their proper movement even though this is something that can least be hidden in the celebration. Therefore the location of the bishop's throne and the chairs of the presiding celebrants and the others with them needs very careful planning. For the need is to bring out, at one and the same time, several things: the fact that these ministers belong entirely to the single assembly; their presidential service of this assembly; their presence around the ambo like the rest of the assembly; and their procession to the altar, unlike the rest of the assembly.

The churches of the Syrians, under the influence of the great Sassanid buildings, have kept their doors at the sides of the nave and not in the façade; I have already mentioned how they have the ambo on a bema in the center of the nave. Although the churches of the Byzantines and Slavs provide an episcopal throne and presbyteral chairs in the sanctuary for occasional use, they arrange the ministers of the altar at the head of the assembly; similarly, they place the two choirs of singers at the head of the assembly, on the two sides of the *solea*. This last is a projection of the altar bema into the nave; it is the primary place of diaconal activity and corresponds to a similar projection that the Syro-Chaldeans call a *qestroma*.

As a result of our uncertainties about the ambo, the plan and general arrangement of the nave are still an unresolved problem for us Westerners after Vatican II. In addition to the improvised arrangements of the presbyteral chairs and even of the episcopal *cathedra* and to the absence of a place for the deacon even in cathedrals, a further indicator of the general uneasiness about proper arrangement is the uncertainty about the place of the cantors and of the lectors who minister from the ambo. The lectors have disappeared from the ancient *schola* around the galleries of the ambo in the nave, a place that functioned as the location of the choir, cantors, and lectors but was structurally the Easter "garden" of the empty tomb (as shown by its iconography). The cantors, for their part, were moved to the stands around the organ, which was attached to the wall or in any case elevated in competition with the vanished ambo. The lectors and cantors, thus likewise separated from the assembly, now await a correct arrangement that will once again make them a fully integral part of the synaxis. And, along with them, the still wandering ministers.

3. Baptistery

By its structure the baptismal font symbolizes the tomb of the risen Christ, into which the catechumens descend in order to die in his death and from which the neophytes arise, risen in his resurrection. It also symbolizes the womb of the Church in which these individuals are reborn in the Spirit. Its function is to provide the bath in the sacramental water of rebirth in the Spirit, of death and resurrection in Christ. The structure and function of the font extend to the baptistery, which turns the baptismal font into the third place that identifies a church.

The baptistery with its font is again obviously one, as are the altar and the ambo. In ambo and baptistery, which are interrelated in various ways, the octagon comes into play (Easter on the eighth day) along with the circle and the concave-convex (the womb filled with the Holy Spirit). In the font, the hexagon also comes into play (the six days of the first creation as type of the work of God in the new creation).

It hardly needs saying that the iconography derives from the history of salvation and baptismal typologies. But it is not useless to recall that the privileged element in the iconography of the baptistery is light: baptism itself is an "illumination" or "enlightenment," and the baptistery is a φωτιστήριον, a "place of illumination."

According as the intention is to highlight one or other aspect of the baptismal mystery, the location of the baptistery is different. Emphasis on purification prefers a baptistery and font separated from the church; emphasis on incorporation into the body of Christ prompts a baptistery-font located at the entrance to the church; emphasis on participation in the death and resurrection of Christ has led to the baptistery-font being joined to the ambo. Easterners still prefer a location in the narthex, the threshold from outside to inside and the link between the inside and the outside.

We Westerners after Vatican II have reacted against the location that has long reduced the baptistery to a simple font (reduction in structure) and of the font to a place of simple washing (reduction in function), but we often let ourselves be limited by the standard of visual participation. As a result, we do not plan a baptistery and we use an ordinary basin, and thus we really celebrate baptism without a baptistery (on the usual elevated platform) and without a font (with a movable vessel). The uncertainty is about a substantial active participation in the liturgy rather than about the "place" of the baptistery. Also, the indications favor the planning of a font for baptism by infusion *and* for baptism by immersion, and they favor the planning of a baptistery as an identifying mark of the church.

This last point is worth dwelling on. If an altar and an ambo are "normal" in churches, a baptistery is "normal" only for cathedrals and parish churches. Yet it is not an abstraction to say that if a church is to be fully identified as a "place," it will become a liturgical "building" in virtue of the three "foundational places" of celebration; it is no accident that even in nonparochial churches a baptistery can be planned. Moreover, only in exceptional cases are new churches not parochial churches, rather than the other way around. Let me return to the subject from another point of view, namely, that of "locating and covering."

To "locate" within the building is to connect the structure with its functions. In our case these relationships become clear from our very perception of the places in question, but because the baptistery is by its nature polyvalent, it is worth our while to review this polyvalency.

In my opinion, the polyvalency flows from the "light" (both theological and architectonic). In the final analysis, even in churches that lack a baptistery, the receptive form of the baptistery, namely, light, is no less an identifying mark of these churches. But there must be a conscious planning. The altar is to the bema as the ambo is to the nave; but this does not mean that the baptismal font must be to the baptistery as the ambo is to the nave and the altar to the bema. Rather, as the ambo is to the nave and the altar to the bema, so the baptistery-font is to the light. In churches the light is designed no less than are the bema and the nave; moreover, the bema and the nave are designed to be in the light. It is the privilege of the light to be emblematically receptive of the baptistery with its font and formally receptive of the entire structure.

The architecture of light plays a determining role in churches both because light plays that role in every kind of architecture and because light marks the identity of nave and ambo in the synaxis and of altar and bema in the church. The subtle relationship which all the Rites reflect in "building" their churches, in erecting their "houses," is the triangulation of bema-nave-light. And the polyvalence of the baptistery and the baptismal font is unified by the all-embracing light. This is the enigma encountered in codifying and decodifying a liturgical building: a process that too many people try to replace with an esoteric sacrality. Even from this point of view, the pointing of the church toward the dawning of the light is not accidental.

To "cover" the building is to complete the construction. The roof faces the floor, and the two bring the walls into harmony. Traditionally the roofs of churches have been trussed or arched. In the case of truly magnificent structures, the peak and the caissons have been gilded, painted, or carved in ways more or less deliberately based on iconography suggested by the ark of Noah, which is a type of the Church, while plaster and stucco have been modeled iconographically on the curvature of heaven over earth. The floor has looked up to the roof with a consistent iconology based on the surrounding shipwrecked world or the paradisal garden in the cosmic Eden. The pavements have been richly crossed by designs showing the dynamics of the assembly: directional passages, circular interlacings, and processional pointers amid stationary carpets. By various forms of the kinds mentioned, roofs and pavements have brought into harmony the walls, the colonnades, the overhead windows, and much else.

And, lo!, the light reappears, for the perfection that brings a subtle harmony to the "royal house," the "house of the kingdom and priests," is the light in which the synaxis vividly reflects, by its very being, the beauty of the wedding of Christ with the Church. The circle of the hours and the cycle of the seasons, along with the by-no-means accidental directedness to the east, is priceless and unique in the way in which it captures the light in the south, in the west, and in the north as material reflections of the beauty of the Church. Mosaics and windows are esthetically attuned to the light and are at the same time superb poetic devices.

II. INTERIORLY

If the plan takes account of all that has been said, there will be architectural interaction between, on the one hand, the liturgical "place" thus identified and, on the other, the other places that are structurally one with it, as well as the accessories that have recovered their simple functional role. In this regard the various Rites behave analogously with ours, but less rigidly. On the other hand, the West has certainly developed these secondary aspects to a much greater extent. It would not be profitable, however, to belittle everything; it is instead enriching to cultivate what is worthwhile in such a way that every environment may use it in its own original way and interchangeably.

1. The Weekday Chapel and the Chapel of Eucharistic Reservation

The need for a chapel independent of the place of assembly but an organic part of the liturgical building is created by the daily eucharistic celebration in which only small groups participate. This need of a place is matched by the demand for a rite that is itself of the everyday. Perhaps the second need even precedes the first: is it really appropriate, for example, to have the Word proclaimed from the ambo for assemblies of a dozen or so participants? The weekday chapel will therefore not have an ambo, and sooner or later the ritual conclusion will be drawn that the daily celebration does not take place at the ambo. This example is self-evident, but the logic at work is very instructive. A weekday chapel is modeled on the *domus ecclesia,* not on the *domus cathedralis.*

One thing is certain: the weekday chapel cannot be assimilated to the chapel where the Eucharist is reserved. As a matter of fact, the daily eucharistic celebration is not very different from the Sunday celebration as far as the permanence of the Eucharist after the celebration is concerned. The theological and devotional language used of eucharistic reservation is well known. In light of it, it is impossible for us today to plan a church without a chapel for eucharistic reservation. This chapel will not have an altar but will be geared to maximizing eucharistic devotion, on the lines set down by the relevant liturgical books. The case is different with existing churches; but even for these a solution should be sought that is as close as possible to the solution for new churches, that is, a chapel that is independent of the assembly hall where the altar is the focal point and everything is organically connected with the altar.

2. *The images of the cross, Mary, and the saints*

The martyr's cross with the crucified Christ on it is *per se* to be solidly fixed in place (or carried); think of how in the East the cross is fixed on the top of the iconostasis. The jeweled cross of Christ's glory, on the other hand, is *per se* to be suspended (or hung); think of the cross that in the East hangs from the triumphal arch. Just as a church is inconceivable without the one or the other of these crosses, so too it cannot have a multiplicity of crosses and/or crucifixes (sculptured, painted, chiseled, or embroidered) if it is not to divide their spiritual impact. Nor can we be enthusiastic about the crucifixes that are attached to the back wall of all the churches and/or the astylar crosses that stand beside all the altars. This kind of solution is unconvincing in any architectural plan. Every church—no longer every altar!—is to have "its" cross.

The image of Mary is "spousal" in relation to the image of the crucified Jesus. All the better if, as in the form classic in the West and even more in the East, it makes visible the Church in its final perfection. In any case, it is an image that reflects the assembly as face to face with its Lord, and does so by the very fact that it is the image of the all-holy woman in whom every kind of holiness is prefigured. It is not sufficient, therefore, that the image of Mary in a church be restricted to representations of some incident or other that has little of the theological pregnancy of the events of salvation or spiritual contemplation of the mystery (such, for example, are images of apparitions). The image of Mary's presence is in fact "connatural" with the presence of the divine Persons to human beings; it is an image of christological, pneumatological, and trinitarian presence.

The images of the saints are part of the overall iconographical program and are a mirror of the assembly, although "patronal" or "titular" saints are to be given priority, especially in churches where their relics rest in Christ. Attention must therefore be given, in planning, not to overturn but rather to bring out the "hierarchies" involved in the mysteries; I am referring to hierarchies in the theological manner of Pseudo-Dionysius, who is in fact recapitulating venerable traditions that extensively inspired the iconographical programs of both East and West.

3. *The Room for the Sacrament of Penance*

This is a new concretization of the penitential dimension that was accommodated in the old narthex. It would be a gain to recapture fully this ancient ancestor and to plan for it anew in a coherent way, with an iconography based on its iconology. Once again, in this we are to follow the lines taken by the relevant liturgical books on penance.

4. *Places That Are Merely Functional*

The most important of these is the sacristy and its attached premises. In our present context, it is recommended that if its ritual functionality is to be suited to the celebration, the sacristy should be planned in such a way as to be accessible from the end of the bema and the front of the nave (also from the transverse nave if there is one, or from the middle of the nave). In other words, new sacristies are to be built into the long axis of the church, not the cross axis, in order to make it possible, without difficulty or contrivances, to enter and exit from solemn celebrations and subordinate services.

Places of this kind include more than the sacristy and its attached premises, but for our purpose no more need be discussed.

III. EXTERNALLY

The outside of a church is all the more authentic the more it translates the inside. This is always in interaction with its figurative metonymy; that is (let us express this representationally with the tools given us by Vatican II), so that *Sacrosanctum Concilium* may be inflected externally along with *Gaudium et spes,* that is, along with the Church's relationship to the world, just as it is conjugated internally along with *Lumen gentium,* that is, with the sacramental constitution of the Church.

1. Architecture and Urban Planning
A liturgical building enters into a dialogue with the city, and even with the territory, in a way that corresponds to the proper relationship between Church and world: the day before yesterday or there yonder in the submissiveness of an imposed silence; yesterday or here in the catalytic action of a carefully chosen pivotal point; today or here with the discreetness of a witness' suggestion; tomorrow or yonder with the dignity of a responsible freedom . . . The prudent and efficacious attitude taken by the Church in the world thus becomes part of the figurative metonymy of a church: it is not the purely stylistic choice between building high or low or the politico-social appropriateness of a western campanile or an eastern *simandra* built of planks, or the backlash either of a ghettoizing secularization or of a demagogy that places everything on the same level—it is none of these that will decide whether the Church sets itself apart or becomes indistinguishable. History, in its own fashion, will synchronize the diachronisms that thus follow one upon another.

The territory, however, makes its own demands, ranging from those made by human nature or external nature around us to the expectations of individuals and cultural communities, and to legislative or bureaucratic requirements, all of them alike making their mark if they are legitimate.

2. The Complex
Do not make the mistake of conceiving the church as a cultic place uprooted and standing by itself. The result of this outlook would probably be a room arranged so as to be multifunctional. Nor should we suppose that the idea of what people today call a "parish complex" is a Western invention after Vatican II. Both the West and the East, in both their cathedral buildings and their monasteries, planned their ecclesial architecture (spontaneously, we might say) to include the needs of evangelization and caritative activity in places that went along with the liturgical hall. What is new to us Westerners after Vatican II is that what we take as a model is not the episcopal complex of the cities nor the monastic complex out in the country but the parish complex of the suburbs. Just as the model celebration is not the cathedral rite or the monastic rite in a form miniaturized to fit needs, but the Sunday celebration of an assembly of about five hundred persons, a presbyter (and a deacon), two acolytes and two servers, a nonprofessional group

of singers (and an organist), and some "extraordinary ministers" of the Eucharist.

The model architecture of a church *hic et nunc* is that which is planned by an experienced and serious professional architect who comes to grips with this celebration of this community.

* * *

On January 6, 1996, the Congregation for the Oriental Churches promulgated an Instruction on the Application of the Liturgical Laws of the Code of Canon Law of the Oriental Churches; chapter 14 of the Instruction was devoted to the "places, actions, and objects" of the liturgy.

We were pleased to see that the course we have followed in our reflection on architecture corresponds to the great tradition of the universal Church.

Not only that, but we also found ourselves in agreement with the conclusion (which we therefore cite explicitly here) on the involvement of the human person in his/her totality as conveying the ultimate meaning of art for the liturgy:

"The human person in his/her totality is enlightened by God and reaches the fullest possible relationship with him through adoption as his child (see John 1:13). . . . No aspect is excluded . . . in fact, each aspect contributes to constituting the spiritual building raised up by the Lord. The human person, who is priest of creation, then associates everything else with himself/herself and so gives inanimate things a voice with which to praise the creator. In the incarnation of the Son of God humanity is assumed by the Word, and the divinity sanctifies and consecrates the universe. Here is to be found the Christian meaning of the spaces, actions, and objects that interact with the believer in divine worship" (Instruction, n. 100).

Bibliography

AA.VV. *Gli spaze della celebrazione rituale.* Milan, 1984.

AA.VV. *Binnale di Venezia: Architettura e spazio sacro nelle modernità.* Milan, 1992.

AA.VV. *Arte e liturgica.* Cinisello Balsamo, 1993.

AA.VV. "Spazio e rito: Aspetti costitutivi dei luoghi della celebrazione cristiana." In *Atti della XXIII Settimana di Studio APL 1994*. Rome, 1996.

Bouyer, L. *Architettura e liturgia.* Magnano, 1994.

Ciampani, P., ed. "Liturgia e architettura." In *Atti del Convegno "Azione liturgica e comunità nell'edificio sacro."* Assisi, 1965.

Cornoldi, A. *L'architettura dell'edificio sacro.* Rome, 1995.

De Carli, C., ed. *Le nuove chiese della diocesi di Milano 1945–1993*. Milan, 1994.

Lukken, G., and M. Searle. *Semiotics and Church: Architecture.* Kempen, 1993.

Lukken, G. "Die architektonischen Dimensionen des Rituals." In L. van Tongeren and Ch. Caspers, eds. *Per visibilia ad invisibilia,* 360–374. Kempen, 1994.

____. "La sémiotique de l'architecture de l'église en tant que sémiotique du visuel." In L. van Tongeren and Ch. Caspers, eds. *Per visibilia ad invisibilia,* 375–394. Kempen, 1994.

Valenziano, C. *Architetti di chiese.* Palermo, 1995.

Zahner, W. *Rudolf Schwarz, Baumeister der neuen Gemeinde: Ein Beitrag zum Gespräch zwischen Liturgietheologie und Architektur in der Liturgischen Bewegung.* Alterberge, 1992.

Cettina Militello

15

A Theology of Liturgical Space

I shall divide my essay into the two areas that call for attention: the biblical and ecclesiological bases, and the more specifically liturgical area. In discussing the latter, I shall bring out the structural and functional peculiarities of Christian cultic space.

My basic thesis is that liturgical space arises from the interaction of, on the one hand, the theological status of the people of God who gather there and, on the other, the place itself, whose theological dynamics support and signify the status of the gathered people. The people of God, united by the Spirit and the Word and called to give praise to the Father through the Son in the Spirit, are one with their house; that is, the house externalizes and renders visible the people's theological status. In short, the church building is a spatial icon of the Church as mystery.[1]

The liturgy celebrated in the church building gives various forms to the emblematic presence of God in the midst of his people. It celebrates the wonders he has performed in history. It looks to him as the ultimate goal of an encounter and a praise which have no end and which the celebration itself anticipates, so that the people on pilgrimage is also in a real sense an eschatological people.

[1] I am concerned, therefore, with different matters than those on which Y. J.-M. Congar focuses in his article " L'Église, ce n'est pas les mures mais les fidèles," *MD* 70 105–114. But his thesis, which he supports with attractive patristic and canonical testimonies, is not opposed to mine. If in fact the Church is something other than the church building (since the Church is indeed the faithful and not the walls), it is necessary for this very reason to ask why we have so naturally used the same word for these two different realities. Congar helps us answer this question, and I shall borrow some basic ideas from him (see his *Il mistero del Tempio* [Turin, 1963]). ET: *The Mystery of the Temple,* trans. R. F. Trevett (Westminster, Md., 1962).

In the spatio-temporal continuum, then, there is accomplished the mystery of the assembly as the mystery of the God who convokes it. It is this that really turns a cosmic space into the human "liturgical place."

I. TOWARD A THEOLOGICAL FOUNDATION

1. *Local Church and Worshiping Assembly*

The etymology of the word "church," as everyone knows, takes us back to the Old Testament *qahal Yahweh,* which the messianic community of salvation reinterpreted in order to make it the basic expression of its own self-consciousness.[2] The ἐκκλησία is the assembly actually gathered here and now, in the immediacy of a space and a time that are experiential and experienced. It is true, of course, that this space and this time are transcended both in memory and eschatologically in accordance with the dynamics of the history of salvation, the mystery of which the assembly celebrates and in doing so experiences and proclaims.

All this is certainly behind the semantic ambivalence created by the fact that the word "church" is also used for the Christian building, with the result that it is sometimes difficult to discern which is predominant: the Church and its mystery or the church understood simply as a building for worship.

On the other hand, the new covenantal community of salvation, like the Old Testament community before it, does not start from an immediate experience of a place of worship but rather reaches this experience after a journey on which it has been open to the suitabilities and solicitations of other cultures.[3] It is, however, in the construction of a building for worship that the mature religious status of both the former and the new people finds expression. In that sense, the Jerusalem temple is emblematic.

2. *The Anthropological Data*

These considerations turn our attention to, even before any theological postulates, the anthropological constants of "place" and of the location in it of the individual and the human community.

[2] K. L. Schmidt, "ἐκκλησία," *TDNT* 3:501–536.

[3] See, e.g., R. de Vaux, *Ancient Israel: Its Life and Institutions,* trans. J. McHugh (New York, 1966) 284–288.

The individual and the multitude of individuals who in unceasing succession make up the community do not experience in this world a natural absence of place and time; rather it is in place and time that their existence, and their consciousness of this existence, matures. This fact calls for keys to significant interpretation. The history of human beings is one with the history of their habitat. Changes in home and city are elements in the fuller development of their values and life-settings. At work here are complex anthropological and cultural dialectics, in addition to psychological and social dynamics that are no less complex.

All this has to do, properly speaking, with the human sciences. If I refer to them, it is in order to recall the constant practice of giving the name " house" to the place of worship. The Old Testament is no exception, for it uses two different words, *bêt* and *hêkal,* which mean "house" and "palace" respectively, both of which the Septuagint translates with the word ἱερόν, "sanctuary," a term that is in fact quite different in meaning.[4]

While place articulates the modes of existence, it is also connected with key events of life, and therefore not only with the experience people have of their fellows but also with the experience they have of the divine Other. In this sense, and according to the saying attributed to Plutarch, the temple or place of worship is even more a human constant than is a person's city or even a person's own house.

The place of worship has a rather varied typology. M. Eliade,[5] G. van der Leeuw,[6] and others have shown how the place of worship responds to symbolic influences that are similar amid cultural variations. Moreover, different though the value given them may be, there is a constant: the search for their meaning. This is all the more so since the very presence of the divinity changes the meaning of the place. Think of the cycles of earth and water, of air and fire, and of their links with the cycle of time; think of the typology of height, of "orientation," of the ways of circumscribing place, of its openness or closed character, of the modalities of inclusion or exclusion of the community that enters it, the human group that experiences there the hidden and

[4] G. Schrenk, "ἱερόν," *TDNT* 3:230–247; O. Michel, "ναός," *TDNT* 4:764–811.

[5] M. Eliade, *Patterns in Comparative Religion,* trans. Rosemary Sheed (New York, 1958; Cleveland, 1963) 367–387.

[6] G. van der Leeuw, *Religion in Essence and Manifestation,* trans. J. E. Turner (London, 1938; New York, 1963) 393–401.

ineffable reality of God. Place, then, like time,[7] combines with the human being and with the human representation of the divine. Human beings experience the otherness of the divine and at the same time celebrate its breakthrough into human space and time.

3. The Biblical Datum

Amid the variations in their religious consciousness and in the course of their gradual understanding of the God of the covenant, who draws near to them, the human beings of the Bible, too, had their ritual places. Think, for example, of Abraham and his altar, which gave expression to his meeting with the one, personal God (see Gen 12:6-7).[8] The recasting by Moses of Israel's religion in light of the deliverance from Egypt and the striking of the Sinai covenant brought an awareness of the simultaneous transcendence and immanence of the God of the covenant to the people who had been set free and redeemed by his intervention.

The contexts in which this God manifested himself now included the gathered assembly and always referred back to the emblematic assembly that had subscribed to the covenant (Exod 19–24). The covenant itself and the acknowledgment of Yahweh as the God of the covenant were the "tent" that protected the "sanctuary" of Israel, which was the tangible sign of the covenant. The ark of the covenant, which expressed the self-consciousness of a nomadic Israel, became the center of the sanctuary of the sedentary Israel, which on gaining possession of the land gave itself a king and cities and experienced both borders and power.[9] In the temple of stone, the spatial arrangement which symbolized the cosmos[10] while changing its meaning and

[7] Eliade, *Patterns,* 388–409; van der Leeuw, *Religion,* 384–387.

[8] de Vaux, *Ancient Israel,* 289–294. The altar erected by Abraham had as its forerunners the cosmic altar of Eden (as is said in the *ODEA,* Introduction, 27) and the altar built by Noah in Genesis 8:20. Between the two, as shown by Genesis 4, there was the offering of a praise that the destruction of the balance achieved in Eden had not called into doubt.

[9] N. Füglister, "Strutture dell'ecclesiologia veterotestamentaria," in J. Feiner and M. Löhrer, eds., *L'evento salvifico nella comunità di Gesù Christo,* Mysterium Salutis 7 (Brescia, 1972) 23–62. On the temple as a religious institution, see De Vaux again, *Ancient Israel,* 310–327. Still basic, however, is Congar, *The Mystery of the Temple;* on the aspect being considered here see especially 21–53. See also G. Bissoli, *Il tempio nella letteratura giudaica e neotestamentaria* (Jerusalem, 1994).

[10] See Congar, *The Mystery of the Temple,* 94–100, but also M. Olivetti, *Il tempio simbolo cosmico* (Rome, 1967).

relating it to the God who gave it its order, Israel bodied forth its national identity, its identity as a people, so that in reality the temple was simply an image of Israel itself in its alternations of grace and sin.[11] It was a structural image of the very being of Israel as "God's people" and his "spouse."

In the temple the spatial dimension of the place of meeting and the temporal dimension of God's salvific interventions in the history of his people were intertwined. As a result, temple and people were in fact correlative categories,[12] and while the temple was the place where Yahweh's Name dwelt, it was also the house where the faithful people gathered.

The loss of the temple, its destruction and ruin, was a tragedy for the people and a punishment on them, even if it promoted the deeper movement of people-temple in the direction of an interiorization of worship and therefore, in a sense, in the direction of a theological identification of the people itself with the temple and all that the temple signified.[13]

The New Testament springs from an extraordinary event: God's presence taking its definitive form in the midst of humanity, an event expressed emblematically in John 1:14: "And the Word became flesh and lived among us, and we have seen his glory."

The incarnation of the Word does away with the imperfect or partial forms of the immanence of the thrice-holy God. He makes his dwelling among this people in concrete flesh, in a concrete place, and in a temporal completion that Galatians 4:4 describes as a fullness. The Incarnation turns this human being himself into the temple of the Most High, his dwelling place. It shows forth the very humanity of the Word as the definitive and symbolic ναός.[14]

It is in this light that we can decipher the aporias involved in the Jesus-temple controversy[15] of which the evangelists tell us. In addition,

[11] Flavius Josephus, *Antiquitates Judaicae* VIII, 3–4, speaks of it as the center of the world, the sanctifier of time and cosmic space, and the imperishable meeting point of sea (vestibule), earth (sanctuary), and heaven (holy of holies).

[12] This is even clearer in New Testament interpretation. See S. Marsili, "Dal tempio locale al tempio spirituale," in the collective work *Il tempio* (Acts of the 18th National Liturgical Week, Monreale, Aug. 28–Sept. 1, 1967; Padua, 1968) 60–63.

[13] Füglister, "Strutture," 73.

[14] Congar, *The Mystery of the Temple,* 112–150.

[15] Symbolic of all this is the "cleansing of the temple" that Jesus carried out (Mark 11:15ff. and par.; John 2:14-18); see Congar, *The Mystery of the Temple,* 120ff.

these aporias link Jesus to the prophetism-temple controversy, in the context of the interiorization of the law and the covenant and, in a spirited dialectic, with the instrumentalizing and externalizing reduction of the covenant to an empty, formal cult.

When read in this light, Jesus' reply to the Samaritan woman in John 4:21, 23 ("Woman, believe me, the hour is coming when you will worship the Father neither on this mountain nor in Jerusalem. . . . But the hour is coming, and is now here, when the true worshipers will worship the Father in spirit and truth"[16]) is a polemical answer within the religious history of Israel and in light of the ways in which Israel's worship was interpreted and in which it became idolatrous.

The christological aspect, that is, the identification of Jesus with the ναός in John 2:19, 21 ("'Destroy this temple and in three days I will raise it up.' . . . But he was speaking of the temple of his body") locates us at another point on the same line. Let us observe, moreover, that of the two terms used in the New Testament for the place of worship, namely, ναός and ἱερόν, only the first, strictly speaking, means "temple," while the second indicates the complex of buildings located within the temple esplanade. Of the two, only ναός will be applied to Christ himself by John. In the setting of the Passion, the Synoptic writers will do the same (see Mark 14:48; Matt 26:61 . . .).

These very convergences show that the problem is not so much one of moving beyond the temple or showing it to be unnecessary in the new spiritual worship that is keyed to adoration of the Father; the problem is rather that of giving christological recognition to the new and definitive temple that is Jesus himself, the Messiah and Savior of his people.

This line of interpretation is already begun in the Apocalypse.[17] There the holy city, the new Jerusalem that comes down from heaven adorned as a bride garbed for her wedding, is said to lack a temple, because God himself and the Lamb are its temple (Rev 21–22, especially 21:22). All this is set in a framework of liturgical celebration (Rev 1:10) that reflects the assembly on the Lord's day. The Church-Bride celebrates the eschatological event; it joins the Spirit in calling on the

[16] See R. Schnackenburg, *The Gospel according to John,* trans. K. Smyth (New York, 1982) 1:434–439. Schnackenburg says that Jesus is also the "place" of the new worship of God, and he stresses the eschatological and religious significance of the expression used in v. 23.

[17] See Congar, *The Mystery of the Temple,* 204ff.

Lord to come (Rev 22:17), and this precisely while it is gathered in a place and celebrating his memory.

All this amounts to saying that if the temple in the truest sense is the humanity of the incarnate Word, if this temple is his body given to death for our sake and raised in the power of the Spirit, and if the community gathered in his name is to remember his death and resurrection until he comes (see Matt 26:26-29; Mark 14:22-25; Luke 22:14-20; 1 Cor 11:23-27), then this can happen only in ways involving place and time, only in the ways in which an assembly gathers that needs walls, roof, garments, words, songs, sounds, light, food—in short, all the things that are part of human experience and apart from which the celebration cannot take place.[18]

Even in celebrating the fulfillment and therefore the transcending of space and time, the Apocalypse has recourse to sensible images in order to signify and express that very fulfillment. Think of the full-bodied, dazzling, bejeweled description of the city, its walls, and its gates; think of the suprasensible form taken by the light and water in it, whose theophanic meaning is nonetheless expressed by the light and water of our spatio-temporal experience (see Rev 21:9–22:5).

In keeping, however, with the developmental line followed by the New Testament, all this acquires its full value in the interiorization of the temple and its identification with the people of God of the new and everlasting covenant. It acquires this value not by eliminating the temple as unnecessary, but by pursuing the increasing depth of meaning that had already interpreted the theological and liturgical status of the people of Israel when united in their holy assembly.[19]

Everyone is familiar with the New Testament passages having to do with the Christian community as temple: 1 Cor 3:16-17; 6:19; 2 Cor 6:16; Eph 2:14-22; 1 Pet 2:4-10. Whereas the passage from 1 Peter explicitly connects the two categories of temple and people, this connection is established in the Pauline writings (except for 2 Cor 6:16) via the category of "the body of the Lord," that is, according to the prison letters, the body that is the Church. But the emblematic passage in Ephesians 2:14ff. not only connects the category of the Lord's body with that of the spiritual temple but also establishes a correspondence and even an identity between the new people made up of Jews and

[18] See L. Bouyer, *Rite and Man: Natural Sacredness and Christian Liturgy*, trans. M. J. Costelloe (Notre Dame, Ind., 1963); S. Maggiani, " Rito/riti," *NDL* 1223–1232.

[19] On the cultic aspect of the *qahal Yahweh* see Füglister, "Strutture," 41–46, 71–74.

gentiles and the body of the Lord. In the eschatological age of salvation, believers in Christ are themselves, in a proper sense, the temple of the Spirit.

The First Letter of Peter exhorts these believers to be built up into a spiritual temple (οἰκός) so that they may be a holy priesthood and may, through Jesus Christ, offer spiritual sacrifices pleasing to God; it also calls to mind the baptismal status of believers as "a chosen race, a royal priesthood, a holy nation, God's own people." Ephesians 2:14-22, on the other hand, joins gentiles and Jews in a unity within the history of salvation, a unity created by him who "has made both groups into one . . . through the cross." The material absence of the word λαός[20] and the presence of the word σῶμα in the second part of the parallel show the connection between the two words "people" and "body" and how the salvation-historical dynamic of the λαός flows into the concrete σῶμα. It is in virtue of their status as people of God, acquired by the cross of Christ, that the author of the Letter to the Ephesians can say of the gentiles, too, that they are no longer strangers and aliens but fellow citizens of the saints and members of the family (οἰκεῖοι) of God, built on the foundation of the apostles and prophets. Jesus Christ himself, for his part, is the cornerstone in whom the entire structure (οἰκοδομή) is joined together and grows into a holy temple (ναός) for the Lord and in whom the gentiles too are being built, by the Spirit, into a dwelling place (κατοικητήριον) for God (see Eph 2:19-22).

4. Local Community and Worshiping Assembly

Since the christological basis for the status of the temple and the identification of the community with the temple are both mediated by the category "body of Christ," our attention is turned to the ecclesiological aspects of "body." Since this term designates the community and the manner in which the community is structured, it defines the community not in an abstract way but with immediate reference to its local coming together.[21] The fact that I earlier invoked some passages

[20] Though the word was to be expected here, since the author had been invoking the Jew-gentile (λαός-ἔθνη) dialectic. The word is in fact used in 2 Corinthians 6:16-17 (a passage reminiscent of Revelation 21:1) in full continuity with the Old Testament tradition. Some Old Testament passages: Lev 26:12; Ezek 37:27; Isa 52:11; 2 Sam 7:14.

[21] On the relationship between local Church and Eucharist see W. Elert, *Eucharist and Church: Fellowship in the First Four Centuries* (St. Louis, 1966); H. Legrand,

of 1 Corinthians as giving expression to the body-temple connection should not make us forget that the same letter sets forth the organizational dynamics of the Church-body, whose many members all contribute to the common κοινονία (1 Cor 12–14). The same letter connects this mystery with participation in the body and blood of the Lord; when the community feeds on this body (in the full sense of "feed"), it is built up into the body of the Lord (1 Cor 10:16-17).

This brings us back once again to the gathering of the local community for the Eucharist (see 1 Cor 11:17-32). It brings us back to the community actually gathered in the place where it assembles in order to body forth its identity and to express its being through the proclamation of the Word and the remembering of the Lord's self-giving for us (this was the necessary condition of our becoming his body).

All this thus brings us back to the local dimension as indispensable for the existence of the community which, by reason of its origin, both historical and theological, is first and foremost a community gathered in a place. In this community, in this actual, present assembly, the ἐκκλησία of the risen Lord is immanent as an interlocal reality. For a structural element of this ἐκκλησία, too, is its presence, in its totality, to every locally gathered community that expresses it completely and fully.[22]

We move, then, from the people to the ναός, by way of the organic and symphonic articulation of the community in its function and by way of the building up of the temple in the expressive setting of the place.

It was basically this motif that made the young community of Jerusalem independent of the temple, once it had overcome any calls for

"Communion ecclésiale et eucharistie aux premiers siècles," *L'Année canonique* 25 (1981) 125–148; J. D. Zizioulas, "La communauté eucharistique et la catholicité de l'Eglise," *Istina* 14 (1969) 66–88. See also B. Forte, *La Chiesa nell'Eucaristia: Per una ecclesiologia eucaristica alla luce del Vaticano II* (Naples, 1975), and the document published by the Joint International Commission for Dialogue between the Roman Catholic Church and the Orthodox Church, "Il mistero della Chiesa e dell'Eucaristia alla luce del mistero della Trinità," *Irén* 55 (1982) 350–362. On these same problems see also: *RL* 59, no. 1 (1972): "Chiesa locale e liturgia"; *MD* 165 (1986): "Réflexions sur l'Eglise locale"; and the collective work *Ecclesiologia e liturgia* (Casale Monferrato, 1982).

[22] Reread *SC* 41, *LG* 23 and 26, *CD* 11, and the relevant literature. See, e.g., the collective works: *L'Eglise de Vatican II* (Paris, 1967); *La liturgie après Vatican II* (Paris, 1967); *La charge pastorale des evêques* (Paris, 1969).

syncretism and any initial uncertainties. It was this that also caused the community to take a one-way path toward the breaking of bread in homes (see Acts 2:46; 20:7).

True enough, the destruction of the Jerusalem temple and the development of a cultic practice that combined elements of novelty and elements borrowed from synagogal and family custom make it difficult to describe without ambiguity the process that, in the course of a century, led the young communities to develop places of worship. But whatever the individual factors at work in this process, the key factor was the connection between ἐκκλησία and place, assembly and place. In the strict sense, then, the community is to be found where it subsists and manifests itself; the place of worship, the *domus ecclesiae,* the "house of the people of God" expresses the theological aspect of this subsistence and self-manifestation.

The house of the people of God is not a temple, because the separatist dynamics of the τέμενος[23] remain alien to it; on the other hand, various terms such as sanctuary, basilica, womb, cathedral, and church can be legitimately, that is, theologically, predicated of it. This house is what it is because it is a *spatial icon of the local Church,* of the one, holy, catholic, and apostolic Church of the risen Lord as subsisting in a place and assembled in a place. It is for this reason that this Church's functional form, that is, the building of stone, continually points to its ministerial role. It is for this reason, too, that it expresses itself and finds its center through the emblematic character of nave and sanctuary and through the reference of these both to the people gathered there and to the mystery that the gathered people celebrate and experience.[24]

II. LITURGICAL SPACE

What has been said thus far makes it clear that to speak of liturgical space is in fact to speak of "place," a particular kind of place that takes its "form" from the liturgy. The Christian building for worship, the "house of the people of God," does not summon up a general idea of space. Like time, space is certainly an a priori, a modality indispensable for our access to an understanding and experience of the real. But if this understanding and experience are to take place, space must

[23] C. Valenziano, *Architetti di chiese* (Palermo, 1995) 60–61.

[24] C. Militello, "Il popolo di Dio tra navata e santuario," in the collective work *Gli spazi della celebrazione rituale* (Milan, 1984) 11–39.

always take concrete form in a complete and well-defined place, with the synergy of structure and function proper to it.

As far as liturgical space is concerned, we must attend in a consistent way to turning this space that is peculiar to and characteristic of the liturgy into a "place." We will see and understand this if we focus our attention on the factor that determines function, namely, the liturgy, and to the element that determines structure, namely, the people of God. In short, liturgical space is precisely that the very arrangement of the "place" mirrors and reflects the people of God that gathers there. Liturgical space is precisely that it functionally allows the assembly to structure itself and perform there not just any action but the action specific to Christian worship. But whether we look at the structure of the place of worship or analyze its function, it is evident that the issue is always the mystery of the Church. Structure and function always and in every case point to a reality that is "theological" or better "ecclesiological."

1. The Place of Worship as an "Image of the Church"

The figurative metonymy[25] that allows the passage back and forth between the Church as mystery and the church as building determines and regulates the very structure of the place of worship. This metonymy is found at work especially in the correspondence between the stones and walls of the building and the living stones and living walls made up of the faithful who constitute the assembly and take advantage of the stones and walls that circumscribe the church as building.

The correlation of living stones—inanimate stones—works out in two ways that are synergetic. A twofold phenomenology—linguistic and architectonic—determines the quality of the place of Christian worship. We are speaking always of a theological quality.

We noticed earlier the multiplicity of names for the Christian cultic building. These are synonyms for the term ἐκκλησία with its structural and structuring theological meaning, and all of them point to the identity of the people of God whom the church as building brings together, this building itself being, in its forms and spatial arrangements, a mirror of the mysterious compenetration between members that is at work within the body of Christ.

[25] Valenziano, *Architetti di chiese*, 68–80.

The church building is first of all a "basilica."[26] It is true enough that on hearing the word we are reminded of the basilica's architectural antecedent: the Roman basilica, a type of building whose characteristics were carried over to some extent to the Christian place of worship. In addition, the Roman basilica, by reason of the civic functions proper to it, was a place of assembly that brought together and received the people of the city for rituals having to do chiefly with the administration of justice. Furthermore, the name "basilica" calls to mind the βασιλεύς, the sovereign, the emperor; it was therefore a place where sovereignty was exercised. In the history of buildings for worship the name "basilica" would subsequently be given to those buildings also that owed their existence to the generosity or patronage of a sovereign, buildings erected due to his devotion.

In the strict and proper sense, however, "basilica" is the name given to a church building when it explicitly highlights the royal status of the people of God who gather there. In point of fact, the people of God is a people of kings and priests (this is the basic theological status assigned to the people of God from Exodus 19:6 down to the hymns of the Apocalypse; see 1:6; 5:10). The house of God's people is the house of a royal people, a holy assembly, a community called upon to exercise there its own royalty, its own royal priesthood.

Few buildings for worship implement this theology as does Justinian's basilica of Hagia Sophia in Constantinople. Here the diaconal royalty of the king and the priestly royalty of the gathered people are reflected and given new expression in the volumetric purity of its forms, walls, design, and mosaic iconography. Hagia Sophia is the "basilica" par excellence, the place where the entire people of God, ministers and faithful, come together in action. It is a place that renders visible the constitutive royalty of the faithful people, who have been made royal through participation in the royalty of Christ, and this in virtue of a powerful anointing by the Spirit.

The term "basilica," which also has a weaker meaning, has been accompanied through history by other designations for the church building. Among these, the one that comes closest to conveying the theological status of the house of God's people (although this fact is not always realized) is the rather common Italian word "duomo." This name, reserved to more important churches and sometimes applied to

[26] Ibid., 202–207.

the cathedral church, really translates the oldest consciousness, the original theological meaning, of the gathering of a community in a place. Derived as it is from the Latin *domus*, this term recalls the original form of the local church, namely, the *domus ecclesia*, the "house-church," which subsequently became the *domus ecclesiae*, the house "of the" church.

I have already several times referred to the Christian place of worship as "the house of the people of God." The point here is not simply to go back to the explicit form of the first building, when Christianity had become a *religio licita*. We must go further upstream, as it were, and recall the celebration of the Eucharist in homes. The walled structure called a house, the building that housed a family, expanded to welcome the family of God that gathered there amid the spontaneity of the Eucharist in the earliest days. The building for worship kept this form when it became in the proper sense a "house of the Church" and manifested the centrality not only of the Eucharist but of baptism.[27]

Independently of the term "duomo," there is no church-as-building that does not continue to be a "house of the people of God." The phrase is one that allows for all the complex interpretations and all the changes that have taken place in the church-as-building. However different the building has become in the course of time, all the architectural typologies remain connected, in one or other way, with this assembling, this coming together, which the walls circumscribe without ever losing their dynamic aspect of welcoming all who gather there.

The church-as-building is the house, the special place, of the faithful people. Its walls, its roof, its design are at the service of the liturgical subjectivities of all who gather there.

The back-and-forth between church-as-building and Church-as-mystery thus remains constant amid such terminological variants as "duomo" and "church-house," in complete consistency with the theological significance of the word οἰκός, which gives expression at once to the subjectivity of those who make it up and to the place where they gather in order to body forth and exercise this theological subjectivity.

[27] It is no accident that the *domus ecclesiae* at Dura Europos has a baptistery as one of its parts.

The mystery of the Church determines the place of worship theologically in the case of other designations as well. Think of the terms "womb" and "cathedral." The former refers to the metaphor of the womb, which was already dear to the Fathers; it refers to the Church as the "mother"[28] from whose "womb" persons are born to new life. Here the building for worship receives a further theological meaning: the spousal fruitfulness of the Church as mystery (her motherhood) gives its name to the church-as-building; the latter becomes a "mother-church"[29] due to its function of bringing new members into itself.

There is no country that does not have its "womb," its mother-church; generally speaking, this is the first church built there, the first to which people usually came for baptism.

Similarly, the "cathedral" church is the one that represents the apostolic root of the community, while the final completeness of the place links the community to the authoritative witnesses of the paschal event. The allusion to the "chair" in the word "cathedral" gives this place of worship an expressiveness peculiar to the ministry of the bishop through which the community is in touch with the apostolic foundation of its faith. There is a strong element of symbolism here that is likewise patristic[30] and is voiced once again in *Sacrosanctum Concilium:* "All should hold in great esteem the liturgical life of the diocese centered around the bishop, especially in his cathedral church; they must be convinced that the preeminent manifestation of the Church is present in the full, active participation of all God's holy people in these liturgical celebrations, especially in the same Eucharist, in a single prayer, at one altar at which the bishop presides, surrounded by his college of priests and by his ministers" (41; *DOL* 41).

The proper names of the place of worship continue, however, to be primarily "church," "basilica," and "duomo." The others, though pregnant with meaning, do not express the entirety of the theological mystery that is inherent in "the house of the people of God." And, on the other hand, the theological structure of the church-as-building,

[28] Ch. Delahaye, *Ecclesia Mater chez les Pères des trois premiers siècles* (Paris, 1964); H. De Lubac, "La maternità della Chiesa," in idem, *Pluralismo di Chiese o unità della Chiesa?* (Brescia, 1973) 135–212.

[29] Chr. Schönborn, " Le temple comme lieu maternel de l'Eglise," *MD* 169 (1987) 25–37.

[30] Ignatius of Antioch, *Ad Magn.* 7; *Ad Phil.* 4; *Ad Smyrn.* 8, cited in *SC* 41.

which is symmetrical with and reflective of the Church-as-mystery, is also subject to changes in architectural forms as well as changes in the Church's image of itself.[31] These changes, too, are reflected visibly in the church-as-building.

Amid the changes in style and in the stress now on this name, now on that, it is possible to see how the essentially communional nature of the Church in its beginnings still pervades, at least ideally, the house of the people of God, the architectural arrangement of which is at the service of this communion. Socio-cultural change in the form of a separation of clergy from laity would determine a different image of the Church, one that again could also be discerned in formal changes in the cultic building. The Church that is *imperatrix et domina* would arrange its spaces differently, interpreting them and making them visible in light of its identification of itself with the kingdom of God in the here and now of its own history. The post-Tridentine Church, which was bent on understanding itself as a *societas hierarchica iuridica inaequalis,* would rid itself not only of the imperative of communion but also of the immediate and monumental evidence of its being called together on the basis of the word. The forgetfulness of the ambo, for example, and the change that took place in the altar point to this profound shift at the level of ecclesiological consciousness. Yet the church-as-building would continue to be the house of God's people and, despite everything, would remain an expression of their subjectivity, even when this was challenged or lulled to sleep.[32]

The change that has taken place since Vatican II and since the rediscovery of an ecclesiology of communion obviously compels a different understanding of the theological status of the people of God and therefore a concrete translation of it in ways that are fully coherent with the two points of reference so strongly emphasized by the Council: the Church itself and the world.

[31] H. Fries, " Mutamenti dell'immagine di Chiesa ed evoluzione storico-dommatica," in *Mysterium Salutis* 7:267–339.

[32] One instance of this was baroque ornamentation, which was so varied depending on place, whether in the regions of Europe or the region of Latin America. Paradoxically, it was this particular form of expression, which was always exuberant and always different according to latitudes and cultures, that showed the indispensable need of correlating the "house of God's people" with the concrete history of the local community and its most unique forms of expression.

The ecclesiology of Vatican II assigns a very special place to the local Church and its concrete coming together.[33] For it is there, in fact, that the mystery of the one holy, catholic, and apostolic Church has its supreme manifestation. This attention to area and place as the setting for the Church's full epiphany in the here and now of history is translated into a newfound correspondence between theological status and the church-as-building. The latter must therefore assume responsibility for the necessary manifestation of the Church-as-mystery and make this Church visible and incarnate it in space and time (a space and time that are, obviously, contextualized and carefully circumscribed). On the other hand, having rediscovered its bonds of solidarity with the world, the church-as-building, while remaining fully related to the Church-as-mystery, cannot shrug off its responsibility to its native cultural context and the specific settings of the place, as rendered authentic by the subjectivities of those who make their dwelling there.[34]

If, according to *Lumen gentium,* leadership in the local Church is to be a source of creativity, an overseer of correspondence and synergy between the people of God who make up that Church and the building as such (whether the latter be adapted or newly built[35]), then analogously, according to *Gaudium et spes,* the place has a priority that is obligatory at the level of mission. The building for worship is located in the human and natural habitat for which it is intended; it must somehow make this habitat its own, somehow ensure an effective osmosis between the theological status of those who directly and immediately profit from it and the status of those others who also profit from it, if not at the level of faith, then at least at the level of needs. The community cannot detach itself from the dialogue that the very church-as-building imposes, if for no other reason than because of its impact on the area.

[33] See H. Legrand, "La realizzazione della Chiesa in un luogo," in B. Lauret and Fr. Refoulé, eds., *Iniziazione alla pratica della teologia. Dogmatica* II (Brescia, 1986) 147–355.

[34] See, e.g., C. Giraudo, "Madagascar: spazio sacro e inculturazione," *Rassegna di Teologia* 34, no. 2 (1994) 131–47; on the general problem see A. Stauffer, "Inculturation et architetture d'église," *MD* 179 (1989) 83–98.

[35] The problem of adaptation is one that affects especially the Old World and is presently the focus of an ideological and theological dispute; no less lively and no less far from satisfactory solutions is the debate over the criteria for the building of new churches. See Valenziano, *Architetti di chiese,* 103–107.

Once again, this discourse remains an eminently theological one. It is a strictly theological solicitation that invokes the visibility of the local Church and therefore asks that the church-as-building be that Church's expression and warranty. No less theological is the demand for a connection between the Church of the place and its habitat in the broadest acceptance of this term. In short, the church-as-building produces a culture, just as the people of God produce a culture. But this cultural product must of necessity be involved in the larger human reality in which the community, though a pilgrim, takes up its dwelling. Otherwise there would be a denial of a constitutive feature of the Church, namely, its existence as a "sacrament," a sign and means of intimate union with God and of unity with the entire human race.

2. *The Place of Worship and Its Liturgical Functioning*

The emphasis placed on the theological status of the people of God and on its harmony with the place of worship is paralleled by another theological polarity that builds up a theology of liturgical space, namely, the "liturgical" functioning proper to this place.

The house of the people of God is not such solely because it reflects the reciprocal relationship between living stones and inanimate stones. Or, rather, it fully reflects this relationship only if the inanimate stones make possible the subjective experience and activity of the living stones.

It is its liturgical function that also identifies the Christian space of worship. A church-building is what it is if the faithful people can gather in it to exercise their royal priesthood, if they can be the subjects there of ritual activity. This activity certainly has as its central action the Eucharist, which is the *culmen et fons* (*SC* 10) of the Church's life, but it also finds expression in the many functions associated with all the sacramental actions and with liturgical praise.

Functionality refers to the unifying poles of the celebration, namely, the table of the Word and the table of the eucharistic Bread; but both of these demand a full use of the place and the mobility of the people of God who gather there. The Eucharist in particular most certainly calls for a people who do not just stand by but who concelebrate.[36]

The space for worship must be planned in a way that fosters a theological transparency.

[36] See Y. J.-M. Congar, "L'Eglise ou communauté chrétienne, subjet intégral de l'action liturgique," in *La liturgie après Vatican II* (Paris, 1967) 241–282.

Liturgical functionality is a matter of stability and movement, silence and speech, proclamation and acclamation. The dynamics of a celebration must be fully possible, fully usable; this means the complete availability of the multi-faceted ministerial activity of the people of God. To correlate the inanimate stones with the living stones is not simply to make them a reflection of the assembly, whether by means of the architectural components or by means of the iconographical program. To effect this correlation means recognizing that the play of architectural forces corresponds to the ecclesiological subsidiarity involved. The stake here is the many-faceted ministerial activity of the people of God. The place of worship must be an emblem in its polarities both within and outside the building.

What is required, then, is a space that is functional for the liturgy, a place in which the proper roles of the bishop, the presbyters, and the deacons, of the lectors and acolytes, the ministers, the cantor and choir, the ministers of the Eucharist, and of those, too, who bring up the gifts, those who welcome and usher in the faithful, and of all other ministers will be shown forth in all their vivid clarity. What is required is a space that takes into account the requirements of all the rites, from initiation to marriage, from the ordination of ministers to the celebration of funerals; a space that takes account of the fact that the faithful are fed not only by the Eucharist but also by the Word of God, which likewise has its own special celebration; a space, finally, that makes possible in a dignified and expressive way the course of conversion, which culminates in the sacramental celebration of penance and that preserves the Eucharist for devotional worship; a space which allows the assembly to experience its own solemn coming together and which in a no less dignified way ensures the weekday gathering; a space that brings together and does not scatter; a space that does not level everything down but brings out all the theological values at work.[37]

[37] On these subjects see *MD* 197 (1994): "L'espace liturgique," and the collective work *Spazio e rito* (Rome, 1996).

Bibliography

AA.VV. "Art et liturgie aujourd'hui." *MD* 169 (1987).

AA.VV. *L'espace liturgique. MD* 197 (1994).

AA.VV. *La dimora di Dio tra gli uomini: Tempio e assemblea.* Rome, 1993.

AA.VV. *Spazio e rito.* Rome, 1996.

Bouyer, L. *Architettura e liturgia.* Magnano, 1994.

Congar, Y. J.-M. *The Mystery of the Temple.* Trans. R. F. Trevett. Westminster, Md., 1962.

____. "L'église, ce n'est pas les mures mais les fidèles." *MD* 70, 105–114.

Congregation for the Oriental Churches, *Instruction for Applying the Liturgical Prescriptions of the Code of Canons of the Eastern Churches* (Jan. 6, 1996) XIV, 102–109.

Leclerq, H. "Eglises." *DACL* IV/2, 2279–3394.

Marsili, S. "Dal tempio locale al tempio spirituale." In *Il tempio,* 51–63. Padua, 1968.

____. "Dedicazione sensa consacrazione." *RL* 66 (1979) 578–601.

Militello, C. "Il populo di Dio tra navata e santuario." In *Gli spazi della celebrazione rituale,* 11–39. Milan, 1984.

Mohrmann, Ch. "Les dénominations de l'eglise en tant qu'édifice en grec et en latin au cours des prémièrs siècles. *RSR* (April, 1962) 155–174.

Régamey, P. R. *Art sacré au XX*[e] *siecle?* Paris, 1952.

Valenziano, C. *Architetti di chiese.* Palermo, 1995.

Subject Index

The following pages list the chief or more commonly treated subjects that are pertinent to the study of liturgical time and space. This index does not contain the names of persons (unless they are primary sources), events, and places recorded in this volume.